COLLEGE GUIDE 2009

PUBLISHING
New York

All career and salary information presented in this book was gathered from the Bureau of Labor Statistics, the U.S. Department of Labor, and the Occupational Outlook Handbook, 2007–08 Edition, published by the U.S. Department of Labor's Bureau of Labor Statistics.

The views of individuals profiled in this book are their own and do not reflect those of the companies for which they work, the schools they attended, or those of Kaplan Publishing, a division of Kaplan, Inc.

This publication is designed to provide accurate and authoritative information in regard to the subject matter covered. It is sold with the understanding that the publisher is not engaged in rendering legal, accounting, or other professional service. If legal advice or other expert assistance is required, the services of a competent professional should be sought.

Published by Kaplan Publishing, a division of Kaplan, Inc.
1 Liberty Plaza, 24th Floor
New York, NY 10006

Printed in the United States of America

August 2008
10 9 8 7 6 5 4 3 2 1

ISBN-13: 978-1-4277-9750-6

Kaplan Publishing books are available at special quantity discounts to use for sales promotions, employee premiums, or educational purposes. Please email our Special Sales Department to order or for more information at kaplanpublishing@kaplan.com, or write to Kaplan Publishing, 1 Liberty Plaza, 24th Floor, New York, NY 10006.

CONTENTS

PLUS 390 MORE SCHOOL POSSIBILITIES

10 HOT GREEN CAREERS

PLUS 25 MORE CAREER POSSIBILITIES!

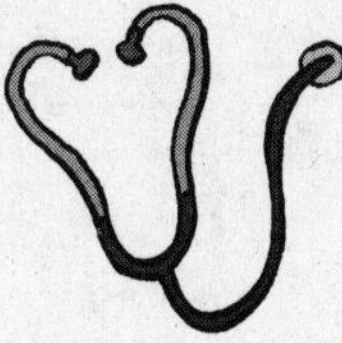

Introduction

Have you ever wondered how successful individuals got where they are? Ever think about how your college choice might fit into your career path? Are you wondering about how to **go green** and help save the environment?

If so, then *Kaplan College Guide* 2009 Edition is the perfect book for you!

Inside this book you'll find just what you need to help define and achieve your college and career goals:

Information on 390 of the most interesting colleges across the country to help you make smart choices about which college is best for you, including:

- Academics
- Admissions
- Costs
- Financial aid
- Student body
- And much more!

An in-depth look at today's 35 hottest careers and what you really want to know about them, including:

- Areas of specialty
- Average salaries
- Educational requirements
- Where the jobs are
- Where to go for more info
- And much more!

Interviews with 145 successful individuals from each career path. They give you the inside scoop on:

- Their college experiences—including what they've learned and what they'd do differently
- What it takes to make it in their chosen career field
- What their jobs are really like
- And much more!

Interested in learning more about what you can do to help improve the environment? *Kaplan College Guide* 2009 Editionalso gives you all the info you need to **go green**!

Green schools: in-depth profiles of 25 environmentally responsible colleges across the country including:

- Green campus projects and initiatives
- Green courses offered
- Green organizations and student groups on campus

Green careers: profiles of today's ten hottest green careers. Wonder what it's like to be a solar energy engineer or a green interior designer? There are so many interesting career options that directly or indirectly help the environment, and after reading about some of them you just might realize that one of them is perfect for you!

Green organizations: a look at organizations that are focused on addressing environmental issues. Interested in volunteering or learning more? Check out their websites for additional information.

Green glossary: a glossary filled with the terms and buzzwords you'll often hear when green issues are discussed. Use this list to help you think—and talk—like a green expert.

How did we come up with our list of the 35 hottest careers? The list was compiled with you in mind—Kaplan surveyed hundreds of prospective undergraduates like you across the country. We then compared these selections against some of the fastest-growing, most competitive industries around the globe today, according to the U.S. Department of Labor. This combination of options helped us come up with a strong balance of intriguing, competitive, and cutting-edge fields that are likely to provide tremendous opportunity and growth over the coming decade.

We hope you enjoy exploring this book and the many wonderful college and career options. Best of luck with discovering the college and career path that's right for you!

Sincerely,

Brandon Jones, Contributing Editor
Kaplan Publishing, Editorial Team

How to Use This Book

There are lots of ways to use *Kaplan College Guide* 2009 Edition—it all depends on what you're looking for. Want to search for colleges that match your needs and goals? Interested in today's hottest careers and how to get them? Feel free to browse through the book any way you want, or use the following guide to help you find what you're looking for.

COLLEGES

The first part of the book has lots of useful information to help you decide which college is right for you.

Start here to learn about 25 cutting-edge green colleges around the country. In addition to being great schools, they're working hard to be environmentally responsible role models. We'll tell you all about what each school is up to and what students can do to help make a difference!

If you already have some schools in mind, or would like to learn more about schools in a specific state, setting, or price range, check out our comprehensive listing of 390 schools, which includes a helpful state and price index.

Not sure what school is right for you? Feel free to browse the listings and learn more about which schools meet your specific needs. You may discover some great options that you hadn't thought about before!

CAREERS 

Interested in learning more about some of the hottest careers out there? In this part of the book, you'll find in-depth profiles of 35 hot career fields with all sorts of useful information. The career fields are divided into two groups—Arts and Humanities and Science—which helps make the book easier to navigate.

Kaplan College Guide 2009 Edition also includes 145 revealing interviews with individuals from our featured career fields. These Q & As are full of good advice and can really give you a sense of what it's like to work in a particular field, as well as some of the academic issues you might want to consider. Some of our featured interviews are anonymous, but the information provided is accurate and we hope it will prove useful as you explore the many career options out there.

Thinking about a career that will allow you to make a real impact on the environment? Check out our ten featured green careers. You'll get a close look at what it's like to work in these fields, as well as some of the environmental issues that are affecting our entire planet. It's a great way to learn more about how you can make a difference!

The information provided in *Kaplan College Guide* is designed to help you define and sharpen your college and career goals, and make more informed life decisions. Have fun on this exciting journey!

25 Cutting–Edge Green Colleges

For additional stats on these schools, look them up in the Profiles of 390 Schools section, beginning on page 53.

Arizona State University

WHAT'S GREEN

GREEN ORGANIZATIONS/STUDENT GROUPS

- **Sustainability Coalition:** This group brings together environmental groups on campus to concentrate environmental efforts.
- **2020 Vision at ASU:** This group pursues renewable energy resources for long-term sustainability.
- **Ecology and Evolutionary Biology Lunch:** The group that lunches together promotes ecological research together!

GREEN CAMPUS PROJECTS/INITIATIVES

- **Undergraduate Student Government Bike Co-op:** To encourage students to ride their bikes instead of drive, the school offers low-cost bike repair and maintenance.
- **Decision Theater:** This high-tech visualization laboratory helps sustainability researchers simulate their proposed environmental solutions.
- **Water Conservation Technology Exchange:** This program is sponsored by the Arizona Water Institute, a consortium of three universities including ASU. It is designed as a way to disseminate technology and ideas pertaining to water conservation.

GREEN COURSES OFFERED

- Sustainable Cities
- International Development and Sustainability
- Sustainable Use of Renewable and Nonrenewable Environmental Resources
- Environment and Society
- Environmental History
- Human Impacts on Ancient Environments

To run a school as large as Arizona State University takes real leadership. And that is exactly what President Michael Crow exemplified when he cofounded the Presidents Climate Commitment, which he also chairs. This kind of action is exactly what makes ASU one of our top green schools.

Although the Presidents Climate Commitment is an important document at ASU and other schools around the country, it is only one aspect of promoting environmental stewardship. With regard to academics, ASU is clearly on board with its College of Sustainability and other environmental courses. But it is what is being done outside of the classroom that is having the most impact.

While ASU's current recycling is only at 15 percent, it is implementing steps to reach 50 percent, a notable feat achieved by Harvard in late 2007. ASU is also focusing on other environmental goals. One of the most significant relates to construction on campus. The school has committed to making all new construction meet silver-level LEED (Leadership in Energy and Environmental Design) ratings. ASU already has a total of eight LEED buildings, one of them certified at the platinum level—the highest LEED rating possible.

The school is also trying to conserve energy by setting thermostats higher in the summer and lower in the winter and turning off lights and computers when they're not in use. And ASU has retrofitted buildings throughout the campus with more energy-efficient lightbulbs, steam pipes, and temperature controls.

INSIDE THE CLASSROOM

Like most large state universities, ASU is more than just a school. In fact, there are 22 different colleges and schools spread out over three cities. The majority of schools are located in Tempe, but there are also colleges in Mesa and Phoenix. Perhaps more difficult than choosing a school is choosing a degree program. ASU offers more than 250 dif-

Tempe, AZ (main campus)
Website: www.asu.edu
Sustainability website: http://asusustainability.asu.edu or http://sustainable.asu.edu/giosmain/index.htm
Email contact address: askasu@asu.edu

ferent undergraduate degrees. One of the newest undergrad programs is the College of Sustainability. Undergraduate-level sustainability courses will be offered for the first time in fall 2008.

Research is also an important element of an undergraduate education at ASU. There is an easily searchable and often-updated resource listing of available programs to choose from. Some examples of research opportunities include a fellowship at the Center for the Study of Religion and Conflicts or an assistantship in the Department of Psychology.

Like students around the United States, ASU students have wonderful opportunities to study abroad. Programs are divided into winter and summer. Winter programs are offered in Argentina, Australia, the Bahamas, Brazil, the Dominican Republic, England, France, India, Mexico, and Thailand. There are even more countries to choose from in the summer programs, including such varied nations as Israel, Ghana, Romania, and Ecuador.

AROUND CAMPUS

As mentioned before, ASU is spread across three cities: Mesa, Phoenix, and Tempe. Tempe is by far the largest campus and is home to the most students. Students who choose to attend ASU are encouraged, but not required, to live on campus their first year.

ASU has found that students who are well integrated into campus life tend to have better retention and graduation rates, and the department of residential life does its best to keep students happy on campus.

There are 15 residence halls on the Tempe campus. The majority of housing is dedicated to first-year students. The campus is divided into four "residential neighborhoods." All students who live in residence halls must purchase a meal plan. There are literally dozens of dining facilities to choose from, which keep students well fed regardless of what plan they select.

STUDENT LIFE

There are more than 51,000 ASU students on the Tempe campus—that is the single largest enrollment on one campus in the entire country. It's no wonder then that students have almost limitless opportunities for socializing and interaction. The Student Organization Resource Center manages more than 450 registered student clubs and organizations. There are clubs for almost any interest, and students are encouraged to start their own clubs.

Greek life is another area in which to find a niche at this massive school. There are five different Greek councils, with dozens of different Greek chapters to choose from. While there are some Greek houses, many students choose to live in regular housing.

Sports are truly a highlight of social life at ASU. There are 20 NCAA Division I varsity teams (9 men's, 11 women's), and they all have achieved success to some degree. Especially high ranked is men's baseball. ASU also has many alumni who play or have played professional baseball and professional football. For those who don't play, watching the Sun Devils is just as fun.

Bates College

WHAT'S GREEN

GREEN ORGANIZATIONS/STUDENT GROUPS

- **Bates Energy Action Movement (BEAM):** This group promotes carbon neutrality on campus.
- **Environmental Coalition (EC):** This group aims to improve environmental behaviors on campus and around the country.
- **Bates Outing Club (BOC):** This is the nation's largest outing club, and it sponsors trips throughout the many beautiful natural areas of New England.

GREEN CAMPUS PROJECTS/INITIATIVES

- **Bates Bike Co-op:** This initiative makes ten bikes available to co-op members to use on campus and around town.
- **Take a Mug/Leave a Mug Program:** The first of its kind in the nation, this program replaces disposable drink cups with reusable ones. Students can return used mugs for clean ones.
- **Clean Sweep:** This massive tag sale ensures that reusable items that students leave behind at the end of the school year do not just end up in a landfill.

GREEN COURSES OFFERED

- Material and Energy Flow in Engineered and Natural Systems
- Environment and Society
- Field Methods in Environmental Science
- Comparative Environmental Politics and Policy
- Environmental Archeology
- Chemical Reactivity in Environmental Systems

It was in February 2007 that Bates president Elaine Tuttle Hansen signed the Presidents Climate Commitment, an act that sets into motion an inventorying of greenhouse gas emissions and the implementation of countless methods for achieving carbon neutrality. Although the signing was quite recent, environmental efforts at Bates are not. Back in 2006, Bates made a major purchase of green energy sysytems, and it has committed to converting to renewable energy on campus.

Other changes on campus are physical reminders of environmentalism. All new construction on campus must reach a minimum silver-level LEED rating, and the new residence hall has achieved that goal. Even the wood used to build these structures is from local, sustainable sources. In addition, dorms are being fitted with double-glazed windows, low-flow shower heads and toilets, and occupancy sensors to reduce waste. At Bates, eco-friendly cleaners are used to keep buildings fresh and sanitary.

Dining services at Bates have also made a concerted effort to embrace environmentally friendly practices. Recently, Bates Dining joined the Green Restaurant Association, which encourages green purchasing. The school also recycles, composts, and donates leftover food to shelters and even gives food scraps to a local pig farm.

INSIDE THE CLASSROOM

Without a doubt, Bates is one of the top liberal arts colleges in the United States. The 1,650 students have 32 majors to choose from, including environmental studies, as well as three so-called "Special Curricular Programs." These are interdisciplinary studies, which allows students to create a personal interdisciplinary major; Japanese studies, which focuses on the language and culture of Japan; and Medical studies guide, which

Lewiston, ME
Website: www.bates.edu
Sustainability website: www.bates.edu/sustainable-bates.xml
Email contact address: admissions@bates.edu

is an advising system for students interested in health professions.

Incoming students have the unique opportunity to take First-Year Seminars. These for credit courses, such as Issues in Oceanography or Intercultural Music Experiences, are limited to 15 students each, and about 90 percent of Bates freshmen participate. This program is also very popular because these courses tend to focus on discussion and debate. And whereas Bates students used to have to complete a core curriculum, they now have more broad general education requirements. The class of 2011 is the first to take part in this new program.

Another unique aspect of a Bates education is the "short term." All Batesies, as students are known, must take at least two short terms (but no more than three) before they graduate. The short term is a special five-week period in May when students can take it a bit easier by studying something slightly less conventional. Some short-term courses involve field trips (studying marine biology on the coast of Maine or theater in New York City) or more extensive travel (learning about art history in Italy or conservation practices in Ecuador).

AROUND CAMPUS

Although students looking for an urban setting might be hesitant to consider Bates, its location, Lewiston-Auburn, is actually ideal. With a population of almost 60,000, these twin cities are the second-largest metropolitan area in Maine. Students who prefer a rural setting will most definitely not be disappointed. A 30-minute drive lands students at the ocean or in the mountains. The gorgeous forest and coastline are perfect for various outdoor activities.

The Bates campus itself blends beautifully into its setting. The meticulously maintained 109-acre campus has an impressive mixture of old and new structures.

STUDENT LIFE

Social life at Bates is pretty active, despite the lack of fraternities and sororities. There are more than 60 different clubs and organizations—many with their own websites so that students can learn more about what they are up to.

Environmental groups on campus have become especially active in recent years, proving that not just the administration but also the students are committed to sustainable practices.

With such beautiful natural surroundings, outdoor activities are very popular. There are 24 varsity sports, and for those who don't play on these intercollegiate teams, there is always a chance to go out and support the Bobcats or just play any of the club and intramural sports available. One IM sport you may never have heard of before is wallyball—a sport that just begs to be Googled.

Berea College

WHAT'S GREEN

GREEN ORGANIZATIONS/STUDENT GROUPS

- **Helping Earth and Learning (HEAL):** This is the only environmental group on campus. As a result, it is extremely active with community cleanups and other environmental practices.

GREEN CAMPUS PROJECTS/INITIATIVES

- **Local Food Initiative:** One of the main objectives of this initiative is to bring more locally grown produce to Berea's campus.
- **10 × 10:** This student-led campaign urges Berea College to purchase 10 percent of its energy from renewable sources by 2010.
- **Berea Bikes:** Like other bike-sharing programs on campuses around the country, Berea Bikes hopes to provide enough blue bikes to students for use on and around campus.

GREEN COURSES OFFERED

- Ecological Architecture
- Ecological Design
- Geographical Information Systems
- Ecology
- Sustainable and Environmental Studies
- Sustainable Appalachia

When a school has its own Ecovillage, you know that it must be committed to green practices. And Berea College is. The Ecovillage is a multipurpose facility with 50 apartments, a laboratory, an ecologically constructed home, a wastewater treatment center, and gardens. The overall purpose of the Ecovillage is to put into practice Berea's sustainability plan and to educate students and the community about environmentally sound practices. Goals include reducing energy use by 75 percent and achieving an overall recycling rate of at least 50 percent. The Commons House, also found in the Ecovillage, is the site of different ecological events and meetings. Although it is not LEED-certified, the Commons House was built with recycled materials and features energy-efficient appliances.

But the Ecovillage is just a small part of what Berea College is doing to achieve sustainability. Back in 2004, Berea's administrative building, Lincoln Hall, became the first LEED-certified building in the entire state of Kentucky. Considering the hall was built back in the late 1800s, it's even more impressive that the renovation achieved this status.

Dining services are getting in on the green act as well. Thanks to the Berea College Educational Farm and Gardens, students can truly enjoy local produce and meat. The school has also made a firm commitment to buy locally whenever possible. To complete the food chain, so to speak, food waste is composted for use in the gardens.

As at other schools, energy is a big issue at Berea. To reduce energy waste, the school has implemented compact fluorescent lightbulbs (CFLs) since 2004, and overall Berea hopes to reduce its energy use yearly. The installation of a new heating plant in 2006 has significantly reduced gas use on campus.

Berea, KY
Website: ***www.berea.edu***
Sustainability website: ***www.berea.edu/sens/default.asp***
Email contact address: N/A

INSIDE THE CLASSROOM

Berea College may not have the name recognition of other Southern schools, such as Duke or Emory, but it does have nationally recognized academics. One of the things that stands out most about Berea is the small class size. The average class at Berea has about 15 students. The school also boasts an impressive student-to-faculty ratio of only 10 to 1. In addition, teaching assistants never instruct courses at Berea; all courses are taught by professors.

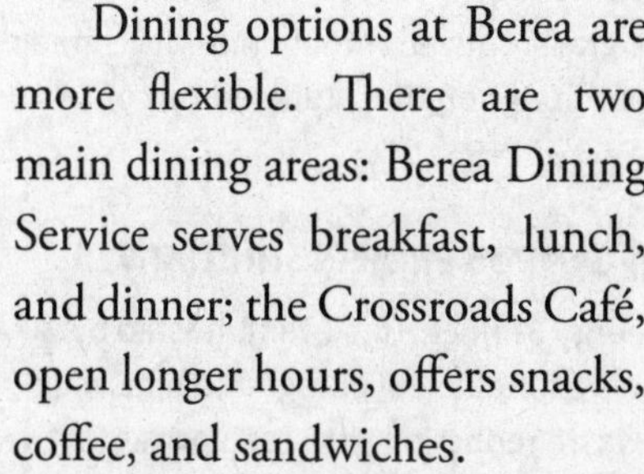

Students have their choice from among 32 different majors. One of Berea's 22 minors is sustainability and environmental studies, a choice that is becoming increasingly popular. And what if students are passionate about a topic that is not included in these majors? Berea offers students the opportunity to create an independent major of their choice. Past independent majors have included Asian studies and peace and justice studies. Finally, five preprofessional programs are offered at Berea. Whereas most majors can be declared during sophomore year, enrollment in one of these programs may be required during freshman year.

AROUND CAMPUS

Berea College is set in the small town (population 10,000) of Berea, Kentucky, which for the last 20 years has been recognized as the Arts and Crafts Capital of Kentucky. The campus itself is beautiful and small—students can get pretty much anywhere on campus in about ten minutes. If students want to go farther, they can take one of the school's free shuttles. During the week, the shuttles go between campus and town, on Friday they run to nearby Richmond, and on Saturdays they run into the city of Lexington.

Dining options at Berea are more flexible. There are two main dining areas: Berea Dining Service serves breakfast, lunch, and dinner; the Crossroads Café, open longer hours, offers snacks, coffee, and sandwiches.

STUDENT LIFE

Student life at Berea is completely unique for two reasons: convocations and the labor program. Whereas students in schools around the United States mostly just have to drag themselves out of bed for class and can spend the rest of their free time as they wish, Berea students are required to attend seven convocations each semester. These convocations include performances and speeches by notable people, so it's not as though they are uninteresting; they are nonetheless mandatory.

But it's not all about work. There are eight men's intercollegiate teams and eight women's intercollegiate teams, and about 65 percent of the student body participates in intramural sports. There are also dozens of student organizations on campus.

Bowdoin College

WHAT'S GREEN

GREEN ORGANIZATIONS/STUDENT GROUPS

- **The Evergreens**: This student group aims to raise environmental awareness on campus.
- **Bowdoin Outing Club**: There are 300 members in this organization, which plans trips to enjoy the natural beauty of Maine.
- **EcoReps**: These student representatives are part of a grassroots attempt to introduce green practices throughout the student body on campus.

GREEN CAMPUS PROJECTS/INITIATIVES

- **Dorm Energy Project**: This event, hosted by Bowdoin's EcoReps, encourages campuswide energy waste reduction with cash prizes to motivate students.
- **CFL Lightbulb Project**: Every year, this project has expanded to increase the use of CFLs (compact fluorescent lightbulbs) throughout the campus. Each bulb saves 75 percent energy over regular lightbulbs.
- **Dump and Run**: In their eagerness to get home for the summer, students at Bowdoin were tossing out their belongings to hasten the moving process. Rather than see perfectly good items go to the dump, Bowdoin started Dump and Run—students can donate unwanted items, which are then sold and the profits donated to local charities.

GREEN COURSES OFFERED

- Marine Environmental Geology
- Behavioral Ecology and Population Biology
- Community, Ecosystem, and Global Change Ecology
- Environmental Law
- Watershed Hydrology
- Telling Environmental Stories

According to current available statistics from the Sustainable Endowments Institute, Bowdoin College is only one of seven schools in the United States that gets 100 percent of its electricity from renewable resources or purchases enough alternative energy credits to offset its fossil fuel–based electricity use. Some buildings are running on alternative fuels, such as biodiesel and even cooking oil from campus dining halls. In addition, the school has signed the Presidents Climate Commitment and the rigorous Maine Governor's Carbon Challenge. The end goal of the challenge is for Bowdoin to reduce its greenhouse emissions to more than 10 percent below its 2002 emission levels.

But Bowdoin's commitment to the environment does not stop at energy sources. New construction, such as the Watson Arena, must meet LEED standards. Two dormitories are LEED-certified, and renovations to The Bricks include measures to increase energy efficiency. Even when Bowdoin demolishes a building, it practices environmentalism. In 2002, a campus house was demolished, and instead of carting the remains off to the landfill, the college recycled or reused almost 100 percent of the waste.

To ensure that sustainable practices are used in dining services, Bowdoin has started its own gardens. Fresh herbs are grown on campus, and in July 2007, a student-run garden became certified organic. In addition, Bowdoin purchases all of its naturally fed beef locally—the school even has its own butcher shop. Waste has been reduced because of alternative packaging and disposal programs, and food scraps are used for compost, which is in turn used in Bowdoin's gardens.

Even the campus bookstore is getting in on the act. Not only does the store sell several eco-friendly products, such as reusable mugs and recycled greeting cards, but practices such as reusing packaging materials and recycling printer cartridges have been put into effect.

Brunswick, ME
Website: www.bowdoin.edu
Sustainability website: www.bowdoin.edu/sustainablebowdoin
Email contact address: admissions@bowdoin.edu

INSIDE THE CLASSROOM

Despite its relatively remote location, Bowdoin College has almost no problem attracting students with its impressive academics. Bowdoin offers more than 600 courses and a choice of more than 30 majors to undergraduates. One major that is increasingly popular, attracting about 45 students per year, is the environmental studies (ES) coordinate major—for example, Spanish/ES or Philosophy/ES. Bowdoin also has several renowned interdisciplinary majors, including art history and visual arts, English and theater, and geology and chemistry—to name a few. Thanks to cutting-edge facilities, most notably its microscale labs, Bowdoin's science departments have excellent reputations.

The quality of academics at any school relies heavily on its faculty. Bowdoin has more than 160 full-time faculty members of which almost 100 percent hold a terminal degree. Because class size is very small, fewer than 20, Bowdoin students receive personalized attention. First-year students are especially integrated into Bowdoin academics by participating in first-year seminars. These required courses for all incoming freshmen are meant to help students think critically and improve research skills.

AROUND CAMPUS

Students who are looking for natural beauty and a rural setting are sure to put Bowdoin at the top of their lists. The 205-acre campus is surrounded by beautiful Maine wilderness. Its location near forests, rivers, and the Atlantic coastline means that the "great outdoors" is as much a part of the campus as anything else.

One of the most popular features of residential life is dining. True to the school's dedication to the environment, food is grown locally and prepared fresh. Whether students dine at either of the two dining halls they are sure to find something delicious to keep them sustained during long hours of studying.

STUDENT LIFE

Because the nearest major city, Portland, is a 30-minute drive from campus, many students opt for spending time in the nearby town of Brunswick. This quaint and quiet Maine town is complete with restaurants, stores, a movie theater, a bowling alley, and bars. Overall, the school's location means that the center of social life is undoubtedly on campus.

Bowdoin students may work hard, but they also play hard—literally. There are 31 varsity teams (men's, women's, and coed). Intramural sports and club sports (including ultimate frisbee) have lots of participants as well.

In addition to the athletics program, more than 100 clubs and organizations cater to interests as varied as breakdancing, math, and yoga.

Carleton College

WHAT'S GREEN

GREEN ORGANIZATIONS/STUDENT GROUPS ON CAMPUS

- **SOPE (Students Organized for the Protection of the Environment):** This group encourages environmental activism and awareness on campus and beyond.
- **Carleton Farm Club:** These students grow organic produce on campus.
- **KFC (Kids for Conservation):** Not limiting themselves to promoting environmentalism among college students, this group extends its message to local elementary schools.

GREEN CAMPUS PROJECTS/INITIATIVES

- **Yellow Bikes and Green Bikes:** The Yellow Bike program fixes up old bicycles, paints them yellow, and provides them to students for use on campus. The Green Bike program, initiated by SOPE, offers students access to bicycles for use off campus. Both programs aim to minimize the need for and use of cars on campus.
- **Green Roof Project:** A green roof is what it sounds like—a roof with green growth on it. The result is energy savings (good insulation) and less water runoff waste.
- **Single-Stream Recycling:** Recycling just got easier—instead of students having to sort their recyclables, Carleton now offers one bin and sorts the items later. This program is expected to result in 30 percent more items being recycled.

GREEN COURSES OFFERED

- Environment and Society: Challenges of the 21st Century
- Environmental Ethics
- Principles of Environmental Chemistry
- Economics of Natural Resources and the Environment
- Biodiversity, Conservation, and Development
- Climate Warming and the Changing Arctic Landscape

The same way everything Midas touched turned to gold, it seems that everything Carleton College touches turns to green. But what makes Carleton such a standout among the schools across the country that are doing so much to improve the environment? Well, to start with, it received the honorable recognition of being both a College Sustainability Leader and an Endowment Sustainability Leader by the Sustainable Endowments Institute.

Some of the practices that helped earn this important recognition include purchasing food from local farmers, composting, and single-stream recycling. Dining services have also gone organic—all of the beef is grass-fed and all of the flour is organic.

The campus buildings themselves are also participating. All new construction will meet LEED standards, and existing buildings have been renovated to reduce energy waste. Currently, the school owns and operates a 1.65-megawatt wind turbine. Although this turbine does not provide the campus with energy directly, it shows Carleton's commitment to investing in alternative energy resources.

When it comes to going green, it couldn't be done without the support of Carleton's students. One of the most notable environmental organizations on campus is SOPE (Students Organized for the Protection of the Environment), which has revolutionized transportation both on and off campus. Through the Yellow Bike and Green Bike Programs, students are allowed to use these free, well-maintained bikes for getting to classes or heading into town. To keep tabs on all the excellent environmental efforts made at the school, Carleton students recently launched the Shrinking Footprints (as in carbon footprint) blog.

Northfield, MN
Website: www.carleton.edu
Sustainability website: http://apps.carleton.edu/campus/sustainability
Email contact address: admissions@acs.carleton.edu

INSIDE THE CLASSROOM

Carleton is a well-respected liberal arts college known for its dedicated staff and for the comprehensive but individual education offered to its students. With 190 of the 200 full-time faculty holding a terminal degree and an impressive student-to-faculty ratio of 9 to 1, it's no wonder that many Carleton graduates go on to receive prestigious fellowships and job opportunities.

To help first-year students embrace a liberal arts education, the first-year seminars, which encourage critical thinking and independence, are offered. Class size is limited for these seminars, but there are a variety of other courses to choose from as well. In addition to the more than 40 majors offered, 15 different special concentrations—from archaeology to—you guessed it—environmental and technology studies are available.

To support what is taught in the classroom, Carleton is home to plenty of academic facilities. The Laurence McKinley Gould Library (Gould or "the Libe" for short) is home to more than half a million books, not counting 8,000 volumes in the special collections.

AROUND CAMPUS

Northfield is only 45 minutes from the twin cities of Minneapolis and St. Paul, which offer everything a certified city dweller could want: theaters, restaurants, sporting events, and shopping. However, many students don't ever feel the need to leave the beautiful Carleton campus. Just one look at the 400-acre Cowling Arboretum, and you will know why Carleton students are so passionate about the environment.

It's a good thing the campus is beautiful, because students are required to live on campus in one of the nine residence halls or 38 residence houses all four years.

STUDENT LIFE

One thing that can be said for Carleton is that it has many traditions. The school year opens with "bubbles"—when faculty blow soap bubbles after the opening convocation. Students get their payback at 10:00 P.M. the night before finals—stressed-out students screech at the top of their lungs during "primal scream."

Athletics are another popular way of relieving stress. There are 19 men's and women's varsity sports—from soccer to synchronized swimming. In addition, there are about a half dozen intramural teams and another 20 or so club sports to choose from.

Clubs and organizations are another popular way to broaden the college experience. There are at least six nature and environmental organizations at Carleton, along with the usual performing arts, political, and religious groups. Students who are looking for a unique organization might try the Moustache Club or the Carleton Anime Club.

Carnegie Mellon University

WHAT'S GREEN

GREEN ORGANIZATIONS/STUDENT GROUPS

- **Sustainable Earth:** This student organization promotes environmental awareness on campus and around Pittsburgh.
- **Solar Splash:** This group builds solar-powered boats to race in competitions.

GREEN CAMPUS PROJECTS/INITIATIVES

- **Recyclemania:** Each year, Carnegie Mellon joins more than 200 other schools and universities in a friendly competition to see which school can recycle the most.
- **Eco-Reps:** This program designates students as Eco-Reps who help educate others on campus about ecological practices.
- **Painless Environmentalism:** This campaign aims to prevent student apathy by advertising effective and simple ways to preserve the environment.

GREEN COURSES OFFERED

- Visualizing the Global Footprint
- Management, Environment, and Ethics
- Sustainability
- Environmental Decision Making
- Environmental Rhetoric
- Economics of the Environment and Natural Resources

One of Carnegie Mellon University's earliest attempts at going green came about back in 1990 when the school initiated an official recycling policy (the school currently recycles about 18 percent of its waste). Eight years later, CMU established the Green Practices Committee, which is comprised of staff, students, and faculty dedicated to making CMU greener every year. In October 2007, CMU took some of its green practices off campus: the school participated in the Solar Decathlon and displayed its solar-powered green building (named TriPod for its three rooms).

Clearly, green building is important to CMU. Currently, the school's building policy requires all new construction to meet a minimum silver-level LEED rating. There are six LEED buildings on campus, with more buildings planned or being built. One literally green feature on four CMU buildings is a green roof, with turf and/or other plants keeping them cooler in the summer and warmer in the winter and protecting the structure.

Carnegie Mellon has made several other advances in making the school more sustainable. One major initiative is the purchasing of wind turbine energy to account for 5 percent of the school's energy needs. To help offset the increased cost of wind energy, the school is planning campuswide conservation efforts. This includes the Sleep Is Good campaign, which encourages students to switch their computer monitors to sleep mode to reduce unnecessary energy waste.

Recently, the school switched its shuttle buses to run on biodiesel, and Facilities Management has purchased several zero-emission electric vehicles for use by its staff.

INSIDE THE CLASSROOM

Although founded in the early 20th century as a technical school, Carnegie Mellon University wasted

Pittsburgh, PA
Website: www.cmu.edu
Sustainability website: www.cmu.edu/greenpractices
Email contact address: undergraduate-admissions@andrew.cmu.edu

no time in broadening its academic programs and establishing itself as a premier educational institution. Indeed, today CMU offers undergraduates an impressive 90 different majors and minors. Carnegie Mellon actually has six different undergraduate colleges, depending on their academic interests. For students who really can't decide, there are even two intercollege degree programs.

Almost all programs provide students with opportunities for hands-on, practical experience. To encourage students to pursue research, CMU offers financial grants to students. The Small Undergraduate Research Grants (SURG) help students to cover research expenses, and summer fellowships give students financial freedom to complete full-time research during the summer break. To further reinforce the importance of student research, CMU holds an annual "Meeting of the Minds," which celebrates and honors undergraduate students who have conducted research projects throughout the year. Top-notch facilities on campus are yet another reason why research is a popular choice for students.

AROUND CAMPUS

Carnegie Mellon's 140-acre campus is located in the Oakland neighborhood of Pittsburgh, five miles from the downtown area. Since 1996, the epicenter of campus life at Carnegie Mellon has undoubtedly been the University Center. The UC not only offers rooms for club and other organization meetings but also provides recreational areas for activities such as racquetball and swimming.

Because CMU is located in a city, the availability of housing is very important. All first-year students are required to live on campus, and thankfully, students are guaranteed housing all four years. One of the newest dorms on campus is the New House, home to more than 250 students, which is the first LEED-certified building on campus.

STUDENT LIFE

When it comes to extracurricular activities, CMU has lots to offer to its students. There are about 225 different student organizations to choose from. For those students who are interested in athletics, CMU offers 17 Division III varsity teams. Intramural sports are also very popular, with the intramural program offering basketball, football, soccer, and badminton, to name a few.

What would college life be without campus traditions? One of the most famous CMU traditions is "painting the Fence" (used as an unofficial campus billboard, the Fence is painted by students only at night, and then they must guard their handiwork until sunrise). Other traditions include the Spring Carnival, which includes buggy races, and during the long winter months, "traying" (using cafeteria trays as sleds).

College of the Atlantic

WHAT'S GREEN

GREEN ORGANIZATIONS/STUDENT GROUPS

- **Outing Club:** This group uses the school's outdoor equipment for trips around the Maine wilderness.
- **Social and Environmental Action (SEA):** This group focuses on direct action in improving environmental practices on campus.
- **World Citizens for Social, Environmental, and Economic Justice:** This student organization aims to achieve justice for all.

GREEN CAMPUS PROJECTS/INITIATIVES

- **Farm to Food:** This program ensures that students eat local, fresh, and sustainable produce.
- **Zero Waste Graduation:** Students and staff plan the entire year so that literally nothing goes to waste during the week of graduation. This includes everything from the reusable containers the celebratory food is shipped in to the compostable plates and utensils.
- **Beech Hill Farm:** This farm, which includes 5 acres of certified organic farmland and 65 acres of forest, doubles as an outdoor classroom for students.

GREEN COURSES OFFERED

- Plants in the Campus Landscape
- Issues in National Park Planning
- Land Use Planning
- Agroecology
- Conservation Biology
- Edible Botany
- River Ecology

Everything at the College of the Atlantic is about as green as it can be. From the education itself to the buildings in which the students learn, COA is making significant efforts to reduce its negative environmental impact.

The newest construction on COA's campus is also set to be the greenest. The Kathryn W. Davis Residence Village—which will soon be the school's largest residence—is being built with dedication to environmentalism. Many of the key features of this residence focus on energy efficiency. Windows are triple-glazed, and the entire building is heavily insulated. The village will also feature composting toilets and other water-conserving methods, such as the reuse of gray water. And of course, compact fluorescent lamps (CFLs) are used wherever possible, and all cleaning supplies are virtually toxin-free.

Even though COA is a small school, classrooms require a lot of supplies. Students can recycle ink cartridges on campus, and the paper used at COA is chlorine- and dioxin-free and comprised of 60 percent postconsumer waste. All other office supplies come from a vendor that recycles and offers products, which come with environmental certifications.

One of the most astonishing green achievements made by the College of the Atlantic is that the school is carbon net zero. While many other American schools have pledged to achieve this feat by 2050, COA made it happen in December 2007—just over a year after making the pledge to achieve this goal—becoming the first school in the United States to succeed. While it is impossible to be carbon zero (no greenhouse gases emitted), since students and faculty need to drive or fly at some point during their time at COA, the school has made immense efforts to offset any emissions produced.

Bar Harbor, ME
Website: www.coa.edu
Sustainability website: www.coa.edu/html/sustainability.htm
Email contact address: inquiry@coa.edu

INSIDE THE CLASSROOM

The College of the Atlantic, quite simply, is not like other institutes of higher education in the United States. That is not to say that it isn't a "real" school—it is accredited by the New England Association of Schools and Colleges. What really makes COA different is the education. It is a very small school, and every student graduates with the same degree—a BA in human ecology, a field of study that focuses on how humans interact with their environment.

At COA, there are no formal majors and no specific academic departments. Instead, courses are divided into three categories: Arts and Design, Environmental Science, and Human Studies. Each of these offers a wide variety of courses, and students are responsible for creating individualized courses of study to receive their degrees.

Some aspects of a COA education are similar to those of other more traditional schools. For example, students can complete independent study projects, they can participate in internships, and they can even study abroad. In fact, almost 63 percent of the student body studied abroad in 2007.

AROUND CAMPUS

A school that places such a heavy emphasis on the environment is completely in sync with the gorgeous natural surroundings at COA. Acadia National Park is nearby, but the campus itself is just as beautiful. It is set on 35 acres of Mount Desert Island near the town of Bar Harbor. The greater campus is also comprised of the 81-acre Beech Hill Organic Farm and Forest, Mount Desert Rock, and Great Duck Island.

As you might imagine, COA makes an effort to make student housing as comfortable and intimate as its education. There are no massive dorms or residence halls at COA. In fact, the largest existing housing facility, Seafox, is home to only 22 students.

STUDENT LIFE

With only 325 students, life at COA is unique. As the school itself promotes, "It's impossible to fade into the woodwork." To keep students engaged, the school plans many student activities. These include concerts and field trips. There are also three student organizations, two of which focus exclusively on environmental issues.

There are no varsity sports at COA, but students are incredibly active. There are club sports such as soccer, volleyball, and basketball, but independent outdoor activities attract the most students. COA offers students kayaks, canoes, and even sailboats to enjoy. Another popular activity is scuba diving, which is taught by the YMCA.

Dartmouth College

WHAT'S GREEN

GREEN ORGANIZATIONS/STUDENT GROUPS

- **The Green Magazine:** This quarterly magazine is written by students for students to keep them informed about environmental issues and sustainability.
- **Sustainable Dartmouth:** This sustainability organization spearheaded the Sustainable Move-In and Move-Out program to reduce solid waste and promote recycling.
- **ECO (Environmental Conservation Organization):** This student group aims to educate the community about recycling, composting, and other environmental initiatives.

GREEN CAMPUS PROJECTS/INITIATIVES

- **Dartmouth Organic Farm:** This student-run organic farm doubles as a teaching and research facility. Students can get their hands dirty year-round.
- **Sustainable Move-In and Move-Out:** This student-led initiative was intended to prevent unnecessary waste. Rather than throw away items, students were encouraged to donate items to be sold for profit, thus saving space in local landfills.
- **The Big Green Bus:** This bus, conceived by Dartmouth students, roams the United States informing citizens about the dependency on and dangers of fossil fuels. The bus actually runs on vegetable oil waste, which is normally thrown away. Oh, and the bus also promotes ultimate frisbee.

GREEN COURSES OFFERED

- Introduction to Environmental Science
- Population, Consumption, & Sustainability
- Eating Is an Agricultural Act
- Conservation of Biodiversity
- Environmental Justice Movements in the USA
- Environment & Politics in Southeast Asia

When your school's nickname is "The Big Green," there's a sort of built-in pressure to perform when it comes to green issues. In 2005, Dartmouth created the Dartmouth Sustainability Initiative to help reduce its negative impact on the environment and promote sound and sustainable environmental practices.

What makes Dartmouth's efforts so remarkable is their variety. Dining halls are composting food waste, and only eggs from cage-free chickens are used on campus. Efforts are also being made to reduce energy waste. Some buildings are being retrofitted for green features, and newly constructed buildings aim to achieve LEED certification.

In addition to the Energy Task Force, student organizations are leading the way to sustainability. Dartmouth's students should be commended for their efforts to reduce waste with the Sustainable Move-In and Sustainable Move-Out, both coordinated by Sustainable Dartmouth. The school's *Green Magazine* works to promote green efforts and awareness, and students have clearly responded well.

INSIDE THE CLASSROOM

Dartmouth, the only Ivy League school to refer to itself as a college, was founded in 1769 and has a long history of providing a high-quality liberal arts education. That reputation is well earned. Nearly 1,600 courses are offered at the college, and there are 29 different departments to choose from.

Students don't shine only in the classroom. The school encourages all of its students to pursue the numerous research opportunities available. The unique "D-plan," which divides the academic year into four quarters corresponding with the seasons, allows students more flexibility when scheduling course work, internships, and other projects.

Hanover, NH
Website: www.dartmouth.edu
Sustainability website: www.dartmouth.edu/~sustain
Email contact address: admissions.office@dartmouth.edu

There is also a robust study abroad program. Undergrads have a choice of 40 Dartmouth programs that span 20 different countries. This makes a Dartmouth education a truly global one.

From this global perspective, on Earth Day 1996, Dartmouth faculty voted to approve a major in Environmental Studies. It was actually a quarter of a century earlier that the Environmental Studies Program (ENVS) first launched at Dartmouth. The program and the major are interdisciplinary, focusing on science, law, economics, history, and other studies relevant to the environment. The program not only has its own library (Hornig) but also its own study abroad opportunity. Each year, 20 Dartmouth undergrads have a chance to complete a program in South Africa. This program is designed to give a real-life setting to the problems and solutions studied on campus.

AROUND CAMPUS

The Dartmouth Green, which was established a year after the school was founded, is both the literal and figurative heart of the Dartmouth College campus. This beautiful five acres is also the setting of the school's yearly events, such as the homecoming bonfire and commencement.

The rest of the 265-acre campus is also stunning. It is home to 200 buildings and facilities, not the least impressive of which are the residential buildings. Eighty-five percent of students live on campus in buildings that are owned, operated, and/or affiliated with Dartmouth. For those who prefer time on their own, a large percentage of rooms are singles—a true luxury on any college campus.

There are several dining facilities on campus. Whether students go to East Wheelock for a late-night pizza or REMIX for a smoothie, they're sure to find something to satisfy their appetites.

STUDENT LIFE

Ivy League schools have a reputation for their academics, but there is so much more to life than studying. Not only is Dartmouth Ivy League, it is also NCAA Division I. There are a total of 34 varsity sports, ranging from football to squash. Also, 21 club sports are offered throughout the year, including kung fu, figure skating, and even ultimate frisbee teams.

For students looking for strictly social outlets, there is the coed, fraternity, and sorority (CFS) community. There are 28 CFS organizations, including 9 sororities, 16 fraternities, and 3 coed organizations.

Numerous clubs and special interest organizations are available as well. If the green organizations don't pique a student's interest, that student can check out the Dartmouth Outdoor Club or the Dartmouth Symphony Orchestra. With over 350 to choose from, students are sure to find a club or organization that meets their needs.

Dickinson College

WHAT'S GREEN

GREEN ORGANIZATIONS/STUDENT GROUPS

- **Dickinson Student Garden/Sustainable Agriculture:** This group is responsible for tending to the Dickinson sustainable garden.
- **EarthNow!:** This organization is dedicated to all aspects of environmentalism on Dickinson's campus.
- **Outing Club:** Since this group enjoys the great outdoors, it indirectly supports environmental conservation.

GREEN CAMPUS PROJECTS/INITIATIVES

- **Caught Green-Handed:** To encourage students who are already doing something to help the environment, a sustainability intern rewards students who are "caught" doing so.
- **Step It Up 2007:** Dickinson joined schools from around the country to unite in an effort to convince Congress to drastically reduce carbon emissions by 2050.
- **Blogging:** Who doesn't have a blog these days? Still, they are as popular and effective as ever, which is why the sustainability office maintains one on its website.

GREEN COURSES OFFERED

- Environment, Culture, and Values
- Environmental Science
- Environmental Geology
- Ecology
- Wild Resource Management
- Analysis and Management of the Aquatic Environment

In 2007, Dickinson College received the prestigious distinction of being one of the Sustainable Endowments Institute's Campus Sustainability Leaders—with good reason. In 2007, Dickinson made great strides with regards to sustainability. In June, Dickinson president William Durdan signed the Presidents Climate Commitment. A short three months later, Dickinson began meeting a full 50 percent of its electricity needs from alternative energy—in this case, wind power. The school also got an impressive number of solar panels installed at Kaufman Hall.

Not only must all major construction on campus meet LEED silver standards, but the special interest residence, Treehouse, is aiming for a gold standard. To reduce energy and solid waste on campus, Dickinson participated in the national RecycleMania competition. Not satisfied to attempt this just once, the school initiated the Green Devil Challenge to see which residence halls, offices, and buildings could reduce utility use by 15 percent. The winner? The entire campus! Every participating team rose to the challenge, making the environment the real winner.

The dining halls at Dickinson are another place where green has taken over. To start, most of the produce served on campus comes from just down the road. About six miles from campus is a 30-acre farm that is home to the Dickinson College Garden. What started in 1999 as a small student farm run by two environmental studies majors is now a thriving space adhering to sustainable agricultural practices.

INSIDE THE CLASSROOM

Dickinson is a well-respected liberal arts college. Students have a choice of 40 different majors, including such

Carlisle, PA
Website: www.dickinson.edu
Sustainability website: www.dickinson.edu/departments/sustainability
Email contact address: admit@dickinson.edu

green topics as environmental studies and environmental science. But that's not all: Dickinson students can also major in such varied subjects as neuroscience, Russian area studies, and religion. Additionally, students can choose to double major or even develop their own unique majors. There are even nine so-called "special programs" in astronomy, film studies, and Japanese, to name a few.

As impressive as the variety of majors at Dickinson is the faculty. There are 208 faculty members, with 95 percent holding a terminal degree. Dickinson students have easy access to this esteemed faculty, as the student-to-teacher ratio is 12 to 1. Small class sizes further encourage interaction with faculty. The average class size at Dickinson is only 18 students.

The opportunity to study off campus is almost always appealing to college students. There are 12 Dickinson-run programs in wide-flung regions, such as Asia, Africa, and Australia.Other interesting options are programs within the United States. For example, students can choose to earn a joint baccalaureate and law degree with the 3-3 program with Penn State School of Law.

AROUND CAMPUS

The town of Carlisle, Pennsylvania, is only slightly older than Dickinson College. With a population of around 20,000, it can hardly be described as a bustling metropolis, but it is lovely. The town is found in central Pennsylvania in the Cumberland Valley. If you're not up on your geography, it might help to know that Carlisle is about a two hour drive to Philadelphia and only a four hour drive to New York City.

The main campus at Dickinson occupies about 90 acres plus another 30 acres of recreational area. First-year students typically have the most structured arrangements, while upper-class students can live in apartment-style housing complete with kitchens.

STUDENT LIFE

Students really have their choice when it comes to how to spend their free time. First, there are about 120 different student clubs and organizations. These include academic, religious, multicultural, and media organizations. Social life is also fleshed out with Greek activities. Fraternities have been on the Dickinson campus for more than 150 years.

Sports are also very popular at Dickinson. There are 21 varsity teams. Some highlights among the ten men's teams are baseball, football, and basketball, and some of the particularly great women's teams are lacrosse, basketball, and cross-country. Students who don't play love to come out and support the Red Devils. Also, 38 different recreational teams include seven club sports, such as ice hockey and equestrian sports.

Duke University

WHAT'S GREEN

GREEN ORGANIZATIONS/STUDENT GROUPS

- **Environmental Alliance:** This group supports environmental issues on campus.
- **Duke Bike Advocates:** This group is unique in that it pairs an experienced rider with a novice so that the inexperienced rider can learn safe bicycle routes to, from, and around campus.
- **Project WILD:** This student-run orientation group shows students how to survive in and appreciate the wilderness.

GREEN CAMPUS PROJECTS/INITIATIVES

- **Low-Flow Giveaway:** In December 2007, Duke University gave away 5,000 low-flow shower heads to any Duke student or employee who wanted one. Each head is designed to save more than 7,000 gallons of water per year.
- **Home Depot Smart Home:** This ten-person residence hall is both dormitory and living lab. Its ecological design makes it a contender for a gold-level LEED rating.
- **Autoflush:** To minimize the school's impact on water resources, the school is investigating the possibility of installing automatic flushing toilets in an effort to reduce water waste.

GREEN COURSES OFFERED

- Environment as Community
- World Trade in Energy
- GIS and Geospatial Analysis
- Economics of the Environment
- Into the Woods: The Duke Forest
- Ethical Challenges of Environmental Conservation

The campus of Duke University has changed a lot in recent years. Several new buildings have been constructed and others renovated. It's important then that since 2003, Duke has committed to having all new construction and major renovations meet LEED certification standards. In fact, the same year that Duke committed to LEED standards, it was honored with having the first LEED-certified dorm renovation in the United States.

Because the university is the largest consumer of water resources in all of Durham, water conservation is a big deal on campus. In late 2007, the school's president sent out an email soliciting tips from students about ways in which water could be conserved. There is even a specific water conservation website (*www.duke.edu/sustainability/water/conservation.html*) where students can report leaks around campus. The end result is that Duke has reduced its water use by 30 million gallons in just one year.

Energy is another area in which Duke hopes to improve. To start, first-year students are provided with free compact fluorescent lightbulbs (CFLs) in exchange for less efficient ones. And after inventorying the school's greenhouse gas emissions, Duke has gone on to investigate ways in which alternative energy sources can be implemented on campus.

Getting around on campus is another way that Duke is going green. Not only have the Duke Bike Advocates had an impact on how students and faculty get around, but also more than 30 of the school's vehicles run on nonfossil fuels.

INSIDE THE CLASSROOM

Duke University was founded in 1924 when a generous endowment helped expand the existing Trinity Col-

Durham, NC
Website: www.duke.edu
Sustainability website: www.duke.edu/sustainability
Email contact address: N/A

lege into Duke University. Today, the university is comprised of nine schools: the Trinity College of Arts and Sciences, the Pratt School of Engineering, the School of Law, the Divinity School, the Graduate School, the School of Medicine, the School of Nursing, the Nicholas School of the Environment and Earth Sciences, and the Fuqua School of Business.

Undergrads at Duke are privy to a top-notch education. There are more than 40 majors and minors to choose from, including environmental sciences and environmental sciences and policy. Prior to graduation, students at Trinity must complete general education requirements, whereas Pratt students, regardless of their specialization, are required to complete basic engineering degree requirements.

Duke feels that studying abroad gives students a global perspective on their learning. The United Kingdom, Italy, Spain, and Australia are among the most popular countries for studying abroad.

AROUND CAMPUS

Durham, North Carolina, has all the charm of a small Southern city, but it is dominated by the sprawling Duke University campus. The entire campus is a whopping 8,610 acres, which include a golf course, three school campuses, a marine lab, and the wonderful Duke Forest. The forest, which alone is 7,200 acres, acts both as a learning lab for Duke students and as a recreation area for hikers, walkers, and picnickers.

If you happen to know anyone who graduated from Duke even ten years ago, that alum would need a guided tour today, because so many new buildings have been completed in the last few years. These buildings join the hundreds of other Duke buildings, such as the nationally renowned libraries and the easily recognizable Duke Chapel.

STUDENT LIFE

Because Duke is, after all, a Southern school, Greek life is big on campus. There are no fewer than 40 different Greek organizations, including various sororities, fraternities, and councils. However, this is just a small fraction of the 300 or so student organizations found at Duke. Whether students' interests lie in politics, activism, cultural affairs, or the arts, they will find other students with similar interests on campus.

One aspect of student life that has earned national renown is athletics. Duke, whose team name is the Blue Devils, participates in 26 NCAA Division I varsity sports. Some of the most notable teams are the nationally recognized men's basketball team, which won the National Championships most recently in 2001, and the women's basketball team, which reached the final four in the 2006 NCAA tournament.

Grand Valley State University

WHAT'S GREEN

GREEN ORGANIZATIONS/STUDENT GROUPS

- **Student Environmental Coalition:** This group works with the Sustainability Office to educate students about sustainability and conservation.
- **Recycling Advocacy Club:** This club works to reduce waste and promote recycling at GVSU.
- **Soil and Water Conservation Society (SWCS):** The SWCS works in the greater community to clean and preserve natural habitats and resources.

GREEN CAMPUS PROJECTS/INITIATIVES

- **The Rapid Bus System:** GVSU has several hybrid-electric buses to transport off-campus students to and from school.
- **Project E!:** This project is spearheaded by one student who is passionate about reducing paper waste by encouraging the proliferation of electronic documents.
- **Energy Conservation Competition:** In November 2007, GVSU communities' energy consumption was monitored and compared to energy consumption in November 2006. The winning community could choose a prize such as an Energy Star appliance or free sustainability training.

GREEN COURSES OFFERED

- Environmental Science
- Environmental and Resource Economics
- Ecology of the Great Lakes
- Environmental Ethics
- Global Environmental Change
- Geology and the Environment

It's easy for big schools with even bigger endowments to ramp up their sustainability programs. But what about schools with significantly smaller endowments which are nonetheless doing their part to improve the environment. Grand Valley State University is one of those schools recognized by the Sustainability Endowments Institute. For its efforts, GVSU earned a 2008 Sustainability Innovator Award.

Obviously, this school is making the most of its endowment. There seems to be no limit to what GVSU is doing to go green. To start, the school has tried to incorporate more environmentally themed courses into its catalog. GVSU even publishes its own "Student Sustainability Guide." There's also a full-time sustainability director at GVSU.

Other GVSU initiatives include the adoption of LEED certification as the standard for all construction on campus. More LEED-certified buildings at the very least mean greater energy efficiency. To reduce energy waste, the school has installed occupancy sensors so that lights do not remain on in unoccupied rooms. Water waste has been drastically reduced thanks to waterless urinals and various low-flow features on toilets and showers.

INSIDE THE CLASSROOM

While Grand Valley State University might not be the most recognized name on our list, it does provide a quality education. There are seven different colleges to choose from: the Padnos College of Engineering and Computing, the Kirkhof College of Nursing, the College of Education, the Seidman College of Business, the College of Health Professions, the College of Interdisciplinary Studies, the College of Community and Public Services, and the College of Liberal Arts and Sciences

Allendale, MI
Website: www.gvsu.edu
Sustainability website: www.gvsu.edu/sustainability
Email contact address: admissions@gvsu.edu

(CLAS). Students also have 69 majors to choose from among 200 areas of study. Whether students want to study German, dance, or behavioral science, they will find it at GVSU.

The dedicated faculty at GVSU is always on hand to help students with their needs. Courses are always taught by professors—never by graduate students. However, the presence of graduate students does provide a great opportunity for undergrads, because undergrads who are looking for a challenge can participate in graduate-level research.

For students who want to see more of the world than Allendale, Michigan, can offer, GVSU has a seemingly unlimited number of study abroad programs—3,900 in all! The Ukraine, Turkey, Egypt—no part of the globe seems to be off-limits.

AROUND CAMPUS

There are two different GVSU campuses. The main one is in Allendale, while the other has a more urban setting in Grand Rapids—as mentioned, a free shuttle links the two. With prime locations near Lake Michigan, the school seems to have a little of everything to offer its students.

One of the biggest selling points of the GVSU campus is the fact that the student residences are some of the newest in the entire state. The traditional-style dorms are set aside for first-year students. There is also apartment-style housing in a choice of five different buildings. There are 11 different suite-style apartments, each housing four students. Finally, there are campus apartments: four campus apartment buildings in Allendale and another two in Grand Rapids. If upper-class students prefer theme housing, they can choose among honors, all-female, art, healthy living, or prelaw housing.

STUDENT LIFE

Louie the Laker, GVSU's mascot, watches over athletics at this NCAA Division II school. There are a total of eight men's varsity teams and another nine women's varsity teams. Football is extremely popular, especially when GVSU is playing its rivals at Ferris State University for the Anchor Bone Trophy. GVSU football won the 2005–06 National Championships, a feat also accomplished by the women's basketball and volleyball teams. Intramural sports, such as bowling, tennis, and golf, are a great alternative to varsity sports.

GVSU is proud to have nearly 300 student organizations to choose from. With areas of interest such as faith, culture, service, and sports, there is literally something for everyone. And what about students who want to go Greek? Well, they will have to narrow their choice to 1 of the 27 different Greek organizations on campus.

Harvard University

WHAT'S GREEN

GREEN ORGANIZATIONS/STUDENT GROUPS ON CAMPUS

- **Environmental Education Program (EnviroEd):** This group brings the message of environmental awareness to local middle school students.
- **Environmental Action Committee:** This group is based on campus but aims to educate the greater community about conservation and sustainability.
- **The Harvard Project for Sustainable Development (HPSD):** This organization promotes discussion about sustainability around the world in less-developed countries.

GREEN CAMPUS PROJECTS/INITIATIVES

- **Harvard Green Campus Initiative (HGCI):** This initiative, which employs 19 full-time staff and 40 part-time students, has a goal to make Harvard a sustainable campus.
- **Campus Energy Reduction Program:** This program, initiated by the HGCI, aims to inform and encourage students regarding energy conservation.
- **Sustainability Course:** This course, which teaches how sustainability can be achieved, is offered to any Harvard student, regardless of enrollment status or school.

GREEN COURSES OFFERED

- Environmental Science for Public Policy
- Environmental Politics
- Ecology and Land-Use Planning
- Conservation Biology
- Environmental Crises and Population Flight
- Global Change and Human Health

A school such as Harvard, which is often labeled with the superlative "the best," certainly has added motivation to be among the best at being green. So it's to the environment's benefit that Harvard has set out to do just that. So far, the results have been stellar. In fact, Harvard is among the top-rated schools for sustainability.

One of the most impressive achievements made by Harvard has been in the realm of recycling. Recycling is nothing new to the campus. In fact, in 2002, 34 percent of its waste was recycled. Those numbers have been steadily growing: a record 49.9 percent was recycled in November 2006, and this record was shattered in October 2007 when more than 50 percent was recycled. Efforts to show students exactly what can be recycled and where remain strong, and the hope remains of reaching a record 60 percent recycling rate.

Numbers and percentages are a great way to show performance and progress, so for the first time, the *Harvard University Fact Book 2007 edition,* contains information on greenhouse gas emissions, LEED-certified buildings (the numbers don't lie, Harvard has several LEED-certified buildings, including one with a platinum rating), water usage, and several other environmental issues. Harvard also garnered attention from the Environmental Protection Agency (EPA) for being one of the Ivy League schools that purchases the most renewable energy.

INSIDE THE CLASSROOM

Harvard is practically synonymous with stellar academics. While getting in may seem like the biggest challenge, graduating is no small feat either. All students must complete the CORE curriculum. The thrust of this curriculum is that students must dedicate 25 percent of their studies to seven disciplines: foreign cultures, historical study, literature and the arts, moral

Cambridge, MA
Website: www.harvard.edu
Sustainability website: www.greencampus.harvard.edu
Email contact address: N/A

reasoning, quantitative reasoning, science, and social analysis.

Aside from completing the CORE curriculum, students must choose a concentration (read: major); there are 41 to choose from. Students also have three unique programs to choose from. For first-year students, there is the Freshman Seminar, which has no letter grades and no exams. This seminar allows students to work closely with one of Harvard's many esteemed faculty members. The House Seminar offers students the opportunity to take a course offered in their residential house. These courses have themes such as nutrition and the public or the art and history of St. Petersburg; upon completion, students receive a letter grade. Finally, extra-departmental courses offer students the opportunity to take a non-CORE course.

The popularity of study abroad programs has skyrocketed in recent years—there has been a 313 percent increase in study abroad participation in the past seven years alone. The programs, particularly popular with language and literature students, take place in such diverse and exciting locations as Brazil, Australia, and China.

AROUND CAMPUS

There's no denying the beauty of Harvard's campus. Thankfully, first-year students are in the center of the action, since freshman dorms are found in the Yard, Apley Court, and the Union Dormitories. After freshman year, things change. Students go on to live in 1 of 12 different houses on campus. Residents live, eat, socialize, study, and even receive their diplomas in their house.

Dining services on campus serve both the students and the local economy. Local farmers and suppliers provide food to the campus. And naturally, any and all food waste at Harvard is composted.

STUDENT LIFE

Harvard students are not just high achievers in academics but also in sports. Harvard is an NCAA Division I school and boasts 20 men's varsity teams and 19 women's varsity teams. Everyone is ready to "go Crimson," especially during The Game. For students, it doesn't need further explanation, but to everyone else, that means the annual Harvard-Yale football game played near the end of each football season. Both club and intramural sports are also popular.

With such strenuous academics, you might think that students have no time for fun. On the contrary, there are hundreds of different clubs, organizations, and activities on campus. Interested in the arts and performance? Students can take their choice. Want to get more involved in government and politics? There is a club for that. They are only limited by their amount of free time.

Massachusetts Institute of Technology (MIT)

WHAT'S GREEN

GREEN ORGANIZATIONS/STUDENT GROUPS ON CAMPUS

- **Students for Global Sustainability:** This group is for both graduate and undergraduate students interested in sustainability and conservation.
- **Energy Club:** This organization studies the particular challenges related to energy sources on Earth.
- **Solar Electrical Vehicle Team:** This student organization builds and races cars that run on alternative energy sources.

GREEN CAMPUS PROJECTS/INITIATIVES

- **Green Living Series:** This is a series of lectures and discussions hosted by the Students for Global Sustainability about ways to integrate sustainable practices into how students live, shop, and eat.
- **Coffee Mug Project:** In an effort to reduce the need for disposable coffee cups, Campus Dining offers free mugs to students and discounts the price of coffee for students with reusable mugs.
- **Free Plants:** If you didn't already know, November 15 is America Recycles Day. It's also the day when MIT students can receive a free plant from the Share a Vital Earth (SAVE) club.

GREEN COURSES OFFERED

- Engineering for Sustainability
- Environmental Chemistry and Biology
- Environmental Health
- Global Change Science
- Environmental Microbiology
- The Earth System

You might expect a high-caliber science and technology school such as Massachusetts Institute of Technology to be on the forefront of efforts to improve sustainability—and you would be correct. MIT has been a pioneer with regards to green practices, which range from recycling to energy conservation to energy production to water conservation and even to retrofitting.

One of the earliest and most notable efforts made by MIT is in the realm of water conservation. There are low-flow toilets and urinals, aerated faucets, and low-flow shower heads throughout buildings on campus. In addition, water that cannot be used for drinking is re-routed to laboratories for alternative uses. Amazingly, in the eight years between 1997 and 2005, MIT reduced its water consumption by an astonishing 60 percent. Most recently, in 2006, MIT implemented a system for capturing rainwater for reuse in irrigation.

MIT is also a green leader in alternative energy and energy conservation. Today, MIT generates 80 percent of its own energy for 100 buildings on campus. This energy comes from a 20-megawatt gas turbine. The unique design of this turbine, which produces both electricity and heat, helped earn MIT the Energy Star Combining Heat and Power Award from the EPA and the U.S. Department of Energy in 2002. In addition to producing its own energy, MIT is serious about conserving it whenever possible. In 2006, the school implemented a plan to retrofit lights to more energy-efficient ones.

Recycling is yet another way MIT is working to conserve the environment. Its recycling has increased three-fold since 2000, and MIT enjoys an impressive 40 percent recycling rate.

Cambridge, MA
Website: www.mit.edu
Sustainability website: web.mit.edu/facilities/environmental
Email contact address: admissions@mit.edu

INSIDE THE CLASSROOM

Massachusetts Institute of Technology is comprised of six schools: the School of Architecture and Planning; the School of Engineering; the School of Humanities, Arts, and Social Sciences; the Sloan School of Management; the School of Science; and the Whitaker College of Health Sciences and Technology. All feature top-notch academics and some of the most impressive faculty in the nation.

Even though MIT is known for math and science, an undergraduate student is exposed to a broad education. By the time students have earned their BS degrees, they will have completed courses in math, science, humanities, arts, and social sciences, as well as in communications.

At MIT, there are several unique opportunities for first-year and undergraduate students. Freshmen can participate in Experimental Study Groups. These groups, comprised of only 50 students, approach education in a "learn by doing" style. Undergraduates can participate in the Undergraduate Research Opportunity Program (UROP) to research such interesting topics as cancer or nanotechnology. Also, Terrascope is a field-research program in the area of environmental issues.

AROUND CAMPUS

MIT's campus in Cambridge is comprised of 168 acres along the Charles River Basin. In 1916, the first group of interconnected buildings opened, and since then, the campus has expanded greatly. In recent years, MIT has seen the construction of several new buildings including the Zesiger Sports Fitness Center. MIT requires silver-level LEED rating for all new construction on campus.

Although not even first-year students are required to live on campus (those who live close enough to commute may do so), many students choose to live on campus. There are 11 institute houses and another 36 fraternity, sorority, and independent-living group houses.

STUDENT LIFE

Although MIT students may have a reputation for being brainy and studious, their social life at MIT is actually quite active. Not only are there 26 nationally affiliated fraternities and 5 nationally affiliated sororities, but there are also literally hundreds of student organizations on campus. Of particular interest to many MIT students is the *How to Get Around MIT* handbook, which aims to help students find the "nooks and crannies" of MIT. Independent Living Groups are another feature of life at MIT. ILCs are small, residential co-ops, although residency is not a requirement. There are five ILCs at MIT.

Not only are athletics a required aspect of an MIT education, but the majority of students voluntarily participate in 1 of the 20 intramural sports offered. There are also 30 club sports on campus. Not only that, but MIT has a whopping 41 NCAA Division III varsity teams.

Middlebury College

WHAT'S GREEN

GREEN ORGANIZATIONS/STUDENT GROUPS

- **Environmental Quality (EQ):** This group promotes environmental awareness at Middlebury.
- **Vermon'ers:** This group is comprised of students who love all aspects of Vermont, including its natural beauty.
- **Slow the Plow:** This group is responsible for the Middlebury College Organic Garden (MCOG).

GREEN CAMPUS PROJECTS/INITIATIVES

- **Middlebury College Organic Garden (MCOG):** This student-run organic garden located behind Bicentennial Hall grows food for campus dining and off-campus food shelters.
- **The Middlebury Green Fund:** Established in 2007, this fund is mean to ensure that environmental progress continues on Middlebury's campus.
- **Howard E. Woodlin Environmental Studies Colloquium Series:** Held weekly at the Hillcrest Environmental Center, this series aims to inform the greater Middlebury community about the importance of the environment and conservation.

GREEN COURSES OFFERED

- Natural Science and the Environment
- Conservation and Environmental Policy
- Nature's Meanings
- Geographic Information Systems
- Environmental Economics
- Human Origins, Culture, and Biodiversity

Middlebury is regarded nationally for its academics, but it has another reason for being renowned. With the creation of the environmental studies major back in 1965, it earned the recognition of being the first American university to offer such an area of study. Today, about 90 students choose this major each year, making it among the most popular at the school.

Not only did Middlebury earn the distinction of being one of the top six College Sustainability Leaders, according to the Sustainability Endowments Institute, but it even included sustainability as part of its mission statement when it was revised in 2006.

Other specific strides made by the school include signing the Presidents Climate Commitment, signing the Talloires Declaration, and hiring a full-time recycling coordinator. Middlebury has also expressed plans to be carbon-neutral by 2016. Other initiatives include lowering thermostats to 68 degrees, using biofuel in campus vehicles, and using a wind turbine at the recycling center. Clearly, the school does not take its environmental responsibility lightly—something that students and the greater community certainly appreciate.

INSIDE THE CLASSROOM

Middlebury College, which was founded in 1800, has a long history of providing an unparalleled education. It consistently ranks as one of the top ten liberal arts schools in the United States, and with good reason—the caliber of the academics is very high.

First-year students are immediately enrolled in a first-year seminar. These courses require a lot of writing, but small class sizes—no more than 15 students each—mean that freshmen are immediately connected with a professor.

Middlebury, VT
Website: www.middlebury.edu
Sustainability website: www.middlebury.edu/administration/enviro
Email contact address: admissions@middlebury.edu

Nearly all professors at Middlebury hold a terminal degree. Graduate students never teach courses, so undergrads have direct access to the talented and dedicated faculty. What's more, with a student-to-teacher ratio of 9 to 1, Middlebury students are almost guaranteed to get personal attention. They also have their choice of more than 40 majors. (Not surprisingly, Environmental Studies has gained popularity in the last few years.)

Many students choose to leave campus at some point to participate in the study abroad program. With over 90 programs in 40 countries to choose from, it's no surprise this option is popular.

AROUND CAMPUS

There's no denying that the Middlebury campus is scenic and gorgeous. It's got mountains, trees, and general Vermont beauty. There are also many highlights on the campus itself.

The Commons are another remarkable feature at Middlebury. There are five Commons: Atwater, Brainerd, Cook, Ross, and Wonnacott. About 400–500 students are enrolled in each Commons, students from each year are in each. In addition, each Commons is made up of a group of residence halls. Each hall also has its own personality and sometimes even a theme. For example, Atwater Commons is home to the Environmental House.

While most college students dread dining on campus, that's not the case at Middlebury. Fresh, local products are served in the dining halls. In addition, the school makes an effort to accommodate dietary restrictions by offering vegetarian, vegan, lactose-free, and low-fat options.

STUDENT LIFE

Although Middlebury is not known for having the most diverse student body, it does offer students a wide array of extracurricular opportunities. The arts are very popular on campus, and the Kevin P. Mahaney '84 Center for the Arts (CFA) is just one of many sites for exhibitions, recitals, and performances on campus.

Sports are just as much of a draw for Middlebury students. An impressive 28 percent of students play for one of the 30 varsity teams—14 men's and 16 women's. Club sports and outdoor activities are also very popular at Middlebury. The Middlebury Mountain Club (MMC) is one of the largest organizations on campus. It plans weekly overnight trips and even offers free equipment rental to students who want to go out on their own.

Student organizations also offer a great variety of options. Whether academic, political, religious, media related, or artistic, there is something for every Middlebury student.

Oberlin College

WHAT'S GREEN

GREEN ORGANIZATIONS/STUDENT GROUPS

- **Environmental Policy Implementation Group (EPIG):** This group aims to help implement Oberlin's environmental policy, which was established in 2004.
- **Local Community Environmental Action (LECA):** This group supports environmental action both on and off campus.
- **Oberlin Student Sierra Coalition:** This organization associates with the ideals and goals of the Sierra Club.

GREEN CAMPUS PROJECTS/INITIATIVES

- **Enviroalums:** This group of environmentally minded alumni want to help the school continue its efforts in making Oberlin a sustainable campus.
- **CityWheels:** This car-sharing company has partnered with Oberlin College to reduce the need for individual vehicles by offering students the chance to rent cars only when they need one.
- **The Lightbulb Brigade:** This is a student-run effort to replace old lightbulbs with high-efficiency ones.

GREEN COURSES OFFERED

- Ecological Design
- Campus Sustainability: A Practicum
- Systems Ecology
- Energy and Society
- Dynamics of Consumption
- Environmental Economics

Although many schools and universities have signed the Presidents Climate Commitment, Oberlin was one of the first four in the United States to do so. But signing the Commitment is just the first step. From there, Oberlin must inventory all its greenhouse gas emissions.

Students are just as involved as administrators in reducing Oberlin's negative environmental impact. Recently, students worked to design Ohio's largest photovoltaic array (solar panel). This helped Oberlin achieve another first—having the first solar-powered college or university academic building in the United States.

When it comes to buildings, Oberlin has left no detail untouched by green. The school has established that all new construction and renovations must meet LEED silver standards. This would include the newly proposed Student Experiment in Ecological Design (SEED) theme house. Oberlin has also switched to using environmentally safe paint and even environmentally friendly cleaners to keep buildings sanitary.

One of the most impressive among many noteworthy efforts is the purchase of green energy for use on campus. In 2004, the school made an agreement to purchase enough alternative energy to meet 50 percent of Oberlin's needs. The school is now researching whether the installation of a wind turbine is possible.

INSIDE THE CLASSROOM

Oberlin College, which was founded in 1833, is actually comprised of two distinct schools: the College of Arts and Sciences (CAS) and the Conservatory of Music. Although most students choose one or the other, Oberlin's unique Double Degree Program allows especially ambitious and dedicated students to earn a degree from each school.

Oberlin, OH
Website: www.oberlin.edu
Sustainability website: www.oberlin.edu/sustainability
Email contact address: college.admissions@oberlin.edu

For the majority of students, though, CAS is where they will study all four years. First-year students have the unique opportunity to participate in first-year seminars (FYS). In these small classes, students work closely with faculty in highly specialized areas of study.

With 47 majors and 42 minors to choose from, one would think that Oberlin students would need all four years on campus to complete their education. However, each semester, about 150 students participate in the study abroad program. Oberlin runs four programs—one each in the United Kingdom, Spain, and Italy and one that spans Western Europe.

AROUND CAMPUS

One of the highlights of the 440-acre Oberlin campus is the Allen Memorial Art Museum. Since it opened in 1917, it has amassed an impressive collection of works from virtually every era and origin. Techies are probably more impressed with the Oberlin Science Center, which is home to a 64-bit supercomputer—the first one found on a liberal arts campus.

There is no shortage of different housing options for those living on campus at Oberlin, with 11 traditional residence halls, nine program houses, four co-ops, and 10 village houses. Within those choices, there are also special interest spaces (for example, 24-hour quiet floors) and theme housing—yes, there is a science fiction–themed house!

While the Oberlin College campus is beautiful, those wanting big-city excitement might not find it here. Thankfully, Cleveland is only 35 miles away, so students don't have to travel far to satisfy their urban urges.

STUDENT LIFE

Because the Conservatory of Music is part of Oberlin College, it should come as no surprise that plenty of music-related activities take place on campus. In fact, there are at least 400 concerts and recitals each year, plus two operas. But not every activity on campus is about music.

Oberlin College has a very active athletics department. There are 20 varsity teams—10 each for men and women. Intramurals are always popular, as are club sports. The variety of club sports really helps Oberlin athletics stand out. Students can be involved in rugby, tumbling, and even scuba diving.

Even though Oberlin is a relatively small school, there are plenty of student organizations to choose from. The Student Union website lists all 142 organizations, but to give you an idea, students can find everything from environmental to Africana to five different co-op organizations on campus.

Oregon State University (OSU)

WHAT'S GREEN

GREEN ORGANIZATIONS/STUDENT GROUPS ON CAMPUS

- **Biodiesel Initiative:** This student organization promotes the use of biodiesel on campus.
- **Environmental Consortium of Sustainable Technology:** This group meets to develop sustainable technology.
- **Range Ecology & Management Club:** This group is for both undergrads and graduate students interested in environmental and sustainability issues.

GREEN CAMPUS PROJECTS/INITIATIVES

- **Sustainable Biofuel Systems for Undeveloped Regions:** This project is spearheaded by the Biodiesel Initiative group. Students are designing and building a system that can produce sustainable fuel to create electricity sources in less-developed countries.
- **Campus Carbon Challenge:** This month-long event in early 2008 aimed to track the ways students reduced their carbon footprint using simple but effective methods and practices.
- **Solar Trailer:** This portable photovoltaic array serves to educate the community about solar energy as well as to power outdoor events, such as concerts, on campus.

GREEN COURSES OFFERED

- Wilderness Resource Stewardship
- 20th Century U.S. Environmental Policy
- Environmental Engineering Fundamentals
- Air Pollution Control
- Sustainable Water Resources Development
- Managing Natural Resources for the Future

Oregon State University has the impressive distinction of being only one of seven schools in the United States that uses 100 percent renewable energy or purchases enough to offset its use of traditional energy sources. This environmentally sound practice goes hand in hand with OSU's signing of the Presidents Climate Commitment. OSU has not taken this commitment lightly, fast-tracking its greenhouse gas emission inventory, which was completed more than a year in advance of its deadline.

When it comes to green building, OSU has also made great strides. All new construction at OSU must meet LEED silver standards. One recent construction project, the Kelley Engineering Center, received a gold standard. This was a landmark achievement, because this is now the highest LEED-rated academic engineering building in the country.

At OSU, Dining Services is also doing its best to go green. Thanks to the Student Sustainability Initiative, composting has increased at OSU. Earth Tubs (a brand of composting containers) and Worm Wigwams (a system of using worms to compost food scraps) can be found at various dining halls around campus. Dining Services has also joined the Oregon Food Alliance, an organization that promotes and supports sustainable agricultural practices. When possible, local produce and meat are purchased and served on campus.

INSIDE THE CLASSROOM

An undergraduate education at Oregon State University begins with the Baccalaureate Core Curriculum. This comprehensive foundation covers five course areas: skills; perspectives; difference, power, and discrimination; synthesis; and writing intensive courses. The Bacc Core is

Corvallis, OR
Website: www.oregonstate.edu
Sustainability website: http://oregonstate.edu/sustainability
Email contact address: osuadmit@oregonstate.edu

designed to produce students who will become educated and aware citizens of the world.

When it comes to environmentalism, OSU's College of Agricultural Sciences, College of Engineering, and College of Forestry lead the way. Undergraduates can major in ecological engineering; environmental economics, policy, and management; environmental engineering; or environmental science. There are also three environmentally themed minors at OSU.

To have students gain a global perspective, OSU has a huge array of study abroad opportunities. Not only can students complete for-credit international internships, but they can choose from about 200 different traditional study abroad programs. There are programs in Bali, Bulgaria, Madagascar, and even the Balkans, to name just a few.

AROUND CAMPUS

Corvallis is a small college town with about 50,000 residents. While the serenity of this town is a big draw for some students, others who are looking for more action will be pleased to know that Portland is only about 90 minutes away.

Oregon State University and the town of Corvallis are set in the scenic Willamette Valley—also home to Oregon's wine country. There are plenty of recreational areas, so hiking, white-water rafting, skiing, and biking are all easily enjoyed. The campus itself is 400 acres of beautiful buildings and open landscapes, which make for an idyllic backdrop for studying and living.

At OSU, there are 14 residence halls (1 is privately managed) and four cooperative houses—one for men and three for women. There are also 14 different themed housing options.

STUDENT LIFE

Students don't have a hard time finding plenty of things to keep them busy outside of class. OSU students have their choice of more than 300 different student organizations. These organizations range from religious groups to performing arts groups, proving there is something for everyone. Greek life is also active at OSU. There are about 30 Greek organizations on campus.

Athletics are big at OSU, too. Not only is it an NCAA Division I school, but OSU is part of the Pacific 10 (Pac 10) Conference. There are seven men's teams and ten women's teams. The OSU Beavers' biggest rivals are the University of Oregon's Ducks—matches between the two are always well attended and hotly contested. In addition to varsity sports, there are 30 intramural sports and 25 club sports on campus.

Pennsylvania State University

WHAT'S GREEN

GREEN ORGANIZATIONS/STUDENT GROUPS

- **Sustainability Coalition:** This university-wide organization unites the efforts of the various environmental student organizations on all Penn State campuses.
- **Eco-Action (Penn State Altoona):** This organization promotes environmental action and awareness.
- **Greener Beaver (Penn State Beaver):** This club promotes discussion of environmental issues that affect the campus and the world.

GREEN CAMPUS PROJECTS/INITIATIVES

- **Solar Decathlon:** In 2007, Penn State was 1 of 20 schools around the world selected by the U.S. Department of Energy to design and build a solar-powered home.
- **American Indian Housing Initiative:** Although this program does not take place on campus, it is supported by Penn State. Its goal is to build sustainable housing on reservations with limited resources.
- **Guide to Green Pennsylvania Businesses and Industries:** Not satisfied with just highlighting improvements on campus, the Center for Sustainability at Penn State has created this database of statewide businesses that embrace sustainability and green practices.

GREEN COURSES OFFERED

- Water Supply and Pollution Control
- Environmental Toxicology
- Wetland Conservation
- Research Methods in Environmental Studies
- Natural Resource Economics
- Sustainable Engineering

Since Pennsylvania State University's history is based on agriculture, it is no shock that the school is assertively pursuing sustainable and environmental practices across all of its schools and campuses. One of the first steps taken by the school was to reduce its greenhouse gas emissions by as much as 17 percent over the next four years.

Individual campuses are doing their part by minimizing solid waste through recycling programs. Waste is also being reduced in dining halls thanks to nascent composting projects. And in an effort to support Pennsylvania-based farmers, food served in campus dining halls comes from local agricultural businesses.

Sports are big at Penn State, and baseball, the school's oldest sport, got a big boost in 2006 with the completion of Medlar Field. Not only is this a state-of-the-art baseball stadium, it's also the first LEED-certified baseball field anywhere in the world. All new construction at Penn State is required to be LEED-certified.

It should come as no surprise that this ecologically sound baseball field is located near the Ecological Systems Laboratory. This lab, which was funded by donations from the class of 2000 and the U.S. Department of Energy, is first and foremost a wastewater treatment facility. It is also home to a variety of plants and fish in an attempt to mimic a natural ecosystem. To live up to its ecological title, the lab gets its energy from ten solar panels installed nearby. Any excess energy is diverted for use in other buildings in the area.

INSIDE THE CLASSROOM

There are 13 different schools at Penn State: the College of Agricultural Sciences, the College of Arts and Architecture, the Smeal College of Business, the College

University Park, PA (main campus)
Website: www.psu.edu
Sustainability website: www.engr.psu.edu/cfs
Email contact address: admissions@psu.edu

of Communications, the College of Earth and Mineral Sciences, the College of Education, the College of Engineering, the College of Health and Human Development, the College of Information Sciences and Technology, the College of the Liberal Arts, the Eberly College of Science, the Graduate School, and the Schreyer Honors College. There are also 20 different undergraduate campuses spread throughout Pennsylvania to choose from.

When it comes to academics, there are plenty of choices for areas of study, majors, and minors. To help first-year students navigate such a large university system, there is even a first-year seminar dedicated entirely to learning about the school and how it can impact a student's future.

But a Penn State education is not just about what students can learn on campus. It has robust study abroad program that spans the globe. Students can also choose from many more Penn State–approved programs.

AROUND CAMPUS

Penn State's University Park campus, located in the heart of Pennsylvania, is the administrative headquarters of all PSU schools. Set in the small city of State College, the campus is close to Mount Nittany, and the area has earned the nickname "Happy Valley."

To help house all of its students, there are five residence halls (North, South, West, East, and Pollock) and four university apartments and suites. Unfortunately, only first-year students are guaranteed housing, but there is a user-friendly off-campus housing website to assist other students in finding a place to live.

Feeding all of those students is another challenge. There are six dining halls, five campus restaurants and snack bars, and also the very popular Penn State Bakery. To minimize waste, Penn State dining facilities have started a composting program.

STUDENT LIFE

Being the 11th school in the Big Ten conference, there's no denying that Penn State has quite a reputation for athletics. There are 27 varsity teams. The 13 women's teams encompass such varied sports as fencing, golf, and swimming and diving. There are 14 men's teams, perhaps the most famous of which is the football team.

The Nittany Lion is the mascot of Penn State athletics. The Nittany Lion "Nittany comes from nearby Mount Nittany" is also the name of Penn State's fight song. But varsity sports are just one aspect of the athletic program. There are also intramural and club sports to choose from.

Greek life is also an important aspect of student life. Each campus has its own chapters, so prospective students are encouraged to investigate each school's campus before applying.

Santa Clara University

WHAT'S GREEN

GREEN ORGANIZATIONS/STUDENT GROUPS

- **Bronco Alumni Environmental Network (BEAN):** This group is for both students and alumni who want to share information about job opportunities and current events in the environmental field.
- **Bottom Line and Beyond (BLAB):** This group approaches sustainability from a business perspective and looks at how environmentalism can be integrated into business practices.
- **Green Club:** This club explores all the ways our daily actions can affect the environment.

GREEN CAMPUS PROJECTS/INITIATIVES

- **RecycleMania:** Along with 200 other schools in the nation, Santa Clara participated in this ten-week recycling competition. SCU came in 12th in the waste-minimization competition.
- **Earth Day:** This annual event hosted by the Green Club features projects such as free bike tune-ups and repairs.
- **Solar Decathlon:** SCU placed an impressive third for its Ripple Home in the 2007 competition.

GREEN COURSES OFFERED

- Conservation Biology
- Restoration Ecology
- Solid Waste Management
- Sustainable Development in Rural Latin America
- Economics of Environment
- Environmental Literature of California

Since Santa Clara University was a pioneer in higher education in California, it should come as no surprise that it is also a pioneer in sustainability. Not only was SCU named a Campus Sustainability Leader by the Sustainable Endowments Institute, but it has committed itself to environmental stewardship, education, and service.

First and foremost, SCU has adopted LEED standards for all new construction and renovation on campus. The Kennedy Commons, built in 2005, was one of the first green academic buildings in the United States. Students have picked up on green design, and they came in third in the prestigious Solar Decathlon in 2007. To make sure that older buildings don't cancel out the good work done by new buildings, SCU is retrofitting many buildings to make them more energy efficient.

Other notable achievements include the seven tons of reusable items donated to the Goodwill by SCU students during move-out, that 90 percent of showers in dorms are low-flow, and that nearly 6.5 million gallons of water are saved through the use of waterless urinals.

Taking advantage of California's many sunny days, SCU has installed a 338-panel solar system on the school's facilities building. To further show its commitment to alternative energy, SCU recently increased its investment in a renewable energy program fivefold. These measures are meant to help SCU achieve a 20 percent reduction in CO_2 emissions below its 1990 emissions level.

INSIDE THE CLASSROOM

One of Santa Clara University's first distinctions was that it was the oldest operating higher education institution in California. Undergrads have their choice of three schools: the College of Arts and Sciences (the school half

Santa Clara, CA
Website: www.scu.edu
Sustainability website: www.scu.edu/sustainability/index.cfm
Email contact address: ugadmissions@scu.edu

of SCU's undergrads attend), the Leavey School of Business, and the School of Engineering.

Santa Clara University is a Jesuit school, and this tradition is upheld today. To ensure that students graduate with a well-rounded Jesuit education, all students must complete a core curriculum. The themes are Laying Foundations, Reaching Out, and Integrating for Leadership. Once the core curriculum is complete, students have a choice of more than 60 majors and programs.

Because SCU is a relatively small school, undergraduate students have a great opportunity to work closely with professors. There are nearly 500 full-time faculty members, and the student-to-faculty ratio is an enviable 12 to 1.

Because one of the themes of an SCU education is reaching out, it's no wonder that the school encourages students to study abroad during their undergraduate career. Students at SCU have a choice of more than 150 different programs in almost 50 countries around the world.

AROUND CAMPUS

Santa Clara University calls itself "The Jesuit University in the Silicon Valley." Its location in this hotbed of technological advances has not affected its 106-acre campus. It undoubtedly has the feel of a small school.

Whether freshmen live on campus or not, they are assigned to a Residential Learning Community. These communities encourage students to live and study together and are designed to help students transition to life at college. After freshman year, students can change their RLC, but their RLC always determines which of the ten undergraduate residence halls they live in.

Students who live on campus have their choice of meal plans, and whether students eat at the Market Square or opt for late-night dining at the Bronco, they will be served local and/or organic food whenever possible.

STUDENT LIFE

SCU is dedicated to keeping its more than 5,000 students active, engaged, and entertained when they are not studying. To help ensure this, there are more than 80 registered student organizations. This includes numerous fraternities and sororities, which have become increasingly popular, with more students rushing and pledging each year.

Athletics are also very popular on campus. SCU is an NCAA Division I school and has 19 varsity teams—9 men's and 10 women's. Students like to come out and support the Broncos, but they also like to participate in 1 of the 12 intramural sports or 19 club sports.

Social life also revolves around the Center for Performing Arts. Each season, the theaters and performance spaces in the center are home to dance, theater, and music events.

Tufts University

WHAT'S GREEN

GREEN ORGANIZATIONS/STUDENT GROUPS

- **Environmental Consciousness Outreach (ECO):** This organization almost single-handedly spearheads student efforts pertaining to environmentalism.

GREEN CAMPUS PROJECTS/INITIATIVES

- **Do It in the Dark:** This annual event led by ECO is a competition among residence halls for who can reduce energy use the most.
- **Think Outside the Bottle:** This is a campaign to get students to think about the environmental impact of drinking bottled water.
- **Wind Energy:** Each year, ECO sells $10 wind power credits in an effort to offset the harmful effects of using nonrenewable energy on campus.

GREEN COURSES OFFERED

- Environmental Biology
- Principles of Conservation Biology
- Politics of Environmental Policy in the United States
- Sustainable Development
- Environment and Technology
- Environmental Chemistry

For more than 15 years now, Tufts University has not been an environmental follower but a leader. The majority of Tufts's green practices were established back in 1990—when most schools hadn't even begun to think about recycling and sustainability.

The years of commitment to the environment have earned Tufts several important distinctions. Recently, *Sierra* magazine named it one of the top green schools in the country, and in 2005, Tufts received the EPA's Climate Protection Award. At the end of 2007, Tufts received another prestigious award, the National Grid's Excellence in Energy Efficiency. Since 2000, Tufts has worked hard to bring its energy use levels back to what they were in 1990—no small task. According to National Grid, Tufts saves itself more than half a million dollars and prevents the emission of more than 3,000 tons of greenhouse gases. One of the most energy-efficient buildings on campus is the LEED-certified Sophia Gordon Hall.

Countless other programs on campus are devoted to sustainability. The school has switched to sustainable landscape practices, drastically reducing the use of pesticides. The school also strives to get its food from local producers. The composting of food waste has resulted in 62 percent less waste going to landfills. Recycling is also prevalent campuswide. Currently, Tufts recycles more than 30 percent of its waste, and students can request free recycle bins for their rooms.

INSIDE THE CLASSROOM

Founded in 1852, Tufts certainly has top-notch academics. The majority of students earn their degrees from the College of Liberal Arts, which offers 60 majors and minors. The tough liberal arts core requirements include courses in humanities, arts, social sciences, math, natural

Medford, MA
Website: www.tufts.edu
Sustainability website: www.tufts.edu/programs/sustainability
Email contact address: admissions.inquiry@ase.tufts.edu

sciences, writing, and foreign language, as well as a course in world civilization. The other option for students is the College of Engineering. Requirements are slightly different for engineering students; they must take a certain number of introductory courses (math, science, English), foundation and concentration courses (science and major-related courses), and humanities and social science courses.

As great and personalized as academics are on campus, a large percentage of students choose to study abroad. In fact, 40 percent of juniors study abroad for one or more semesters. Altogether, Tufts runs ten programs; these are in Chile, China, Ghana, Hong Kong, Japan, the United Kingdom, Spain, France, and Germany.

AROUND CAMPUS

Although Tufts has its veterinary school in Grafton and its medical and biomedical schools in Boston, the main campus is in Medford. While this is a strictly residential area with a beautiful, serene campus, it is only five miles from Boston. Students appreciate the proximity to the big city and all that it offers, but they also appreciate being able to return to the serenity of the Medford campus.

Whether they like it or not, all first-year students are required to live on campus. Hill, Tilton, and Houston Halls are exclusively for first-year students, but other halls are mixed years. There are a variety of other housing options as well. For example, Richardson House is all-female, and other buildings have all-female floors or blocks of rooms.

STUDENT LIFE

With about 8,500 students, Tufts is an active campus. There are more than 200 student clubs and organizations, ranging from such interests as geology to kite boarding. One activity in particular that is popular is a cappella singing. In total, there are a half dozen a cappella groups at Tufts. The most popular organization at Tufts is the Leonard Carmichael Society. With more than 1,000 students, this group hosts community service events throughout the year.

Athletics are popular at most colleges, but at Tufts, the school seems to be known more for its mascot than its actual teams. The bizarre history of the mascot is this: Jumbo was the star elephant in the Barnum and Bailey circus. After he was hit by a train and killed in 1885, his stuffed hide was donated to Tufts by P. T. Barnum, an original trustee of the college. Jumbo stood in Barnum Hall until destroyed by a fire in 1975. Today, his ashes remain on campus in a peanut butter jar. The odd team name, the Jumbos hasn't deterred the athletics program; there are 12 men's varsity teams, 14 women's varsity teams, and two coed teams (golf, sailing).

University of California

WHAT'S GREEN

GREEN ORGANIZATIONS/STUDENT GROUPS

- **The Environmental Coalition (ECo)**: This Berkeley organization brings together all environmental groups on campus.
- **California Student Sustainability Coalition (CSSC)**: This group, based in Davis, aims to promote sustainability within the UC system.
- **One Earth One Justice (OEOJ)**: This San Diego–based group highlights environmental injustice around the world.

GREEN CAMPUS PROJECTS/INITIATIVES

- **Recycling for Scholarships**: At UC—Merced, a recycling program has become a way to fund the scholarship program. Proceeds from recycling are collected in this newly created scholarship fund.
- **Student Affairs Innovation Projects**: This UC—Irvine program allows students to propose a project, such as improving resource efficiency.
- **Green Idea Challenge**: At UC—Riverside, GIVE (Green Institute for Village Empowerment) is sponsoring a competition for the best new green ideas. The winner will receive $500.

GREEN COURSES OFFERED

- Conservation and the Human Predicament (UC—San Diego)
- Environmental Perils (UC—San Diego)
- Ecological Field Methods (UC—Santa Cruz)
- Community Ecology (UC—Santa Cruz)
- Quantitative Thinking Environmental Studies (UC—Santa Barbara)
- Solar and Renewable Energy (UC—Santa Barbara)

Despite, or perhaps because of, the UC system's massive size, it has become a leader in green initiatives across its ten campuses. While the entire school system has signed on to the Presidents Climate Commitment, individual campuses have adopted their own school-specific environmental policies.

But really, it's what the UC system has done as a whole that earns it a spot in the top 10 of our 25 greenest schools. In 2007, the UC system earned the distinction of Campus Sustainability Leader from the Sustainability Endowments Institute, and it received an Environmental Achievement Award from the U.S. Environmental Protection Agency for its achievements in the realm of environmental sustainability.

Systemwide, UC schools have committed to making all new construction LEED certified. Currently, eight of the ten campuses are inventorying their greenhouse emissions, and by 2010, all schools have committed to buying at least 20 percent of their energy from renewable resources.

Two other realms in which UC schools achieve and compete for accolades are food and transportation. Because California has so much arable land, it's no wonder that many schools already buy locally. But the added distinction of buying organic is the next goal for UC schools. UC–Santa Cruz purchases 25 percent of its produce from local organic farmers. Not to be outdone, UC–Berkeley serves only all-organic greens at its dining hall salad bars.

With so many students, staff, and faculty commuting to and from school, one might expect terrible traffic and pollution. However, to offset these problems, UC schools are providing alternative transportation solutions. In particular, students at both UC–Santa Barbara and UC–

There are ten schools in the UC system. Please visit the main UC website for further information.
Website: www.universityofcalifornia.edu
Sustainability website: www.universityofcalifornia.edu/environment/environment.html
Email contact address: ucinfo@ucapplication.net

Santa Cruz can use public transportation free of cost. And in a city where everyone seems to have a car, UC–San Diego has more than 200 electric vehicles and another 30 hybrid vehicles for campus use. And, all of UC–Irvine's shuttles run entirely on biodiesel.

INSIDE THE CLASSROOM

The University of California system was established in 1889, with 38 students and ten teachers.

Today, the UC system has ten universities: UC–Berkeley (the oldest and original), UC–Davis, UC–Irvine, UC–Los Angeles, UC–Merced, UC–Riverside, UC–San Diego,UC–San Francisco, UC–Santa Barbara, and UC–Santa Cruz.

As you might expect, each school has its own character and reputation. However, regardless of which campus students choose, they will have a more challenging time choosing from the seemingly endless majors and courses of study offered at each one. Faculty at UC schools are notorious for being the top of their field, so students can expect excellence—it will be expected of them.

AROUND CAMPUS

Some people think that California is unofficially two states: Northern California and Southern California. It's true, there is a difference between the two "states," so schools vary depending on where they are located. For example, students who envision themselves on the beach during the winter should take a look at Irvine, L.A., Riverside, Santa Barbara, or San Diego. If students can't see themselves enjoying an endless summer and want something that could be described as more rural, Davis, Merced, and Santa Cruz would be good options. Berkeley, on the other hand, is embedded within a funky, progressive, urban Bay Area neighborhood. Again, no matter where students go, each campus has excellent facilities, buildings, libraries, gyms, and classrooms.

STUDENT LIFE

With about 214,000 students across ten campuses, there is an average of more than 20,000 students per campus. Surely there is something to do wherever UC students choose to go. Each of the schools has hundreds of student organizations of every type. Athletics are big, too. Who hasn't heard of the fierce rivalry between the UC–Berkeley Bears and the Stanford Cardinals football teams? That annual matchup is known simply as "The Big Game." UCLA also has renowned teams. In 2007, UCLA Bruin Chris Horton was named First-Team All-American by the *Sporting News*. UC–Santa Barbara probably has a reputation closest to being a party school, but its academics are also rigorous.

University of New Hampshire

WHAT'S GREEN

GREEN ORGANIZATIONS/STUDENT GROUPS

- **New Hampshire Outing Club**: Because this group enjoys the great outdoors, they indirectly focus on preserving the environment.
- **Student Environmental Action Coalition**: This group focuses on environmental education and activism.
- **Wildlife Society**: This student organization focuses on preserving the environment as it pertains to wildlife.

GREEN CAMPUS PROJECTS/INITIATIVES

- **UNH Organic Garden**: This garden, established and maintained by the Organic Garden Club, helps promote sustainable farming practices.
- **Powering Down**: College campuses are veritable ghost towns during the Thanksgiving holiday, so students, staff, and faculty are encouraged to turn off or unplug everything they can while they are away. This program saved more than $7,000 in energy costs.
- **Student Waste Watch Challenge**: This campuswide competition encourages students to minimize energy and water waste. The three residence buildings that show the greatest decrease win.

GREEN COURSES OFFERED

- Global Biological Change
- Wildlife Ecology
- Contemporary Conservation Issues and Environmental Awareness
- Forest Ecosystems and Environmental Change
- How to Change the World: Engaging Students and Community Partners in Collaborative Research
- The Real Dirt

The University of New Hampshire takes environmental stewardship very seriously, and this commitment shows in the depth and breadth of its practices and initiatives. The school's Office of Sustainability was established back in 1997, so compared to many schools, UNH has had a head start in sustainability. As you might expect, UNH has signed both the Presidents Climate Challenge and the Talloires Declaration.

One campus service that really stands out when it comes to sustainability is dining. First, Dining Services aims to buy as much food as it can from local and responsible vendors. UNH serves cage-free eggs, local honey, local apples, fair-trade coffee, and even produce from UNH's organic garden. In addition, the dining service pulps and composts its food waste, saves used cooking oil for it to be made into biodiesel, distributes reusable drinking mugs to first-year students, recycles, and has installed waterless urinals in various bathrooms.

Although the school does not require LEED certification for its new construction, the school has received Energy Star ratings for eight of its buildings. UNH has also made great efforts in reducing energy waste and finding alternative energy sources. Its cogeneration (COGEN) plant reduced greenhouse gas emissions by more than 20 percent. Never one to rest on its laurels, the school has now committed to becoming the first American university to use landfill gas as its main source of energy in 2008. The use of landfill gas is expected to lower greenhouse gas emissions by a staggering 67 percent below what they were in 2005.

INSIDE THE CLASSROOM

The University of New Hampshire was founded in 1866. Now, more than 140 years later, it has earned an excellent reputation for the education it provides among

Durham, NH
Website: www.unh.edu
Sustainability website: www.sustainableunh.unh.edu/
Email contact address: admissions@unh.edu

its seven schools. Although the number one major at UNH is "undeclared liberal arts," the school offers more than 100 different majors.

UNH boasts almost 1,250 faculty members, most of them full-time, and the student-to-faculty ratio is an impressive 17 to 1. One way in which UNH students are encouraged to get involved with faculty is through the undergraduate Research Opportunities Program (UROP). The school helps fund undergraduate research awards and summer undergraduate research fellowships and even offers grants to help offset the cost for traveling and presenting research around the country.

Every year, hundreds of UNH students seek broader horizons by participating in the study abroad program. UNH manages 16 programs around the world in countries such as Austria, Mexico, Guatemala, Hungary, and France. There are six more exchange programs around the world, and UNH students can choose from another 28 programs that are approved by UNH.

AROUND CAMPUS

The small city of Durham is the backdrop of the University of New Hampshire. However, the heart of the school is definitely the Memorial Union Building (MUB). The MUB just celebrated its 50th birthday in 2007, and it continues to offer students a place to catch a movie, somewhere to shop, and a meeting point for social engagements.

When it comes to housing, UNH students have loads of options. Campus housing is divided into three areas. Furthermore, students have a choice among several themed housing options. First-year students can choose between the First Year Experience or the Alexander Advantage. There are ten other mixed-year theme houses, including chem-free and international. Finally, there are three living/learning floors, where students live and take classes together.

STUDENT LIFE

Compared to a state university such as UCLA, UNH is fairly small, but there is still plenty to do on campus. Greek life attracts about 10 percent of the student body. About 1,000 students are members of one of the eight fraternities or six sororities on campus. There are also lots of clubs to join. Whether students are interested in sign language, mechanical engineering, or animal rights, they will find a club that is right for them. And if they don't find something of interest from among the 200-plus existing clubs, students are free to start their own.

While winter means cold weather in New Hampshire, it also means ice hockey season. There are both men's and women's ice hockey teams, and students scramble to see the Wildcats play. Altogether, there are 20 varsity sports, 20 intramural sports, and another 27 club sports that take advantage of UNH's many athletic facilities.

University of North Carolina—Chapel Hill

WHAT'S GREEN

GREEN ORGANIZATIONS/STUDENT GROUPS

- **Carolina Environmental Student Alliance:** The goal of this organization is to raise environmental awareness on campus.
- **Student Environmental Action Coalition (SEAC):** SEAC hopes to increase student involvement in going green.
- **Environmental Law Project:** This is a sort of pre-professional organization for those interested in pursuing a career in environmental law.

GREEN CAMPUS PROJECTS/INITIATIVES

- **ICARE (I Called About Renewable Energy):** This campaign, which was spearheaded by the Student Environmental Action Coalition, encouraged students to call their state representatives and senators to get them to support renewable energy bills. Thanks in part to ICARE, the Renewable Energy and Efficiency Portfolio Standard passed in 2007.
- **Focus the Nation:** UNC has joined this national campaign to raise awareness among college students and the general population about environmental and global warming issues.
- **Green Games:** Like the national RecycleMania, UNC hosted its own green competition to see which residence hall could conserve the most energy and water.

GREEN COURSES OFFERED

- Environment and Society
- Environmental Science
- Ecology
- International Environmental Politics
- Biodiversity Conservation
- Environmental Advocacy

When it comes to being green, UNC—Chapel Hill is leading the way in an effort to improve sustainability statewide. First, UNC—Chapel Hill's Chancellor Moeser has signed the Presidents Climate Commitment and has vowed to make UNC carbon-neutral by 2050. Being carbon-neutral will be the fruition of many coordinated efforts with many benefits.

Because UNC has so much construction under way, implementing LEED standards for buildings is crucial. Several buildings are under construction on campus, and three of them are aiming to achieve the highest LEED rating: platinum. The buildings themselves make a positive contribution to the school. For example, at the FedEx Global Education Center, rainwater is collected and used for irrigation or flushing toilets.

UNC has also explored and developed alternative energy projects. In fall 2007, students had a solar-powered water heater to thank for their hot showers in the morning. Another campus addition is a five million gallon thermal storage tank. To keep electricity use to a minimum during peak daytime hours, the tank holds chilled water at night and releases it throughout the day.

UNC is promoting energy conservation across the campus. Students are encouraged to set their computers to sleep mode and to keep lights turned off when rooms are not in use. UNC also promotes the use of CFLs (compact fluorescent lightbulbs) in all fixtures, further increasing campus energy efficiency.

INSIDE THE CLASSROOM

The University of North Carolina is the oldest public education institution in the United States; the first school opened in 1795. Today, the University of North

Chapel Hill, NC
Website: www.unc.edu
Sustainability website: sustainability.unc.edu
Email contact address: unchelp@admissions.unc.edu

Carolina system is comprised of 16 different campuses with more than 180,000 students. A total of 300 majors are offered.

UNC—Chapel Hill offers students 84 courses of study. Most students attend the College of Arts and Sciences (CAS), which is the largest school and awards half the degrees for undergraduates. There are 42 academic departments to choose from.

UNC students must complete a core curriculum known as General Education. This underwent some changes in 2006, and the new program is divided into three sections: Foundations, Approaches, and Connections. CAS students pursuing a BA must complete additional courses in either a distributive or integrative option.

Perhaps due to the emphasis on connections in UNC education, every year more and more students choose to study abroad. More than a third of students now go abroad, and that number is expected to increase by 10 percent each year.

AROUND CAMPUS

Since UNC—Chapel Hill is the original campus of the UNC system, it is highlighted here. The Chapel Hill campus is 729 acres dotted with massive oak trees, beautifully manicured quads, and brick pathways. Given its long history, it should be no wonder that UNC is home to two national historic landmarks: Old East and the Playmakers Theatre. Old East is also noted for being one of the oldest state university buildings in the country.

However, having all of these old buildings on campus does not mean that UNC is outdated. On the contrary, between 2000 and 2007, UNC completed a staggering 68 building projects. This does not include the other 40 projects that are currently underway or the 60 that are in the design stage.

STUDENT LIFE

UNC—Chapel Hill is home to more than 600 student organizations. This means that students with interest in activism, religion, politics, dance, or just about anything else will be able to find a community on campus. There are also a seemingly endless array of Greek fraternities and sororities to choose from, including 12 religious and multicultural ones.

One of the most dominant aspects of student life at UNC is athletics. There are 14 women's varsity teams and 12 men's varsity teams. Athletics and athletes are so popular at UNC that the school had to institute an autograph request policy, and season tickets for football go on sale a year in advance!

University of Vermont

WHAT'S GREEN

GREEN ORGANIZATIONS/STUDENT GROUPS

- **Consortium for Ecological Living (CEL):** This group strives to find ecologically sound ways of building and living.
- **Student Environmental Educators Doing Something (SEEDS):** The organization takes lessons about improving the environment off campus and into local elementary schools.
- **Vermont Student Environmental Program (VSTEP):** The students in this group aim to disseminate information about environmental programs and practices on campus.

GREEN CAMPUS PROJECTS/INITIATIVES

- **RecycleMania:** This is a national competition to see which campus can recycle the most.
- **Pasture Network Program:** This program is run by the Center for Sustainable Agriculture and promotes sustainable grazing for livestock.
- **Biodiesel Buses:** Since an environmental studies student first suggested using biodiesel in the school's buses in 2002, UVM has continued to use some form of alternative energy sources for its fleet.

GREEN COURSES OFFERED

- Environmental History of North America
- Introduction to Landscape Restoration
- Ecological Landscape Design
- Environmental Law
- Environmental Ethics
- Global Environmental Assessment

Perhaps its Vermont's natural beauty that inspires educators and students alike to dedicate so much time to preserving it. Regardless of the motivation, UVM is doing a significant amount to improve the environment.

When it comes to education, UVM offers students not one but three different environmental degrees: environmental studies, environmental engineering, and environmental sciences. Specifically, the Rubenstein School of Environment and Natural Resources is there to educate students and to make innovations in environmental practices. But what is UVM itself doing?

Well, the UVM mission statement and that of virtually every department it encompasses make some mention of preserving the environment. To make this mission statement come true, the school has established the UVM Recycling and Solid Waste Program. In 2007, UVM was named "Outstanding College/University Recycling Program of the Year" by the National Recycling Coalition. To ensure that recycling remains on the forefront of students' minds, each residence hall employs an Eco-Rep, who promotes recycling and environmental awareness.

Because UVM has such a large campus, transportation is an issue. The school encourages students to walk and discourages driving by offering free public transportation. Buildings on campus are also getting a green face lift. All new buildings and any renovated buildings must meet at least a silver-level LEED rating.

One building striving to achieve this certification is the Dudley H. Davis Center, which was designed to drastically reduce unnecessary energy and water waste.

INSIDE THE CLASSROOM

Founded in 1791, the University of Vermont is one of the oldest schools in New England. However, UVM is

Burlington, VT
Website: www.uvm.edu
Sustainability website: www.uvm.edu/greening
Email contact address: admissions@uvm.edu

more than just a school. In fact, there are eight different undergraduate schools to choose from: the College of Agriculture and Life Sciences, the College of Arts and Sciences, the College of Education and Social Services, the College of Engineering and Mathematical Sciences, the College of Nursing and Health Sciences, the School of Business Administration, the Honors College, and most notably for green issues, the Rubenstein School of Environment and Natural Resources.

The quantity of colleges does not affect quality, but it does mean that undergrads have a wide variety of majors and courses to choose from. Nearly 100 different bachelor's programs and almost 1,800 courses are available. UVM's dedicated faculty members are poised to impart their expertise to students.

Students looking for academic opportunities outside of Burlington have the opportunity to study abroad. The Office of International Education helps students, mostly juniors, find an accredited program. Take a cue from past students who have studied in Africa, Asia, Europe, Latin America, and the Middle East.

AROUND CAMPUS

The UVM campus is gorgeous. Its 460 acres overlooking Lake Champlain are based at the foot of the Green Mountains. UVM also holds plenty of off-campus land, including four research farms and even the top of nearby Mount Mansfield.

UVM students usually live in one of 29 residence halls or in one of nine fraternity houses or five sorority houses. There are also plenty of dining options—11 in all. And to support Vermont farmers, about 30 percent of food served in the halls comes from local growers.

STUDENT LIFE

UVM is not only known for being environmental, it's also known for having very active students. So it's not surprising that sports are one of the most popular student activities. There are a total of 20 NCAA Division I sports teams—nine men's and 11 women's (go Catamounts!). Club sports are also very popular, as are classic intramural sports such as ultimate frisbee and flag football.

Greek life is another draw for student participation. There are 14 Greek organizations on campus—nine fraternities and five sororities. About eight percent of UVM students choose to pledge a Greek organization.

UVM also boasts more than 100 clubs and organizations. Some students want to join the nationally recognized debate team or write for the school newspaper—why not do both at UVM? And of course, there are always the environmental clubs on campus—a half dozen to choose from.

University of Washington

WHAT'S GREEN

GREEN ORGANIZATIONS/STUDENT GROUPS

- **Earth Club:** This student organization encourages environmental responsibility on campus.
- **International Forestry Students Association (IFSA):** This group focuses on forestry and its preservation around the world.
- **American Water Resources Association:** This organization discusses issues related to water resources.

GREEN CAMPUS PROJECTS/INITIATIVES

- **Classroom and Conference Room Recycling:** This program prevents students from making excuses that recycling is a hassle. Three bins, one for paper, one for bottles and cans, and one for waste, have been placed in classrooms and conference rooms to encourage recycling around campus.
- **UW BaSiC Initiative:** This program helps plan and build sustainable communities in marginalized areas.
- **Udall Legacy Bus Tour:** This cross-country bus tour began in Washington, D.C., and ended in Tucson, Arizona. Along the way, the bus made 22 stops throughout the country to educate citizens about environmentalism as it relates to the American Indian community.

GREEN COURSES OFFERED

- Society and Sustainable Environments
- Sustainable Pacific Northwest Ecosystems
- Principals of Sustainability
- Environmental and Resource Assessment
- Restoration Design
- Wildlife Biology and Conservation

When your school is recognized as an Overall Sustainability Leader by the Sustainability Endowments Institute, you know you must be doing something right. Since UW President Emmert signed the Presidents Climate Commitment, the school has completed its greenhouse gas emissions inventory and pledged to make improvements. The changes since then have been remarkable. The University of Washington is one of only seven schools in the United States that purchase 100 percent of their energy from renewable resources (e.g., wind, solar, geothermal) or offset fossil fuel–based electricity by investing in renewable energy.

Efforts are campuswide in other areas as well. For example, Dining Services at UW purchases as much produce as it can from local farmers. Students get the freshest goods, and the local agricultural economy is boosted.

Recycling is an area where UW particularly excels. Its current rate of recycling is 44 percent, which is extremely high. The school doesn't want to give students any excuses not to recycle, so it taps into students' competitive nature by hosting RecycleMania competitions to see who can recycle the most.

Students also get in on the act of environmentalism with lightbulb exchanges. Students can swap their energy-inefficient bulbs for CFLs (compact fluorescent lightbulbs), which use 75 percent less energy. To date, the school has purchased about 4,000 CFLs to distribute on campus.

What green college campus would be complete without LEED-certified buildings? Like other schools, UW has committed to achieving LEED certification with all new buildings and renovations. Currently, UW has four LEED buildings on campus.

Seattle, WA (main campus)
Website: www.washington.edu
Sustainability website: www.washington.edu/about/environmentalstewardship

INSIDE THE CLASSROOM

UW has three campuses—Seattle, Bothell, and Tacoma—and 17 different colleges and schools. It is also considered one of the premier research universities in the country.

Undergrads have their choice of several schools, including the College of Arts and Sciences, the College of Architecture and Urban Planning, the Michael G. Foster School of Business, and the renowned College of Forest Resources. Students shouldn't feel limited to any particular field; the College of Arts and Sciences alone offers more than 50 different majors.

The study abroad program at UW is especially robust. There are more than 300 programs and exchange opportunities to choose from. And students are not limited to standard Western European locations like Spain and Italy. Tunisia, Cambodia, and Bosnia are all home to UW programs.

AROUND CAMPUS

Although there are campuses in Bothell and Tacoma, the main campus is in the amazing city of Seattle. Students have plenty of social and cultural opportunities in this mellow but bustling metropolis, and campus life can be just as exciting.

Although housing is not guaranteed at UW, many students who can do so choose to live on campus. Each of the nine residence halls has its distinct personality. Upper-class students may choose Hansee Hall, 2104 House, or the student apartments at Stevens Court.

Dining has an excellent reputation at UW. The ease and convenience of "debit card dining" is popular, since students pay for exactly what they eat. There are plenty of dining options on campus. Better yet, the produce is mostly local, and the beef is 100 percent natural. Students also have vegan, vegetarian, and kosher options. Finally, to help students stay awake during long study hours, there are more than 20 espresso bars to choose from on campus.

STUDENT LIFE

No doubt about it: The University of Washington is a BIG school. But that doesn't mean that students have a hard time finding their niches on campus. There are around 500 student organizations, covering just about every interest students might have. Greek life is another option to build a social circle, with about 16 sororities and 29 fraternities to choose from.

Sports are another great outlet for students. There are great club sports like archery and kayaking. The Intramural Athletics Center (IMA) has spectacular facilities. There are 13 tennis courts, saunas, and even an indoor climbing center. Without a doubt, though, it's the 21 (ten men's, 11 women's) varsity sports that garner the most attention. When it comes to athletics, there's plenty of school spirit for the Huskies. There's even a Dawg Channel so students can follow their favorite teams.

Yale University

WHAT'S GREEN

GREEN ORGANIZATIONS/STUDENT GROUPS

- **Yale Student Environmental Coalition (YSEC):** This student group, founded in 1986, promotes environmental stewardship on campus and in New Haven.
- **Society for Conservation Biology:** This group promotes ecology and conservation through the relatively new science of conservation biology.
- **Social and Community-Oriented Practice on the Environment (SCOPE):** This group is dedicated to strengthening the connection between social sciences and the environment.

GREEN CAMPUS PROJECTS/INITIATIVES

- **Harvest:** This preorientation program for incoming Yale freshmen promotes sustainability before students ever set foot on campus. Students spend time on organic farms throughout Connecticut to learn about the importance of sustainable practices.
- **Environmental Education Project:** This outreach program is aimed at New Haven fifth-graders. Leaders of this project gathered environmental lesson plans to offer throughout area schools to increase awareness of global warming and other environmental issues.
- **Climate Campaign 2006–2007:** Each year, the Yale Student Environmental Coalition spearheads different projects. During this school year, the focus was the use of alternative energy sources to offset Yale's use of greenhouse gas–producing energy sources.

GREEN COURSES OFFERED

- Environmental Politics and Law
- Global Environmental History
- Community Ecology
- Environmental Hydrology
- Sustainability
- Environmental Archaeology in the Near East

When you visit Yale's Office of Sustainability's website (www.yale.edu/sustainability), it's clear that the school has really ramped up to become a leader among schools in the United States. But it's not just a cool website that makes Yale University a sustainability leader—it's also the programs and efforts being made by the school to reduce its negative impact on the environment.

To start, there are four LEED-certified buildings on campus. One of the most impressive is the Malone Center, which serves as the engineering research building. It received a gold-level rating in 2006 for its use of recycled and/or sustainable materials, its water conservation features, and its impressive energy efficiency. In addition, building on campus not only strives to meet LEED standards but also places a heavy emphasis on energy efficiency.

When it comes to recycling, Yale is determined to make improvements. A Deskside Recycling Program has been implemented to achieve an overall level of 40 percent. The program places two bins, one for recycling, one for nonrecyclable waste, next to every desk in every office on campus. By making recycling as accessible as possible and by further educating the campus about what can and should be recycled, Yale is on target to improve.

Other initiatives being implemented and supported on campus include the use of local food in dining halls as part of the Yale Sustainable Food Project and the use of a hydrogen fuel cell, which is meant to produce zero-emission electricity.

INSIDE THE CLASSROOM

While Yale has many traditions in its long history, the foremost is an excellent education. At Yale, the under-

New Haven, CT
Website: www.yale.edu
Sustainability website: www.yale.edu/sustainability
Email contact address: undergraduate.admissions@yale.edu

graduate program is referred to as Yale College. This school offers an impressive 77 different majors, including one in environmental studies. With 906 tenured faculty members, as well as another 2,500 faculty members, students can easily take advantage of the brilliant minds on campus.

Because the world seems to be getting smaller every day, it's no wonder that many Yale students choose to study abroad during their college career. Yale thoroughly encourages students to do so, and there are plenty of countries to choose from. Currently, Yale offers programs in 11 African countries, ten Latin American and Caribbean countries, five Asian countries, four Oceanic countries, 16 European countries, five Middle Eastern countries, and two United Kingdom countries.

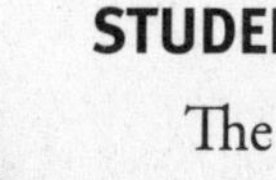

AROUND CLASSROOM

The Yale campus is New Haven's biggest tourist attraction. The beautiful main campus is 320 acres (with another 600 or so acres of athletic fields, golf courses, and nature reserves) and is home to 275 buildings. And even though New York City is just a Metro-North train ride away, there is definitely something special about the campus that keeps the tourists and students coming.

At Yale, all first- and second-year students are required to live on campus. The school's unique residential college system is a longstanding tradition. Students are assigned to 1 of 12 colleges, and they live and dine in those colleges until graduation. First-year students live in Silliman, in Timothy Dwight, or in one of the eight dormitories on the Old Campus. Although there are no single-occupancy rooms and no air-conditioning, more than 85 percent of students choose to live on campus.

STUDENT LIFE

The vast majority of Yale students are from out of state. This broad spectrum of backgrounds and interests are reflected in the 200 or so registered student organizations. Whether students want to belly dance, join a Greek-letter organization, or save the environment, Yale has an organization for them.

Yale is best known for being an Ivy League school, but it is also a reputable NCAA Division I school with 35 varsity teams—16 men's, 18 women's, and one coed (sailing) team. About 20 percent of students participate in varsity sports, while about 50 percent participate in one of the hundreds of intramural events that take place throughout the year.

An interesting fact about Yale athletics comes from its mascot, the oldest team mascot in the United States, Handsome Dan the Bulldog. Handsome Dan was established as mascot back in 1890, and Yale is now on real-live bulldog Handsome Dan the 16th.

Plus 390 More School Possibilities

Kaplan College Guide 2009 Edition has information on 390 schools throughout the country. At press time, this was the most current information available. For listings marked "Unavailable," information was not available at the time of publication. For listings marked "N/A," information is not publicly reported by the school. For the most up-to-the-minute and accurate information, please contact chosen schools.

Largest School Libraries (by number of volumes)

Harvard University	15,391,906
Yale University	11,389,504
University of Illinois, Urbana	10,191,895
University of Toronto	10,032,197
University of California, Berkeley	9,812,997

ABILENE CHRISTIAN UNIVERSITY

Abilene, TX

info@admissions.acu.edu; www.acu.edu

General Info: Private, Church Of Christ, University, Four-year, Coed, College Board member, Regionally Accredited. Residential campus, Small city (50,000–249,999), Urban setting. Academic Calendar: Semester.

Student Body: Full-Time Undergrads: 4,166. Men: 45%, Women: 55%. Total Undergrad Population: Native American or Native Alaskan: 0%. Asian American or Pacific Islander: 1%. African American: 8%. Latino: 5%. Caucasian: 81%. International: 2%. Out-of-State: 19%. Total all graduate and professional students: 545.

Academics: Full-Time Faculty: Unavailable.

Admissions: Regular Application Deadline: 8/1. Priority Application Deadline: Unavailable. Early Decision Deadline: Unavailable. Transfer Priority Deadline: 5/15. Financial Aid Deadline: Unavailable. Total Number of Students Applied: Unavailable. Percent Admitted: 52%. Number Enrolled: 1,030. Test Scores (Middle 50%): SAT Critical Reading: 480–620. SAT Math: 490–630. SAT Writing: Unavailable. ACT Comp: 20–27. HS Rank of Entering Freshmen: Top 10%: 21%. Top 25%: 49%. Avg. HS GPA: Unavailable.

Cost: Tuition and Fees: In-State: $16,330. Out-of-State: $16,330. Room and Board: $6,129.

Inst. Aid: FT Undergrads Receiving Aid: Unavailable. Avg. Amount per Student: Unavailable.

ADAMS STATE COLLEGE

Alamosa, CO

ascadmit@adams.edu; www.adams.edu

General Info: Public, Liberal Arts College, Four-year, Coed, North Central Association of Colleges and Schools, Regionally Accredited, Hispanic serving. Rural setting, Small town (2,500–9,999), Residential campus. Academic Calendar: Semester.

Student Body: Full-Time Undergrads: 2,308. Men: 47%, Women: 53%. Total Undergrad Population: Native American or Native Alaskan: 2%. Asian American or Pacific Islander: 1%. African American: 9%. Latino: 33%. Caucasian: 52%. International: 0%. Out-of-State: 11%. Total all graduate and professional students: 2,591.

Academics: Graduation Rates: 16% within 4 years. 30% within 6 years.

Admissions: Regular Application Deadline: No closing date. Priority Application Deadline: 8/1. Early Decision Deadline: Unavailable. Transfer Priority Deadline: Unavailable. Financial Aid Deadline: 4/15. Total Number of Students Applied: Unavailable. Number Admitted: 1,113. Number Enrolled: 507. Test Scores (Middle 50%): SAT Critical Reading: 413–540. SAT Math: 423–540. SAT Writing: Unavailable. ACT Comp: 17–21. HS Rank of Entering Freshmen: Top 10%: 6%. Top 25%: 20%. Avg. HS GPA: 2.92.

Cost: Tuition and Fees: In-State: $3,171. Out-of-State: $9,597. Room and Board: $6,310.

Inst. Aid: FT Undergrads Receiving Aid: Unavailable. Avg. Amount per Student: Unavailable.

ADELPHI UNIVERSITY

Garden City, NY

admissions@adelphi.edu; www.adelphi.edu

General Info: Private, University, Four-year, Coed, Regionally Accredited, College Board member. Suburban setting, Large town (10,000–49,999), Commuter campus. Academic Calendar: Semester.

Student Body: Full-Time Undergrads: 4,930. Men: 29%, Women: 71%. Total Undergrad Population: Native American or Native Alaskan: 0%. Asian American or Pacific Islander: 6%. African American: 12%. Latino: 8%. Caucasian: 59%. International: 5%. Out-of-State: 12%. Total all graduate and professional students: 3,123.

Academics: Full-Time Faculty: 280.

Admissions: Regular Application Deadline: 3/1. Priority Application Deadline: Unavailable. Early Decision Deadline: 12/1. Transfer Priority Deadline: Unavailable. Financial Aid Deadline: Unavailable. Total Number of Students Applied: Unavailable. Percent Admitted: 68%. Number Enrolled: 839. Test Scores (Middle 50%): SAT Critical Reading: 480–580. SAT Math: 490–590. SAT Writing: 480–590. ACT Comp: 20–25. HS Rank of Entering Freshmen: Top 10%: 17%. Top 25%: 48%. Avg. HS GPA: Unavailable.

Cost: Tuition and Fees: In-State: $20,900. Out-of-State: $20,900. Room and Board: $9,500.

Inst. Aid: FT Undergrads Receiving Aid: Unavailable. Avg. Amount per Student: Unavailable.

AGNES SCOTT COLLEGE

Decatur, GA

admission@agnesscott.edu; www.agnesscott.edu

General Info: College Board member, Four-year, Liberal Arts College, Presbyterian Church (USA), Private, Regionally Accredited, Women Only. Urban setting, Very large city (over 500,000), Residential campus. Academic Calendar: Semester.

Student Body: Full-Time Undergrads. Men: 0%, Women: 100%. Part-Time Undergrads: Men: 0%, Women: 1%. Total Undergrad Population: Native American or Native Alaskan: 0.2%. Asian American or Pacific Islander: 5%. African American: 21%. Latino: 4%. Caucasian: 54%. International: 5%. Out-of-State: 46%. Living Off-Campus: 14%. Total all graduate and professional students: 7.

Academics: Full-Time Faculty: 84. With PhD: 77. Percentage completing two or more majors: 21%. Graduation Rates: 64% within 4 years. 69% within 6 years.

Admissions: Regular Application Deadline: 3/1. Priority Application Deadline: 3/1. Early Decision Deadline: Unavailable. Transfer Priority Deadline: 3/1. Financial Aid Deadline: 2/15. Total Number of Students Applied: 18. Number Admitted: 721. Number Enrolled: 218. Number accepting place on waitlist: 4. Number of waitlisted students admitted: 2. Number applied early decision: 49. Early decision admitted: 19. Test Scores (Middle 50%): SAT Critical Reading: 550–680. SAT Math: 500–610. SAT Writing: 550–650. ACT Comp: 22–29. HS Rank of Entering Freshmen: Top 10%: 41%. Top 25%: 73%. Avg. HS GPA: 3.65.

Cost: Tuition and Fees: In-State: $28,200. Out-of-State: $28,200. Room and Board: $9,850.

Inst. Aid: FT Undergrads Receiving Aid: 801. Avg. Amount per Student: $28,138. Freshmen Receiving Non-Need Scholarship or Grant: 64. Avg. Amount per Student: $15,673.

Graduates: No. of companies recruiting on campus: 26. Percentage of grads accepting a job at time of graduation: 30%. Alumni Giving %: 42%.

ALBION COLLEGE

Albion, MI

admissions@albion.edu; www.albion.edu

General Info: Private, Liberal Arts College, Four-year, United Methodist Church, Coed, Regionally Accredited, College Board member. Rural setting, Small town (2,500–9,999), Residential campus. Academic Calendar: Semester.

Student Body: Full-Time Undergrads: 1,941. Men: 44%, Women: 56%. Total Undergrad Population: Native American or Native Alaskan: 1%. Asian American or Pacific Islander: 3%. African American: 4%. Latino: 1%. Caucasian: 89%. International: 2%. Out-of-State: 10%.

Academics: Full-Time Faculty: 139.

Admissions: Regular Application Deadline: 12/1. Priority Application Deadline: Unavailable. Early Decision Deadline: Unavailable. Transfer Priority Deadline: Unavailable. Financial Aid Deadline: Unavailable. Total Number of Students Applied: Unavailable. Percent Admitted: 82%. Number Enrolled: 571. Test Scores (Middle 50%): SAT Critical Reading: 520–645. SAT Math: 540–670. SAT Writing: Unavailable. ACT Comp: 22–27. HS Rank of Entering Freshmen: Top 10%: 30%. Top 25%: 64%. Avg. HS GPA: Unavailable.

Cost: Tuition and Fees: In-State: $26,122. Out-of-State: $26,122. Room and Board: $7,408.

Inst. Aid: FT Undergrads Receiving Aid: Unavailable. Avg. Amount per Student: Unavailable.

ALFRED UNIVERSITY

Alfred, NY

admissions@alfred.edu; www.alfred.edu

General Info: Coed, College Board member, College of Art, College of Business, College of Engineering, Four-year, Liberal Arts College, Middle States Association of Colleges and Schools, Nondenominational, Private, Regionally Accredited, University. Rural setting, Rural community (under 2,500), Residential campus. Academic Calendar: Semester.

Student Body: Full-Time Undergrads: 1,863. Men: 48%, Women: 52%. Total Undergrad Population: Native American or Native Alaskan: 0%. Asian American or Pacific Islander: 2%. African American: 4%. Latino: 2.5%. Caucasian: 63%. International: 1%. Out-of-State: 35%. Living Off-Campus: 33%. Total all graduate and professional students: 406.

Academics: Full-Time Faculty: 172. Graduation Rate: 64% within 6 years.

Admissions: Regular Application Deadline: 2/1. Priority Application Deadline: 2/1. Early Decision Deadline: 12/1. Financial Aid Deadline: Unavailable. Total Number of Students Applied: Unavailable. Percent Admitted: 78%. Number Enrolled: Unavailable. Test Scores (Middle 50%): SAT Critical Reading: 490–610. SAT Math: 500–620. SAT Writing: 480–590. ACT Comp: 22–27. HS Rank of Entering Freshmen: Top 10%: 18%. Top 25%: 46%. Avg. HS GPA: 3.13.

Cost: Tuition and Fees: In-State: $23,428. Out-of-State: $23,428. Room and Board: $10,796.

Inst. Aid: FT Undergrads Receiving Aid: 323. Avg. Amount per Student: $19,135.

ALLEGHENY COLLEGE

Meadville, PA

admissions@allegheny.edu; www.allegheny.edu

General Info: Private, Liberal Arts College, Four-year, United Methodist Church, Coed, Regionally Accredited, College Board member. Rural setting, Large town (10,000–49,999), Residential campus. Academic Calendar: Semester.

Student Body: Full-Time Undergrads: 2,100. Men: 46%, Women: 54%. Total Undergrad Population: Native American or Native Alaskan: 0%. Asian American or Pacific Islander: 2%. African American: 2%. Latino: 2%. Caucasian: 93%. International: 1%. Out-of-State: 37%.

Academics: Full-Time Faculty: 137.

Admissions: Regular Application Deadline: 2/15. Priority Application Deadline: Unavailable. Early Decision Deadline: 11/15. Financial Aid Deadline: Unavailable. Total Number of Students Applied: Unavailable. Percent Admitted: 63%. Number Enrolled: 570. Test Scores (Middle 50%): SAT Critical Reading: 550–660. SAT Math: 560–650. SAT Writing: Unavailable. ACT Comp: 23–28. HS Rank of Entering Freshmen: Top 10%: 41%. Top 25%: 75%. Avg. HS GPA: Unavailable.

Cost: Tuition and Fees: In-State: $30,000. Out-of-State: $30,000. Room and Board: $7,500.

Inst. Aid: FT Undergrads Receiving Aid: Unavailable. Avg. Amount per Student: Unavailable.

Presidents & Their Colleges

John Adams—Harvard University

Thomas Jefferson—College of William & Mary

Woodrow Wilson—Princeton University

Ulysses S. Grant—United States Military Academy

Bill Clinton—Yale University

AMERICAN UNIVERSITY

Washington, DC
admissions@american.edu; www.american.edu

General Info: Private, University, Four-year, United Methodist Church, Coed, Regionally Accredited, College Board member. Suburban setting, Very large city (over 500,000), Residential campus. Academic Calendar: Semester.

Student Body: Full-Time Undergrads: 5,866. Men: 34%, Women: 66%. Total Undergrad Population: Native American or Native Alaskan: 1%. Asian American or Pacific Islander: 5%. African American: 3%. Latino: 4%. Caucasian: 70%. International: 2%. Out-of-State: 90%. Total all graduate and professional students: 3,740.

Academics: Full-Time Faculty: 594.

Admissions: Regular Application Deadline: 1/15. Priority Application Deadline: Unavailable. Early Decision Deadline: 11/15. Transfer Priority Deadline: 3/1. Financial Aid Deadline: 2/15. Total Number of Students Applied: Unavailable. Percent Admitted: 53%. Number Enrolled: 1,396. Test Scores (Middle 50%): SAT Critical Reading: 590–700. SAT Math: 580–670. SAT Writing: 590–680. ACT Comp: 25–30. HS Rank of Entering Freshmen: Top 10%: 47%. Top 25%: 82%. Avg. HS GPA: Unavailable.

Cost: Tuition and Fees: In-State: $29,673. Out-of-State: $29,673. Room and Board: $11,240.

Inst. Aid: FT Undergrads Receiving Aid: Unavailable. Avg. Amount per Student: Unavailable.

AMHERST COLLEGE

Amherst, MA
admission@amherst.edu; www.amherst.edu

General Info: Private, Liberal Arts College, Four-year, Coed, Regionally Accredited, College Board member. Rural setting, Large town (10,000–49,999), Residential campus. Academic Calendar: Semester.

Student Body: Full-Time Undergrads: 1,648. Men: 50%, Women: 50%. Total Undergrad Population: Native American or Native Alaskan: 0%. Asian American or Pacific Islander: 12%. African American: 10%. Latino: 9%. Caucasian: 44%. International: 7%. Out-of-State: 90%. Living Off-Campus: 2%.

Academics: Full-Time Faculty: 177.

Admissions: Regular Application Deadline: 1/1. Priority Application Deadline: Unavailable. Early Decision Deadline: 11/15. Fall Transfer Deadline: 11/1. Spring Transfer Deadline: 3/1. Transfer Priority Deadline: Unavailable. Financial Aid Deadline: 2/15. Total Number of Students Applied: Unavailable. Number Admitted: Unavailable. Number Enrolled: 433. Test Scores (Middle 50%): SAT Critical Reading: 670–770. SAT Math: 660–760. SAT Writing: 660–760. ACT Comp: 28–33. HS Rank of Entering Freshmen: Top 10%: 87%. Top 25%: 95%. Avg. HS GPA: Unavailable.

Cost: Tuition and Fees: In-State: $35,580. Out-of-State: $35,580. Room and Board: $9,420.

Inst. Aid: FT Undergrads Receiving Aid: 873. Avg. Amount per Student: $36,398.

APPALACHIAN STATE UNIVERSITY

Boone, NC
admissions@appstate.edu; www.appstate.edu

General Info: Public, University, Four-year, Coed, Southern Association of Colleges and Schools, Regionally Accredited, College Board member. Rural setting, Large town

(10,000–49,999), Residential campus. Academic Calendar: Semester.

Student Body: Full-Time Undergrads: 13,447. Men: 48%, Women: 52%. Total Undergrad Population: Native American or Native Alaskan: 0%. Asian American or Pacific Islander: 2%. African American: 4%. Latino: 2%. Caucasian: 88%. International: 0%. Out-of-State: 12%. Total all graduate and professional students: 1,670.

Academics: Full-Time Faculty: 710.

Admissions: Regular Application Deadline: 1/31. Priority Application Deadline: Unavailable. Early Decision Deadline: 11/15. Transfer Priority Deadline: Unavailable. Financial Aid Deadline: Unavailable. Total Number of Students Applied: Unavailable. Percent Admitted: 69%. Number Enrolled: 2,711. Test Scores (Middle 50%): SAT Critical Reading: 510–600. SAT Math: 530–620. SAT Writing: 480–580. ACT Comp: 20–25. HS Rank of Entering Freshmen: Top 10%: 16%. Top 25%: 50%. Avg. HS GPA: Unavailable.

Cost: Tuition and Fees: In-State: $4,081. Out-of-State: $13,823. Room and Board: $5,760.

Inst. Aid: FT Undergrads Receiving Aid: Unavailable. Avg. Amount per Student: Unavailable.

Offbeat Colleges Courses

"Art of Walking"—Center College

"The Horror Film in Context"—Bowdoin College

"Maple Syrup"—Alfred University

"Philosophy and Star Trek"—Georgetown University

"The American Vacation"—University of Iowa

ARIZONA STATE UNIVERSITY

Tempe, AZ

ugradinq@asu.edu; www.asu.edu

General Info: Coed, College Board member, Four-year, North Central Association of Colleges and Schools, Public, Regionally Accredited, University. Suburban setting, Small city (50,000–249,999), Commuter campus. Academic Calendar: Semester.

Student Body: Full-Time Undergrads: 32,865. Men: 50.8%, Women: 49.2%. Part-Time Undergrads: Men: 47.8%, Women: 52.2%. Total Undergrad Population: Native American or Native Alaskan: 2.1%. Asian American or Pacific Islander: 5.9%. African American: 3.7%. Latino: 13.5%. Caucasian: 67.5%. International: 2.7%. Out-of-State: 27%. Living Off-Campus: 17.3%. % In Fraternities: 7%. % In Sororities: 6%. Total all graduate and professional students: 9,855.

Academics: Full-Time Faculty: 1,799. With PhD: 1,445. Graduation Rates: 29.4% within 4 years. 56% within 6 years.

Admissions: Regular Application Deadline: 2/2. Priority Application Deadline: 12/1. Transfer Priority Deadline: 6/1. Total Number of Students Applied: 20,290. Number Admitted: 19,259. Number Enrolled: 7,740. Test Scores (Middle 50%): SAT Critical Reading: 470–600. SAT Math: 490–620. SAT Writing: Unavailable. ACT Comp: 20–26. HS Rank of Entering Freshmen: Top 10%: 27%. Top 25%: 52.4%. Avg. HS GPA: 3.34.

Cost: Tuition and Fees: In-State: $5,409. Out-of-State: $17,697. Room and Board: $8,790.

Inst. Aid: FT Undergrads Receiving Aid: 11,705. Avg. Amount per Student: $8,792. Freshmen Receiving Non-Need Scholarship or Grant: 1,719. Avg. Amount per Student: $6,616.

Graduates: No. of companies recruiting on campus: 1,773. Alumni Giving %: 11.9%.

ARMSTRONG ATLANTIC STATE UNIVERSITY

Savannah, GA

adm-info@mail.armstrong.edu; www.armstrong.edu

General Info: Public, University, Four-year, Coed, Southern Association of Colleges and Schools, Regionally Accredited, College Board member. Suburban setting, Small city (50,000–249,999), Commuter campus. Academic Calendar: Semester.

Student Body: Full-Time Undergrads: 6,086. Men: 31%, Women: 68%. Total Undergrad Population: Native American or Native Alaskan: 0%. Asian American or Pacific Islander: 2%. African American: 19%. Latino: 4%. Caucasian: 63%. International: 4%. Out-of-State: 4%. Total all graduate and professional students: 642.

Academics: Full-Time Faculty: 224.

Admissions: Regular Application Deadline: 6/30. Priority Application Deadline: Unavailable. Early Decision Deadline: Unavailable. Transfer Priority Deadline: Unavailable. Financial Aid Deadline: Unavailable. Total Number of Students Applied: Unavailable. Percent Admitted: 64%. Number Enrolled: 1,936. Test Scores (Middle 50%): SAT Critical Reading: 470–630. SAT Math: 460–620. SAT Writing: Unavailable. ACT Comp: 18–22. HS Rank of Entering Freshmen: Top 10%: Unavailable. Top 25%: Unavailable. Avg. HS GPA: Unavailable.

Cost: Tuition and Fees: In-State: $3,074. Out-of-State: $10,756. Room and Board: $0.

Inst. Aid: FT Undergrads Receiving Aid: Unavailable. Avg. Amount per Student: Unavailable.

AUBURN UNIVERSITY

Auburn, AL
admissions@auburn.edu; www.auburn.edu

General Info: Public, University, Four-year, Coed, Regionally Accredited, Southern Association of Colleges and Schools, College Board member. Suburban setting, Large town (10,000–49,999), Commuter campus. Academic Calendar: Semester.

Student Body: Full-Time Undergrads: 20,302. Men: 50%, Women: 50%. Total Undergrad Population: Native American or Native Alaskan: 1%. Asian American or Pacific Islander: 2%. African American: 8%. Latino: 2%. Caucasian: 81%. International: 0%. Out-of-State: 1%. Total all graduate and professional students: 3,245.

Academics: Full-Time Faculty: 1,176.

Admissions: Regular Application Deadline: 5/1. Priority Application Deadline: Unavailable. Early Decision Deadline: 11/1. Transfer Priority Deadline: Rolling. Financial Aid Deadline: Unavailable. Total Number of Students Applied: Unavailable. Percent Admitted: 72%. Number Enrolled: 4,092. Test Scores (Middle 50%): SAT Critical Reading: 500–600. SAT Math: 520–630. SAT Writing: Unavailable. ACT Comp: 22–27. HS Rank of Entering Freshmen: Top 10%: 36%. Top 25%: 59%. Avg. HS GPA: Unavailable.

Cost: Tuition and Fees: In-State: $5,496. Out-of-State: $15,496. Room and Board: $7,564.

Inst. Aid: FT Undergrads Receiving Aid: Unavailable. Avg. Amount per Student: Unavailable.

Notable School Newspapers

Yale Daily News—Yale University

The Tar Heel—University of North Carolina

The Daily Pennsylvanian—University of Pennsylvania

AUSTIN COLLEGE

Sherman, TX
admission@austincollege.edu; www.austincollege.edu

General Info: Private, Liberal Arts College, Teachers College/College of Education, Four-year, Presbyterian Church (USA), Coed, Regionally Accredited, College Board member. Suburban setting, Small city (50,000–249,999), Residential campus. Academic Calendar: 4-1-4.

Student Body: Full-Time Undergrads: 1,370. Men: 46%, Women: 54%. Total Undergrad Population: Native American or Native Alaskan: 1%. Asian American or Pacific Islander: 13%. African American: 3%. Latino: 8%. Caucasian: 74%. International: 1%. Out-of-State: 7%. Total all graduate and professional students: 33.

Academics: Full-Time Faculty: 92.

Admissions: Regular Application Deadline: 3/1. Priority Application Deadline: 1/15. Early Decision Deadline: 12/1. Transfer Priority Deadline: 1/15. Financial Aid Deadline: Unavailable. Total Number of Students Applied: Unavailable. Percent Admitted: 76%. Number Enrolled: 304. Test Scores (Middle 50%): SAT Critical Reading: 560–670. SAT Math: 580–670. SAT Writing: Unavailable. ACT Comp: 23–28. HS Rank of Entering Freshmen: Top 10%: 48%. Top 25%: 78%. Avg. HS GPA: Unavailable.

Cost: Tuition and Fees: In-State: $23,355. Out-of-State: $23,355. Room and Board: $7,741.

Inst. Aid: FT Undergrads Receiving Aid: Unavailable. Avg. Amount per Student: Unavailable.

AZUSA PACIFIC UNIVERSITY

Azusa, CA
admissions@apu.edu; www.apu.edu

General Info: Coed, College Board member, Four-year, Interdenominational, Private, Regionally Accredited, University, Western Association of Schools and Colleges. Suburban setting, Small city (50,000–249,999), Residential campus. Academic Calendar: Semester.

Student Body: Full-Time Undergrads: 4,060. Men: 39%, Women: 61%. Total Undergrad Population: Native American or Native Alaskan: 1%. Asian American or Pacific Islander: 7%. African American: 5%. Latino: 14%. Caucasian: 63%. International: 2%. Out-of-State: 19%. Total all graduate and professional students: 3,220.

Academics: Full-Time Faculty: 333. Graduation Rates: 52% within 4 years. 64% within 6 years.

Admissions: Regular Application Deadline: 2/15. Priority Application Deadline: Unavailable. Early Decision Deadline: Unavailable. Transfer Priority Deadline: 1/1. Financial Aid Deadline: 3/2. Total Number of Students Applied: 3,229. Number Admitted: 2,370. Number Enrolled: 855. Test Scores (Middle 50%): SAT Critical Reading: 510–610. SAT Math: 500–610. SAT Writing: Unavailable. ACT Comp: 21–27. HS Rank of Entering Freshmen: Top 10%: 27%. Top 25%: 57%. Avg. HS GPA: 3.6.

Cost: Tuition and Fees: In-State: $24,430. Out-of-State: $24,430. Room and Board: $3,976.

Inst. Aid: FT Undergrads Receiving Aid: Unavailable. Avg. Amount per Student: $19,684.

BABSON COLLEGE

Babson Park, MA

ugradadmission@babson.edu; www.babson.edu

General Info: Private, College of Business, Four-year, Coed, Regionally Accredited, College Board member. Suburban setting, Large town (10,000–49,999), Residential campus. Academic Calendar: Semester.

Student Body: Full-Time Undergrads: 1,776. Men: 60%, Women: 40%. Total Undergrad Population: Native American or Native Alaskan: 0%. Asian American or Pacific Islander: 11%. African American: 3%. Latino: 7%. Caucasian: 45%. International: 16%. Out-of-State: 0%. Total all graduate and professional students: 1,583.

Academics: Full-Time Faculty: 152.

Admissions: Regular Application Deadline: 1/15. Priority Application Deadline: 11/15. Early Decision Deadline: 11/15. Transfer Priority Deadline: Unavailable. Financial Aid Deadline: 2/15. Total Number of Students Applied: Unavailable. Percent Admitted: 37%. Number Enrolled: 435. Test Scores (Middle 50%): SAT Critical Reading: 530–630. SAT Math: 600–690. SAT Writing: 560–640. ACT Comp: 25–29. HS Rank of Entering Freshmen: Top 10%: 52%. Top 25%: 91%. Avg. HS GPA: Unavailable.

Cost: Tuition and Fees: In-State: $34,112. Out-of-State: $32,256. Room and Board: $11,222.

Inst. Aid: FT Undergrads Receiving Aid: Unavailable. Avg. Amount per Student: Unavailable.

BALL STATE UNIVERSITY

Muncie, IN

askus@bsu.edu; www.bsu.edu

General Info: Public, University, Four-year, Coed, Regionally Accredited, North Central Association of Colleges and Schools, College Board member. Suburban setting, Small city (50,000–249,999), Residential campus. Academic Calendar: Semester.

Student Body: Full-Time Undergrads: 16,063. Men: 49%, Women: 51%. Total Undergrad Population: Native American or Native Alaskan: 0%. Asian American or Pacific Islander: 1%. African American: 8%. Latino: 2%. Caucasian: 87%. International: 0%. Out-of-State: 7%. Total all graduate and professional students: 2,948.

Academics: Full-Time Faculty: 910.

Admissions: Regular Application Deadline: Unavailable. Priority Application Deadline: 3/1. Early Decision Deadline: Unavailable. Transfer Priority Deadline: Unavailable. Financial Aid Deadline: Unavailable. Total Number of Students Applied: Unavailable. Percent Admitted: 79%. Number Enrolled: 3,953. Test Scores (Middle 50%): SAT Critical Reading: 460–560. SAT Math: 470–570. SAT Writing: 450–550. ACT Comp: 19–25. HS Rank of Entering Freshmen: Top 10%: 14%. Top 25%: 41%. Avg. HS GPA: Unavailable.

Cost: Tuition and Fees: In-State: $6,810. Out-of-State: $17,186. Room and Board: $6,898.

Inst. Aid: FT Undergrads Receiving Aid: Unavailable. Avg. Amount per Student: Unavailable.

Funny School Mascots

Sammy the Banana Slug—UC Santa Cruz

Artie the Fighting Artichoke—Scottsdale Community College

Boll Weevil—University of Arkansas Monticello

Gorlok (a mythical creature with parts from a buffalo, cheetah and Saint Bernard)—Webster University

Billiken (an elf-like creature with pointed ears) —St. Louis University

BARD COLLEGE

Annandale-on-Hudson, NY

admissions@bard.edu; www.bard.edu

General Info: Private, Liberal Arts College, Four-year, Episcopal Church, Coed, Regionally Accredited, College Board member. Residential campus, Small town (2,500–9,999), Suburban setting. Academic Calendar: Semester.

Student Body: Full-Time Undergrads: 1,641. Men: 43%, Women: 57%. Total Undergrad Population: Native American or Native Alaskan: 1%. Asian American or Pacific Islander: 4%. African American: 4%. Latino: 3%. Caucasian: 73%. International: 10%. Out-of-State: 70%. Total all graduate and professional students: 1,583.

Academics: Full-Time Faculty: 136.

Admissions: Regular Application Deadline: 1/15. Priority Application Deadline: Unavailable. Early Decision Deadline: 11/1. Transfer Priority Deadline: 3/15. Financial Aid

Deadline: Unavailable. Total Number of Students Applied: Unavailable. Percent Admitted: 29%. Number Enrolled: 498. Test Scores (Middle 50%): SAT Critical Reading: Unavailable. SAT Math: 640–690. SAT Writing: 680–740. HS Rank of Entering Freshmen: Top 10%: 59%. Top 25%: 85%. Avg. HS GPA: Unavailable.

Cost: Tuition and Fees: In-State: $35,784. Out-of-State: $34,782. Room and Board: $10,346.

Inst. Aid: FT Undergrads Receiving Aid: Unavailable. Avg. Amount per Student: Unavailable.

BARNARD COLLEGE

New York, NY

admissions@barnard.edu; www.barnard.edu

General Info: Private, Liberal Arts College, Four-year, Women Only, Regionally Accredited, College Board member. Urban setting, Very large city (over 500,000), Residential campus. Academic Calendar: Semester.

Student Body: Full-Time Undergrads: 2,389. Men: 0%, Women: 100%. Total Undergrad Population: Native American or Native Alaskan: 0%. Asian American or Pacific Islander: 18%. African American: 3%. Latino: 9%. Caucasian: 66%. International: 3%. Out-of-State: 66%.

Academics: Full-Time Faculty: 193.

Admissions: Regular Application Deadline: 1/1. Priority Application Deadline: Unavailable. Early Decision Deadline: 11/15. Transfer Priority Deadline: Unavailable. Financial Aid Deadline: 2/1. Total Number of Students Applied: Unavailable. Percent Admitted: 26%. Number Enrolled: 556. Test Scores (Middle 50%): SAT Critical Reading: 640–740. SAT Math: 640–710. SAT Writing: 640–740. ACT Comp: 29–31. HS Rank of Entering Freshmen: Top 10%: 83%. Top 25%: 99%. Avg. HS GPA: Unavailable.

Cost: Tuition and Fees: In-State: $33,078. Out-of-State: $33,078. Room and Board: $11,392.

Inst. Aid: FT Undergrads Receiving Aid: Unavailable. Avg. Amount per Student: Unavailable.

BASTYR UNIVERSITY

Kenmore, WA

admiss@bastyr.edu; www.bastyr.edu

General Info: Private, College of Health Sciences, University, Two-year, upper division, Coed, Regionally Accredited. Suburban setting, Small city (50,000–249,999), Commuter campus. Academic Calendar: Quarter.

Student Body: Full-Time Undergrads: Unavailable. Men: 19%, Women: 81%. Total all graduate and professional students: 863.

Academics: Full-Time Faculty: 51.

Admissions: Regular Application Deadline: 3/15. Priority Application Deadline: Unavailable. Early Decision Deadline: Unavailable. Transfer Priority Deadline: 3/15. Financial Aid Deadline: Unavailable. Total Number of Students Applied: Unavailable. Percent Admitted: 77%. Number Enrolled: Unavailable. Test Scores (Middle 50%): SAT Critical Reading: Unavailable. SAT Math: Unavailable. SAT Writing: Unavailable. HS Rank of Entering Freshmen: Top 10%: Unavailable. Top 25%: Unavailable. Avg. HS GPA: Unavailable.

Cost: Tuition and Fees: In-State: $16,365. Out-of-State: $15,990. Room and Board: $15,084.

Inst. Aid: FT Undergrads Receiving Aid: Unavailable. Avg. Amount per Student: Unavailable.

BATES COLLEGE

Lewiston, ME

admissions@bates.edu; www.bates.edu

General Info: Coed, College Board member, Four-year, Liberal Arts College, New England Association of Colleges and Schools, Private, Regionally Accredited. Residential campus, Small city (50,000–249,999), Urban setting. Academic Calendar: 4-4-1.

Student Body: Full-Time Undergrads: 1,660. Men: 48.4%, Women: 51.6%. Total Undergrad Population: Native American or Native Alaskan: 0.5%. Asian American or Pacific Islander: 5.6%. African American: 2.8%. Latino: 2.4%. Caucasian: 80.7%. International: 5.3%. Out-of-State: 90%. Living Off-Campus: 8%.

Academics: Full-Time Faculty: 162.

Admissions: Regular Application Deadline: 1/1. Priority Application Deadline: Unavailable. Early Decision Deadline: 11/15. Fall Transfer Deadline: 3/1. Spring Transfer Deadline: 11/1. Transfer Priority Deadline: Unavailable. Financial Aid Deadline: 2/1. Total Number of Students Applied: 4,434. Number Admitted: 1,312. Number Enrolled: 445. Test Scores (Middle 50%): SAT Critical Reading: 635–710. SAT Math: 630–700. SAT Writing: Unavailable. HS Rank of Entering Freshmen: Top 10%: 55%. Top 25%: 86%. Avg. HS GPA: Unavailable.

Cost: Tuition and Fees: In-State: $44,350. Out-of-State: $44,350. Room and Board: $1,150.

Inst. Aid: FT Undergrads Receiving Aid: 656. Avg. Amount per Student: $30,341.

BAYLOR UNIVERSITY

Waco, TX

admissions@baylor.edu; www.baylor.edu

General Info: Baptist, Coed, College Board member, Four-year, Private, Regionally Accredited, University. Urban setting, Small city (50,000–249,999), Residential campus. Academic Calendar: Semester.

Student Body: Full-Time Undergrads: 11,831. Men: 41.5%, Women: 58.5%. Part-Time Undergrads. Men: 41.8%, Women: 58.2%. Total Undergrad Population: Native American or Native Alaskan: 0.7%. Asian American or Pacific Islander: 7%. African American: 7.5%. Latino: 10.3%. Caucasian: 70.9%. International: 1.8%. Out-of-State: 17%. Living Off-Campus: 64%. 13% in Fraternities. 17% in Sororities. Total all graduate and professional students: 14,174.

Academics: Full-Time Faculty: 813. With PhD: 655. Graduation Rates: 48% within 4 years. 72% within 6 years.

Admissions: Regular Application Deadline: 2/1. Priority Application Deadline: 11/1. Early Decision Deadline: Unavailable. Financial Aid Deadline: 5/30. Total Number of Students Applied: 26,514. Number Admitted: 11,668. Number Enrolled: 2,732. Test Scores (Middle 50%): SAT Critical Reading: 550–650. SAT Math: 560–660. SAT Writing: 540–640. ACT Comp: 23–28. HS Rank of Entering Freshmen: Top 10%: 45%. Top 25%: 76%. Avg. HS GPA: Unavailable.

Cost: Tuition and Fees: In-State: $26,234. Out-of-State: $26,234. Room and Board: $6,966.

Inst. Aid: Avg. Amount per Student: $15,591.

BELMONT UNIVERSITY

Nashville, TN

buadmission@mail.belmont.edu; www.belmont.edu

General Info: Private, University, Four-year, Baptist, Coed, Regionally Accredited. Urban setting, Very large city (over 500,000), Residential campus. Academic Calendar: Semester.

Student Body: Full-Time Undergrads: 3,448. Men: 42%, Women: 58%. Total Undergrad Population: Native American or Native Alaskan: 0%. Asian American or Pacific Islander: 2%. African American: 4%. Latino: 2%. Caucasian: 90%. International: 1%. Out-of-State: 64%. Total all graduate and professional students: 707.

Academics: Full-Time Faculty: 214.

Admissions: Regular Application Deadline: 8/1. Priority Application Deadline: Unavailable. Early Decision Deadline: Unavailable. Financial Aid Deadline: Unavailable. Total Number of Students Applied: Unavailable. Percent Admitted: 69%. Number Enrolled: 792. Test Scores (Middle 50%): SAT Critical Reading: 540–640. SAT Math: 530–640. SAT Writing: Unavailable. ACT Comp: 23–28. HS Rank of Entering Freshmen: Top 10%: 36%. Top 25%: 67%. Avg. HS GPA: Unavailable.

Cost: Tuition and Fees: In-State: $18,420. Out-of-State: $18,420. Room and Board: $7,076.

Inst. Aid: FT Undergrads Receiving Aid: Unavailable.

BELOIT COLLEGE

Beloit, WI

admiss@beloit.edu; www.beloit.edu

General Info: Private, Liberal Arts College, Four-year, Coed, Regionally Accredited, College Board member. Urban setting, Large town (10,000–49,999), Residential campus. Academic Calendar: Semester.

Student Body: Full-Time Undergrads: 1,250. Men: 40%, Women: 60%. Total Undergrad Population: Native American or Native Alaskan: 0%. Asian American or Pacific Islander: 2%. African American: 3%. Latino: 4%. Caucasian: 83%. International: 5%. Out-of-State: 80%.

Academics: Full-Time Faculty: 103.

Admissions: Regular Application Deadline: 4/1. Priority Application Deadline: Unavailable. Early Decision Deadline: Unavailable. Financial Aid Deadline: Unavailable. Total Number of Students Applied: Unavailable. Percent Admitted: 67%. Number Enrolled: 347. Test Scores (Middle 50%): SAT Critical Reading: 600–730. SAT Math: 560–650. SAT Writing: Unavailable. ACT Comp: 25–29. HS Rank of Entering Freshmen: Top 10%: 37%. Top 25%: 64%. Avg. HS GPA: Unavailable.

Cost: Tuition and Fees: In-State: $28,350. Out-of-State: $28,350. Room and Board: $6,162.

Inst. Aid: FT Undergrads Receiving Aid: Unavailable. Avg. Amount per Student: Unavailable.

BENNINGTON COLLEGE

Bennington, VT

admissions@bennington.edu; www.bennington.edu

General Info: Accrediting Council for Independent Colleges and Schools, Coed, College Board member, Four-year, Liberal Arts College, New England Association of Colleges and Schools, Nondenominational, Private, Regionally Accredited. Rural setting, Large town (10,000–49,999), Residential campus. Academic Calendar: Semester.

Student Body: Full-Time Undergrads: 523. Men: 32%, Women: 68%. Total Undergrad Population: Native American or Native Alaskan: 0.2%. Asian American or Pacific Islander: 2%. African American: 2%. Latino: 2%. Caucasian: 84%. International: 3%. Out-of-State: 96%. Total all graduate and professional students: 140.

Academics: Full-Time Faculty: 60. With PhD: 23. Graduation Rates: 52% within 4 years. 59% within 6 years.

Admissions: Regular Application Deadline: 1/3. Priority Application Deadline: Unavailable. Early Decision Deadline: 11/15. Fall Transfer Deadline: 8/1. Spring Transfer Deadline: 12/1. Transfer Priority Deadline: 3/15 for Fall, 11/1 for Spring. Financial Aid Deadline: Unavailable. To-

Oldest American Schools

Harvard University – founded 1636

University of Pennsylvania – founded 1779

William and Mary – founded 1779

tal Number of Students Applied: 1,008. Number Admitted: 69. Number Enrolled: 201. Number accepting place on waitlist: 10. Number applied early decision: 73. Early decision admitted: 53. Test Scores (Middle 50%): SAT Critical Reading: 580–700. SAT Math: 540–630. SAT Writing: 580–690. ACT Comp: 25–29. HS Rank of Entering Freshmen: Top 10%: 28%. Top 25%: 69%. Avg. HS GPA: 3.4.

Cost: Tuition and Fees: In-State: $37,280. Out-of-State: $37,280. Room and Board: $10,680.

Inst. Aid: FT Undergrads Receiving Aid: 396. Avg. Amount per Student: $29,528. Freshmen Receiving Non-Need Scholarship or Grant: 20. Avg. Amount per Student: $22,833.

Graduates: Alumni Giving %: 24%.

Competitive Schools (percent of applicants accepted)

Juilliard School	7%
Curtis Institute of Music	7%
Yale University	9%
Harvard University	9%
Cooper Union	10%

BENTLEY COLLEGE

Waltham, MA

ugadmission@bentley.edu; www.bentley.edu

General Info: Coed, College Board member, College of Business, Four-year, New England Association of Colleges and Schools, Nondenominational, Private, Regionally Accredited. Suburban setting, Small city (50,000–249,999), Residential campus. Academic Calendar: Semester.

Student Body: Full-Time Undergrads: 3,994. Men: 59%, Women: 41%. Part-Time Undergrads. Men: 3%, Women: 2.6%. Total Undergrad Population: Native American or Native Alaskan: 0%. Asian American or Pacific Islander: 8%. African American: 3%. Latino: 4.4%. Caucasian: 65%. International: 7.5%. Out-of-State: 60%. Living Off-Campus: 20%. Total all graduate and professional students: 1,393.

Academics: Full-Time Faculty: 267. With PhD: 299. Graduation Rates: 78% within 4 years. 87% within 6 years.

Admissions: Regular Application Deadline: 1/15. Priority Application Deadline: Unavailable. Early Decision Deadline: 11/15. Transfer Priority Deadline: 5/1. Financial Aid Deadline: 2/1. Total Number of Students Applied: 6,689. Number Admitted: 2,531. Number Enrolled: 931. Test Scores (Middle 50%): SAT Critical Reading: 550–630. SAT Math: 600–680. SAT Writing: 550–640. ACT Comp: 24–29. HS Rank of Entering Freshmen: Top 10%: 42.1%. Top 25%: 80.5%. Avg. HS GPA: Unavailable.

Cost: Tuition and Fees: In-State: $33,030. Out-of-State: $33,030. Room and Board: $11,320.

Inst. Aid: FT Undergrads Receiving Aid: 2,053.

BEREA COLLEGE

Berea, KY

admissions@berea.edu; www.berea.edu

General Info: Private, Liberal Arts College, Four-year, Coed, Regionally Accredited, College Board member. Rural setting, Small town (2,500–9,999), Residential campus. Academic Calendar: 4-1-4.

Student Body: Full-Time Undergrads: 1,582. Men: 40%, Women: 60%. Total Undergrad Population: Native American or Native Alaskan: 0%. Asian American or Pacific Islander: 1%. African American: 19%. Latino: 1%. Caucasian: 69%. International: 8%. Out-of-State: 54%.

Academics: Full-Time Faculty: 128. Graduation Rate: 30% within 4 years.

Admissions: Regular Application Deadline: 4/30. Priority Application Deadline: n/a. Transfer Priority Deadline: Unavailable. Financial Aid Deadline: 3/1. Total Number of Students Applied: 2,083. Number Admitted: 597. Number Enrolled: 421. Test Scores (Middle 50%): SAT Critical Reading: Unavailable. SAT Math: Unavailable. SAT Writing: Unavailable. HS Rank of Entering Freshmen: Top 10%: 26%. Top 25%: 67%. Avg. HS GPA: 3.42.

Cost: Tuition and Fees: In-State: Unavailable. Out-of-State: Unavailable. Room and Board: Unavailable.

Inst. Aid: FT Undergrads Receiving Aid: 1,527. Avg. Amount per Student: $29,504.

BERRY COLLEGE

Mount Berry, GA

admissions@berry.edu; www.berry.edu

General Info: Coed, College Board member, Four-year, Liberal Arts College, Private, Regionally Accredited, Southern Association of Colleges and Schools. Suburban setting, Large town (10,000–49,999), Residential campus. Academic Calendar: Semester.

Student Body: Full-Time Undergrads: 1,829. Total Undergrad Population: Native American or Native Alaskan: 0.2%.

Asian American or Pacific Islander: 1.6%. African American: 3.3%. Latino: 23%. Caucasian: 88.8%. International: 2.1%. Out-of-State: 16.6%. Living Off-Campus: 23%. Total all graduate and professional students: 121.

Academics: Full-Time Faculty: 145. With PhD: 134. Percentage completing two or more majors: 4.7%. Graduation Rates: 48% within 4 years. 61% within 6 years.

Admissions: Regular Application Deadline: 7/25. Priority Application Deadline: 2/1. Early Decision Deadline: Unavailable. Transfer Priority Deadline: 2/1. Financial Aid Deadline: Unavailable. Total Number of Students Applied: 1,813. Number Admitted: 1,278. Number Enrolled: Unavailable. Test Scores (Middle 50%): SAT Critical Reading: 510–620. SAT Math: 510–610. ACT Comp: 23–29. HS Rank of Entering Freshmen: Top 10%: 34%. Top 25%: 65%. Avg. HS GPA: 3.61.

Cost: Tuition and Fees: In-State: $22,370. Out-of-State: $22,370. Room and Board: $7,978.

Inst. Aid: FT Undergrads Receiving Aid: 1,723. Avg. Amount per Student: $17,716. Freshmen Receiving Non-Need Scholarship or Grant: 201. Avg. Amount per Student: $21,268.

Graduates: No. of companies recruiting on campus: 56. Percentage of grads accepting a job at time of graduation: 44.6%. Alumni Giving %: 24.5%.

Big Sports Schools

Notre Dame—most NCAA football championships (11 wins)

UCLA—most NCAA men's basketball championships (11 wins)

Michigan—largest college football stadium

BIRMINGHAM-SOUTHERN COLLEGE

Birmingham, AL

admission@bsc.edu; www.bsc.edu

General Info: Private, Liberal Arts College, Four-year, United Methodist Church, Coed, Regionally Accredited, College Board member. Urban setting, Very large city (over 500,000), Residential campus. Academic Calendar: 4-1-4.

Student Body: Full-Time Undergrads: 1,294. Men: 36%, Women: 64%. Total Undergrad Population: Native American or Native Alaskan: 1%. Asian American or Pacific Islander: 2%. African American: 14%. Latino: 1%. Caucasian: 78%. International: 0%. Out-of-State: 33%. Total all graduate and professional students: 49.

Academics: Full-Time Faculty: 96.

Admissions: Regular Application Deadline: Rolling. Priority Application Deadline: 1/15. Early Decision Deadline: Unavailable. Transfer Priority Deadline: Unavailable. Financial Aid Deadline: Unavailable. Total Number of Students Applied: Unavailable. Percent Admitted: 57%. Number Enrolled: 292. Test Scores (Middle 50%): SAT Critical Reading: 530–660. SAT Math: 520–630. SAT Writing: 520–650. ACT Comp: 23–28. HS Rank of Entering Freshmen: Top 10%: 31%. Top 25%: 64%. Avg. HS GPA: Unavailable.

Cost: Tuition and Fees: In-State: $23,040. Out-of-State: $23,040. Room and Board: $7,740.

Inst. Aid: FT Undergrads Receiving Aid: Unavailable. Avg. Amount per Student: Unavailable.

BOISE STATE UNIVERSITY

Boise, ID

bsuinfo@boisestate.edu; www.boisestate.edu

General Info: Coed, College Board member, Four-year, Northwest Association of Schools and Colleges, Public, Regionally Accredited, Technical College, University, Western Association of Schools and Colleges. Commuter campus, Residential campus, Small city (50,000–249,999), Urban setting. Academic Calendar: Semester.

Student Body: Full-Time Undergrads: 17,040. Men: 47%, Women: 53%. Total Undergrad Population: Native American or Native Alaskan: 1.1%. Asian American or Pacific Islander: 3.2%. African American: 1.4%. Latino: 6.2%. Caucasian: 81%. International: 1.8%. Out-of-State: 11%. Total all graduate and professional students: 1,850.

Academics: Full-Time Faculty: 622. Graduation Rates: 7% within 4 years. 28% within 6 years.

Admissions: Regular Application Deadline: 6/30. Priority Application Deadline: 2/15. Early Decision Deadline: Unavailable. Transfer Priority Deadline: Unavailable. Financial Aid Deadline: Unavailable. Total Number of Students Applied: 5,132. Number Admitted: 3,014. Number Enrolled: 2,280. Test Scores (Middle 50%): SAT Critical Reading: 460–590. SAT Math: 460–593. SAT Writing: Unavailable. ACT Comp: 17–25. HS Rank of Entering Freshmen: Top 10%: 12%. Top 25%: 35.1%. Avg. HS GPA: 3.3.

Cost: Tuition and Fees: In-State: $4,632. Out-of-State: $13,208. Room and Board: $6,140.

Inst. Aid: FT Undergrads Receiving Aid: Unavailable. Avg. Amount per Student: Unavailable.

BOSTON COLLEGE

Chestnut Hill, MA
www.bc.edu

General Info: Private, University, Four-year, Roman Catholic Church, Society of Jesus (Jesuits), Coed, Regionally Accredited, College Board member. Suburban setting, Small city (50,000–249,999), Residential campus. Academic Calendar: Semester.

Student Body: Full-Time Undergrads: 9,081. Men: 48%, Women: 52%. Total Undergrad Population: Native American or Native Alaskan: 0%. Asian American or Pacific Islander: 9%. African American: 6%. Latino: 6%. Caucasian: 74%. International: 2%. Out-of-State: 74%. Total all graduate and professional students: 4,642.

Academics: Full-Time Faculty: 717.

Admissions: Regular Application Deadline: 1/2. Priority Application Deadline: Unavailable. Early Decision Deadline: 11/1. Transfer Priority Deadline: Unavailable. Financial Aid Deadline: Unavailable. Total Number of Students Applied: Unavailable. Number Admitted: Unavailable. Number Enrolled: 2,291. Test Scores (Middle 50%): SAT Critical Reading: 610–700. SAT Math: 640–720. SAT Writing: 610–700. HS Rank of Entering Freshmen: Top 10%: 80%. Top 25%: 95%. Avg. HS GPA: Unavailable.

Cost: Tuition and Fees: In-State: $35,674. Out-of-State: $33,506. Room and Board: $11,060.

Inst. Aid: FT Undergrads Receiving Aid: Unavailable. Avg. Amount per Student: Unavailable.

BOSTON UNIVERSITY

Boston, MA
admissions@bu.edu; www.bu.edu

General Info: Private, University, Four-year, Coed, Regionally Accredited, College Board member. Urban setting, Very large city (over 500,000), Residential campus. Academic Calendar: Semester.

Student Body: Full-Time Undergrads: 18,521. Men: 36.6%, Women: 55.2%. Total Undergrad Population: Native American or Native Alaskan: 0%. Asian American or Pacific Islander: 14%. African American: 3%. Latino: 7%. Caucasian: 58%. International: 6%. Out-of-State: 81%. Total all graduate and professional students: 10,970.

Academics: Full-Time Faculty: 1,454.

Admissions: Regular Application Deadline: 1/1. Priority Application Deadline: Unavailable. Early Decision Deadline: 11/1. Transfer Priority Deadline: Unavailable. Financial Aid Deadline: 2/15. Total Number of Students Applied: 33,930. Number Admitted: 19,888. Number Enrolled: 4,163. Test Scores (Middle 50%): SAT Critical Reading: 580–680. SAT Math: 600–690. SAT Writing: 590–690. ACT Comp: 25–29. HS Rank of Entering Freshmen: Top 10%: 58%. Top 25%: 87%. Avg. HS GPA: Unavailable.

Cost: Tuition and Fees: In-State: $36,540. Out-of-State: $36,540. Room and Board: $10,950.

Inst. Aid: FT Undergrads Receiving Aid: 6,799. Avg. Amount per Student: $29,723.

BOWDOIN COLLEGE

Brunswick, ME
admissions@bowdoin.edu; www.bowdoin.edu

General Info: Coed, College Board member, Four-year, Liberal Arts College, New England Association of Colleges and Schools, Private, Regionally Accredited. Suburban setting, Large town (10,000–49,999), Residential campus. Academic Calendar: Semester.

Student Body: Full-Time Undergrads: 1,734. Men: 48%, Women: 52%. Part-Time Undergrads: Men: 33%, Women: 67%. Total Undergrad Population: Native American or Native Alaskan: 1%. Asian American or Pacific Islander: 13%. African American: 6%. Latino: 7%. Caucasian: 68%. International: 3%. Out-of-State: 88. Living Off-Campus: 8%.

Academics: Full-Time Faculty: 166. Percentage completing two or more majors: 23%.

Admissions: Regular Application Deadline: 1/1. Priority Application Deadline: Unavailable. Early Decision Deadline: 11/15. Transfer Priority Deadline: Unavailable. Financial Aid Deadline: 2/15. Total Number of Students Applied: 5,961. Number Admitted: 1,130. Number Enrolled: 476. Number applied early decision: 710. Early decision admitted: 211. Test Scores (Middle 50%): SAT Critical Reading: 650–740. SAT Math: 650–730. SAT Writing: 650–730. ACT Comp: 29–33. HS Rank of Entering Freshmen: Top 10%: 85%. Top 25%: 99%. Avg. HS GPA: Unavailable.

Cost: Tuition and Fees: In-State: $35,990. Out-of-State: $35,990. Room and Board: $9,890.

Inst. Aid: FT Undergrads Receiving Aid: Unavailable. Avg. Amount per Student: Unavailable.

Graduates: Percentage of grads accepting a job at time of graduation: 60%.

BOWLING GREEN STATE UNIVERSITY

Huron, OH
fireadm@bgsu.edu; www.firelands.bgsu.edu

General Info: Public, Branch Campus, Two-year, Coed, Regionally Accredited, North Central Association of Colleges and Schools. Rural setting, Small town (2,500–9,999), Commuter campus. Academic Calendar: Semester.

Student Body: Full-Time Undergrads: 16,085. Men: 45%, Women: 55%. Total Undergrad Population: Native American or Native Alaskan: 0%. Asian American or Pacific Islander: 0%. African American: 5%. Latino: 2%. Caucasian: 86%. International: 0%. Out-of-State: 0%. Total all graduate and professional students: 40.

Academics: Full-Time Faculty: 875.

Admissions: Regular Application Deadline: 7/15. Priority Application Deadline: Unavailable. Early Decision Deadline: Unavailable. Transfer Priority Deadline: Unavailable. Financial Aid Deadline: Unavailable. Total Number of Students Applied: Unavailable. Percent Admitted: 89%. Number Enrolled: 3,598. Test Scores (Middle 50%): SAT Critical Reading: 440–560. SAT Math: 450–570. SAT Writing: Unavailable. ACT Comp: 19–24. HS Rank of Entering Freshmen: Top 10%: 14%. Top 25%: 36%. Avg. HS GPA: Unavailable.

Cost: Tuition and Fees: In-State: $4,228. Out-of-State: $11,536.

Inst. Aid: FT Undergrads Receiving Aid: Unavailable. Avg. Amount per Student: Unavailable.

BRADLEY UNIVERSITY

Peoria, IL

admissions@bradley.edu; www.bradley.edu

General Info: Private, University, Four-year, Coed, Regionally Accredited, College Board member. Urban setting, Large city (250,000–499,999), Residential campus. Academic Calendar: Semester.

Student Body: Full-Time Undergrads: 5,315. Men: 43%, Women: 57%. Total Undergrad Population: Native American or Native Alaskan: 0%. Asian American or Pacific Islander: 4%. African American: 6%. Latino: 3%. Caucasian: 85%. International: 0%. Out-of-State: 13%. Total all graduate and professional students: 811.

Academics: Full-Time Faculty: 326.

Admissions: Regular Application Deadline: 8/1. Priority Application Deadline: 3/1. Early Decision Deadline: Unavailable. Transfer Priority Deadline: Unavailable. Financial Aid Deadline: Unavailable. Total Number of Students Applied: Unavailable. Percent Admitted: 83%. Number Enrolled: 1,075. Test Scores (Middle 50%): SAT Critical Reading: 520–620. SAT Math: 550–650. SAT Writing: Unavailable. ACT Comp: 22–27. HS Rank of Entering Freshmen: Top 10%: 28%. Top 25%: 59%. Avg. HS GPA: Unavailable.

Cost: Tuition and Fees: In-State: $20,078. Out-of-State: $20,078. Room and Board: $6,750.

Inst. Aid: FT Undergrads Receiving Aid: Unavailable. Avg. Amount per Student: Unavailable.

BRANDEIS UNIVERSITY

Waltham, MA

admissions@brandeis.edu; www.brandeis.edu

General Info: Private, University, Four-year, Coed, Regionally Accredited, College Board member. Suburban setting, Small city (50,000–249,999), Residential campus. Academic Calendar: Semester.

Student Body: Full-Time Undergrads: 3,304. Men: 44%, Women: 55.5%. Part-Time Undergrads. Men: 0.1%, Women: 0.4%. Total Undergrad Population: Native American or Native Alaskan: 1%. Asian American or Pacific Islander: 9%. African American: 4%. Latino: 4%. Caucasian: 57%. International: 7%. Out-of-State: 75%. Living Off-Campus: 23%. Total all graduate and professional students: 2,100.

Academics: Full-Time Faculty: 352. Graduation Rates: 84% within 4 years. 96% within 6 years.

Admissions: Regular Application Deadline: 1/15. Priority Application Deadline: Unavailable. Early Decision Deadline: 11/15. Transfer Priority Deadline: Unavailable. Financial Aid Deadline: Unavailable. Total Number of Students Applied: 7,562. Number Admitted: 2,601. Number Enrolled: 701. Number accepting place on waitlist: 414. Number of waitlisted students admitted: 105. Number applied early decision: 359. Early decision admitted: 204. Test Scores (Middle 50%): SAT Critical Reading: 675. SAT Math: 685. SAT Writing: Unavailable. ACT Comp: 30. HS Rank of Entering Freshmen: Top 10%: 79%. Top 25%: 96%. Avg. HS GPA: 3.8.

Cost: Tuition and Fees: In-State: $36,122. Out-of-State: $36,122. Room and Board: $10,354.

Inst. Aid: FT Undergrads Receiving Aid: 1,519. Avg. Amount per Student: $27,315. Freshmen Receiving Non-Need Scholarship or Grant: 128. Avg. Amount per Student: $17,940.

"Greek" Colleges

- Clearwater Christian College
- Washington and Lee University
- Ohio Valley University
- DePauw University
- Sewanee University of the South

BRIGHAM YOUNG UNIVERSITY

Provo, UT

admissions@byu.edu; www.byu.edu

General Info: Coed, College Board member, Four-year, Northwest Association of Schools and Colleges, Private, Regionally Accredited, University, Church Of Jesus Christ Of Latter Day Saints. Suburban setting, Small city (50,000–249,999), Residential campus. Academic Calendar: Semester.

Student Body: Full-Time Undergrads: 30,520. Men: 51%, Women: 49%. Total Undergrad Population: Native American or Native Alaskan: 0%. Asian American or Pacific Islander: 4%. African American: 0%. Latino: 3%. Caucasian:

Great Dorms

Dobie Center—University of Texas Austin

Watterson Towers—Illinois State University

Bowles Hall—UC Berkeley

90%. International: 0%. Out-of-State: 72. Total all graduate and professional students: 2,800.

Academics: Full-Time Faculty: 1,321.

Admissions: Regular Application Deadline: 2/1. Priority Application Deadline: 12/1. Early Decision Deadline: Unavailable. Transfer Priority Deadline: Unavailable. Financial Aid Deadline: 4/15. Total Number of Students Applied: Unavailable. Percent Admitted: 70%. Number Enrolled: 5,367. Test Scores (Middle 50%): SAT Critical Reading: 550–660. SAT Math: 570–670. SAT Writing: Unavailable. ACT Comp: 25–29. HS Rank of Entering Freshmen: Top 10%: Unavailable. Top 25%: Unavailable. Avg. HS GPA: Unavailable.

Cost: Tuition and Fees: In-State: $4,080. Out-of-State: $4,080. Room and Board: $6,460.

Inst. Aid: FT Undergrads Receiving Aid: Unavailable. Avg. Amount per Student: Unavailable.

BROWN UNIVERSITY

Providence, RI

admission_undergraduate@brown.edu; www.brown.edu

General Info: Private, Liberal Arts College, University, Four-year, Coed, Regionally Accredited, College Board member. Urban setting, Small city (50,000–249,999), Residential campus. Academic Calendar: Semester.

Student Body: Full-Time Undergrads: 6,010. Men: 49%, Women: 51%. Total Undergrad Population: Native American or Native Alaskan: 0%. Asian American or Pacific Islander: 14%. African American: 7%. Latino: 8%. Caucasian: 50%. International: 7%. Out-of-State: 0%. Total all graduate and professional students: 1,734.

Academics: Full-Time Faculty: 728.

Admissions: Regular Application Deadline: 1/1. Priority Application Deadline: Unavailable. Early Decision Deadline: 11/1. Transfer Priority Deadline: Unavailable. Financial Aid Deadline: 2/1. Total Number of Students Applied: Unavailable. Percent Admitted: 14%. Number Enrolled: 1,469. Test Scores (Middle 50%): SAT Critical Reading: 670–760. SAT Math: 680–770. SAT Writing: 650–760. ACT Comp: 27–33. HS Rank of Entering Freshmen: Top 10%: 91%. Top 25%: 99%. Avg. HS GPA: Unavailable.

Cost: Tuition and Fees: In-State: $34,620. Out-of-State: $34,620. Room and Board: $9,134.

Inst. Aid: FT Undergrads Receiving Aid: Unavailable. Avg. Amount per Student: $28,995.

BRYANT UNIVERSITY

Smithfield, RI

admission@bryant.edu; www.bryant.edu

General Info: Private, College of Business, Liberal Arts College, Four-year, Coed, Regionally Accredited, College Board member. Suburban setting, Large town (10,000–49,999), Residential campus. Academic Calendar: Semester.

Student Body: Full-Time Undergrads: 3,200. Men: 54%, Women: 46%. Total Undergrad Population: Native American or Native Alaskan: 0%. Asian American or Pacific Islander: 3%. African American: 4%. Latino: 4%. Caucasian: 83%. International: 4%. Out-of-State: 91%. Total all graduate and professional students: 383.

Academics: Full-Time Faculty: 133.

Admissions: Regular Application Deadline: 2/1. Priority Application Deadline: Unavailable. Early Decision Deadline: 11/15. Transfer Priority Deadline: 4/1. Financial Aid Deadline: Unavailable. Total Number of Students Applied: Unavailable. Percent Admitted: 44%. Number Enrolled: 808. Test Scores (Middle 50%): SAT Critical Reading: 500–580. SAT Math: 540–620. SAT Writing: 510–590. ACT Comp: 21–25. HS Rank of Entering Freshmen: Top 10%: 18%. Top 25%: 56%. Avg. HS GPA: Unavailable.

Cost: Tuition and Fees: In-State: $26,099. Out-of-State: $26,099. Room and Board: $10,293.

Inst. Aid: FT Undergrads Receiving Aid: Unavailable. Avg. Amount per Student: Unavailable.

BRYN MAWR COLLEGE

Bryn Mawr, PA

admissions@brynmawr.edu; www.brynmawr.edu

General Info: College Board member, Four-year, Liberal Arts College, Private, Regionally Accredited, Women Only. Suburban setting, Very large city (over 500,000), Residential campus. Academic Calendar: Semester.

Student Body: Full-Time Undergrads: 1,378. Men: 0%, Women: 100%. Part-Time Undergrads: Men: 0%, Women: 100%. Total Undergrad Population: Native American or Native Alaskan: 0.1%. Asian American or Pacific Islander: 11.7%. African American: 6.1%. Latino: 3.4%. Caucasian: 46.6%. International: 7.1%. Out-of-State: 82%. Living Off-Campus: 5%. Total all graduate and professional students: 503.

Academics: Full-Time Faculty: 153. With PhD: 136. Percentage completing two or more majors: 15%. Graduation Rate: 80% within 4 years.

Admissions: Regular Application Deadline: 1/15. Priority Application Deadline: Unavailable. Early Decision Deadline: 11/15. Transfer Priority Deadline: Unavailable. Financial Aid Deadline: 2/4. Total Number of Students Applied: 2,106. Number Admitted: 958. Number Enrolled: 358. Number accepting place on waitlist: 200. Number of waitlisted students admitted: 20. Test Scores (Middle 50%): SAT Critical Reading: 620–730. SAT Math: 580–690. SAT Writing: 620–720. ACT Comp: 26–30. HS Rank of Entering Freshmen: Top 10%: 62%. Top 25%: 91%. Avg. HS GPA: Unavailable.

Cost: Tuition and Fees: In-State: $35,700. Out-of-State: $35,700. Room and Board: $11,520.

Inst. Aid: FT Undergrads Receiving Aid: 53. Avg. Amount per Student: Unavailable.

Graduates: Percentage of grads accepting a job at time of graduation: 49%. Alumni Giving %: 43.3%.

BUCKNELL UNIVERSITY

Lewisburg, PA
admissions@bucknell.edu; www.bucknell.edu

General Info: Private, University, Four-year, Coed, Regionally Accredited, College Board member. Rural setting, Small town (2,500–9,999), Residential campus. Academic Calendar: Semester.

Student Body: Full-Time Undergrads: 3,400. Men: 50%, Women: 50%. Part-Time Undergrads: unavailable. Total Undergrad Population: Native American or Native Alaskan: 0%. Asian American or Pacific Islander: 4%. African American: 4%. Latino: 3%. Caucasian: 85%. International: 2%. Out-of-State: 77%. Total all graduate and professional students: 157.

Academics: Full-Time Faculty: 317. Graduation Rates: 86% within 4 years. 89% within 6 years.

Admissions: Regular Application Deadline: 1/15. Priority Application Deadline: Unavailable. Early Decision Deadline: 11/15. Transfer Priority Deadline: Unavailable. Financial Aid Deadline: 1/1. Total Number of Students Applied: Unavailable. Percent Admitted: 33%. Number Enrolled: 923. Test Scores (Middle 50%): SAT Critical Reading: 600–690. SAT Math: 630–710. SAT Writing: 600–690. ACT Comp: 27–31. HS Rank of Entering Freshmen: Top 10%: 72%. Top 25%: 93%. Avg. HS GPA: Unavailable.

Cost: Tuition and Fees: In-State: $39,434. Out-of-State: $39,434. Room and Board: $8,728.

Inst. Aid: FT Undergrads Receiving Aid: Unavailable. Avg. Amount per Student: Unavailable.

BUTLER UNIVERSITY

Indianapolis, IN
admission@butler.edu; go.butler.edu

General Info: Coed, College Board member, Four-year, Nondenominational, North Central Association of Colleges and Schools, Private, Regionally Accredited, University. Residential campus, Suburban setting, Very large city (over 500,000), 12 minutes from downtown Indianapolis. Academic Calendar: Semester.

Student Body: Full-Time Undergrads: 3,872. Men: 37%, Women: 63%. Part-Time Undergrads: 2%. Total Undergrad Population: Native American or Native Alaskan: 0.2%. Asian American or Pacific Islander: 2.2%. African American: 3.2%. Latino: 1.7%. Caucasian: 86%. International: 3.1%. Out-of-State: 44%. Living Off-Campus: 33%. Total all graduate and professional students: 576.

Academics: Full-Time Faculty: 373. With PhD: 248. Percentage completing two or more majors: 14%. Graduation Rates: 56% within 4 years. 70% within 6 years.

Admissions: Regular Application Deadline: 3/1. Priority Application Deadline: 12/1. Early Decision Deadline: Unavailable. Transfer Priority Deadline: 8/15. Financial Aid Deadline: 8/1. Total Number of Students Applied: 5,265. Number Admitted: 3,987. Number Enrolled: 965. Test Scores (Middle 50%): SAT Critical Reading: 530–630. SAT Math: 540–650. SAT Writing: Unavailable. ACT Comp: 25–29. HS Rank of Entering Freshmen: Top 10%: 48.5%. Top 25%: 78.6%. Avg. HS GPA: 3.7.

Cost: Tuition and Fees: In-State: $26,070. Out-of-State: $26,070. Room and Board: $8,735.

Inst. Aid: FT Undergrads Receiving Aid: 3,268. Avg. Amount per Student: Unavailable.

Graduates: No. of companies recruiting on campus: 200. Percentage of grads accepting a job at time of graduation: 61%. Alumni Giving %: 24%.

CALIFORNIA INSTITUTE OF TECHNOLOGY

Pasadena, CA
ugadmissions@caltech.edu; www.caltech.edu

General Info: Private, University, Four-year, Coed, Regionally Accredited, College Board member. Suburban setting, Small city (50,000–249,999), Residential campus. Academic Calendar: Quarter.

Student Body: Full-Time Undergrads: 864. Men: 71%, Women: 29%. Total Undergrad Population: Native American or Native Alaskan: 1%. Asian American or Pacific Islander: 38%. African American: 1%. Latino: 5%. Caucasian: 43%. International: 9%. Out-of-State: 65. Total all graduate and professional students: 1,220.

Academics: Full-Time Faculty: 284. With PhD: 278.

Admissions: Regular Application Deadline: 1/1. Priority Application Deadline: Unavailable. Early Decision Deadline: 11/1. Transfer Priority Deadline: Unavailable. Financial Aid Deadline: 1/15. Total Number of Students Applied: 3,597. Number Admitted: 607. Number Enrolled: Unavailable. Number accepting place on waitlist: 164. Number of waitlisted students admitted: 30. Test Scores (Middle 50%): SAT Critical Reading: 700–780. SAT Math: 770–800. SAT Writing: 680–770. ACT Comp: 32–35. HS Rank of Entering Freshmen: Top 10%: 99%. Top 25%: 100%. Avg. HS GPA: Unavailable.

Cost: Tuition and Fees: In-State: $31,437. Out-of-State: $31,437. Room and Board: $10,146.

Inst. Aid: FT Undergrads Receiving Aid: Unavailable. Avg. Amount per Student: Unavailable.

Graduates: Alumni Giving %: 28%.

CALIFORNIA POLYTECHNIC STATE UNIVERSITY

San Luis Obispo, CA

admissions@calpoly.edu; www.calpoly.edu

General Info: Public, University, Four-year, Coed, Western Association of Schools and Colleges, Regionally Accredited, College Board member. Suburban setting, Large town (10,000–49,999), Residential campus. Academic Calendar: Quarter.

Student Body: Full-Time Undergrads: 17,488. Men: 52%, Women: 48%. Total Undergrad Population: Native American or Native Alaskan: 1%. Asian American or Pacific Islander: 12%. African American: 1%. Latino: 9%. Caucasian: 68%. Total all graduate and professional students: 987.

Academics: Full-Time Faculty: 726.

Admissions: Regular Application Deadline: 11/30. Priority Application Deadline: Unavailable. Early Decision Deadline: 10/31. Transfer Priority Deadline: Unavailable. Financial Aid Deadline: Unavailable. Total Number of Students Applied: Unavailable. Percent Admitted: 45%. Number Enrolled: 4,294. Test Scores (Middle 50%): SAT Critical Reading: 520–630. SAT Math: 570–670. SAT Writing: Unavailable. ACT Comp: 23–28. HS Rank of Entering Freshmen: Top 10%: 37%. Top 25%: 76%. Avg. HS GPA: Unavailable.

Cost: Tuition and Fees: In-State: $4,350. Out-of-State: $14,520. Room and Board: $8,430.

Inst. Aid: FT Undergrads Receiving Aid: Unavailable. Avg. Amount per Student: Unavailable.

Schools with Great Food Options

Dickinson College

University of Southern California

College of the Atlantic

CALIFORNIA STATE UNIVERSITY–CHICO

Chico, CA

info@csuchico.edu; www.csuchico.edu

General Info: Public, Liberal Arts College, University, Four-year, Coed, Regionally Accredited, Western Association of Schools and Colleges, College Board member. Rural setting, Small city (50,000–249,999), Residential campus. Academic Calendar: Semester.

Student Body: Full-Time Undergrads: 16,250. Men: 46%, Women: 54%. Total Undergrad Population: Native American or Native Alaskan: 1%. Asian American or Pacific Islander: 7%. African American: 3%. Latino: 13%. Caucasian: 63%. International: 1%. Out-of-State: 1%. Total all graduate and professional students: 1,393.

Academics: Full-Time Faculty: 499.

Admissions: Regular Application Deadline: 11/30. Priority Application Deadline: Unavailable. Early Decision Deadline: Unavailable. Transfer Priority Deadline: 10/1. Financial Aid Deadline: Unavailable. Total Number of Students Applied: Unavailable. Percent Admitted: 87%. Number Enrolled: 2,300. Test Scores (Middle 50%): SAT Critical Reading: 460–570. SAT Math: 470–580. SAT Writing: Unavailable. ACT Comp: 19–23. HS Rank of Entering Freshmen: Top 10%: 35%. Top 25%: 76%. Avg. HS GPA: Unavailable.

Cost: Tuition and Fees: In-State: $3,402. Out-of-State: $13,572. Room and Board: $8,560.

Inst. Aid: FT Undergrads Receiving Aid: Unavailable. Avg. Amount per Student: Unavailable.

CALIFORNIA STATE UNIVERSITY–LONG BEACH

Long Beach, CA

eslb@csulb.edu; www.csulb.edu

General Info: Public, University, Four-year, Coed, Regionally Accredited, Western Association of Schools and Colleges, College Board member. Suburban setting, Large city (250,000–499,999), Commuter campus. Academic Calendar: Semester.

Student Body: Full-Time Undergrads: 28,514. Men: 37%, Women: 63%. Total Undergrad Population: Native American or Native Alaskan: 1%. Asian American or Pacific Islander: 24%. African American: 6%. Latino: 28%. Caucasian: 31%. International: 3%. Out-of-State: 1%. Total all graduate and professional students: 6,033.

Academics: Graduation Rates: 12% within 4 years. 45% within 6 years.

Admissions: Regular Application Deadline: 11/30. Priority Application Deadline: Unavailable. Early Decision Deadline: Unavailable. Transfer Priority Deadline: 11/30. Financial Aid Deadline: Unavailable. Total Number of Students Applied: 42,815. Number Admitted: 22,131. Number Enrolled: 4,464. Test Scores (Middle 50%): SAT Critical Reading: 450–560. SAT Math: 470–580. SAT Writing: Unavailable. ACT Comp: 17–23. HS Rank of Entering Freshmen: Top 10%: Unavailable. Top 25%: 84%. Avg. HS GPA: 3.40.

Cost: Tuition and Fees: In-State: $2,864. Out-of-State: $13,034. Room and Board: $6,648.

Inst. Aid: FT Undergrads Receiving Aid: 64%. Avg. Amount per Student: Unavailable.

CALIFORNIA STATE UNIVERSITY–SAN JOSE

San Jose, CA

outreach@sjsu.edu; www.sjsu.edu/

General Info: Public University, Four-year, Coed. Academic Calendar: Semester.

Student Body: Full-Time Undergrads: 17,189. Men: Unavailable, Women: Unavailable.

Academics: Full-Time Faculty: 1,688. Graduation Rate: 41.3% within 6 years.

Admissions: Regular Application Deadline: 2/1. Priority Application Deadline: 10/1. Financial Aid Deadline: 3/2. Total Number of Students Applied: 9,164. Number Admitted: 5,983. Number Enrolled: 2,671. Test Scores (Middle 50%): SAT Critical Reading: Unavailable. SAT Math: Unavailable. SAT Writing: Unavailable. ACT Comp: Unavailable. HS Rank of Entering Freshmen: Top 10%: Unavailable. Top 25%: Unavailable. Avg. HS GPA: 3.13.

Cost: Tuition and Fees: $8,690. In-State: Unavailable. Out-of-State: Unavailable. Room and Board: $9,505.

Inst. Aid: FT Undergrads Receiving Aid: Unavailable. Avg. Amount per Student: Unavailable.

CALVIN COLLEGE

Grand Rapids, MI

admissions@calvin.edu; www.calvin.edu

General Info: Coed, College Board member, Four-year, Liberal Arts College, North Central Association of Colleges and Schools, Private, Regionally Accredited, Christian Reformed Church. Suburban setting, Large city (250,000–499,999), Residential campus. Academic Calendar: 4-1-4.

Student Body: Full-Time Undergrads: 4,200. Men: 46%, Women: 54%. Total Undergrad Population: Native American or Native Alaskan: 0%. Asian American or Pacific Islander: 4%. African American: 1.5%. Latino: 2%. Caucasian: 81%. International: 7.5%. Out-of-State: 48%. Living Off-Campus: 44%. Total all graduate and professional students: 71.

Academics: Full-Time Faculty: 322. With PhD: 266. Graduation Rate: 74% within 6 years.

Admissions: Regular Application Deadline: 8/15. Priority Application Deadline: 12/1. Early Decision Deadline: Unavailable. Fall Transfer Deadline: 8/15. Spring Transfer Deadline: 1/15. Financial Aid Deadline: Unavailable. Total Number of Students Applied: 2,277. Number Admitted: 2,169. Number Enrolled: 1,124. Number accepting place on waitlist: 50. Number of waitlisted students admitted: 30. Test Scores (Middle 50%): SAT Critical Reading: 530–650. SAT Math: 540–650. SAT Writing: Unavailable. ACT Comp: 23–28. HS Rank of Entering Freshmen: Top 10%: 26%. Top 25%: 51%. Avg. HS GPA: 3.6.

Cost: Tuition and Fees: In-State: $22,940. Out-of-State: $22,940. Room and Board: $7,970.

Inst. Aid: FT Undergrads Receiving Aid: 4,011. Avg. Amount per Student: $16,200. Freshmen Receiving Non-Need Scholarship or Grant: 222. Avg. Amount per Student: $10,500.

Graduates: No. of companies recruiting on campus: 50. Alumni Giving %: 31%.

Unique Majors

Environmental Justice—St. Thomas University

Astrobiology—Arizona State University

Peace and Conflict Studies—UC Berkeley

Turfgrass Management—Ohio State University

Three Languages—University of Delaware

CANISIUS COLLEGE

Buffalo, NY

admissions@canisius.edu; www.canisius.edu

General Info: Private, Liberal Arts College, Teachers College/College of Education, Four-year, Roman Catholic Church, Society of Jesus (Jesuits), Coed, Regionally Accredited, College Board member. Urban setting, Large city (250,000–499,999), Residential campus. Academic Calendar: Semester.

Student Body: Full-Time Undergrads: 2,898. Men: 47%, Women: 53%. Total Undergrad Population: Native American or Native Alaskan: 1%. Asian American or Pacific Islander: 1%. African American: 8%. Latino: 3%. Caucasian: 80%. International: 3%. Out-of-State: 9%. Total all graduate and professional students: 1,389.

Academics: Full-Time Faculty: 215.

Admissions: Regular Application Deadline: 5/1. Priority Application Deadline: Unavailable. Early Decision Deadline: 11/15. Transfer Priority Deadline: Unavailable. Financial Aid Deadline: Unavailable. Total Number of Students

Most Nobel Prize Affiliations

Columbia University—87 affiliations

Harvard University—82 affiliations

University of Chicago—81 affiliations

MIT—72 affiliations

University of California Berkeley—61 affiliations

Applied: Unavailable. Percent Admitted: 77%. Number Enrolled: 753. Test Scores (Middle 50%): SAT Critical Reading: 490–590. SAT Math: 510–610. SAT Writing: Unavailable. ACT Comp: 21–25. HS Rank of Entering Freshmen: Top 10%: 22%. Top 25%: 51%. Avg. HS GPA: Unavailable.

Cost: Tuition and Fees: In-State: $24,857. Out-of-State: $24,857. Room and Board: $9,480.

Inst. Aid: FT Undergrads Receiving Aid: Unavailable. Avg. Amount per Student: Unavailable.

CARLETON COLLEGE

Northfield, MN

admissions@carleton.edu; www.carleton.edu

General Info: Coed, College Board member, Four-year, Liberal Arts College, Private, Regionally Accredited. Rural setting, Large town (10,000–49,999), Residential campus. Academic Calendar: Trimester.

Student Body: Full-Time Undergrads: 2,005. Men: 47.5%, Women: 52.5%. Total Undergrad Population: Native American or Native Alaskan: 1%. Asian American or Pacific Islander: 10%. African American: 4%. Latino: 5%. Caucasian: 73%. International: 6%. Out-of-State: 77%. Living Off-Campus: 11%.

Academics: Full-Time Faculty: 227. With PhD: 202. Graduation Rates: 90% within 4 years. 93% within 6 years.

Admissions: Regular Application Deadline: 1/15. Priority Application Deadline: Unavailable. Early Decision Deadline: 11/15. Transfer Priority Deadline: Unavailable. Financial Aid Deadline: 2/15. Total Number of Students Applied: 4,850. Number Admitted: 1,444. Number Enrolled: 509. Test Scores (Middle 50%): SAT Critical Reading: 670–750. SAT Math: 660–740. SAT Writing: 650–740. ACT Comp: 29–33. HS Rank of Entering Freshmen: Top 10%: 74%. Top 25%: 92%. Avg. HS GPA: Unavailable.

Cost: Tuition and Fees: In-State: $37,860. Out-of-State: $37,860. Room and Board: $9,978.

Inst. Aid: FT Undergrads Receiving Aid: 1,083. Avg. Amount per Student: $29,601.

CARNEGIE MELLON UNIVERSITY

Pittsburgh, PA

undergraduate-admissions@andrew.cmu.edu; www.cmu.edu

General Info: Coed, College Board member, Four-year, Private, Regionally Accredited, University. Urban setting, Large city (250,000–499,999), Residential campus. Academic Calendar: Semester.

Student Body: Full-Time Undergrads: 5,758. Men: 61%, Women: 39%. Total Undergrad Population: Native American or Native Alaskan: 1%. Asian American or Pacific Islander: 24%. African American: 5%. Latino: 4%. Caucasian: 39%. International: 14%. Out-of-State: 77%. Living Off-Campus: 20%. Total all graduate and professional students: 4,644.

Academics: Full-Time Faculty: 822.

Admissions: Regular Application Deadline: 1/1. Priority Application Deadline: Unavailable. Early Decision Deadline: 11/1. Fall Transfer Deadline: 3/1. Spring Transfer Deadline: 11/1. Transfer Priority Deadline: Unavailable. Financial Aid Deadline: 5/1. Total Number of Students Applied: 22,356. Number Admitted: 6,259. Number Enrolled: 1,436. Number applied early decision: 995. Early decision admitted: 226. Test Scores (Middle 50%): SAT Critical Reading: Unavailable. SAT Math: Unavailable. SAT Writing: Unavailable. HS Rank of Entering Freshmen: Top 10%: 73%. Top 25%: 94%. Avg. HS GPA: 3.63.

Cost: Tuition and Fees: In-State: $39,750. Out-of-State: $39,750. Room and Board: $10,050.

Inst. Aid: FT Undergrads Receiving Aid: Unavailable. Avg. Amount per Student: $24,724.

Graduates: No. of companies recruiting on campus: 800. Percentage of grads accepting a job at time of graduation: 99%.

CASE WESTERN RESERVE UNIVERSITY

Cleveland, OH

admission@case.edu; www.case.edu

General Info: Private, University, Four-year, Coed, Regionally Accredited, College Board member. Urban setting, Very large city (over 500,000), Residential campus. Academic Calendar: Semester.

Student Body: Full-Time Undergrads: 4,080. Men: 59%, Women: 41%. Total Undergrad Population: Native American or Native Alaskan: 0%. Asian American or Pacific Islander: 20%. African American: 7%. Latino: 2%. Caucasian: 62%. International: 3%. Out-of-State: 54%. Total all graduate and professional students: 3,928.

Academics: Full-Time Faculty: 696.

Admissions: Regular Application Deadline: 1/15. Priority Application Deadline: Unavailable. Early Decision Deadline: 11/1. Transfer Priority Deadline: Unavailable. Financial Aid Deadline: Unavailable. Total Number of Students Applied: Unavailable. Percent Admitted: 67%. Number Enrolled: 1,015. Test Scores (Middle 50%): SAT Critical Reading: 600–700. SAT Math: 630–730. SAT Writing: 590–680. ACT Comp: 26–31. HS Rank of Entering Freshmen: Top 10%: 68%. Top 25%: 93%. Avg. HS GPA: Unavailable.

Cost: Tuition and Fees: In-State: $33,908. Out-of-State: $31,738. Room and Board: $9,938.

Inst. Aid: FT Undergrads Receiving Aid: Unavailable. Avg. Amount per Student: Unavailable.

CATHOLIC UNIVERSITY OF AMERICA

Washington, DC

cua-admissions@cua.edu; www.cua.edu

General Info: Coed, College Board member, Four-year, Liberal Arts College, Private, Regionally Accredited, Roman Catholic Church, University. Urban setting, Very large city (over 500,000), Residential campus. Academic Calendar: Semester.

Student Body: Full-Time Undergrads: 3,123. Men: 46%, Women: 54%. Total Undergrad Population: Native American or Native Alaskan: 0%. Asian American or Pacific Islander: 4%. African American: 5%. Latino: 6%. Caucasian: 71%. International: 1%. Out-of-State: 99%. Total all graduate and professional students: 2,059.

Academics: Full-Time Faculty: 344.

Admissions: Regular Application Deadline: 2/15. Priority Application Deadline: Unavailable. Early Decision Deadline: 11/15. Financial Aid Deadline: 4/15. Total Number of Students Applied: Unavailable. Percent Admitted: 81%. Number Enrolled: 857. Test Scores (Middle 50%): SAT Critical Reading: 520–620. SAT Math: 520–620. SAT Writing: Unavailable. ACT Comp: 22–27. HS Rank of Entering Freshmen: Top 10%: 25%. Top 25%: 53%. Avg. HS GPA: 3.5.

Cost: Tuition and Fees: In-State: $28,990. Out-of-State: $30,670. Room and Board: $10,808.

Inst. Aid: FT Undergrads Receiving Aid: Unavailable. Avg. Amount per Student: Unavailable.

CENTENARY COLLEGE OF LOUISIANA

Shreveport, LA

tcrowley@centenary.edu; www.centenary.edu

General Info: Private, Liberal Arts College, Four-year, United Methodist Church, Coed, Regionally Accredited, College Board member. Suburban setting, Small city (50,000–249,999), Residential campus. Academic Calendar: Semester.

Student Body: Full-Time Undergrads: 904. Men: 41%, Women: 59%. Total Undergrad Population: Native American or Native Alaskan: 1%. Asian American or Pacific Islander: 1%. African American: 5%. Latino: 6%. Caucasian: 85%. International: 1%. Out-of-State: 57%. Total all graduate and professional students: 140.

Academics: Full-Time Faculty: 73.

Admissions: Regular Application Deadline: 2/15. Priority Application Deadline: 1/15. Early Decision Deadline: 12/1. Transfer Priority Deadline: Unavailable. Financial Aid Deadline: Unavailable. Total Number of Students Applied: Unavailable. Percent Admitted: 64%. Number Enrolled: 233. Test Scores (Middle 50%): SAT Critical Reading: 510–650. SAT Math: 500–630. SAT Writing: Unavailable. ACT Comp: 23–28. HS Rank of Entering Freshmen: Top 10%: 36%. Top 25%: 67%. Avg. HS GPA: Unavailable.

Cost: Tuition and Fees: In-State: $20,950. Out-of-State: $19,760. Room and Board: $6,990.

Inst. Aid: FT Undergrads Receiving Aid: Unavailable. Avg. Amount per Student: Unavailable.

CENTRE COLLEGE

Danville, KY

admission@centre.edu; www.centre.edu

General Info: Private, Liberal Arts College, Four-year, Presbyterian Church (USA), Coed, Regionally Accredited, College Board member. Suburban setting, Large town (10,000–49,999), Residential campus. Academic Calendar: 4-1-4.

Student Body: Full-Time Undergrads: 1,150. Men: 47%, Women: 53%. Total Undergrad Population: Native Ameri-

Large International Student Bodies (Percentage of Student Body)

Brigham Young University–Hawaii	48%
New School (NY)	22%
Mount Holyoke College (MA)	17%
College of the Atlantic (ME)	16%
Florida Institute of Technology (FL)	16%

can or Native Alaskan: 0%. Asian American or Pacific Islander: 2%. African American: 3%. Latino: 2%. Caucasian: 90%. International: 2%. Out-of-State: 44%. Living Off-Campus: 2%.

Academics: Graduation Rates: 80% within 4 years. 80% within 6 years.

Admissions: Regular Application Deadline: 2/1. Priority Application Deadline: Unavailable. Early Decision Deadline: Unavailable. Financial Aid Deadline: 3/1. Total Number of Students Applied: 2,200. Number Admitted: 1,300. Number Enrolled: Unavailable. Test Scores (Middle 50%): SAT Critical Reading: 570–690. SAT Math: 570–650. SAT Writing: Unavailable. ACT Comp: 26–30. HS Rank of Entering Freshmen: Top 10%: 60%. Top 25%: 84%. Avg. HS GPA: 3.65.

Cost: Tuition and Fees: In-State: $29,600. Room and Board: $7,400.

Inst. Aid: FT Undergrads Receiving Aid: 676. Avg. Amount per Student: Unavailable.

CHATHAM UNIVERSITY

Pittsburgh, PA

admissions@chatham.edu; www.chatham.edu

General Info: College Board member, Four-year, Middle States Association of Colleges and Schools, Private, Regionally Accredited, University, Women Only. Urban setting, Large city (250,000–499,999), Residential campus. Academic Calendar: 4-4-1.

Student Body: Full-Time Undergrads: Unavailable. Men: 0%, Women: 100%. Total Undergrad Population: Native American or Native Alaskan: 0.3%. Asian American or Pacific Islander: 1.5%. African American: 8%. Latino: 1.5%. Caucasian: 64.2%. International: 6.4%. Out-of-State: 19%. Total all graduate and professional students: 985.

Academics: Full-Time Faculty: 85. Graduation Rates: 51.4% within 4 years. 48.1% within 6 years.

Admissions: Regular Application Deadline: 8/1. Priority Application Deadline: 3/15. Early Decision Deadline: N/A. Transfer Priority Deadline: Rolling admission. Financial Aid Deadline: 5/1. Total Number of Students Applied: Unavailable. Percent Admitted: 61%. Number Enrolled: 117. Test Scores (Middle 50%): SAT Critical Reading: 480–583. SAT Math: 440–563. SAT Writing: Unavailable. ACT Comp: 21–26. HS Rank of Entering Freshmen: Top 10%: 18%. Top 25%: 41%. Avg. HS GPA: Unavailable.

Cost: Tuition and Fees: In-State: $25,216. Out-of-State: $25,216. Room and Board: $7,892.

Inst. Aid: FT Undergrads Receiving Aid: Unavailable. Avg. Amount per Student: Unavailable.

CITADEL, THE MILITARY COLLEGE OF SOUTH CAROLINA

Charleston, SC

admissions@citadel.edu; www.citadel.edu

General Info: Public, Military College, Four-year, Coed, Regionally Accredited, Southern Association of Colleges and Schools, College Board member. Urban setting, Large city (250,000–499,999), Residential campus. Academic Calendar: Semester.

Student Body: Full-Time Undergrads: 1,964. Men: 95%, Women: 5%. Total Undergrad Population: Native American or Native Alaskan: 0%. Asian American or Pacific Islander: 4%. African American: 8%. Latino: 4%. Caucasian: 82%. International: 2%. Out-of-State: 55%. Total all graduate and professional students: 1,068.

Academics: Full-Time Faculty: 157.

Admissions: Regular Application Deadline: Rolling. Priority Application Deadline: Unavailable. Early Decision Deadline: 10/1. Transfer Priority Deadline: Unavailable. Financial Aid Deadline: 3/1. Total Number of Students Applied: Unavailable. Percent Admitted: 75%. Number Enrolled: 538. Test Scores (Middle 50%): SAT Critical Reading: 490–590. SAT Math: 510–610. SAT Writing: 20–23. ACT Comp: 20–24. HS Rank of Entering Freshmen: Top 10%: 9%. Top 25%: 31%. Avg. HS GPA: 3.1.

Cost: Tuition and Fees: In-State: $8,000. Out-of-State: $20,500. Room and Board: $5,765.

Inst. Aid: FT Undergrads Receiving Aid: 994. Avg. Amount per Student: $10,969. Freshmen Receiving Non-Need Scholarship or Grant: 199. Avg. Amount per Student: $57.

Graduates: No. of companies recruiting on campus: 150. Percentage of grads accepting a job at time of graduation: 95%.

CITY UNIVERSITY OF NEW YORK–BARUCH COLLEGE

New York, NY

admissions@baruch.cuny.edu; www.baruch.cuny.edu

General Info: Coed, Public. Very large city (over 500,000). Academic Calendar: Semester.

Student Body: Full-Time Undergrads: 12,796. Men: 47%, Women: 53%.

Academics: Full-Time Faculty: 473.

Admissions: Regular Application Deadline: 2/1. Priority Application Deadline: Unavailable. Early Decision Deadline: 12/1. Financial Aid Deadline: Unavailable. Total Number of Students Applied: Unavailable. Percent Admitted: 36%. Number Enrolled: 1,508. Test Scores (Middle 50%): SAT Critical Reading: 460–570. SAT Math: 530–630. ACT Comp: Unavailable. HS Rank of Entering Freshmen: Top 10%: 28%. Top 25%: 59%. Avg. HS GPA: Unavailable.

Cost: Tuition and Fees: In-State: $4,349.

Inst. Aid: FT Undergrads Receiving Aid: Unavailable. Avg. Amount per Student: Unavailable.

CITY UNIVERSITY OF NEW YORK–BROOKLYN COLLEGE

Brooklyn, NY

adminqry@brooklyn.cuny.edu; www.brooklyn.cuny.edu

General Info: Public, Liberal Arts College, Four-year, Coed, Regionally Accredited, Middle States Association of Colleges and Schools. Urban setting, Very large city (over 500,000), Commuter campus. Academic Calendar: Semester.

Student Body: Full-Time Undergrads: 12,111. Men: 40%, Women: 60%. Total Undergrad Population: Native American or Native Alaskan: 0%. Asian American or Pacific Islander: 20%. African American: 18%. Latino: 13%. Caucasian: 43%. International: 6%. Out-of-State: 1%. Total all graduate and professional students: 3,917.

Academics: Full-Time Faculty: 515. Graduation Rates: 18% within 4 years. 44% within 6 years.

Admissions: Regular Application Deadline: 3/15. Priority Application Deadline: Unavailable. Early Decision Deadline: Unavailable. Transfer Priority Deadline: Unavailable. Financial Aid Deadline: Unavailable. Total Number of Students Applied: Unavailable. Percent Admitted: 45%. Number Enrolled: 1,379. Test Scores (Middle 50%): SAT Critical Reading: 450–560. SAT Math: 490–580. SAT Writing: Unavailable. ACT Comp: Unavailable. HS Rank of Entering Freshmen: Top 10%: 14%. Top 25%: 45%. Avg. HS GPA: Unavailable.

Cost: Tuition and Fees: In-State: $4,377. Out-of-State: $11,177.

Inst. Aid: FT Undergrads Receiving Aid: Unavailable. Avg. Amount per Student: Unavailable.

CITY UNIVERSITY OF NEW YORK–JOHN JAY COLLEGE OF CRIMINAL JUSTICE

New York, NY

admiss@jjay.cuny.edu; www.jjay.cuny.edu

General Info: Public, Liberal Arts College, Four-year, Coed, Regionally Accredited, Middle States Association of Colleges and Schools, Hispanic serving. Urban setting, Very large city (over 500,000), Commuter campus. Academic Calendar: Semester.

Student Body: Full-Time Undergrads: 12,784. Men: 44%, Women: 56%. Total Undergrad Population: Native American or Native Alaskan: 0%. Asian American or Pacific Islander: 8%. African American: 22%. Latino: 43%. Caucasian: 23%. International: 4%. Out-of-State: 7%. Total all graduate and professional students: 1,861.

Academics: Full-Time Faculty: 341.

Admissions: Regular Application Deadline: Rolling. Priority Application Deadline: Unavailable. Early Decision Deadline: Unavailable. Transfer Priority Deadline: Unavailable. Financial Aid Deadline: Unavailable. Total Number of Students Applied: Unavailable. Percent Admitted: 82%. Number Enrolled: 2,704. Test Scores (Middle 50%): SAT Critical Reading: 420–520. SAT Math: 420–510. SAT Writing: 370–420. HS Rank of Entering Freshmen: Top 10%: Unavailable. Top 25%: Unavailable. Avg. HS GPA: Unavailable.

Cost: Tuition and Fees: In-State: $4,279. Out-of-State: $11,079. Room and Board: Unavailable.

Inst. Aid: FT Undergrads Receiving Aid: 58%. Avg. Amount per Student: $3,544.

Schools with Great Locations

New York University

University of Wisconsin

UC Santa Cruz

University of Colorado

CITY UNIVERSITY OF NEW YORK–LEHMAN COLLEGE

Bronx, NY

enroll@lehman.cuny.edu; www.lehman.edu

General Info: Public, Liberal Arts College, Four-year, Coed, Regionally Accredited, Middle States Association of Colleges and Schools, College Board member, Hispanic serving. Urban setting, Very large city (over 500,000), Commuter campus. Academic Calendar: Semester.

Student Body: Full-Time Undergrads: 8,747. Men: 26%, Women: 74%. Total Undergrad Population: Native American or Native Alaskan: 0%. Asian American or Pacific Islander: 5%. African American: 27%. Latino: 55%. Caucasian: 7%. International: 6%. Out-of-State: 1%. Living Off-Campus: 100%. Total all graduate and professional students: 2,067.

Academics: Full-Time Faculty: 95.

Admissions: Regular Application Deadline: 8/15. Priority Application Deadline: 2/15. Early Decision Deadline: Unavailable. Financial Aid Deadline: Unavailable. Total Number of Students Applied: Unavailable. Number Admitted: Unavailable. Number Enrolled: Unavailable. Test Scores (Middle 50%): SAT Critical Reading: 380–480. SAT Math: 380–480. SAT Writing: Unavailable. HS Rank of Entering Freshmen: Top 10%: Unavailable. Top 25%: Unavailable. Avg. HS GPA: Unavailable.

Cost: Tuition and Fees: In-State: $4,290. Out-of-State: $11,090.

Inst. Aid: FT Undergrads Receiving Aid: Unavailable. Avg. Amount per Student: Unavailable.

CITY UNIVERSITY OF NEW YORK–QUEENS COLLEGE

Flushing, NY

vincent@qc1.qc.edu; www.qc.cuny.edu

General Info: Public, Liberal Arts College, Four-year, Coed, Regionally Accredited, Middle States Association of Colleges and Schools, College Board member. Urban setting, Very large city (over 500,000), Commuter campus. Academic Calendar: Semester.

Student Body: Full-Time Undergrads: 13,019. Men: 40%, Women: 60%. Total Undergrad Population: Native American or Native Alaskan: 0%. Asian American or Pacific Islander: 20%. African American: 7%. Latino: 16%. Caucasian: 48%. International: 9%. Out-of-State: 1%. Total all graduate and professional students: 4,620.

Academics: Full-Time Faculty: 581.

Admissions: Regular Application Deadline: 1/1. Priority Application Deadline: 2/1. Early Decision Deadline: Unavailable. Transfer Priority Deadline: 3/1. Financial Aid Deadline: Unavailable. Total Number of Students Applied: Unavailable. Percent Admitted: 43%. Number Enrolled: Unavailable. Test Scores (Middle 50%): SAT Critical Reading: 440–550. SAT Math: 480–580. SAT Writing: Unavailable. ACT Comp: 24. HS Rank of Entering Freshmen: Top 10%: Unavailable. Top 25%: Unavailable. Avg. HS GPA: Unavailable.

Cost: Tuition and Fees: In-State: $4,377. Out-of-State: $11,177.

Inst. Aid: FT Undergrads Receiving Aid: Unavailable. Avg. Amount per Student: Unavailable.

Schools with Strong Religious Ties

University of Notre Dame—Catholicism

Brandeis University—Judaism

Brigham Young University—Mormon

CLAREMONT MCKENNA COLLEGE

Claremont, CA

admission@claremontmckenna.edu; www.claremontmckenna.edu

General Info: Private, Liberal Arts College, Four-year, Coed, Regionally Accredited, College Board member. Suburban setting, Large town (10,000–49,999), Residential campus. Academic Calendar: Semester.

Student Body: Full-Time Undergrads: 1,150. Men: 55%, Women: 45%. Total Undergrad Population: Native American or Native Alaskan: 0%. Asian American or Pacific Islander: 13%. African American: 3%. Latino: 16%. Caucasian: 54%. International: 2%. Out-of-State: 51%.

Academics: Full-Time Faculty: 124.

Admissions: Regular Application Deadline: 1/2. Priority Application Deadline: Unavailable. Early Decision Deadline: 11/15. Fall Transfer Deadline: 4/1. Transfer Priority Deadline: Unavailable. Financial Aid Deadline: Unavailable. Total Number of Students Applied: Unavailable. Percent Admitted: 22%. Number Enrolled: 296. Test Scores (Middle 50%): SAT Critical Reading: 630–730. SAT Math: 640–740. SAT Writing: 700. ACT Comp: 31. HS Rank of Entering Freshmen: Top 10%: 93%. Top 25%: 98%. Avg. HS GPA: Unavailable.

Cost: Tuition and Fees: In-State: $33,210. Out-of-State: $33,210. Room and Board: $10,740.

Inst. Aid: FT Undergrads Receiving Aid: Unavailable. Avg. Amount per Student: Unavailable.

CLARK UNIVERSITY

Worcester, MA

admissions@clarku.edu; www.clarku.edu

General Info: Coed, College Board member, Four-year, Liberal Arts College, Private, Regionally Accredited, University. Urban setting, Small city (50,000–249,999), Residential campus. Academic Calendar: Semester.

Student Body: Full-Time Undergrads. Men: 37%, Women: 63%. Total Undergrad Population: Native American or Native Alaskan: 1%. Asian American or Pacific Islander: 4%. African American: 2%. Latino: 2%. Caucasian: 69%. International: 8%. Out-of-State: 70%. Living Off-Campus: 1%. Total all graduate and professional students: 714.

Academics: Full-Time Faculty: 173. With PhD: 167. Percentage completing two or more majors: 18%. Graduation Rates: 69% within 4 years. 76% within 6 years.

Admissions: Regular Application Deadline: 1/15. Priority Application Deadline: Unavailable. Early Decision Deadline: 11/15. Transfer Priority Deadline: Unavailable. Financial Aid Deadline: 2/1. Total Number of Students Applied: 5,201. Number Admitted: 2,918. Number Enrolled: Unavailable. Number accepting place on waitlist: 28. Number of waitlisted students admitted: 7. Test Scores (Middle 50%): SAT Critical Reading: 553–660. SAT Math: 543–650. SAT Writing: Unavailable. ACT Comp: 24–28. HS Rank of Entering Freshmen: Top 10%: 32%. Top 25%: 74%. Avg. HS GPA: 3.47.

Cost: Tuition and Fees: In-State: $33,900. Out-of-State: $6,650. Room and Board: $3,900.

Inst. Aid: FT Undergrads Receiving Aid: 1,145. Avg. Amount per Student: Unavailable.

Graduates: No. of companies recruiting on campus: 60. Alumni Giving %: 23%.

CLEMSON UNIVERSITY

Clemson, SC

cuadmissions@clemson.edu; www.clemson.edu

General Info: Public, University, Four-year, Coed, Regionally Accredited, Southern Association of Colleges and Schools, College Board member. Rural setting, Large town (10,000–49,999), Residential campus. Academic Calendar: Semester.

Student Body: Full-Time Undergrads: 14,096. Men: 54%, Women: 46%. Total Undergrad Population: Native American or Native Alaskan: 0%. Asian American or Pacific Islander: 2%. African American: 8%. Latino: 1%. Caucasian: 82%. International: 1%. Out-of-State: 32%. Total all graduate and professional students: 3,137.

Academics: Full-Time Faculty: 1,082.

Admissions: Regular Application Deadline: 5/7. Priority Application Deadline: 12/1. Early Decision Deadline: Unavailable. Transfer Priority Deadline: Unavailable. Financial Aid Deadline: Unavailable. Total Number of Students Applied: Unavailable. Percent Admitted: 55%. Number Enrolled: 2,812. Test Scores (Middle 50%): SAT Critical Reading: 540–640. SAT Math: 590–680. SAT Writing: Unavailable. ACT Comp: 24–29. HS Rank of Entering Freshmen: Top 10%: 47%. Top 25%: 72%. Avg. HS GPA: Unavailable.

Cost: Tuition and Fees: In-State: $9,400. Out-of-State: $19,824. Room and Board: $5,874.

Inst. Aid: FT Undergrads Receiving Aid: Unavailable. Avg. Amount per Student: Unavailable.

COE COLLEGE

Cedar Rapids, IA

admission@coe.edu; www.coe.edu

General Info: Coed, College Board member, Four-year, Liberal Arts College, Presbyterian Church (USA), Private, Regionally Accredited. Urban setting, Small city (50,000–249,999), Residential campus. Academic Calendar: Semester.

Student Body: Full-Time Undergrads: 1,300. Men: 45%, Women: 55%. Part-Time Undergrads. Men: 44%, Women: 56%. Total Undergrad Population: Native American or Native Alaskan: 1%. Asian American or Pacific Islander: 1%. African American: 2%. Latino: 2%. Caucasian: 89%. International: 4%. Out-of-State: 43%. Living Off-Campus: 12%. % In Fraternities: 21%. % In Sororities: 21%. Total all graduate and professional students: 16.

Academics: Full-Time Faculty: 88. Percentage completing two or more majors: 40%. Graduation Rates: 64% within 4 years. 71% within 6 years.

Admissions: Regular Application Deadline: 3/1. Priority Application Deadline: 12/10. Early Decision Deadline: Unavailable. Transfer Priority Deadline: Unavailable. Financial Aid Deadline: Unavailable. Total Number of Students Applied: 2,087. Number Admitted: 1,321. Number Enrolled: 397. Test Scores (Middle 50%): SAT Critical Reading: 528–633. SAT Math: 570–673. SAT Writing: 510–623. ACT Comp: 23–28. HS Rank of Entering Freshmen: Top 10%: 32%. Top 25%: 67%. Avg. HS GPA: 3.6.

Cost: Tuition and Fees: In-State: $27,400. Out-of-State: $27,400. Room and Board: $6,890.

Inst. Aid: FT Undergrads Receiving Aid: Unavailable. Avg. Amount per Student: Unavailable.

Graduates: Percentage of grads accepting a job at time of graduation: 72%.

COLBY COLLEGE

Waterville, ME

admissions@colby.edu; www.colby.edu

General Info: Private, Liberal Arts College, Four-year, Coed, Regionally Accredited, College Board member. Urban setting, Large town (10,000–49,999), Residential campus. Academic Calendar: 4-1-4.

Student Body: Full-Time Undergrads: 1,871. Men: 46%, Women: 54%. Total Undergrad Population: Native American or Native Alaskan: 1%. Asian American or Pacific Islander: 11%. African American: 3%. Latino: 3%. Caucasian: 75%. International: 7%. Out-of-State: 91%.

Academics: Full-Time Faculty: 161.

Admissions: Regular Application Deadline: 1/1. Priority Application Deadline: Unavailable. Early Decision Deadline: 11/15. Transfer Priority Deadline: Unavailable. Financial Aid Deadline: Unavailable. Total Number of Students Applied: Unavailable. Percent Admitted: 33%. Number Enrolled: 475. Test Scores (Middle 50%): SAT Critical Reading: 630–720. SAT Math: 640–720. SAT Writing: 610–710. ACT Comp: 27–31. HS Rank of Entering Freshmen: Top 10%: 67%. Top 25%: 92%. Avg. HS GPA: Unavailable.

Cost: Tuition and Fees: In-State: $44,080. Out-of-State: Unavailable. Room and Board: $700.

Inst. Aid: FT Undergrads Receiving Aid: Unavailable. Avg. Amount per Student: Unavailable.

COLGATE UNIVERSITY

Hamilton, NY

admission@mail.colgate.edu; www.colgate.edu

General Info: Private, Liberal Arts College, Four-year, Coed, Regionally Accredited, College Board member. Rural setting, Small town (2,500–9,999), Residential campus. Academic Calendar: Semester.

Strong Co-op Programs

University of Cincinnati

University of Waterloo

Northeastern University

Student Body: Full-Time Undergrads: 2,750. Men: 44%, Women: 56%. Total Undergrad Population: Native American or Native Alaskan: 1%. Asian American or Pacific Islander: 6%. African American: 5%. Latino: 5%. Caucasian: 73%. International: 5%. Out-of-State: 75%. Living Off-Campus: 7%. Total all graduate and professional students: 6.

Academics: Full-Time Faculty: 245. Percentage completing two or more majors: 25%. Graduation Rates: 90% within 4 years. 90% within 6 years.

Admissions: Regular Application Deadline: 1/15. Priority Application Deadline: Unavailable. Early Decision Deadline: 11/15. Transfer Priority Deadline: Unavailable. Financial Aid Deadline: 1/15. Total Number of Students Applied: 8,759. Number Admitted: 2,242. Number Enrolled: Unavailable. Number accepting place on waitlist: 469. Number of waitlisted students admitted: 44. Test Scores (Middle 50%): SAT Critical Reading: 620–720. SAT Math: 630–710. SAT Writing: Unavailable. ACT Comp: 29–32. HS Rank of Entering Freshmen: Top 10%: 64%. Top 25%: 83%. Avg. HS GPA: 3.6.

Cost: Tuition and Fees: In-State: $37,660. Out-of-State: $37,660. Room and Board: $9,170.

Inst. Aid: FT Undergrads Receiving Aid: 951. Avg. Amount per Student: Unavailable.

COLLEGE OF CHARLESTON

Charleston, SC

admissions@cofc.edu; www.cofc.edu

General Info: Coed, College Board member, Four-year, Liberal Arts College, Public, Regionally Accredited, Southern Association of Colleges and Schools. Urban setting, Large city (250,000–499,999), Residential campus. Academic Calendar: Semester.

Student Body: Full-Time Undergrads: 9,923. Men: 35.6%, Women: 64.4%. Part-Time Undergrads. Men: 41.4%, Women: 58.6%. Total Undergrad Population: Native American or Native Alaskan: 0.3%. Asian American or Pacific Islander: 1.6%. African American: 7%. Latino: 1.9%. Caucasian: 82.8%. International: 1.6%. Out-of-State: 38%. Living Off-Campus: 66.2%. % In Fraternities: 14.4%. % In Sororities: 18.2%. Total all graduate and professional students: 1,393.

Academics: Full-Time Faculty: 522. With PhD: 449. Graduation Rates: 50.6% within 4 years. 61.2% within 6 years.

Admissions: Regular Application Deadline: 4/1. Priority Application Deadline: 11/1. Early Decision Deadline: Unavailable. Transfer Priority Deadline: Unavailable. Financial Aid Deadline: Unavailable. Total Number of Students Applied: 8,941. Number Admitted: 5,775. Number Enrolled: 2,064. Number accepting place on waitlist: 256. Number of waitlisted students admitted: 79. Number applied early decision: 4,390. Early decision admitted: 2,665. Test Scores (Middle 50%): SAT Critical Reading: 570–650. SAT Math: 570–650. ACT Comp: 23–26. HS Rank of Entering Freshmen: Top 10%: 26.7%. Top 25%: 60.2%. Avg. HS GPA: 3.82.

Cost: Tuition and Fees: In-State: $7,778. Out-of-State: $18,732. Room and Board: $8,495.

Inst. Aid: FT Undergrads Receiving Aid: 3,254. Avg. Amount per Student: $11,492. Freshmen Receiving Non-Need Scholarship or Grant: 233. Avg. Amount per Student: $4,944.

Graduates: No. of companies recruiting on campus: 231. Alumni Giving %: 27%.

COLLEGE OF NEW JERSEY

Ewing, NJ

tcnjinfo@tcnj.edu; www.tcnj.edu

General Info: Public, Liberal Arts College, Four-year, Coed, Regionally Accredited, Middle States Association of Colleges and Schools. Suburban setting, Large town (10,000–49,999), Residential campus. Academic Calendar: Semester.

Student Body: Full-Time Undergrads: 5,910. Men: 42%, Women: 58%. Total Undergrad Population: Native American or Native Alaskan: 0%. Asian American or Pacific Islander: 9%. African American: 7%. Latino: 11%. Caucasian: 64%. International: 0%. Out-of-State: 5%. Total all graduate and professional students: 840.

Academics: Full-Time Faculty: 332.

Admissions: Regular Application Deadline: 2/15. Priority Application Deadline: Unavailable. Early Decision Deadline: 11/15. Transfer Priority Deadline: 2/15. Financial Aid Deadline: 10/1. Total Number of Students Applied: Unavailable. Percent Admitted: 44%. Number Enrolled: 1,270. Test Scores (Middle 50%): SAT Critical Reading: 570–670. SAT Math: 590–700. SAT Writing: 560–760. ACT Comp: Unavailable. HS Rank of Entering Freshmen: Top 10%: 68%. Top 25%: 93%. Avg. HS GPA: Unavailable.

Cost: Tuition and Fees: In-State: $10,553. Out-of-State: $17,099. Room and Board: $8,843.

Inst. Aid: FT Undergrads Receiving Aid: Unavailable. Avg. Amount per Student: Unavailable.

COLLEGE OF THE ATLANTIC

Bar Harbor, ME

inquiry@coa.edu; www.coa.edu

General Info: Private, Liberal Arts College, Four-year, Coed, Regionally Accredited. Rural setting, Small town (2,500–9,999), Residential campus. Academic Calendar: 3 ten-week terms.

Student Body: Full-Time Undergrads: 341. Men: 36%, Women: 64%. Part-Time Undergrads. Men: 39%, Women: 61%. Total Undergrad Population: Native American or Native Alaskan: 0%. Asian American or Pacific Islander: 0%. African American: 0%. Latino: 1%. Caucasian: 23%. International: 13%. Out-of-State: 80%. Living Off-Campus: 60%. Total all graduate and professional students: 8.

Academics: Full-Time Faculty: 26. With PhD: 22. Graduation Rates: 48% within 4 years. 56% within 6 years.

Admissions: Regular Application Deadline: 2/15. Priority Application Deadline: 2/15. Early Decision Deadline: 12/1. Transfer Priority Deadline: 4/1. Financial Aid Deadline: 2/15. Total Number of Students Applied: 305. Number Admitted: 235. Number Enrolled: Unavailable. Test Scores (Middle 50%): SAT Critical Reading: 647. SAT Math: 589. SAT Writing: 631. ACT Comp: 26–29. HS Rank of Entering Freshmen: Top 10%: 33%. Top 25%: 52%. Avg. HS GPA: 3.49.

Cost: Tuition and Fees: In-State: $30,990. Out-of-State: $30,990. Room and Board: $8,490.

Inst. Aid: FT Undergrads Receiving Aid: 247. Avg. Amount per Student: $27,041.

COLLEGE OF THE HOLY CROSS

Worcester, MA

admissions@holycross.edu; www.holycross.edu

General Info: Coed, College Board member, Four-year, Liberal Arts College, Private, Regionally Accredited, Roman Catholic Church, Society of Jesus (Jesuits). Suburban setting, Small city (50,000–249,999), Residential campus. Academic Calendar: Semester.

Student Body: Full-Time Undergrads: 2,700. Men: 44.3%, Women: 55.7%. Part-Time Undergrads. Men: 50%, Women: 50%. Total Undergrad Population: Native American or Native Alaskan: 0.5%. Asian American or Pacific Islander: 5.4%. African American: 4.4%. Latino: 5.5%. Caucasian: 70.7%. International: 1%. Out-of-State: 60.8%. Living Off-Campus: 10.2%.

Academics: Full-Time Faculty: 240. With PhD: 225. Percentage completing two or more majors: 13.5%. Graduation Rates: 88% within 4 years. 92% within 6 years.

Admissions: Regular Application Deadline: 1/15. Priority Application Deadline: Unavailable. Early Decision Deadline: 12/15. Fall Transfer Deadline: 5/1. Spring Transfer Deadline: 11/1. Transfer Priority Deadline: Unavailable. Financial Aid Deadline: 2/1. Total Number of Students Applied: 7,066. Number Admitted: 2,331. Number Enrolled: 719. Number accepting place on waitlist: 296. Number of waitlisted students admitted: 43. Number applied early decision: 469. Early decision admitted: 251. Test Scores (Middle 50%): SAT Critical Reading: 590–690. SAT Math: 620–690. SAT Writing: Unavailable. HS Rank of Entering Freshmen: Top 10%: 65%. Top 25%: 97%. Avg. HS GPA: Unavailable.

Cost: Tuition and Fees: In-State: $37,242. Out-of-State: $37,242. Room and Board: $10,260.

Inst. Aid: FT Undergrads Receiving Aid: 1,537. Avg. Amount per Student: $27,856. Freshmen Receiving Non-Need Scholarship or Grant: 14. Avg. Amount per Student: $38,183.

Graduates: No. of companies recruiting on campus: 47. Percentage of grads accepting a job at time of graduation: 65%. Alumni Giving %: 53%.

Celebrity Colleges

Jon Stewart—College of William and Mary

Adam Sandler—New York University

Tiger Woods—Stanford University

Natalie Portman—Harvard University

COLLEGE OF THE OZARKS

Point Lookout, MO

admiss4@cofo.edu; www.cofo.edu

General Info: Coed, Four-year, Liberal Arts College, Nondenominational, Private, Regionally Accredited. Rural setting, Small town (2,500–9,999), Residential campus. Academic Calendar: Semester.

Student Body: Full-Time Undergrads: 1,345. Men: 55%, Women: 45%. Total Undergrad Population: Native American or Native Alaskan: 2%. Asian American or Pacific Islander: 0%. African American: 1%. Latino: 1%. Caucasian: 95%. International: 1%. Out-of-State: 37%.

Academics: Full-Time Faculty: 81. Percentage completing two or more majors: 2%. Graduation Rates: 52% within 4 years. 63% within 6 years.

Admissions: Regular Application Deadline: 3/15. Priority Application Deadline: 2/15. Early Decision Deadline: Unavailable. Transfer Priority Deadline: 2/15. Financial Aid Deadline: Unavailable. Total Number of Students Applied: 2,709. Number Admitted: 321. Number Enrolled: 1,377.

Number accepting place on waitlist: 425. Number of waitlisted students admitted: 15. Test Scores (Middle 50%): SAT Critical Reading: Unavailable. SAT Math: Unavailable. SAT Writing: Unavailable. ACT Comp: 22. HS Rank of Entering Freshmen: Top 10%: 14%. Top 25%: 52%. Avg. HS GPA: 3.5.

Cost: Tuition and Fees: $15,680. In-State: Unavailable. Out-of-State: Unavailable. Room and Board: $4,700.

Inst. Aid: FT Undergrads Receiving Aid: 1,424. Avg. Amount per Student: $15,227. Freshmen Receiving Non-Need Scholarship or Grant: 50. Avg. Amount per Student: $11,074.

Graduates: Percentage of grads accepting a job at time of graduation: 75%.

COLLEGE OF WILLIAM AND MARY

Williamsburg, VA
admission@wm.edu; www.wm.edu

General Info: Public, University, Four-year, Coed, Regionally Accredited, Southern Association of Colleges and Schools, College Board member. Suburban setting, Large town (10,000–49,999), Residential campus. Academic Calendar: Semester.

Student Body: Full-Time Undergrads: 5,500. Men: 46%, Women: 54%. Total Undergrad Population: Native American or Native Alaskan: 1%. Asian American or Pacific Islander: 6%. African American: 7%. Latino: 5%. Caucasian: 67%. International: 4%. Out-of-State: 33%. Living Off-Campus: 25%. % In Fraternities: 24%. % In Sororities: 27%. Total all graduate and professional students: 1,380.

Academics: Full-Time Faculty: 594. Graduation Rates: 81% within 4 years. 91% within 6 years.

Admissions: Regular Application Deadline: 1/1. Priority Application Deadline: Unavailable. Early Decision Deadline: 11/1. Spring Transfer Deadline: 11/1. Transfer Priority Deadline: Unavailable. Financial Aid Deadline: 3/15. Total Number of Students Applied: Unavailable. Number Admitted: Unavailable. Number Enrolled: Unavailable. Test Scores (Middle 50%): SAT Critical Reading: 630–730. SAT Math: 630–710. SAT Writing: Unavailable. ACT Comp: 28–31. HS Rank of Entering Freshmen: Top 10%: 79%. Top 25%: 96%. Avg. HS GPA: Unavailable.

Cost: Tuition and Fees: In-State: $8,490. Out-of-State: $25,048. Room and Board: $6,932.

Inst. Aid: FT Undergrads Receiving Aid: Unavailable. Avg. Amount per Student: Unavailable.

COLORADO COLLEGE

Colorado Springs, CO
admission@coloradocollege.edu;
www.coloradocollege.edu

General Info: Coed, College Board member, Four-year, Liberal Arts College, North Central Association of Colleges and Schools, Private, Regionally Accredited. Urban setting, Large city (250,000–499,999), Residential campus. Academic Calendar: Unavailable.

Student Body: Full-Time Undergrads: 1,928. Men: 46.3%, Women: 53.7%. Part-Time Undergrads: Men: 52.6%, Women: 47.4%. Total Undergrad Population: Native American or Native Alaskan: 0.8%. Asian American or Pacific Islander: 5.1%. African American: 1.9%. Latino: 6.7%. Caucasian: 79.1%. International: 2.5%. Out-of-State: 74%. % In Fraternities: 12%. % In Sororities: 15%. Total all graduate and professional students: 22.

Academics: Full-Time Faculty: 176. Graduation Rates: 77% within 4 years. 83% within 6 years.

Admissions: Regular Application Deadline: 1/15. Priority Application Deadline: Unavailable. Early Decision Deadline: 11/15. Transfer Priority Deadline: Unavailable. Financial Aid Deadline: 2/15. Total Number of Students Applied: 4,853. Number Admitted: 1,540. Number Enrolled: 524. Test Scores (Middle 50%): SAT Critical Reading: 610–700. SAT Math: 620–690. SAT Writing: 600–700. ACT Comp: 27–31. HS Rank of Entering Freshmen: Top 10%: 60%. Top 25%: 92%. Avg. HS GPA: Unavailable.

Cost: Tuition and Fees: In-State: $35,844. Out-of-State: $35,844. Room and Board: $9,096.

Inst. Aid: FT Undergrads Receiving Aid: Unavailable. Avg. Amount per Student: Unavailable.

COLORADO SCHOOL OF MINES

Golden, CO
admit@mines.edu; www.mines.edu

General Info: Public, College of Engineering, University, Four-year, Coed, Regionally Accredited, North Central Association of Colleges and Schools, College Board member. Suburban setting, Large town (10,000–49,999), Residential campus. Academic Calendar: Semester.

Student Body: Full-Time Undergrads: 3,100. Men: 76%, Women: 24%. Total Undergrad Population: Native American or Native Alaskan: 1%. Asian American or Pacific Is-

Politically-Inclined Schools

George Washington University

Brigham Young University

Hampshire College

United States Air Force Academy

lander: 5%. African American: 1%. Latino: 8%. Caucasian: 76%. International: 3%. Out-of-State: 25%. Total all graduate and professional students: 833.

Academics: Full-Time Faculty: 215.

Admissions: Regular Application Deadline: 5/1. Priority Application Deadline: Unavailable. Early Decision Deadline: Unavailable. Transfer Priority Deadline: 5/1. Financial Aid Deadline: Unavailable. Total Number of Students Applied: Unavailable. Percent Admitted: 84%. Number Enrolled: 760. Test Scores (Middle 50%): SAT Critical Reading: 540–640. SAT Math: 600–690. SAT Writing: Unavailable. ACT Comp: 25–29. HS Rank of Entering Freshmen: Top 10%: 48%. Top 25%: 81%. Avg. HS GPA: Unavailable.

Cost: Tuition and Fees: In-State: $9,656. Out-of-State: $22,250. Room and Board: $7,100.

Inst. Aid: FT Undergrads Receiving Aid: Unavailable. Avg. Amount per Student: Unavailable.

Largest Universities (By Enrollment)

The Ohio State University—52,586 students

University of Florida—51,913 students

Arizona State University—51,481 students

University of Minnesota—50,880 students

University of Texas at Austin—50,201 students

COLUMBIA UNIVERSITY

New York, NY
ugrad-ask@columbia.edu;
www.studentaffairs.columbia.edu/admissions

General Info: Coed, College Board member, College of Engineering, Four-year, Liberal Arts College, Nondenominational, Private, Regionally Accredited, University. Urban setting, Very large city (over 500,000), Residential campus. Academic Calendar: Semester.

Student Body: Full-Time Undergrads: 5,602. Men: 53%, Women: 47%. Total Undergrad Population: Native American or Native Alaskan: 1%. Asian American or Pacific Islander: 18%. African American: 9%. Latino: 10%. Caucasian: 42%. International: 11%. Out-of-State: 75%. Living Off-Campus: 6%.

Academics: Full-Time Faculty: 844. Graduation Rates: 87% within 4 years. 94% within 6 years.

Admissions: Regular Application Deadline: 1/2. Priority Application Deadline: Unavailable. Early Decision Deadline: 11/1. Transfer Priority Deadline: Unavailable. Financial Aid Deadline: 2/10. Total Number of Students Applied: 21,342. Number Admitted: 2,255. Number Enrolled: 1,333. Number applied early decision: 2,438. Early decision admitted: 599. Test Scores (Middle 50%): SAT Critical Reading: 680–760. SAT Math: 680–780. SAT Writing: 670–760. ACT Comp: 30–34. HS Rank of Entering Freshmen: Top 10%: 94%. Top 25%: 99%. Avg. HS GPA: 3.9.

Cost: Tuition and Fees: In-State: $35,516. Out-of-State: $35,516. Room and Board: $9,938.

Inst. Aid: FT Undergrads Receiving Aid: 2,635. Avg. Amount per Student: $33,064.

CONNECTICUT COLLEGE

New London, CT
admission@conncoll.edu; www.conncoll.edu

General Info: Private, Liberal Arts College, Four-year, Coed, Regionally Accredited, College Board member. Suburban setting, Large town (10,000–49,999), Residential campus. Academic Calendar: Semester.

Student Body: Full-Time Undergrads: 1,900. Men: 40%, Women: 60%. Total Undergrad Population: Native American or Native Alaskan: 0%. Asian American or Pacific Islander: 4%. African American: 4%. Latino: 5%. Caucasian: 76%. International: 4%. Out-of-State: 83%. Living Off-Campus: 1%. Total all graduate and professional students: 12.

Academics: Full-Time Faculty: 171. Percentage completing two or more majors: 40%. Graduation Rates: 84% within 4 years. 88% within 6 years.

Admissions: Regular Application Deadline: 1/1. Priority Application Deadline: Unavailable. Early Decision Deadline: 11/15. Transfer Priority Deadline: 4/1. Financial Aid Deadline: 1/15. Total Number of Students Applied: Unavailable. Percent Admitted: 38%. Number Enrolled: 490. Number of waitlisted students admitted: 30. Test Scores (Middle 50%): SAT Critical Reading: 630–720. SAT Math: 610–690. SAT Writing: 630–720. ACT Comp: 25-29. HS Rank of Entering Freshmen: Top 10%: 60%. Top 25%: 93%. Avg. HS GPA: Unavailable.

Cost: Tuition and Fees: In-State: $46,675. Out-of-State: Unavailable. Room and Board: $800.

Inst. Aid: FT Undergrads Receiving Aid: Unavailable. Avg. Amount per Student: Unavailable.

COOPER UNION FOR THE ADVANCEMENT OF SCIENCE AND ART

New York, NY
admissions@cooper.edu; www.cooper.edu

General Info: Private, College of Art, College of Engineering, Four-year, Coed, Regionally Accredited, College Board member. Urban setting, Very large city (over 500,000), Commuter campus. Academic Calendar: Semester.

Student Body: Full-Time Undergrads: 920. Men: 60%, Women: 40%. Total Undergrad Population: Native American or Native Alaskan: 0.5%. Asian American or Pacific Islander: 26%. African American: 6%. Latino: 9%. Caucasian: 46%. International: 11%. Out-of-State: 40%. Total all graduate and professional students: 48.

Academics: Full-Time Faculty: 52. Graduation Rates: 77% within 4 years. 86% within 6 years.

Admissions: Regular Application Deadline: 1/1. Priority Application Deadline: Unavailable. Early Decision Deadline: 12/1. Transfer Priority Deadline: Unavailable. Financial Aid Deadline: 6/1. Total Number of Students Applied: Unavailable. Percent Admitted: 10%. Number Enrolled: 202. Test Scores (Middle 50%): SAT Critical Reading: 600–700. SAT Math: 640–770. SAT Writing: Unavailable. ACT Comp: 28–33. HS Rank of Entering Freshmen: Top 10%: 85%. Top 25%: 100%. Avg. HS GPA: Unavailable.

Cost: Tuition and Fees: In-State: $0. Out-of-State: $0. Room and Board: $13,900.

Inst. Aid: FT Undergrads Receiving Aid: Unavailable. Avg. Amount per Student: Unavailable.

CORNELL COLLEGE

Mount Vernon, IA
admissions@cornellcollege.edu; www.cornellcollege.edu

General Info: Private, Liberal Arts College, Four-year, United Methodist Church, Coed, Regionally Accredited, College Board member. Residential campus, Small town (2,500–9,999), 20 miles from two cities. Academic Calendar: Unavailable.

Student Body: Full-Time Undergrads: 1,121. Men: 48%, Women: 52%. Total Undergrad Population: Native American or Native Alaskan: 1%. Asian American or Pacific Islander: 3%. African American: 7%. Latino: 4%. Caucasian: 72%. International: 3%. Out-of-State: 72%. Living Off-Campus: 10%. % In Fraternities: 30%. % In Sororities: 30%.

Academics: Full-Time Faculty: 94. Graduation Rates: 60% within 4 years. 67% within 6 years.

Admissions: Regular Application Deadline: 3/1. Priority Application Deadline: 12/1. Early Decision Deadline: Unavailable. Transfer Priority Deadline: 12/1. Financial Aid Deadline: 3/1. Total Number of Students Applied: Unavailable. Percent Admitted: 62%. Number Enrolled: 248. Test Scores (Middle 50%): SAT Critical Reading: 560–670. SAT Math: 540–670. SAT Writing: 510–630. ACT Comp: 24–29. HS Rank of Entering Freshmen: Top 10%: Unavailable. Top 25%: Unavailable. Avg. HS GPA: Unavailable.

Cost: Tuition and Fees: In-State: $27,670. Out-of-State: $27,670. Room and Board: $7,220.

Inst. Aid: FT Undergrads Receiving Aid: Unavailable. Avg. Amount per Student: Unavailable.

CORNELL UNIVERSITY

Ithaca, NY
admissions@cornell.edu; www.cornell.edu

General Info: Private, University, Four-year, Coed, Regionally Accredited, College Board member. Rural setting, Large town (10,000–49,999), Residential campus. Academic Calendar: Semester.

Student Body: Full-Time Undergrads: 13,510. Men: 51%, Women: 49%. Total Undergrad Population: Native American or Native Alaskan: 1%. Asian American or Pacific Islander: 15%. African American: 6%. Latino: 6%. Caucasian: 40%. International: 8%. Out-of-State: 68%. Total all graduate and professional students: 5,181.

Academics: Full-Time Faculty: 1,728.

Admissions: Regular Application Deadline: 1/1. Priority Application Deadline: Unavailable. Early Decision Deadline: 11/1. Transfer Priority Deadline: Unavailable. Financial Aid Deadline: 2/11. Total Number of Students Applied: 33. Number Admitted: 6,735. Number Enrolled: Unavailable. Test Scores (Middle 50%): SAT Critical Reading: Unavailable. SAT Math: Unavailable. SAT Writing: Unavailable. HS Rank of Entering Freshmen: Top 10%: Unavailable. Top 25%: Unavailable. Avg. HS GPA: Unavailable.

Cost: Tuition and Fees: In-State: $32,981. Out-of-State: $32,981. Room and Board: $10,726.

Inst. Aid: FT Undergrads Receiving Aid: 5,171. Avg. Amount per Student: $28,577.

CREIGHTON UNIVERSITY

Omaha, NE
admissions@creighton.edu; www.creighton.edu

General Info: Private, University, Four-year, Roman Catholic Church, Society of Jesus (Jesuits), Coed, Regionally Accredited, College Board member. Residential campus, Urban setting, Very large city (over 500,000). Academic Calendar: Semester.

Student Body: Full-Time Undergrads: 3,817. Men: 40%, Women: 60%. Total Undergrad Population: Native American or Native Alaskan: 1%. Asian American or Pacific Islander: 11%. African American: 3%. Latino: 5%. Caucasian: 78%. International: 1%. Out-of-State: 70%. Living Off-Campus: 96%. Total all graduate and professional students: 543.

Academics: Full-Time Faculty: 501. With PhD: 434. Graduation Rates: 60% within 4 years. 75% within 6 years.

Admissions: Regular Application Deadline: 2/1. Priority Application Deadline: 12/1. Early Decision Deadline: N/A. Transfer Priority Deadline: 3/1. Financial Aid Deadline: 3/1. Total Number of Students Applied: 4,274. Number Admitted: 3,476. Number Enrolled: Unavailable. Number accepting place on waitlist: 101. Number of waitlisted students admitted: 17. Test Scores (Middle 50%): SAT Critical Reading: 530–640. SAT Math: 550–660. SAT Writing: 520–640. ACT Comp: 24–30. HS Rank of Entering Freshmen: Top 10%: 43%. Top 25%: 74%. Avg. HS GPA: 3.78.

Cost: Tuition and Fees: In-State: $27,282. Out-of-State: $27,282. Room and Board: $8,516.

Inst. Aid: FT Undergrads Receiving Aid: 3,111. Avg. Amount per Student: Unavailable.

Graduates: No. of companies recruiting on campus: 220. Percentage of grads accepting a job at time of graduation: 58%. Alumni Giving %: 29%.

CULINARY INSTITUTE OF AMERICA

Hyde Park, NY

admissions@culinary.edu; www.ciachef.edu

General Info: Private, Culinary Arts, Four-year, Coed, Accrediting Commission of Career Schools and Colleges of Technology, Regionally Accredited, Candidate for accreditation. Suburban setting, Large town (10,000–49,999), Residential campus. Academic Calendar: Continuous.

Student Body: Full-Time Undergrads: 2,742. Men: 57%, Women: 43%. Out-of-State: 77%.

Academics: Full-Time Faculty: 125.

Admissions: Regular Application Deadline: June. Priority Application Deadline: Unavailable. Early Decision Deadline: December. Financial Aid Deadline: Unavailable. Total Number of Students Applied: Unavailable. Number Admitted: Unavailable. Number Enrolled: Unavailable. Test Scores (Middle 50%): SAT Critical Reading: Unavailable. SAT Math: Unavailable. SAT Writing: Unavailable. HS Rank of Entering Freshmen: Top 10%: 8%. Top 25%: 22%. Avg. HS GPA: Unavailable.

Cost: Tuition and Fees: In-State: $19,180. Out-of-State: $19,180. Room and Board: $8,990.

Inst. Aid: FT Undergrads Receiving Aid: Unavailable. Avg. Amount per Student: $8,500.

DARTMOUTH COLLEGE

Hanover, NH

admissions.office@dartmouth.edu; www.dartmouth.edu

General Info: Coed, College Board member, Four-year, Liberal Arts College, Private, Regionally Accredited, University. Large town (10,000–49,999), Residential campus, Rural setting. Academic Calendar: Quarter.

Student Body: Full-Time Undergrads: 4,164. Men: 50%, Women: 50%. Part-Time Undergrads. Men: 50%, Women: 50%. Total Undergrad Population: Native American or Native Alaskan: 3.4%. Asian American or Pacific Islander: 14.3%. African American: 7.6%. Latino: 7.1%. Caucasian: 54%. International: 9.1%. Out-of-State: 97%. Living Off-Campus: 14%. Total all graduate and professional students: 1,685.

Academics: Full-Time Faculty: 540. With PhD: 509. Graduation Rate: 94% within 6 years.

Admissions: Regular Application Deadline: 1/1. Priority Application Deadline: Unavailable. Early Decision Deadline: 11/1. Transfer Priority Deadline: Unavailable. Financial Aid Deadline: 2/1. Total Number of Students Applied: 16,538. Number Admitted: 2,189. Number Enrolled: 1,116. Number accepting place on waitlist: 1,381. Number of waitlisted students admitted: 797. Test Scores (Middle 50%): SAT Critical Reading: 660–770. SAT Math: 670–780. SAT Writing: 660–770. ACT Comp: 29–34. HS Rank of Entering Freshmen: Top 10%: 91%. Top 25%: Unavailable. Avg. HS GPA: Unavailable.

Cost: Tuition and Fees: In-State: $34,965. Out-of-State: $34,965. Room and Board: $10,518.

Inst. Aid: FT Undergrads Receiving Aid: 2,082. Avg. Amount per Student: $31,803.

Graduates: Alumni Giving %: 53%.

Big Party Schools

University of Wisconsin

University of Florida

Washington and Lee University

University of Texas—Austin

Ohio State University

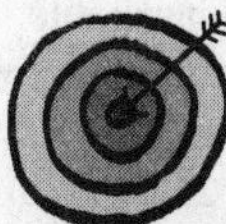

DAVIDSON COLLEGE

Davidson, NC

admission@davidson.edu; www.davidson.edu

General Info: Private, Liberal Arts College, Four-year, Presbyterian Church (USA), Coed, Regionally Accredited, College Board member. Suburban setting, Small town (2,500–9,999), Residential campus. Academic Calendar: Semester.

Student Body: Full-Time Undergrads: 1,700. Men: 50%, Women: 50%. Total Undergrad Population: Native American or Native Alaskan: 1%. Asian American or Pacific Islander: 3%. African American: 6%. Latino: 4%. Caucasian: 75%. International: 4%. Out-of-State: 81%. Living Off-Campus: 9%.

Popular Liberal Arts Schools

St. Thomas Aquinas College

Berea College

Principia College

Williams College

Amherst College

Wellesley College

Skidmore College

Academics: Full-Time Faculty: 167. With PhD: 161. Percentage completing two or more majors: 4%. Graduation Rates: 91% within 4 years. 92% within 6 years.

Admissions: Regular Application Deadline: 1/2. Priority Application Deadline: Unavailable. Early Decision Deadline: 11/15. Financial Aid Deadline: 1/2. Total Number of Students Applied: 3,992. Number Admitted: 1,127. Number Enrolled: Unavailable. Test Scores (Middle 50%): SAT Critical Reading: 678. SAT Math: 677. SAT Writing: Unavailable. ACT Comp: 30. HS Rank of Entering Freshmen: Top 10%: 83%. Top 25%: 98%. Avg. HS GPA: 4.1.

Cost: Tuition and Fees: In-State: $33,148. Out-of-State: $33,148. Room and Board: $9,471.

Inst. Aid: FT Undergrads Receiving Aid: 565. Avg. Amount per Student: Unavailable.

Graduates: No. of companies recruiting on campus: 812. Percentage of grads accepting a job at time of graduation: 67%. Alumni Giving %: 60%.

DEEP SPRINGS COLLEGE

Dyer, NV

apcom@deepsprings.edu; www.deepsprings.edu

General Info: Private, Liberal Arts College, Two-year, Men Only, Regionally Accredited. Rural setting, Rural community (under 2,500), Residential campus. Academic Calendar: Continuous.

Student Body: Full-Time Undergrads: 26. Men: 100%, Women: 0%. Out-of-State: 83%.

Academics: Full-Time Faculty: 8.

Admissions: Regular Application Deadline: 11/15. Priority Application Deadline: Unavailable. Early Decision Deadline: Unavailable. Transfer Priority Deadline: Unavailable. Financial Aid Deadline: Unavailable. Total Number of Students Applied: Unavailable. Percent Admitted: 7%. Number Enrolled: Unavailable. Test Scores (Middle 50%): SAT Critical Reading: 750–800. SAT Math: 710–750. SAT Writing: Unavailable. ACT Comp: Unavailable. HS Rank of Entering Freshmen: Top 10%: Unavailable. Top 25%: Unavailable. Avg. HS GPA: Unavailable.

Cost: Tuition and Fees: In-State: Unavailable. Out-of-State: Unavailable. Room and Board: Unavailable.

Inst. Aid: FT Undergrads Receiving Aid: Unavailable. Avg. Amount per Student: Unavailable.

DELAWARE VALLEY COLLEGE

Doylestown, PA

admitme@devalcol.edu; www.delval.edu

General Info: Private, Agricultural and Technical College, Liberal Arts College, Four-year, Coed, Regionally Accredited, College Board member. Suburban setting, Large town (10,000–49,999), Residential campus. Academic Calendar: Semester.

Student Body: Full-Time Undergrads. Men: 42%, Women: 58%. Total Undergrad Population: Native American or Native Alaskan: 0%. Asian American or Pacific Islander: 2%. African American: 3%. Latino: 2%. Caucasian: 87%. Out-of-State: 44%. Total all graduate and professional students: 135.

Admissions: Regular Application Deadline: Unavailable. Priority Application Deadline: Unavailable. Early Decision Deadline: Unavailable. Transfer Priority Deadline: Unavailable. Financial Aid Deadline: Unavailable. Total Number of Students Applied: Unavailable. Number Admitted: Unavailable. Number Enrolled: Unavailable. Test Scores (Middle 50%): SAT Critical Reading: 450–550. SAT Math: 460–560. SAT Writing: 435–540. ACT Comp: 21–25. HS Rank of Entering Freshmen: Top 10%: Unavailable. Top 25%: Unavailable. Avg. HS GPA: Unavailable.

Cost: Tuition and Fees: In-State: $24,710. Out-of-State: $24,710. Room and Board: $8,964.

DENISON UNIVERSITY

Granville, OH

admissions@denison.edu; www.denison.edu

General Info: Coed, College Board member, Four-year, Liberal Arts College, Nondenominational, Private, Regionally Accredited. Suburban setting, Small town (2,500–9,999), Residential campus. Academic Calendar: Semester.

Student Body: Full-Time Undergrads: 2,100. Men: 44%, Women: 56%. Total Undergrad Population: Native American or Native Alaskan: 1%. Asian American or Pacific Islander: 4%. African American: 7%. Latino: 3%. Caucasian: 80%. International: 5%. Out-of-State: 68%. % In Fraternities: 26%. % In Sororities: 39%.

Academics: Full-Time Faculty: 164. Percentage completing two or more majors: 21.6%. Graduation Rates: 79.6% within 4 years. 78.7% within 6 years.

Admissions: Regular Application Deadline: 1/15. Priority Application Deadline: 12/15. Early Decision Deadline: 11/1. Fall Transfer Deadline: 6/1. Spring Transfer Deadline: 12/1. Transfer Priority Deadline: Unavailable. Financial Aid Deadline: Unavailable. Total Number of Students Applied: Unavailable. Percent Admitted: 39%. Number Enrolled: 573. Test Scores (Middle 50%): SAT Critical Reading: 580–690. SAT Math: 580–670. SAT Writing: Unavailable. ACT Comp: 28-31. HS Rank of Entering Freshmen: Top 10%: 54%. Top 25%: 80%. Avg. HS GPA: Unavailable.

Cost: Tuition and Fees: In-State: $32,160. Out-of-State: $32,160. Room and Board: $8,570.

Inst. Aid: FT Undergrads Receiving Aid: Unavailable. Avg. Amount per Student: Unavailable.

DEPAUL UNIVERSITY

Chicago, IL

admitdpu@depaul.edu; www.depaul.edu

General Info: Private, University, Four-year, Roman Catholic Church, Coed, Regionally Accredited, College Board member. Urban setting, Very large city (over 500,000), Residential campus. Academic Calendar: Quarter.

Student Body: Full-Time Undergrads: 14,893. Men: 44%, Women: 56%. Total Undergrad Population: Native American or Native Alaskan: 0%. Asian American or Pacific Islander: 8%. African American: 8%. Latino: 13%. Caucasian: 65%. International: 1%. Out-of-State: 29%. Total all graduate and professional students: 7,229.

Academics: Full-Time Faculty: 850.

Admissions: Regular Application Deadline: Unavailable. Priority Application Deadline: 2/1. Early Decision Deadline: Unavailable. Financial Aid Deadline: Unavailable. Total Number of Students Applied: Unavailable. Percent Admitted: 70%. Number Enrolled: 2,537. Test Scores (Middle 50%): SAT Critical Reading: Unavailable. SAT Math: 510–620. SAT Writing: Unavailable. ACT Comp: Unavailable. HS Rank of Entering Freshmen: Top 10%: 20%. Top 25%: 48%. Avg. HS GPA: Unavailable.

Cost: Tuition and Fees: In-State: $22,365. Room and Board: $10,392.

Inst. Aid: FT Undergrads Receiving Aid: Unavailable. Avg. Amount per Student: Unavailable.

DEPAUW UNIVERSITY

Greencastle, IN

admission@depauw.edu; www.depauw.edu

General Info: Coed, College Board member, College of Music, Four-year, Liberal Arts College, Private, Regionally Accredited, United Methodist Church. Rural setting, Small town (2,500–9,999), Residential campus. Academic Calendar: 4-1-4.

Student Body: Full-Time Undergrads: 2,326. Men: 44%, Women: 56%. Total Undergrad Population: Native American or Native Alaskan: 0.5%. Asian American or Pacific Islander: 2%. African American: 7%. Latino: 3%. Caucasian: 77.5%. International: 60%. Out-of-State: 43%.

Academics: Full-Time Faculty: 211. Graduation Rates: 82% within 4 years. 81% within 6 years.

Admissions: Regular Application Deadline: 2/1. Priority Application Deadline: Unavailable. Early Decision Deadline: 11/1. Transfer Priority Deadline: Unavailable. Financial Aid Deadline: 2/15. Total Number of Students Applied: Unavailable. Percent Admitted: 68%. Number Enrolled: 596. Test Scores (Middle 50%): SAT Critical Reading: 560–660. SAT Math: 570–660. SAT Writing: 550–650. ACT Comp: 25–29. HS Rank of Entering Freshmen: Top 10%: 50%. Top 25%: 83%. Avg. HS GPA: Unavailable.

Cost: Tuition and Fees: In-State: $27,780. Out-of-State: $27,780. Room and Board: $7,800.

Inst. Aid: FT Undergrads Receiving Aid: Unavailable. Avg. Amount per Student: Unavailable.

DICKINSON COLLEGE

Carlisle, PA

admit@dickinson.edu; www.dickinson.edu

General Info: Private, Liberal Arts College, Four-year, Coed, Regionally Accredited, College Board member. Suburban setting, Large town (10,000–49,999), Residential campus. Academic Calendar: Semester.

Student Body: Full-Time Undergrads: 2,381. Men: 44.7%, Women: 55.3%. Total Undergrad Population: Native American or Native Alaskan: 0%. Asian American or Pacific Islander: 4%. African American: 5%. Latino: 4%. Caucasian: 77%. International: 6%. Out-of-State: 76%.

Academics: Full-Time Faculty: 188.

Admissions: Regular Application Deadline: 2/1. Priority Application Deadline: Unavailable. Early Decision Deadline: 11/15. Transfer Priority Deadline: Unavailable. Financial Aid Deadline: 2/1. Total Number of Students Applied: 5,844. Number Admitted: 2,442. Number Enrolled: 621. Test Scores (Middle 50%): SAT Critical Reading: Unavailable. SAT Math: Unavailable. SAT Writing: Unavailable. HS Rank of Entering Freshmen: Top 10%: 48%. Top 25%: 79%. Avg. HS GPA: Unavailable.

Cost: Tuition and Fees: In-State: $37,900. Out-of-State: $37,900. Room and Board: $9,600.

Inst. Aid: FT Undergrads Receiving Aid: 1,025. Avg. Amount per Student: $28,455.

DIGIPEN INSTITUTE OF TECHNOLOGY

Redmond, WA

admissions@digipen.edu; www.digipen.edu

General Info: Proprietary, College of Art, College of Engineering, Four-year, Coed, Accrediting Commission of Career Schools and Colleges of Technology. Suburban setting, Large town (10,000–49,999), Commuter campus. Academic Calendar: Semester.

Student Body: Full-Time Undergrads: 687. Men: 92%, Women: 8%. Total all graduate and professional students: 58.

Academics: Full-Time Faculty: 36. Graduation Rates: 55% within 4 years.

Admissions: Regular Application Deadline: Rolling. Priority Application Deadline: 2/1. Early Decision Deadline: Unavailable. Transfer Priority Deadline: Unavailable. Financial Aid Deadline: Unavailable. Total Number of Students Applied: Unavailable. Number Admitted: Unavailable. Number Enrolled: 300. Test Scores (Middle 50%): SAT Critical Reading: 515–640. SAT Math: 540–660. SAT Writing: Unavailable. ACT Comp: 22–28. HS Rank of Entering Freshmen: Top 10%: Unavailable. Top 25%: Unavailable. Avg. HS GPA: Unavailable.

Cost: Tuition and Fees: In-State: $19,040. Out-of-State: $19,040. Room and Board: $0.

DREW UNIVERSITY

Madison, NJ

cadm@drew.edu; www.drew.edu

General Info: Private, Liberal Arts College, University, Four-year, United Methodist Church, Coed, Regionally Accredited, College Board member. Suburban setting, Large town (10,000–49,999), Residential campus. Academic Calendar: Semester.

Student Body: Full-Time Undergrads: 1,608. Men: 34%, Women: 66%. Total Undergrad Population: Native American or Native Alaskan: 1%. Asian American or Pacific Islander: 5%. African American: 10%. Latino: 8%. Caucasian: 62%. International: 2%. Out-of-State: 41%. Total all graduate and professional students: 764.

Academics: Full-Time Faculty: 148.

Admissions: Regular Application Deadline: 2/15. Priority Application Deadline: Unavailable. Early Decision Deadline: 12/1. Transfer Priority Deadline: Unavailable. Financial Aid Deadline: 2/15. Total Number of Students Applied: Unavailable. Percent Admitted: 64%. Number Enrolled: 391. Test Scores (Middle 50%): SAT Critical Reading: 530–650. SAT Math: 530–630. SAT Writing: 530–640. ACT Comp: 24–28. HS Rank of Entering Freshmen: Top 10%: 36%. Top 25%: 66%. Avg. HS GPA: Unavailable.

Cost: Tuition and Fees: In-State: $33,054. Out-of-State: $33,054. Room and Board: $9,001.

DREXEL UNIVERSITY

Philadelphia, PA

enroll@drexel.edu; www.drexel.edu

General Info: Private, University, Four-year, Coed, Regionally Accredited, College Board member. Urban setting, Very large city (over 500,000), Commuter campus. Academic Calendar: Quarter.

Student Body: Full-Time Undergrads: 12,906. Men: 61%, Women: 39%. Total Undergrad Population: Native American or Native Alaskan: 0%. Asian American or Pacific Islander: 13%. African American: 5%. Latino: 4%. Caucasian: 65%. International: 6%. Out-of-State: 51%. Total all graduate and professional students: 5,093.

Academics: Full-Time Faculty: 723.

Admissions: Regular Application Deadline: 3/1. Priority Application Deadline: Unavailable. Early Decision Deadline: Unavailable. Transfer Priority Deadline: 8/15. Financial Aid Deadline: 3/1. Total Number of Students Applied: Unavailable. Percent Admitted: 82%. Number Enrolled: 2,457. Test Scores (Middle 50%): SAT Critical Reading: 530–630. SAT Math: 550–660. SAT Writing: Unavailable. HS Rank of Entering Freshmen: Top 10%: 30%. Top 25%: 59%. Avg. HS GPA: Unavailable.

Cost: Tuition and Fees: In-State: $25,450. Out-of-State: $25,450. Room and Board: $12,015.

Inst. Aid: FT Undergrads Receiving Aid: Unavailable. Avg. Amount per Student: Unavailable.

DUKE UNIVERSITY

Durham, NC

askduke@admiss.duke.edu; www.duke.edu

General Info: Private, University, Four-year, United Methodist Church, Coed, Regionally Accredited, College Board member. Suburban setting, Small city (50,000–249,999), Residential campus. Academic Calendar: Semester.

Student Body: Full-Time Undergrads: 6,197. Men: 52%, Women: 48%. Total Undergrad Population: Native American or Native Alaskan: 1%. Asian American or Pacific Islander: 18%. African American: 9%. Latino: 6%. Caucasian: 53%. International: 6%. Out-of-State: 85%. Total all graduate and professional students: 5,699.

Academics: Full-Time Faculty: 964.

Admissions: Regular Application Deadline: 1/2. Priority Application Deadline: Unavailable. Early Decision Deadline: 11/1. Transfer Priority Deadline: Unavailable. Financial Aid Deadline: 3/1. Total Number of Students Applied: Unavailable. Percent Admitted: 22%. Number Enrolled: 1,683. Test Scores (Middle 50%): SAT Critical Reading: 690–770. SAT Math: 690–780. SAT Writing: Unavailable. ACT Comp: 29–34. HS Rank of Entering Freshmen: Top 10%: 87%. Top 25%: 98%. Avg. HS GPA: Unavailable.

Cost: Tuition and Fees: In-State: $33,963. Out-of-State: $33,963. Room and Board: $9,699.

Inst. Aid: FT Undergrads Receiving Aid: Unavailable. Avg. Amount per Student: $28,532.

DUQUESNE UNIVERSITY

Pittsburgh, PA

admissions@duq.edu; www.duq.edu

General Info: Private, University, Four-year, Roman Catholic Church, Coed, Regionally Accredited, College Board member. Urban setting, Large city (250,000–499,999), Residential campus. Academic Calendar: Semester.

Student Body: Full-Time Undergrads: 5,751. Men: 42%, Women: 58%. Total Undergrad Population: Native American or Native Alaskan: 0%. Asian American or Pacific Islander: 2%. African American: 2%. Latino: 2%. Caucasian: 88%. International: 2%. Out-of-State: 23%. Total all graduate and professional students: 3,079.

Academics: Full-Time Faculty: 442.

Admissions: Regular Application Deadline: 7/1. Priority Application Deadline: 11/1. Early Decision Deadline: 11/1. Transfer Priority Deadline: 12/1. Financial Aid Deadline: 5/1. Total Number of Students Applied: Unavailable. Percent Admitted: 72%. Number Enrolled: 1,325. Test Scores (Middle 50%): SAT Critical Reading: 510–600. SAT Math: 520–620. SAT Writing: 510–600. ACT Comp: 21–26. HS Rank of Entering Freshmen: Top 10%: 28%. Top 25%: 57%. Avg. HS GPA: Unavailable.

Cost: Tuition and Fees: In-State: $22,665. Out-of-State: $22,665. Room and Board: $8,296.

Inst. Aid: FT Undergrads Receiving Aid: Unavailable. Avg. Amount per Student: Unavailable.

Notable Financial Aid Programs

Princeton University

Cooper Union

Thomas Aquinas College

Stanford University

Claremont McKenna College

EAST CAROLINA UNIVERSITY

Greenville, NC

admis@mail.ecu.edu; www.ecu.edu

General Info: Public, University, Four-year, Coed, Regionally Accredited, Southern Association of Colleges and Schools, College Board member. Urban setting, Small city (50,000–249,999), Residential campus. Academic Calendar: Semester.

Student Body: Full-Time Undergrads: 17,728. Men: 39%, Women: 61%. Total Undergrad Population: Native American or Native Alaskan: 1%. Asian American or Pacific Islander: 2%. African American: 14%. Latino: 2%. Caucasian: 78%. Out-of-State: 16%. Total all graduate and professional students: 5,150.

Academics: Full-Time Faculty: 1,539. With PhD: 73%. Graduation Rate: 54% within 6 years.

Admissions: Regular Application Deadline: Rolling. Early Decision Deadline: Unavailable. Transfer Priority Deadline: Unavailable. Financial Aid Deadline: Unavailable. Total Number of Students Applied: 3,206. Number Admitted: 2,938. Number Enrolled: 1,667. Test Scores (Middle 50%): SAT Critical Reading: 460–560. SAT Math: 480–570. SAT Writing: Unavailable. ACT Comp: 18–22.

Cost: Tuition and Fees: In-State: $4,003. Out-of-State: $14,517. Room and Board: $6,640.

Inst. Aid: FT Undergrads Receiving Aid: Unavailable. Avg. Amount per Student: Unavailable.

EASTERN KENTUCKY UNIVERSITY

Richmond, KY

admissions@eku.edu; www.eku.edu

General Info: Public, University, Four-year, Coed, Regionally Accredited, Southern Association of Colleges and Schools, College Board member. Rural setting, Large town (10,000–49,999), Residential campus. Academic Calendar: Semester.

Student Body: Full-Time Undergrads: 13,623. Men: 43%, Women: 57%. Total Undergrad Population: Native American or Native Alaskan: 0%. Asian American or Pacific Islander: 1%. African American: 5%. Latino: 1%. Caucasian: 92%. International: 0%. Out-of-State: 17%. Total all graduate and professional students: 2,140.

Academics: Full-Time Faculty: 556.

Admissions: Regular Application Deadline: 8/1. Priority Application Deadline: Unavailable. Early Decision Deadline: Unavailable. Transfer Priority Deadline: Unavailable. Financial Aid Deadline: Unavailable. Total Number of Students Applied: Unavailable. Percent Admitted: 72%. Number Enrolled: 2,441. Test Scores (Middle 50%): SAT Critical Reading: Unavailable. SAT Math: 440–550. SAT Writing: Unavailable. ACT Comp: 18–23. HS Rank of Entering Freshmen: Top 10%: Unavailable. Top 25%: Unavailable. Avg. HS GPA: Unavailable.

Cost: Tuition and Fees: In-State: $5,194. Out-of-State: $14,538. Room and Board: $5,140.

Inst. Aid: FT Undergrads Receiving Aid: Unavailable. Avg. Amount per Student: Unavailable.

Highest Acceptance Rates (100% of Applicants Accepted in 2007)

Glenville State College (WV)

Golden Gate University (CA)

Lake Erie College (OH)

Mountain State University (WV)

Shawnee State University (OH)

EASTERN MICHIGAN UNIVERSITY

Ypsilanti, MI

admissions@emich.edu; www.emich.edu

General Info: Public, University, Four-year, Coed, Regionally Accredited, North Central Association of Colleges and Schools, College Board member. Urban setting, Small city (50,000–249,999), Residential campus. Academic Calendar: Semester.

Student Body: Full-Time Undergrads: 18,245. Men: 41%, Women: 59%. Total Undergrad Population: Native American or Native Alaskan: 0%. Asian American or Pacific Islander: 2%. African American: 25%. Latino: 3%. Caucasian: 64%. International: 1%. Out-of-State: 11%. Total all graduate and professional students: 4,649.

Academics: Full-Time Faculty: 764.

Admissions: Regular Application Deadline: 8/1. Priority Application Deadline: Unavailable. Early Decision Deadline: Unavailable. Transfer Priority Deadline: Unavailable. Financial Aid Deadline: Unavailable. Total Number of Students Applied: Unavailable. Percent Admitted: 79%. Number Enrolled: 2,347. Test Scores (Middle 50%): SAT Critical Reading: 440–580. SAT Math: 450–580. SAT Writing: Unavailable. ACT Comp: 18–24. HS Rank of Entering Freshmen: Top 10%: 10%. Top 25%: 33%. Avg. HS GPA: Unavailable.

Cost: Tuition and Fees: In-State: $6,935. Out-of-State: $18,290. Room and Board: $6,610.

Inst. Aid: FT Undergrads Receiving Aid: Unavailable. Avg. Amount per Student: Unavailable.

ECKERD COLLEGE

St. Petersburg, FL

admissions@eckerd.edu; www.eckerd.edu

General Info: Coed, College Board member, Four-year, Liberal Arts College, Presbyterian Church (USA), Private, Southern Association of Colleges and Schools. Suburban setting, Large city (250,000–499,999), Residential campus. Academic Calendar: 4-1-4.

Student Body: Full-Time Undergrads: 1,750. Men: 42%, Women: 58%. Part-Time Undergrads. Men: 1%, Women: 1%. Total Undergrad Population: Native American or Native Alaskan: 0%. Asian American or Pacific Islander: 2%. African American: 3%. Latino: 4%. Caucasian: 77%. International: 3%. Out-of-State: 75%. Living Off-Campus: 24%.

Academics: Full-Time Faculty: 113. With PhD: 100. Percentage completing two or more majors: 17%. Graduation Rates: 53% within 4 years. 58% within 6 years.

Admissions: Regular Application Deadline: 4/1. Priority Application Deadline: Unavailable. Early Decision Deadline: Unavailable. Transfer Priority Deadline: 3/1. Financial Aid Deadline: Unavailable. Total Number of Students Applied: 3,118. Number Admitted: 2,086. Number Enrolled: Unavailable. Number accepting place on waitlist: 111. Number of waitlisted students admitted: 35. Test Scores (Middle 50%): SAT Critical Reading: 510–610. SAT Math: 500–610. SAT Writing: 500–600. ACT Comp: 22–27. HS Rank of Entering Freshmen: Top 10%: 17%. Top 25%: 45%. Avg. HS GPA: 3.3.

Cost: Tuition and Fees: In-State: $30,304. Out-of-State: $30,304. Room and Board: $8,754.

Inst. Aid: FT Undergrads Receiving Aid: 1,698. Avg. Amount per Student: Unavailable.

Graduates: No. of companies recruiting on campus: 250. Percentage of grads accepting a job at time of graduation: 33%. Alumni Giving %: 35%.

ELON UNIVERSITY

Elon, NC

admissions@elon.edu; www.elon.edu

General Info: Private, Liberal Arts College, University, Four-year, United 96, Coed, Regionally Accredited, College Board member. Suburban setting, Large town (10,000–49,999), Residential campus. Academic Calendar: 4-1-4.

Student Body: Full-Time Undergrads: 4,850. Men: 40.3%, Women: 57.6%. Part-Time Undergrads. Men: 0.8%, Women: 1.3%. Total Undergrad Population: Native American or Native Alaskan: 0.2%. Asian American or Pacific Islander: 1.1%. African American: 6%. Latino: 2.2%. Caucasian: 82.8%. International: 2.1%. Out-of-State: 72%. Living Off-Campus: 42%. % In Fraternities: 18%. % In Sororities: 31%. Total all graduate and professional students: 517.

Academics: Full-Time Faculty: 311. With PhD: 264. Percentage completing two or more majors: 10%. Graduation Rates: 65.8% within 4 years. 72.6% within 6 years.

Admissions: Regular Application Deadline: 1/10. Priority Application Deadline: Unavailable. Early Decision Deadline: 11/1. Transfer Priority Deadline: 6/1. Financial Aid Deadline: Unavailable. Total Number of Students Applied: 9,380. Number Admitted: 3,870. Number Enrolled: Unavailable. Number accepting place on waitlist: 1,211. Number of waitlisted students admitted: 39. Test Scores (Middle 50%): SAT Critical Reading: 560–650. SAT Math: 570–660. SAT Writing: 560–660. ACT Comp: 24-28. HS Rank of Entering Freshmen: Top 10%: 29%. Top 25%: 66%. Avg. HS GPA: 3.95.

Cost: Tuition and Fees: In-State: $24,076. Out-of-State: $24,076. Room and Board: $7,770.

Inst. Aid: FT Undergrads Receiving Aid: 2,165. Avg. Amount per Student: Unavailable.

Graduates: No. of companies recruiting on campus: 250. Percentage of grads accepting a job at time of graduation: 78%. Alumni Giving %: 25%.

EMBRY-RIDDLE AERONAUTICAL UNIVERSITY

Daytona Beach, FL

ecinfo@erau.edu; www.embryriddle.edu

General Info: Private, University, Four-year, Coed, Regionally Accredited. Urban setting, Small city (50,000–249,999), Commuter campus. Academic Calendar: Semester.

Student Body: Full-Time Undergrads: 12,782. Men: 91%, Women: 9%. Total Undergrad Population: Native American or Native Alaskan: 0%. Asian American or Pacific Islander: 3%. African American: 10%. Latino: 7%. Caucasian: 60%. International: 1%. Total all graduate and professional students: 4,044.

Academics: Full-Time Faculty: 336.

Admissions: Regular Application Deadline: Unavailable. Priority Application Deadline: Unavailable. Early Decision Deadline: Unavailable. Transfer Priority Deadline: Unavailable. Financial Aid Deadline: Unavailable. Total Number of Students Applied: Unavailable. Number Admitted: Unavailable. Number Enrolled: Unavailable. Test Scores (Middle 50%): SAT Critical Reading: Unavailable. SAT Math: Unavailable. SAT Writing: Unavailable. ACT Comp: Unavailable. HS Rank of Entering Freshmen: Top 10%: 20%. Top 25%: 48%. Avg. HS GPA: Unavailable.

Cost: Tuition and Fees: In-State: $24,420. Out-of-State: $24,420. Room and Board: $6,900.

Inst. Aid: FT Undergrads Receiving Aid: Unavailable. Avg. Amount per Student: Unavailable.

EMERSON COLLEGE

Boston, MA

admission@emerson.edu; www.emerson.edu

General Info: Coed, College Board member, Four-year, New England Association of Colleges and Schools, Private, Regionally Accredited. Urban setting, Very large city (over 500,000), Residential campus. Academic Calendar: Semester.

Student Body: Full-Time Undergrads: 3,402. Men: 44%, Women: 56%. Part-Time Undergrads. Men: 38%, Women: 62%. Total Undergrad Population: Native American or Native Alaskan: 0.6%. Asian American or Pacific Islander: 4.7%. African American: 2.6%. Latino: 7.1%. Caucasian: 75.8%. International: 2.4%. Out-of-State: 78%. Living Off-Campus: 51%. % In Fraternities: 2%. % In Sororities: 2%. Total all graduate and professional students: 904.

Academics: Full-Time Faculty: 159. With PhD: 114. Graduation Rates: 66% within 4 years. 72% within 6 years.

Admissions: Regular Application Deadline: 1/5. Priority Application Deadline: Unavailable. Early Decision Deadline: Unavailable. Transfer Priority Deadline: 3/15. Financial Aid Deadline: Unavailable. Total Number of Students Applied: 4,981. Number Admitted: 2,221. Number Enrolled: Unavailable. Number accepting place on waitlist: 281. Number of waitlisted students admitted: 4. Test Scores (Middle 50%): SAT Critical Reading: 590–680. SAT Math: 550–650. SAT Writing: 580–670. ACT Comp: 25-29. HS Rank of Entering Freshmen: Top 10%: 42%. Top 25%: 79%. Avg. HS GPA: 3.6.

Cost: Tuition and Fees: In-State: $28,352. Out-of-State: $28,352. Room and Board: $11,832.

Inst. Aid: FT Undergrads Receiving Aid: 2,073. Avg. Amount per Student: $15,280. Freshmen Receiving Non-Need Scholarship or Grant: 164. Avg. Amount per Student: $12,800.

Graduates: No. of companies recruiting on campus: 200. Percentage of grads accepting a job at time of graduation: 75%. Alumni Giving %: 20%.

Strong Community Service Schools

Chaminade University of Honolulu

University of Colorado at Boulder

Otterbein College

University of Pennsylvania

University of Redlands

Syracuse University

EMORY UNIVERSITY

Atlanta, GA

admiss@learnlink.emory.edu; www.emory.edu

General Info: Private, University, Four-year, United Methodist Church, Coed, Regionally Accredited, College Board member. Suburban setting, Very large city (over 500,000), Residential campus. Academic Calendar: Semester.

Student Body: Full-Time Undergrads: 6,646. Men: 43%, Women: 57%. Total Undergrad Population: Native American or Native Alaskan: 0%. Asian American or Pacific Islander: 17%. African American: 9%. Latino: 4%. Caucasian: 53%. International: 6%. Out-of-State: 83%. Total all graduate and professional students: 3,980.

Academics: Full-Time Faculty: 1,236.

Admissions: Regular Application Deadline: 1/15. Priority Application Deadline: Unavailable. Early Decision Deadline: 11/1. Financial Aid Deadline: 4/1. Total Number of Students Applied: Unavailable. Percent Admitted: 37%. Number Enrolled: 1,665. Test Scores (Middle 50%): SAT Critical Reading: 640–730. SAT Math: 660–740. SAT Writing: Unavailable. ACT Comp: 29–33. HS Rank of Entering Freshmen: Top 10%: 88%. Top 25%: 95%. Avg. HS GPA: Unavailable.

Cost: Tuition and Fees: In-State: $32,100. Out-of-State: $32,506. Room and Board: $9,938.

Inst. Aid: FT Undergrads Receiving Aid: Unavailable. Avg. Amount per Student: Unavailable.

EMPORIA STATE UNIVERSITY

Emporia, KS

go2esu@emporia.edu; www.emporia.edu

General Info: Public, Teachers College/College of Education, University, Four-year, Coed, Regionally Accredited, North Central Association of Colleges and Schools. Suburban setting, Large town (10,000–49,999), Residential campus. Academic Calendar: Semester.

Student Body: Full-Time Undergrads: 4,458. Men: 39%, Women: 61%. Total Undergrad Population: Native American or Native Alaskan: 0%. Asian American or Pacific Islander: 1%. African American: 4%. Latino: 7%. Caucasian: 80%. International: 5%. Out-of-State: 8%. Total all graduate and professional students: 2,034.

Academics: Full-Time Faculty: 259. Graduation Rates: 23% within 4 years. 44% within 6 years.

Admissions: Regular Application Deadline: Rolling. Priority Application Deadline: Unavailable. Early Decision Deadline: Unavailable. Transfer Priority Deadline: Unavailable. Financial Aid Deadline: Unavailable. Total Number of Students Applied: Unavailable. Percent Admitted: 80%. Number Enrolled: 769. Test Scores (Middle 50%): SAT Critical Reading: Unavailable. SAT Math: Unavailable. SAT Writing: Unavailable. ACT Comp: 19–24. HS Rank of Entering Freshmen: Top 10%: Unavailable. Top 25%: Unavailable. Avg. HS GPA: Unavailable.

Cost: Tuition and Fees: In-State: $3,926. Out-of-State: $11,976. Room and Board: $5,582.

Inst. Aid: FT Undergrads Receiving Aid: Unavailable. Avg. Amount per Student: Unavailable.

EUGENE LANG COLLEGE–THE NEW SCHOOL FOR LIBERAL ARTS

New York, NY

Lang@newschool.edu; www.lang.edu

General Info: Private, Liberal Arts College, Four-year, Coed, Regionally Accredited, College Board member. Urban setting, Very large city (over 500,000), Commuter campus. Academic Calendar: Semester.

Student Body: Full-Time Undergrads: 1,164. Men: 32%, Women: 68%. Total Undergrad Population: Native American or Native Alaskan: 1%. Asian American or Pacific Islander: 7%. African American: 4%. Latino: 9%. Caucasian: 59%. International: 4%. Out-of-State: 76%.

Academics: Full-Time Faculty: 49.

Admissions: Regular Application Deadline: 2/1. Priority Application Deadline: Unavailable. Early Decision Deadline: 11/15. Fall Transfer Deadline: 5/15. Transfer Priority Deadline: Unavailable. Financial Aid Deadline: Unavailable. Total Number of Students Applied: Unavailable. Percent Admitted: 63%. Number Enrolled: 283. Test Scores (Middle 50%): SAT Critical Reading: 610. SAT Math: 560–670. SAT Writing: 550–660. ACT Comp: 22–28. HS Rank of Entering Freshmen: Top 10%: 13%. Top 25%: 58%. Avg. HS GPA: Unavailable.

Cost: Tuition and Fees: In-State: $30,270. Out-of-State: $29,210. Room and Board: $11,750.

Inst. Aid: FT Undergrads Receiving Aid: Unavailable. Avg. Amount per Student: Unavailable.

Great Engineering Schools

Massachusetts Institute of Technology

California Institute of Technology

Stanford University

University of California—Berkeley

EVERGREEN STATE COLLEGE

Olympia, WA
admissions@evergreen.edu; www.evergreen.edu

General Info: Coed, College Board member, Four-year, Liberal Arts College, Northwest Association of Schools and Colleges, Public, Regionally Accredited. Commuter campus, Residential campus, Rural setting, Small city (50,000–249,999). Academic Calendar: Quarter.

Student Body: Full-Time Undergrads: 4,124. Men: 48%, Women: 52%. Part-Time Undergrads. Men: 4%, Women: 7%. Total Undergrad Population: Native American or Native Alaskan: 4%. Asian American or Pacific Islander: 5%. African American: 4%. Latino: 5%. Caucasian: 67%. International: 0.37%. Out-of-State: 24%. Living Off-Campus: 78%. Total all graduate and professional students: 304.

Academics: Full-Time Faculty: 158. With PhD: 177. Graduation Rates: 42% within 4 years. 58% within 6 years.

Admissions: Regular Application Deadline: 3/1. Priority Application Deadline: 3/1. Early Decision Deadline: Unavailable. Transfer Priority Deadline: 3/1. Financial Aid Deadline: Unavailable. Total Number of Students Applied: 3,163. Number Admitted: 3,076. Number Enrolled: Unavailable. Test Scores (Middle 50%): SAT Critical Reading: Unavailable. SAT Math: Unavailable. SAT Writing: Unavailable. HS Rank of Entering Freshmen: Top 10%: Unavailable. Top 25%: Unavailable. Avg. HS GPA: 3.06.

Cost: Tuition and Fees: In-State: $4,897. Out-of-State: $15,567. Room and Board: $8,052.

Inst. Aid: FT Undergrads Receiving Aid: 2,049. Avg. Amount per Student: Unavailable.

Graduates: No. of companies recruiting on campus: 175.

FAIRFIELD UNIVERSITY

Fairfield, CT
admis@mail.fairfield.edu; www.fairfield.edu

General Info: Private, University, Four-year, Roman Catholic Church, Society of Jesus (Jesuits), Coed, Regionally Accredited, College Board member. Suburban setting, Small city (50,000–249,999), Residential campus. Academic Calendar: Semester.

Student Body: Full-Time Undergrads: 4,008. Men: 40%, Women: 60%. Total Undergrad Population: Native American or Native Alaskan: 1%. Asian American or Pacific Islander: 4%. African American: 4%. Latino: 9%. Caucasian: 81%. International: 1%. Out-of-State: 80%. Total all graduate and professional students: 1,083.

Academics: Full-Time Faculty: 226. Graduation Rates: 79% within 4 years. 81% within 6 years.

Admissions: Regular Application Deadline: 1/15. Financial Aid Deadline: 2/15. Total Number of Students Applied: Unavailable. Percent Admitted: 61%. Number Enrolled: 899. Test Scores (Middle 50%): SAT Critical Reading: 540–630. SAT Math: 550–640. SAT Writing: 780–780. ACT Comp: 23–27. HS Rank of Entering Freshmen: Top 10%: Unavailable. Top 25%: Unavailable. Avg. HS GPA: Unavailable.

Strong Writing Programs

University of Iowa

Knox University

Columbia University

Cost: Tuition and Fees: In-State: $35,510. Out-of-State: $35,510. Room and Board: $10,850.

Inst. Aid: FT Undergrads Receiving Aid: Unavailable. Avg. Amount per Student: Unavailable.

FASHION INSTITUTE OF TECHNOLOGY

New York, NY
fitinfo@fitnyc.edu; www.fitnyc.edu

General Info: Public, College of Art, College of Business, Liberal Arts College, Four-year, Coed, Regionally Accredited, Middle States Association of Colleges and Schools, College Board member. Urban setting, Very large city (over 500,000), Commuter campus. Academic Calendar: Semester.

Student Body: Full-Time Undergrads: 9,825. Men: 13%, Women: 87%. Total Undergrad Population: Native American or Native Alaskan: 0%. Asian American or Pacific Islander: 7%. African American: 7%. Latino: 11%. Caucasian: 57%. International: 4%. Out-of-State: 39%. Total all graduate and professional students: 185.

Academics: Full-Time Faculty: 223.

Admissions: Regular Application Deadline: 2/15. Priority Application Deadline: 1/1. Early Decision Deadline: 11/1. Transfer Priority Deadline: 1/1. Financial Aid Deadline: Unavailable. Total Number of Students Applied: Unavailable. Percent Admitted: 43%. Number Enrolled: 1,021. Test Scores (Middle 50%): SAT Critical Reading: Unavailable. SAT Math: Unavailable. SAT Writing: Unavailable. ACT Comp: Unavailable. HS Rank of Entering Freshmen: Top 10%: 13%. Top 25%: 45%. Avg. HS GPA: Unavailable.

Cost: Tuition and Fees: In-State: $3,494. Out-of-State: $9,642. Room and Board: $9,213.

Inst. Aid: FT Undergrads Receiving Aid: Unavailable. Avg. Amount per Student: Unavailable.

Great Collegiate Sports Teams (2007 Division I Champions)

Football (Men)—Louisiana State University

Basketball (Men)—University of Florida

Basketball (Women)—University of Tennessee

Baseball (Men)—Oregon State

Softball (Women)—University of Arizona

FERRIS STATE UNIVERSITY

Big Rapids, MI
admissions@ferris.edu; www.ferris.edu

General Info: Public, University, Four-year, Coed, Regionally Accredited, North Central Association of Colleges and Schools, College Board member. Rural setting, Large town (10,000–49,999), Residential campus. Academic Calendar: Semester.

Student Body: Full-Time Undergrads: 11,409. Men: 54%, Women: 46%. Total Undergrad Population: Native American or Native Alaskan: 2%. Asian American or Pacific Islander: 2%. African American: 5%. Latino: 2%. Caucasian: 78%. International: 1%. Out-of-State: 6%. Total all graduate and professional students: 518.

Academics: Full-Time Faculty: 545.

Admissions: Regular Application Deadline: Rolling. Priority Application Deadline: Unavailable. Early Decision Deadline: Unavailable. Transfer Priority Deadline: Unavailable. Financial Aid Deadline: Unavailable. Total Number of Students Applied: Unavailable. Percent Admitted: 76%. Number Enrolled: 2,201. Test Scores (Middle 50%): SAT Critical Reading: Unavailable. SAT Math: Unavailable. SAT Writing: Unavailable. ACT Comp: 18–24. HS Rank of Entering Freshmen: Top 10%: Unavailable. Top 25%: Unavailable. Avg. HS GPA: Unavailable.

Cost: Tuition and Fees: In-State: $7,342. Out-of-State: $14,782. Room and Board: $7,220.

Inst. Aid: FT Undergrads Receiving Aid: Unavailable. Avg. Amount per Student: Unavailable.

FISK UNIVERSITY

Nashville, TN
admit@fisk.edu; www.fisk.edu

General Info: Private, Liberal Arts College, Four-year, United 96, Coed, Regionally Accredited, College Board member, Historically black. Urban setting, Very large city (over 500,000), Residential campus. Academic Calendar: Semester.

Student Body: Full-Time Undergrads: 864. Men: 27%, Women: 73%. Total Undergrad Population: Native American or Native Alaskan: 0%. Asian American or Pacific Islander: 1%. African American: 95%. Latino: 0%. Caucasian: 0%. International: 2%. Out-of-State: 70%. Total all graduate and professional students: 56.

Academics: Full-Time Faculty: 52. Graduation Rates: 54% within 4 years. 71% within 6 years.

Admissions: Regular Application Deadline: 3/1. Priority Application Deadline: 1/6. Early Decision Deadline: Unavailable. Transfer Priority Deadline: Unavailable. Financial Aid Deadline: 7/1. Total Number of Students Applied: Unavailable. Percent Admitted: 80%. Number Enrolled: 178. Test Scores (Middle 50%): SAT Critical Reading: 450–560. SAT Math: 440–540. SAT Writing: 480–560. ACT Comp: 20–22. HS Rank of Entering Freshmen: Top 10%: 20%. Top 25%: 45%. Avg. HS GPA: 3.3.

Cost: Tuition and Fees: In-State: $15,140. Out-of-State: $15,140. Room and Board: $7,730.

Inst. Aid: FT Undergrads Receiving Aid: Unavailable. Avg. Amount per Student: Unavailable.

Graduates: No. of companies recruiting on campus: 30.

FLAGLER COLLEGE

St. Augustine, FL
admiss@flagler.edu; www.flagler.edu

General Info: Private, Liberal Arts College, Four-year, Coed, Regionally Accredited, College Board member. Suburban setting, Large town (10,000–49,999), Residential campus. Academic Calendar: Semester.

Student Body: Full-Time Undergrads: 2,246. Men: 39%, Women: 61%. Total Undergrad Population: Native American or Native Alaskan: 0%. Asian American or Pacific Islander: 0%. African American: 2%. Latino: 4%. Caucasian: 89%. International: 0%. Out-of-State: 35%.

Academics: Full-Time Faculty: 74. Graduation Rates: 44% within 4 years. 55% within 6 years.

Admissions: Regular Application Deadline: 3/1. Priority Application Deadline: Unavailable. Early Decision Deadline: 12/1. Transfer Priority Deadline: 1/15. Financial Aid Deadline: Unavailable. Total Number of Students Applied: Unavailable. Percent Admitted: 26%. Number Enrolled: 481. Test Scores (Middle 50%): SAT Critical Reading: 520–610. SAT Math: 510–590. SAT Writing: 520–600. ACT Comp: 22–26. HS Rank of Entering Freshmen: Top 10%: 16%. Top 25%: 51%. Avg. HS GPA: Unavailable.

Cost: Tuition and Fees: In-State: $12,520. Out-of-State: $12,520. Room and Board: $6,810.

Inst. Aid: FT Undergrads Receiving Aid: Unavailable. Avg. Amount per Student: Unavailable.

FLORIDA STATE UNIVERSITY

Tallahassee, FL

admissions@admin.fsu.edu; www.fsu.edu

General Info: Public, University, Four-year, Coed, Regionally Accredited, Southern Association of Colleges and Schools, College Board member. Urban setting, Small city (50,000–249,999), Residential campus. Academic Calendar: Semester.

Student Body: Full-Time Undergrads: 31,347. Men: 42%, Women: 58%. Total Undergrad Population: Native American or Native Alaskan: 1%. Asian American or Pacific Islander: 3%. African American: 9%. Latino: 12%. Caucasian: 74%. International: 0%. Out-of-State: 12%. Total all graduate and professional students: 7,583.

Academics: Full-Time Faculty: 1,265.

Admissions: Regular Application Deadline: 3/1. Priority Application Deadline: 11/1. Early Decision Deadline: Unavailable. Transfer Priority Deadline: Unavailable. Financial Aid Deadline: Unavailable. Total Number of Students Applied: Unavailable. Percent Admitted: 59%. Number Enrolled: 6,176. Test Scores (Middle 50%): SAT Critical Reading: 530–620. SAT Math: 540–630. SAT Writing: 510–600. ACT Comp: 23–27. HS Rank of Entering Freshmen: Top 10%: 26%. Top 25%: 61%. Avg. HS GPA: Unavailable.

Cost: Tuition and Fees: In-State: $3,307. Out-of-State: $17,355. Room and Board: $7,078.

Inst. Aid: FT Undergrads Receiving Aid: Unavailable. Avg. Amount per Student: Unavailable.

FORDHAM UNIVERSITY

Bronx, NY

enroll@fordham.edu; www.fordham.edu

General Info: Private, University, Four-year, Roman Catholic Church, Society of Jesus (Jesuits), Coed, Regionally Accredited, College Board member. Urban setting, Very large city (over 500,000), Residential campus. Academic Calendar: Semester.

Student Body: Full-Time Undergrads: 6,500. Men: 43%, Women: 57%. Part-Time Undergrads. Men: 37.5%, Women: 62.5%. Total Undergrad Population: Native American or Native Alaskan: 0.3%. Asian American or Pacific Islander: 6%. African American: 6%. Latino: 12%. Caucasian: 56%. International: 2%. Out-of-State: 45.1%. Living Off-Campus: 43.8%. Total all graduate and professional students: 6,796.

Academics: Full-Time Faculty: 686. With PhD: 657. Graduation Rates: 72% within 4 years. 80% within 6 years.

Admissions: Regular Application Deadline: 1/15. Priority Application Deadline: Unavailable. Early Decision Deadline: Unavailable. Fall Transfer Deadline: 7/1. Spring Transfer Deadline: 12/1. Transfer Priority Deadline: 7/1. Financial Aid Deadline: 2/1. Total Number of Students Applied: 22,035. Number Admitted: 9,281. Number Enrolled: 1,784. Number accepting place on waitlist: 1,187. Number of waitlisted students admitted: 104. Test Scores (Middle 50%): SAT Critical Reading: 570–670. SAT Math: 560–660. SAT Writing: Unavailable. ACT Comp: 25-29. HS Rank of Entering Freshmen: Top 10%: 42.5%. Top 25%: 78.2%. Avg. HS GPA: 3.68.

Cost: Tuition and Fees: In-State: $31,800. Out-of-State: $31,800. Room and Board: $12,300.

Inst. Aid: FT Undergrads Receiving Aid: 4,485. Avg. Amount per Student: $25,258. Freshmen Receiving Non-Need Scholarship or Grant: 182. Avg. Amount per Student: $9,259.

Graduates: No. of companies recruiting on campus: 300. Percentage of grads accepting a job at time of graduation: 72%. Alumni Giving %: 22%.

FRANKLIN & MARSHALL COLLEGE

Lancaster, PA

admission@fandm.edu; www.fandm.edu

General Info: Private, Liberal Arts College, Four-year, Coed, Regionally Accredited, College Board member. Suburban setting, Small city (50,000–249,999), Residential campus. Academic Calendar: Semester.

Student Body: Full-Time Undergrads: 2,028. Men: 48%, Women: 52%. Total Undergrad Population: Native American or Native Alaskan: 0%. Asian American or Pacific Islander: 5%. African American: 5%. Latino: 5%. Caucasian: 61%. International: 9%. Out-of-State: 71%.

Academics: Full-Time Faculty: 175.

Admissions: Regular Application Deadline: 2/1. Priority Application Deadline: Unavailable. Early Decision Deadline: 11/15. Transfer Priority Deadline: Unavailable. Financial Aid Deadline: 3/1. Total Number of Students Applied: Unavailable. Percent Admitted: 46%. Number Enrolled: 524. Test Scores (Middle 50%): SAT Critical Reading: 580–670. SAT Math: 600–690. SAT Writing: Unavailable. ACT Comp: Unavailable. HS Rank of Entering Freshmen: Top 10%: 54%. Top 25%: 83%. Avg. HS GPA: Unavailable.

Cost: Tuition and Fees: In-State: $34,450. Out-of-State: $34,450. Room and Board: $8,540.

Inst. Aid: FT Undergrads Receiving Aid: Unavailable. Avg. Amount per Student: Unavailable.

FRANKLIN W. OLIN COLLEGE OF ENGINEERING

Needham, MA

info@olin.edu; www.olin.edu

General Info: Private, College of Engineering, Four-year, Coed, Regionally Accredited. Suburban setting, Large town (10,000–49,999), Residential campus. Academic Calendar: Semester.

Student Body: Full-Time Undergrads: 304. Men: 54%, Women: 46%.

Academics: Full-Time Faculty: 27.

Admissions: Regular Application Deadline: 1/1. Priority Application Deadline: Unavailable. Transfer Priority Deadline: Unavailable. Financial Aid Deadline: Unavailable. Total Number of Students Applied: Unavailable. Percent Admitted: 44%. Number Enrolled: 75. Test Scores (Middle 50%): SAT Critical Reading: Unavailable. SAT Math: Unavailable. SAT Writing: Unavailable. ACT Comp: Unavailable. HS Rank of Entering Freshmen: Top 10%: 94%. Top 25%: 100%. Avg. HS GPA: Unavailable.

Cost: Tuition and Fees: In-State: $35,000. Out-of-State: $35,000.

Inst. Aid: FT Undergrads Receiving Aid: Unavailable. Avg. Amount per Student: Unavailable.

FURMAN UNIVERSITY

Greenville, SC

admissions@furman.edu; www.furman.edu

General Info: Private, Liberal Arts College, Four-year, Coed, Regionally Accredited, College Board member. Suburban setting, Small city (50,000–249,999), Residential campus. Academic Calendar: 3-2-3.

Student Body: Full-Time Undergrads: 2,551. Men: 44%, Women: 56%. Total Undergrad Population: Native American or Native Alaskan: 0%. Asian American or Pacific Islander: 2%. African American: 7%. Latino: 1%. Caucasian: 85%. International: 1%. Out-of-State: 72%. Total all graduate and professional students: 251.

Academics: Full-Time Faculty: 228.

Admissions: Regular Application Deadline: 1/15. Priority Application Deadline: Unavailable. Early Decision Deadline: 11/15. Transfer Priority Deadline: Unavailable. Financial Aid Deadline: 1/15. Total Number of Students Applied: Unavailable. Percent Admitted: 56%. Number Enrolled: 683. Test Scores (Middle 50%): SAT Critical Reading: 590–690. SAT Math: 590–690. SAT Writing: Unavailable. ACT Comp: 25–31. HS Rank of Entering Freshmen: Top 10%: 64%. Top 25%: 87%. Avg. HS GPA: Unavailable.

Cost: Tuition and Fees: In-State: $31,040. Out-of-State: $28,840. Room and Board: $8,064.

Inst. Aid: FT Undergrads Receiving Aid: Unavailable. Avg. Amount per Student: Unavailable.

GEORGE MASON UNIVERSITY

Fairfax, VA

admissions@gmu.edu; www.gmu.edu

General Info: Public, University, Four-year, Coed, Regionally Accredited, Southern Association of Colleges and Schools, College Board member. Suburban setting, Large town (10,000–49,999), Residential campus. Academic Calendar: Semester.

Student Body: Full-Time Undergrads: 17,529. Men: 46%, Women: 54%. Total Undergrad Population: Native American or Native Alaskan: 0%. Asian American or Pacific Islander: 18%. African American: 6%. Latino: 6%. Caucasian: 53%. International: 2%. Out-of-State: 20%. Total all graduate and professional students: 10,906.

Academics: Full-Time Faculty: 1,028.

Admissions: Regular Application Deadline: 1/15. Priority Application Deadline: 12/1. Early Decision Deadline: 11/15. Transfer Priority Deadline: Unavailable. Financial Aid Deadline: Unavailable. Total Number of Students Applied: Unavailable. Percent Admitted: 61%. Number Enrolled: 2,458. Test Scores (Middle 50%): SAT Critical Reading: 500–600. SAT Math: 510–610. SAT Writing: 490–590. ACT Comp: 20–25. HS Rank of Entering Freshmen: Top 10%: 15%. Top 25%: 48%. Avg. HS GPA: Unavailable.

Cost: Tuition and Fees: In-State: $6,408. Out-of-State: $18,552. Room and Board: $6,750.

Inst. Aid: FT Undergrads Receiving Aid: Unavailable. Avg. Amount per Student: $8,394.

GEORGE WASHINGTON UNIVERSITY

Washington, DC

gwadm@gwu.edu; www.gwu.edu

General Info: Private, University, Four-year, Coed, Regionally Accredited, College Board member. Urban setting, Very large city (over 500,000), Residential campus. Academic Calendar: Semester.

Student Body: Full-Time Undergrads: 9,839. Men: 43%, Women: 57%. Total Undergrad Population: Native American or Native Alaskan: 0%. Asian American or Pacific Islander: 10%. African American: 6%. Latino: 6%. Caucasian: 65%. International: 4%. Out-of-State: 99%. Total all graduate and professional students: 11,022.

Academics: Full-Time Faculty: 826.

Admissions: Regular Application Deadline: 1/10. Priority Application Deadline: 12/1. Early Decision Deadline: 12/1. Transfer Priority Deadline: Unavailable. Financial Aid Deadline: 2/1. Total Number of Students Applied: Unavailable. Percent Admitted: 37%. Number Enrolled: 2,623. Test Scores (Middle 50%): SAT Critical Reading: 600–700. SAT Math: 600–690. SAT Writing: Unavailable. ACT Comp: Unavailable. HS Rank of Entering Freshmen: Top 10%: 63%. Top 25%: 88%. Avg. HS GPA: Unavailable.

Cost: Tuition and Fees: In-State: $37,820. Out-of-State: $37,820. Room and Board: $11,100.

Inst. Aid: FT Undergrads Receiving Aid: Unavailable. Avg. Amount per Student: Unavailable.

GEORGETOWN UNIVERSITY

Washington, DC

georgetown.edu; www.georgetown.edu

General Info: Private, University, Four-year, Roman Catholic Church, Society of Jesus (Jesuits), Coed, Regionally Accredited, College Board member. Urban setting, Very large city (over 500,000), Residential campus. Academic Calendar: Semester.

Student Body: Full-Time Undergrads: 6,853. Men: 46%, Women: 54%. Total Undergrad Population: Native American or Native Alaskan: 0%. Asian American or Pacific Islander: 8%. African American: 8%. Latino: 8%. Caucasian: 65%. International: 4%. Out-of-State: 99%. Total all graduate and professional students: 4,490.

Academics: Full-Time Faculty: 700.

Admissions: Regular Application Deadline: 1/10. Priority Application Deadline: Unavailable. Early Decision Deadline: 11/1. Transfer Priority Deadline: Unavailable. Financial Aid Deadline: 2/1. Total Number of Students Applied: Unavailable. Percent Admitted: 22%. Number Enrolled: 1,588. Test Scores (Middle 50%): SAT Critical Reading: 640–750. SAT Math: 650–740. SAT Writing: Unavailable. ACT Comp: 27–32. HS Rank of Entering Freshmen: Top 10%: 84%. Top 25%: 96%. Avg. HS GPA: Unavailable.

Cost: Tuition and Fees: In-State: $33,352. Out-of-State: $33,934. Room and Board: $10,930.

Inst. Aid: FT Undergrads Receiving Aid: Unavailable. Avg. Amount per Student: $27,330.

Top Undergraduate Business Programs

University of Pennsylvania—Wharton

New York University—Stern

Notre Dame—Mendoza

University of Virginia—McIntire

GEORGIA INSTITUTE OF TECHNOLOGY

Atlanta, GA
admission@gatech.edu; www.gatech.edu

General Info: Public, University, Four-year, Coed, Regionally Accredited, Southern Association of Colleges and Schools, College Board member. Urban setting, Very large city (over 500,000), Residential campus. Academic Calendar: Semester.

Student Body: Full-Time Undergrads: 12,361. Men: 71%, Women: 29%. Total Undergrad Population: Native American or Native Alaskan: 0%. Asian American or Pacific Islander: 17%. African American: 6%. Latino: 4%. Caucasian: 68%. International: 4%. Out-of-State: 34%. Total all graduate and professional students: 5,575.

Academics: Full-Time Faculty: 845.

Admissions: Regular Application Deadline: 1/15. Priority Application Deadline: Unavailable. Early Decision Deadline: Unavailable. Transfer Priority Deadline: 2/1. Financial Aid Deadline: 3/1. Total Number of Students Applied: Unavailable. Percent Admitted: 69%. Number Enrolled: 2,837. Test Scores (Middle 50%): SAT Critical Reading: 590–680. SAT Math: 640–720. SAT Writing: 570–660. ACT Comp: 26–30. HS Rank of Entering Freshmen: Top 10%: 54%. Top 25%: 83%. Avg. HS GPA: Unavailable.

Cost: Tuition and Fees: In-State: $4,926. Out-of-State: $20,272. Room and Board: $7,094.

Inst. Aid: FT Undergrads Receiving Aid: Unavailable. Avg. Amount per Student: Unavailable.

GETTYSBURG COLLEGE

Gettysburg, PA
admiss@gettysburg.edu; www.gettysburg.edu

General Info: Coed, College Board member, Four-year, Liberal Arts College, Private, Regionally Accredited. Suburban setting, Large town (10,000–49,999), Residential campus. Academic Calendar: Semester.

Student Body: Full-Time Undergrads: 2,600. Men: 46%, Women: 54%. Total Undergrad Population: Native American or Native Alaskan: 0%. Asian American or Pacific Islander: 1%. African American: 5%. Latino: 3%. Caucasian: 82%. International: 2%. Out-of-State: 75%.

Academics: Full-Time Faculty: 187.

Admissions: Regular Application Deadline: 2/1. Priority Application Deadline: Unavailable. Early Decision Deadline: 11/15. Transfer Priority Deadline: 4/15. Financial Aid Deadline: 2/15. Total Number of Students Applied: Unavailable. Percent Admitted: 41%. Number Enrolled: 729. Test Scores (Middle 50%): SAT Critical Reading: 620–690. SAT Math: 600–670. SAT Writing: Unavailable. ACT Comp: Unavailable. HS Rank of Entering Freshmen: Top 10%: 66%. Top 25%: 89%. Avg. HS GPA: Unavailable.

Cost: Tuition and Fees: In-State: $37,600. Out-of-State: $37,600. Room and Board: $9,100.

Inst. Aid: FT Undergrads Receiving Aid: Unavailable. Avg. Amount per Student: Unavailable.

GONZAGA UNIVERSITY

Spokane, WA
mcculloh@gu.gonzaga.edu; www.gonzaga.edu

General Info: Private, Liberal Arts College, University, Four-year, Roman Catholic Church, Society of Jesus (Jesuits), Coed, Regionally Accredited, College Board member. Urban setting, Large city (250,000–499,999), Residential campus. Academic Calendar: Semester.

Student Body: Full-Time Undergrads: 4,100. Men: 46%, Women: 54%. Total Undergrad Population: Native American or Native Alaskan: 1%. Asian American or Pacific Islander: 6%. African American: 1%. Latino: 5%. Caucasian: 83%. International: 1%. Out-of-State: 55%. Total all graduate and professional students: 1,780.

Academics: Full-Time Faculty: 311.

Admissions: Regular Application Deadline: 2/1. Priority Application Deadline: Unavailable. Early Decision Deadline: 11/15. Transfer Priority Deadline: 3/1. Financial Aid Deadline: 6/30. Total Number of Students Applied: Unavailable. Percent Admitted: 67%. Number Enrolled: 977. Test Scores (Middle 50%): SAT Critical Reading: 530–650. SAT Math: 550–650. SAT Writing: Unavailable. ACT Comp: 23–29. HS Rank of Entering Freshmen: Top 10%: 44%. Top 25%: 75%. Avg. HS GPA: Unavailable.

Cost: Tuition and Fees: In-State: $25,012. Out-of-State: $25,012. Room and Board: $7,220.

Inst. Aid: FT Undergrads Receiving Aid: Unavailable. Avg. Amount per Student: Unavailable.

GOSHEN COLLEGE

Goshen, IN

admission@goshen.edu; www.goshen.edu

General Info: Private, Liberal Arts College, Four-year, Mennonite Church, Coed, Regionally Accredited. Rural setting, Large town (10,000–49,999), Residential campus. Academic Calendar: Semester.

Student Body: Full-Time Undergrads: 951. Men: 40%, Women: 60%. Total Undergrad Population: Native American or Native Alaskan: 0%. Asian American or Pacific Islander: 2%. African American: 4%. Latino: 7%. Caucasian: 84%. International: 3%. Out-of-State: 59%. Total all graduate and professional students: 5.

Academics: Full-Time Faculty: 64.

Admissions: Regular Application Deadline: Unavailable. Priority Application Deadline: 2/1. Early Decision Deadline: Unavailable. Transfer Priority Deadline: Unavailable. Financial Aid Deadline: Unavailable. Total Number of Students Applied: Unavailable. Percent Admitted: 76%. Number Enrolled: 206. Test Scores (Middle 50%): SAT Critical Reading: 490–640. SAT Math: 500–620. SAT Writing: 460–600. ACT Comp: 22–27. HS Rank of Entering Freshmen: Top 10%: 30%. Top 25%: 60%. Avg. HS GPA: Unavailable.

Cost: Tuition and Fees: In-State: $22,300. Out-of-State: $22,300. Room and Board: $7,400.

Inst. Aid: FT Undergrads Receiving Aid: Unavailable. Avg. Amount per Student: $17,198.

GOUCHER COLLEGE

Baltimore, MD

admissions@goucher.edu; www.goucher.edu

General Info: Private, Liberal Arts College, Four-year, Coed, Regionally Accredited, College Board member. Suburban setting, Small city (50,000–249,999), Residential campus. Academic Calendar: Semester.

Student Body: Full-Time Undergrads: 1,350. Men: 33%, Women: 67%. Total Undergrad Population: Native American or Native Alaskan: 1%. Asian American or Pacific Islander: 2%. African American: 5%. Latino: 3%. Caucasian: 72%. Out-of-State: 76%. Total all graduate and professional students: 864.

Academics: Full-Time Faculty: 130.

Admissions: Regular Application Deadline: 2/1. Priority Application Deadline: Unavailable. Early Decision Deadline: Unavailable. Transfer Priority Deadline: 5/15. Financial Aid Deadline: 2/15. Total Number of Students Applied: Unavailable. Percent Admitted: 70%. Number Enrolled: 508. Test Scores (Middle 50%): SAT Critical Reading: 560–670. SAT Math: 530–630. SAT Writing: Unavailable. ACT Comp: 23–27. HS Rank of Entering Freshmen: Top 10%: 28%. Top 25%: 60%. Avg. HS GPA: Unavailable.

Cost: Tuition and Fees: In-State: $31,082. Out-of-State: $29,325. Room and Board: $9,840.

Inst. Aid: FT Undergrads Receiving Aid: Unavailable. Avg. Amount per Student: Unavailable.

Largest School Endowments (2007)

Harvard University	$34.9 billion
Yale University	$22.5 billion
Stanford University	$17.2 billion
Princeton University	$15.8 billion
The University of Texas (system-wide)	$15.6 billion

GRAND VALLEY STATE UNIVERSITY

Allendale, MI
go2gvsu@gvsu.edu; www.gvsu.edu

General Info: Public, University, Four-year, Coed, North Central Association of Colleges and Schools, Regionally Accredited, College Board member. Large town (10,000–49,999), Residential campus, Suburban setting. Academic Calendar: Semester.

Student Body: Full-Time Undergrads: 19,806. Men: 39.8%, Women: 60.2%. Part-Time Undergrads. Men: 39.5%, Women: 60.5%. Total Undergrad Population: Native American or Native Alaskan: 0.6%. Asian American or Pacific Islander: 3.2%. African American: 5.1%. Latino: 3.2%. Caucasian: 85.2%. International: 0.8%. Out-of-State: 3.9%. Total all graduate and professional students: 3,658.

Academics: Full-Time Faculty: 941. With PhD: 648. Graduation Rates: 19.1% within 4 years. 52.4% within 6 years.

Admissions: Regular Application Deadline: Unavailable. Priority Application Deadline: Unavailable. Early Decision Deadline: Unavailable. Transfer Priority Deadline: 2/1. Financial Aid Deadline: Unavailable. Total Number of Students Applied: 13,435. Number Admitted: 9,335. Number Enrolled: 3,452. Test Scores (Middle 50%): SAT Critical Reading: 490–600. SAT Math: 500–610. SAT Writing: 480–580. ACT Comp: 22–26. HS Rank of Entering Freshmen: Top 10%: 24%. Top 25%: 60%. Avg. HS GPA: 3.57.

Cost: Tuition and Fees: In-State: $7,240. Out-of-State: $12,510. Room and Board: $6,880.

Inst. Aid: FT Undergrads Receiving Aid: 10,950. Avg. Amount per Student: $8,430. Freshmen Receiving Non-Need Scholarship or Grant: 1,450. Avg. Amount per Student: $3,250.

Graduates: Alumni Giving %: 8.9%.

GRINNELL COLLEGE

Grinnell, IA
askgrin@grinnell.edu; www.grinnell.edu

General Info: Coed, College Board member, Four-year, Liberal Arts College, Nondenominational, North Central Association of Colleges and Schools, Private. Rural setting, Small town (2,500–9,999), Residential campus. Academic Calendar: Semester.

Student Body: Full-Time Undergrads: 1,500. Men: 46%, Women: 54%. Total Undergrad Population: Native American or Native Alaskan: 0.7%. Asian American or Pacific Islander: 8%. African American: 5.2%. Latino: 6.3%. Caucasian: 59.6%. International: 13.4%. Out-of-State: 76%.

Academics: Full-Time Faculty: 165. With PhD: 171. Percentage completing two or more majors: 21.4%. Graduation Rates: 78% within 4 years. 87% within 6 years.

Admissions: Regular Application Deadline: 1/20. Priority Application Deadline: Unavailable. Early Decision Deadline: 11/20. Transfer Priority Deadline: Unavailable. Financial Aid Deadline: 2/1. Total Number of Students Applied: 3,077. Number Admitted: 1,534. Number Enrolled: Unavailable. Number accepting place on waitlist: 279. Number of waitlisted students admitted: 16. Test Scores (Middle 50%): SAT Critical Reading: 610–750. SAT Math: 620–740. SAT Writing: Unavailable. ACT Comp: 29–33. HS Rank of Entering Freshmen: Top 10%: 66%. Top 25%: 93%. Avg. HS GPA: Unavailable.

Cost: Tuition and Fees: In-State: $33,910. Out-of-State: $33,910. Room and Board: $8,030.

Inst. Aid: FT Undergrads Receiving Aid: 267. Avg. Amount per Student: $26,136.

Haunted Colleges?

Huntingdon College—The Red Lady Of Pratt

University of Notre Dame—The Ghost of George Gipp

Illinois State University—Angie Milner's Ghost

GROVE CITY COLLEGE

Grove City, PA
admissions@gcc.edu; www.gcc.edu

General Info: Private, Liberal Arts College, Four-year, Presbyterian Church (USA), Coed, Regionally Accredited, College Board member. Rural setting, Small town (2,500–9,999), Residential campus. Academic Calendar: Semester.

Student Body: Full-Time Undergrads: 2,465. Men: 49%, Women: 51%. Total Undergrad Population: Native American or Native Alaskan: 0%. Asian American or Pacific Islander: 3%. African American: 1%. Latino: 1%. Caucasian: 94%. International: 0%. Out-of-State: 50%.

Academics: Full-Time Faculty: 140. Graduation Rates: 78% within 4 years. 82% within 6 years.

Admissions: Regular Application Deadline: 2/1. Priority Application Deadline: Unavailable. Early Decision Deadline: 11/15. Financial Aid Deadline: 4/15. Total Number of Students Applied: Unavailable. Percent Admitted: 57%. Number Enrolled: 674. Test Scores (Middle 50%): SAT Critical Reading: 566–702. SAT Math: 574–691. SAT Writing: Unavailable. ACT Comp: 25–30. HS Rank of Entering Freshmen: Top 10%: 52%. Top 25%: 83%. Avg. HS GPA: Unavailable.

Great Freshman Housing

Illinois Wesleyan University

New York University

Smith College

Bryn Mawr College

Cost: Tuition and Fees: In-State: $11,500. Out-of-State: $11,500. Room and Board: $6,134.

Inst. Aid: FT Undergrads Receiving Aid: Unavailable. Avg. Amount per Student: $3,371.

GUILFORD COLLEGE

Greensboro, NC
admission@guilford.edu; www.guilford.edu

General Info: Private, Liberal Arts College, Four-year, Society Of Friends (Quaker), Coed, Regionally Accredited, College Board member. Suburban setting, Small city (50,000–249,999), Residential campus. Academic Calendar: Semester.

Student Body: Full-Time Undergrads: 2,687. Men: 49%, Women: 51%.

Academics: Full-Time Faculty: 126.

Admissions: Regular Application Deadline: 2/15. Priority Application Deadline: Unavailable. Early Decision Deadline: Unavailable. Transfer Priority Deadline: 6/1. Financial Aid Deadline: Unavailable. Total Number of Students Applied: Unavailable. Percent Admitted: 73%. Number Enrolled: 430. Test Scores (Middle 50%): SAT Critical Reading: 520–630. SAT Math: 500–610. SAT Writing: Unavailable. ACT Comp: 20–26. HS Rank of Entering Freshmen: Top 10%: 14%. Top 25%: 44%. Avg. HS GPA: Unavailable.

Cost: Tuition and Fees: In-State: $23,020. Out-of-State: $23,020. Room and Board: $6,690.

Inst. Aid: FT Undergrads Receiving Aid: Unavailable. Avg. Amount per Student: Unavailable.

GUSTAVUS ADOLPHUS COLLEGE

St. Peter, MN
admission@gustavus.edu; www.gustavus.edu

General Info: Private, Liberal Arts College, Four-year, Evangelical Lutheran Church in America, Coed, Regionally Accredited, College Board member. Rural setting, Small town (2,500–9,999), Residential campus. Academic Calendar: 4-1-4.

Student Body: Full-Time Undergrads: 2,572. Men: 42%, Women: 58%. Total Undergrad Population: Native American or Native Alaskan: 0%. Asian American or Pacific Islander: 5%. African American: 2%. Latino: 2%. Caucasian: 88%. International: 1%. Out-of-State: 20%.

Academics: Full-Time Faculty: 187.

Admissions: Regular Application Deadline: Rolling. Priority Application Deadline: Unavailable. Early Decision Deadline: Unavailable. Transfer Priority Deadline: 4/1. Financial Aid Deadline: 4/15. Total Number of Students Applied: Unavailable. Percent Admitted: 79%. Number Enrolled: 662. Test Scores (Middle 50%): SAT Critical Reading: 520–670. SAT Math: 540–670. SAT Writing: Unavailable. ACT Comp: 23–28. HS Rank of Entering Freshmen: Top 10%: 41%. Top 25%: 71%. Avg. HS GPA: Unavailable.

Cost: Tuition and Fees: In-State: $26,700. Out-of-State: $26,700. Room and Board: $6,400.

Inst. Aid: FT Undergrads Receiving Aid: Unavailable. Avg. Amount per Student: Unavailable.

HAMILTON COLLEGE

Clinton, NY
admission@hamilton.edu; www.hamilton.edu

General Info: Private, Liberal Arts College, Four-year, Coed, Regionally Accredited, College Board member. Rural setting, Small town (2,500–9,999), Residential campus. Academic Calendar: Semester.

Student Body: Full-Time Undergrads: 1,775. Men: 50%, Women: 50%. Total Undergrad Population: Native American or Native Alaskan: 1%. Asian American or Pacific Islander: 8%. African American: 5%. Latino: 4%. Caucasian: 69%. International: 5%. Out-of-State: 67%.

Academics: Full-Time Faculty: 173.

Admissions: Regular Application Deadline: 1/1. Priority Application Deadline: Unavailable. Early Decision Deadline: 11/15. Transfer Priority Deadline: 4/15. Financial Aid Deadline: 1/1. Total Number of Students Applied: Unavailable. Number Admitted: Unavailable. Number Enrolled: Unavailable. Test Scores (Middle 50%): SAT Critical Reading: 630–740. SAT Math: 630–720. SAT Writing: Unavailable. HS Rank of Entering Freshmen: Top 10%: Unavailable. Top 25%: Unavailable. Avg. HS GPA: Unavailable.

Cost: Tuition and Fees: In-State: $36,860. Out-of-State: $34,980. Room and Board: $9,350.

Inst. Aid: FT Undergrads Receiving Aid: Unavailable. Avg. Amount per Student: Unavailable.

HAMILTON COLLEGE

Omaha, NE
jhorner@hamiltonomaha.edu; www.hamiltonia.edu

General Info: Proprietary, Coed. Setting: Very large city (over 500,000). Academic Calendar: Quarter.

Student Body: Full-Time Undergrads: Unavailable. Men: Unavailable, Women: Unavailable.

Academics: Full-Time Faculty: 173.

Admissions: Regular Application Deadline: Unavailable. Priority Application Deadline: Unavailable. Early Decision Deadline: Unavailable. Financial Aid Deadline: Unavailable. Total Number of Students Applied: Unavailable. Number Admitted: Unavailable. Number Enrolled: Unavailable. Test Scores (Middle 50%): SAT Critical Reading: Unavailable. SAT Math: Unavailable. SAT Writing: Unavailable. HS Rank of Entering Freshmen: Top 10%: 70%. Top 25%: 91%. Avg. HS GPA: Unavailable.

Cost: Tuition and Fees: In-State: $33,150. Out-of-State: $33,150. Room and Board: $8,310.

Inst. Aid: FT Undergrads Receiving Aid: Unavailable. Avg. Amount per Student: Unavailable.

HAMPDEN-SYDNEY COLLEGE

Hampden-Sydney, VA
hsapp@hsc.edu; www.hsc.edu

General Info: Private, Liberal Arts College, Four-year, Presbyterian Church (USA), Men Only, Regionally Accredited, College Board member. Rural setting, Rural community (under 2,500), Residential campus. Academic Calendar: Semester.

Student Body: Full-Time Undergrads: 1,060. Men: 100%, Women: 0%. Total Undergrad Population: Native American or Native Alaskan: 0.2%. Asian American or Pacific Islander: 0.8%. African American: 5.4%. Latino: 1.2%. Caucasian: 90.8%. International: 1.5%. Out-of-State: 35%.

Academics: Full-Time Faculty: 97. With PhD: 93. Percentage completing two or more majors: 20%. Graduation Rates: 67.2% within 4 years. 67.5% within 6 years.

Admissions: Regular Application Deadline: 3/1. Priority Application Deadline: Unavailable. Early Decision Deadline: 11/15. Financial Aid Deadline: Unavailable. Total Number of Students Applied: 1,470. Number Admitted: 984. Test Scores (Middle 50%): SAT Critical Reading: 510–600. SAT Math: 515-630. SAT Writing: 480–590. ACT Comp: 20–26. HS Rank of Entering Freshmen: Top 10%: 8.6%. Top 25%: 20%. Avg. HS GPA: 3.26.

Cost: Tuition and Fees: In-State: $28,144. Out-of-State: $28,144. Room and Board: $91,448.

Inst. Aid: FT Undergrads Receiving Aid: Unavailable. Avg. Amount per Student: $18,564.

Graduates: No. of companies recruiting on campus: 40. Percentage of grads accepting a job at time of graduation: 25%. Alumni Giving %: 48.3%.

HAMPSHIRE COLLEGE

Amherst, MA
admissions@hampshire.edu; www.hampshire.edu

General Info: Private, Liberal Arts College, Four-year, Coed, Regionally Accredited, College Board member. Rural setting, Large town (10,000–49,999), Residential campus. Academic Calendar: 4-1-4.

Student Body: Full-Time Undergrads: 1,448. Men: 38%, Women: 62%. Total Undergrad Population: Native American or Native Alaskan: 1%. Asian American or Pacific Islander: 2%. African American: 4%. Latino: 7%. Caucasian: 66%. International: 2%. Out-of-State: 85%.

Academics: Full-Time Faculty: 115.

Admissions: Regular Application Deadline: 1/15. Priority Application Deadline: 11/15. Early Decision Deadline: 11/15. Transfer Priority Deadline: Unavailable. Financial Aid Deadline: 2/1. Total Number of Students Applied: Unavailable. Percent Admitted: 56%. Number Enrolled: Unavailable. Test Scores (Middle 50%): SAT Critical Reading: 610–700. SAT Math: 540–660. SAT Writing: 600–690. ACT Comp: 26–29. HS Rank of Entering Freshmen: Top 10%: 28%. Top 25%: 63%. Avg. HS GPA: Unavailable.

Cost: Tuition and Fees: In-State: $37,789. Out-of-State: $37,789. Room and Board: $10,080.

Inst. Aid: FT Undergrads Receiving Aid: Unavailable. Avg. Amount per Student: $28,725.

HAMPTON UNIVERSITY

Hampton, VA
admit@hamptonu.edu; www.hamptonu.edu

General Info: Private, University, Four-year, Coed, Regionally Accredited, College Board member, Historically black. Urban setting, Small city (50,000–249,999), Residential campus. Academic Calendar: Semester.

Student Body: Full-Time Undergrads: 5,135. Men: 37%, Women: 63%. Total Undergrad Population: Native American or Native Alaskan: 0%. Asian American or Pacific Islander: 0%. African American: 98%. Latino: 0%. Caucasian: 1%. International: 0%. Out-of-State: 68%. Total all graduate and professional students: 784.

Academics: Full-Time Faculty: 323.

Admissions: Regular Application Deadline: 4/15. Priority Application Deadline: Unavailable. Early Decision Deadline: Unavailable. Transfer Priority Deadline: Unavailable. Financial Aid Deadline: Unavailable. Total Number of Students Applied: Unavailable. Percent Admitted: 37%. Number Enrolled: Unavailable. Test Scores (Middle 50%): SAT Critical Reading: 480–550. SAT Math: 460–600. SAT Writing: Unavailable. ACT Comp: 17–26. HS Rank of Entering Freshmen: Top 10%: 20%. Top 25%: 54%. Avg. HS GPA: Unavailable.

Cost: Tuition and Fees: In-State: $14,818. Out-of-State: $14,818. Room and Board: $6,746.

Inst. Aid: FT Undergrads Receiving Aid: Unavailable. Avg. Amount per Student: Unavailable.

HANOVER COLLEGE

Hanover, IN
admission@hanover.edu; www.hanover.edu

General Info: Private, Liberal Arts College, Four-year, Presbyterian Church (USA), Coed, Regionally Accredited, College Board member. Rural setting, Rural community (under 2,500), Residential campus. Academic Calendar: 4-1-4.

Student Body: Full-Time Undergrads: 975. Men: 52%, Women: 48%. Total Undergrad Population: Native American or Native Alaskan: 1%. Asian American or Pacific Islander: 1%. African American: 1%. Latino: 1%. Caucasian: 90%. International: 1%. Out-of-State: 38%.

Academics: Full-Time Faculty: 95.

Admissions: Regular Application Deadline: Rolling. Priority Application Deadline: Unavailable. Early Decision Deadline: Unavailable. Financial Aid Deadline: Unavailable. Total Number of Students Applied: Unavailable. Number Admitted: Unavailable. Number Enrolled: Unavailable. Test Scores (Middle 50%): SAT Critical Reading: 520–640. SAT Math: 510–640. ACT Comp: 23–28. HS Rank of Entering Freshmen: Top 10%: 44%. Top 25%: 80%. Avg. HS GPA: Unavailable.

Cost: Tuition and Fees: In-State: $22,200. Out-of-State: $22,200. Room and Board: $6,800.

Inst. Aid: FT Undergrads Receiving Aid: Unavailable. Avg. Amount per Student: Unavailable.

HARVARD COLLEGE

Cambridge, MA
college@fas.harvard.edu; www.college.harvard.edu

General Info: Private, University, Four-year, Coed, Regionally Accredited, College Board member. Urban setting, Small city (50,000–249,999), Residential campus. Academic Calendar: Semester.

Student Body: Full-Time Undergrads: 6,715. Men: 50%, Women: 50%. Total Undergrad Population: Native American or Native Alaskan: 1%. Asian American or Pacific Islander: 19%. African American: 9%. Latino: 7%. Caucasian: 47%. International: 9%. Out-of-State: 86%. Total all graduate and professional students: 9,960.

Academics: Full-Time Faculty: 1,592.

Admissions: Regular Application Deadline: 1/1. Priority Application Deadline: Unavailable. Early Decision Deadline: Unavailable. Transfer Priority Deadline: Unavailable. Financial Aid Deadline: 2/1. Total Number of Students Applied: Unavailable. Percent Admitted: 9%. Number Enrolled: 2,058. Test Scores (Middle 50%): SAT Critical Reading: 700–790. SAT Math: 700–790. SAT Writing: 700–790. ACT Comp: 30–34. HS Rank of Entering Freshmen: Top 10%: 96%. Top 25%: 99%. Avg. HS GPA: Unavailable.

Cost: Tuition and Fees: In-State: $30,275. Out-of-State: Unavilable. Room and Board: $9,946.

Inst. Aid: FT Undergrads Receiving Aid: Unavailable. Avg. Amount per Student: Unavailable.

HARVEY MUDD COLLEGE

Claremont, CA
admission@hmc.edu; www.hmc.edu

General Info: Private, College of Engineering, Liberal Arts College, Four-year, Coed, Regionally Accredited, College Board member. Suburban setting, Small city (50,000–249,999), Residential campus. Academic Calendar: Semester.

Student Body: Full-Time Undergrads: 735. Men: 67%, Women: 33%. Total Undergrad Population: Native American or Native Alaskan: 0%. Asian American or Pacific Islander: 18%. African American: 2%. Latino: 6%. Caucasian: 43%. International: 5%. Out-of-State: 55%.

Academics: Full-Time Faculty: 79.

Admissions: Regular Application Deadline: 1/15. Priority Application Deadline: Unavailable. Early Decision Deadline: 11/15. Financial Aid Deadline: Unavailable. Total Number of Students Applied: Unavailable. Number Admitted: Unavailable. Number Enrolled: Unavailable. Test Scores (Middle 50%): SAT Critical Reading: 690–760. SAT Math: 740–800. SAT Writing: 680–760. HS Rank of Entering Freshmen: Top 10%: Unavailable. Top 25%: Unavailable. Avg. HS GPA: Unavailable.

Cost: Tuition and Fees: In-State: $34,891. Out-of-State: $34,891. Room and Board: $11,415.

Inst. Aid: FT Undergrads Receiving Aid: 85%. Avg. Amount per Student: Unavailable.

HASTINGS COLLEGE

Hastings, NE
mmolliconi@hastings.edu; www.hastings.edu

General Info: Coed, College Board member, Four-year, Liberal Arts College, North Central Association of Colleges and Schools, Presbyterian Church (USA), Private, Regionally Accredited. Suburban setting, Large town (10,000–49,999), Residential campus. Academic Calendar: 4-1-4.

Student Body: Full-Time Undergrads: 1,093. Men: 58%, Women: 42%. Total Undergrad Population: Native American or Native Alaskan: 0%. Asian American or Pacific Islander: 1%. African American: 2%. Latino: 4%. Caucasian: 92%. International: 1%. Out-of-State: 34%. Total all graduate and professional students: 44.

Academics: Full-Time Faculty: 79.

Admissions: Regular Application Deadline: Rolling. Priority Application Deadline: Unavailable. Early Decision Deadline: Unavailable. Transfer Priority Deadline: 3/1. Financial Aid Deadline: Unavailable. Total Number of Students Applied: Unavailable. Percent Admitted: 81%. Number Enrolled: 263. Test Scores (Middle 50%): SAT Critical Reading: 500–600. SAT Math: 490–605. SAT Writing: Unavailable. ACT Comp: 20–26. HS Rank of Entering Freshmen: Top 10%: 14%. Top 25%: 37%. Avg. HS GPA: Unavailable.

Cost: Tuition and Fees: In-State: $18,302. Out-of-State: $18,302. Room and Board: $5,148.

Inst. Aid: FT Undergrads Receiving Aid: Unavailable. Avg. Amount per Student: $13,338.

HAVERFORD COLLEGE

Haverford, PA

admission@haverford.edu; www.haverford.edu

General Info: Coed, College Board member, Four-year, Liberal Arts College, Private, Regionally Accredited. Large town (10,000–49,999), Residential campus, Suburban setting, 8 miles from downtown Philadelphia. Academic Calendar: Semester.

Student Body: Full-Time Undergrads: 1,168. Men: 45%, Women: 55%. Total Undergrad Population: Native American or Native Alaskan: 0.6%. Asian American or Pacific Islander: 14.2%. African American: 8.9%. Latino: 9.8%. Caucasian: 63.6%. International: 6%. Out-of-State: 89%.

Academics: Full-Time Faculty: 112. With PhD: 106. Graduation Rates: 92% within 4 years. 94% within 6 years.

Admissions: Regular Application Deadline: 1/15. Priority Application Deadline: Unavailable. Early Decision Deadline: 11/15. Transfer Priority Deadline: Unavailable. Financial Aid Deadline: 1/31. Total Number of Students Applied: 3,492. Number Admitted: 878. Number Enrolled: Unavailable. Test Scores (Middle 50%): SAT Critical Reading: 650–750. SAT Math: 640–740. SAT Writing: 650–750. ACT Comp: Unavailable. HS Rank of Entering Freshmen: Top 10%: 89%. Top 25%: 99%. Avg. HS GPA: Unavailable.

Cost: Tuition and Fees: In-State: $37,175. Out-of-State: $37,175. Room and Board: $11,450.

Inst. Aid: FT Undergrads Receiving Aid: 642. Avg. Amount per Student: $28,531.

Graduates: Alumni Giving %: 53%.

HAWAII PACIFIC UNIVERSITY

Honolulu, HI

admissions@hpu.edu; www.hpu.edu

General Info: Private, Liberal Arts College, University, Four-year, Coed, Regionally Accredited, College Board member. Urban setting, Large city (250,000–499,999), Commuter campus. Academic Calendar: Semester.

Student Body: Full-Time Undergrads: 6,856. Men: 35%, Women: 65%. Total Undergrad Population: Native American or Native Alaskan: 1%. Asian American or Pacific Islander: 39%. African American: 4%. Latino: 5%. Caucasian: 39%. International: 9%. Out-of-State: 53%. Total all graduate and professional students: 1,224.

Academics: Full-Time Faculty: 238.

Admissions: Regular Application Deadline: Rolling. Priority Application Deadline: 3/1. Early Decision Deadline: Unavailable. Transfer Priority Deadline: 8/15. Financial Aid Deadline: Unavailable. Total Number of Students Applied: Unavailable. Number Admitted: Unavailable. Number Enrolled: Unavailable. Test Scores (Middle 50%): SAT Critical Reading: 420–550. SAT Math: 430–560. SAT Writing: 350–540. ACT Comp: 17–24. HS Rank of Entering Freshmen: Top 10%: 22%. Top 25%: 50%. Avg. HS GPA: Unavailable.

Cost: Tuition and Fees: In-State: $12,312. Out-of-State: $12,312. Room and Board: $9,840.

Inst. Aid: FT Undergrads Receiving Aid: Unavailable. Avg. Amount per Student: Unavailable.

Great Career Service Programs

Northeastern University

Notre Dame University

Sweet Briar College

Penn State University—University Park

New York University

HENDRIX COLLEGE

Conway, AR

adm@hendrix.edu; www.hendrix.edu

General Info: Private, Liberal Arts College, Four-year, United Methodist Church, Coed, Regionally Accredited, College Board member. Suburban setting, Small city (50,000–249,999), Residential campus. Academic Calendar: Semester.

Student Body: Full-Time Undergrads: 1,094. Men: 44%, Women: 56%. Total Undergrad Population: Native American or Native Alaskan: 1%. Asian American or Pacific Islander: 4%. African American: 6%. Latino: 3%. Caucasian: 81%. International: 1%. Out-of-State: 49%. Total all graduate and professional students: 7.

Academics: Full-Time Faculty: 85.

Admissions: Regular Application Deadline: Rolling. Priority Application Deadline: 12/1. Early Decision Deadline: Unavailable. Transfer Priority Deadline: 7/15. Financial Aid Deadline: Unavailable. Total Number of Students Applied: Unavailable. Percent Admitted: 80%. Number Enrolled: 645. Test Scores (Middle 50%): SAT Critical Reading: 560–690. SAT Math: 560–660. ACT Comp: 25–31. HS Rank of Entering Freshmen: Top 10%: 37%. Top 25%: 73%. Avg. HS GPA: Unavailable.

Cost: Tuition and Fees: In-State: $22,916. Out-of-State: $22,916. Room and Board: $6,738.

Inst. Aid: FT Undergrads Receiving Aid: Unavailable. Avg. Amount per Student: Unavailable.

HOBART AND WILLIAM SMITH COLLEGES

Geneva, NY

admissions@hws.edu; www.hws.edu

General Info: Private, Liberal Arts College, Four-year, Coed, Regionally Accredited, College Board member. Suburban setting, Large town (10,000–49,999), Residential campus. Academic Calendar: Semester.

Student Body: Full-Time Undergrads: 1,928. Men: 48%, Women: 52%. Total Undergrad Population: Native American or Native Alaskan: 0%. Asian American or Pacific Islander: 3%. African American: 5%. Latino: 3%. Caucasian: 88%. International: 1%. Out-of-State: 60%. Total all graduate and professional students: 15.

Academics: Full-Time Faculty: 156.

Admissions: Regular Application Deadline: 2/1. Priority Application Deadline: Unavailable. Early Decision Deadline: 11/15. Financial Aid Deadline: 2/1. Total Number of Students Applied: Unavailable. Percent Admitted: 65%. Number Enrolled: 594. Test Scores (Middle 50%): SAT Critical Reading: 530–640. SAT Math: 540–630. SAT Writing: Unavailable. ACT Comp: Unavailable. HS Rank of Entering Freshmen: Top 10%: 31%. Top 25%: 45%. Avg. HS GPA: Unavailable.

Cost: Tuition and Fees: In-State: $34,688. Out-of-State: $34,688. Room and Board: $8,828.

Inst. Aid: FT Undergrads Receiving Aid: Unavailable. Avg. Amount per Student: Unavailable.

Schools with Work-Intensive Reputations

California Institute of Technology

Reed College

University of Chicago

HOFSTRA UNIVERSITY

Hempstead, NY

admitme@hofstra.edu; www.hofstra.edu

General Info: Coed, College Board member, Four-year, Middle States Association of Colleges and Schools, New York State Board of Regents, Private, Regionally Accredited, University. Suburban setting, Large city (250,000–499,999), Residential campus. Academic Calendar: 4-1-4.

Student Body: Full-Time Undergrads: 7,762. Men: 47%, Women: 53%. Part-Time Undergrads. Men: 54%, Women: 46%. Total Undergrad Population: Native American or Native Alaskan: 1%. Asian American or Pacific Islander: 5%. African American: 7%. Latino: 6%. Caucasian: 66%. International: 2%. Out-of-State: 50%. Living Off-Campus: 21%. % In Fraternities: 9%. % In Sororities: 9%. Total all graduate and professional students: 4,046.

Academics: Full-Time Faculty: 544. With PhD: 675. Percentage completing two or more majors: 10%. Graduation Rates: 35% within 4 years. 54% within 6 years.

Admissions: Regular Application Deadline: Rolling admission. Priority Application Deadline: Unavailable. Early Decision Deadline: 11/15. Transfer Priority Deadline: Unavailable. Financial Aid Deadline: Unavailable. Total Number of Students Applied: 18,471. Number Admitted: 9,986. Number Enrolled: 1,735. Number accepting place on waitlist: 752. Number of waitlisted students admitted: 176. Test Scores (Middle 50%): SAT Critical Reading: 540–530. SAT Math: 550–630. SAT Writing: Unavailable. ACT Comp: 23-26. HS Rank of Entering Freshmen: Top 10%: 26%. Top 25%: 56%. Avg. HS GPA: 3.37.

Cost: Tuition and Fees: In-State: $26,730. Out-of-State: $26,730. Room and Board: $10,300.

Inst. Aid: FT Undergrads Receiving Aid: Unavailable. Avg. Amount per Student: $11,270.

Graduates: No. of companies recruiting on campus: 322. Percentage of grads accepting a job at time of graduation: 65%.

HOLLINS UNIVERSITY

Roanoke, VA

huadm@hollins.edu; www.hollins.edu

General Info: Private, Liberal Arts College, University, Four-year, Women Only, Regionally Accredited, College Board member. Suburban setting, Small city (50,000–249,999), Residential campus. Academic Calendar: 4-1-4.

Student Body: Full-Time Undergrads: 799. Men: 0%, Women: 100%. Total Undergrad Population: Native American or Native Alaskan: 1%. Asian American or Pacific Islander: 3%. African American: 10%. Latino: 5%. Caucasian: 77%. International: 5%. Out-of-State: 58%. Total all graduate and professional students: 262.

Academics: Full-Time Faculty: 68.

Admissions: Regular Application Deadline: 2/15. Priority Application Deadline: Unavailable. Early Decision Deadline: 12/1. Transfer Priority Deadline: Unavailable. Financial Aid Deadline: Unavailable. Total Number of Students Applied: Unavailable. Percent Admitted: 84%. Number Enrolled: 194. Test Scores (Middle 50%): SAT Critical Reading: 500–670. SAT Math: 470–600. ACT Comp: 21–28. HS Rank of Entering Freshmen: Top 10%: 19%. Top 25%: 55%. Avg. HS GPA: Unavailable.

Cost: Tuition and Fees: In-State: $24,325. Out-of-State: $24,325. Room and Board: $8,650.

Inst. Aid: FT Undergrads Receiving Aid: Unavailable. Avg. Amount per Student: $22,225.

HOWARD UNIVERSITY

Washington, DC

admissions@howard.edu; www.howard.edu

General Info: Private, University, Four-year, Coed, Regionally Accredited, College Board member, Historically black. Urban setting, Very large city (over 500,000), Residential campus. Academic Calendar: Semester.

Student Body: Full-Time Undergrads: 7,164. Men: 33%, Women: 67%. Total Undergrad Population: Native American or Native Alaskan: 0%. Asian American or Pacific Islander: 1%. African American: 92%. Latino: 0%. Caucasian: 0%. International: 7%. Out-of-State: 93%. Total all graduate and professional students: 1,940.

Academics: Full-Time Faculty: 1,068.

Admissions: Regular Application Deadline: Unavailable. Priority Application Deadline: Unavailable. Early Decision Deadline: 11/1. Transfer Priority Deadline: Unavailable. Financial Aid Deadline: 8/15. Total Number of Students Applied: 7,603. Number Admitted: 4,080. Number Enrolled: Unavailable. Test Scores (Middle 50%): SAT Critical Reading: 460–680. SAT Math: 450–690. SAT Writing: Unavailable. ACT Comp: 19–28. HS Rank of Entering Freshmen: Top 10%: Unavailable. Top 25%: Unavailable. Avg. HS GPA: Unavailable.

Cost: Tuition and Fees: In-State: $13,215. Out-of-State: $13,215. Room and Board: $6,522.

Inst. Aid: FT Undergrads Receiving Aid: 6,314. Avg. Amount per Student: $16,473.

HUNTER COLLEGE

New York, NY

admissions@hunter.cuny.edu; www.hunter.cuny.edu

General Info: Coed, Public. Academic Calendar: Semester.

Student Body: Full-Time Undergrads: 14,382. Men: 32%, Women: 68%.

Academics: Full-Time Faculty: 635.

Admissions: Regular Application Deadline: 3/15. Priority Application Deadline: Unavailable. Early Decision Deadline: Unavailable. Transfer Priority Deadline: 3/15. Financial Aid Deadline: Unavailable. Total Number of Students Applied: Unavailable. Percent Admitted: 34%. Number Enrolled: 3,258. Test Scores (Middle 50%): SAT Critical Reading: 490–580. SAT Math: 500–600. SAT Writing: Unavailable. HS Rank of Entering Freshmen: Top 10%: 22%. Top 25%: 49%. Avg. HS GPA: Unavailable.

Cost: Tuition and Fees: In-State: $4,349. Out-of-State: Unavailable. Room and Board: Unavailable.

Inst. Aid: FT Undergrads Receiving Aid: Unavailable. Avg. Amount per Student: $6,476.

Great Gendered Colleges

Smith College (Women)

Wellesley College (Women)

Hampden-Sydney College (Men)

Morehouse College (Men)

ILLINOIS INSTITUTE OF TECHNOLOGY

Chicago, IL

admission@iit.edu; www.iit.edu

General Info: Coed, College Board member, College of Engineering, Four-year, Private, Regionally Accredited, University. Residential campus, Urban setting, Very large city (over 500,000). Academic Calendar: Semester.

Student Body: Full-Time Undergrads: 2,124. Men: 79%, Women: 21%. Part-Time Undergrads. Men: 5%, Women: 1%. Total Undergrad Population: Native American or Native Alaskan: 0%. Asian American or Pacific Islander: 14%. African American: 4%. Latino: 7%. Caucasian: 50%. International: 16%. Out-of-State: 34%. Living Off-Campus: 47%. % In Fraternities: 13%. % In Sororities: 15%. Total all graduate and professional students: 4,833.

Academics: Full-Time Faculty: 359. Percentage completing two or more majors: 3%. Graduation Rates: 40% within 4 years. 67% within 6 years.

Admissions: Regular Application Deadline: Rolling Admission. Priority Application Deadline: 11/15, 1/15. Early Decision Deadline: None. Fall Transfer Deadline: 7/1. Spring Transfer Deadline: 11/1. Transfer Priority Deadline: Unavailable. Financial Aid Deadline: Unavailable. Total Number of Students Applied: 4,383. Number Admitted: 2,474. Number Enrolled: 521. Test Scores (Middle 50%): SAT Critical Reading: 543–670. SAT Math: 620–710. SAT Writing: 530–640. ACT Comp: 25–30. HS Rank of Entering Freshmen: Top 10%: 43%. Top 25%: 72%. Avg. HS GPA: 3.77.

Cost: Tuition and Fees: In-State: $26,709. Out-of-State: $26,709. Room and Board: $9,226.

Inst. Aid: FT Undergrads Receiving Aid: Unavailable. Avg. Amount per Student: Unavailable.

ILLINOIS WESLEYAN UNIVERSITY

Bloomington, IL

iwuadmit@iwu.edu; www.iwu.edu

General Info: Coed, College Board member, Four-year, Liberal Arts College, Private, Regionally Accredited, University. Suburban setting, Small city (50,000–249,999), Residential campus. Academic Calendar: 4-4-1.

Student Body: Full-Time Undergrads: 2,137. Men: 40%, Women: 60%. Total Undergrad Population: Native American or Native Alaskan: 1%. Asian American or Pacific Islander: 5%. African American: 6%. Latino: 3%. Caucasian: 81%. International: 3%. Out-of-State: 12%. Living Off-Campus: 18%.

Academics: Full-Time Faculty: 170.

Admissions: Regular Application Deadline: Rolling. Priority Application Deadline: Unavailable. Early Decision Deadline: Unavailable. Financial Aid Deadline: 3/1. Total Number of Students Applied: Unavailable. Percent Admitted: 52%. Number Enrolled: 552. Test Scores (Middle 50%): SAT Critical Reading: 580–680. SAT Math: 580–680. ACT Comp: 26–30. HS Rank of Entering Freshmen: Top 10%: 47%. Top 25%: 81%. Avg. HS GPA: Unavailable.

Cost: Tuition and Fees: In-State: $32,260. Out-of-State: $32,260. Room and Board: $7,350.

Inst. Aid: FT Undergrads Receiving Aid: Unavailable. Avg. Amount per Student: Unavailable.

Great Study Abroad Programs

Tufts University

New York University

University of Illinois

American University

INDIANA UNIVERSITY OF PENNSYLVANIA

Indiana, PA

admissions_inquiry@iup.edu; www.iup.edu

General Info: Public, University, Four-year, Coed, Regionally Accredited, Middle States Association of Colleges and Schools, College Board member. Rural setting, Large town (10,000–49,999), Residential campus. Academic Calendar: Semester.

Student Body: Full-Time Undergrads: 11,976. Men: 45%, Women: 55%. Total Undergrad Population: Native American or Native Alaskan: 0%. Asian American or Pacific Islander: 1%. African American: 13%. Latino: 2%. Caucasian: 80%. International: 1%. Out-of-State: 5%. Total all graduate and professional students: 2,272.

Academics: Full-Time Faculty: 778.

Admissions: Regular Application Deadline: Rolling. Priority Application Deadline: Unavailable. Early Decision Deadline: Unavailable. Transfer Priority Deadline: Unavailable. Financial Aid Deadline: 4/15. Total Number of Students Applied: Unavailable. Percent Admitted: 71%. Number Enrolled: 2,568. Test Scores (Middle 50%): SAT Critical Reading: 430–530. SAT Math: 430–530. SAT Writing: Unavailable. HS Rank of Entering Freshmen: Top 10%: 7%. Top 25%: 22%. Avg. HS GPA: Unavailable.

Cost: Tuition and Fees: In-State: $6,390. Out-of-State: $14,013. Room and Board: $5,162.

Inst. Aid: FT Undergrads Receiving Aid: Unavailable. Avg. Amount per Student: $8,137.

INDIANA UNIVERSITY BLOOMINGTON

Bloomington, IN

iuadmit@indiana.edu; www.iub.edu

General Info: Public, University, Four-year, Coed, Regionally Accredited, North Central Association of Colleges and Schools, College Board member. Urban setting, Small city (50,000–249,999), Residential campus. Academic Calendar: Semester.

Student Body: Full-Time Undergrads: 29,562. Men: 36%, Women: 64%. Total Undergrad Population: Native American or Native Alaskan: 0%. Asian American or Pacific Islander: 4%. African American: 5%. Latino: 2%. Caucasian: 83%. International: 3%. Out-of-State: 37%. Total all graduate and professional students: 7,481.

Academics: Full-Time Faculty: 1,865.

Admissions: Regular Application Deadline: No closing date. Priority Application Deadline: 2/1. Early Decision Deadline: Unavailable. Transfer Priority Deadline: 2/1. Financial Aid Deadline: Unavailable. Total Number of Students Applied: Unavailable. Percent Admitted: 80%. Number Enrolled: 7,260. Test Scores (Middle 50%): SAT Critical Reading: 400–510. SAT Math: 390–510. SAT Writing: Unavailable. ACT Comp: 16-22. HS Rank of Entering Freshmen: Top 10%: 25%. Top 25%: 57%. Avg. HS GPA: Unavailable.

Cost: Tuition and Fees: In-State: $7,837. Out-of-State: $20,472. Room and Board: $6,138.

Inst. Aid: FT Undergrads Receiving Aid: Unavailable. Avg. Amount per Student: Unavailable.

IONA COLLEGE

New Rochelle, NY
icad@iona.edu; www.iona.edu

General Info: Private, College of Business, Liberal Arts College, Four-year, Roman Catholic Church, Coed, Regionally Accredited, College Board member. Suburban setting, Small city (50,000–249,999), Commuter campus. Academic Calendar: Semester.

Student Body: Full-Time Undergrads: 3,100. Men: 45%, Women: 55%. Total Undergrad Population: Native American or Native Alaskan: 0%. Asian American or Pacific Islander: 2%. African American: 5%. Latino: 10%. Caucasian: 67%. International: 2%. Out-of-State: 25%. Total all graduate and professional students: 791.

Academics: Full-Time Faculty: 176.

Admissions: Regular Application Deadline: 2/15. Priority Application Deadline: Unavailable. Early Decision Deadline: 12/1. Transfer Priority Deadline: Unavailable. Financial Aid Deadline: 4/15. Total Number of Students Applied: Unavailable. Percent Admitted: 60%. Number Enrolled: 906. Test Scores (Middle 50%): SAT Critical Reading: 520–620. SAT Math: 530–620. SAT Writing: Unavailable. HS Rank of Entering Freshmen: Top 10%: 31%. Top 25%: 54%. Avg. HS GPA: Unavailable.

Cost: Tuition and Fees: In-State: $23,218. Out-of-State: $23,218. Room and Board: $10,298.

Inst. Aid: FT Undergrads Receiving Aid: Unavailable. Avg. Amount per Student: $15,293.

IOWA STATE UNIVERSITY

Ames, IA
admissions@iastate.edu; www.iastate.edu

General Info: Public, University, Four-year, Coed, Regionally Accredited, North Central Association of Colleges and Schools, College Board member. Urban setting, Small city (50,000–249,999), Residential campus. Academic Calendar: Semester.

Student Body: Full-Time Undergrads: 20,440. Men: 55%, Women: 45%. Total Undergrad Population: Native American or Native Alaskan: 0%. Asian American or Pacific Islander: 4%. African American: 3%. Latino: 3%. Caucasian: 85%. International: 2%. Out-of-State: 28%. Total all graduate and professional students: 4,583.

Academics: Full-Time Faculty: 1,419.

Admissions: Regular Application Deadline: 7/1. Priority Application Deadline: Unavailable. Early Decision Deadline: Unavailable. Transfer Priority Deadline: Unavailable. Financial Aid Deadline: Unavailable. Total Number of Students Applied: Unavailable. Number Admitted: Unavailable. Number Enrolled: Unavailable. Test Scores (Middle 50%): SAT Critical Reading: 510–640. SAT Math: 540–690. SAT Writing: Unavailable. ACT Comp: 22–27. HS Rank of Entering Freshmen: Top 10%: 24%. Top 25%: 52%. Avg. HS GPA: Unavailable.

Cost: Tuition and Fees: In-State: $5,860. Out-of-State: $16,354. Room and Board: $6,445.

Inst. Aid: FT Undergrads Receiving Aid: Unavailable. Avg. Amount per Student: $9,199.

Great Film and Acting Schools

American Film Institute

Cinematic Arts at University of Southern California

New York University— Tisch School of the Arts

School of Motion Pictures, Television and Recording Arts at Florida State University

Theater, Film and Television at University of California–Los Angeles

ITHACA COLLEGE

Ithaca, NY
admission@ithaca.edu; www.ithaca.edu

General Info: Private, College of Health Sciences, Liberal Arts College, Four-year, Coed, Regionally Accredited, College Board member. Suburban setting, Large town (10,000–49,999), Residential campus. Academic Calendar: Semester.

Student Body: Full-Time Undergrads: 6,028. Men: 46%, Women: 54%. Total Undergrad Population: Native American or Native Alaskan: 1%. Asian American or Pacific Islander: 4%. African American: 3%. Latino: 3%. Caucasian: 76%. International: 1%. Out-of-State: 56%. Total all graduate and professional students: 381.

Academics: Full-Time Faculty: 442.

Admissions: Regular Application Deadline: 2/1. Priority Application Deadline: Unavailable. Early Decision Deadline: 11/1. Financial Aid Deadline: Unavailable. Total Number of Students Applied: Unavailable. Percent Admitted: 69%. Number Enrolled: 1,521. Test Scores (Middle 50%): SAT Critical Reading: 530–640. SAT Math: 540–640. SAT Writing: Unavailable. ACT Comp: Unavailable. HS Rank of Entering Freshmen: Top 10%: 29%. Top 25%: 64%. Avg. HS GPA: Unavailable.

Cost: Tuition and Fees: In-State: $26,832. Out-of-State: $26,832. Room and Board: $10,728.

Inst. Aid: FT Undergrads Receiving Aid: Unavailable. Avg. Amount per Student: $22,875.

JAMES MADISON UNIVERSITY

Harrisonburg, VA

admissions@jmu.edu; www.jmu.edu

General Info: Public, University, Four-year, Coed, Regionally Accredited, Southern Association of Colleges and Schools, College Board member. Rural setting, Large town (10,000–49,999), Residential campus. Academic Calendar: Semester.

Student Body: Full-Time Undergrads: 15,687. Men: 39%, Women: 61%. Total Undergrad Population: Native American or Native Alaskan: 0%. Asian American or Pacific Islander: 5%. African American: 5%. Latino: 2%. Caucasian: 82%. International: 1%. Out-of-State: 33%. Total all graduate and professional students: 1,380.

Academics: Full-Time Faculty: 831.

Admissions: Regular Application Deadline: 1/15. Priority Application Deadline: 11/1. Early Decision Deadline: Unavailable. Transfer Priority Deadline: Unavailable. Financial Aid Deadline: Unavailable. Total Number of Students Applied: Unavailable. Percent Admitted: 63%. Number Enrolled: 3,748. Test Scores (Middle 50%): SAT Critical Reading: 520–610. SAT Math: 530–620. SAT Writing: 520–610. ACT Comp: 21–26. HS Rank of Entering Freshmen: Top 10%: 31%. Top 25%: 78%. Avg. HS GPA: Unavailable.

Cost: Tuition and Fees: In-State: $6,666. Out-of-State: $17,386. Room and Board: $6,836.

Inst. Aid: FT Undergrads Receiving Aid: Unavailable. Avg. Amount per Student: $6,693.

JOHNS HOPKINS UNIVERSITY

Baltimore, MD

gotojhu@jhu.edu; www.jhu.edu

General Info: Coed, College Board member, Four-year, Middle States Association of Colleges and Schools, Private, Regionally Accredited, University. Urban setting, Very large city (over 500,000), Residential campus. Academic Calendar: 4-1-4.

Student Body: Full-Time Undergrads: 4,478. Men: 54%, Women: 46%. Total Undergrad Population: Native American or Native Alaskan: 0.6%. Asian American or Pacific Islander: 24.9%. African American: 6.4%. Latino: 6.5%. Caucasian: 45.8%. International: 5.3%. Out-of-State: 85%. Living Off-Campus: 40%. % In Fraternities: 24%. % In Sororities: 23%. Total all graduate and professional students: 1,666.

Academics: Full-Time Faculty: 447. Graduation Rates: 84% within 4 years. 91% within 6 years.

Admissions: Regular Application Deadline: 1/1. Priority Application Deadline: Unavailable. Early Decision Deadline: 11/15. Fall Transfer Deadline: 3/15. Financial Aid Deadline: 3/1. Total Number of Students Applied: 14,848. Number Admitted: 3,603. Number Enrolled: 1,206. Number accepting place on waitlist: 1,319. Number of waitlisted students admitted: 46. Number applied early decision: 997. Early decision admitted: 446. Test Scores (Middle 50%): SAT Critical Reading: 630–730. SAT Math: 660–770. SAT Writing: 630–730. ACT Comp: 28-33. HS Rank of Entering Freshmen: Top 10%: 82%. Top 25%: 97%. Avg. HS GPA: 3.7.

Cost: Tuition and Fees: In-State: $37,700. Out-of-State: $37,700. Room and Board: $11,578.

Inst. Aid: FT Undergrads Receiving Aid: 2,066. Avg. Amount per Student: $28,765. Freshmen Receiving Non-Need Scholarship or Grant: 81. Avg. Amount per Student: $27,471.

Graduates: Percentage of grads accepting a job at time of graduation: 45%.

JOHNSON & WALES UNIVERSITY

Providence, RI

admissions.pvd@jwu.edu; www.jwu.edu

General Info: Private, University, Four-year, Coed, Regionally Accredited, College Board member. Urban setting, Small city (50,000–249,999), Residential campus. Academic Calendar: Quarter.

Student Body: Full-Time Undergrads: 9,349. Men: 49%, Women: 51%. Total Undergrad Population: Native American or Native Alaskan: 0%. Asian American or Pacific Islander: 3%. African American: 9%. Latino: 7%. Caucasian: 62%. International: 1%. Out-of-State: 22%. Total all graduate and professional students: 961.

Academics: Full-Time Faculty: 282.

Admissions: Regular Application Deadline: Rolling. Priority Application Deadline: Unavailable. Early Decision Deadline: Unavailable. Transfer Priority Deadline: Unavailable. Financial Aid Deadline: Unavailable. Total Number of Students Applied: Unavailable. Number Admitted: Unavailable. Number Enrolled: Unavailable. Test Scores (Middle 50%): SAT Critical Reading: 400–520. SAT Math: 400–520. SAT Writing: Unavailable. ACT Comp: Unavailable. HS Rank of Entering Freshmen: Top 10%: Unavailable. Top 25%: Unavailable. Avg. HS GPA: Unavailable.

Cost: Tuition and Fees: In-State: $21,714. Out-of-State: $21,714. Room and Board: $7,650–9,600.

Inst. Aid: FT Undergrads Receiving Aid: Unavailable. Avg. Amount per Student: Unavailable.

JUILLIARD SCHOOL

New York, NY
admissions@juilliard.edu; www.juilliard.edu

General Info: Private, College of Music, College of Performing Arts, Four-year, Coed, Regionally Accredited. Urban setting, Very large city (over 500,000), Commuter campus. Academic Calendar: Semester.

Student Body: Full-Time Undergrads: Approximately 800. Men: Unavailable, Women: Unavailable. Total Undergrad Population: Native American or Native Alaskan: 0.2%. Asian American or Pacific Islander: 19.6%. African American: 9.4%. Latino: 4.8%. Caucasian: 66%. International: 24.8%. Total all graduate and professional students: 298.

Academics: Full-Time Faculty: 115.

Admissions: Regular Application Deadline: 12/1. Priority Application Deadline: Unavailable. Early Decision Deadline: Unavailable. Transfer Priority Deadline: Unavailable. Financial Aid Deadline: 3/1. Total Number of Students Applied: Unavailable. Number Admitted: Unavailable. Number Enrolled: Unavailable. Test Scores (Middle 50%): SAT Critical Reading:–Not required. SAT Math:–Not required. SAT Writing:–Not required. ACT Comp:–Not required. HS Rank of Entering Freshmen: Top 10%: Unavailable. Top 25%: Unavailable. Avg. HS GPA: Unavailable.

Cost: Tuition and Fees: In-State: $28,640. Out-of-State: $28,640. Room and Board: $11,250.

Inst. Aid: FT Undergrads Receiving Aid: Unavailable. Avg. Amount per Student: Unavailable.

KALAMAZOO COLLEGE

Kalamazoo, MI
admission@kzoo.edu; www.kzoo.edu

General Info: Private, Liberal Arts College, Four-year, Coed, Regionally Accredited, College Board member. Suburban setting, Small city (50,000–249,999), Residential campus. Academic Calendar: Quarter.

Student Body: Full-Time Undergrads: 1,345. Men: 45%, Women: 55%. Total Undergrad Population: Native American or Native Alaskan: 0%. Asian American or Pacific Islander: 6%. African American: 4%. Latino: 4%. Caucasian: 77%. International: 1%. Out-of-State: 30%. Living Off-Campus: 23%.

Academics: Full-Time Faculty: 95. With PhD: 90. Graduation Rates: 73% within 4 years. 78% within 6 years.

Admissions: Regular Application Deadline: 2/1. Priority Application Deadline: 12/1. Early Decision Deadline: 11/15. Transfer Priority Deadline: 5/1. Financial Aid Deadline: 2/15. Total Number of Students Applied: 2,090. Number Admitted: 1,310. Number Enrolled: Unavailable. Number accepting place on waitlist: 130. Number of waitlisted students admitted: 28. Test Scores (Middle 50%): SAT Critical Reading: 580–690. SAT Math: 570–680. ACT Comp: 26–30. HS Rank of Entering Freshmen: Top 10%: 44%. Top 25%: 75%. Avg. HS GPA: 3.63.

Strong ROTC Programs

Texas A&M

Boston College

University of Illinois

Cost: Tuition and Fees: In-State: $28,716. Out-of-State: $28,716. Room and Board: $7,122.

Inst. Aid: FT Undergrads Receiving Aid: Unavailable. Avg. Amount per Student: Unavailable.

KANSAS STATE UNIVERSITY

Manhattan, KS
kstate@ksu.edu; www.k-state.edu

General Info: Public, Technical College, University, Four-year, Coed, Regionally Accredited, North Central Association of Colleges and Schools, College Board member. Commuter campus, Large town (10,000–49,999), Residential campus, Suburban setting. Academic Calendar: Semester.

Student Body: Full-Time Undergrads: 18,545. Men: 52.2%, Women: 47.8%. Part-Time Undergrads. Men: 47%, Women: 53%. Total Undergrad Population: Native American or Native Alaskan: 0.06%. Asian American or Pacific Islander: 1.3%. African American: 3.3%. Latino: 3%. Caucasian: 85.96%. International: 2%. Out-of-State: 13%. Living Off-Campus: 63%. % In Fraternities: 20%. % In Sororities: 20%. Total all graduate and professional students: 4,787.

Academics: Full-Time Faculty: 944. With PhD: 704. Graduation Rates: 24.6% within 4 years. 57.3% within 6 years.

Admissions: Regular Application Deadline: Unavailable. Priority Application Deadline: Unavailable. Early Decision Deadline: Unavailable. Transfer Priority Deadline: Unavailable. Financial Aid Deadline: Unavailable. Total Number of Students Applied: Unavailable. Number Admitted: Unavailable. Number Enrolled: 23,332. Test Scores (Middle 50%): SAT Critical Reading: Unavailable. SAT Math: Unavailable. SAT Writing: Unavailable. ACT Comp: 21–28. HS Rank of Entering Freshmen: Top 10%: 0%. Top 25%: 62%. Avg. HS GPA: Unavailable.

Cost: Tuition and Fees: In-State: $5,625. Out-of-State: $15,360. Room and Board: $6,084.

Reputable Music Programs

Curtis Institute of Music

Cleveland Institute

San Francisco Conservatory of Music

Colburn School of Music

New England Conservatory

Inst. Aid: FT Undergrads Receiving Aid: 8,351. Avg. Amount per Student: $6,825. Freshmen Receiving Non-Need Scholarship or Grant: 521. Avg. Amount per Student: $3,449.

Graduates: Alumni Giving %: 26.8%.

KENT STATE UNIVERSITY

Kent, OH

admissions@kent.edu; www.kent.edu

General Info: Public, University, Four-year, Coed, Regionally Accredited, North Central Association of Colleges and Schools, College Board member. Suburban setting, Large town (10,000–49,999), Residential campus. Academic Calendar: Semester.

Student Body: Full-Time Undergrads: 18,136. Men: 39%, Women: 61%. Total Undergrad Population: Native American or Native Alaskan: 1%. Asian American or Pacific Islander: 2%. African American: 10%. Latino: 2%. Caucasian: 81%. International: 1%. Out-of-State: 12%. Total all graduate and professional students: 4,561.

Academics: Full-Time Faculty: 856.

Admissions: Regular Application Deadline: Rolling. Priority Application Deadline: Unavailable. Early Decision Deadline: Unavailable. Transfer Priority Deadline: 7/1. Financial Aid Deadline: Unavailable. Total Number of Students Applied: Unavailable. Number Admitted: Unavailable. Number Enrolled: 8,039. Test Scores (Middle 50%): SAT Critical Reading: 460–580. SAT Math: 460–580. SAT Writing: Unavailable. ACT Comp: 18–24. HS Rank of Entering Freshmen: Top 10%: 12%. Top 25%: 32%. Avg. HS GPA: Unavailable.

Cost: Tuition and Fees: In-State: $8,430. Out-of-State: $15,862. Room and Board: $7,200.

Inst. Aid: FT Undergrads Receiving Aid: Unavailable. Avg. Amount per Student: Unavailable.

KENYON COLLEGE

Gambier, OH

admissions@kenyon.edu; www.kenyon.edu

General Info: Coed, College Board member, Four-year, Liberal Arts College, Nondenominational, Private, Regionally Accredited. Rural setting, Rural community (under 2,500), Residential campus. Academic Calendar: Semester.

Student Body: Full-Time Undergrads: 1,646. Men: 51%, Women: 49%. Part-Time Undergrads. Men: 0.1%, Women: 0.5%. Total Undergrad Population: Native American or Native Alaskan: 0.5%. Asian American or Pacific Islander: 4.5%. African American: 3.9%. Latino: 2.8%. Caucasian: 81.5%. International: 3.3%. Out-of-State: 80%. Living Off-Campus: 2%.

Academics: Full-Time Faculty: 152. With PhD: 149. Percentage completing two or more majors: 21.9%. Graduation Rates: 82% within 4 years. 84% within 6 years.

Admissions: Regular Application Deadline: 1/15. Priority Application Deadline: 1/15. Early Decision Deadline: 11/15, 1/15. Transfer Priority Deadline: 4/15. Financial Aid Deadline: 2/15. Total Number of Students Applied: 4,626. Number Admitted: 1,352. Number Enrolled: Unavailable. Number accepting place on waitlist: 378. Number of waitlisted students admitted: 10. Test Scores (Middle 50%): SAT Critical Reading: 630–730. SAT Math: 610–690. SAT Writing: 630–710. ACT Comp: 28-32. HS Rank of Entering Freshmen: Top 10%: 73%. Top 25%: 94%. Avg. HS GPA: 3.86.

Cost: Tuition and Fees: In-State: $39,080. Out-of-State: $39,080. Room and Board: $6,590.

Inst. Aid: FT Undergrads Receiving Aid: 742. Avg. Amount per Student: Unavailable.

Graduates: No. of companies recruiting on campus: 46. Percentage of grads accepting a job at time of graduation: 78%. Alumni Giving %: 40%.

KETTERING UNIVERSITY

Flint, MI

admissions@kettering.edu; www.kettering.edu

General Info: Private, College of Engineering, University, Four-year, Coed, Regionally Accredited, College Board member. Urban setting, Small city (50,000–249,999), Residential campus. Academic Calendar: Semester.

Student Body: Full-Time Undergrads: 2,290. Men: 84%, Women: 16%. Total Undergrad Population: Native American or Native Alaskan: 1%. Asian American or Pacific Islander: 3%. African American: 7%. Latino: 2%. Caucasian: 77%. International: 1%. Out-of-State: 26%. Total all graduate and professional students: 519.

Academics: Full-Time Faculty: 140.

Admissions: Regular Application Deadline: Rolling. Priority Application Deadline: Unavailable. Early Decision Deadline: Unavailable. Financial Aid Deadline: Unavailable. Total Number of Students Applied: Unavailable. Percent Admitted: 71%. Number Enrolled: 495. Test Scores (Middle 50%): SAT Critical Reading: 520–610. SAT Math: 610–680. SAT Writing: Unavailable. ACT Comp: 24–28. HS Rank of Entering Freshmen: Top 10%: 31%. Top 25%: 62%. Avg. HS GPA: Unavailable.

Cost: Tuition and Fees: In-State: $24,908. Out-of-State: $24,908. Room and Board: $5,608.

Inst. Aid: FT Undergrads Receiving Aid: Unavailable. Avg. Amount per Student: $15,433.

KNOX COLLEGE

Galesburg, IL

admission@knox.edu; www.knox.edu

General Info: Private, Liberal Arts College, Four-year, Coed, Regionally Accredited, College Board member. Rural setting, Large town (10,000–49,999), Residential campus. Academic Calendar: Trimester.

Student Body: Full-Time Undergrads: 1,351. Men: 44%, Women: 56%. Total Undergrad Population: Native American or Native Alaskan: 2%. Asian American or Pacific Islander: 8%. African American: 5%. Latino: 4%. Caucasian: 70%. International: 6%. Out-of-State: 51%.

Academics: Full-Time Faculty: 97.

Admissions: Regular Application Deadline: 2/1. Priority Application Deadline: Unavailable. Early Decision Deadline: 12/1. Transfer Priority Deadline: 4/1. Financial Aid Deadline: Unavailable. Total Number of Students Applied: Unavailable. Percent Admitted: 74%. Number Enrolled: 407. Test Scores (Middle 50%): SAT Critical Reading: 580–690. SAT Math: 540–670. SAT Writing: 560–690. ACT Comp: 25–30. HS Rank of Entering Freshmen: Top 10%: 34%. Top 25%: 68%. Avg. HS GPA: Unavailable.

Cost: Tuition and Fees: In-State: $27,900. Out-of-State: $27,900. Room and Board: $5,925.

Inst. Aid: FT Undergrads Receiving Aid: Unavailable. Avg. Amount per Student: $22,948.

LAFAYETTE COLLEGE

Easton, PA

admissions@lafayette.edu; www.lafayette.edu

General Info: Private, College of Engineering, Liberal Arts College, Four-year, Presbyterian Church (USA), Coed, Regionally Accredited, College Board member. Suburban setting, Large town (10,000–49,999), Residential campus. Academic Calendar: Semester.

Student Body: Full-Time Undergrads. Men: 54%, Women: 46%. Total Undergrad Population: Native American or Native Alaskan: 0%. Asian American or Pacific Islander: 4%. African American: 6%. Latino: 5%. Caucasian: 81%. International: 4%. Out-of-State: 73%.

Academics: Full-Time Faculty: 188.

Admissions: Regular Application Deadline: 1/1. Priority Application Deadline: Unavailable. Early Decision Deadline: 1/1. Transfer Priority Deadline: 5/1. Financial Aid Deadline: 2/15. Total Number of Students Applied: Unavailable. Percent Admitted: 37%. Number Enrolled: 597. Test Scores (Middle 50%): SAT Critical Reading: 580–670. SAT Math: 620–710. SAT Writing: 580–670. ACT Comp: 24–29. HS Rank of Entering Freshmen: Top 10%: 63%. Top 25%: 90%. Avg. HS GPA: Unavailable.

Cost: Tuition and Fees: In-State: $33,811. Out-of-State: $33,811. Room and Board: $10,377.

Inst. Aid: FT Undergrads Receiving Aid: Unavailable. Avg. Amount per Student: $28,257.

LAKE FOREST COLLEGE

Lake Forest, IL

admissions@lakeforest.edu; www.lakeforest.edu

General Info: Coed, College Board member, Four-year, Liberal Arts College, Private, Regionally Accredited. Suburban setting, Large town (10,000–49,999), Residential campus. Academic Calendar: Semester.

Student Body: Full-Time Undergrads: 1,413. Men: 42%, Women: 58%. Total Undergrad Population: Native American or Native Alaskan: 0%. Asian American or Pacific Islander: 5%. African American: 4%. Latino: 6%. Caucasian: 77%. International: 8%. Out-of-State: 60%. Living Off-Campus: 20%. Total all graduate and professional students: 20.

Academics: Full-Time Faculty: 89.

Admissions: Regular Application Deadline: 2/15. Priority Application Deadline: Unavailable. Early Decision Deadline: 12/1. Transfer Priority Deadline: 6/15. Financial Aid Deadline: Unavailable. Total Number of Students Applied: Unavailable. Percent Admitted: 63%. Number Enrolled: 386. Test Scores (Middle 50%): SAT Critical Reading: 560–660. SAT Math: 540–660. SAT Writing: 540–640. ACT Comp: 24–29. HS Rank of Entering Freshmen: Top 10%: 32%. Top 25%: 54%. Avg. HS GPA: 3.47.

Cost: Tuition and Fees: In-State: $30,600. Out-of-State: $30,600. Room and Board: $7,326.

Inst. Aid: FT Undergrads Receiving Aid: Unavailable. Avg. Amount per Student: Unavailable.

LEHIGH UNIVERSITY

Bethlehem, PA

admissions@lehigh.edu; www.lehigh.edu

General Info: Coed, College Board member, Four-year, Private, Regionally Accredited, University. Suburban setting, Small city (50,000–249,999), Residential campus. Academic Calendar: Semester.

Student Body: Full-Time Undergrads: 4,743. Men: 58%, Women: 42%. Part-Time Undergrads. Men: 1.6%, Women: 0.4%. Total Undergrad Population: Native American or Native Alaskan: 0%. Asian American or Pacific Islander: 6.4%. African American: 4.5%. Latino: 6.1%. Caucasian: 72.4%. International: 2.7%. Out-of-State: 75%. Living Off-Campus: 1%. % In Fraternities: 35%. % In Sororities: 38%. Total all graduate and professional students: 2,089.

Academics: Full-Time Faculty: 430. With PhD: 436. Percentage completing two or more majors: 7.3%. Graduation Rates: 72% within 4 years. 83% within 6 years.

Admissions: Regular Application Deadline: 1/1. Priority Application Deadline: Unavailable. Early Decision Deadline: 11/15. Transfer Priority Deadline: 4/1. Financial Aid Deadline: 2/15. Total Number of Students Applied: 12,155. Number Admitted: 3,882. Number Enrolled: 1,166. Number accepting place on waitlist: 1,096. Number of waitlisted students admitted: 72. Number applied early decision: 827. Early decision admitted: 481. Test Scores (Middle 50%): SAT Critical Reading: 600–680. SAT Math: 640–710. HS Rank of Entering Freshmen: Top 10%: 93%. Top 25%: 99%. Avg. HS GPA: Unavailable.

Cost: Tuition and Fees: In-State: $37,250. Out-of-State: $37,250. Room and Board: $9,770.

Inst. Aid: FT Undergrads Receiving Aid: 2,067. Avg. Amount per Student: $29,498. Freshmen Receiving Non-Need Scholarship or Grant: 95. Avg. Amount per Student: $10,799.

Graduates: No. of companies recruiting on campus: 275. Percentage of grads accepting a job at time of graduation: 64%. Alumni Giving %: 32%.

LEWIS & CLARK COLLEGE

Portland, OR

admissions@lclark.edu; www.lclark.edu

General Info: Private, Liberal Arts College, Four-year, Coed, Regionally Accredited, College Board member. Urban setting, Very large city (over 500,000), Residential campus. Academic Calendar: Semester.

Student Body: Full-Time Undergrads: 1,985. Men: 38%, Women: 62%. Total Undergrad Population: Native American or Native Alaskan: 1%. Asian American or Pacific Islander: 7%. African American: 2%. Latino: 5%. Caucasian: 61%. International: 6%. Out-of-State: 81%. Total all graduate and professional students: 937.

Academics: Full-Time Faculty: 205.

Admissions: Regular Application Deadline: 2/1. Priority Application Deadline: Unavailable. Early Decision Deadline: 11/1. Transfer Priority Deadline: 2/1. Financial Aid Deadline: Unavailable. Total Number of Students Applied: Unavailable. Percent Admitted: 58%. Number Enrolled: 509. Test Scores (Middle 50%): SAT Critical Reading: 620–700. SAT Math: 590–680. SAT Writing: Unavailable. ACT Comp: 26–30. HS Rank of Entering Freshmen: Top 10%: 42%. Top 25%: 78%. Avg. HS GPA: Unavailable.

Cost: Tuition and Fees: In-State: $29,772. Out-of-State: $29,772. Room and Board: $8,048.

Inst. Aid: FT Undergrads Receiving Aid: Unavailable. Avg. Amount per Student: $26,051.

LOUISIANA STATE UNIVERSITY AND AGRICULTURAL AND MECHANICAL COLLEGE

Baton Rouge, LA

admissions@lsu.edu; www.lsu.edu

General Info: Public, Agricultural and Technical College, University, Four-year, Coed, Regionally Accredited, Southern Association of Colleges and Schools, College Board member. Urban setting, Large city (250,000–499,999), Commuter campus. Academic Calendar: Semester.

Student Body: Full-Time Undergrads: 25,705. Men: 47%, Women: 53%. Total Undergrad Population: Native American or Native Alaskan: 0%. Asian American or Pacific Islander: 3%. African American: 9%. Latino: 3%. Caucasian: 82%. International: 1%. Out-of-State: 17%. Total all graduate and professional students: 4,507.

Academics: Full-Time Faculty: 1,293.

Admissions: Regular Application Deadline: 4/15. Priority Application Deadline: 11/15. Early Decision Deadline: Unavailable. Transfer Priority Deadline: Unavailable. Financial Aid Deadline: Unavailable. Total Number of Students Applied: Unavailable. Number Admitted: Unavailable. Number Enrolled: 4,508. Test Scores (Middle 50%): SAT Critical Reading: 520–630. SAT Math: 540–660. SAT Writing: Unavailable. ACT Comp: 22–27. HS Rank of Entering Freshmen: Top 10%: 23%. Top 25%: 50%. Avg. HS GPA: Unavailable.

Cost: Tuition and Fees: In-State: $4,449. Out-of-State: $12,749. Room and Board: $6,498.

Inst. Aid: FT Undergrads Receiving Aid: Unavailable. Avg. Amount per Student: $9,366.

Reputable Programs in Television

University of Southern California

New York University

Dodge College at Chapman University

School of Motion Pictures, Television and Recording Arts at Florida State University

LOYOLA COLLEGE IN MARYLAND

Baltimore, MD
www.loyola.edu

General Info: Private, College of Business, Liberal Arts College, Four-year, Roman Catholic Church, Society of Jesus (Jesuits), Coed, Regionally Accredited, College Board member. Urban setting, Very large city (over 500,000), Residential campus. Academic Calendar: Semester.

Student Body: Full-Time Undergrads: 3,556. Men: 41%, Women: 59%. Total Undergrad Population: Native American or Native Alaskan: 0%. Asian American or Pacific Islander: 3%. African American: 4%. Latino: 3%. Caucasian: 86%. International: 1%. Out-of-State: 83%. Total all graduate and professional students: 2,631.

Academics: Full-Time Faculty: 305.

Admissions: Regular Application Deadline: 1/15. Priority Application Deadline: Unavailable. Early Decision Deadline: Unavailable. Transfer Priority Deadline: 7/15. Financial Aid Deadline: 2/15. Total Number of Students Applied: Unavailable. Percent Admitted: 47%. Number Enrolled: 898. Test Scores (Middle 50%): SAT Critical Reading: 560–650. SAT Math: 570–660. SAT Writing: Unavailable. ACT Comp: 24–28. HS Rank of Entering Freshmen: Top 10%: 35%. Top 25%: 74%. Avg. HS GPA: Unavailable.

Cost: Tuition and Fees: In-State: $32,370. Out-of-State: $32,370. Room and Board: $10,350.

Inst. Aid: FT Undergrads Receiving Aid: Unavailable. Avg. Amount per Student: $21,375.

LOYOLA MARYMOUNT UNIVERSITY

Los Angeles, CA
admissions@lmu.edu; www.lmu.edu

General Info: Private, University, Four-year, Roman Catholic Church, Society of Jesus (Jesuits), Coed, Regionally Accredited, College Board member. Suburban setting, Very large city (over 500,000), Residential campus. Academic Calendar: Semester.

Student Body: Full-Time Undergrads: 5,724. Men: 45%, Women: 55%. Total Undergrad Population: Native American or Native Alaskan: 1%. Asian American or Pacific Islander: 12%. African American: 9%. Latino: 21%. Caucasian: 56%. International: 1%. Out-of-State: 26%. Total all graduate and professional students: 1,797.

Academics: Full-Time Faculty: Unavailable.

Admissions: Regular Application Deadline: Unavailable. Priority Application Deadline: Unavailable. Early Decision Deadline: Unavailable. Transfer Priority Deadline: 6/1. Financial Aid Deadline: 3/2. Total Number of Students Applied: Unavailable. Number Admitted: Unavailable. Number Enrolled: Unavailable. Test Scores (Middle 50%): SAT Critical Reading: 530–630. SAT Math: 540–640. SAT Writing: Unavailable. ACT Comp: 22–27. HS Rank of Entering Freshmen: Top 10%: Unavailable. Top 25%: Unavailable. Avg. HS GPA: Unavailable.

Great Fine Arts Programs

Rhode Island School of Design

Cooper Union

Pratt Institute

Yale School of Art

Cost: Tuition and Fees: In-State: $29,834. Out-of-State: $29,834. Room and Board: $11,074.

Inst. Aid: FT Undergrads Receiving Aid: Unavailable. Avg. Amount per Student: Unavailable.

LOYOLA UNIVERSITY NEW ORLEANS

New Orleans, LA
admit@loyno.edu; www.loyno.edu

General Info: Private, Liberal Arts College, University, Four-year, Roman Catholic Church, Society of Jesus (Jesuits), Coed, Regionally Accredited, College Board member. Urban setting, Large city (250,000–499,999), Residential campus. Academic Calendar: Semester.

Student Body: Full-Time Undergrads: 3,556. Men: 41%, Women: 59%. Total Undergrad Population: Native American or Native Alaskan: 0%. Asian American or Pacific Islander: 7%. African American: 12%. Latino: 12%. Caucasian: 60%. International: 2%. Out-of-State: 44%. Total all graduate and professional students: 1,931.

Academics: Full-Time Faculty: 305.

Admissions: Regular Application Deadline: 1/15. Priority Application Deadline: Unavailable. Early Decision Deadline: Unavailable. Transfer Priority Deadline: 7/15. Financial Aid Deadline: Unavailable. Total Number of Students Applied: Unavailable. Percent Admitted: 47%. Number Enrolled: 898. Test Scores (Middle 50%): SAT Critical Reading: 550–690. SAT Math: 530–630. SAT Writing: Unavailable. ACT Comp: 23–28. HS Rank of Entering Freshmen: Top 10%: 35%. Top 25%: 74%. Avg. HS GPA: Unavailable.

Cost: Tuition and Fees: In-State: $25,632. Out-of-State: $25,632. Room and Board: $9,028.

Inst. Aid: FT Undergrads Receiving Aid: Unavailable. Avg. Amount per Student: Unavailable.

Beautiful Campuses

Colgate University

University of Virginia

Dartmouth College

Hanover College

Princeton University

Bucknell University

Susquehanna University

Pepperdine University

Cornell University

MACALESTER COLLEGE

St. Paul, MN

admissions@macalester.edu; www.macalester.edu

General Info: Coed, College Board member, Four-year, Liberal Arts College, Presbyterian Church (USA), Private, Regionally Accredited. Residential campus, Urban setting, Very large city (over 500,000). Academic Calendar: Semester.

Student Body: Full-Time Undergrads: 1,884. Men: 42%, Women: 58%. Total Undergrad Population: Native American or Native Alaskan: 1%. Asian American or Pacific Islander: 9%. African American: 4.5%. Latino: 4%. Caucasian: 69%. International: 11%. Out-of-State: 78%. Living Off-Campus: 33%.

Academics: Full-Time Faculty: 157. With PhD: 181. Percentage completing two or more majors: 23.8%. Graduation Rates: 83% within 4 years. 86% within 6 years.

Admissions: Regular Application Deadline: 1/15. Priority Application Deadline: Unavailable. Early Decision Deadline: 11/15. Transfer Priority Deadline: Unavailable. Financial Aid Deadline: Unavailable. Total Number of Students Applied: 4,967. Number Admitted: 2,015. Number Enrolled: 501. Number accepting place on waitlist: 177. Number of waitlisted students admitted: 33. Test Scores (Middle 50%): SAT Critical Reading: 630–740. SAT Math: 630–710. SAT Writing: 620–720. ACT Comp: 28–33. HS Rank of Entering Freshmen: Top 10%: 66.31%. Top 25%: 90.32%. Avg. HS GPA: 0.

Cost: Tuition and Fees: In-State: $36,304. Out-of-State: $36,304. Room and Board: $8,472.

Inst. Aid: FT Undergrads Receiving Aid: 1,258. Avg. Amount per Student: $26,820.

Graduates: No. of companies recruiting on campus: 75. Percentage of grads accepting a job at time of graduation: 45%. Alumni Giving %: 67%.

MANHATTANVILLE COLLEGE

Purchase, NY

admissions@mville.edu; www.manhattanville.edu

General Info: Coed, College Board member, Four-year, Liberal Arts College, Middle States Association of Colleges and Schools, New York State Board of Regents, Private, Regionally Accredited, Teachers College/College of Education. Suburban setting, Small town (2,500–9,999), Residential campus. Academic Calendar: Semester.

Student Body: Full-Time Undergrads: 1,831. Men: 35%, Women: 65%. Total Undergrad Population: Native American or Native Alaskan: 1%. Asian American or Pacific Islander: 3%. African American: 10%. Latino: 16%. Caucasian: 57%. International: 9%. Out-of-State: 40%. Living Off-Campus: 24%. Total all graduate and professional students: 1,181.

Academics: Full-Time Faculty: 94. Graduation Rate: 65% within 4 years.

Admissions: Regular Application Deadline: 3/1. Priority Application Deadline: 3/1. Early Decision Deadline: 12/1. Transfer Priority Deadline: 3/1. Financial Aid Deadline: 3/1. Total Number of Students Applied: Unavailable. Percent Admitted: 53%. Number Enrolled: Unavailable. Test Scores (Middle 50%): SAT Critical Reading: 500–620. SAT Math: 500–610. ACT Comp: 20–25. HS Rank of Entering Freshmen: Top 10%: 21%. Top 25%: 47%. Avg. HS GPA: Unavailable.

Cost: Tuition and Fees: In-State: $31,620. Out-of-State: $31,620. Room and Board: $13,040.

Inst. Aid: FT Undergrads Receiving Aid: Unavailable. Avg. Amount per Student: $25,039.

MARIST COLLEGE

Poughkeepsie, NY

admission@marist.edu; www.marist.edu

General Info: Private, Liberal Arts College, Four-year, Coed, Regionally Accredited, College Board member. Suburban setting, Small city (50,000–249,999), Residential campus. Academic Calendar: Semester.

Student Body: Full-Time Undergrads: 4,479. Men: 42%, Women: 58%. Total Undergrad Population: Native American or Native Alaskan: 0%. Asian American or Pacific Islander: 3%. African American: 2%. Latino: 4%. Caucasian:

81%. International: 0%. Out-of-State: 48%. Total all graduate and professional students: 854.

Academics: Full-Time Faculty: 204.

Admissions: Regular Application Deadline: 2/15. Priority Application Deadline: Unavailable. Early Decision Deadline: 11/15. Transfer Priority Deadline: Unavailable. Financial Aid Deadline: 5/1. Total Number of Students Applied: Unavailable. Percent Admitted: 49%. Number Enrolled: 1,038. Test Scores (Middle 50%): SAT Critical Reading: 530–610. SAT Math: 540–630. SAT Writing: 530–620. ACT Comp: 20–26. HS Rank of Entering Freshmen: Top 10%: 26%. Top 25%: 78%. Avg. HS GPA: Unavailable.

Cost: Tuition and Fees: In-State: $22,676. Out-of-State: $22,576. Room and Board: $9,790.

Inst. Aid: FT Undergrads Receiving Aid: Unavailable. Avg. Amount per Student: $14,291.

MARLBORO COLLEGE

Marlboro, VT

admissions@marlboro.edu; www.marlboro.edu

General Info: Private, Liberal Arts College, Four-year, Coed, Regionally Accredited, College Board member. Rural setting, Rural community (under 2,500), Residential campus. Academic Calendar: Semester.

Student Body: Full-Time Undergrads: 324. Men: 53%, Women: 47%. Total Undergrad Population: Native American or Native Alaskan: 1%. Asian American or Pacific Islander: 6%. African American: 0%. Latino: 4%. Caucasian: 87%. International: 1%. Out-of-State: 90%.

Academics: Full-Time Faculty: 35.

Admissions: Regular Application Deadline: 3/1. Priority Application Deadline: Unavailable. Early Decision Deadline: 12/1. Financial Aid Deadline: Unavailable. Total Number of Students Applied: Unavailable. Number Admitted: Unavailable. Number Enrolled: Unavailable. Test Scores (Middle 50%): SAT Critical Reading: Unavailable. SAT Math: Unavailable. SAT Writing: Unavailable. ACT Comp: Unavailable. HS Rank of Entering Freshmen: Top 10%: 33%. Top 25%: 62%. Avg. HS GPA: Unavailable.

Cost: Tuition and Fees: In-State: $28,350. Out-of-State: $ 28,350. Room and Board: $8,600.

Inst. Aid: FT Undergrads Receiving Aid: Unavailable. Avg. Amount per Student: Unavailable.

MARQUETTE UNIVERSITY

Milwaukee, WI

admissions@marquette.edu; www.marquette.edu/explore/

General Info: Coed, College Board member, Four-year, Private, Regionally Accredited, Roman Catholic Church, Society of Jesus (Jesuits), University. Urban setting, Very large city (over 500,000), Residential campus. Academic Calendar: Semester.

Small Schools (Under 500 Students)

Webb Institute

The Curtis Institute of Music

San Francisco Conservatory of Music

Thomas Aquinas College

College of the Atlantic

Student Body: Full-Time Undergrads: 8,010. Men: 45%, Women: 55%. Part-Time Undergrads. Men: 50%, Women: 50%. Total Undergrad Population: Native American or Native Alaskan: 2%. Asian American or Pacific Islander: 5%. African American: 5%. Latino: 5%. Caucasian: 83%. International: 3%. Out-of-State: 60%. Living Off-Campus: 3%. Total all graduate and professional students: 3,865.

Academics: Full-Time Faculty: 525. With PhD: 500. Percentage completing two or more majors: 45%. Graduation Rates: 80% within 4 years. 85% within 6 years.

Admissions: Regular Application Deadline: 12/1. Priority Application Deadline: 12/1. Early Decision Deadline: N/A. Transfer Priority Deadline: N/A. Financial Aid Deadline: 2/1. Total Number of Students Applied: 15,500. Number Admitted: 8,250. Number Enrolled: Unavailable. Number accepting place on waitlist: 900. Number of waitlisted students admitted: 425. Test Scores (Middle 50%): SAT Critical Reading: 520–700. SAT Math: 520–700. SAT Writing: 520–700. ACT Comp: 24-29. HS Rank of Entering Freshmen: Top 10%: 40%. Top 25%: 75%. Avg. HS GPA: 3.6.

Cost: Tuition and Fees: $26,678. In-State: Unavailable. Out-of-State: Unavailable. Room and Board: $8,590.

Inst. Aid: FT Undergrads Receiving Aid: Unavailable. Avg. Amount per Student: Unavailable.

Graduates: No. of companies recruiting on campus: 225. Percentage of grads accepting a job at time of graduation: 64%.

MERCER UNIVERSITY

Macon, GA

admissions@mercer.edu; www.mercer.edu

General Info: Private, University, Four-year, Baptist, Coed, Regionally Accredited, College Board member. Suburban setting, Small city (50,000–249,999), Residential campus. Academic Calendar: Semester.

Student Body: Full-Time Undergrads: 2,301. Men: 49%, Women: 51%. Total Undergrad Population: Native American or Native Alaskan: 0%. Asian American or Pacific Islander: 6%. African American: 16%. Latino: 2%. Caucasian: 68%. International: 1%. Out-of-State: 23%. Total all graduate and professional students: 1,313.

Academics: Full-Time Faculty: 345.

Admissions: Regular Application Deadline: 6/1. Priority Application Deadline: Unavailable. Early Decision Deadline: Unavailable. Transfer Priority Deadline: 8/1. Financial Aid Deadline: Unavailable. Total Number of Students Applied: Unavailable. Percent Admitted: 74%. Number Enrolled: 566. Test Scores (Middle 50%): SAT Critical Reading: 530–630. SAT Math: 550–640. SAT Writing: 520–620. ACT Comp: 22–27. HS Rank of Entering Freshmen: Top 10%: 48%. Top 25%: 74%. Avg. HS GPA: Unavailable.

Cost: Tuition and Fees: In-State: $25,256. Out-of-State: $25,256. Room and Board: $7,710.

Inst. Aid: FT Undergrads Receiving Aid: Unavailable. Avg. Amount per Student: $26,194.

MERRIMACK COLLEGE

North Andover, MA

admission@merrimack.edu; www.merrimack.edu

General Info: Private, College of Business, Liberal Arts College, Four-year, Roman Catholic Church, Coed, Regionally Accredited, College Board member. Suburban setting, Large town (10,000–49,999), Residential campus. Academic Calendar: Semester.

Student Body: Full-Time Undergrads: 2,213. Men: 52%, Women: 48%. Total Undergrad Population: Native American or Native Alaskan: 0%. Asian American or Pacific Islander: 3%. African American: 2%. Latino: 5%. Caucasian: 78%. International: 1%. Out-of-State: 21%. Total all graduate and professional students: 38.

Academics: Full-Time Faculty: 133.

Admissions: Regular Application Deadline: 2/1. Priority Application Deadline: Unavailable. Early Decision Deadline: 11/15. Transfer Priority Deadline: 7/1. Financial Aid Deadline: 2/1. Total Number of Students Applied: Unavailable. Percent Admitted: 72%. Number Enrolled: 532. Test Scores (Middle 50%): SAT Critical Reading: 520–580. SAT Math: 530–590. SAT Writing: Unavailable. ACT Comp: 19–26. HS Rank of Entering Freshmen: Top 10%: 19%. Top 25%: 44%. Avg. HS GPA: Unavailable.

Cost: Tuition and Fees: In-State: $27,070. Out-of-State: $27,070. Room and Board: $10,705.

Inst. Aid: FT Undergrads Receiving Aid: Unavailable. Avg. Amount per Student: $18,625.

MIAMI UNIVERSITY

Oxford, OH

admission@muohio.edu; www.muohio.edu

General Info: Coed, College Board member, Four-year, North Central Association of Colleges and Schools, Public, Regionally Accredited, University. Rural setting, Small town (2,500–9,999), Residential campus. Academic Calendar: Semester.

Student Body: Full-Time Undergrads: 14,385. Men: 46%, Women: 54%. Total Undergrad Population: Native American or Native Alaskan: 1%. Asian American or Pacific Islander: 3%. African American: 3%. Latino: 2%. Caucasian: 85%. International: 1%. Out-of-State: 37%. Living Off-Campus: 52%. % In Fraternities: 20%. % In Sororities: 25%. Total all graduate and professional students: 1,367.

Academics: Full-Time Faculty: 842. Graduation Rates: 67% within 4 years. 81% within 6 years.

Admissions: Regular Application Deadline: 2/1. Priority Application Deadline: 12/1. Early Decision Deadline: 11/1. Transfer Priority Deadline: Unavailable. Financial Aid Deadline: Unavailable. Total Number of Students Applied: 15,925. Number Admitted: 12,012. Number Enrolled: 3,479. Test Scores (Middle 50%): SAT Critical Reading: 540–640. SAT Math: 570–660. SAT Writing: Unavailable. ACT Comp: 24–29. HS Rank of Entering Freshmen: Top 10%: 35%. Top 25%: 72%. Avg. HS GPA: Unavailable.

Cost: Tuition and Fees: In-State: $11,443. Out-of-State: $25,307. Room and Board: $8,998.

Inst. Aid: FT Undergrads Receiving Aid: Unavailable. Avg. Amount per Student: $17,660.

MICHIGAN STATE UNIVERSITY

East Lansing, MI

admis@msu.edu; www.msu.edu

General Info: Public, University, Four-year, Coed, Regionally Accredited, North Central Association of Colleges and Schools, College Board member. Suburban setting, Small city (50,000–249,999), Residential campus. Academic Calendar: Semester.

Student Body: Full-Time Undergrads: 32,767. Men: 44%, Women: 56%. Total Undergrad Population: Native American or Native Alaskan: 1%. Asian American or Pacific Islander: 6%. African American: 9%. Latino: 3%. Caucasian: 77%. International: 4%. Out-of-State: 12%. Total all graduate and professional students: 8,099.

Academics: Full-Time Faculty: 2,411.

Admissions: Regular Application Deadline: No closing date. Priority Application Deadline: Unavailable. Early Decision Deadline: Unavailable. Transfer Priority Deadline: Unavailable. Financial Aid Deadline: Unavailable. Total Number of Students Applied: Unavailable. Percent Admitted: 73%. Number Enrolled: 7,308. Test Scores (Middle

50%): SAT Critical Reading: 500–630. SAT Math: 530–600. SAT Writing: 490–610. ACT Comp: 22–27. HS Rank of Entering Freshmen: Top 10%: 26%. Top 25%: 64%. Avg. HS GPA: Unavailable.

Cost: Tuition and Fees: In-State: $8,793. Out-of-State: $21,438. Room and Board: $6,044.

Inst. Aid: FT Undergrads Receiving Aid: Unavailable. Avg. Amount per Student: $9,798.

MICHIGAN TECHNOLOGICAL UNIVERSITY

Houghton, MI

mtu4u@mtu.edu; www.admissions.mtu.edu

General Info: Public, University, Four-year, Coed, Regionally Accredited, North Central Association of Colleges and Schools. Residential campus, Rural setting, Small town (2,500–9,999). Academic Calendar: Semester.

Student Body: Full-Time Undergrads: 5,614. Men: 82%, Women: 18%. Total Undergrad Population: Native American or Native Alaskan: 0.7%. Asian American or Pacific Islander: 0.9%. African American: 2.1%. Latino: 1.2%. Caucasian: 85.2%. International: 4.9%. Out-of-State: 21.1%. Total all graduate and professional students: 912.

Academics: Full-Time Faculty: 360. Graduation Rates: 25.9% within 4 years. 60.5% within 6 years.

Admissions: Regular Application Deadline: No closing date. Priority Application Deadline: 1/15. Early Decision Deadline: N/A. Transfer Priority Deadline: 1/15. Financial Aid Deadline: Unavailable. Total Number of Students Applied: Unavailable. Percent Admitted: 85%. Number Enrolled: 1,324. Test Scores (Middle 50%): SAT Critical Reading: 530–650. SAT Math: 590–690. SAT Writing: 500–620. ACT Comp: 23-28. HS Rank of Entering Freshmen: Top 10%: 30.1%. Top 25%: 61.1%. Avg. HS GPA: Unavailable.

Cost: Tuition and Fees: In-State: $9,828. Out-of-State: $21,588. Room and Board: $7,315.

Inst. Aid: FT Undergrads Receiving Aid: Unavailable. Avg. Amount per Student: $8,711.

MIDDLEBURY COLLEGE

Middlebury, VT

admissions@middlebury.edu; www.middlebury.edu

General Info: Private, Liberal Arts College, Four-year, Coed, Regionally Accredited, College Board member. Rural setting, Small town (2,500–9,999), Residential campus. Academic Calendar: 4-1-4.

Student Body: Full-Time Undergrads: 2,450. Men: 49%, Women: 51%. Total Undergrad Population: Native American or Native Alaskan: 1%. Asian American or Pacific Islander: 10%. African American: 4%. Latino: 7%. Caucasian: 62%. International: 11%. Out-of-State: 96%. Living Off-Campus: 2%.

Academics: Full-Time Faculty: 249.

Admissions: Regular Application Deadline: 1/1. Priority Application Deadline: Unavailable. Early Decision Deadline: 11/15. Transfer Priority Deadline: Unavailable. Financial Aid Deadline: 1/1. Total Number of Students Applied: 7,185. Number Admitted: 1,479. Number Enrolled: Unavailable. Number accepting place on waitlist: 589. Test Scores (Middle 50%): SAT Critical Reading: 650–750. SAT Math: 650–740. SAT Writing: 650–740. ACT Comp: 29–32. HS Rank of Entering Freshmen: Top 10%: 82%. Top 25%: 0%. Avg. HS GPA: Unavailable.

Cost: Tuition and Fees: In-State: $49,210. Out-of-State: Unavailable. Room and Board: Unavailable.

Inst. Aid: FT Undergrads Receiving Aid: 255. Avg. Amount per Student: $30,439.

Great Midwest Universities

Drake University

Bradley University

Truman State University

Creighton University

Xavier University

MILLS COLLEGE

Oakland, CA

admission@mills.edu; www.mills.edu

General Info: College Board member, Four-year, Liberal Arts College, Private, Regionally Accredited, Western Association of Schools and Colleges, Women Only. Urban setting, Large city (250,000–499,999), Residential campus. Academic Calendar: Semester.

Student Body: Full-Time Undergrads: 881. Men: 0%, Women: 100%. Part-Time Undergrads. Men: 0%, Women: 7%. Total Undergrad Population: Native American or Native Alaskan: 1%. Asian American or Pacific Islander: 8%. African American: 9%. Latino: 14%. Caucasian: 43%. International: 2%. Out-of-State: 27%. Living Off-Campus: 5%. Total all graduate and professional students: 506.

Academics: Full-Time Faculty: 90. With PhD: 106. Graduation Rates: 44% within 4 years. 57% within 6 years.

Admissions: Regular Application Deadline: 2/1. Priority Application Deadline: 2/1. Early Decision Deadline: Unavailable. Fall Transfer Deadline: 8/1. Spring Transfer Deadline: 12/15. Transfer Priority Deadline: 3/2. Financial Aid Deadline: 2/15. Total Number of Students Applied: Unavailable. Number Admitted: Unavailable. Number Enrolled: Unavailable. Test Scores (Middle 50%): SAT Critical Reading: 520–640. SAT Math: 490–610. SAT Writing: 500–630. ACT Comp: 19–27. HS Rank of Entering Freshmen: Top 10%: 40%. Top 25%: 50%. Avg. HS GPA: 3.61.

Cost: Tuition and Fees: In-State: $34,170. Out-of-State: $34,170. Room and Board: $11,270.

Inst. Aid: FT Undergrads Receiving Aid: 679. Avg. Amount per Student: $27,195. Freshmen Receiving Non-Need Scholarship or Grant: 19. Avg. Amount per Student: $25,650.

Graduates: Alumni Giving %: 26%.

Great Northern Universities

Providence College

Fairfield University

Rochester Institute of Technology

Villanova University

St. Joseph's University

MILLSAPS COLLEGE

Jackson, MS

admissions@millsaps.edu; www.millsaps.edu

General Info: Private, College of Business, Liberal Arts College, Four-year, United Methodist Church, Coed, Regionally Accredited. Urban setting, Large city (250,000–499,999), Residential campus. Academic Calendar: Semester.

Student Body: Full-Time Undergrads: 1,085. Men: 54%, Women: 46%. Total Undergrad Population: Native American or Native Alaskan: 0%. Asian American or Pacific Islander: 3%. African American: 15%. Latino: 1%. Caucasian: 81%. International: 1%. Out-of-State: 60%. Total all graduate and professional students: 69.

Academics: Full-Time Faculty: 92. Graduation Rates: 63% within 4 years. 71% within 6 years.

Admissions: Regular Application Deadline: Rolling. Priority Application Deadline: Unavailable. Early Decision Deadline: 1/8. Financial Aid Deadline: Unavailable. Total Number of Students Applied: Unavailable. Percent Admitted: 82%. Number Enrolled: 258. Test Scores (Middle 50%): SAT Critical Reading: 540–680. SAT Math: 540–650. SAT Writing: Unavailable. ACT Comp: 23–30. HS Rank of Entering Freshmen: Top 10%: 38%. Top 25%: 63%. Avg. HS GPA: Unavailable.

Cost: Tuition and Fees: In-State: $23,214. Out-of-State: $23,214. Room and Board: $8,800.

Inst. Aid: FT Undergrads Receiving Aid: Unavailable. Avg. Amount per Student: $18,185.

MASSACHUSETTS INSTITUTE OF TECHNOLOGY

Cambridge, MA

admissions@mit.edu; web.mit.edu

General Info: Coed, College Board member, Four-year, Private, Regionally Accredited, University. Residential campus, Small city (50,000–249,999), Urban setting. Academic Calendar: 4-1-4.

Student Body: Full-Time Undergrads: 4,068. Men: 56%, Women: 44%. Total Undergrad Population: Native American or Native Alaskan: 1%. Asian American or Pacific Islander: 28%. African American: 8%. Latino: 12%. Caucasian: 37%. International: 8%. Out-of-State: 91.6%. Total all graduate and professional students: 6,126.

Academics: Full-Time Faculty: 1,191.

Admissions: Regular Application Deadline: 1/1. Priority Application Deadline: Unavailable. Early Decision Deadline: 11/1. Transfer Priority Deadline: Unavailable. Financial Aid Deadline: 2/1. Total Number of Students Applied: Unavailable. Percent Admitted: 13%. Number Enrolled: 1,002. Test Scores (Middle 50%): SAT Critical Reading: 660–760. SAT Math: 720–800. SAT Writing: Unavailable. ACT Comp: 30–34. HS Rank of Entering Freshmen: Top 10%: 97%. Top 25%: 100%. Avg. HS GPA: Unavailable.

Cost: Tuition and Fees: In-State: $34,986. Out-of-State: $34,986. Room and Board: $10,400.

Inst. Aid: FT Undergrads Receiving Aid: Unavailable. Avg. Amount per Student: Unavailable.

MONTANA STATE UNIVERSITY

Havre, MT

admissions@msun.edu; www.msun.edu

General Info: Public, Liberal Arts College, University, Four-year, Coed, Regionally Accredited, Northwest Association of Schools and Colleges. Rural setting, Large town (10,000–49,999), Commuter campus. Academic Calendar: Semester.

Student Body: Full-Time Undergrads: 1,279. Men: Unavailable, Women: Unavailable. Total Undergrad Population: 1,279. Out-of-State: 10%.

Academics: Full-Time Faculty: 534.

Admissions: Regular Application Deadline: No closing date. Priority Application Deadline: Unavailable. Early Decision Deadline: Unavailable. Transfer Priority Deadline: Unavailable. Financial Aid Deadline: Unavailable. Total Number of Students Applied: Unavailable. Number Admitted: Unavailable. Number Enrolled: Unavailable. Test Scores (Middle 50%): SAT Critical Reading: 420–510. SAT Math: 400–500. SAT Writing: Unavailable. ACT Comp: 16–21. HS Rank of Entering Freshmen: Top 10%: 17%. Top 25%: 41%. Avg. HS GPA: Unavailable.

Cost: Tuition and Fees: In-State: $4,324. Out-of-State: $13,798. Room and Board: $5,142.

Inst. Aid: FT Undergrads Receiving Aid: Unavailable. Avg. Amount per Student: Unavailable.

MORAVIAN COLLEGE

Bethlehem, PA

admissions@moravian.edu; www.moravian.edu

General Info: Private, Liberal Arts College, Four-year, Moravian Church In America, Coed, Regionally Accredited, College Board member. Suburban setting, Small city (50,000–249,999), Residential campus. Academic Calendar: Semester.

Student Body: Full-Time Undergrads: 1,543. Men: 41%, Women: 59%. Total Undergrad Population: Native American or Native Alaskan: 0%. Asian American or Pacific Islander: 2%. African American: 2%. Latino: 2%. Caucasian: 92%. International: 1%. Out-of-State: 50%. Total all graduate and professional students: 162.

Academics: Full-Time Faculty: 118.

Admissions: Regular Application Deadline: 2/15. Priority Application Deadline: Unavailable. Early Decision Deadline: 1/15. Transfer Priority Deadline: 5/1. Financial Aid Deadline: 3/15. Total Number of Students Applied: Unavailable. Percent Admitted: 65%. Number Enrolled: 375. Test Scores (Middle 50%): SAT Critical Reading: 510–600. SAT Math: 510–610. SAT Writing: 500–590. ACT Comp: Unavailable. HS Rank of Entering Freshmen: Top 10%: 31%. Top 25%: 64%. Avg. HS GPA: Unavailable.

Cost: Tuition and Fees: In-State: $26,775. Out-of-State: $26,775. Room and Board: $7,760.

Inst. Aid: FT Undergrads Receiving Aid: Unavailable. Avg. Amount per Student: $18,668.

MOREHOUSE COLLEGE

Atlanta, GA

admissions@morehouse.edu; www.morehouse.edu

General Info: Private, Liberal Arts College, Four-year, Men Only, Regionally Accredited, College Board member, Historically black. Urban setting, Very large city (over 500,000), Residential campus. Academic Calendar: Semester.

Student Body: Full-Time Undergrads. Men: 100%, Women: 0%. Total Undergrad Population: Native American or Native Alaskan: 0%. Asian American or Pacific Islander: 0%. African American: 89%. Latino: 0%. Caucasian: 0%. International: 9%. Out-of-State: 72%.

Academics: Full-Time Faculty: 76.

Admissions: Regular Application Deadline: 2/15. Priority Application Deadline: 11/1. Early Decision Deadline: Unavailable. Transfer Priority Deadline: Unavailable. Financial Aid Deadline: 4/1. Total Number of Students Applied: Unavailable. Percent Admitted: 55%. Number Enrolled: 654. Test Scores (Middle 50%): SAT Critical Reading: 480–580. SAT Math: 480–590. SAT Writing: Unavailable. ACT Comp: 20–24. HS Rank of Entering Freshmen: Top 10%: 18%. Top 25%: 41%. Avg. HS GPA: Unavailable.

Cost: Tuition and Fees: In-State: $17,536. Out-of-State: $17,536. Room and Board: $9,454.

Inst. Aid: FT Undergrads Receiving Aid: Unavailable. Avg. Amount per Student: $4,525.

MOUNT HOLYOKE COLLEGE

South Hadley, MA

admission@mtholyoke.edu; www.mtholyoke.edu

General Info: Private, Liberal Arts College, Four-year, Women Only, Regionally Accredited, College Board member. Suburban setting, Large town (10,000–49,999), Residential campus. Academic Calendar: Semester.

Student Body: Full-Time Undergrads: 2,149. Men: 0%, Women: 100%. Part-Time Undergrads. Men: 6%, Women: 94%. Total Undergrad Population: Native American or Native Alaskan: 1%. Asian American or Pacific Islander: 12%. African American: 5%. Latino: 5%. Caucasian: 50%. International: 16%. Out-of-State: 75%. Living Off-Campus: 7%. Total all graduate and professional students: 3.

Academics: Full-Time Faculty: 208. With PhD: 180. Percentage completing two or more majors: 18%. Graduation Rates: 78% within 4 years. 81% within 6 years.

Admissions: Regular Application Deadline: 1/15. Priority Application Deadline: Unavailable. Early Decision Deadline: 11/15. Fall Transfer Deadline: 5/15. Spring Transfer Deadline: 11/1. Transfer Priority Deadline: 2/15. Financial Aid Deadline: 2/1. Total Number of Students Applied: 3,194. Number Admitted: 1,671. Number Enrolled: 522. Number accepting place on waitlist: 178. Number applied early decision: 225. Early decision admitted: 119. Test Scores (Middle 50%): SAT Critical Reading: 640–730. SAT Math: 590–690. SAT Writing: 630–710. ACT Comp: 26–30. HS Rank of Entering Freshmen: Top 10%: 55%. Top 25%: 86%. Avg. HS GPA: 3.67.

Cost: Tuition and Fees: In-State: $37,460. Out-of-State: $37,460. Room and Board: $11,020.

Inst. Aid: FT Undergrads Receiving Aid: 1,367. Avg. Amount per Student: $31,077. Freshmen Receiving Non-Need Scholarship or Grant: 38. Avg. Amount per Student: $16,184.

Graduates: No. of companies recruiting on campus: 45. Percentage of grads accepting a job at time of graduation: 65%. Alumni Giving %: 44%.

Great Southern Universities

Stetson University

Belmont University

Samford University

Rollins College

Mercer University

MUHLENBERG COLLEGE

Allentown, PA

admissions@muhlenberg.edu; www.muhlenberg.edu

General Info: Coed, College Board member, Evangelical Lutheran Church In America, Four-year, Liberal Arts College, Private, Regionally Accredited. Suburban setting, Small city (50,000–249,999), Residential campus. Academic Calendar: Semester.

Student Body: Full-Time Undergrads: 2,500. Men: 42%, Women: 58%. Part-Time Undergrads. Men: 33%, Women: 67%. Total Undergrad Population: Native American or Native Alaskan: 0.2%. Asian American or Pacific Islander: 2.3%. African American: 2.2%. Latino: 3.7%. Caucasian: 89.4%. International: 0.2%. Out-of-State: 70%. Living Off-Campus: 8%. % In Fraternities: 14%. % In Sororities: 17%.

Academics: Full-Time Faculty: 161. With PhD: 124. Percentage completing two or more majors: 32%. Graduation Rates: 78.8% within 4 years. 83.3% within 6 years.

Admissions: Regular Application Deadline: 2/15. Priority Application Deadline: Unavailable. Early Decision Deadline: Unavailable. Transfer Priority Deadline: 6/15. Financial Aid Deadline: 2/15. Total Number of Students Applied: 4,703. Number Admitted: 1,750. Number Enrolled: 551. Number accepting place on waitlist: 541. Number of waitlisted students admitted: 41. Number applied early decision: 420. Early decision admitted: 283. Test Scores (Middle 50%): SAT Critical Reading: 550–650. SAT Math: 560–660. SAT Writing: 560–660. ACT Comp: 24-29. HS Rank of Entering Freshmen: Top 10%: 47%. Top 25%: 80%. Avg. HS GPA: 3.41.

Cost: Tuition and Fees: In-State: $35,125. Out-of-State: $35,125. Room and Board: $8,060.

Inst. Aid: FT Undergrads Receiving Aid: 974. Avg. Amount per Student: $21,496. Freshmen Receiving Non-Need Scholarship or Grant: 171. Avg. Amount per Student: $70,585.

Graduates: No. of companies recruiting on campus: 74. Alumni Giving %: 35%.

NEW COLLEGE OF FLORIDA

Sarasota, FL

admissions@ncf.edu; www.ncf.edu

General Info: Public, Liberal Arts College, Four-year, Coed, Regionally Accredited, Southern Association of Colleges and Schools, College Board member. Suburban setting, Small city (50,000–249,999), Residential campus. Academic Calendar: 4-1-4.

Student Body: Full-Time Undergrads: 750. Men: 37%, Women: 63%. Total Undergrad Population: Native American or Native Alaskan: 1%. Asian American or Pacific Islander: 2%. African American: 2%. Latino: 9%. Caucasian: 81%. International: 1%. Out-of-State: 35%.

Academics: Full-Time Faculty: 65.

Admissions: Regular Application Deadline: 12/1. Priority Application Deadline: Unavailable. Early Decision Deadline: Unavailable. Financial Aid Deadline: Unavailable. Total Number of Students Applied: Unavailable. Percent Admitted: 49%. Number Enrolled: 175. Test Scores (Middle 50%): SAT Critical Reading: 650–740. SAT Math: 600–690. SAT Writing: 610–690. ACT Comp: 26–30. HS Rank of Entering Freshmen: Top 10%: 44%. Top 25%: 80%. Avg. HS GPA: Unavailable.

Cost: Tuition and Fees: In-State: $3,111. Out-of-State: $16,650. Room and Board: $6,564.

Inst. Aid: FT Undergrads Receiving Aid: Unavailable. Avg. Amount per Student: $11,662.

NEW MEXICO INSTITUTE OF MINING AND TECHNOLOGY

Socorro, NM

admission@admin.nmt.edu; www.nmt.edu

General Info: Coed, College Board member, College of Engineering, Four-year, North Central Association of Colleges and Schools, Public, Regionally Accredited, Technical College. Rural setting, Small town (2,500–9,999), Residential campus. Academic Calendar: Semester.

Student Body: Full-Time Undergrads: 1,336. Men: 67%, Women: 33%. Total Undergrad Population: Native American or Native Alaskan: 2%. Asian American or Pacific Islander: 2%. African American: 2%. Latino: 27%. Caucasian: 66%. International: 1%. Out-of-State: 16%. Total all graduate and professional students: 510.

Academics: Full-Time Faculty: 121. Graduation Rates: 22% within 4 years. 54% within 6 years.

Admissions: Regular Application Deadline: Rolling. Priority Application Deadline: Unavailable. Early Decision Deadline: Unavailable. Transfer Priority Deadline: 3/1. Financial Aid Deadline: 2/1. Total Number of Students Applied: Unavailable. Number Admitted: Unavailable. Number Enrolled: Unavailable. Number accepting place on waitlist: Unavailable. Test Scores (Middle 50%): SAT Critical Reading: 550–670. SAT Math: 570–670. SAT Writing: Unavailable. ACT Comp: 23–29. HS Rank of Entering Freshmen: Top 10%: Unavailable. Top 25%: Unavailable. Avg. HS GPA: 3.65.

Cost: Tuition and Fees: In-State: $3,971. Out-of-State: $11,405. Room and Board: $5,090.

Inst. Aid: FT Undergrads Receiving Aid: Unavailable. Avg. Amount per Student: Unavailable.

NEW SCHOOL UNIVERSITY

New York, NY
www.newschool.edu

General Info: Academic Calendar: Unavailable.

Student Body: Full-Time Undergrads: 5,262. Men: 28%, Women: 72%.

Academics: Full-Time Faculty: 333.

Admissions: Regular Application Deadline: Rolling. Priority Application Deadline: Unavailable. Early Decision Deadline: 11/15. Transfer Priority Deadline: Unavailable. Financial Aid Deadline: Unavailable. Total Number of Students Applied: 4,945. Number Admitted: 2,649. Number Enrolled: 1,002. Test Scores (Middle 50%): SAT Critical Reading: 500–630. SAT Math: 490–610. SAT Writing: 510–620. ACT Comp: 21–26. HS Rank of Entering Freshmen: Top 10%: Unavailable. Top 25%: Unavailable. Avg. HS GPA: 3.27.

Cost: Tuition and Fees: Unavailable.

Inst. Aid: FT Undergrads Receiving Aid: 3,150. Avg. Amount per Student: $20,552.

NEW YORK SCHOOL OF INTERIOR DESIGN

New York, NY
admissions@nysid.edu; www.nysid.edu

General Info: Private, College of Art, Four-year, Coed. Urban setting, Very large city (over 500,000), Commuter campus. Academic Calendar: Semester.

Student Body: Full-Time Undergrads: 724. Men: 0%, Women: 100%. Total Undergrad Population: Native American or Native Alaskan: 0%. Asian American or Pacific Islander: 13%. African American: 13%. Latino: 17%. Caucasian: 43%. Out-of-State: 39%. Total all graduate and professional students: 15.

Academics: Full-Time Faculty: Unavailable.

Admissions: Regular Application Deadline: No closing date. Priority Application Deadline: 3/1. Early Decision Deadline: Unavailable. Financial Aid Deadline: Unavailable. Total Number of Students Applied: Unavailable. Number Admitted: Unavailable. Number Enrolled: Unavailable. Test Scores (Middle 50%): SAT Critical Reading: Unavailable. SAT Math: Unavailable. SAT Writing: Unavailable. ACT Comp: Unavailable. HS Rank of Entering Freshmen: Top 10%: Unavailable. Top 25%: Unavailable. Avg. HS GPA: Unavailable.

Cost: Tuition and Fees: In-State: $18,820. Out-of-State: $18,820. Room and Board: Unavailable.

Inst. Aid: FT Undergrads Receiving Aid: Unavailable. Avg. Amount per Student: Unavailable.

Great Western Universities

University of Portland

Loyola Marymount University

Gonzaga University

Trinity University

Whitworth College

NEW YORK UNIVERSITY

New York, NY
admissions@nyu.edu; www.nyu.edu

General Info: Private, University, Four-year, Coed, Regionally Accredited, College Board member. Urban setting, Very large city (over 500,000), Residential campus. Academic Calendar: Semester.

Student Body: Full-Time Undergrads: 20,965. Men: 38%, Women: 62%. Part-Time Undergrads. Men: 38%, Women: 62%. Total Undergrad Population: Native American or Native Alaskan: 0%. Asian American or Pacific Islander: 18%. African American: 4%. Latino: 7%. Caucasian: 49%. International: 0%. Out-of-State: 72%. Living Off-Campus: 47%. % In Fraternities: 2%. % In Sororities: 2%. Total all graduate and professional students: 16,477.

Academics: Full-Time Faculty: 2,132.

Admissions: Regular Application Deadline: 1/15. Priority Application Deadline: Unavailable. Early Decision Deadline: 11/1. Transfer Priority Deadline: 4/1. Financial Aid Deadline: 2/15. Total Number of Students Applied: 34,389. Number Admitted: 12,615. Number Enrolled: 4,892. Number of waitlisted students admitted: 12. Test Scores (Middle 50%): SAT Critical Reading: 620–710. SAT Math: 620–720. SAT Writing: 620–710. ACT Comp: 28–31. HS Rank of Entering Freshmen: Top 10%: 66%. Top 25%: 93%. Avg. HS GPA: 3.59.

Cost: Tuition and Fees: In-State: $33,420. Out-of-State: $33,420. Room and Board: $11,780.

Inst. Aid: FT Undergrads Receiving Aid: 10,035. Avg. Amount per Student: $22,207.

NORTH CAROLINA SCHOOL OF THE ARTS

Winston-Salem, NC

admissions@ncarts.edu; www.ncarts.edu

General Info: Public, College of Art, College of Performing Arts, Four-year, Coed, Regionally Accredited, Southern Association of Colleges and Schools, College Board member. Suburban setting, Small city (50,000–249,999), Residential campus. Academic Calendar: Trimester.

Student Body: Full-Time Undergrads: 716. Men: 53%, Women: 47%. Total Undergrad Population: Native American or Native Alaskan: 1%. Asian American or Pacific Islander: 1%. African American: 11%. Latino: 6%. Caucasian: 79%. International: 2%. Out-of-State: 62%. Total all graduate and professional students: 118.

Academics: Full-Time Faculty: 140.

Admissions: Regular Application Deadline: 3/1. Priority Application Deadline: Unavailable. Early Decision Deadline: Unavailable. Transfer Priority Deadline: 3/1. Financial Aid Deadline: Unavailable. Total Number of Students Applied: Unavailable. Percent Admitted: 49%. Number Enrolled: 178. Test Scores (Middle 50%): SAT Critical Reading: Unavailable. SAT Math: Unavailable. SAT Writing: Unavailable. ACT Comp: Unavailable. HS Rank of Entering Freshmen: Top 10%: Unavailable. Top 25%: Unavailable. Avg. HS GPA: Unavailable.

Cost: Tuition and Fees: In-State: $4,679. Out-of-State: $15,959. Room and Board: $6,139.

Inst. Aid: FT Undergrads Receiving Aid: Unavailable. Avg. Amount per Student: $9,884.

NORTH CAROLINA STATE UNIVERSITY

Raleigh, NC

undergrad_admissions@ncsu.edu; www.ncsu.edu

General Info: Public, University, Four-year, Coed, Regionally Accredited, Southern Association of Colleges and Schools, College Board member. Urban setting, Large city (250,000–499,999), Residential campus. Academic Calendar: Semester.

Student Body: Full-Time Undergrads: 23,730. Men: 56%, Women: 44%. Total Undergrad Population: Native American or Native Alaskan: 0%. Asian American or Pacific Islander: 5%. African American: 9%. Latino: 2%. Caucasian: 80%. International: 1%. Out-of-State: 8%. Total all graduate and professional students: 7,096.

Academics: Full-Time Faculty: 1,652. Graduation Rates: 42% within 4 years. 70% within 6 years.

Admissions: Regular Application Deadline: 2/1. Priority Application Deadline: Unavailable. Early Decision Deadline: 11/1. Transfer Priority Deadline: Unavailable. Financial Aid Deadline: Unavailable. Total Number of Students Applied: Unavailable. Percent Admitted: 61%. Number Enrolled: 4,668. Test Scores (Middle 50%): SAT Critical Reading: 520–620. SAT Math: 560–650. SAT Writing: 510–610. ACT Comp: 22–27. HS Rank of Entering Freshmen: Top 10%: 34%. Top 25%: 75%. Avg. HS GPA: Unavailable.

Cost: Tuition and Fees: In-State: $5,286. Out-of-State: $17,584. Room and Board: $7,982.

Inst. Aid: FT Undergrads Receiving Aid: Unavailable. Avg. Amount per Student: Unavailable.

NORTHEASTERN UNIVERSITY

Boston, MA

admissions@neu.edu; www.northeastern.edu

General Info: Private, University, Four-year, Coed, Regionally Accredited, College Board member. Urban setting, Very large city (over 500,000), Residential campus. Academic Calendar: Semester.

Student Body: Full-Time Undergrads: 15,195. Men: 50%, Women: 50%. Total Undergrad Population: Native American or Native Alaskan: 0%. Asian American or Pacific Islander: 8%. African American: 6%. Latino: 5%. Caucasian: 60%. International: 4%. Out-of-State: 65%. Total all graduate and professional students: 4,780.

Academics: Full-Time Faculty: 873.

Admissions: Regular Application Deadline: 1/15. Priority Application Deadline: 11/15. Early Decision Deadline: Unavailable. Transfer Priority Deadline: 5/1. Financial Aid Deadline: 2/15. Total Number of Students Applied: Unavailable. Percent Admitted: 45%. Number Enrolled: 2,955. Test Scores (Middle 50%): SAT Critical Reading: 560–650. SAT Math: 590–680. SAT Writing: Unavailable. ACT Comp:

Where Do Pulitzer Prize Winners Study?

Toni Morrison—Howard University

Roger Ebert—University of Illinois at Urbana–Champaign

Arthur Miller—University of Michigan

John Updike—Harvard University

24–28. HS Rank of Entering Freshmen: Top 10%: 38%. Top 25%: 76%. Avg. HS GPA: Unavailable.

Cost: Tuition and Fees: In-State: $32,149. Out-of-State: $30,309. Room and Board: $11,010.

Inst. Aid: FT Undergrads Receiving Aid: Unavailable. Avg. Amount per Student: $17,553.

NORTHERN ARIZONA UNIVERSITY

Flagstaff, AZ

undergraduate.admissions@nau.edu; www.nau.edu

General Info: Public, University, Four-year, Coed, Regionally Accredited, North Central Association of Colleges and Schools, College Board member. Rural setting, Small city (50,000–249,999), Residential campus. Academic Calendar: Semester.

Student Body: Full-Time Undergrads: 14,562. Men: 41%, Women: 59%. Total Undergrad Population: Native American or Native Alaskan: 5%. Asian American or Pacific Islander: 3%. African American: 3%. Latino: 11%. Caucasian: 74%. International: 1%. Out-of-State: 26%. Total all graduate and professional students: 5,908.

Academics: Full-Time Faculty: 774.

Admissions: Regular Application Deadline: No closing date. Priority Application Deadline: 3/1. Early Decision Deadline: Unavailable. Transfer Priority Deadline: 3/1. Financial Aid Deadline: Unavailable. Total Number of Students Applied: 15,486. Number Admitted: 11,629. Number Enrolled: 2,931. Test Scores (Middle 50%): SAT Critical Reading: 490–590. SAT Math: 450–530. SAT Writing: 460–540. ACT Comp: 20–25. HS Rank of Entering Freshmen: Top 10%: Unavailable. Top 25%: Unavailable. Avg. HS GPA: 3.4.

Cost: Tuition and Fees: In-State: $4,546. Out-of-State: $13,487. Room and Board: $6,260.

Inst. Aid: FT Undergrads Receiving Aid: 1,102. Avg. Amount per Student: $7,575.

NORTHWESTERN UNIVERSITY

Evanston, IL

ug-admission@northwestern.edu; www.northwestern.edu

General Info: Coed, College Board member, Four-year, Private, Regionally Accredited, University. Suburban setting, Small city (50,000–249,999), Residential campus. Academic Calendar: Quarter.

Student Body: Full-Time Undergrads: 7,826. Men: 48%, Women: 52%. Total Undergrad Population: Native American or Native Alaskan: 0%. Asian American or Pacific Islander: 19%. African American: 5%. Latino: 7%. Caucasian: 57.7%. International: 5%. Out-of-State: 75%. Total all graduate and professional students: 9,307.

Academics: Full-Time Faculty: 938.

Admissions: Regular Application Deadline: 1/1. Priority Application Deadline: Unavailable. Early Decision Deadline: 11/1. Transfer Priority Deadline: Unavailable. Financial Aid Deadline: 2/15. Total Number of Students Applied: Unavailable. Percent Admitted: 30%. Number Enrolled: 1,952. Test Scores (Middle 50%): SAT Critical Reading: 670–750. SAT Math: 680–770. SAT Writing: Unavailable. ACT Comp: 30–34. HS Rank of Entering Freshmen: Top 10%: Unavailable. Top 25%: 0%. Avg. HS GPA: Unavailable.

Cost: Tuition and Fees: In-State: $36,756. Out-of-State: $36,756. Room and Board: $11,295.

Inst. Aid: FT Undergrads Receiving Aid: Unavailable. Avg. Amount per Student: Unavailable.

Where Do Fields Medal Winners (Mathematics) Study?

Curtis T. McMullen—Williams College

Edward Witten—Brandeis University

William Thurston—New College of Florida

OBERLIN COLLEGE

Oberlin, OH

college.admissions@oberlin.edu; www.oberlin.edu

General Info: Private, College of Music, Liberal Arts College, Four-year, Coed, Regionally Accredited, College Board member. Rural setting, Small town (2,500–9,999), Residential campus. Academic Calendar: 4-1-4.

Student Body: Full-Time Undergrads: 2,829. Men: 44%, Women: 56%. Total Undergrad Population: Native American or Native Alaskan: 1%. Asian American or Pacific Islander: 8%. African American: 6%. Latino: 5%. Caucasian: 77%. International: 6%. Out-of-State: 91%. Total all graduate and professional students: 12.

Academics: Full-Time Faculty: 275. Graduation Rate: 82% within 6 years.

Admissions: Regular Application Deadline: 1/15. Priority Application Deadline: Unavailable. Early Decision Deadline: 11/15. Fall Transfer Deadline: 3/15. Spring Transfer Deadline: 11/15. Transfer Priority Deadline: Unavailable. Financial Aid Deadline: 2/15. Total Number of Students Applied: 7,014. Number Admitted: 2,193. Number Enrolled: 745. Number accepting place on waitlist: 666. Number of waitlisted students admitted: 18. Number applied early decision: 342. Early decision admitted: 204. Test Scores (Middle 50%): SAT Critical Reading: 640–750. SAT Math: 610–710. SAT Writing: 630–730. ACT Comp: 26-32. HS Rank of Entering Freshmen: Top 10%: 68%. Top 25%: 92%. Avg. HS GPA: 3.6.

Cost: Tuition and Fees: In-State: $36,064. Out-of-State: $36,064. Room and Board: $9,280.

Inst. Aid: FT Undergrads Receiving Aid: 1,491. Avg. Amount per Student: $29,326.

OCCIDENTAL COLLEGE

Los Angeles, CA

admission@oxy.edu; www.oxy.edu

General Info: Private, Liberal Arts College, Four-year, Nondenominational, Coed, Regionally Accredited, College Board member, Hispanic serving. Suburban setting, Very large city (over 500,000), Residential campus. Academic Calendar: Semester.

Student Body: Full-Time Undergrads: 1,850. Men: 45%, Women: 55%. Total Undergrad Population: Out-of-State: 53%. Total all graduate and professional students: 21.

Academics: Full-Time Faculty: 157. With PhD: 140. Percentage completing two or more majors: 6%.

Admissions: Regular Application Deadline: 1/10. Priority Application Deadline: Unavailable. Early Decision Deadline: 11/15. Transfer Priority Deadline: Unavailable. Financial Aid Deadline: 2/1. Total Number of Students Applied: 5,272. Number Admitted: 2,328. Number Enrolled: Unavailable. Number accepting place on waitlist: 234. Number of waitlisted students admitted: 26. Test Scores (Middle 50%): SAT Critical Reading: 590–700. SAT Math: 600–690. SAT Writing: 585–690. ACT Comp: 26–30. HS Rank of Entering Freshmen: Top 10%: 57%. Top 25%: 89%. Avg. HS GPA: Unavailable.

Cost: Tuition and Fees: In-State: $36,160. Out-of-State: $36,160. Room and Board: $10,270.

Inst. Aid: FT Undergrads Receiving Aid: 1,334. Avg. Amount per Student: Unavailable.

Graduates: Alumni Giving %: 45%.

OHIO STATE UNIVERSITY

Columbus, OH

askabuckeye@osu.edu; www.osu.edu

General Info: Public, University, Four-year, Coed, Regionally Accredited, North Central Association of Colleges and Schools, College Board member. Urban setting, Very large city (over 500,000), Residential campus. Academic Calendar: Quarter.

Student Body: Full-Time Undergrads: 38,479. Men: 53%, Women: 47%. Total Undergrad Population: Native American or Native Alaskan: 0%. Asian American or Pacific Islander: 6%. African American: 6%. Latino: 3%. Caucasian: 81%. International: 1%. Out-of-State: 14%. Total all graduate and professional students: 10,083.

Academics: Full-Time Faculty: 3,012.

Admissions: Regular Application Deadline: 2/1. Priority Application Deadline: Unavailable. Early Decision Deadline: Unavailable. Transfer Priority Deadline: Unavailable. Financial Aid Deadline: Unavailable. Total Number of Students Applied: Unavailable. Percent Admitted: 68%. Number Enrolled: 6,280. Test Scores (Middle 50%): SAT Critical Reading: 530–640. SAT Math: 560–670. SAT Writing: 520–630. ACT Comp: 24–29. HS Rank of Entering Freshmen: Top 10%: 43%. Top 25%: 80%. Avg. HS GPA: Unavailable.

Cost: Tuition and Fees: In-State: $8,667. Out-of-State: $20,562. Room and Board: $7,035.

Inst. Aid: FT Undergrads Receiving Aid: Unavailable. Avg. Amount per Student: Unavailable.

OHIO UNIVERSITY

Zanesville, OH

ouzservices@ohio.edu; www.zanesville.ohiou.edu

General Info: Public, Branch Campus, Four-year, Coed, Regionally Accredited, North Central Association of Colleges and Schools. Rural setting, Large town (10,000–49,999), Commuter campus. Academic Calendar: Quarter.

Student Body: Full-Time Undergrads: 1,849. Men: 33%, Women: 67%. Total Undergrad Population: Native American or Native Alaskan: 0%. Asian American or Pacific Islander: 0%. African American: 3%. Latino: 0%. Caucasian: 96%. Total all graduate and professional students: 56.

Academics: Full-Time Faculty: 2,290.

Admissions: Regular Application Deadline: Rolling. Priority Application Deadline: 2/1. Early Decision Deadline: Unavailable. Transfer Priority Deadline: Unavailable. Financial Aid Deadline: Unavailable. Total Number of Students Applied: Unavailable. Percent Admitted: 85%. Number Enrolled: 5,041. Test Scores (Middle 50%): SAT Critical Reading: 490–600. SAT Math: 490–600. SAT Writing: 480–590. HS Rank of Entering Freshmen: Top 10%: 15%. Top 25%: 42%. Avg. HS GPA: Unavailable.

Cost: Tuition and Fees: In-State: $4,581. Out-of-State: $8,904. Room and Board: $0.

Inst. Aid: FT Undergrads Receiving Aid: Unavailable. Avg. Amount per Student: Unavailable.

OKLAHOMA STATE UNIVERSITY

Stillwater, OK

admissions@okstate.edu; okstate.edu

General Info: Public, University, Four-year, Coed, Regionally Accredited, North Central Association of Colleges and Schools, College Board member. Suburban setting, Small city (50,000–249,999), Residential campus. Academic Calendar: Semester.

Student Body: Full-Time Undergrads: 18,909. Men: 51%, Women: 49%. Total Undergrad Population: Native American or Native Alaskan: 9%. Asian American or Pacific Islander: 1%. African American: 4%. Latino: 2%. Caucasian: 82%. International: 1%. Out-of-State: 22%. Total all graduate and professional students: 4,262.

Academics: Full-Time Faculty: 1,020.

Admissions: Regular Application Deadline: 6/1. Priority Application Deadline: Unavailable. Early Decision Deadline: Unavailable. Transfer Priority Deadline: Unavailable. Financial Aid Deadline: Unavailable. Total Number of Students Applied: Unavailable. Percent Admitted: 87%. Number Enrolled: 3,236. Test Scores (Middle 50%): SAT Critical Reading: 490–610. SAT Math: 510–640. SAT Writing: Unavailable. ACT Comp: 22–27. HS Rank of Entering Freshmen: Top 10%: 27%. Top 25%: 55%. Avg. HS GPA: Unavailable.

Cost: Tuition and Fees: In-State: $4,997. Out-of-State: $13,569. Room and Board: $6,015.

Inst. Aid: FT Undergrads Receiving Aid: Unavailable. Avg. Amount per Student: $8,867.

OLD DOMINION UNIVERSITY

Norfolk, VA

admit@odu.edu; www.odu.edu

General Info: Public, University, Four-year, Coed, Regionally Accredited, Southern Association of Colleges and Schools, College Board member. Urban setting, Small city (50,000–249,999), Commuter campus. Academic Calendar: Semester.

Student Body: Full-Time Undergrads: 15,464. Men: 46%, Women: 54%. Total Undergrad Population: Native American or Native Alaskan: 0%. Asian American or Pacific Islander: 6%. African American: 23%. Latino: 4%. Caucasian: 58%. International: 2%. Out-of-State: 12%. Total all graduate and professional students: 6,161.

Academics: Full-Time Faculty: 663.

Admissions: Regular Application Deadline: 3/15. Priority Application Deadline: Unavailable. Early Decision Deadline: 12/1. Financial Aid Deadline: 3/15. Total Number of Students Applied: Unavailable. Percent Admitted: 69%. Number Enrolled: 2,099. Test Scores (Middle 50%): SAT Critical Reading: 480–570. SAT Math: 490–580. SAT Writing: 460–560. ACT Comp: 19–22. HS Rank of Entering Freshmen: Top 10%: 14%. Top 25%: 46%. Avg. HS GPA: Unavailable.

Cost: Tuition and Fees: In-State: $6,098. Out-of-State: $16,658. Room and Board: $6,640.

Inst. Aid: FT Undergrads Receiving Aid: Unavailable. Avg. Amount per Student: Unavailable.

ORAL ROBERTS UNIVERSITY

Tulsa, OK

admissions@oru.edu; www.oru.edu

General Info: Private, Liberal Arts College, University, Four-year, Nondenominational, Coed, Regionally Accredited, College Board member. Suburban setting, Large city (250,000–499,999), Residential campus. Academic Calendar: Semester.

Student Body: Full-Time Undergrads: 3,999. Men: 44%, Women: 56%. Total Undergrad Population: Out-of-State: 71%.

Academics: Full-Time Faculty: 179.

Admissions: Regular Application Deadline: No closing date. Priority Application Deadline: Unavailable. Early Decision Deadline: Unavailable. Transfer Priority Deadline: Unavailable. Financial Aid Deadline: Unavailable. Total Number of Students Applied: Unavailable. Percent Admitted: 67%. Number Enrolled: Unavailable. Test Scores (Middle 50%): SAT Critical Reading: 480–610. SAT Math: 480–600. SAT Writing: Unavailable. ACT Comp: 20–26. HS Rank of Entering Freshmen: Top 10%: 27%. Top 25%: 53%. Avg. HS GPA: Unavailable.

Cost: Tuition and Fees: In-State: $16,670. Out-of-State: $16,670. Room and Board: $7,060.

Inst. Aid: FT Undergrads Receiving Aid: Unavailable. Avg. Amount per Student: Unavailable.

Colleges of Vice Presidents

Al Gore—Harvard University

Dan Quayle—Depauw University

Walter Mondale—University of Minnesota

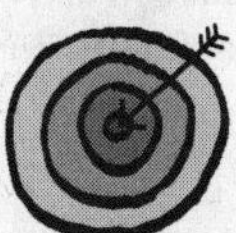

OREGON STATE UNIVERSITY

Corvallis, OR

osuadmit@orst.edu; www.oregonstate.edu

General Info: Public, University, Four-year, Coed, Regionally Accredited, Northwest Association of Schools and Colleges, College Board member. Suburban setting, Small city (50,000–249,999), Residential campus. Academic Calendar: Quarter.

Student Body: Full-Time Undergrads: 15,829. Men: Unavailable, Women: Unavailable. Total Undergrad Population: Native American or Native Alaskan: 1%. Asian American or Pacific Islander: 8%. African American: 1%. Latino: 4%. Caucasian: 78%. International: 1%. Out-of-State: 10%.

Academics: Full-Time Faculty: 760.

Admissions: Regular Application Deadline: 2/1. Priority Application Deadline: Unavailable. Early Decision Deadline: Unavailable. Transfer Priority Deadline: Unavailable. Financial Aid Deadline: 5/1. Total Number of Students Applied: Unavailable. Percent Admitted: 90%. Number Enrolled: 2,798. Test Scores (Middle 50%): SAT Critical Reading: 470–590. SAT Math: 490–610. SAT Writing: Unavailable. ACT Comp: 20–26. HS Rank of Entering Freshmen: Top 10%: 18%. Top 25%: 46%. Avg. HS GPA: Unavailable.

Cost: Tuition and Fees: In-State: $5,643. Out-of-State: $17,559. Room and Board: $7,494.

Inst. Aid: FT Undergrads Receiving Aid: Unavailable. Avg. Amount per Student: Unavailable.

PACIFIC LUTHERAN UNIVERSITY

Tacoma, WA

admission@plu.edu; www.plu.edu

General Info: Private, University, Four-year, Evangelical Lutheran Church In America, Coed, Regionally Accredited, College Board member. Suburban setting, Large city (250,000–499,999), Residential campus. Academic Calendar: 4-1-4.

Student Body: Full-Time Undergrads: 3,107. Men: 36%, Women: 64%. Total Undergrad Population: Native American or Native Alaskan: 1%. Asian American or Pacific Islander: 8%. African American: 2%. Latino: 2%. Caucasian: 72%. International: 2%. Out-of-State: 29%. Living Off-Campus: 9%. Total all graduate and professional students: 300.

Academics: Full-Time Faculty: 237.

Admissions: Regular Application Deadline: Rolling. Priority Application Deadline: 1/31. Early Decision Deadline: Unavailable. Transfer Priority Deadline: 2/15. Financial Aid Deadline: Unavailable. Total Number of Students Applied: Unavailable. Percent Admitted: 74%. Number Enrolled: 670. Test Scores (Middle 50%): SAT Critical Reading: 480–610. SAT Math: 490–590. SAT Writing: Unavailable. ACT Comp: 21–28. HS Rank of Entering Freshmen: Top 10%: 32%. Top 25%: 68%. Avg. HS GPA: Unavailable.

Cost: Tuition and Fees: In-State: $23,450. Out-of-State: $23,450. Room and Board: $7,135.

Inst. Aid: FT Undergrads Receiving Aid: Unavailable. Avg. Amount per Student: Unavailable.

PAUL SMITH'S COLLEGE

Paul Smiths, NY

admiss@paulsmiths.edu; www.paulsmiths.edu

General Info: Private, Liberal Arts College, Four-year, Coed, Regionally Accredited. Rural setting, Rural community (under 2,500), Residential campus. Academic Calendar: Semester.

Student Body: Full-Time Undergrads: 850. Men: 70%, Women: 30%. Total Undergrad Population: Native American or Native Alaskan: 0%. Asian American or Pacific Islander: 1%. African American: 3%. Latino: 2%. Caucasian: 94%. International: 0%. Out-of-State: 40%.

Academics: Full-Time Faculty: 64.

Admissions: Regular Application Deadline: 7/15. Priority Application Deadline: Unavailable. Early Decision Deadline: Unavailable. Financial Aid Deadline: Unavailable. Total Number of Students Applied: Unavailable. Percent Admitted: 84%. Number Enrolled: 308. Test Scores (Middle 50%): SAT Critical Reading: Unavailable. SAT Math: Unavailable. SAT Writing: Unavailable. ACT Comp: Unavailable. HS Rank of Entering Freshmen: Top 10%: Unavailable. Top 25%: Unavailable. Avg. HS GPA: Unavailable.

Cost: Tuition and Fees: In-State: $17,490. Out-of-State: $17,490. Room and Board: $7,420.

Inst. Aid: FT Undergrads Receiving Aid: Unavailable. Avg. Amount per Student: $14,752.

PENN STATE UNIVERSITY AT UNIVERSITY PARK

University Park, PA

admissions@psu.edu; www.psu.edu

General Info: Public, University, Four-year, Coed, Middle States Association of Colleges and Schools, Regionally Accredited, College Board member. Suburban setting, Large town (10,000–49,999), Residential campus. Academic Calendar: Semester.

Student Body: Full-Time Undergrads: 36,815. Men: 55%, Women: 45%. Total Undergrad Population: Native American or Native Alaskan: 0%. Asian American or Pacific Islander: 6%. African American: 4%. Latino: 3%. Caucasian: 85%. International: 2%. Out-of-State: 28%. Total all graduate and professional students: 6,437.

Academics: Full-Time Faculty: 2,233.

Inventors and Their Colleges

Douglas Engelbart (computer mouse)—Oregon State University

Robert H. Goddard (liquid-fueled rocket)—Worcester Polytechnic Institute

Jack Kilby (handheld calculator)—University of Illinois at Urbana-Champaign

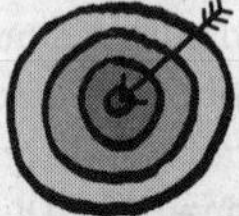

Admissions: Regular Application Deadline: 11/30. Priority Application Deadline: Unavailable. Early Decision Deadline: Unavailable. Transfer Priority Deadline: Unavailable. Financial Aid Deadline: Unavailable. Total Number of Students Applied: 39,551. Number Admitted: 20,156. Number Enrolled: 6,483. Test Scores (Middle 50%): SAT Critical Reading: 520–620. SAT Math: 560–660. SAT Writing: Unavailable. HS Rank of Entering Freshmen: Top 10%: 40%. Top 25%: 78%. Avg. HS GPA: 3.58.

Cost: Tuition and Fees: In-State: $12,164. Out-of-State: $22,712. Room and Board: $7,400.

Inst. Aid: FT Undergrads Receiving Aid: 17,029. Avg. Amount per Student: $9,035.

PEPPERDINE UNIVERSITY

Malibu, CA
admission-seaver@pepperdine.edu;
www.pepperdine.edu

General Info: Private, Liberal Arts College, University, Four-year, Church Of Christ, Coed, Regionally Accredited, College Board member. Suburban setting, Small city (50,000–249,999), Residential campus. Academic Calendar: Semester.

Student Body: Full-Time Undergrads: 3,297. Men: 46%, Women: 54%. Total Undergrad Population: Native American or Native Alaskan: 2%. Asian American or Pacific Islander: 7%. African American: 7%. Latino: 10%. Caucasian: 66%. International: 5%. Out-of-State: 48%. Total all graduate and professional students: 3,597.

Academics: Full-Time Faculty: 400.

Admissions: Regular Application Deadline: 1/15. Priority Application Deadline: 11/15. Early Decision Deadline: Unavailable. Transfer Priority Deadline: 11/15. Financial Aid Deadline: 2/15. Total Number of Students Applied: Unavailable. Percent Admitted: 28%. Number Enrolled: 794. Test Scores (Middle 50%): SAT Critical Reading: 560–670. SAT Math: 570–680. SAT Writing: Unavailable. ACT Comp: 24–29. HS Rank of Entering Freshmen: Top 10%: 43%. Top 25%: 76%. Avg. HS GPA: Unavailable.

Cost: Tuition and Fees: In-State: $32,740. Out-of-State: $32,740. Room and Board: $9,500.

Inst. Aid: FT Undergrads Receiving Aid: Unavailable. Avg. Amount per Student: $33,161.

PITZER COLLEGE

Claremont, CA
admission@pitzer.edu; www.pitzer.edu

General Info: Private, Liberal Arts College, Four-year, Coed, Regionally Accredited, College Board member. Suburban setting, Large town (10,000–49,999), Residential campus. Academic Calendar: Semester.

Student Body: Full-Time Undergrads: 950. Men: 40%, Women: 57%. Total Undergrad Population: Native American or Native Alaskan: 0%. Asian American or Pacific Islander: 10%. African American: 6%. Latino: 14%. Caucasian: 43%. International: 3%. Out-of-State: 51%.

Academics: Full-Time Faculty: 65.

Admissions: Regular Application Deadline: 1/1. Priority Application Deadline: Unavailable. Early Decision Deadline: Unavailable. Transfer Priority Deadline: Unavailable. Financial Aid Deadline: 2/1. Total Number of Students Applied: Unavailable. Percent Admitted: 37%. Number Enrolled: 240. Test Scores (Middle 50%): SAT Critical Reading: 570–680. SAT Math: 560–650. SAT Writing: Unavailable. HS Rank of Entering Freshmen: Top 10%: 45%. Top 25%: 75%. Avg. HS GPA: Unavailable.

Cost: Tuition and Fees: In-State: $34,500. Out-of-State: $34,500. Room and Board: $10,930.

Inst. Aid: FT Undergrads Receiving Aid: Unavailable. Avg. Amount per Student: Unavailable.

POMONA COLLEGE

Claremont, CA
admissions@pomona.edu; www.pomona.edu

General Info: Coed, College Board member, Four-year, Liberal Arts College, Private, Regionally Accredited. Suburban setting, Large town (10,000–49,999), Residential campus. Academic Calendar: Semester.

Student Body: Full-Time Undergrads: 1,500. Men: 50%, Women: 50%. Total Undergrad Population: Native American or Native Alaskan: 1%. Asian American or Pacific Islander: 16%. African American: 10%. Latino: 12%. Caucasian: 50%. International: 3%. Out-of-State: 69%.

Academics: Full-Time Faculty: Unavailable.

Admissions: Regular Application Deadline: 1/2. Priority Application Deadline: Unavailable. Early Decision Deadline: 11/1. Transfer Priority Deadline: Unavailable. Financial Aid Deadline: 2/1. Total Number of Students Applied: Unavailable. Percent Admitted: 17%. Number Enrolled: 378. Test Scores (Middle 50%): SAT Critical Reading: 690–770. SAT Math: 690–760. SAT Writing: 680–750. ACT Comp: 29–34. HS Rank of Entering Freshmen: Top 10%: Unavailable. Top 25%: Unavailable. Avg. HS GPA: Unavailable.

Cost: Tuition and Fees: In-State: $33,932. Out-of-State: $33,932. Room and Board: $11,748.

Inst. Aid: FT Undergrads Receiving Aid: Unavailable. Avg. Amount per Student: Unavailable.

PORTLAND STATE UNIVERSITY

Portland, OR
admissions@pdx.edu; www.pdx.edu

General Info: Public, University, Four-year, Coed, Regionally Accredited, Northwest Association of Schools and Colleges, College Board member. Urban setting, Very large city (over 500,000). Academic Calendar: Quarter.

Student Body: Full-Time Undergrads: 17,348. Men: 46%, Women: 54%. Total Undergrad Population: Native American or Native Alaskan: 1%. Asian American or Pacific Is-

Top Pre-Med Colleges

Harvard University

Stanford University

UC–Berkeley

UCLA

UVA

lander: 12%. African American: 3%. Latino: 5%. Caucasian: 62%. International: 4%. Out-of-State: 17%. Total all graduate and professional students: 6,149.

Academics: Full-Time Faculty: 739.

Admissions: Regular Application Deadline: No closing date. Priority Application Deadline: 6/1. Early Decision Deadline: Unavailable. Transfer Priority Deadline: 6/1. Financial Aid Deadline: Unavailable. Total Number of Students Applied: Unavailable. Percent Admitted: 91%. Number Enrolled: 1,493. Test Scores (Middle 50%): SAT Critical Reading: 460–590. SAT Math: 470–580. ACT Comp: 20–25. HS Rank of Entering Freshmen: Top 10%: Unavailable. Top 25%: Unavailable. Avg. HS GPA: Unavailable.

Cost: Tuition and Fees: In-State: $5,211. Out-of-State: $17,436. Room and Board: $7,177.

Inst. Aid: FT Undergrads Receiving Aid: Unavailable. Avg. Amount per Student: Unavailable.

PRINCETON UNIVERSITY

Princeton, NJ

uaoffice@Princeton.edu; www.princeton.edu

General Info: Private, University, Four-year, Coed, Regionally Accredited, College Board member. Suburban setting, Large town (10,000–49,999), Residential campus. Academic Calendar: Semester.

Student Body: Full-Time Undergrads: 4,760. Men: 53%, Women: 47%. Total Undergrad Population: Native American or Native Alaskan: 1%. Asian American or Pacific Islander: 13%. African American: 10%. Latino: 7%. Caucasian: 60%. International: 9%. Out-of-State: 84%. Total all graduate and professional students: 2,010.

Academics: Full-Time Faculty: 720.

Admissions: Regular Application Deadline: 1/1. Priority Application Deadline: Unavailable. Early Decision Deadline: 11/1. Transfer Priority Deadline: Unavailable. Financial Aid Deadline: Unavailable. Total Number of Students Applied: Unavailable. Number Admitted: Unavailable. Number Enrolled: 1,230. Test Scores (Middle 50%): SAT Critical Reading: 680–800. SAT Math: 690–790. SAT Writing: 680–770. ACT Comp: 30–34. HS Rank of Entering Freshmen: Top 10%: 94%. Top 25%: 99%. Avg. HS GPA: Unavailable.

Cost: Tuition and Fees: In-State: $33,000. Out-of-State: $33,000. Room and Board: $10,980.

Inst. Aid: FT Undergrads Receiving Aid: Unavailable. Avg. Amount per Student: Unavailable.

PROVIDENCE COLLEGE

Providence, RI

pcadmiss@providence.edu; www.providence.edu

General Info: Private, Liberal Arts College, Four-year, Roman Catholic Church, Coed, Regionally Accredited, College Board member. Residential campus, Small city (50,000–249,999), Urban setting. Academic Calendar: Semester.

Student Body: Full-Time Undergrads: 3,981. Men: 44%, Women: 56%. Total Undergrad Population: Native American or Native Alaskan: 0%. Asian American or Pacific Islander: 3%. African American: 2%. Latino: 2%. Caucasian: 83%. International: 1%. Out-of-State: 90%. Total all graduate and professional students: 837.

Academics: Full-Time Faculty: 295.

Admissions: Regular Application Deadline: 1/15. Priority Application Deadline: 4/1. Early Decision Deadline: 11/1. Transfer Priority Deadline: 4/1. Financial Aid Deadline: 2/1. Total Number of Students Applied: Unavailable. Percent Admitted: 48%. Number Enrolled: 1,027. Test Scores (Middle 50%): SAT Critical Reading: 540–640. SAT Math: 560–650. SAT Writing: 560–650. ACT Comp: 23–28. HS Rank of Entering Freshmen: Top 10%: 45%. Top 25%: 83%. Avg. HS GPA: Unavailable.

Cost: Tuition and Fees: In-State: $30,800. Out-of-State: $30,800. Room and Board: $10,810.

Inst. Aid: FT Undergrads Receiving Aid: Unavailable. Avg. Amount per Student: Unavailable.

PURDUE UNIVERSITY

West Lafayette, IN

admissions@purdue.edu; www.purdue.edu

General Info: Public, University, Four-year, Coed, Regionally Accredited, North Central Association of Colleges and Schools, College Board member. Suburban setting, Small city (50,000–249,999), Residential campus. Academic Calendar: Semester.

Student Body: Full-Time Undergrads: 31,186. Men: 58%, Women: 42%. Part-Time Undergrads. Men: 2%, Women: 3%. Total Undergrad Population: Native American or Native Alaskan: 0.5%. Asian American or Pacific Islander: 5.9%. African American: 4.1%. Latino: 3.2%. Caucasian: 73.5%. International: 12.8%. Out-of-State: 41%. Living

Off-Campus: 65%. Total all graduate and professional students: 7,916.

Academics: Full-Time Faculty: 2,387. With PhD: 1,777. Percentage completing two or more majors: 3%. Graduation Rates: 40% within 4 years. 71% within 6 years.

Admissions: Regular Application Deadline: Rolling Admissions begin 9/15. Priority Application Deadline: Unavailable. Early Decision Deadline: Unavailable. Financial Aid Deadline: Unavailable. Total Number of Students Applied: 25,929. Percent Admitted: 85%. Number Enrolled: 8,097. Test Scores (Middle 50%): SAT Critical Reading: 490–600. SAT Math: 530–650. SAT Writing: Unavailable. ACT Comp: 22–28. HS Rank of Entering Freshmen: Top 10%: 27%. Top 25%: 58%. Avg. HS GPA: 3.5.

Cost: Tuition and Fees: In-State: $7,317. Out-of-State: $22,791. Room and Board: $7,530.

Inst. Aid: FT Undergrads Receiving Aid: 23,897. Avg. Amount per Student: $ 12,720.

Graduates: Percentage of grads accepting a job at time of graduation: 76.6%. Alumni Giving %: 15.1%.

QUINNIPIAC UNIVERSITY

Hamden, CT

admissions@quinnipiac.edu; www.quinnipiac.edu

General Info: Private, University, Four-year, Coed, Regionally Accredited, College Board member. Suburban setting, Small city (50,000–249,999), Residential campus. Academic Calendar: Semester.

Student Body: Full-Time Undergrads: 5,422. Men: 40%, Women: 60%. Total Undergrad Population: Out-of-State: 75%. Total all graduate and professional students: 1,061.

Academics: Full-Time Faculty: 290.

Admissions: Regular Application Deadline: 2/1. Priority Application Deadline: Unavailable. Early Decision Deadline: Unavailable. Transfer Priority Deadline: 4/1. Financial Aid Deadline: Unavailable. Total Number of Students Applied: Unavailable. Percent Admitted: 58%. Number Enrolled: 1,425. Test Scores (Middle 50%): SAT Critical Reading: 540–610. SAT Math: 560–630. SAT Writing: Unavailable. ACT Comp: 23–27. HS Rank of Entering Freshmen: Top 10%: 22%. Top 25%: 55%. Avg. HS GPA: Unavailable.

Cost: Tuition and Fees: In-State: $28,720. Out-of-State: $28,720. Room and Board: $11,200.

Inst. Aid: FT Undergrads Receiving Aid: Unavailable. Avg. Amount per Student: $15,201.

RANDOLPH-MACON COLLEGE

Ashland, VA

admissions@rmc.edu; www.rmc.edu

General Info: Private, Liberal Arts College, Four-year, United Methodist Church, Coed, Regionally Accredited, College Board member. Suburban setting, Small town (2,500–9,999), Residential campus. Academic Calendar: 4-1-4.

Famous Athletes and Their Colleges

Michael Jordan—University of North Carolina

Joe Montana—University of Notre Dame

Michelle Wie—Stanford University

Student Body: Full-Time Undergrads: 1,150. Men: 43%, Women: 57%. Total Undergrad Population: Native American or Native Alaskan: 1%. Asian American or Pacific Islander: 3%. African American: 7%. Latino: 2%. Caucasian: 87%. International: 1%. Out-of-State: 30%.

Academics: Full-Time Faculty: 72.

Admissions: Regular Application Deadline: 3/1. Priority Application Deadline: 2/1. Early Decision Deadline: 12/1. Transfer Priority Deadline: 2/1. Financial Aid Deadline: 3/1. Total Number of Students Applied: Unavailable. Percent Admitted: 58%. Number Enrolled: 398. Test Scores (Middle 50%): SAT Critical Reading: 490–590. SAT Math: 490–590. SAT Writing: 480–580. HS Rank of Entering Freshmen: Top 10%: 32%. Top 25%: 68%. Avg. HS GPA: Unavailable.

Cost: Tuition and Fees: In-State: $25,345. Out-of-State: $25,345. Room and Board: $7,695.

Inst. Aid: FT Undergrads Receiving Aid: Unavailable. Avg. Amount per Student: $20,122.

REED COLLEGE

Portland, OR

admission@reed.edu; www.reed.edu

General Info: Private, Liberal Arts College, Four-year, Coed, Northwest Association of Schools and Colleges, Regionally Accredited, College Board member. Suburban setting, Very large city (over 500,000), Residential campus. Academic Calendar: Semester.

Student Body: Full-Time Undergrads: 1,407. Men: 45%, Women: 55%. Total Undergrad Population: Native American or Native Alaskan: 2%. Asian American or Pacific Islander: 8%. African American: 3%. Latino: 6%. Caucasian: 61%. International: 5%. Out-of-State: 93%. Total all graduate and professional students: 29.

Academics: Full-Time Faculty: 119.

Admissions: Regular Application Deadline: 1/15. Priority Application Deadline: Unavailable. Early Decision Deadline: 11/15. Transfer Priority Deadline: 3/1. Financial Aid Deadline: 1/15. Total Number of Students Applied: Unavailable. Percent Admitted: 40%. Number Enrolled: 377. Test Scores (Middle 50%): SAT Critical Reading: 660–750. SAT Math: 620–710. SAT Writing: 640–730. ACT Comp: 28–32. HS Rank of Entering Freshmen: Top 10%: 67%. Top 25%: 89%. Avg. HS GPA: Unavailable.

Cost: Tuition and Fees: In-State: $36,420. Out-of-State: $34,530. Room and Board: $9,460.

Inst. Aid: FT Undergrads Receiving Aid: Unavailable. Avg. Amount per Student: $31,201.

RENSSELAER POLYTECHNIC INSTITUTE

Troy, NY
admissions@rpi.edu; www.rpi.edu

General Info: Private, University, Four-year, Coed, Regionally Accredited, College Board member. Suburban setting, Small city (50,000–249,999), Residential campus. Academic Calendar: Semester.

Student Body: Full-Time Undergrads: 5,193. Men: 75%, Women: 25%. Total Undergrad Population: Native American or Native Alaskan: 0%. Asian American or Pacific Islander: 12%. African American: 3%. Latino: 5%. Caucasian: 76%. International: 1%. Out-of-State: 61%. Total all graduate and professional students: 2,240.

Academics: Full-Time Faculty: 393.

Admissions: Regular Application Deadline: 1/1. Priority Application Deadline: Unavailable. Early Decision Deadline: 11/1. Financial Aid Deadline: 2/15. Total Number of Students Applied: Unavailable. Percent Admitted: 67%. Number Enrolled: 1,270. Test Scores (Middle 50%): SAT Critical Reading: 580–680. SAT Math: 640–740. SAT Writing: 560–660. ACT Comp: 25–29. HS Rank of Entering Freshmen: Top 10%: 62%. Top 25%: 95%. Avg. HS GPA: Unavailable.

Cost: Tuition and Fees: In-State: $35,878. Out-of-State: $33,496. Room and Board: $10,420.

Inst. Aid: FT Undergrads Receiving Aid: Unavailable. Avg. Amount per Student: $27,220.

RHODE ISLAND SCHOOL OF DESIGN

Providence, RI
admissions@risd.edu; www.risd.edu

General Info: Private, College of Art, Four-year, Coed, Regionally Accredited, College Board member. Urban setting, Small city (50,000–249,999), Residential campus. Academic Calendar: 4-1-4.

Student Body: Full-Time Undergrads: 1,863. Men: 35%, Women: 65%. Total Undergrad Population: Native American or Native Alaskan: 1%. Asian American or Pacific Islander: 14%. African American: 2%. Latino: 5%. Caucasian: 40%. International: 13%. Out-of-State: 94%. Total all graduate and professional students: 380.

Academics: Full-Time Faculty: 146.

Admissions: Regular Application Deadline: 2/15. Priority Application Deadline: Unavailable. Early Decision Deadline: Unavailable. Transfer Priority Deadline: Unavailable. Financial Aid Deadline: 2/15. Total Number of Students Applied: Unavailable. Percent Admitted: 33%. Number Enrolled: 422. Test Scores (Middle 50%): SAT Critical Reading: 530–650. SAT Math: 570–680. SAT Writing: Unavailable. ACT Comp: Unavailable. HS Rank of Entering Freshmen: Top 10%: 50%. Top 25%: 79%. Avg. HS GPA: Unavailable.

Cost: Tuition and Fees: In-State: $33,118. Out-of-State: $31,430. Room and Board: $9,860.

Inst. Aid: FT Undergrads Receiving Aid: Unavailable. Avg. Amount per Student: $12,050.

RHODES COLLEGE

Memphis, TN
adminfo@rhodes.edu; www.rhodes.edu

General Info: Private, Liberal Arts College, Four-year, Presbyterian Church (USA), Coed, Regionally Accredited, College Board member. Urban setting, Very large city (over 500,000), Residential campus. Academic Calendar: Semester.

Student Body: Full-Time Undergrads: 1,687. Men: 41%, Women: 57.6%. Total Undergrad Population: Native American or Native Alaskan: 0.2%. Asian American or Pacific Islander: 5%. African American: 5.8%. Latino: 1.6%. Caucasian: 81.9%. International: 0.7%. Out-of-State: 73%. Living Off-Campus: 24%. % In Fraternities: 45%. % In Sororities: 51%. Total all graduate and professional students: 13.

Strong Political Science Schools

Georgetown University

George Washington University

Columbia University

University of Chicago

Academics: Full-Time Faculty: 137. With PhD: 147. Graduation Rates: 70% within 4 years. 74.4% within 6 years.

Admissions: Regular Application Deadline: No closing date. Priority Application Deadline: 1/15. Early Decision Deadline: 11/1. Transfer Priority Deadline: 1/15. Financial Aid Deadline: 1/15. Total Number of Students Applied: 3,709. Number Admitted: 1,887. Number Enrolled: 454. Number accepting place on waitlist: 178. Number of waitlisted students admitted: 45. Number applied early decision: 140. Early decision admitted: 67. Test Scores (Middle 50%): SAT Critical Reading: 590–690. SAT Math: 590–690. SAT Writing: Unavailable. ACT Comp: 26–30. HS Rank of Entering Freshmen: Top 10%: 51%. Top 25%: 83%. Avg. HS GPA: 3.81.

Cost: Tuition and Fees: In-State: $30,342. Out-of-State: $30,342. Room and Board: $7,468.

Inst. Aid: FT Undergrads Receiving Aid: 659. Avg. Amount per Student: $22,891. Freshmen Receiving Non-Need Scholarship or Grant: 180. Avg. Amount per Student: $11,891.

Extensive Services for Disabled Individuals

University of Illinois, Urbana-Champaign

Wayne State University

Florida State University

University of California–Berkeley

RICE UNIVERSITY

Houston, TX

admi@rice.edu; www.rice.edu

General Info: Private, University, Four-year, Coed, Regionally Accredited, College Board member. Urban setting, Very large city (over 500,000), Residential campus. Academic Calendar: Semester.

Student Body: Full-Time Undergrads: 3,001. Men: 51%, Women: 49%. Total Undergrad Population: Native American or Native Alaskan: 1%. Asian American or Pacific Islander: 19%. African American: 7%. Latino: 12%. Caucasian: 52%. International: 5%. Out-of-State: 54%. Living Off-Campus: 23%. Total all graduate and professional students: 2,144.

Academics: Full-Time Faculty: 567. With PhD: 546. Percentage completing two or more majors: 25%.

Admissions: Regular Application Deadline: 1/2. Priority Application Deadline: Unavailable. Early Decision Deadline: 11/1. Fall Transfer Deadline: 03/15. Spring Transfer Deadline: 10/15. Transfer Priority Deadline: Unavailable. Financial Aid Deadline: Unavailable. Total Number of Students Applied: 8,968. Number Admitted: 2,251. Number Enrolled: 742. Number applied early decision: 520. Early decision admitted: 156. Test Scores (Middle 50%): SAT Critical Reading: 640–750. SAT Math: 670–780. SAT Writing: 640–730. ACT Comp: 29–34. HS Rank of Entering Freshmen: Top 10%: 83%. Top 25%: 95%. Avg. HS GPA: Unavailable.

Cost: Tuition and Fees: In-State: $29,960. Out-of-State: $29,960. Room and Board: $10,725.

Inst. Aid: FT Undergrads Receiving Aid: 1,008. Avg. Amount per Student: $20,721.

Graduates: Alumni Giving %: 34%.

RIPON COLLEGE

Ripon, WI

adminfo@ripon.edu; www.ripon.edu

General Info: Private, Liberal Arts College, Four-year, Coed, Regionally Accredited, College Board member. Rural setting, Small town (2,500–9,999), Residential campus. Academic Calendar: Semester.

Student Body: Full-Time Undergrads: 1,000. Men: 42%, Women: 58%. Total Undergrad Population: Native American or Native Alaskan: 1%. Asian American or Pacific Islander: 1%. African American: 2%. Latino: 3%. Caucasian: 86%. International: 2%. Out-of-State: 29%. Living Off-Campus: 90%.

Academics: Full-Time Faculty: 52. Percentage completing two or more majors: 40%.

Admissions: Regular Application Deadline: 8/1. Priority Application Deadline: 12/15. Early Decision Deadline: Unavailable. Transfer Priority Deadline: Unavailable. Financial Aid Deadline: Unavailable. Total Number of Students Applied: Unavailable. Percent Admitted: 78%. Number Enrolled: 264. Test Scores (Middle 50%): SAT Critical Reading: 490–620. SAT Math: 480–610. SAT Writing: Unavailable. ACT Comp: 21–28. HS Rank of Entering Freshmen: Top 10%: 22%. Top 25%: 57%. Avg. HS GPA: 3.0.

Cost: Tuition and Fees: In-State: $23,048. Out-of-State: $23,048. Room and Board: $6,410.

Inst. Aid: FT Undergrads Receiving Aid: Unavailable. Avg. Amount per Student: Unavailable.

Graduates: Alumni Giving %: 40%.

ROCHESTER INSTITUTE OF TECHNOLOGY

Rochester, NY
admissions@rit.edu; www.rit.edu

General Info: Private, University, Four-year, Coed, Regionally Accredited, College Board member. Suburban setting, Large city (250,000–499,999), Residential campus. Academic Calendar: Quarter.

Student Body: Full-Time Undergrads: 13,140. Men: 71%, Women: 29%. Total Undergrad Population: Out-of-State: 50%. Total all graduate and professional students: 2,417.

Academics: Full-Time Faculty: 947.

Admissions: Regular Application Deadline: 2/1. Priority Application Deadline: Unavailable. Early Decision Deadline: 12/1. Financial Aid Deadline: 3/1. Total Number of Students Applied: Unavailable. Number Admitted: Unavailable. Number Enrolled: Unavailable. Test Scores (Middle 50%): SAT Critical Reading: 530–630. SAT Math: 570–670. SAT Writing: Unavailable. ACT Comp: 23–28. HS Rank of Entering Freshmen: Top 10%: Unavailable. Top 25%: Unavailable. Avg. HS GPA: Unavailable.

Cost: Tuition and Fees: In-State: $25,011. Out-of-State: $25,011. Room and Board: $8,748.

Inst. Aid: FT Undergrads Receiving Aid: Unavailable. Avg. Amount per Student: Unavailable.

ROLLINS COLLEGE

Winter Park, FL
admission@rollins.edu; www.rollins.edu

General Info: Private, Liberal Arts College, Four-year, Coed, Regionally Accredited, College Board member. Suburban setting, Large town (10,000–49,999), Residential campus. Academic Calendar: Semester.

Student Body: Full-Time Undergrads: 1,720. Men: 40%, Women: 60%. Total Undergrad Population: Native American or Native Alaskan: 0%. Asian American or Pacific Islander: 5%. African American: 3%. Latino: 10%. Caucasian: 73%. International: 2%. Out-of-State: 54%. Total all graduate and professional students: 734.

Academics: Full-Time Faculty: 195.

Admissions: Regular Application Deadline: 2/15. Priority Application Deadline: Unavailable. Early Decision Deadline: 11/15. Transfer Priority Deadline: 4/1. Financial Aid Deadline: 3/1. Total Number of Students Applied: Unavailable. Percent Admitted: 56%. Number Enrolled: 501. Test Scores (Middle 50%): SAT Critical Reading: 550–630. SAT Math: 550–630. SAT Writing: Unavailable. ACT Comp: 23–27. HS Rank of Entering Freshmen: Top 10%: 65%. Top 25%: 35%. Avg. HS GPA: Unavailable.

Cost: Tuition and Fees: In-State: $30,860. Out-of-State: $30,860. Room and Board: $9,626.

Inst. Aid: FT Undergrads Receiving Aid: Unavailable. Avg. Amount per Student: $30,213.

ROSE-HULMAN INSTITUTE OF TECHNOLOGY

Terre Haute, IN
admis.ofc@rose-hulman.edu; www.rose-hulman.edu

General Info: Private, College of Engineering, Four-year, Coed, Regionally Accredited, College Board member. Suburban setting, Small city (50,000–249,999), Residential campus. Academic Calendar: Quarter.

Student Body: Full-Time Undergrads: 1,862. Men: 79%, Women: 21%. Total Undergrad Population: Native American or Native Alaskan: 0%. Asian American or Pacific Islander: 4%. African American: 1%. Latino: 1%. Caucasian: 93%. International: 1%. Out-of-State: 61%. Total all graduate and professional students: 101.

Academics: Full-Time Faculty: 154.

Admissions: Regular Application Deadline: 3/1. Priority Application Deadline: Unavailable. Early Decision Deadline: Unavailable. Transfer Priority Deadline: Unavailable. Financial Aid Deadline: Unavailable. Total Number of Students Applied: Unavailable. Percent Admitted: 72%. Number Enrolled: 525. Test Scores (Middle 50%): SAT Critical Reading: 570–670. SAT Math: 640–720. SAT Writing: 540–640. ACT Comp: 27–31. HS Rank of Entering Freshmen: Top 10%: 63%. Top 25%: 93%. Avg. HS GPA: Unavailable.

Cost: Tuition and Fees: In-State: $30,768. Out-of-State: $29,040. Room and Board: $8,343.

Inst. Aid: FT Undergrads Receiving Aid: Unavailable. Avg. Amount per Student: $25,411.

RUTGERS, THE STATE UNIVERSITY OF NEW JERSEY

New Brunswick, NJ
admissions@ugadm.rutgers.edu; www.rutgers.edu

General Info: Public, University, Four-year, Coed, Regionally Accredited, Middle States Association of Colleges and Schools. Urban setting, Large city (250,000–499,999), Commuter campus. Academic Calendar: Semester.

Student Body: Full-Time Undergrads: 6,503. Men: 44%, Women: 56%. Total Undergrad Population: Native American or Native Alaskan: 0%. Asian American or Pacific Islander: 28%. African American: 15%. Latino: 19%. Caucasian: 30%. International: 2%. Out-of-State: 7%. Total all graduate and professional students: 2,885.

Academics: Full-Time Faculty: 467.

Admissions: Regular Application Deadline: 4/15. Priority Application Deadline: Unavailable. Early Decision Deadline: Unavailable. Transfer Priority Deadline: 1/15. Financial Aid Deadline: Unavailable. Total Number of Students Applied: Unavailable. Percent Admitted: 46%. Number Enrolled: 1,211. Test Scores (Middle 50%): SAT Critical Reading: 480–570. SAT Math: 510–620. SAT Writing: 490–580. HS Rank of Entering Freshmen: Top 10%: 30%. Top 25%: 64%. Avg. HS GPA: Unavailable.

Cost: Tuition and Fees: In-State: $9,958. Out-of-State: $18,039. Room and Board: $9,312.

Inst. Aid: FT Undergrads Receiving Aid: Unavailable. Avg. Amount per Student: $11,960.

SAINT MICHAEL'S COLLEGE

Colchester, VT

admission@smcvt.edu; www.smcvt.edu

General Info: Coed, College Board member, Four-year, Liberal Arts College, Private, Regionally Accredited, Roman Catholic Church. Large town (10,000–49,999), Residential campus, Suburban setting, Less than 3 miles from the city of Burlington. Academic Calendar: Semester.

Student Body: Full-Time Undergrads: 1,992. Men: 46%, Women: 54%. Total Undergrad Population: Native American or Native Alaskan: 0%. Asian American or Pacific Islander: 1%. African American: 1%. Latino: 1%. Caucasian: 94%. International: 2%. Out-of-State: 80%. Total all graduate and professional students: 600.

Academics: Full-Time Faculty: 150. With PhD: 125.

Admissions: Regular Application Deadline: 2/1. Priority Application Deadline: 11/1. Early Decision Deadline: Unavailable. Fall Transfer Deadline: 11/1. Spring Transfer Deadline: 3/15. Transfer Priority Deadline: Unavailable. Financial Aid Deadline: 2/15. Total Number of Students Applied: 3,605. Number Admitted: 2,500. Number Enrolled: Unavailable. Test Scores (Middle 50%): SAT Critical Reading: 530–630. SAT Math: 530–630. SAT Writing: 530–630. ACT Comp: 24-26. HS Rank of Entering Freshmen: Top 10%: 26%. Top 25%: 57%. Avg. HS GPA: 3.2.

Cost: Tuition and Fees: In-State: $31,675. Out-of-State: $31,675. Room and Board: $7,960.

Inst. Aid: FT Undergrads Receiving Aid: Unavailable. Avg. Amount per Student: Unavailable.

Graduates: No. of companies recruiting on campus: 100.

SALISBURY UNIVERSITY

Salisbury, MD

admissions@salisbury.edu; www.salisbury.edu

General Info: Public, Liberal Arts College, University, Four-year, Coed, Regionally Accredited, Middle States Association of Colleges and Schools, College Board member. Rural setting, Large town (10,000–49,999), Residential campus. Academic Calendar: 4-1-4.

Student Body: Full-Time Undergrads: 6,791. Men: 43%, Women: 57%. Total Undergrad Population: Native American or Native Alaskan: 0%. Asian American or Pacific Islander: 3%. African American: 12%. Latino: 3%. Caucasian: 80%. International: 1%. Out-of-State: 17%. Total all graduate and professional students: 592.

Academics: Full-Time Faculty: 337.

Admissions: Regular Application Deadline: 1/15. Priority Application Deadline: 12/1. Early Decision Deadline: Unavailable. Transfer Priority Deadline: Unavailable. Financial Aid Deadline: 3/1. Total Number of Students Applied: Unavailable. Percent Admitted: 55%. Number Enrolled: 956. Test Scores (Middle 50%): SAT Critical Reading: 510–590. SAT Math: 510–600. SAT Writing: 500–580. ACT Comp: 20–25. HS Rank of Entering Freshmen: Top 10%: 18%. Top 25%: 50%. Avg. HS GPA: Unavailable.

Cost: Tuition and Fees: In-State: $6,412. Out-of-State: $14,306. Room and Board: $7,246.

Inst. Aid: FT Undergrads Receiving Aid: Unavailable. Avg. Amount per Student: Unavailable.

Conservative Colleges

Grove City College

Brigham Young University

Wheaton College

SAMFORD UNIVERSITY

Birmingham, AL

admiss@samford.edu; www.samford.edu

General Info: Private, University, Four-year, Southern Baptist Convention, Coed, Regionally Accredited, College Board member. Suburban setting, Very large city (over 500,000), Residential campus. Academic Calendar: 4-1-4.

Student Body: Full-Time Undergrads: 2,882. Men: 40%, Women: 60%. Total Undergrad Population: Native American or Native Alaskan: 0%. Asian American or Pacific Islander: 1%. African American: 5%. Latino: 1%. Caucasian: 92%. Out-of-State: 63%. Total all graduate and professional students: 457.

Academics: Full-Time Faculty: 280.

Admissions: Regular Application Deadline: 5/1. Priority Application Deadline: 3/1. Early Decision Deadline: Unavailable. Transfer Priority Deadline: 3/1. Financial Aid Deadline: Unavailable. Total Number of Students Applied: Unavailable. Percent Admitted: 86%. Number Enrolled: 644. Test Scores (Middle 50%): SAT Critical Reading: 510–630. SAT Math: 520–630. SAT Writing: Unavailable. ACT Comp: 22–27. HS Rank of Entering Freshmen: Top 10%: 40%. Top 25%: 65%. Avg. HS GPA: Unavailable.

Cost: Tuition and Fees: In-State: $19,300. Out-of-State: $19,300. Room and Board: $6,297.

Inst. Aid: FT Undergrads Receiving Aid: Unavailable. Avg. Amount per Student: Unavailable.

SAN DIEGO STATE UNIVERSITY

San Diego, CA
admissions@sdsu.edu; www.sdsu.edu

General Info: Public, University, Four-year, Coed, Regionally Accredited, Western Association of Schools and Colleges, College Board member, Hispanic serving. Urban setting, Very large city (over 500,000), Commuter campus. Academic Calendar: Semester.

Student Body: Full-Time Undergrads: 28,527. Men: 39%, Women: 61%. Total Undergrad Population: Native American or Native Alaskan: 1%. Asian American or Pacific Islander: 18%. African American: 4%. Latino: 21%. Caucasian: 48%. International: 1%. Out-of-State: 5%. Total all graduate and professional students: 5,843.

Academics: Full-Time Faculty: 919.

Admissions: Regular Application Deadline: 11/30. Priority Application Deadline: Unavailable. Early Decision Deadline: Unavailable. Transfer Priority Deadline: Unavailable. Financial Aid Deadline: Unavailable. Total Number of Students Applied: Unavailable. Percent Admitted: 44%. Number Enrolled: 4,670. Test Scores (Middle 50%): SAT Critical Reading: 480–580. SAT Math: 500–600. SAT Writing: Unavailable. ACT Comp: 20–25. HS Rank of Entering Freshmen: Top 10%: Unavailable. Top 25%: Unavailable. Avg. HS GPA: Unavailable.

Cost: Tuition and Fees: In-State: $3,122. Out-of-State: $13,292. Room and Board: $10,093.

Inst. Aid: FT Undergrads Receiving Aid: Unavailable. Avg. Amount per Student: $6,100.

Liberal Colleges

Bard College

Reed College

Sarah Lawrence College

SANTA CLARA UNIVERSITY

Santa Clara, CA
www.scu.edu

General Info: Private, University, Four-year, Roman Catholic Church, Society of Jesus (Jesuits), Coed, Regionally Accredited, College Board member. Suburban setting, Small city (50,000–249,999), Residential campus. Academic Calendar: Quarter.

Student Body: Full-Time Undergrads: 4,613. Men: 45%, Women: 55%. Total Undergrad Population: Native American or Native Alaskan: 0%. Asian American or Pacific Islander: 16%. African American: 3%. Latino: 12%. Caucasian: 52%. International: 2%. Out-of-State: 44%. Total all graduate and professional students: 2,392.

Academics: Full-Time Faculty: 447.

Admissions: Regular Application Deadline: 1/15. Priority Application Deadline: Unavailable. Early Decision Deadline: Unavailable. Financial Aid Deadline: Unavailable. Total Number of Students Applied: Unavailable. Percent Admitted: 66%. Number Enrolled: 1,339. Test Scores (Middle 50%): SAT Critical Reading: Unavailable. SAT Math: 560–670. SAT Writing: 550–650. ACT Comp: 24–29. HS Rank of Entering Freshmen: Top 10%: 40%. Top 25%: 72%. Avg. HS GPA: Unavailable.

Cost: Tuition and Fees: In-State: $30,900. Out-of-State: $30,900. Room and Board: $10,380.

Inst. Aid: FT Undergrads Receiving Aid: Unavailable. Avg. Amount per Student: Unavailable.

SARAH LAWRENCE COLLEGE

Bronxville, NY
slcadmit@sarahlawrence.edu; www.sarahlawrence.edu

General Info: Private, Liberal Arts College, Four-year, Coed, Regionally Accredited, College Board member. Suburban setting, Small city (50,000–249,999), Residential campus. Academic Calendar: Semester.

Student Body: Full-Time Undergrads: 1,391. Men: 25%, Women: 75%. Total Undergrad Population: Native American or Native Alaskan: 1%. Asian American or Pacific Islander: 4%. African American: 4%. Latino: 5%. Caucasian: 68%. International: 2%. Out-of-State: 82%. Total all graduate and professional students: 318.

Academics: Full-Time Faculty: 188.

Admissions: Regular Application Deadline: 1/1. Priority Application Deadline: Unavailable. Early Decision Deadline: 11/15. Transfer Priority Deadline: 3/1. Financial Aid Deadline: 2/1. Total Number of Students Applied: Unavailable. Percent Admitted: 46%. Number Enrolled: 382. Test Scores (Middle 50%): SAT Critical Reading: Unavailable. SAT Math: Unavailable. SAT Writing: Unavailable. HS Rank of Entering Freshmen: Top 10%: 33%. Top 25%: 72%. Avg. HS GPA: Unavailable.

Cost: Tuition and Fees: In-State: $36,088. Out-of-State: $36,088. Room and Board: $12,152.

Inst. Aid: FT Undergrads Receiving Aid: Unavailable. Avg. Amount per Student: $27,188.

SAVANNAH COLLEGE OF ART AND DESIGN

Savannah, GA

admission@scad.edu; www.scad.edu

General Info: Coed, College Board member, College of Art, Four-year, Private, Regionally Accredited, Southern Association of Colleges and Schools. Commuter campus, Small city (50,000–249,999), Urban setting. Academic Calendar: Quarter.

Student Body: Full-Time Undergrads: 6,913. Men: 45%, Women: 55%. Part-Time Undergrads. Men: 46%, Women: 54%. Total Undergrad Population: Native American or Native Alaskan: 0.32%. Asian American or Pacific Islander: 2.03%. African American: 5.21%. Latino: 3%. Caucasian: 38.17%. International: 7.33%. Out-of-State: 81%. Living Off-Campus: 63%. Total all graduate and professional students: 1,323.

Academics: Full-Time Faculty: 423. With PhD: 86. Percentage completing two or more majors: 3%. Graduation Rates: 58% within 4 years. 65% within 6 years.

Admissions: Regular Application Deadline: 8/1. Priority Application Deadline: 4/1. Early Decision Deadline: N/A. Fall Transfer Deadline: 8/1. Spring Transfer Deadline: 12/1. Transfer Priority Deadline: 4/15. Financial Aid Deadline: 8/1. Total Number of Students Applied: 6,426. Number Admitted: 3,460. Number Enrolled: 1,603. Test Scores (Middle 50%): SAT Critical Reading: 500–600. SAT Math: 480–590. SAT Writing: 480–590. ACT Comp: 21-27. HS Rank of Entering Freshmen: Top 10%: 20%. Top 25%: 38%. Avg. HS GPA: 3.34.

Cost: Tuition and Fees: In-State: $25,965. Out-of-State: $25,965. Room and Board: $10,585.

Inst. Aid: FT Undergrads Receiving Aid: 3,407. Avg. Amount per Student: $12,500. Freshmen Receiving Non-Need Scholarship or Grant: 782. Avg. Amount per Student: $10,000.

Graduates: No. of companies recruiting on campus: 100.

SCHOOL OF THE ART INSTITUTE OF CHICAGO

Chicago, IL

admiss@artic.edu; www.artic.edu/saic/

General Info: Private, College of Art, Four-year, Coed, Regionally Accredited, College Board member. Urban setting, Very large city (over 500,000), Commuter campus. Academic Calendar: Semester.

Student Body: Full-Time Undergrads: 2,008. Men: 33%, Women: 67%. Total Undergrad Population: Native American or Native Alaskan: 1%. Asian American or Pacific Islander: 11%. African American: 3%. Latino: 8%. Caucasian: 58%. International: 16%. Out-of-State: 81%. Total all graduate and professional students: 580.

Academics: Full-Time Faculty: 124.

Admissions: Regular Application Deadline: 3/15. Priority Application Deadline: 2/1. Early Decision Deadline: Unavailable. Transfer Priority Deadline: 3/1. Financial Aid Deadline: Unavailable. Total Number of Students Applied: Unavailable. Number Admitted: Unavailable. Number Enrolled: Unavailable. Test Scores (Middle 50%): SAT Critical Reading: Unavailable. SAT Math: Unavailable. SAT Writing: Unavailable. HS Rank of Entering Freshmen: Top 10%: Unavailable. Top 25%: Unavailable. Avg. HS GPA: Unavailable.

Cost: Tuition and Fees: In-State: $30,750. Out-of-State: $30,750. Room and Board: $7,200.

Inst. Aid: FT Undergrads Receiving Aid: Unavailable. Avg. Amount per Student: $17,189.

SCHOOL OF THE MUSEUM OF FINE ARTS

Boston, MA

admissions@smfa.edu; www.smfa.edu

General Info: Private, College of Art, Four-year, Coed. Urban setting, Very large city (over 500,000), Commuter campus. Academic Calendar: Semester.

Student Body: Full-Time Undergrads: 634. Men: 36%, Women: 64%. Total Undergrad Population: Native American or Native Alaskan: 0%. Asian American or Pacific Islander: 1%. African American: 0%. Latino: 4%. Caucasian: 70%. International: 5%. Out-of-State: 76%. Total all graduate and professional students: 99.

Academics: Full-Time Faculty: 51.

Admissions: Regular Application Deadline: 2/1. Priority Application Deadline: 2/1. Early Decision Deadline: Unavailable. Fall Transfer Deadline: 3/1. Transfer Priority Deadline: 3/1. Financial Aid Deadline: Unavailable. Total Number of Students Applied: Unavailable. Percent Admitted: 78%. Number Enrolled: 123. Test Scores (Middle 50%): SAT Critical Reading: 510–630. SAT Math: 470–560. SAT Writing: 490–620. ACT Comp: 23–27. HS Rank of Entering Freshmen: Top 10%: Unavailable. Top 25%: Unavailable. Avg. HS GPA: Unavailable.

Cost: Tuition and Fees: In-State: $26,244. Out-of-State: $26,244. Room and Board: $0.

Inst. Aid: FT Undergrads Receiving Aid: Unavailable. Avg. Amount per Student: $14,877.

SCRIPPS COLLEGE

Claremont, CA

admission@scrippscollege.edu; www.scrippscollege.edu

General Info: College Board member, Four-year, Liberal Arts College, Private, Regionally Accredited, Women Only. Suburban setting, Large town (10,000–49,999), Residential campus. Academic Calendar: Semester.

Student Body: Full-Time Undergrads: 869. Men: 0%, Women: 100%. Total Undergrad Population: Native American or Native Alaskan: 1%. Asian American or Pacific Islander: 13%. African American: 4%. Latino: 8%. Caucasian: 51%. International: 1%. Out-of-State: 59%. Living Off-Campus: 5%. Total all graduate and professional students: 21.

College World Series (Baseball) Champions

2003: Rice University

2004: Cal State Fullerton

2005: University of Texas at Austin

2006: Oregon State University

2007: Oregon State University

Academics: Full-Time Faculty: 62.

Admissions: Regular Application Deadline: 1/1. Priority Application Deadline: Unavailable. Early Decision Deadline: 11/1 or 1/1. Fall Transfer Deadline: 4/1. Spring Transfer Deadline: 11/1. Transfer Priority Deadline: Unavailable. Financial Aid Deadline: 2/1. Total Number of Students Applied: 1,969. Number Admitted: 844. Number Enrolled: 227. Number accepting place on waitlist: 201. Test Scores (Middle 50%): SAT Critical Reading: 650–740. SAT Math: 630–700. SAT Writing: Unavailable. ACT Comp: 27–30. HS Rank of Entering Freshmen: Top 10%: 72%. Top 25%: 95%. Avg. HS GPA: 4.

Cost: Tuition and Fees: In-State: $37,736. Out-of-State: $37,736. Room and Board: $11,500.

Inst. Aid: FT Undergrads Receiving Aid: 359. Avg. Amount per Student: $30,842. Freshmen Receiving Non-Need Scholarship or Grant: 10. Avg. Amount per Student: $17,818.

Graduates: Alumni Giving %: 52.8%.

SEATTLE UNIVERSITY

Seattle, WA
admissions@seattleu.edu; www.seattleu.edu

General Info: Private, University, Four-year, Roman Catholic Church, Society of Jesus (Jesuits), Coed, Regionally Accredited, College Board member. Urban setting, Very large city (over 500,000), Residential campus. Academic Calendar: Quarter.

Student Body: Full-Time Undergrads: 4,160. Men: 39%, Women: 61%. Total Undergrad Population: Native American or Native Alaskan: 1%. Asian American or Pacific Islander: 23%. African American: 5%. Latino: 7%. Caucasian: 58%. International: 1%. Out-of-State: 50%. Total all graduate and professional students: 1,744.

Academics: Full-Time Faculty: 387.

Admissions: Regular Application Deadline: No closing date. Priority Application Deadline: 2/1. Early Decision Deadline: 11/15. Transfer Priority Deadline: 3/1. Financial Aid Deadline: Unavailable. Total Number of Students Applied: Unavailable. Percent Admitted: 68%. Number Enrolled: 761. Test Scores (Middle 50%): SAT Critical Reading: 580–670. SAT Math: 580–670. SAT Writing: Unavailable. ACT Comp: 25-29. HS Rank of Entering Freshmen: Top 10%: 63%. Top 25%: 32%. Avg. HS GPA: Unavailable.

Cost: Tuition and Fees: In-State: $24,615. Out-of-State: $24,615. Room and Board: $8,703.

Inst. Aid: FT Undergrads Receiving Aid: Unavailable. Avg. Amount per Student: $21,431.

SETON HALL UNIVERSITY

South Orange, NJ
thehall@shu.edu; www.shu.edu

General Info: Coed, College Board member, Four-year, Private, Regionally Accredited, Roman Catholic Church, University. Suburban setting, Large town (10,000–49,999), Residential campus. Academic Calendar: Semester.

Student Body: Full-Time Undergrads: 5,300. Men: 48%, Women: 52%. Total Undergrad Population: Native American or Native Alaskan: 0%. Asian American or Pacific Islander: 7%. African American: 9%. Latino: 10%. Caucasian: 55%. International: 1%. Out-of-State: 30%. Total all graduate and professional students: 4,500.

Academics: Full-Time Faculty: 860.

Admissions: Regular Application Deadline: 3/1. Priority Application Deadline: Unavailable. Early Decision Deadline: Unavailable. Fall Transfer Deadline: 6/1. Spring Transfer Deadline: 12/1. Transfer Priority Deadline: 6/1. Financial Aid Deadline: Unavailable. Total Number of Students Applied: Unavailable. Number Admitted: Unavailable. Number Enrolled: Unavailable. Test Scores (Middle 50%): SAT Critical Reading: 550–600. SAT Math: 550–600. SAT Writing: 550–600. ACT Comp: 23–25. HS Rank of Entering Freshmen: Top 10%: Unavailable. Top 25%: Unavailable. Avg. HS GPA: 3.2.

Cost: Tuition and Fees: In-State: $29,630. Out-of-State: $29,630. Room and Board: $11,360.

Inst. Aid: FT Undergrads Receiving Aid: Unavailable. Avg. Amount per Student: Unavailable.

SEWANEE–THE UNIVERSITY OF THE SOUTH

Sewanee, TN

General Info: Coed, Private, University. Small town (2,500–9,999). Academic Calendar: Semester

Student Body: Full-Time Undergrads: 1,518. Men: 51%, Women: 49%.

Academics: Full-Time Faculty: 132.

Admissions: Regular Application Deadline: 2/1. Priority Application Deadline: Unavailable. Early Decision Deadline: 11/15. Financial Aid Deadline: Unavailable. Total Number of Students Applied: Unavailable. Percent Admitted: 71%. Number Enrolled: 412. Test Scores (Middle 50%): SAT Critical Reading: 570–670. SAT Math: 560–650. SAT Writing: 570–670. ACT Comp: 25-29. HS Rank of Entering Freshmen: Top 10%: 42%. Top 25%: 78%. Avg. HS GPA: Unavailable.

Cost: Tuition and Fees: In-State: $30,438. Out-of-State: $30,438. Room and Board: $8,780.

Inst. Aid: FT Undergrads Receiving Aid: Unavailable. Avg. Amount per Student: $24,809.

SIMMONS COLLEGE

Boston, MA

ugadm@simmons.edu; www.simmons.edu

General Info: Private, Liberal Arts College, Four-year, Women Only, Regionally Accredited, College Board member. Urban setting, Large city (250,000–499,999), Residential campus. Academic Calendar: Semester.

Student Body: Full-Time Undergrads: 2,072. Men: 0%, Women: 100%. Part-Time Undergrads. Men: 0%, Women: 48%. Total Undergrad Population: Native American or Native Alaskan: 1%. Asian American or Pacific Islander: 6%. African American: 6%. Latino: 3%. Caucasian: 78%. International: 3%. Out-of-State: 40%. Total all graduate and professional students: 2,661.

Academics: Full-Time Faculty: 206.

Admissions: Regular Application Deadline: 2/1. Priority Application Deadline: 2/1. Early Decision Deadline: Unavailable. Fall Transfer Deadline: 4/1. Spring Transfer Deadline: 11/15. Financial Aid Deadline: 3/1. Total Number of Students Applied: 2,937. Number Admitted: 1,686. Number Enrolled: 479. Number accepting place on waitlist: 22. Number of waitlisted students admitted: 1. Test Scores (Middle 50%): SAT Critical Reading: 500–600. SAT Math: 480–590. SAT Writing: 510–610. ACT Comp: 21-26. HS Rank of Entering Freshmen: Top 10%: 18%. Top 25%: 58%. Avg. HS GPA: 3.17.

Cost: Tuition and Fees: In-State: $29,120. Out-of-State: $29,120. Room and Board: $11,500.

Inst. Aid: FT Undergrads Receiving Aid: Unavailable. Avg. Amount per Student: Unavailable.

SKIDMORE COLLEGE

Saratoga Springs, NY

admissions@skidmore.edu; www.skidmore.edu

General Info: Private, Liberal Arts College, Four-year, Coed, Regionally Accredited, College Board member. Suburban setting, Large town (10,000–49,999), Residential campus. Academic Calendar: Semester.

Student Body: Full-Time Undergrads: 2,759. Men: 42%, Women: 58%. Total Undergrad Population: Native American or Native Alaskan: 1%. Asian American or Pacific Islander: 9%. African American: 3%. Latino: 4%. Caucasian: 64%. International: 3%. Out-of-State: 68%. Total all graduate and professional students: 57.

Academics: Full-Time Faculty: 228.

Admissions: Regular Application Deadline: 1/15. Priority Application Deadline: Unavailable. Early Decision Deadline: 11/15. Transfer Priority Deadline: Unavailable. Financial Aid Deadline: 1/15. Total Number of Students Applied: Unavailable. Percent Admitted: 39%. Number Enrolled: 673. Test Scores (Middle 50%): SAT Critical Reading: 580–680. SAT Math: 580–670. SAT Writing: 580–680. ACT Comp: 25–29. HS Rank of Entering Freshmen: Top 10%: 46%. Top 25%: 78%. Avg. HS GPA: Unavailable.

Cost: Tuition and Fees: In-State: $34,694. Out-of-State: $34,694. Room and Board: $9,556.

Inst. Aid: FT Undergrads Receiving Aid: Unavailable. Avg. Amount per Student: $29,198.

SMITH COLLEGE

Northampton, MA

admission@smith.edu; www.smith.edu

General Info: Private, Liberal Arts College, Four-year, Women Only, Regionally Accredited, College Board member. Suburban setting, Large town (10,000–49,999), Residential campus. Academic Calendar: Semester.

Student Body: Full-Time Undergrads: 2,634. Men: 0%, Women: 100%. Total Undergrad Population: Native American or Native Alaskan: 0%. Asian American or Pacific Islander: 13%. African American: 8%. Latino: 8%. Caucasian: 42%. International: 7%. Out-of-State: 82%. Total all graduate and professional students: 87.

Academics: Full-Time Faculty: 285.

Heisman Trophy Winners

2003: Jason White—University of Oklahoma

2004: Matt Leinart—USC

2005: Reggie Bush—USC

2006: Troy Smith—Ohio State University

2007: Tim Tebow—University of Florida

Admissions: Regular Application Deadline: 1/15. Priority Application Deadline: Unavailable. Early Decision Deadline: 11/15. Transfer Priority Deadline: 2/1. Financial Aid Deadline: 2/15. Total Number of Students Applied: Unavailable. Percent Admitted: 52%. Number Enrolled: 674. Test Scores (Middle 50%): SAT Critical Reading: 580–700. SAT Math: 560–670. SAT Writing: 640–730. ACT Comp: 25–29. HS Rank of Entering Freshmen: Top 10%: 61%. Top 25%: 91%. Avg. HS GPA: Unavailable.

Cost: Tuition and Fees: In-State: $33,940. Room and Board: $11,420.

Inst. Aid: FT Undergrads Receiving Aid: Unavailable. Avg. Amount per Student: Unavailable. Avg. Amount per Student: $32,307.

SOUTHERN METHODIST UNIVERSITY

Dallas, TX

enrol_serv@smu.edu; www.smu.edu

General Info: Private, University, Four-year, United Methodist Church, Coed, Regionally Accredited, College Board member. Suburban setting, Large town (10,000–49,999), Residential campus. Academic Calendar: Semester.

Student Body: Full-Time Undergrads: 6,296. Men: 45%, Women: 55%. Total Undergrad Population: Native American or Native Alaskan: 1%. Asian American or Pacific Islander: 6%. African American: 4%. Latino: 6%. Caucasian: 78%. International: 5%. Out-of-State: 49%. Total all graduate and professional students: 3,402.

Academics: Full-Time Faculty: 603.

Admissions: Regular Application Deadline: 1/15. Priority Application Deadline: Unavailable. Early Decision Deadline: Unavailable. Transfer Priority Deadline: 6/1. Financial Aid Deadline: Unavailable. Total Number of Students Applied: Unavailable. Percent Admitted: 54%. Number Enrolled: 1,371. Test Scores (Middle 50%): SAT Critical Reading: 560–650. SAT Math: 580–670. SAT Writing: 550–650. ACT Comp: 24–29. HS Rank of Entering Freshmen: Top 10%: 35%. Top 25%: 64%. Avg. HS GPA: Unavailable.

Cost: Tuition and Fees: In-State: $30,880. Out-of-State: $30,880. Room and Board: $10,995.

Inst. Aid: FT Undergrads Receiving Aid: Unavailable. Avg. Amount per Student: $25,764.

SOUTHWESTERN UNIVERSITY

Georgetown, TX

admission@southwestern.edu; www.southwestern.edu

General Info: Private, Liberal Arts College, Four-year, United Methodist Church, Coed, Regionally Accredited, College Board member. Residential campus, Small city (50,000–249,999), Suburban setting. Academic Calendar: Semester.

Student Body: Full-Time Undergrads: 1,310. Men: 36%, Women: 64%. Total Undergrad Population: Native American or Native Alaskan: 0%. Asian American or Pacific Islander: 4%. African American: 4%. Latino: 14%. Caucasian: 77%. International: 2%. Out-of-State: 8%. Living Off-Campus: 10%.

Academics: Full-Time Faculty: 125. Graduation Rates: 70% within 4 years. 80% within 6 years.

Admissions: Regular Application Deadline: 2/1. Priority Application Deadline: Unavailable. Early Decision Deadline: 11/1. Transfer Priority Deadline: 4/1. Financial Aid Deadline: 3/1. Total Number of Students Applied: 1,916. Number Admitted: 1,289. Number Enrolled: Unavailable. Test Scores (Middle 50%): SAT Critical Reading: 555–670. SAT Math: 560–665. SAT Writing: Unavailable. ACT Comp: 23–29. HS Rank of Entering Freshmen: Top 10%: 50%. Top 25%: 85%. Avg. HS GPA: 3.5.

Cost: Tuition and Fees: In-State: $27,490. Out-of-State: $27,490. Room and Board: $8,000.

Inst. Aid: FT Undergrads Receiving Aid: Unavailable. Avg. Amount per Student: Unavailable.

Graduates: No. of companies recruiting on campus: 50. Alumni Giving %: 35%.

SPELMAN COLLEGE

Atlanta, GA

admiss@spelman.edu; www.spelman.edu

General Info: Private, Liberal Arts College, Four-year, Women Only, Regionally Accredited, College Board member, Historically black. Urban setting, Very large city (over 500,000), Residential campus. Academic Calendar: Semester.

Student Body: Full-Time Undergrads: 2,236. Men: 0%, Women: 100%. Total Undergrad Population: Native American or Native Alaskan: 0%. Asian American or Pacific Islander: 0%. African American: 98%. Latino: 0%. Caucasian: 0%. International: 1%. Out-of-State: 79%.

Academics: Full-Time Faculty: 172.

Admissions: Regular Application Deadline: 2/1. Priority Application Deadline: Unavailable. Early Decision Deadline: 11/1. Transfer Priority Deadline: Unavailable. Financial Aid Deadline: Unavailable. Total Number of Students Applied: 5,656. Number Admitted: 1,866. Number Enrolled: 553. Test Scores (Middle 50%): SAT Critical Reading: 500–590. SAT Math: 480–570. ACT Comp: 20–24. HS Rank of Entering Freshmen: Top 10%: 40%. Top 25%: 73%. Avg. HS GPA: 3.59.

Cost: Tuition and Fees: In-State: $17,005. Out-of-State: $17,005. Room and Board: $8,750.

Inst. Aid: FT Undergrads Receiving Aid: 1,650. Avg. Amount per Student: $7,000.

ST. ANSELM COLLEGE

Manchester, NH

admission@anselm.edu; www.anselm.edu

General Info: Private, College of Nursing, Liberal Arts College, Four-year, Roman Catholic Church, Coed, Regionally Accredited, College Board member. Suburban setting,

Small city (50,000–249,999), Residential campus. Academic Calendar: Semester.

Student Body: Full-Time Undergrads: 2,000. Men: 43%, Women: 57%. Total Undergrad Population: Native American or Native Alaskan: 0%. Asian American or Pacific Islander: 2%. African American: 1%. Latino: 1%. Caucasian: 79%. International: 1%. Out-of-State: 80%.

Academics: Full-Time Faculty: 131.

Admissions: Regular Application Deadline: No closing date. Priority Application Deadline: Unavailable. Early Decision Deadline: 11/15. Transfer Priority Deadline: 5/1. Financial Aid Deadline: Unavailable. Total Number of Students Applied: Unavailable. Percent Admitted: 73%. Number Enrolled: 572. Test Scores (Middle 50%): SAT Critical Reading: 510–600. SAT Math: 510–600. SAT Writing: Unavailable. ACT Comp: 21–26. HS Rank of Entering Freshmen: Top 10%: 15%. Top 25%: 45%. Avg. HS GPA: Unavailable.

Cost: Tuition and Fees: In-State: $26,100. Out-of-State: $26,100. Room and Board: $9,620.

Inst. Aid: FT Undergrads Receiving Aid: Unavailable. Avg. Amount per Student: $18,915.

NCAA Women's Division I Basketball Champions

2004: University of Connecticut

2005: Baylor University

2006: University of Maryland

2007: University of Tennessee

2008: University of Tennessee

Graduates: No. of companies recruiting on campus: 8. Percentage of grads accepting a job at time of graduation: 30%. Alumni Giving %: 30%.

ST. JOHN'S COLLEGE–ANNAPOLIS

Annapolis, MD

admissions@sjca.edu; www.stjohnscollege.edu

General Info: Coed, College Board member, Four-year, Liberal Arts College, Middle States Association of Colleges and Schools, Private, Regionally Accredited. Urban setting, Large town (10,000–49,999), Residential campus. Academic Calendar: Semester.

Student Body: Full-Time Undergrads: 489. Men: 53%, Women: 47%. Total Undergrad Population: Native American or Native Alaskan: 1%. Asian American or Pacific Islander: 3%. African American: 1%. Latino: 3%. Caucasian: 89%. International: 5%. Out-of-State: 80%. Living Off-Campus: 25%. Total all graduate and professional students: 90.

Academics: Full-Time Faculty: 75. With PhD: 61. Graduation Rates: 61% within 4 years. 74% within 6 years.

Admissions: Regular Application Deadline: No closing date. Priority Application Deadline: 3/1. Early Decision Deadline: Unavailable. Transfer Priority Deadline: 3/1. Financial Aid Deadline: Unavailable. Total Number of Students Applied: 441. Number Admitted: 356. Number Enrolled: 143. Test Scores (Middle 50%): SAT Critical Reading: 660–770. SAT Math: 580–680. SAT Writing: Unavailable. HS Rank of Entering Freshmen: Top 10%: 32%. Top 25%: 66%. Avg. HS GPA: Unavailable.

Cost: Tuition and Fees: In-State: $38,854. Out-of-State: $38,854. Room and Board: $9,284.

Inst. Aid: FT Undergrads Receiving Aid: 300. Avg. Amount per Student: $26,241. Freshmen Receiving Non-Need Scholarship or Grant: 89. Avg. Amount per Student: $28,400.

ST. JOHN'S COLLEGE–SANTA FE

Santa Fe, NM

admissions@sjcsf.edu; www.stjohnscollege.edu

General Info: Coed, College Board member, Four-year, Liberal Arts College, Middle States Association of Colleges and Schools, North Central Association of Colleges and Schools, Private, Regionally Accredited. Suburban setting, Small city (50,000–249,999), Residential campus. Academic Calendar: Semester.

Student Body: Full-Time Undergrads: 436. Men: 60%, Women: 40%. Total Undergrad Population: Native American or Native Alaskan: 1%. Asian American or Pacific Islander: 3%. African American: 1%. Latino: 5%. Caucasian: 86%. International: 3%. Out-of-State: 93.6%. Living Off-Campus: 75%. Total all graduate and professional students: 96.

Academics: Full-Time Faculty: 67. With PhD: 61. Graduation Rates: 54% within 4 years. 64% within 6 years.

Admissions: Regular Application Deadline: Rolling. Priority Application Deadline: 3/1. Early Decision Deadline: Unavailable. Fall Transfer Deadline: Rolling. Spring Transfer Deadline: Rolling. Transfer Priority Deadline: 3/1. Financial Aid Deadline: Rolling. Total Number of Students Applied: 344. Number Admitted: 270. Number Enrolled: 134. Test Scores (Middle 50%): SAT Critical Reading: 620–730. SAT Math: 570–680. SAT Writing: Unavailable. ACT Comp: 25–30. HS Rank of Entering Freshmen: Top 10%: 28%. Top 25%: 64%. Avg. HS GPA: Unavailable.

Oldest College Graduate

In 2007, a Kansas resident received her degree from Fort Hays State University at the age of 95!

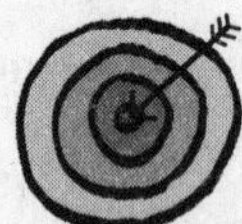

Cost: Tuition and Fees: In-State: $38,854. Out-of-State: $338,854. Room and Board: $9,283.

Inst. Aid: FT Undergrads Receiving Aid: 282. Avg. Amount per Student: $24,858.

ST. LAWRENCE UNIVERSITY

Canton, NY

admissions@stlawu.edu; www.stlawu.edu

General Info: Coed, College Board member, Four-year, Liberal Arts College, Private, Regionally Accredited. Rural setting, Small town (2,500–9,999), Residential campus. Academic Calendar: Semester.

Student Body: Full-Time Undergrads: 2,182. Men: 47%, Women: 53%. Part-Time Undergrads. Men: 0.5%, Women: 0.5%. Total Undergrad Population: Native American or Native Alaskan: 0.5%. Asian American or Pacific Islander: 1.8%. African American: 2.1%. Latino: 4.6%. Caucasian: 71%. International: 5%. Out-of-State: 55%. Living Off-Campus: 1%. Total all graduate and professional students: 121.

Academics: Full-Time Faculty: 167. Percentage completing two or more majors: 25%. Graduation Rate: 78.2% within 4 years.

Admissions: Regular Application Deadline: 2/1. Priority Application Deadline: Unavailable. Early Decision Deadline: 11/15. Financial Aid Deadline: 2/1. Total Number of Students Applied: 4,645. Number Admitted: 2,030. Number Enrolled: Unavailable. Number accepting place on waitlist: 151. Test Scores (Middle 50%): SAT Critical Reading: 560–640. SAT Math: 560–640. SAT Writing: 560–650. ACT Comp: 25–29. HS Rank of Entering Freshmen: Top 10%: 34.7%. Top 25%: 74.3%. Avg. HS GPA: Unavailable.

Cost: Tuition and Fees: In-State: $37,675. Out-of-State: $37,675. Room and Board: $9,645.

Inst. Aid: FT Undergrads Receiving Aid: 1,367. Avg. Amount per Student: Unavailable.

Graduates: Alumni Giving %: 35.7%.

ST. LOUIS UNIVERSITY

St. Louis, MO

admitme@slu.edu; www.slu.edu

General Info: Private, University, Four-year, Roman Catholic Church, Society of Jesus (Jesuits), Coed, Regionally Accredited, College Board member. Urban setting, Very large city (over 500,000), Residential campus. Academic Calendar: Semester.

Student Body: Full-Time Undergrads: 7,479. Men: 41%, Women: 59%. Total Undergrad Population: Native American or Native Alaskan: 0%. Asian American or Pacific Islander: 7%. African American: 6%. Latino: 4%. Caucasian: 71%. International: 1%. Out-of-State: 60%. Total all graduate and professional students: 2,937.

Academics: Full-Time Faculty: 616.

Admissions: Regular Application Deadline: Rolling. Priority Application Deadline: 11/1. Early Decision Deadline: Unavailable. Transfer Priority Deadline: 11/1. Financial Aid Deadline: Unavailable. Total Number of Students Applied: Unavailable. Percent Admitted: 67%. Number Enrolled: 1,514. Test Scores (Middle 50%): SAT Critical Reading: 530–640. SAT Math: 550–660. SAT Writing: Unavailable. ACT Comp: 24–29. HS Rank of Entering Freshmen: Top 10%: 36%. Top 25%: 66%. Avg. HS GPA: Unavailable.

Cost: Tuition and Fees: In-State: $26,648. Out-of-State: $26,648. Room and Board: $8,230.

Inst. Aid: FT Undergrads Receiving Aid: Unavailable. Avg. Amount per Student: $19,061.

ST. MARY'S COLLEGE OF CALIFORNIA

Moraga, CA

smcadmit@stmarys_ca.edu; www.stmarys-ca.edu

General Info: Private, Liberal Arts College, Four-year, Roman Catholic Church, Coed, Regionally Accredited, College Board member. Suburban setting, Large town (10,000–49,999), Residential campus. Academic Calendar: 4-1-4.

Student Body: Full-Time Undergrads: 2,835. Men: 36%, Women: 64%. Total Undergrad Population: Native American or Native Alaskan: 1%. Asian American or Pacific Islander: 14%. African American: 8%. Latino: 21%. Caucasian: 50%. International: 1%. Out-of-State: 15%. Total all graduate and professional students: 1,127.

Academics: Full-Time Faculty: 213.

Admissions: Regular Application Deadline: 2/15. Priority Application Deadline: Unavailable. Early Decision Deadline: 11/15. Transfer Priority Deadline: 2/1. Financial Aid Deadline: 3/2. Total Number of Students Applied: Unavailable. Percent Admitted: 59%. Number Enrolled: 611. Test Scores (Middle 50%): SAT Critical Reading: 480–590. SAT Math: 480–600. SAT Writing: Unavailable. HS Rank of Entering Freshmen: Top 10%: 59%. Top 25%: 66%. Avg. HS GPA: Unavailable.

Cost: Tuition and Fees: In-State: $29,050. Out-of-State: $29,050. Room and Board: $10,566.

Inst. Aid: FT Undergrads Receiving Aid: Unavailable. Avg. Amount per Student: $29,417.

ST. MARY'S COLLEGE OF MARYLAND

St. Mary's City, MD

admissions@smcm.edu; www.smcm.edu

General Info: Public, Liberal Arts College, Four-year, Coed, Regionally Accredited, Middle States Association of Colleges and Schools, College Board member. Rural setting, Rural community (under 2,500), Residential campus. Academic Calendar: Semester.

Student Body: Full-Time Undergrads: 1,948. Men: 42%, Women: 58%. Total Undergrad Population: Native American or Native Alaskan: 0%. Asian American or Pacific Islander: 5%. African American: 8%. Latino: 7%. Caucasian: 75%. International: 1%. Out-of-State: 21%. Total all graduate and professional students: 9.

Academics: Full-Time Faculty: 139.

Admissions: Regular Application Deadline: 1/15. Priority Application Deadline: 12/1. Early Decision Deadline: 12/1. Transfer Priority Deadline: Unavailable. Financial Aid Deadline: 3/1. Total Number of Students Applied: Unavailable. Percent Admitted: 56%. Number Enrolled: 488. Test Scores (Middle 50%): SAT Critical Reading: 570–680. SAT Math: 560–660. SAT Writing: Unavailable. HS Rank of Entering Freshmen: Top 10%: 46%. Top 25%: 79%. Avg. HS GPA: Unavailable.

Cost: Tuition and Fees: In-State: $11,710. Out-of-State: $21,280. Room and Board: $8,520.

Inst. Aid: FT Undergrads Receiving Aid: Unavailable. Avg. Amount per Student: $4,000.

ST. OLAF COLLEGE

Northfield, MN

admissions@stolaf.edu; www.stolaf.edu

General Info: Private, Liberal Arts College, Four-year, Evangelical Lutheran Church In America, Coed, Regionally Accredited, College Board member. Rural setting, Large town (10,000–49,999), Residential campus. Academic Calendar: 4-1-4.

Student Body: Full-Time Undergrads: 3,000. Men: 45%, Women: 55%. Total Undergrad Population: Native American or Native Alaskan: 0%. Asian American or Pacific Islander: 5%. African American: 1%. Latino: 2%. Caucasian: 87%. International: 1%. Out-of-State: 43%.

Academics: Full-Time Faculty: 195.

Admissions: Regular Application Deadline: 1/15. Priority Application Deadline: Unavailable. Early Decision Deadline: 11/1. Transfer Priority Deadline: Unavailable. Financial Aid Deadline: 2/1. Total Number of Students Applied: Unavailable. Percent Admitted: 65%. Number Enrolled: 793. Test Scores (Middle 50%): SAT Critical Reading: 580–700. SAT Math: 590–700. SAT Writing: Unavailable. ACT Comp: 25–30. HS Rank of Entering Freshmen: Top 10%: 51%. Top 25%: 83%. Avg. HS GPA: Unavailable.

Youngest College Graduate

In 1994, a 10-year-old graduated with a bachelor's degree in anthropology from the University of South Alabama.

Cost: Tuition and Fees: In-State: $30,600. Out-of-State: $30,600. Room and Board: $7,900.

Inst. Aid: FT Undergrads Receiving Aid: Unavailable. Avg. Amount per Student: $22,416.

STANFORD UNIVERSITY

Stanford, CA

admission@stanford.edu; www.stanford.edu

General Info: Coed, College Board member, Four-year, Private, Regionally Accredited, University, Western Association of Schools and Colleges. Suburban setting, Small city (50,000–249,999), Residential campus. Academic Calendar: Quarter.

Student Body: Full-Time Undergrads: 6,584. Men: 51.5%, Women: 48.5%. Total Undergrad Population: Native American or Native Alaskan: 2%. Asian American or Pacific Islander: 24%. African American: 10%. Latino: 11%. Caucasian: 41%. International: 6%. Out-of-State: 56%. Total all graduate and professional students: 10,285.

Academics: Full-Time Faculty: 1,028.

Admissions: Regular Application Deadline: 12/15. Priority Application Deadline: Unavailable. Early Decision Deadline: Unavailable. Transfer Priority Deadline: Unavailable. Financial Aid Deadline: Unavailable. Total Number of Students Applied: 23,958. Number Admitted: 2,464. Number Enrolled: 1,722. Test Scores (Middle 50%): SAT Critical Reading: Unavailable. SAT Math: Unavailable. SAT Writing: Unavailable. HS Rank of Entering Freshmen: Top 10%: 91%. Top 25%: 98%. Avg.

Cost: Tuition and Fees: In-State: $32,994. Out-of-State: $32,994. Room and Board: $10,367.

Inst. Aid: FT Undergrads Receiving Aid: 2,977. Avg. Amount per Student: $31,515.

Schools for Organic Agriculture Majors

University of Florida

Washington State University

STATE UNIVERSITY OF NEW YORK AT ALBANY

Albany, NY

ugadmissions@albany.edu; www.albany.edu

General Info: Public, University, Four-year, Coed, Regionally Accredited, Middle States Association of Colleges and Schools, College Board member. Suburban setting, Small city (50,000–249,999), Residential campus. Academic Calendar: Semester.

Student Body: Full-Time Undergrads: 12,457. Men: 50%, Women: 50%. Total Undergrad Population: Native American or Native Alaskan: 0%. Asian American or Pacific Islander: 6%. African American: 10%. Latino: 9%. Caucasian: 56%. International: 2%. Out-of-State: 7%. Total all graduate and professional students: 4,977.

Academics: Full-Time Faculty: 631.

Admissions: Regular Application Deadline: 3/1. Priority Application Deadline: Unavailable. Early Decision Deadline: 12/1. Transfer Priority Deadline: 3/1. Financial Aid Deadline: 4/15. Total Number of Students Applied: Unavailable. Percent Admitted: 56%. Number Enrolled: 2,414. Test Scores (Middle 50%): SAT Critical Reading: 490–580. SAT Math: 510–610. SAT Writing: Unavailable. ACT Comp: 21–26. HS Rank of Entering Freshmen: Top 10%: 14%. Top 25%: 31%. Avg. HS GPA: Unavailable.

Cost: Tuition and Fees: In-State: $5,939. Out-of-State: $12,199. Room and Board: $8,605.

Inst. Aid: FT Undergrads Receiving Aid: Unavailable. Avg. Amount per Student: $8,763.

STATE UNIVERSITY OF NEW YORK AT BINGHAMTON

Binghamton, NY

admit@binghamton.edu; www.binghamton.edu

General Info: Public, University, Four-year, Coed, Regionally Accredited, Middle States Association of Colleges and Schools, College Board member. Suburban setting, Small city (50,000–249,999), Residential campus. Academic Calendar: Semester.

Student Body: Full-Time Undergrads: 11,174. Men: 52%, Women: 48%. Part-Time Undergrads. Men: 55%, Women: 45%. Total Undergrad Population: Native American or Native Alaskan: 0%. Asian American or Pacific Islander: 13%. African American: 6%. Latino: 9%. Caucasian: 49%. International: 10%. Out-of-State: 9%. Living Off-Campus: 44%. % In Fraternities: 8%. % In Sororities: 9%. Total all graduate and professional students: 2,844.

Academics: Full-Time Faculty: 575.

Admissions: Regular Application Deadline: Rolling. Priority Application Deadline: 12/1. Transfer Priority Deadline: 2/15. Financial Aid Deadline: 3/1. Total Number of Students Applied: 25,242. Number Admitted: 9,799. Number Enrolled: 2,218. Number accepting place on waitlist: 664. Number of waitlisted students admitted: 97. Test Scores (Middle 50%): SAT Critical Reading: 560–660. SAT Math: 600–690. SAT Writing: Unavailable. ACT Comp: 26–29. HS Rank of Entering Freshmen: Top 10%: 49%. Top 25%: 85%. Avg. HS GPA: 3.7.

Cost: Tuition and Fees: In-State: $4,350. Out-of-State: $10,610. Room and Board: $10,090.

Inst. Aid: FT Undergrads Receiving Aid: 4,904. Avg. Amount per Student: $12,403. Freshmen Receiving Non-Need Scholarship or Grant: 291.

Graduates: No. of companies recruiting on campus: 400.

STATE UNIVERSITY OF NEW YORK AT BUFFALO

Buffalo, NY

admissions@buffalostate.edu; www.buffalostate.edu

General Info: Public, Liberal Arts College, Teachers College/College of Education, Four-year, Coed, Regionally Accredited, Middle States Association of Colleges and Schools, College Board member. Urban setting, Large city (250,000–499,999), Commuter campus. Academic Calendar: Semester.

Student Body: Full-Time Undergrads: 9,314. Men: 40%, Women: 60%. Total Undergrad Population: Native American or Native Alaskan: 0%. Asian American or Pacific Islander: 2%. African American: 17%. Latino: 6%. Caucasian: 61%. International: 0%. Out-of-State: 1%. Total all graduate and professional students: 1,906.

Academics: Full-Time Faculty: 1,748.

Admissions: Regular Application Deadline: 11/30. Priority Application Deadline: Unavailable. Early Decision Deadline: 11/15. Transfer Priority Deadline: Unavailable. Financial Aid Deadline: 5/1. Total Number of Students Applied: Unavailable. Percent Admitted: 55%. Number Enrolled: 3,471. Test Scores (Middle 50%): SAT Critical Reading: 450–540. SAT Math: 450–550. SAT Writing: Unavailable. ACT Comp: Unavailable. HS Rank of Entering Freshmen: Top 10%: 34%. Top 25%: 59%. Avg. HS GPA: Unavailable.

Cost: Tuition and Fees: In-State: $5,285. Out-of-State: $11,545. Room and Board: $7,500.

Inst. Aid: FT Undergrads Receiving Aid: Unavailable. Avg. Amount per Student: Unavailable.

STATE UNIVERSITY OF NEW YORK AT GENESEO

Geneseo, NY

admissions@geneseo.edu; www.geneseo.edu

General Info: Public, Liberal Arts College, Four-year, Coed, Regionally Accredited, Middle States Association of Colleges and Schools, College Board member. Rural setting, Small town (2,500–9,999), Residential campus. Academic Calendar: Semester.

Student Body: Full-Time Undergrads: Men: 41%, Women: 59%. Total Undergrad Population: Native American or Native Alaskan: 1%. Asian American or Pacific Islander: 8%. African American: 2%. Latino: 5%. Caucasian: 67%. International: 2%. Out-of-State: 1%.

Academics: Full-Time Faculty: 260.

Admissions: Regular Application Deadline: 1/15. Priority Application Deadline: Unavailable. Early Decision Deadline: 11/15. Transfer Priority Deadline: Unavailable. Financial Aid Deadline: 2/15. Total Number of Students Applied: Unavailable. Percent Admitted: 41%. Number Enrolled: 1,080. Test Scores (Middle 50%): SAT Critical Reading: 600–670. SAT Math: 620–680. SAT Writing: Unavailable. ACT Comp: 26–29. HS Rank of Entering Freshmen: Top 10%: 54%. Top 25%: 89%. Avg. HS GPA: Unavailable.

Cost: Tuition and Fees: In-State: $5,560. Out-of-State: $11,820. Room and Board: $8,488.

Inst. Aid: FT Undergrads Receiving Aid: Unavailable. Avg. Amount per Student: $9,055.

STATE UNIVERSITY OF NEW YORK AT NEW PALTZ

New Paltz, NY

admissions@newpaltz.edu; www.newpaltz.edu

General Info: Public, Liberal Arts College, Four-year, Coed, Regionally Accredited, Middle States Association of Colleges and Schools, College Board member. Suburban setting, Large town (10,000–49,999), Residential campus. Academic Calendar: Semester.

Student Body: Full-Time Undergrads: 6,263. Men: 32%, Women: 68%. Total Undergrad Population: Native American or Native Alaskan: 0%. Asian American or Pacific Islander: 4%. African American: 8%. Latino: 10%. Caucasian: 59%. International: 2%. Out-of-State: 5%. Total all graduate and professional students: 1,496.

Academics: Full-Time Faculty: 305.

Admissions: Regular Application Deadline: 4/1. Priority Application Deadline: Unavailable. Early Decision Deadline: 11/15. Transfer Priority Deadline: Unavailable. Financial Aid Deadline: Unavailable. Total Number of Students Applied: Unavailable. Percent Admitted: 45%. Number Enrolled: 999. Test Scores (Middle 50%): SAT Critical Reading: 510–600. SAT Math: 520–610. SAT Writing: Unavailable. HS Rank of Entering Freshmen: Top 10%: Unavailable. Top 25%: Unavailable. Avg. HS GPA: Unavailable.

Cost: Tuition and Fees: In-State: $5,340. Out-of-State: $11,600. Room and Board: $7,630.

Inst. Aid: FT Undergrads Receiving Aid: Unavailable. Avg. Amount per Student: $2,040.

STATE UNIVERSITY OF NEW YORK AT PURCHASE

Purchase, NY

admissn@purchase.edu; www.purchase.edu

General Info: Public, Four-year, Coed, Regionally Accredited, Middle States Association of Colleges and Schools. Suburban setting, Large town (10,000–49,999), Residential campus. Academic Calendar: Semester.

Student Body: Full-Time Undergrads: 3,754. Men: 46%, Women: 54%. Total Undergrad Population: Native American or Native Alaskan: 1%. Asian American or Pacific Islander: 3%. African American: 8%. Latino: 10%. Caucasian: 60%. International: 1%. Out-of-State: 23%. Total all graduate and professional students: 147.

Academics: Full-Time Faculty: 144.

Admissions: Regular Application Deadline: 6/1. Priority Application Deadline: 3/1. Early Decision Deadline: 11/1. Transfer Priority Deadline: Unavailable. Financial Aid Deadline: Unavailable. Total Number of Students Applied: Unavailable. Number Admitted: Unavailable. Number Enrolled: Unavailable. Test Scores (Middle 50%): SAT Critical Reading: 510–620. SAT Math: 480–590. SAT Writing: Unavailable. HS Rank of Entering Freshmen: Top 10%: 9%. Top 25%: 29%. Avg. HS GPA: Unavailable.

Cost: Tuition and Fees: In-State: $5,699. Out-of-State: $11,959. Room and Board: $9,078.

Inst. Aid: FT Undergrads Receiving Aid: Unavailable. Avg. Amount per Student: $7,076.

Schools for Environmental Science Majors

SUNY—College of Environmental Science and Forestry

Yale University

Barnard College

Rutgers University

STATE UNIVERSITY OF NEW YORK AT STONY BROOK

Stony Brook, NY

enroll@stonybrook.edu; www.stonybrook.edu

General Info: Public, University, Four-year, Coed, Regionally Accredited, Middle States Association of Colleges and Schools, College Board member. Suburban setting, Large town (10,000–49,999), Residential campus. Academic Calendar: Semester.

Student Body: Full-Time Undergrads: 14,847. Men: 51%, Women: 49%. Total Undergrad Population: Native American or Native Alaskan: 0%. Asian American or Pacific Islander: 22%. African American: 9%. Latino: 9%. Caucasian: 35%. International: 5%. Out-of-State: 7%. Total all graduate and professional students: 7,675.

Academics: Full-Time Faculty: 909.

Admissions: Regular Application Deadline: 4/1. Priority Application Deadline: Unavailable. Early Decision Deadline: 11/15. Transfer Priority Deadline: 4/15. Financial Aid Deadline: Unavailable. Total Number of Students Applied: Unavailable. Percent Admitted: 47%. Number Enrolled: 2,708. Test Scores (Middle 50%): SAT Critical Reading: 540–620. SAT Math: 590–680. SAT Writing: 520–620. ACT Comp: Unavailable. HS Rank of Entering Freshmen: Top 10%: 33%. Top 25%: 69%. Avg. HS GPA: Unavailable.

Cost: Tuition and Fees: In-State: $5,631. Out-of-State: $11,891. Room and Board: $8,424.

Inst. Aid: FT Undergrads Receiving Aid: Unavailable. Avg. Amount per Student: Unavailable.

STATE UNIVERSITY OF NEW YORK COLLEGE OF ENVIRONMENTAL SCIENCE AND FORESTRY

Syracuse, NY

esfinfo@esf.edu; www.esf.edu

General Info: Public, Liberal Arts College, University, Four-year, Coed, Regionally Accredited, Middle States Association of Colleges and Schools, College Board member. Urban setting, Small city (50,000–249,999), Residential campus. Academic Calendar: Semester.

Student Body: Full-Time Undergrads: 1,544. Men: 64%, Women: 36%. Total Undergrad Population: Native American or Native Alaskan: 0%. Asian American or Pacific Islander: 3%. African American: 1%. Latino: 2%. Caucasian: 92%. International: 0%. Out-of-State: 10%. Total all graduate and professional students: 525.

Academics: Full-Time Faculty: 128.

Admissions: Regular Application Deadline: 1/15. Priority Application Deadline: Unavailable. Early Decision Deadline: Unavailable. Transfer Priority Deadline: 12/1. Financial Aid Deadline: Unavailable. Total Number of Students Applied: Unavailable. Number Admitted: Unavailable. Number Enrolled: 260. Test Scores (Middle 50%): SAT Critical Reading: 480–590. SAT Math: 500–600. SAT Writing: Unavailable. ACT Comp: 21–24. HS Rank of Entering Freshmen: Top 10%: 22%. Top 25%: 52%. Avg. HS GPA: Unavailable.

Cost: Tuition and Fees: In-State: $5,068. Out-of-State: $11,360. Room and Board: $18,520.

Inst. Aid: FT Undergrads Receiving Aid: Unavailable. Avg. Amount per Student: Unavailable.

STETSON UNIVERSITY

DeLand, FL

admissions@stetson.edu; www.stetson.edu

General Info: Private, University, Four-year, Coed, Regionally Accredited, College Board member. Suburban setting, Large town (10,000–49,999), Residential campus. Academic Calendar: Semester.

Student Body: Full-Time Undergrads: 2,273. Men: 40%, Women: 60%. Total Undergrad Population: Native American or Native Alaskan: 0%. Asian American or Pacific Islander: 2%. African American: 8%. Latino: 10%. Caucasian: 71%. International: 3%. Out-of-State: 19%. Total all graduate and professional students: 432.

Academics: Full-Time Faculty: 195.

Admissions: Regular Application Deadline: 3/15. Priority Application Deadline: Unavailable. Early Decision Deadline: 11/1. Transfer Priority Deadline: 3/15. Financial Aid Deadline: Unavailable. Total Number of Students Applied: Unavailable. Percent Admitted: 65%. Number Enrolled: 567. Test Scores (Middle 50%): SAT Critical Reading: 500–620. SAT Math: 500–610. SAT Writing: Unavailable. ACT Comp: 21–27. HS Rank of Entering Freshmen: Top 10%: Unavailable. Top 25%: Unavailable. Avg. HS GPA: Unavailable.

Cost: Tuition and Fees: In-State: $28,780. Out-of-State: $28,780. Room and Board: $7,968.

Inst. Aid: FT Undergrads Receiving Aid: Unavailable. Avg. Amount per Student: Unavailable.

Interested in Hydrology?

University of California, Davis

University of Wisconsin

University of Florida

University of Arizona

STONEHILL COLLEGE

Easton, MA

admissions@stonehill.edu; www.stonehill.edu

General Info: Coed, College Board member, Four-year, Liberal Arts College, Private, Regionally Accredited, Roman Catholic Church. Suburban setting, Large town (10,000–49,999), Residential campus. Academic Calendar: Semester.

Student Body: Full-Time Undergrads: 2,371. Men: 40%, Women: 60%. Total Undergrad Population: Native American or Native Alaskan: 0%. Asian American or Pacific Islander: 1%. African American: 3%. Latino: 5%. Caucasian: 91%. International: 0%. Out-of-State: 47%. Total all graduate and professional students: 15.

Academics: Full-Time Faculty: 135.

Admissions: Regular Application Deadline: 1/15. Priority Application Deadline: Unavailable. Early Decision Deadline: 11/1. Transfer Priority Deadline: Unavailable. Financial Aid Deadline: 2/1. Total Number of Students Applied: Unavailable. Percent Admitted: 54%. Number Enrolled: 594. Test Scores (Middle 50%): SAT Critical Reading: 530–620. SAT Math: 560–630. SAT Writing: Unavailable. ACT Comp: 23–27. HS Rank of Entering Freshmen: Top 10%: 50%. Top 25%: 91%. Avg. HS GPA: Unavailable.

Cost: Tuition and Fees: In-State: $27,080. Out-of-State: $27,080. Room and Board: $11,040.

Inst. Aid: FT Undergrads Receiving Aid: Unavailable. Avg. Amount per Student: Unavailable.

SUSQUEHANNA UNIVERSITY

Selinsgrove, PA

suadmiss@susqu.edu; www.susqu.edu

General Info: Coed, College Board member, Evangelical Lutheran Church In America, Four-year, Liberal Arts College, Middle States Association of Colleges and Schools, New York State Board of Regents, Private, Regionally Accredited, University. Suburban setting, Small town (2,500–9,999), Residential campus. Academic Calendar: Semester.

Student Body: Full-Time Undergrads: 1,900. Men: 45.2%, Women: 52.1%. Part-Time Undergrads. Men: 0.9%, Women: 1.8%. Total Undergrad Population: Native American or Native Alaskan: 0.01%. Asian American or Pacific Islander: 2%. African American: 3%. Latino: 2%. Caucasian: 90%. International: 1%. Out-of-State: 43%. Living Off-Campus: 33%. % In Fraternities: 20%. % In Sororities: 25%.

Academics: Full-Time Faculty: 121. With PhD: 112. Percentage completing two or more majors: 12%. Graduation Rates: 79% within 4 years. 82% within 6 years.

Admissions: Regular Application Deadline: 3/1. Priority Application Deadline: Unavailable. Early Decision Deadline: 11/15. Fall Transfer Deadline: 7/1. Spring Transfer Deadline: 5/1. Transfer Priority Deadline: 5/1. Financial Aid Deadline: 5/1. Total Number of Students Applied: 2,792. Number Admitted: 2,042. Number Enrolled: 593. Number accepting place on waitlist: 68. Number of waitlisted students admitted: 14. Number applied early decision: 212. Early decision admitted: 170. Test Scores (Middle 50%): SAT Critical Reading: 520–610. SAT Math: 530–610. SAT Writing: 510–610. ACT Comp: 22–27. HS Rank of Entering Freshmen: Top 10%: 34.3%. Top 25%: 60.5%. Avg. HS GPA: Unavailable.

Cost: Tuition and Fees: In-State: $31,080. Out-of-State: $31,080. Room and Board: $8,400.

Inst. Aid: FT Undergrads Receiving Aid: 1,250. Avg. Amount per Student: $21,943. Freshmen Receiving Non-Need Scholarship or Grant: 182. Avg. Amount per Student: $14,438.

Graduates: No. of companies recruiting on campus: 82. Percentage of grads accepting a job at time of graduation: 78%. Alumni Giving %: 23%.

SWARTHMORE COLLEGE

Swarthmore, PA

admissions@swarthmore.edu; www.swarthmore.edu

General Info: Private, Liberal Arts College, Four-year, Coed, Regionally Accredited, College Board member. Suburban setting, Small town (2,500–9,999), Residential campus. Academic Calendar: Semester.

Student Body: Full-Time Undergrads: 1,484. Men: 48%, Women: 52%. Total Undergrad Population: Native American or Native Alaskan: 1%. Asian American or Pacific Islander: 17%. African American: 9%. Latino: 10%. Caucasian: 44%. International: 7%. Out-of-State: 87%.

Academics: Full-Time Faculty: 168. Graduation Rates: 91% within 4 years. 94% within 6 years.

Admissions: Regular Application Deadline: 1/2. Priority Application Deadline: Unavailable. Early Decision Deadline: 11/15. Transfer Priority Deadline: Unavailable. Financial Aid Deadline: 2/15. Total Number of Students Applied: Unavailable. Percent Admitted: 19%. Number Enrolled: 371. Test Scores (Middle 50%): SAT Critical Reading: 680–780. SAT Math: 680–760. SAT Writing: 680–760. ACT Comp: 27–33. HS Rank of Entering Freshmen: Top 10%: 88%. Top 25%: 95%. Avg. HS GPA: Unavailable.

Cost: Tuition and Fees: In-State: $34,564. Out-of-State: $34,564. Room and Board: $10,816.

Inst. Aid: FT Undergrads Receiving Aid: Unavailable. Avg. Amount per Student: Unavailable.

SWEET BRIAR COLLEGE

Sweet Briar, VA

admissions@sbc.edu; www.sbc.edu

General Info: Private, Liberal Arts College, Four-year, Women Only, Regionally Accredited, College Board member. Rural setting, Rural community (under 2,500), Residential campus. Academic Calendar: Semester.

Student Body: Full-Time Undergrads: 739. Men: 0%, Women: 100%. Total Undergrad Population: Native American or Native Alaskan: 1%. Asian American or Pacific Islander: 0%. African American: 4%. Latino: 3%. Caucasian: 88%.

International: 0%. Out-of-State: 57%. Total all graduate and professional students: 12.

Academics: Full-Time Faculty: 64.

Admissions: Regular Application Deadline: 2/1. Priority Application Deadline: 2/1. Early Decision Deadline: 12/1. Transfer Priority Deadline: Unavailable. Financial Aid Deadline: Unavailable. Total Number of Students Applied: Unavailable. Percent Admitted: 80%. Number Enrolled: 181. Test Scores (Middle 50%): SAT Critical Reading: 510–640. SAT Math: 470–595. SAT Writing: 500–600. ACT Comp: 21–26. HS Rank of Entering Freshmen: Top 10%: 25%. Top 25%: 64%. Avg. HS GPA: Unavailable.

Cost: Tuition and Fees: In-State: $25,015. Out-of-State: $25,015. Room and Board: $10,040.

Inst. Aid: FT Undergrads Receiving Aid: Unavailable. Avg. Amount per Student: Unavailable.

SYRACUSE UNIVERSITY

Syracuse, NY
orange@syr.edu; www.syr.edu

General Info: Coed, College Board member, Four-year, Middle States Association of Colleges and Schools, Private, Regionally Accredited, University, Extensive Doctoral/Research University. Urban setting, Small city (50,000–249,999), Residential campus. Academic Calendar: Semester.

Student Body: Full-Time Undergrads: 12,144. Men: 45%, Women: 55%. Part-Time Undergrads. Men: 62%, Women: 38%. Total Undergrad Population: Native American or Native Alaskan: 0.7%. Asian American or Pacific Islander: 10.8%. African American: 8%. Latino: 7.2%. Caucasian: 60.2%. International: 4.3%. Out-of-State: 58%. Living Off-Campus: 1%. % In Fraternities: 15%. % In Sororities: 26%. Total all graduate and professional students: 5,881.

Academics: Full-Time Faculty: 906. With PhD: 793. Percentage completing two or more majors: 10%. Graduation Rates: 70.6% within 4 years. 81.5% within 6 years.

Admissions: Regular Application Deadline: 1/1. Priority Application Deadline: Unavailable. Early Decision Deadline: 11/15. Fall Transfer Deadline: 1/1. Spring Transfer Deadline: 11/15. Transfer Priority Deadline: 1/1. Financial Aid Deadline: 2/1. Total Number of Students Applied: 21,219. Number Admitted: 10,744. Number Enrolled: 3,098. Number accepting place on waitlist: 1,761. Number of waitlisted students admitted: 197. Number applied early decision: 757. Early decision admitted: 607. Test Scores (Middle 50%): SAT Critical Reading: 540–650. SAT Math: 570–680. SAT Writing: Unavailable. ACT Comp: 24–29. HS Rank of Entering Freshmen: Top 10%: 42%. Top 25%: 70%. Avg. HS GPA: 3.6.

Cost: Tuition and Fees: In-State: $32,180. Out-of-State: $32,180. Room and Board: $11,520.

Inst. Aid: FT Undergrads Receiving Aid: 7,094. Avg. Amount per Student: $24,200. Freshmen Receiving Non-Need Scholarship or Grant: 390. Avg. Amount per Student: $9,440.

Graduates: Percentage of grads accepting a job at time of graduation: 79%.

TEMPLE UNIVERSITY

Philadelphia, PA
tuadm@temple.edu; www.temple.edu

General Info: Public, University, Four-year, Coed, Regionally Accredited, Middle States Association of Colleges and Schools, College Board member. Urban setting, Very large city (over 500,000), Commuter campus. Academic Calendar: Semester.

Student Body: Full-Time Undergrads: 24,674. Men: 45%, Women: 55%. Total Undergrad Population: Native American or Native Alaskan: 0%. Asian American or Pacific Islander: 11%. African American: 18%. Latino: 4%. Caucasian: 58%. International: 2%. Out-of-State: 29%. Total all graduate and professional students: 6,098.

Academics: Full-Time Faculty: 1,253.

Admissions: Regular Application Deadline: 4/1. Priority Application Deadline: Unavailable. Early Decision Deadline: Unavailable. Transfer Priority Deadline: Unavailable. Financial Aid Deadline: 3/1. Total Number of Students Applied: Unavailable. Percent Admitted: 60%. Number Enrolled: 4,043. Test Scores (Middle 50%): SAT Critical Reading: 490–590. SAT Math: 500–600. SAT Writing: 480–580. ACT Comp: 20–25. HS Rank of Entering Freshmen: Top 10%: 18%. Top 25%: 50%. Avg. HS GPA: Unavailable.

Cost: Tuition and Fees: In-State: $10,180. Out-of-State: $18,224. Room and Board: $8,230.

Inst. Aid: FT Undergrads Receiving Aid: Unavailable. Avg. Amount per Student: Unavailable.

TEXAS A&M UNIVERSITY

College Station, TX
admissions@tamu.edu; www.tamu.edu

General Info: Public, University, Four-year, Coed, Regionally Accredited, Southern Association of Colleges and Schools, College Board member. Rural setting, Small city (50,000–249,999), Residential campus. Academic Calendar: Semester.

Student Body: Full-Time Undergrads: 36,082. Men: 53%, Women: 47%. Total Undergrad Population: Native American or Native Alaskan: 1%. Asian American or Pacific Islander: 4%. African American: 3%. Latino: 12%. Caucasian: 79%. International: 1%. Out-of-State: 5%. Total all graduate and professional students: 8,291.

Academics: Full-Time Faculty: 1,922.

Admissions: Regular Application Deadline: 2/1. Priority Application Deadline: Unavailable. Early Decision Deadline: 11/15. Transfer Priority Deadline: Unavailable. Financial Aid Deadline: Unavailable. Total Number of Students Applied: Unavailable. Percent Admitted: 77%. Number Enrolled: 7,804. Test Scores (Middle 50%): SAT Critical Reading: 520–630. SAT Math: 560–660. SAT Writing: 500–610.

ACT Comp: 23–28. HS Rank of Entering Freshmen: Top 10%: 46%. Top 25%: 77%. Avg. HS GPA: Unavailable.

Cost: Tuition and Fees: In-State: $6,966. Out-of-State: $15,216. Room and Board: $7,660.

Inst. Aid: FT Undergrads Receiving Aid: Unavailable. Avg. Amount per Student: Unavailable.

TEXAS CHRISTIAN UNIVERSITY

Fort Worth, TX

frogmail@tcu.edu; www.tcu.edu

General Info: Private, University, Four-year, Christian Church (Disciples Of Christ), Coed, Regionally Accredited, College Board member. Suburban setting, Large city (250,000–499,999), Residential campus. Academic Calendar: Semester.

Student Body: Full-Time Undergrads: 7,267. Men: 41%, Women: 59%. Total Undergrad Population: Native American or Native Alaskan: 1%. Asian American or Pacific Islander: 4%. African American: 5%. Latino: 9%. Caucasian: 75%. International: 3%. Out-of-State: 24%. Total all graduate and professional students: 1,308.

Academics: Full-Time Faculty: 478.

Admissions: Regular Application Deadline: 2/15. Priority Application Deadline: 11/15. Early Decision Deadline: Unavailable. Transfer Priority Deadline: 4/15. Financial Aid Deadline: 5/1. Total Number of Students Applied: Unavailable. Percent Admitted: 63%. Number Enrolled: 1,649. Test Scores (Middle 50%): SAT Critical Reading: 520–620. SAT Math: 540–640. SAT Writing: Unavailable. ACT Comp: 23–28. HS Rank of Entering Freshmen: Top 10%: 28%. Top 25%: 64%. Avg. HS GPA: Unavailable.

Cost: Tuition and Fees: In-State: $24,868. Out-of-State: $24,868. Room and Board: $7,400.

Inst. Aid: FT Undergrads Receiving Aid: Unavailable. Avg. Amount per Student: Unavailable.

TEXAS TECH UNIVERSITY

Lubbock, TX

admissions@ttu.edu; www.gototexastech.com

General Info: Public, University, Four-year, Coed, Regionally Accredited, Southern Association of Colleges and Schools, College Board member. Residential campus, Small city (50,000–249,999). Academic Calendar: Semester.

Student Body: Full-Time Undergrads: 22,851. Men: 52%, Women: 48%. Total Undergrad Population: Native American or Native Alaskan: 1%. Asian American or Pacific Islander: 3%. African American: 4%. Latino: 12%. Caucasian: 80%. International: 1%. Out-of-State: 5%. Total all graduate and professional students: 4,443.

Academics: Full-Time Faculty: 1,046.

Admissions: Regular Application Deadline: 5/1. Priority Application Deadline: Unavailable. Early Decision Deadline: Unavailable. Transfer Priority Deadline: Unavailable. Financial Aid Deadline: Unavailable. Total Number of Students Applied: Unavailable. Percent Admitted: 70%. Number Enrolled: 3,743. Test Scores (Middle 50%): SAT Critical Reading: 500–590. SAT Math: 520–620. SAT Writing: 470–570. ACT Comp: 21–26. HS Rank of Entering Freshmen: Top 10%: 22%. Top 25%: 55%. Avg. HS GPA: Unavailable.

Cost: Tuition and Fees: In-State: $6,759. Out-of-State: $14,589. Room and Board: $6,720.

Inst. Aid: FT Undergrads Receiving Aid: Unavailable. Avg. Amount per Student: Unavailable.

Schools with Green Buildings

Pacific Lutheran University

Seattle University

Western Washington University

TRINITY COLLEGE

Hartford, CT

admissions.office@trincoll.edu; www.trincoll.edu

General Info: Private, Liberal Arts College, Four-year, Coed, Regionally Accredited, College Board member. Urban setting, Large city (250,000–499,999), Residential campus. Academic Calendar: Semester.

Student Body: Full-Time Undergrads: 2,353. Men: 52%, Women: 48%. Total Undergrad Population: Native American or Native Alaskan: 0%. Asian American or Pacific Islander: 6%. African American: 6%. Latino: 6%. Caucasian: 65%. International: 2%. Out-of-State: 85%. Total all graduate and professional students: 175.

Academics: Full-Time Faculty: 183.

Admissions: Regular Application Deadline: 1/1. Priority Application Deadline: Unavailable. Early Decision Deadline: 11/15. Transfer Priority Deadline: Unavailable. Financial Aid Deadline: 2/1. Total Number of Students Applied: Unavailable. Percent Admitted: 43%. Number Enrolled: 609. Test Scores (Middle 50%): SAT Critical Reading: 600–690. SAT Math: 610–700. SAT Writing: 600–700. ACT Comp: 27–29. HS Rank of Entering Freshmen: Top 10%: 53%. Top 25%: 89%. Avg. HS GPA: Unavailable.

Cost: Tuition and Fees: In-State: $35,130. Out-of-State: $35,130. Room and Board: $8,970.

Inst. Aid: FT Undergrads Receiving Aid: Unavailable. Avg. Amount per Student: Unavailable.

TRINITY UNIVERSITY

San Antonio, TX

admissions@trinity.edu; www.trinity.edu

General Info: Private, Liberal Arts College, Four-year, Presbyterian Church (USA), Coed, Regionally Accredited, College Board member. Urban setting, Very large city (over 500,000), Residential campus. Academic Calendar: Semester.

Student Body: Full-Time Undergrads: 2,693. Men: 46%, Women: 54%. Total Undergrad Population: Native American or Native Alaskan: 1%. Asian American or Pacific Islander: 7%. African American: 3%. Latino: 10%. Caucasian: 60%. International: 6%. Out-of-State: 17%. Total all graduate and professional students: 226.

Academics: Full-Time Faculty: 240.

Admissions: Regular Application Deadline: 2/1. Priority Application Deadline: Unavailable. Early Decision Deadline: 11/1. Transfer Priority Deadline: Unavailable. Financial Aid Deadline: 4/1. Total Number of Students Applied: Unavailable. Percent Admitted: 61%. Number Enrolled: 633. Test Scores (Middle 50%): SAT Critical Reading: 580–680. SAT Math: 610–690. SAT Writing: Unavailable. ACT Comp: 26–31. HS Rank of Entering Freshmen: Top 10%: 49%. Top 25%: 84%. Avg. HS GPA: Unavailable.

Cost: Tuition and Fees: In-State: $24,131. Out-of-State: $24,131. Room and Board: $8,198.

Inst. Aid: FT Undergrads Receiving Aid: Unavailable. Avg. Amount per Student: Unavailable.

TRUMAN STATE UNIVERSITY

Kirksville, MO

admissions@truman.edu; admissions.truman.edu

General Info: Public, Liberal Arts College, University, Four-year, Coed, Regionally Accredited, North Central Association of Colleges and Schools, College Board member. Rural setting, Large town (10,000–49,999), Residential campus. Academic Calendar: Semester.

Student Body: Full-Time Undergrads: 5,391. Men: 39%, Women: 61%. Total Undergrad Population: Native American or Native Alaskan: 1%. Asian American or Pacific Islander: 3%. African American: 6%. Latino: 3%. Caucasian: 81%. International: 3%. Out-of-State: 21%. Total all graduate and professional students: 238.

Academics: Full-Time Faculty: 240.

Admissions: Regular Application Deadline: 3/1. Priority Application Deadline: Unavailable. Early Decision Deadline: Unavailable. Financial Aid Deadline: Unavailable. Total Number of Students Applied: Unavailable. Percent Admitted: 81%. Number Enrolled: 1,444. Test Scores (Middle 50%): SAT Critical Reading: 550–680. SAT Math: 540–660. SAT Writing: Unavailable. ACT Comp: 25–30. HS Rank of Entering Freshmen: Top 10%: 51%. Top 25%: 83%. Avg. HS GPA: Unavailable.

Cost: Tuition and Fees: In-State: $6,092. Out-of-State: $10,522. Room and Board: $5,790.

Inst. Aid: FT Undergrads Receiving Aid: Unavailable. Avg. Amount per Student: Unavailable.

TUFTS UNIVERSITY

Medford, MA

admissions.inquiry@ase.tufts.edu; www.tufts.edu

General Info: Private, University, Four-year, Coed, Regionally Accredited, College Board member. Suburban setting, Small city (50,000–249,999), Residential campus. Academic Calendar: Semester.

Student Body: Full-Time Undergrads: 5,035. Men: 50%, Women: 50%. Total Undergrad Population: Native American or Native Alaskan: 0%. Asian American or Pacific Islander: 12%. African American: 6%. Latino: 6%. Caucasian: 57%. International: 6%. Out-of-State: 79%. Total all graduate and professional students: 4,723.

Some U.S. Green Building Council members (there are hundreds!)

- Arizona State University
- Clemson University
- Dartmouth College
- Duke University
- Kansas State University
- Penn State University
- Purdue University
- Stanford University
- University of Kentucky
- University of Oklahoma

Academics: Full-Time Faculty: 1,210. With PhD: 989. Graduation Rates: 84% within 4 years. 89% within 6 years.

Admissions: Regular Application Deadline: 1/1. Priority Application Deadline: Unavailable. Early Decision Deadline: 11/1. Transfer Priority Deadline: Unavailable. Financial Aid Deadline: 2/15. Total Number of Students Applied: 15,365. Number Admitted: 4,229. Number Enrolled: 1,373. Number applied early decision: 1,321. Early decision admitted: 422. Test Scores (Middle 50%): SAT Critical Reading: 670–750. SAT Math: 670–740. SAT Writing: 670–740. ACT Comp: 30–32. HS Rank of Entering Freshmen: Top 10%: 80%. Top 25%: 95%. Avg. HS GPA: Unavailable.

Cost: Tuition and Fees: In-State: $38,840. Out-of-State: $38,840. Room and Board: $10,518.

Inst. Aid: FT Undergrads Receiving Aid: 1,963. Avg. Amount per Student: $27,828.

Graduates: Alumni Giving %: 22%.

Top Media Studies Programs

UC Berkeley

Tufts University

Louisiana State University – Baton Rouge

TULANE UNIVERSITY

New Orleans, LA

undergrad.admission@tulane.edu; www.tulane.edu

General Info: Private, University, Four-year, Coed, Regionally Accredited, College Board member. Urban setting, Very large city (over 500,000), Residential campus. Academic Calendar: Semester.

Student Body: Full-Time Undergrads: 6,533. Men: 48%, Women: 52%. Total Undergrad Population: Native American or Native Alaskan: 2%. Asian American or Pacific Islander: 5%. African American: 10%. Latino: 4%. Caucasian: 76%. International: 7%. Out-of-State: 86%. Living Off-Campus: 30%. Total all graduate and professional students: 2,305.

Academics: Full-Time Faculty: 1,132. Percentage completing two or more majors: 40%.

Admissions: Regular Application Deadline: 1/15. Priority Application Deadline: 11/1. Early Decision Deadline: N/A. Financial Aid Deadline: 2/1. Total Number of Students Applied: Unavailable. Number Admitted: 8,000. Number Enrolled: Unavailable. Test Scores (Middle 50%): SAT Critical Reading: 610–725. SAT Math: 610–700. SAT Writing: 590–680. ACT Comp: 27–31. HS Rank of Entering Freshmen: Top 10%: 80%. Top 25%: 98%. Avg. HS GPA: 3.7.

Cost: Tuition and Fees: In-State: $38,664. Out-of-State: $34,896. Room and Board: $9,330.

Inst. Aid: FT Undergrads Receiving Aid: Unavailable. Avg. Amount per Student: Unavailable.

TUSKEGEE UNIVERSITY

Tuskegee, AL

adm@tuskegee.edu; www.tuskegee.edu

General Info: Private, Liberal Arts College, University, Four-year, Coed, Regionally Accredited, College Board member, Historically black. Rural setting, Small town (2,500–9,999), Residential campus. Academic Calendar: Semester.

Student Body: Full-Time Undergrads: 2,299. Men: 43%, Women: 57%. Total Undergrad Population: Native American or Native Alaskan: 0%. Asian American or Pacific Islander: 0%. African American: 86%. Latino: 0%. Caucasian: 0%. International: 1%. Out-of-State: 52%. Total all graduate and professional students: 186.

Academics: Full-Time Faculty: 252.

Admissions: Regular Application Deadline: 6/15. Priority Application Deadline: Unavailable. Early Decision Deadline: Unavailable. Transfer Priority Deadline: 5/15. Financial Aid Deadline: 3/31. Total Number of Students Applied: Unavailable. Percent Admitted: 59%. Number Enrolled: 697. Test Scores (Middle 50%): SAT Critical Reading: 390–500. SAT Math: 380–490. SAT Writing: Unavailable. ACT Comp: 16–21. HS Rank of Entering Freshmen: Top 10%: 20%. Top 25%: 59%. Avg. HS GPA: Unavailable.

Cost: Tuition and Fees: In-State: $12,985. Out-of-State: $12,985. Room and Board: $7,110.

Inst. Aid: FT Undergrads Receiving Aid: Unavailable. Avg. Amount per Student: Unavailable.

UNION COLLEGE

Schenectady, NY

admissions@union.edu; www.union.edu

General Info: Private, College of Engineering, Liberal Arts College, Four-year, Coed, Regionally Accredited, College Board member. Urban setting, Small city (50,000–249,999), Residential campus. Academic Calendar: Trimester.

Student Body: Full-Time Undergrads: 2,000. Men: 48%, Women: 52%. Total Undergrad Population: Native American or Native Alaskan: 0%. Asian American or Pacific Islander: 5%. African American: 3%. Latino: 4%. Caucasian: 84%. International: 3%. Out-of-State: 64%.

Academics: Full-Time Faculty: 182.

Admissions: Regular Application Deadline: 1/15. Priority Application Deadline: Unavailable. Early Decision Deadline: 11/15. Transfer Priority Deadline: Unavailable. Financial Aid Deadline: 2/1. Total Number of Students Applied: Unavailable. Percent Admitted: 43%. Number Enrolled: Unavailable. Test Scores (Middle 50%): SAT Critical Reading: 550–650. SAT Math: 580–670. SAT Writing: Unavailable. ACT Comp: 24–29. HS Rank of Entering Freshmen: Top 10%: 62%. Top 25%: 87%. Avg. HS GPA: Unavailable.

Cost: Tuition and Fees: In-State: $46,245. Out-of-State: Unavailable. Room and Board: $0.

Inst. Aid: FT Undergrads Receiving Aid: Unavailable. Avg. Amount per Student: Unavailable.

UNITED STATES COAST GUARD ACADEMY

New London, CT

www.uscga.edu; amy.l.miller.uscga.edu

General Info: Public, College of Engineering, Military College, Maritime College, Four-year, Coed, Regionally Accredited, New England Association of Colleges and Schools, College Board member. Suburban setting, Small city (50,000–249,999), Residential campus. Academic Calendar: Semester.

Student Body: Full-Time Undergrads: 950. Men: 70%, Women: 30%. Total Undergrad Population: Native American or Native Alaskan: 1%. Asian American or Pacific Islander: 4%. African American: 5%. Latino: 8%. Caucasian: 81%. International: 2%. Out-of-State: 97%.

Academics: Full-Time Faculty: 100.

Admissions: Regular Application Deadline: 3/1. Priority Application Deadline: Unavailable. Early Decision Deadline: Unavailable. Transfer Priority Deadline: Unavailable. Financial Aid Deadline: Unavailable. Total Number of Students Applied: Unavailable. Percent Admitted: 24%. Number Enrolled: 274. Test Scores (Middle 50%): SAT Critical Reading: 570–670. SAT Math: 610–680. SAT Writing: Unavailable. ACT Comp: 27–31. HS Rank of Entering Freshmen: Top 10%: 47%. Top 25%: 86%. Avg. HS GPA: Unavailable.

Cost: Tuition and Fees: In-State: Unavailable. Out-of-State: Unavailable. Room and Board: Unavailable.

Inst. Aid: FT Undergrads Receiving Aid: Unavailable. Avg. Amount per Student: Unavailable.

UNITED STATES MERCHANT MARINE ACADEMY

Kings Point, NY

admissions@usmma.edu; www.usmma.edu

General Info: Public, College of Engineering, Military College, Maritime College, Four-year, Coed, Regionally Accredited, Middle States Association of Colleges and Schools, College Board member. Suburban setting, Large town (10,000–49,999), Residential campus. Academic Calendar: Trimester.

Student Body: Full-Time Undergrads: 950. Men: 81%, Women: 19%. Total Undergrad Population: Native American or Native Alaskan: 0%. Asian American or Pacific Islander: 0%. African American: 0%. Latino: 0%. Caucasian: 0%. International: 0%. Out-of-State: 86%.

Academics: Full-Time Faculty: 85.

Admissions: Regular Application Deadline: Unavailable. Priority Application Deadline: Unavailable. Early Decision Deadline: 11/1. Transfer Priority Deadline: Unavailable. Financial Aid Deadline: 5/1. Total Number of Students Applied: Unavailable. Percent Admitted: 28%. Number Enrolled: Unavailable. Test Scores (Middle 50%): SAT Critical Reading: 540–640. SAT Math: 595–660. SAT Writing: Unavailable. ACT Comp: 25–29. HS Rank of Entering Freshmen: Top 10%: 26%. Top 25%: 64%. Avg. HS GPA: Unavailable.

Cost: Tuition and Fees: In-State: Unavailable. Out-of-State: Unavailable. Room and Board: Unavailable.

Inst. Aid: FT Undergrads Receiving Aid: Unavailable. Avg. Amount per Student: Unavailable.

Famous Writers' Schools

Nathaniel Hawthorne—Bowdoin College

Edgar Allan Poe—University of Virginia

Emily Dickinson—Mount Holyoke College

Elizabeth Bishop—Vassar College

Ezra Pound—Hamilton College

F. Scott Fitzgerald—Princeton University

Kurt Vonnegut—Cornell University

Thomas Pynchon—Cornell

Toni Morrison—Howard University

Joyce Carol Oates—Syracuse University

JD Salinger—New York University

Chuch Palahniuk—University of Oregon

UNITED STATES MILITARY ACADEMY

West Point, NY

admissions@usma.edu; www.usma.edu

General Info: Public, College of Engineering, Military College, Four-year, Coed, Regionally Accredited, Middle States Association of Colleges and Schools, College Board member. Rural setting, Small town (2,500–9,999), Residential campus. Academic Calendar: Semester.

Student Body: Full-Time Undergrads: Men: 86%, Women: 14%. Total Undergrad Population: Native American or Native Alaskan: 1%. Asian American or Pacific Islander: 6%. African American: 8%. Latino: 8%. Caucasian: 74%. International: 2%. Out-of-State: 92%.

Academics: Full-Time Faculty: Unavailable.

Admissions: Regular Application Deadline: Unavailable. Priority Application Deadline: Unavailable. Early Decision Deadline: Unavailable. Transfer Priority Deadline: Unavailable. Financial Aid Deadline: Unavailable. Total Number of Students Applied: 10,838. Number Admitted: 1,305. Number Enrolled: Unavailable. Test Scores (Middle 50%): SAT Critical Reading: 570–680. SAT Math: 590–680. SAT Writing: Unavailable. ACT Comp: 26–29. HS Rank of Entering Freshmen: Top 10%: 92%. Top 25%: 99%. Avg. HS GPA: Unavailable.

Cost: Tuition and Fees: In-State: Unavailable. Out-of-State: Unavailable. Room and Board: Unavailable.

Inst. Aid: FT Undergrads Receiving Aid: Unavailable. Avg. Amount per Student: Unavailable.

UNITED STATES NAVAL ACADEMY

Annapolis, MD

webmail@usna.edu; www.usna.edu

General Info: Public, Military College, Four-year, Coed, Regionally Accredited, Middle States Association of Colleges and Schools, College Board member. Urban setting, Large town (10,000–49,999), Residential campus. Academic Calendar: Semester.

Student Body: Full-Time Undergrads: 4,479. Men: 81%, Women: 19%. Total Undergrad Population: Native American or Native Alaskan: 3%. Asian American or Pacific Islander: 4%. African American: 6%. Latino: 10%. Caucasian: 76%. International: 1%. Out-of-State: 95%.

Academics: Full-Time Faculty: 514.

Admissions: Regular Application Deadline: 3/1. Priority Application Deadline: Unavailable. Early Decision Deadline: Unavailable. Transfer Priority Deadline: Unavailable. Financial Aid Deadline: Unavailable. Total Number of Students Applied: Unavailable. Percent Admitted: 12%. Number Enrolled: 1,191. Test Scores (Middle 50%): SAT Critical Reading: 570–680. SAT Math: 620–700. SAT Writing: Unavailable. HS Rank of Entering Freshmen: Top 10%: 63%. Top 25%: 80%. Avg. HS GPA: Unavailable.

Cost: Tuition and Fees: In-State: $0. Out-of-State: $0. Room and Board: $0.

Inst. Aid: FT Undergrads Receiving Aid: Unavailable. Avg. Amount per Student: Unavailable.

UNIVERSITY OF ALABAMA

Tuscaloosa, AL

admissions@ua.edu; www.ua.edu

General Info: Public, University, Four-year, Coed, Regionally Accredited, Southern Association of Colleges and Schools, College Board member. Suburban setting, Small city (50,000–249,999), Residential campus. Academic Calendar: Semester.

Student Body: Full-Time Undergrads: 17,553. Men: 45%, Women: 55%. Total Undergrad Population: Native American or Native Alaskan: 1%. Asian American or Pacific Islander: 1%. African American: 9%. Latino: 4%. Caucasian: 85%. International: 1%. Out-of-State: 34%. Total all graduate and professional students: 3,781.

Academics: Full-Time Faculty: 893.

Admissions: Regular Application Deadline: 5/1. Priority Application Deadline: Unavailable. Early Decision Deadline: Unavailable. Transfer Priority Deadline: Unavailable. Financial Aid Deadline: Unavailable. Total Number of Students Applied: Unavailable. Percent Admitted: 70%. Number Enrolled: 3,706. Test Scores (Middle 50%): SAT Critical Reading: 500–630. SAT Math: 500–630. SAT Writing: Unavailable. ACT Comp: 21–27. HS Rank of Entering Freshmen: Top 10%: 32%. Top 25%: 51%. Avg. HS GPA: Unavailable.

Cost: Tuition and Fees: In-State: $5,278. Out-of-State: $15,294. Room and Board: $5,380.

Inst. Aid: FT Undergrads Receiving Aid: Unavailable. Avg. Amount per Student: Unavailable.

School Mottos

University of Pennsylvania—"Laws without morals are useless"

Dartmouth College—"A voice of one crying out in the wilderness"

Seton Hall University—"Whatever risk, yet go forward"

Famous Harvard Graduates

Cotton Mather (1678): minister

John Adams (1754): 2nd president

Ralph Waldo Emerson (1821): transcendentalist poet

Sumner Redstone (1944): Viacom chairman

Natalie Portman (2003): actress

UNIVERSITY OF ARIZONA

Tucson, AZ

appinfo@arizona.edu; www.arizona.edu

General Info: Public, University, Four-year, Coed, Regionally Accredited, North Central Association of Colleges and Schools, College Board member. Urban setting, Very large city (over 500,000), Residential campus. Academic Calendar: Semester.

Student Body: Full-Time Undergrads: 28,442. Men: 47%, Women: 53%. Total Undergrad Population: Native American or Native Alaskan: 3%. Asian American or Pacific Islander: 7%. African American: 3%. Latino: 17%. Caucasian: 65%. International: 2%. Out-of-State: 37%. Total all graduate and professional students: 7,105.

Academics: Full-Time Faculty: 1,412.

Admissions: Regular Application Deadline: 4/1. Priority Application Deadline: Unavailable. Early Decision Deadline: Unavailable. Transfer Priority Deadline: Unavailable. Financial Aid Deadline: Unavailable. Total Number of Students Applied: Unavailable. Percent Admitted: 80%. Number Enrolled: 5,785. Test Scores (Middle 50%): SAT Critical Reading: 490–600. SAT Math: 500–630. SAT Writing: Unavailable. ACT Comp: 20–26. HS Rank of Entering Freshmen: Top 10%: 34%. Top 25%: 61%. Avg. HS GPA: Unavailable.

Cost: Tuition and Fees: In-State: $4,754. Out-of-State: $14,960. Room and Board: $7,850.

Inst. Aid: FT Undergrads Receiving Aid: Unavailable. Avg. Amount per Student: Unavailable.

UNIVERSITY OF ARKANSAS

Fayetteville, AR

uofa@uark.edu; www.uark.edu

General Info: Public, University, Four-year, Coed, Regionally Accredited, North Central Association of Colleges and Schools, College Board member. Urban setting, Small city (50,000–249,999), Residential campus. Academic Calendar: Semester.

Student Body: Full-Time Undergrads: 14,350. Men: 50%, Women: 50%. Part-Time Undergrads. Men: 7.5%, Women: 7%. Total Undergrad Population: Native American or Native Alaskan: 2%. Asian American or Pacific Islander: 3%. African American: 5%. Latino: 3%. Caucasian: 80%. International: 5%. Out-of-State: 33%. Living Off-Campus: 12.6%. Total all graduate and professional students: 3,700.

Academics: Full-Time Faculty: 852. With PhD: 780. Graduation Rate: 58% within 6 years.

Admissions: Regular Application Deadline: 8/15. Priority Application Deadline: Unavailable. Early Decision Deadline: Unavailable. Transfer Priority Deadline: Unavailable. Financial Aid Deadline: Unavailable. Total Number of Students Applied: 10,230. Number Admitted: 6,262. Number Enrolled: Unavailable. Test Scores (Middle 50%): SAT Critical Reading: 510–630. SAT Math: 520–650. SAT Writing: Unavailable. ACT Comp: 23–29. HS Rank of Entering Freshmen: Top 10%: 31.7%. Top 25%: 62%. Avg. HS GPA: 3.

Cost: Tuition and Fees: In-State: $4,772. Out-of-State: $13. Room and Board: $7,017.

Inst. Aid: FT Undergrads Receiving Aid: Unavailable. Avg. Amount per Student: Unavailable.

UNIVERSITY OF CALIFORNIA–BERKELEY

Berkeley, CA

ouars@uclink.berkeley.edu; www.berkeley.edu

General Info: Public, University, Four-year, Coed, Regionally Accredited, Western Association of Schools and Colleges, College Board member. Urban setting, Small city (50,000–249,999), Residential campus. Academic Calendar: Semester.

Student Body: Full-Time Undergrads: 23,107. Men: 46%, Women: 54%. Total Undergrad Population: Native American or Native Alaskan: 0%. Asian American or Pacific Islander: 47%. African American: 3%. Latino: 10%. Caucasian: 30%. International: 2%. Out-of-State: 7%.

Academics: Full-Time Faculty: 1,545.

Admissions: Regular Application Deadline: 11/30. Priority Application Deadline: Unavailable. Early Decision Deadline: Unavailable. Transfer Priority Deadline: Unavailable. Financial Aid Deadline: 3/2. Total Number of Students Applied: Unavailable. Percent Admitted: 24%. Number Enrolled: 4,157. Test Scores (Middle 50%): SAT Critical Reading: 580–710. SAT Math: 620–740. SAT Writing: 590–710. ACT Comp: Unavailable. HS Rank of Entering Freshmen: Top 10%: 99%. Top 25%: 100%. Avg. HS GPA: Unavailable.

Cost: Tuition and Fees: In-State: $7,149. Out-of-State: $25,338. Room and Board: $13,848.

Inst. Aid: FT Undergrads Receiving Aid: Unavailable. Avg. Amount per Student: Unavailable.

UNIVERSITY OF CALIFORNIA–DAVIS

Davis, CA
undergraduateadmissions@ucdavis.edu;
www.ucdavis.edu

General Info: Public, University, Four-year, Coed, Regionally Accredited, Western Association of Schools and Colleges, College Board member. Suburban setting, Small city (50,000–249,999), Residential campus. Academic Calendar: Quarter.

Student Body: Full-Time Undergrads: 23,118. Men: 45%, Women: 55%. Part-Time Undergrads. Men: 52%, Women: 48%. Total Undergrad Population: Native American or Native Alaskan: 0.7%. Asian American or Pacific Islander: 40.8%. African American: 3%. Latino: 11.9%. Caucasian: 34.9%. International: 1.9%. Out-of-State: 3%. Total all graduate and professional students: 4,094.

Academics: Full-Time Faculty: 1,595. With PhD: 1,850. Graduation Rates: 43% within 4 years. 79% within 6 years.

Admissions: Regular Application Deadline: 11/30. Priority Application Deadline: Unavailable. Early Decision Deadline: Unavailable. Transfer Priority Deadline: Unavailable. Financial Aid Deadline: Unavailable. Total Number of Students Applied: Unavailable. Number Admitted: 26,064. Number Enrolled: Unavailable. Test Scores (Middle 50%): SAT Critical Reading: 490– 630. SAT Math: 540–660. SAT Writing: 500–630. ACT Comp: 20–27. HS Rank of Entering Freshmen: Top 10%: 95%. Top 25%: 100%. Avg. HS GPA: 374.

Cost: Tuition and Fees: In-State: $8,124. Out-of-State: $27,774. Room and Board: $11,533.

Inst. Aid: FT Undergrads Receiving Aid: 10,557. Avg. Amount per Student: Unavailable.

Graduates: Alumni Giving %: 13%.

UNIVERSITY OF CALIFORNIA–IRVINE

Irvine, CA
admissions@uci.edu; www.uci.edu

General Info: Public, University, Four-year, Coed, Western Association of Schools and Colleges, Regionally Accredited, College Board member. Suburban setting, Small city (50,000–249,999), Residential campus. Academic Calendar: Quarter.

Student Body: Full-Time Undergrads: 19,930. Men: 47%, Women: 53%. Total Undergrad Population: Native American or Native Alaskan: 0%. Asian American or Pacific Islander: 52%. African American: 2%. Latino: 11%. Caucasian: 26%. International: 1%. Out-of-State: 3%. Total all graduate and professional students: 4,065.

Academics: Full-Time Faculty: 966.

Admissions: Regular Application Deadline: 11/30. Priority Application Deadline: Unavailable. Early Decision Deadline: Unavailable. Transfer Priority Deadline: 11/30. Financial Aid Deadline: 3/1. Total Number of Students Applied: 39,956. Number Admitted: 22,220. Number Enrolled: 4,900. Test Scores (Middle 50%): SAT Critical Reading: 540–630. SAT Math: 570–680. SAT Writing: Unavailable. HS Rank of Entering Freshmen: Top 10%: Unavailable. Top 25%: Unavailable. Avg. HS GPA: 3.92.

Cost: Tuition and Fees: In-State: $6,794. Out-of-State: $25,478. Room and Board: $0.

Inst. Aid: FT Undergrads Receiving Aid: Unavailable. Avg. Amount per Student: Unavailable.

UNIVERSITY OF CALIFORNIA–LOS ANGELES

Los Angeles, CA
ugadm@saonet.ucla.edu; www.ucla.edu

General Info: Public, University, Four-year, Coed, Regionally Accredited, Western Association of Schools and Colleges, College Board member. Urban setting, Very large city (over 500,000), Residential campus. Academic Calendar: Quarter.

Student Body: Full-Time Undergrads: 24,811. Men: 41%, Women: 59%. Total Undergrad Population: Native American or Native Alaskan: 0%. Asian American or Pacific Islander: 41%. African American: 3%. Latino: 14%. Caucasian: 33%. International: 2%. Out-of-State: 4%. Total all graduate and professional students: 10,492.

Academics: Full-Time Faculty: 1,890.

Admissions: Regular Application Deadline: 11/30. Priority Application Deadline: Unavailable. Early Decision Deadline: Unavailable. Transfer Priority Deadline: Unavailable. Financial Aid Deadline: 3/2. Total Number of Students Applied: Unavailable. Percent Admitted: 26%. Number Enrolled: Unavailable. Test Scores (Middle 50%): SAT Critical Reading: 570–690. SAT Math: 600–720. SAT Writing: 590–700. ACT Comp: 24–30. HS Rank of Entering Freshmen: Top 10%: 97%. Top 25%: 100%. Avg. HS GPA: Unavailable.

Cost: Tuition and Fees: In-State: $6,522. Out-of-State: $25,206. Room and Board: $12,312.

Inst. Aid: FT Undergrads Receiving Aid: Unavailable. Avg. Amount per Student: Unavailable.

UNIVERSITY OF CALIFORNIA–SAN DIEGO

La Jolla, CA
admissionsinfo@ucsd.edu; www.ucsd.edu

General Info: Public, Coed. Setting: Large Town. Academic Calendar: Quarter.

Student Body: Full-Time Undergrads: 20,679. Men: 49%, Women: 51%.

Academics: Full-Time Faculty: 965.

Admissions: Regular Application Deadline: 11/30. Priority Application Deadline: Unavailable. Early Decision Deadline: Unavailable. Financial Aid Deadline: Unavailable. Total Number of Students Applied: Unavailable. Percent Admitted: 42%. Number Enrolled: Unavailable. Test Scores (Middle 50%): SAT Critical Reading: 540–660. SAT Math: 590–700. SAT Writing: Unavailable. ACT Comp: 23–29. HS Rank of Entering Freshmen: Top 10%: 99%. Top 25%: 100%. Avg. HS GPA: Unavailable.

Cost: Tuition and Fees: In-State: $6,888. Out-of-State: $6,888. Room and Board: $9,657.

Inst. Aid: FT Undergrads Receiving Aid: Unavailable. Avg. Amount per Student: Unavailable.

UNIVERSITY OF CALIFORNIA–SANTA BARBARA

Santa Barbara, CA
appinfo@sa.ucsb.edu; www.ucsb.edu

General Info: Public, University, Four-year, Coed, Regionally Accredited, Western Association of Schools and Colleges, College Board member. Suburban setting, Small city (50,000–249,999), Residential campus. Academic Calendar: Quarter.

Student Body: Full-Time Undergrads: 18,077. Men: 43%, Women: 57%. Total Undergrad Population: Native American or Native Alaskan: 1%. Asian American or Pacific Islander: 17%. African American: 3%. Latino: 20%. Caucasian: 53%. International: 1%. Out-of-State: 2%. Total all graduate and professional students: 2,939.

Academics: Full-Time Faculty: 919.

Admissions: Regular Application Deadline: 11/30. Priority Application Deadline: Unavailable. Early Decision Deadline: Unavailable. Transfer Priority Deadline: Unavailable. Financial Aid Deadline: 5/31. Total Number of Students Applied: Unavailable. Percent Admitted: 53%. Number Enrolled: 3,876. Test Scores (Middle 50%): SAT Critical Reading: 530–650. SAT Math: 560–670. SAT Writing: Unavailable. ACT Comp: 22–28. HS Rank of Entering Freshmen: Top 10%: Unavailable. Top 25%: Unavailable. Avg. HS GPA: Unavailable.

Cost: Tuition and Fees: In-State: $7,010. Out-of-State: $25,694. Room and Board: $10,577.

Inst. Aid: FT Undergrads Receiving Aid: Unavailable. Avg. Amount per Student: Unavailable.

UNIVERSITY OF CALIFORNIA–SANTA CRUZ

Santa Cruz, CA
admissions@ucsc.edu; www.ucsc.edu

General Info: Public, University, Four-year, Coed, Western Association of Schools and Colleges, Regionally Accredited, College Board member. Suburban setting, Small city (50,000–249,999), Residential campus. Academic Calendar: Quarter.

Student Body: Full-Time Undergrads: 13,482. Men: 47%, Women: 53%. Total Undergrad Population: Native American or Native Alaskan: 1%. Asian American or Pacific Islander: 21%. African American: 2%. Latino: 15%. Caucasian: 53%. International: 1%. Out-of-State: 4%. Total all graduate and professional students: 1,387.

Academics: Full-Time Faculty: 554.

Admissions: Regular Application Deadline: 11/30. Priority Application Deadline: Unavailable. Early Decision Deadline: Unavailable. Transfer Priority Deadline: 11/1. Financial Aid Deadline: 3/2. Total Number of Students Applied: Unavailable. Percent Admitted: 80%. Number Enrolled: 3,350. Test Scores (Middle 50%): SAT Critical Reading: 520–630. SAT Math: 530–640. SAT Writing: 510–620. ACT Comp: 22–28. HS Rank of Entering Freshmen: Top 10%: 90%. Top 25%: 100%. Avg. HS GPA: Unavailable.

Cost: Tuition and Fees: In-State: $7,017. Out-of-State: $25,701. Room and Board: $11,805.

Inst. Aid: FT Undergrads Receiving Aid: Unavailable. Avg. Amount per Student: Unavailable.

UNIVERSITY OF CHICAGO

Chicago, IL
questions@phoenix.uchicago.edu; www.uchicago.edu

General Info: Private, Liberal Arts College, University, Four-year, Coed, Regionally Accredited, College Board member. Urban setting, Very large city (over 500,000), Residential campus. Academic Calendar: Quarter.

Student Body: Full-Time Undergrads: 4,671. Men: 50%, Women: 50%. Total Undergrad Population: Native American or Native Alaskan: 0%. Asian American or Pacific Islander: 14%. African American: 4%. Latino: 7%. Caucasian: 48%. International: 7%. Out-of-State: 83%. Total all graduate and professional students: 6,209.

Academics: Full-Time Faculty: 1,055.

Admissions: Regular Application Deadline: 1/2. Priority Application Deadline: Unavailable. Early Decision Deadline: Unavailable. Financial Aid Deadline: 2/1. Total Number of Students Applied: Unavailable. Percent Admitted: 38%. Number Enrolled: 1,259. Test Scores (Middle 50%): SAT Critical Reading: 670–770. SAT Math: 650–760. SAT Writing: Unavailable. ACT Comp: 28-33. HS Rank of Entering Freshmen: Top 10%: 80%. Top 25%: 97%. Avg. HS GPA: Unavailable.

Cost: Tuition and Fees: In-State: $34,005. Out-of-State: $34,005. Room and Board: $10,608.

Inst. Aid: FT Undergrads Receiving Aid: Unavailable. Avg. Amount per Student: Unavailable. %.

UNIVERSITY OF CINCINNATI

Cincinnati, OH
admissions@uc.edu; www.uc.edu

General Info: Public, University, Four-year, Coed, North Central Association of Colleges and Schools, Regionally Accredited, College Board member. Urban setting, Large city (250,000–499,999), Commuter campus. Academic Calendar: Quarter.

Student Body: Full-Time Undergrads: 20,085. Men: 51%, Women: 49%. Total Undergrad Population: Native American or Native Alaskan: 0%. Asian American or Pacific Islander: 2%. African American: 14%. Latino: 1%. Caucasian: 77%. International: 1%. Out-of-State: 9%. Total all graduate and professional students: 7,365.

Academics: Full-Time Faculty: 2,925.

Admissions: Regular Application Deadline: 8/1. Priority Application Deadline: Unavailable. Early Decision Deadline: Unavailable. Transfer Priority Deadline: Unavailable. Financial Aid Deadline: Unavailable. Total Number of Students Applied: Unavailable. Number Admitted: Unavailable. Number Enrolled: 3,750. Test Scores (Middle 50%): SAT Critical Reading: 410–520. SAT Math: 400–520. SAT Writing: 470–590. ACT Comp: 21–27. HS Rank of Entering Freshmen: Top 10%: 19%. Top 25%: 48%. Avg. HS GPA: Unavailable.

Cost: Tuition and Fees: In-State: $9,399. Out-of-State: $23,922. Room and Board: $8,799.

Inst. Aid: FT Undergrads Receiving Aid: Unavailable. Avg. Amount per Student: Unavailable.

UNIVERSITY OF COLORADO AT BOULDER

Boulder, CO

apply@colorado.edu; www.colorado.edu

General Info: Public, University, Four-year, Coed, Regionally Accredited, North Central Association of Colleges and Schools, College Board member. Suburban setting, Small city (50,000–249,999), Residential campus. Academic Calendar: Semester.

Student Body: Full-Time Undergrads: 25,495. Men: 53%, Women: 47%. Total Undergrad Population: Native American or Native Alaskan: 1%. Asian American or Pacific Islander: 7%. African American: 1%. Latino: 7%. Caucasian: 79%. International: 1%. Out-of-State: 41%. Total all graduate and professional students: 4,728.

Academics: Full-Time Faculty: 1,248.

Admissions: Regular Application Deadline: 1/15. Priority Application Deadline: Unavailable. Early Decision Deadline: Unavailable. Transfer Priority Deadline: Unavailable. Financial Aid Deadline: Unavailable. Total Number of Students Applied: Unavailable. Percent Admitted: 88%. Number Enrolled: 5,645. Test Scores (Middle 50%): SAT Critical Reading: 520–630. SAT Math: 540–650. SAT Writing: Unavailable. ACT Comp: 23–28. HS Rank of Entering Freshmen: Top 10%: 23%. Top 25%: 54%. Avg. HS GPA: Unavailable.

Cost: Tuition and Fees: In-State: $5,643. Out-of-State: $23,539. Room and Board: $8,300.

Inst. Aid: FT Undergrads Receiving Aid: Unavailable. Avg. Amount per Student: Unavailable.

Want to Be an Architect?

Columbia University

Cooper Union

Princeton University

UNIVERSITY OF CONNECTICUT

Storrs, CT

beahusky@uconnvm.uconn.edu; www.uconn.edu

General Info: Public, University, Four-year, Coed, Regionally Accredited, New England Association of Colleges and Schools, College Board member. Rural setting, Large town (10,000–49,999), Residential campus. Academic Calendar: Semester.

Student Body: Full-Time Undergrads: 16,112. Men: 45%, Women: 55%. Total Undergrad Population: Native American or Native Alaskan: 0%. Asian American or Pacific Islander: 8%. African American: 6%. Latino: 6%. Caucasian: 68%. International: 1%. Out-of-State: 28%. Total all graduate and professional students: 6,180.

Academics: Full-Time Faculty: 975.

Admissions: Regular Application Deadline: 2/1. Priority Application Deadline: Unavailable. Early Decision Deadline: Unavailable. Transfer Priority Deadline: 2/1. Financial Aid Deadline: Unavailable. Total Number of Students Applied: Unavailable. Percent Admitted: 51%. Number Enrolled: 3,243. Test Scores (Middle 50%): SAT Critical Reading: 540–630. SAT Math: 550–650. SAT Writing: Unavailable. ACT Comp: 23–27. HS Rank of Entering Freshmen: Top 10%: 37%. Top 25%: 80%. Avg. HS GPA: Unavailable.

Cost: Tuition and Fees: In-State: $8,362. Out-of-State: $21,562. Room and Board: $8,266.

Inst. Aid: FT Undergrads Receiving Aid: Unavailable. Avg. Amount per Student: Unavailable.

UNIVERSITY OF DALLAS

Irving, TX

ugadmis@udallas.edu; www.udallas.edu

General Info: Private, Liberal Arts College, University, Four-year, Roman Catholic Church, Coed, Regionally Accredited, College Board member. Urban setting, Small city

Guess Who Didn't Go to College!

Walt Disney: animator and producer

Dave Thomas: Wendy's restaurant founder

Larry and Andy Wachowski: filmmakers (The Matrix)

(50,000–249,999), Residential campus. Academic Calendar: Semester.

Student Body: Full-Time Undergrads: 1,188. Men: 46%, Women: 54%. Total Undergrad Population: Native American or Native Alaskan: 1%. Asian American or Pacific Islander: 8%. African American: 2%. Latino: 16%. Caucasian: 67%. International: 1%. Out-of-State: 49%. Total all graduate and professional students: 1,753.

Academics: Full-Time Faculty: 116.

Admissions: Regular Application Deadline: 3/1. Priority Application Deadline: Unavailable. Early Decision Deadline: Unavailable. Transfer Priority Deadline: Unavailable. Financial Aid Deadline: 7/1. Total Number of Students Applied: Unavailable. Percent Admitted: 85%. Number Enrolled: 256. Test Scores (Middle 50%): SAT Critical Reading: 560–690. SAT Math: 540–650. SAT Writing: Unavailable. ACT Comp: 24–29. HS Rank of Entering Freshmen: Top 10%: 34%. Top 25%: 66%. Avg. HS GPA: Unavailable.

Cost: Tuition and Fees: In-State: $23,219. Out-of-State: $23,219. Room and Board: $7,615.

Inst. Aid: FT Undergrads Receiving Aid: Unavailable. Avg. Amount per Student: Unavailable.

UNIVERSITY OF DAYTON

Dayton, OH

admission@udayton.edu; www.udayton.edu

General Info: Private, University, Four-year, Roman Catholic Church, Coed, Regionally Accredited, College Board member. Suburban setting, Small city (50,000–249,999), Residential campus. Academic Calendar: Semester.

Student Body: Full-Time Undergrads: 7,473. Men: 50%, Women: 50%. Total Undergrad Population: Native American or Native Alaskan: 0%. Asian American or Pacific Islander: 1%. African American: 3%. Latino: 2%. Caucasian: 91%. International: 1%. Out-of-State: 38%. Total all graduate and professional students: 2,580.

Academics: Full-Time Faculty: 446.

Admissions: Regular Application Deadline: 1/1. Priority Application Deadline: Unavailable. Early Decision Deadline: Unavailable. Financial Aid Deadline: Unavailable. Total Number of Students Applied: Unavailable. Percent Admitted: 79%. Number Enrolled: 1,981. Test Scores (Middle 50%): SAT Critical Reading: 510–620. SAT Math: 530–650. SAT Writing: Unavailable. ACT Comp: 23–28. HS Rank of Entering Freshmen: Top 10%: 24%. Top 25%: 50%. Avg. HS GPA: Unavailable.

Cost: Tuition and Fees: In-State: $23,970. Out-of-State: $23,970. Room and Board: $7,190.

Inst. Aid: FT Undergrads Receiving Aid: Unavailable. Avg. Amount per Student: Unavailable.

UNIVERSITY OF DELAWARE

Newark, DE

admissions@udel.edu; www.admissions.udel.edu

General Info: Public, University, Four-year, Coed, Regionally Accredited, Middle States Association of Colleges and Schools, College Board member. Suburban setting, Large town (10,000–49,999), Residential campus. Academic Calendar: 4-1-4.

Student Body: Full-Time Undergrads: 15,849. Men: 42%, Women: 58%. Total Undergrad Population: Native American or Native Alaskan: 0%. Asian American or Pacific Islander: 4%. African American: 5%. Latino: 5%. Caucasian: 82%. International: 0%. Out-of-State: 69%. Total all graduate and professional students: 3,446.

Academics: Full-Time Faculty: 1,117.

Admissions: Regular Application Deadline: 1/15. Priority Application Deadline: 12/1. Early Decision Deadline: N/A. Fall Transfer Deadline: 5/1. Spring Transfer Deadline: 11/1. Transfer Priority Deadline: 5/1. Financial Aid Deadline: 3/15. Total Number of Students Applied: Unavailable. Percent Admitted: 47%. Number Enrolled: 3,500. Test Scores (Middle 50%): SAT Critical Reading: 540–640. SAT Math: 560–660. SAT Writing: 540–650. ACT Comp: 23–28. HS Rank of Entering Freshmen: Top 10%: 39%. Top 25%: 80%. Avg. HS GPA: Unavailable.

Cost: Tuition and Fees: In-State: $7,740. Out-of-State: $18,450. Room and Board: $7,366.

Inst. Aid: FT Undergrads Receiving Aid: Unavailable. Avg. Amount per Student: Unavailable.

UNIVERSITY OF DENVER

Denver, CO

admission@du.edu; www.du.edu

General Info: Coed, College Board member, Four-year, North Central Association of Colleges and Schools, Private, Regionally Accredited, University. Urban setting, Very large city (over 500,000), Residential campus. Academic Calendar: Quarter.

Student Body: Full-Time Undergrads: 4,673. Men: 47%, Women: 53%. Total Undergrad Population: Native American or Native Alaskan: 1.5%. Asian American or Pacific Islander: 5.4%. African American: 2.5%. Latino: 6%. Caucasian: 64.1%. International: 4.5%. Out-of-State: 56%. Living Off-Campus: 6%. Total all graduate and professional students: 5,768.

Academics: Full-Time Faculty: 574. Graduation Rate: 74% within 6 years.

Admissions: Regular Application Deadline: 1/15. Priority Application Deadline: Unavailable. Early Decision Deadline: Unavailable. Transfer Priority Deadline: Unavailable. Financial Aid Deadline: Unavailable. Total Number of Students Applied: 5,072. Number Admitted: 3,755. Number Enrolled: Unavailable. Number accepting place on waitlist: 279. Number of waitlisted students admitted: 92. Test Scores (Middle 50%): SAT Critical Reading: 530–640. SAT Math: 540–640. SAT Writing: Unavailable. ACT Comp: 23–28. HS Rank of Entering Freshmen: Top 10%: 35%. Top 25%: 66%. Avg. HS GPA: 3.59.

Cost: Tuition and Fees: In-State: $32,976. Out-of-State: $32,976. Room and Board: $9,670.

Inst. Aid: FT Undergrads Receiving Aid: Unavailable. Avg. Amount per Student: Unavailable.

UNIVERSITY OF FLORIDA

Gainesville, FL

www.ufl.edu

General Info: Public, University, Four-year, Coed, Regionally Accredited, Southern Association of Colleges and Schools, College Board member. Suburban setting, Small city (50,000–249,999), Residential campus. Academic Calendar: Semester.

Student Body: Full-Time Undergrads: 35, 110. Men: 43%, Women: 57%. Total Undergrad Population: Native American or Native Alaskan: 0%. Asian American or Pacific Islander: 8%. African American: 13%. Latino: 14%. Caucasian: 59%. International: 1%. Out-of-State: 6%. Total all graduate and professional students: 11,439.

Academics: Full-Time Faculty: 2,229.

Admissions: Regular Application Deadline: 1/14. Priority Application Deadline: Unavailable. Early Decision Deadline: 10/1. Transfer Priority Deadline: Unavailable. Financial Aid Deadline: Unavailable. Total Number of Students Applied: Unavailable. Percent Admitted: 48%. Number Enrolled: 7,241. Test Scores (Middle 50%): SAT Critical Reading: 560–670. SAT Math: 580–690. SAT Writing: Unavailable. ACT Comp: 24–29. HS Rank of Entering Freshmen: Top 10%: 21%. Top 25%: 90%. Avg. HS GPA: Unavailable.

Cost: Tuition and Fees: In-State: $3,206. Out-of-State: $17,791. Room and Board: $6,590.

Inst. Aid: FT Undergrads Receiving Aid: Unavailable. Avg. Amount per Student: Unavailable.

UNIVERSITY OF GEORGIA

Athens, GA

adm-info@uga.edu; www.uga.edu

General Info: Public, University, Four-year, Coed, Regionally Accredited, Southern Association of Colleges and Schools, College Board member. Suburban setting, Small city (50,000–249,999), Commuter campus. Academic Calendar: Semester.

Student Body: Full-Time Undergrads: 25,437. Men: 38%, Women: 62%. Total Undergrad Population: Native American or Native Alaskan: 0%. Asian American or Pacific Islander: 7%. African American: 8%. Latino: 2%. Caucasian: 81%. International: 1%. Out-of-State: 15%. Total all graduate and professional students: 6,918.

Academics: Full-Time Faculty: 1,691.

Admissions: Regular Application Deadline: 1/15. Priority Application Deadline: 10/15. Early Decision Deadline: Unavailable. Transfer Priority Deadline: Unavailable. Financial Aid Deadline: Unavailable. Total Number of Students Applied: Unavailable. Percent Admitted: 58%. Number Enrolled: 5,047. Test Scores (Middle 50%): SAT Critical Reading: 570–660. SAT Math: 570–660. SAT Writing: 550–650. ACT Comp: 25–29. HS Rank of Entering Freshmen: Top 10%: 52%. Top 25%: 84%. Avg. HS GPA: Unavailable.

Cost: Tuition and Fees: In-State: $5,622. Out-of-State: $20,726. Room and Board: $7,292.

Inst. Aid: FT Undergrads Receiving Aid: Unavailable. Avg. Amount per Student: Unavailable.

UNIVERSITY OF HAWAII AT MANOA

Honolulu, HI

ar-info@hawaii.edu; www.manoa.hawaii.edu

General Info: Public, University, Four-year, Coed, Western Association of Schools and Colleges, Regionally Accredited, College Board member. Urban setting, Very large city

Interested in a Career in Advertising?

Dartmouth College

University of Alabama–Tuscaloosa

Virginia Commonwealth University

(over 500,000), Commuter campus. Academic Calendar: Semester.

Student Body: Full-Time Undergrads: 14,351. Men: 45%, Women: 55%. Total Undergrad Population: Native American or Native Alaskan: 1%. Asian American or Pacific Islander: 65%. African American: 1%. Latino: 3%. Caucasian: 27%. International: 3%. Out-of-State: 25%. Total all graduate and professional students: 5,679.

Academics: Full-Time Faculty: 1,086.

Admissions: Regular Application Deadline: 6/1. Priority Application Deadline: 8/1. Early Decision Deadline: Unavailable. Financial Aid Deadline: Unavailable. Total Number of Students Applied: Unavailable. Percent Admitted: 68%. Number Enrolled: 2,555. Test Scores (Middle 50%): SAT Critical Reading: 480–580. SAT Math: 510–610. SAT Writing: 470–560. ACT Comp: 21–25. HS Rank of Entering Freshmen: Top 10%: 25%. Top 25%: 61%. Avg. HS GPA: Unavailable.

Cost: Tuition and Fees: In-State: $5,390. Out-of-State: $14,684. Room and Board: $7,184.

Inst. Aid: FT Undergrads Receiving Aid: Unavailable. Avg. Amount per Student: Unavailable.

UNIVERSITY OF HOUSTON

Victoria, TX
admission@uhv.edu; www.uhv.edu

General Info: Public, University, Two-year, upper division, Coed, Regionally Accredited, Southern Association of Colleges and Schools. Urban setting, Small city (50,000–249,999), Commuter campus. Academic Calendar: Semester.

Student Body: Full-Time Undergrads: 1,315. Men: 31%, Women: 69%.

Academics: Full-Time Faculty: 1,218.

Admissions: Regular Application Deadline: Rolling. Priority Application Deadline: Unavailable. Early Decision Deadline: Unavailable. Transfer Priority Deadline: Unavailable. Financial Aid Deadline: Unavailable. Total Number of Students Applied: Unavailable. Number Admitted: Unavailable. Number Enrolled: Unavailable. Test Scores (Middle 50%): SAT Critical Reading: Unavailable. SAT Math: Unavailable. SAT Writing: Unavailable. ACT Comp: Unavailable. HS Rank of Entering Freshmen: Top 10%: 21%. Top 25%: 50%. Avg. HS GPA: Unavailable.

Cost: Tuition and Fees: In-State: $4,680. Out-of-State: $12,930. Room and Board: $0.

Inst. Aid: FT Undergrads Receiving Aid: Unavailable. Avg. Amount per Student: Unavailable.

UNIVERSITY OF ILLINOIS AT URBANA-CHAMPAIGN

Champaign, IL
ugradadmissions@uiuc.edu; www.uiuc.edu

General Info: Public, University, Four-year, Coed, Regionally Accredited, North Central Association of Colleges and Schools, College Board member. Urban setting, Small city (50,000–249,999), Residential campus. Academic Calendar: Semester.

Student Body: Full-Time Undergrads: 30,381. Men: 53%, Women: 47%. Total Undergrad Population: Native American or Native Alaskan: 0%. Asian American or Pacific Islander: 13%. African American: 7%. Latino: 7%. Caucasian: 67%. International: 4%. Out-of-State: 11%. Total all graduate and professional students: 10,000.

Academics: Full-Time Faculty: 2,978.

Admissions: Regular Application Deadline: 1/1. Priority Application Deadline: 11/15. Early Decision Deadline: Unavailable. Transfer Priority Deadline: 3/1. Financial Aid Deadline: Unavailable. Total Number of Students Applied: Unavailable. Percent Admitted: 65%. Number Enrolled: 7,172. Test Scores (Middle 50%): SAT Critical Reading: 540–670. SAT Math: 620–740. SAT Writing: Unavailable. ACT Comp: 26–31. HS Rank of Entering Freshmen: Top 10%: 55%. Top 25%: 96%. Avg. HS GPA: Unavailable.

Cost: Tuition and Fees: In-State: $9,882. Out-of-State: $23,968. Room and Board: $7,716.

Inst. Aid: FT Undergrads Receiving Aid: Unavailable. Avg. Amount per Student: Unavailable.

UNIVERSITY OF INDIANAPOLIS

Indianapolis, IN
admissions@uindy.edu; www.uindy.edu

General Info: Private, Liberal Arts College, University, Four-year, United Methodist Church, Coed, Regionally Accredited, College Board member. Urban setting, Very large city

Like English, Writing or Publishing?

UC Berkeley

New York University

Oberlin College

Rutgers University

Emerson College

(over 500,000), Residential campus. Academic Calendar: Semester.

Student Body: Full-Time Undergrads: 3,352. Men: 32%, Women: 68%. Total Undergrad Population: Native American or Native Alaskan: 0%. Asian American or Pacific Islander: 1%. African American: 8%. Latino: 2%. Caucasian: 85%. International: 2%. Out-of-State: 6%. Total all graduate and professional students: 1,037.

Academics: Full-Time Faculty: 166.

Admissions: Regular Application Deadline: Rolling. Priority Application Deadline: Unavailable. Early Decision Deadline: Unavailable. Financial Aid Deadline: 3/1. Total Number of Students Applied: Unavailable. Percent Admitted: 78%. Number Enrolled: 727. Test Scores (Middle 50%): SAT Critical Reading: 450–550. SAT Math: 460–570. SAT Writing: Unavailable. ACT Comp: 19–24. HS Rank of Entering Freshmen: Top 10%: 20%. Top 25%: 54%. Avg. HS GPA: Unavailable.

Cost: Tuition and Fees: In-State: $18,850. Out-of-State: $18,850. Room and Board: $7,380.

Inst. Aid: FT Undergrads Receiving Aid: Unavailable. Avg. Amount per Student: Unavailable.

UNIVERSITY OF IOWA

Iowa City, IA

admissions@uiowa.edu; www.uiowa.edu

General Info: Public, University, Four-year, Coed, Regionally Accredited, North Central Association of Colleges and Schools, College Board member. Urban setting, Small city (50,000–249,999), Residential campus. Academic Calendar: Semester.

Student Body: Full-Time Undergrads: 20,738. Men: 47%, Women: 53%. Part-Time Undergrads. Men: 41%, Women: 59%. Total Undergrad Population: Native American or Native Alaskan: 1%. Asian American or Pacific Islander: 4%. African American: 2%. Latino: 3%. Caucasian: 85%. International: 2%. Out-of-State: 38%. Living Off-Campus: 30%. Total all graduate and professional students: 8,210.

Academics: Full-Time Faculty: 1,559. With PhD: 1,509. Graduation Rates: 40% within 4 years. 66% within 6 years.

Admissions: Regular Application Deadline: 4/1 for fall semester. Priority Application Deadline: Not applicable. Early Decision Deadline: Not applicable. Transfer Priority Deadline: Not applicable. Financial Aid Deadline: 3/1. Total Number of Students Applied: 14,678. Number Admitted: 12,209. Number Enrolled: Unavailable. Number accepting place on waitlist: 140. Test Scores (Middle 50%): SAT Critical Reading: 520–650. SAT Math: 540–670. SAT Writing: Unavailable. ACT Comp: 23–27. HS Rank of Entering Freshmen: Top 10%: 23.35%. Top 25%: 54.46%. Avg. HS GPA: 3.0.

Cost: Tuition and Fees: In-State: $6,544. Out-of-State: $20,658. Room and Board: $7,673.

Interested in a Career in Finance or Business?

University of Pennsylvania–Wharton

New York University–Stern

Dartmouth University–Tuck

Inst. Aid: FT Undergrads Receiving Aid: Unavailable. Avg. Amount per Student: Unavailable.

Graduates: No. of companies recruiting on campus: 300.

UNIVERSITY OF KANSAS

Lawrence, KS

adm@ku.edu; www.ku.edu

General Info: Public, University, Four-year, Coed, Regionally Accredited, North Central Association of Colleges and Schools, College Board member. Urban setting, Small city (50,000–249,999), Commuter campus. Academic Calendar: Semester.

Student Body: Full-Time Undergrads: 20,828. Men: 50.1%, Women: 49.9%. Total Undergrad Population: Native American or Native Alaskan: 1%. Asian American or Pacific Islander: 5%. African American: 3%. Latino: 3%. Caucasian: 83%. International: 2%. Out-of-State: 28%. Total all graduate and professional students: 6,085.

Academics: Full-Time Faculty: 1,218.

Admissions: Regular Application Deadline: Unavailable. Priority Application Deadline: 12/1. Early Decision Deadline: Unavailable. Transfer Priority Deadline: 1/15. Financial Aid Deadline: Unavailable. Total Number of Students Applied: 10,367. Number Admitted: 9,554. Number Enrolled: 4,084. Test Scores (Middle 50%): SAT Critical Reading: Unavailable. SAT Math: Unavailable. SAT Writing: Unavailable. ACT Comp: 22–28. HS Rank of Entering Freshmen: Top 10%: 28%. Top 25%: 60%. Avg. HS GPA: 3.41.

Cost: Tuition and Fees: In-State: $6,390. Out-of-State: $16,800. Room and Board: $6,144.

Inst. Aid: FT Undergrads Receiving Aid: 7,083. Avg. Amount per Student: $8,117.

Want to Be a Chef?

Institute of Culinary Education

California Culinary Academy

Culinary Institute at Hyde Park

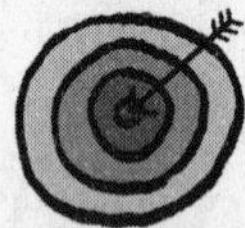

UNIVERSITY OF KENTUCKY

Lexington, KY

admisso@uky.edu; www.uky.edu

General Info: Public, University, Four-year, Coed, Regionally Accredited, Southern Association of Colleges and Schools, College Board member. Urban setting, Large city (250,000–499,999), Commuter campus. Academic Calendar: Semester.

Student Body: Full-Time Undergrads: 18,702. Men: 47%, Women: 53%. Total Undergrad Population: Native American or Native Alaskan: 0%. Asian American or Pacific Islander: 3%. African American: 4%. Latino: 1%. Caucasian: 90%. International: 0%. Out-of-State: 20%. Total all graduate and professional students: 5,485.

Academics: Full-Time Faculty: 1,211.

Admissions: Regular Application Deadline: 2/15. Priority Application Deadline: Unavailable. Early Decision Deadline: Unavailable. Transfer Priority Deadline: Unavailable. Financial Aid Deadline: Unavailable. Total Number of Students Applied: Unavailable. Percent Admitted: 82%. Number Enrolled: 3,825. Test Scores (Middle 50%): SAT Critical Reading: 510–630. SAT Math: 520–640. SAT Writing: Unavailable. ACT Comp: 22–27. HS Rank of Entering Freshmen: Top 10%: 28%. Top 25%: 57%. Avg. HS GPA: Unavailable.

Cost: Tuition and Fees: In-State: $6,510. Out-of-State: $13,970. Room and Board: $5,560.

Inst. Aid: FT Undergrads Receiving Aid: Unavailable. Avg. Amount per Student: Unavailable.

UNIVERSITY OF MAINE

Orono, ME

um-admit@maine.edu; www.go.umaine.edu

General Info: Public, University, Four-year, Coed, Regionally Accredited, New England Association of Colleges and Schools, College Board member. Rural setting, Large town (10,000–49,999), Residential campus. Academic Calendar: Semester.

Student Body: Full-Time Undergrads: 9,179. Men: 51%, Women: 49%. Total Undergrad Population: Native American or Native Alaskan: 2%. Asian American or Pacific Islander: 1%. African American: 1%. Latino: 1%. Caucasian: 92%. International: 2%. Out-of-State: 18%. Total all graduate and professional students: 2,256.

Academics: Full-Time Faculty: 496.

Admissions: Regular Application Deadline: 5/1. Priority Application Deadline: Unavailable. Early Decision Deadline: Unavailable. Transfer Priority Deadline: Unavailable. Financial Aid Deadline: Unavailable. Total Number of Students Applied: Unavailable. Percent Admitted: 80%. Number Enrolled: Unavailable. Test Scores (Middle 50%): SAT Critical Reading: 480–590. SAT Math: 490–600. SAT Writing: Unavailable. ACT Comp: 20–25. HS Rank of Entering Freshmen: Top 10%: 22%. Top 25%: 52%. Avg. HS GPA: Unavailable.

Cost: Tuition and Fees: In-State: $7,464. Out-of-State: $18,414. Room and Board: $7,125.

Inst. Aid: FT Undergrads Receiving Aid: Unavailable. Avg. Amount per Student: Unavailable.

UNIVERSITY OF MARY WASHINGTON

Fredericksburg, VA

admit@umw.edu; www.umw.edu

General Info: Public, Liberal Arts College, University, Four-year, Coed, Regionally Accredited, Southern Association of Colleges and Schools, College Board member. Suburban setting, Small city (50,000–249,999), Residential campus. Academic Calendar: Semester.

Student Body: Full-Time Undergrads: 4,183. Men: 33%, Women: 67%. Total Undergrad Population: Native American or Native Alaskan: 0%. Asian American or Pacific Islander: 5%. African American: 3%. Latino: 3%. Caucasian: 67%. International: 0%. Out-of-State: 36%. Total all graduate and professional students: 679.

Academics: Full-Time Faculty: Unavailable.

Admissions: Regular Application Deadline: 2/1. Priority Application Deadline: 1/15. Early Decision Deadline: Unavailable. Transfer Priority Deadline: Unavailable. Financial Aid Deadline: Unavailable. Total Number of Students Applied: Unavailable. Percent Admitted: 71%. Number Enrolled: 870. Test Scores (Middle 50%): SAT Critical Reading: 580–670. SAT Math: 560–640. SAT Writing: Unavailable. ACT Comp: 25–29. HS Rank of Entering Freshmen: Top 10%: 38%. Top 25%: 83%. Avg. HS GPA: Unavailable.

Cost: Tuition and Fees: In-State: $6,494. Out-of-State: $16,968. Room and Board: $6,606.

Inst. Aid: FT Undergrads Receiving Aid: Unavailable. Avg. Amount per Student: Unavailable.

UNIVERSITY OF MARYLAND–BALTIMORE COUNTY

Baltimore, MD

admissions@umbc.edu; www.umbc.edu

General Info: Public, University, Four-year, Coed, Regionally Accredited, Middle States Association of Colleges and Schools, College Board member. Suburban setting, Large city (250,000–499,999), Residential campus. Academic Calendar: 4-1-4.

Student Body: Full-Time Undergrads: 9,464. Men: 54%, Women: 46%. Part-Time Undergrads. Men: 8%, Women: 8%. Total Undergrad Population: Native American or Native Alaskan: 0.5%. Asian American or Pacific Islander: 21%. African American: 16%. Latino: 4%. Caucasian: 53%. International: 4%. Out-of-State: 11%. Living Off-Campus: 66.5%. % In Fraternities: 4.2%. % In Sororities: 4.1%. Total all graduate and professional students: 2,577.

Academics: Full-Time Faculty: 473. With PhD: 505. Graduation Rates: 28% within 4 years. 56% within 6 years.

Admissions: Regular Application Deadline: 2/1. Priority Application Deadline: 11/1. Early Decision Deadline: Unavailable. Fall Transfer Deadline: 5/31. Spring Transfer Deadline: 12/15. Transfer Priority Deadline: 3/15. Financial Aid Deadline: 2/14. Total Number of Students Applied: 5,836. Number Admitted: 4,024. Number Enrolled: 1,437. Number accepting place on waitlist: 263. Number of waitlisted students admitted: 126. Test Scores (Middle 50%): SAT Critical Reading: 520–640. SAT Math: 560–660. SAT Writing: 520–630. ACT Comp: 22–27. HS Rank of Entering Freshmen: Top 10%: 28.3%. Top 25%: 58.6%. Avg. HS GPA: 3.6.

Cost: Tuition and Fees: In-State: $8,780. Out-of-State: $17,512. Room and Board: $8,720.

Inst. Aid: FT Undergrads Receiving Aid: 3,568. Avg. Amount per Student: $9,527. Freshmen Receiving Non-Need Scholarship or Grant: 117. Avg. Amount per Student: $4,233.

UNIVERSITY OF MARYLAND–COLLEGE PARK

College Park, MD

um-admit@umd.edu; www.admissions.umd.edu

General Info: Coed, College Board member, Four-year, Middle States Association of Colleges and Schools, Public, Regionally Accredited, University. Commuter campus, Large town (10,000–49,999), Residential campus, Suburban setting. Academic Calendar: Semester.

Student Body: Full-Time Undergrads: 25,104. Men: 52%, Women: 46%. Part-Time Undergrads. Men: 8%, Women: 8%. Total Undergrad Population: Native American or Native Alaskan: 0%. Asian American or Pacific Islander: 14%. African American: 13%. Latino: 5%. Caucasian: 56%. International: 3%. Out-of-State: 28%. Living Off-Campus: 55%. % In Fraternities: 14%. % In Sororities: 14%. Total all graduate and professional students: 10,157.

Academics: Full-Time Faculty: 1,536. Graduation Rate: 79.8% within 6 years.

Admissions: Regular Application Deadline: 1/20. Priority Application Deadline: 12/1. Early Decision Deadline: Unavailable. Fall Transfer Deadline: 6/1. Spring Transfer Deadline: 11/15. Transfer Priority Deadline: 3/1. Financial Aid Deadline: Unavailable. Total Number of Students Applied: 28,000. Number Admitted: 10,437. Number Enrolled: 4,050. Test Scores (Middle 50%): SAT Critical Reading: 580–670. SAT Math: 600–700. SAT Writing: Unavailable. HS Rank of Entering Freshmen: Top 10%: 71%. Top 25%: Unavailable. Avg. HS GPA: Unavailable.

Cost: Tuition and Fees: In-State: $7,969. Out-of-State: $22,208. Room and Board: $8,854.

Inst. Aid: FT Undergrads Receiving Aid: Unavailable. Avg. Amount per Student: Unavailable.

UNIVERSITY OF MASSACHUSETTS AMHERST

Amherst, MA

mail@admissions.umass.edu; www.umass.edu

General Info: Public, University, Four-year, Coed, Regionally Accredited, New England Association of Colleges and Schools, College Board member. Suburban setting, Large town (10,000–49,999), Residential campus. Academic Calendar: Semester.

Student Body: Full-Time Undergrads: 19,823. Men: 49%, Women: 51%. Total Undergrad Population: Native American or Native Alaskan: 0%. Asian American or Pacific Islander: 9%. African American: 5%. Latino: 4%. Caucasian: 73%. International: 1%. Out-of-State: 23%. Total all graduate and professional students: 5,770.

Academics: Full-Time Faculty: 1,148.

Admissions: Regular Application Deadline: 1/15. Priority Application Deadline: Unavailable. Early Decision Deadline: Unavailable. Transfer Priority Deadline: Unavailable. Financial Aid Deadline: Unavailable. Total Number of Students Applied: Unavailable. Percent Admitted: 71%. Number Enrolled: 4,458. Test Scores (Middle 50%): SAT Critical Reading: 510–620. SAT Math: 530–640. SAT Writing: Unavailable. ACT Comp: Unavailable. HS Rank of Entering Freshmen: Top 10%: 19%. Top 25%: 51%. Avg. HS GPA: Unavailable.

Cost: Tuition and Fees: In-State: $9,595. Out-of-State: $19,317. Room and Board: $7,255.

Inst. Aid: FT Undergrads Receiving Aid: Unavailable. Avg. Amount per Student: Unavailable.

UNIVERSITY OF MIAMI

Coral Gables, FL

admission@miami.edu; www.miami.edu

General Info: Private, University, Four-year, Coed, Regionally Accredited, College Board member, Hispanic serving. Suburban setting, Small city (50,000–249,999), Commuter campus. Academic Calendar: Semester.

Student Body: Full-Time Undergrads: 10,509. Men: 49%, Women: 51%. Total Undergrad Population: Native American or Native Alaskan: 0%. Asian American or Pacific Islander: 5%. African American: 8%. Latino: 17%. Caucasian: 53%. International: 5%. Out-of-State: 55%. Total all graduate and professional students: 3,175.

Academics: Full-Time Faculty: 872.

Admissions: Regular Application Deadline: 2/1. Priority Application Deadline: Unavailable. Early Decision Deadline: 11/1. Transfer Priority Deadline: 3/1. Financial Aid Deadline: Unavailable. Total Number of Students Applied: Unavailable. Percent Admitted: 40%. Number Enrolled: 2,047. Test Scores (Middle 50%): SAT Critical Reading: 580–670. SAT Math: 600–690. SAT Writing: 550–660. ACT Comp: 26–31. HS Rank of Entering Freshmen: Top 10%: 62%. Top 25%: 89%. Avg. HS GPA: Unavailable.

Cost: Tuition and Fees: In-State: $34,890. Out-of-State: $34,890. Room and Board: $9,334.

Inst. Aid: FT Undergrads Receiving Aid: Unavailable. Avg. Amount per Student: Unavailable.

UNIVERSITY OF MICHIGAN–ANN ARBOR

Ann Arbor, MI

ugadmiss@umich.edu; www.umich.edu

General Info: Public, University, Four-year, Coed, Regionally Accredited, North Central Association of Colleges and Schools, College Board member. Suburban setting, Small city (50,000–249,999), Residential campus. Academic Calendar: Trimester.

Student Body: Full-Time Undergrads: 25,555. Men: 50%, Women: 50%. Part-Time Undergrads. Men: 51%, Women: 49%. Total Undergrad Population: Native American or Native Alaskan: 0%. Asian American or Pacific Islander: 12%. African American: 6%. Latino: 5%. Caucasian: 66%. International: 0%. Out-of-State: 34%. Living Off-Campus: 37%. % In Fraternities: 15%. % In Sororities: 17%. Total all graduate and professional students: 11,946.

Academics: Full-Time Faculty: 2,367.

Admissions: Regular Application Deadline: 2/1. Priority Application Deadline: Unavailable. Early Decision Deadline: Unavailable. Transfer Priority Deadline: Unavailable. Financial Aid Deadline: 4/30. Total Number of Students Applied: 27,474. Number Admitted: 13,826. Number Enrolled: 5,955. Number accepting place on waitlist: 2,067. Test Scores (Middle 50%): SAT Critical Reading: 590–690. SAT Math: 630–730. SAT Writing: Unavailable. ACT Comp: 27–31. HS Rank of Entering Freshmen: Top 10%: 92%. Top 25%: 99%. Avg. HS GPA: Unavailable.

Cost: Tuition and Fees: In-State: $9,723. Out-of-State: $29,131. Room and Board: $7,808.

Inst. Aid: FT Undergrads Receiving Aid: 2,428. Avg. Amount per Student: $8,211.

UNIVERSITY OF MINNESOTA–TWIN CITIES

Minneapolis–St. Paul , MN

admissions@tc.umn.edu; www.umn.edu

General Info: Public, University, Four-year, Coed, Regionally Accredited, North Central Association of Colleges and Schools, College Board member. Urban setting, Very large city (over 500,000), Residential campus. Academic Calendar: Semester.

Student Body: Full-Time Undergrads: 32,767. Men: 46%, Women: 54%. Total Undergrad Population: Native American or Native Alaskan: 1%. Asian American or Pacific Islander: 10%. African American: 5%. Latino: 2%. Caucasian: 79%. International: 1%. Out-of-State: 33%. Total all graduate and professional students: 14,883.

Academics: Full-Time Faculty: 1,680.

Admissions: Regular Application Deadline: Rolling. Priority Application Deadline: 12/15. Early Decision Deadline: Unavailable. Transfer Priority Deadline: 3/1. Financial Aid Deadline: Unavailable. Total Number of Students Applied: Unavailable. Percent Admitted: 71%. Number Enrolled: 5,276. Test Scores (Middle 50%): SAT Critical Reading: 540–660. SAT Math: 570–690. SAT Writing: Unavailable. ACT Comp: 23–28. HS Rank of Entering Freshmen: Top 10%: 34%. Top 25%: 74%. Avg. HS GPA: Unavailable.

Cost: Tuition and Fees: In-State: $9,373. Out-of-State: $21,003. Room and Board: $6,824.

Inst. Aid: FT Undergrads Receiving Aid: Unavailable. Avg. Amount per Student: Unavailable.

UNIVERSITY OF MISSOURI–COLUMBIA

Columbia, MO

mu4u@missouri.edu; www.missouri.edu

General Info: Public, University, Four-year, Coed, Regionally Accredited, North Central Association of Colleges and Schools, College Board member. Suburban setting, Small city (50,000–249,999), Residential campus. Academic Calendar: Semester.

Student Body: Full-Time Undergrads: 21,551. Men: 47%, Women: 53%. Total Undergrad Population: Native American or Native Alaskan: 0%. Asian American or Pacific Islander: 3%. African American: 7%. Latino: 2%. Caucasian: 82%. International: 1%. Out-of-State: 19%. Total all graduate and professional students: 5,600.

Academics: Full-Time Faculty: 1,066.

Admissions: Regular Application Deadline: Rolling. Priority Application Deadline: 5/1. Early Decision Deadline: Unavailable. Financial Aid Deadline: Unavailable. Total Number of Students Applied: Unavailable. Percent Admitted: 78%. Number Enrolled: 4,838. Test Scores (Middle 50%): SAT Critical Reading: 530–650. SAT Math: 540–650. SAT Writing: Unavailable. ACT Comp: 23–28. HS Rank of Entering Freshmen: Top 10%: 27%. Top 25%: 57%. Avg. HS GPA: Unavailable.

Cost: Tuition and Fees: In-State: $7,784. Out-of-State: $18,050. Room and Board: $7,000.

Inst. Aid: FT Undergrads Receiving Aid: Unavailable. Avg. Amount per Student: Unavailable.

UNIVERSITY OF MISSOURI–ROLLA

Rolla, MO

admissions@umr.edu; www.umr.edu

General Info: Public, College of Engineering, University, Four-year, Coed, Regionally Accredited, North Central Association of Colleges and Schools, College Board member. Rural setting, Large town (10,000–49,999), Residential campus. Academic Calendar: Semester.

Student Body: Full-Time Undergrads: 4,515. Men: 77%, Women: 23%. Total Undergrad Population: Native American or Native Alaskan: 0%. Asian American or Pacific Islander: 2%. African American: 4%. Latino: 2%. Caucasian: 88%. International: 2%. Out-of-State: 21%. Total all graduate and professional students: 1,289.

Academics: Full-Time Faculty: 336.

Admissions: Regular Application Deadline: 7/1. Priority Application Deadline: Unavailable. Early Decision Deadline: Unavailable. Transfer Priority Deadline: 5/1. Financial Aid Deadline: Unavailable. Total Number of Students Applied: Unavailable. Percent Admitted: 90%. Number Enrolled: 962. Test Scores (Middle 50%): SAT Critical Reading: 520–710. SAT Math: 590–720. SAT Writing: Unavailable. ACT Comp: 24–30. HS Rank of Entering Freshmen: Top 10%: 39%. Top 25%: 69%. Avg. HS GPA: Unavailable.

Cost: Tuition and Fees: In-State: $7,899. Out-of-State: $18,165. Room and Board: $6,255.

Inst. Aid: FT Undergrads Receiving Aid: Unavailable. Avg. Amount per Student: Unavailable.

UNIVERSITY OF NEBRASKA–LINCOLN

Lincoln, NE

admissions@unl.edu; www.unl.edu

General Info: Public, University, Four-year, Coed, Regionally Accredited, North Central Association of Colleges and Schools, College Board member. Urban setting, Small city (50,000–249,999), Residential campus. Academic Calendar: Semester.

Student Body: Full-Time Undergrads: 17,371. Men: 53%, Women: 47%. Total Undergrad Population: Native American or Native Alaskan: 1%. Asian American or Pacific Islander: 3%. African American: 3%. Latino: 4%. Caucasian: 85%. International: 1%. Out-of-State: 18%. Total all graduate and professional students: 4,336.

Academics: Full-Time Faculty: 1,048.

Admissions: Regular Application Deadline: 5/1. Priority Application Deadline: Unavailable. Early Decision Deadline: Unavailable. Transfer Priority Deadline: Unavailable. Financial Aid Deadline: Unavailable. Total Number of Students Applied: Unavailable. Percent Admitted: 73%. Number Enrolled: 3,831. Test Scores (Middle 50%): SAT Critical Reading: 510–650. SAT Math: 530–670. SAT Writing: Unavailable. ACT Comp: 22–28. HS Rank of Entering Freshmen: Top 10%: 27%. Top 25%: 54%. Avg. HS GPA: Unavailable.

Want to Be a Lawyer or Judge?

University of Chicago

Yale University

Harvard University

New York University

Columbia University

Cost: Tuition and Fees: In-State: $6,316. Out-of-State: $16,336. Room and Board: $6,653.

Inst. Aid: FT Undergrads Receiving Aid: Unavailable. Avg. Amount per Student: Unavailable.

UNIVERSITY OF NEVADA

Reno, NV

asknevada@unr.edu; www.unr.edu

General Info: Public, University, Four-year, Coed, Regionally Accredited, Northwest Association of Schools and Colleges, College Board member. Large city (250,000–499,999), Residential campus, Urban setting. Academic Calendar: Semester.

Student Body: Full-Time Undergrads: 13,134. Men: 45%, Women: 55%. Total Undergrad Population: Native American or Native Alaskan: 1%. Asian American or Pacific Islander: 7%. African American: 4%. Latino: 8%. Caucasian: 67%. International: 2%. Out-of-State: 20%. Total all graduate and professional students: 3,312.

Academics: Full-Time Faculty: 489.

Admissions: Regular Application Deadline: No closing date. Priority Application Deadline: 3/1. Early Decision Deadline: Unavailable. Transfer Priority Deadline: Unavailable. Financial Aid Deadline: Unavailable. Total Number of Students Applied: Unavailable. Percent Admitted: 86%. Number Enrolled: 2,361. Test Scores (Middle 50%): SAT Critical Reading: 450–570. SAT Math: 470–590. SAT Writing: Unavailable. ACT Comp: 20–25. HS Rank of Entering Freshmen: Top 10%: Unavailable. Top 25%: Unavailable. Avg. HS GPA: Unavailable.

Cost: Tuition and Fees: In-State: $3,684. Out-of-State: $13,595. Room and Board: $8,199.

Inst. Aid: FT Undergrads Receiving Aid: Unavailable. Avg. Amount per Student: Unavailable.

UNIVERSITY OF NEVADA

Las Vegas, NV

undergraduate.recruitment@unlv.edu; www.unlv.edu

General Info: Public, University, Four-year, Coed, Northwest Association of Schools and Colleges, Regionally Accredited, College Board member. Urban setting, Very large city (over 500,000), Commuter campus. Academic Calendar: Semester.

Student Body: Full-Time Undergrads: 21,853. Men: 44%, Women: 56%. Total Undergrad Population: Native American or Native Alaskan: 1%. Asian American or Pacific Islander: 20%. African American: 9%. Latino: 15%. Caucasian: 48%. International: 1%. Out-of-State: 19%. Total all graduate and professional students: 5,281.

Academics: Full-Time Faculty: 851.

Admissions: Regular Application Deadline: 2/1. Priority Application Deadline: Unavailable. Early Decision Deadline: Unavailable. Transfer Priority Deadline: Unavailable. Financial Aid Deadline: Unavailable. Total Number of Students Applied: Unavailable. Percent Admitted: 75%. Number Enrolled: 2,510. Test Scores (Middle 50%): SAT Critical Reading: 450–550. SAT Math: 450–580. SAT Writing: Unavailable. ACT Comp: 19–24. HS Rank of Entering Freshmen: Top 10%: 18%. Top 25%: 44%. Avg. HS GPA: Unavailable.

Cost: Tuition and Fees: In-State: $3,732. Out-of-State: $13,643. Room and Board: $8,857.

Inst. Aid: FT Undergrads Receiving Aid: Unavailable. Avg. Amount per Student: Unavailable.

Want to Be a Journalist?

Syracuse University

University of Maryland

New York University

University of North Carolina

UNIVERSITY OF NEW HAMPSHIRE

Durham, NH

admissions@unh.edu; www.unh.edu

General Info: Public, University, Four-year, Coed, Regionally Accredited, New England Association of Colleges and Schools, College Board member. Rural setting, Small town (2,500–9,999), Residential campus. Academic Calendar: Semester.

Student Body: Full-Time Undergrads: 12,067. Men: 44%, Women: 56%. Total Undergrad Population: Native American or Native Alaskan: 0%. Asian American or Pacific Islander: 0%. African American: 0%. Latino: 0%. Caucasian: 0%. International: 0%. Out-of-State: 46%. Total all graduate and professional students: 3,035.

Academics: Full-Time Faculty: 636.

Admissions: Regular Application Deadline: 2/1. Priority Application Deadline: Unavailable. Early Decision Deadline: Unavailable. Transfer Priority Deadline: Unavailable. Financial Aid Deadline: 3/1. Total Number of Students Applied: 14,382. Number Admitted: 8,479. Number Enrolled: Unavailable. Test Scores (Middle 50%): SAT Critical Reading: Unavailable. SAT Math: Unavailable. SAT Writing: Unavailable. HS Rank of Entering Freshmen: Top 10%: 24%. Top 25%: 66%. Avg. HS GPA: Unavailable.

Cost: Tuition and Fees: In-State: $8,810. Out-of-State: $21,770. Room and Board: $8,168.

Inst. Aid: FT Undergrads Receiving Aid: 4,209. Avg. Amount per Student: $16,852.

UNIVERSITY OF NEW MEXICO

Albuquerque, NM

apply@unm.edu; www.unm.edu

General Info: Public, University, Four-year, Coed, Regionally Accredited, North Central Association of Colleges and Schools, College Board member, Hispanic serving. Urban setting, Very large city (over 500,000), Commuter campus. Academic Calendar: Semester.

Student Body: Full-Time Undergrads: 18,199. Men: 42%, Women: 58%. Total Undergrad Population: Native American or Native Alaskan: 5%. Asian American or Pacific Islander: 5%. African American: 4%. Latino: 37%. Caucasian: 46%. International: 1%. Out-of-State: 0%.

Academics: Full-Time Faculty: 885.

Admissions: Regular Application Deadline: 3/1. Priority Application Deadline: Unavailable. Early Decision Deadline: Unavailable. Transfer Priority Deadline: Unavailable. Financial Aid Deadline: Unavailable. Total Number of Students Applied: Unavailable. Number Admitted: Unavailable. Number Enrolled: 3,026. Test Scores (Middle 50%): SAT Critical Reading: 470–600. SAT Math: 470–590. SAT Writing: Unavailable. ACT Comp: 19–25. HS Rank of Entering Freshmen: Top 10%: 21%. Top 25%: 48%. Avg. HS GPA: Unavailable.

Cost: Tuition and Fees: In-State: $4,361. Out-of-State: $14,258. Room and Board: $6,680.

Inst. Aid: FT Undergrads Receiving Aid: Unavailable. Avg. Amount per Student: Unavailable.

UNIVERSITY OF NORTH CAROLINA AT CHAPEL HILL

Chapel Hill, NC

unchelp@admissions.unc.edu; www.unc.edu

General Info: Public, University, Four-year, Coed, Regionally Accredited, Southern Association of Colleges and Schools, College Board member. Suburban setting, Large town (10,000–49,999), Residential campus. Academic Calendar: Semester.

Student Body: Full-Time Undergrads: 17,628. Men: 41.3%, Women: 58.7%. Total Undergrad Population: Native American or Native Alaskan: 1%. Asian American or Pacific Islander: 7%. African American: 12%. Latino: 5%. Caucasian: 70%. International: 1%. Out-of-State: 15%. Total all graduate and professional students: 8,254.

Academics: Full-Time Faculty: 1,514.

Admissions: Regular Application Deadline: 1/15. Priority Application Deadline: Unavailable. Early Decision Deadline: Unavailable. Transfer Priority Deadline: Unavailable. Financial Aid Deadline: Unavailable. Total Number of Students Applied: 20,090. Number Admitted: 6,999. Number Enrolled: 3,893. Test Scores (Middle 50%): SAT Critical Reading: Unavailable. SAT Math: Unavailable. SAT Writing: Unavailable. HS Rank of Entering Freshmen: Top 10%: 76.45%. Top 25%: 95.42%. Avg. HS GPA: 4.42.

Cost: Tuition and Fees: In-State: $3,705. Out-of-State: $19,353. Room and Board: $7,090.

Inst. Aid: FT Undergrads Receiving Aid: 5,232. Avg. Amount per Student: $11,394.

UNIVERSITY OF NORTH DAKOTA

Grand Forks, ND

enrollmentservices@mail.und.nodak.edu; www.und.edu

General Info: Public, University, Four-year, Coed, Regionally Accredited, North Central Association of Colleges and Schools. Urban setting, Small city (50,000–249,999), Residential campus. Academic Calendar: Semester.

Student Body: Full-Time Undergrads: 10,376. Men: 53%, Women: 47%. Total Undergrad Population: Native American or Native Alaskan: 2%. Asian American or Pacific Islander: 1%. African American: 0%. Latino: 1%. Caucasian: 93%. International: 1%. Out-of-State: 56%. Total all graduate and professional students: 1,978.

Academics: Full-Time Faculty: 668.

Admissions: Regular Application Deadline: Rollng admission. Priority Application Deadline: 2/5. Early Decision Deadline: Unavailable. Transfer Priority Deadline: Unavailable. Financial Aid Deadline: Unavailable. Total Number of Students Applied: Unavailable. Percent Admitted: 74%. Number Enrolled: 1,900. Test Scores (Middle 50%): SAT Critical Reading: N/A. SAT Math: N/A. SAT Writing: N/A. ACT Comp: 20–25. HS Rank of Entering Freshmen: Top 10%: 16%. Top 25%: 38%. Avg. HS GPA: Unavailable.

Want to Be a Librarian?

Syracuse University

University of Illinois at Urbana-Champaign

University of North Carolina at Chapel Hill

Cost: Tuition and Fees: In-State: $6,060. Out-of-State: $14,454. Room and Board: $5,140.

Inst. Aid: FT Undergrads Receiving Aid: Unavailable. Avg. Amount per Student: Unavailable.

UNIVERSITY OF NOTRE DAME

South Bend, IN

admissions@nd.edu; www.nd.edu

General Info: Private, University, Four-year, Roman Catholic Church, Coed, Regionally Accredited, College Board member. Suburban setting, Small city (50,000–249,999), Residential campus. Academic Calendar: Semester.

Student Body: Full-Time Undergrads: 8,338. Men: 53%, Women: 47%. Total Undergrad Population: Native American or Native Alaskan: 1%. Asian American or Pacific Islander: 8%. African American: 5%. Latino: 11%. Caucasian: 73%. International: 3%. Out-of-State: 93%. Total all graduate and professional students: 2,646.

Academics: Full-Time Faculty: 964.

Admissions: Regular Application Deadline: 12/31. Priority Application Deadline: Unavailable. Early Decision Deadline: Unavailable. Transfer Priority Deadline: Unavailable. Financial Aid Deadline: 2/15. Total Number of Students Applied: Unavailable. Percent Admitted: 27%. Number Enrolled: 2,000+. Test Scores (Middle 50%): SAT Critical Reading: 630–740. SAT Math: 660–760. SAT Writing: 580–710. ACT Comp: 30–33. HS Rank of Entering Freshmen: Top 10%: 86%. Top 25%: 97%. Avg. HS GPA: Unavailable.

Cost: Tuition and Fees: In-State: $35,187. Out-of-State: $35,187. Room and Board: $9,290.

Inst. Aid: FT Undergrads Receiving Aid: Unavailable. Avg. Amount per Student: Unavailable.

Want a Career in Politics?

Harvard University

Stanford University

Georgetown University

University of Michigan

Bowdoin College

UNIVERSITY OF OKLAHOMA

Norman, OK

admrec@ou.edu; www.ou.edu

General Info: Public, University, Four-year, Coed, Regionally Accredited, North Central Association of Colleges and Schools, College Board member. Suburban setting, Small city (50,000–249,999), Residential campus. Academic Calendar: Semester.

Student Body: Full-Time Undergrads: 20,580. Men: 48%, Women: 52%. Total Undergrad Population: Native American or Native Alaskan: 8%. Asian American or Pacific Islander: 6%. African American: 6%. Latino: 5%. Caucasian: 74%. International: 1%. Out-of-State: 0%. Total all graduate and professional students: 6,695.

Academics: Full-Time Faculty: 1,346.

Admissions: Regular Application Deadline: 4/1. Priority Application Deadline: Unavailable. Early Decision Deadline: Unavailable. Financial Aid Deadline: Unavailable. Total Number of Students Applied: Unavailable. Percent Admitted: 91%. Number Enrolled: 3,342. Test Scores (Middle 50%): SAT Critical Reading: Unavailable. SAT Math: Unavailable. SAT Writing: Unavailable. ACT Comp: 23–28. HS Rank of Entering Freshmen: Top 10%: 35%. Top 25%: 68%. Avg. HS GPA: Unavailable.

Cost: Tuition and Fees: In-State: $5,710. Out-of-State: $13,999. Room and Board: $6,863.

Inst. Aid: FT Undergrads Receiving Aid: Unavailable. Avg. Amount per Student: Unavailable.

UNIVERSITY OF OREGON

Eugene, OR

uoadmit@uoregon.edu; www.uoregon.edu

General Info: Public, University, Four-year, Coed, Regionally Accredited, Northwest Association of Schools and Colleges, College Board member. Urban setting, Small city (50,000–249,999), Residential campus. Academic Calendar: Quarter.

Student Body: Full-Time Undergrads: 16,529. Men: 46%, Women: 54%. Total Undergrad Population: Native American or Native Alaskan: 1%. Asian American or Pacific Islander: 7%. African American: 2%. Latino: 4%. Caucasian: 76%. International: 4%. Out-of-State: 32%. Total all graduate and professional students: 3,290.

Academics: Full-Time Faculty: 785.

Admissions: Regular Application Deadline: 1/15. Priority Application Deadline: 11/1. Early Decision Deadline: Unavailable. Transfer Priority Deadline: Unavailable. Financial Aid Deadline: 6/30. Total Number of Students Applied: Unavailable. Percent Admitted: 88%. Number Enrolled: 3,352. Test Scores (Middle 50%): SAT Critical Reading: 490–610. SAT Math: 500–610. SAT Writing: Unavailable. ACT Comp: Unavailable. HS Rank of Entering Freshmen: Top 10%: 25%. Top 25%: 58%. Avg. HS GPA: Unavailable.

Cost: Tuition and Fees: In-State: $5,970. Out-of-State: $18,768. Room and Board: $7,827.

Inst. Aid: FT Undergrads Receiving Aid: Unavailable. Avg. Amount per Student: Unavailable.

UNIVERSITY OF PENNSYLVANIA

Philadelphia, PA

info@admissions.ugao.upenn.edu; www.upenn.edu

General Info: Private, University, Four-year, Coed, Regionally Accredited, College Board member. Urban setting, Very large city (over 500,000), Residential campus. Academic Calendar: Semester.

Student Body: Full-Time Undergrads: 10,138. Men: 49%, Women: 51%. Total Undergrad Population: Native American or Native Alaskan: 0%. Asian American or Pacific Islander: 16%. African American: 8%. Latino: 6%. Caucasian: 43%. International: 14%. Out-of-State: 81%. Total all graduate and professional students: 6,712.

Academics: Full-Time Faculty: 1,990.

Admissions: Regular Application Deadline: 1/1. Priority Application Deadline: Unavailable. Early Decision Deadline: 11/1. Transfer Priority Deadline: Unavailable. Financial Aid Deadline: Unavailable. Total Number of Students Applied: Unavailable. Percent Admitted: 18%. Number Enrolled: 2,373. Test Scores (Middle 50%): SAT Critical Reading: 650–740. SAT Math: 680–770. SAT Writing: 650–740. ACT Comp: 29–33. HS Rank of Entering Freshmen: Top 10%: 94%. Top 25%: 99%. Avg. HS GPA: Unavailable.

Cost: Tuition and Fees: In-State: $34,156. Out-of-State: $34,156. Room and Board: $9,804.

Inst. Aid: FT Undergrads Receiving Aid: Unavailable. Avg. Amount per Student: Unavailable.

UNIVERSITY OF PITTSBURGH

Pittsburgh, PA
oafa@pitt.edu; www.pitt.edu

General Info: Public, University, Four-year, Coed, Regionally Accredited, Middle States Association of Colleges and Schools, College Board member. Urban setting, Large city (250,000–499,999), Residential campus. Academic Calendar: Semester.

Student Body: Full-Time Undergrads: 17,024. Men: 46%, Women: 54%. Total Undergrad Population: Native American or Native Alaskan: 0%. Asian American or Pacific Islander: 5%. African American: 9%. Latino: 1%. Caucasian: 82%. International: 0%. Out-of-State: 21%. Total all graduate and professional students: 7,718.

Academics: Full-Time Faculty: 3,655.

Admissions: Regular Application Deadline: Rolling. Priority Application Deadline: Unavailable. Early Decision Deadline: Unavailable. Transfer Priority Deadline: Unavailable. Financial Aid Deadline: 6/1. Total Number of Students Applied: Unavailable. Percent Admitted: 56%. Number Enrolled: Unavailable. Test Scores (Middle 50%): SAT Critical Reading: 560–660. SAT Math: 570–670. SAT Writing: Unavailable. ACT Comp: 24–29. HS Rank of Entering Freshmen: Top 10%: 43%. Top 25%: 80%. Avg. HS GPA: Unavailable.

Cost: Tuition and Fees: In-State: $12,138. Out-of-State: $21,456. Room and Board: $7,800.

Inst. Aid: FT Undergrads Receiving Aid: Unavailable. Avg. Amount per Student: Unavailable.

UNIVERSITY OF PUGET SOUND

Tacoma, WA
admission@ups.edu; www.ups.edu

General Info: Coed, College Board member, Four-year, Liberal Arts College, Private, Regionally Accredited, University. Suburban setting, Small city (50,000–249,999), Residential campus. Academic Calendar: Semester.

Student Body: Full-Time Undergrads: 2,576. Men: 40.53%, Women: 57.9%. Part-Time Undergrads. Men: 0.94%, Women: 0.63%. Total Undergrad Population: Native American or Native Alaskan: 1.5%. Asian American or Pacific Islander: 9.2%. African American: 2.7%. Latino: 3.8%. Caucasian: 73.7%. International: 0.4%. Out-of-State: 68.3%. Living Off-Campus: 41.1%. % In Fraternities: 23%. % In Sororities: 22%. Total all graduate and professional students: 260.

Academics: Full-Time Faculty: 224. With PhD: 196. Percentage completing two or more majors: 13.3%. Graduation Rates: 67.9% within 4 years. 76.6% within 6 years.

Admissions: Regular Application Deadline: 1/15. Priority Application Deadline: 1/15. Early Decision Deadline: 11/15–1/02. Fall Transfer Deadline: 3/1. Spring Transfer Deadline: 11/1. Transfer Priority Deadline: 3/1. Financial Aid Deadline: Unavailable. Total Number of Students Applied: 5,273. Number Admitted: 3,502. Number Enrolled: 644. Number accepting place on waitlist: 75. Number of waitlisted students admitted: 29. Number applied early decision: 128. Early decision admitted: 114. Test Scores (Middle 50%): SAT Critical Reading: 570–690. SAT Math: 550–660. SAT Writing: 560–660. ACT Comp: 25–29.75. HS Rank of Entering Freshmen: Top 10%: 40.2%. Top 25%: 69.3%. Avg. HS GPA: 3.54.

Cost: Tuition and Fees: In-State: $33,780. Out-of-State: $33,780. Room and Board: $8,760.

Inst. Aid: FT Undergrads Receiving Aid: 2,207. Avg. Amount per Student: $25,089. Freshmen Receiving Non-Need Scholarship or Grant: 143. Avg. Amount per Student: $6,335.

Graduates: No. of companies recruiting on campus: 122. Percentage of grads accepting a job at time of graduation: 30%. Alumni Giving %: 19.37%.

UNIVERSITY OF REDLANDS

Redlands, CA
admissions@redlands.edu; www.redlands.edu

General Info: Private, Liberal Arts College, University, Four-year, Coed, Regionally Accredited, College Board member. Suburban setting, Small city (50,000–249,999), Residential campus. Academic Calendar: 4-1-4.

Student Body: Full-Time Undergrads: 2,313. Men: 41%, Women: 59%. Total Undergrad Population: Native American or Native Alaskan: 0%. Asian American or Pacific Islander: 7%. African American: 2%. Latino: 11%. Caucasian: 55%. International: 1%. Out-of-State: 37%. Total all graduate and professional students: 94.

Academics: Full-Time Faculty: 165.

Admissions: Regular Application Deadline: 2/1. Priority Application Deadline: Unavailable. Early Decision Deadline: Unavailable. Transfer Priority Deadline: 12/15. Financial Aid Deadline: Unavailable. Total Number of Students Applied: Unavailable. Percent Admitted: 65%. Number Enrolled: 613. Test Scores (Middle 50%): SAT Critical Reading: 540–630. SAT Math: 540–630. SAT Writing: Unavailable. ACT Comp: 22–26. HS Rank of Entering Freshmen: Top 10%: 32%. Top 25%: 69%. Avg. HS GPA: Unavailable.

Cost: Tuition and Fees: In-State: $28,776. Out-of-State: $28,776. Room and Board: $9,360.

Inst. Aid: FT Undergrads Receiving Aid: Unavailable. Avg. Amount per Student: Unavailable.

UNIVERSITY OF RHODE ISLAND

Kingston, RI
admission@uri.edu; www.uri.edu

General Info: Public, University, Four-year, Coed, Regionally Accredited, New England Association of Colleges and Schools, College Board member. Rural setting, Small town (2,500–9,999), Commuter campus. Academic Calendar: Semester.

Student Body: Full-Time Undergrads: 11,546. Men: 44%, Women: 56%. Total Undergrad Population: Native American or Native Alaskan: 0%. Asian American or Pacific Islander: 3%. African American: 4%. Latino: 5%. Caucasian: 76%. International: 0%. Out-of-State: 47%. Total all graduate and professional students: 2,996.

Academics: Full-Time Faculty: 668.

Admissions: Regular Application Deadline: 3/1. Priority Application Deadline: Unavailable. Early Decision Deadline: Unavailable. Transfer Priority Deadline: 5/1. Financial Aid Deadline: Unavailable. Total Number of Students Applied: Unavailable. Percent Admitted: 77%. Number Enrolled: 2,323. Test Scores (Middle 50%): SAT Critical Reading: 500–600. SAT Math: 520–620. SAT Writing: Unavailable. ACT Comp: Unavailable. HS Rank of Entering Freshmen: Top 10%: 21%. Top 25%: Unavailable. Avg. HS GPA: Unavailable.

Cost: Tuition and Fees: In-State: $7,724. Out-of-State: $21,424. Room and Board: $9,199.

Inst. Aid: FT Undergrads Receiving Aid: Unavailable. Avg. Amount per Student: Unavailable.

UNIVERSITY OF RICHMOND

University of Richmond, VA
admissions@richmond.edu; www.richmond.edu

General Info: Coed, College Board member, Four-year, Liberal Arts College, Nondenominational, Private, Regionally Accredited, Southern Association of Colleges and Schools, University. Suburban setting, Very large city (over 500,000), Residential campus. Academic Calendar: Semester.

Student Body: Full-Time Undergrads: 2,857. Men: 49%, Women: 51%. Total Undergrad Population: Native American or Native Alaskan: 0%. Asian American or Pacific Islander: 4%. African American: 6%. Latino: 3%. Caucasian: 75%. International: 5%. Out-of-State: 84%. Living Off-Campus: 8%. % In Fraternities: 28%. % In Sororities: 43%. Total all graduate and professional students: 167.

Academics: Full-Time Faculty: 286. With PhD: 263. Graduation Rates: 81% within 4 years. 86% within 6 years.

Admissions: Regular Application Deadline: 1/15. Priority Application Deadline: Unavailable. Early Decision Deadline: 11/15. Transfer Priority Deadline: 2/15. Financial Aid Deadline: 2/15. Total Number of Students Applied: 6,649. Number Admitted: 2,654. Number Enrolled: 810. Number accepting place on waitlist: 710. Number of waitlisted students admitted: 66. Number applied early decision: 288. Early decision admitted: 164. Test Scores (Middle 50%): SAT Critical Reading: 590–690. SAT Math: 610–690. SAT Writing: 590–690. ACT Comp: 27-31. HS Rank of Entering Freshmen: Top 10%: 61.8%. Top 25%: 88.7%. Avg. HS GPA: Unavailable.

Cost: Tuition and Fees: In-State: $38,850. Out-of-State: $38,850. Room and Board: $8,200.

Inst. Aid: FT Undergrads Receiving Aid: 418. Avg. Amount per Student: Unavailable.

UNIVERSITY OF ROCHESTER

Rochester, NY
admit@admissions.rochester.edu; www.rochester.edu

General Info: Coed, College Board member, Four-year, Private, Regionally Accredited, University. Suburban setting, Large city (250,000–499,999), Residential campus. Academic Calendar: Semester.

Student Body: Full-Time Undergrads: 4,696. Men: 51%, Women: 49%. Part-Time Undergrads. Men: 22%, Women: 78%. Total Undergrad Population: Native American or Native Alaskan: 0%. Asian American or Pacific Islander: 10%. African American: 4%. Latino: 4%. Caucasian: 59%. International: 5%. Out-of-State: 44%. Living Off-Campus: 14%. % In Fraternities: 19%. % In Sororities: 20%. Total all graduate and professional students: 4,203.

Academics: Full-Time Faculty: 521. With PhD: 438. Graduation Rates: 70% within 4 years. 81% within 6 years.

Admissions: Regular Application Deadline: 1/1. Priority Application Deadline: Unavailable. Early Decision Deadline: 11/1. Fall Transfer Deadline: 6/1. Spring Transfer Deadline: 11/1. Transfer Priority Deadline: Unavailable. Financial Aid Deadline: 2/1. Total Number of Students Applied: 11,676. Number Admitted: 4,815. Number Enrolled: 1,062. Number accepting place on waitlist: 390. Number applied early decision: 652. Early decision admitted: 266. Test Scores (Middle 50%): SAT Critical Reading: 600–700. SAT Math: 630–720. SAT Writing: Unavailable. ACT Comp: 27-31. HS Rank of Entering Freshmen: Top 10%: 72%. Top 25%: 95%. Avg. HS GPA: 3.7.

Cost: Tuition and Fees: In-State: $36,410. Out-of-State: $36,410. Room and Board: $10,810.

Inst. Aid: FT Undergrads Receiving Aid: 2,236. Avg. Amount per Student: $28,668. Freshmen Receiving Non-Need Scholarship or Grant: 388. Avg. Amount per Student: $9,620.

Graduates: No. of companies recruiting on campus: 1,055. Percentage of grads accepting a job at time of graduation: 32.5%. Alumni Giving %: 17.6%.

UNIVERSITY OF SCRANTON

Scranton, PA
admissions@scranton.edu; www.scranton.edu

General Info: Private, Liberal Arts College, University, Four-year, Roman Catholic Church, Society of Jesus (Jesuits), Coed, Regionally Accredited, College Board member. Urban setting, Small city (50,000–249,999), Residential campus. Academic Calendar: Semester.

Student Body: Full-Time Undergrads: 3,999. Men: 40%, Women: 60%. Total Undergrad Population: Native American or Native Alaskan: 0%. Asian American or Pacific Islander: 3%. African American: 1%. Latino: 4%. Caucasian: 81%. International: 1%. Out-of-State: 57%. Total all graduate and professional students: 1,354.

Academics: Full-Time Faculty: 263.

Admissions: Regular Application Deadline: 3/15. Priority Application Deadline: Unavailable. Early Decision Deadline: Unavailable. Transfer Priority Deadline: Unavailable. Financial Aid Deadline: Unavailable. Total Number of Students Applied: Unavailable. Percent Admitted: 70%. Number Enrolled: 981. Test Scores (Middle 50%): SAT Critical Reading: 510–600. SAT Math: 510–610. SAT Writing: Unavailable. ACT Comp: Unavailable. HS Rank of Entering Freshmen: Top 10%: 26%. Top 25%: 57%. Avg. HS GPA: Unavailable.

Cost: Tuition and Fees: In-State: $25,938. Out-of-State: $25,938. Room and Board: $10,224.

Inst. Aid: FT Undergrads Receiving Aid: Unavailable. Avg. Amount per Student: Unavailable.

UNIVERSITY OF SOUTH CAROLINA AT COLUMBIA
Columbia, SC
admissions-ugrad@sc.edu; www.sc.edu

General Info: Coed, Four-year, Public, Regionally Accredited, University. Small city (50,000–249,999). Academic Calendar: Semester.

Student Body: Full-Time Undergrads: 27,390. Men: 45%, Women: 55%.

Academics: Full-Time Faculty: 1,231.

Admissions: Regular Application Deadline: 12/1. Priority Application Deadline: Unavailable. Early Decision Deadline: Unavailable. Financial Aid Deadline: Unavailable. Total Number of Students Applied: Unavailable. Percent Admitted: 63%. Number Enrolled: 3,680. Test Scores (Middle 50%): SAT Critical Reading: 520–620. SAT Math: 540–640. SAT Writing: Unavailable. ACT Comp: Unavailable. HS Rank of Entering Freshmen: Top 10%: 29%. Top 25%: 63%. Avg. HS GPA: Unavailable.

Cost: Tuition and Fees: In-State: $7,808. Out-of-State: Unavailable. Room and Board: $6,520.

Inst. Aid: FT Undergrads Receiving Aid: Unavailable. Avg. Amount per Student: Unavailable.

UNIVERSITY OF SOUTH DAKOTA
Vermillion, SD
admission@usd.edu; www.usd.edu

General Info: Public, University, Four-year, Coed, Regionally Accredited, North Central Association of Colleges and Schools, College Board member. Rural setting, Small town (2,500–9,999), Residential campus. Academic Calendar: Semester.

Student Body: Full-Time Undergrads: 6,468. Men: 40%, Women: 60%. Total Undergrad Population: Native American or Native Alaskan: 3%. Asian American or Pacific Islander: 1%. African American: 2%. Latino: 1%. Caucasian: 87%. International: 0%. Out-of-State: 30%. Total all graduate and professional students: 1,773.

Academics: Full-Time Faculty: 285.

Want to Be a Psychologist?

Stanford University

University of Michigan – Ann Arbor

Yale University

Admissions: Regular Application Deadline: Rolling. Priority Application Deadline: Unavailable. Early Decision Deadline: Unavailable. Transfer Priority Deadline: Unavailable. Financial Aid Deadline: Unavailable. Total Number of Students Applied: Unavailable. Percent Admitted: 86%. Number Enrolled: 1,035. Test Scores (Middle 50%): SAT Critical Reading: 460–580. SAT Math: 470–620. SAT Writing: Unavailable. ACT Comp: 20–25. HS Rank of Entering Freshmen: Top 10%: 13%. Top 25%: 35%. Avg. HS GPA: Unavailable.

Cost: Tuition and Fees: In-State: $5,072. Out-of-State: $6,263. Room and Board: $4,964.

Inst. Aid: FT Undergrads Receiving Aid: Unavailable. Avg. Amount per Student: Unavailable.

UNIVERSITY OF SOUTH FLORIDA
Tampa, FL
admissions@admin.usf.edu; www.usf.edu

General Info: Public, University, Four-year, Coed, Regionally Accredited, Southern Association of Colleges and Schools, College Board member. Urban setting, Very large city (over 500,000), Commuter campus. Academic Calendar: Semester.

Student Body: Full-Time Undergrads: 34,077. Men: 41%, Women: 59%. Total Undergrad Population: Native American or Native Alaskan: 0%. Asian American or Pacific Islander: 7%. African American: 10%. Latino: 15%. Caucasian: 63%. International: 1%. Out-of-State: 5%. Total all graduate and professional students: 8,740.

Academics: Full-Time Faculty: 1,660.

Admissions: Regular Application Deadline: Rolling. Priority Application Deadline: 4/15. Early Decision Deadline: Unavailable. Transfer Priority Deadline: 7/1. Financial Aid Deadline: Unavailable. Total Number of Students Applied: Unavailable. Number Admitted: Unavailable. Number Enrolled: Unavailable. Test Scores (Middle 50%): SAT Critical Reading: 500–600. SAT Math: 510–610. SAT Writing: 470–570. ACT Comp: 22–26. HS Rank of Entering Freshmen: Top 10%: 27%. Top 25%: 64%. Avg. HS GPA: Unavailable.

Cost: Tuition and Fees: In-State: $3,416. Out-of-State: $16,115. Room and Board: $7,180.

Inst. Aid: FT Undergrads Receiving Aid: Unavailable. Avg. Amount per Student: Unavailable.

UNIVERSITY OF SOUTHERN CALIFORNIA

Los Angeles, CA

admitusc@usc.edu; www.usc.edu

General Info: Private, University, Four-year, Coed, Regionally Accredited, College Board member. Urban setting, Very large city (over 500,000), Residential campus. Academic Calendar: Semester.

Student Body: Full-Time Undergrads: 16,500. Men: 48%, Women: 52%. Total Undergrad Population: Native American or Native Alaskan: 1%. Asian American or Pacific Islander: 22%. African American: 6%. Latino: 13%. Caucasian: 47%. International: 9%. Out-of-State: 47%. % In Fraternities: 15%. % In Sororities: 15%. Total all graduate and professional students: 16,071.

Academics: Full-Time Faculty: 3,200.

Admissions: Regular Application Deadline: 1/10. Priority Application Deadline: 12/10. Early Decision Deadline: Unavailable. Transfer Priority Deadline: Unavailable. Financial Aid Deadline: 1/20. Total Number of Students Applied: Unavailable. Percent Admitted: 25%. Number Enrolled: 2,763. Test Scores (Middle 50%): SAT Critical Reading: 630–720. SAT Math: 650–740. SAT Writing: 640–720. ACT Comp: 28–32. HS Rank of Entering Freshmen: Top 10%: 86%. Top 25%: 97%. Avg. HS GPA: Unavailable.

Cost: Tuition and Fees: In-State: $33,888. Out-of-State: $33,888. Room and Board: $10,144.

Inst. Aid: FT Undergrads Receiving Aid: Unavailable. Avg. Amount per Student: Unavailable.

Want to Be a Teacher?

Stanford University

UCLA

Vanderbilt University

UNIVERSITY OF TENNESSEE–KNOXVILLE

Knoxville, TN

admissions@utk.edu; www.utk.edu

General Info: Coed, College Board member, Four-year, Public, Regionally Accredited, Southern Association of Colleges and Schools, University. Urban setting, Large city (250,000–499,999), Residential campus. Academic Calendar: Semester.

Student Body: Full-Time Undergrads: 20,400. Men: 50%, Women: 50%. Total Undergrad Population: Native American or Native Alaskan: 0%. Asian American or Pacific Islander: 3%. African American: 10%. Latino: 2%. Caucasian: 84%. International: 0%. Out-of-State: 13%. Total all graduate and professional students: 6,022.

Academics: Full-Time Faculty: 1,397.

Admissions: Regular Application Deadline: 2/1. Priority Application Deadline: Unavailable. Early Decision Deadline: 11/1. Transfer Priority Deadline: Unavailable. Financial Aid Deadline: Unavailable. Total Number of Students Applied: Unavailable. Number Admitted: Unavailable. Number Enrolled: Unavailable. Test Scores (Middle 50%): SAT Critical Reading: 520–630. SAT Math: 530–640. SAT Writing: Unavailable. ACT Comp: 24–29. HS Rank of Entering Freshmen: Top 10%: 41%. Top 25%: 68%. Avg. HS GPA: Unavailable.

Cost: Tuition and Fees: In-State: $5,932. Out-of-State: $17,874. Room and Board: $6,358.

Inst. Aid: FT Undergrads Receiving Aid: Unavailable. Avg. Amount per Student: Unavailable.

UNIVERSITY OF TENNESSEE–MARTIN

Martin, TN

admitme@utm.edu; www.utm.edu

General Info: Public, University, Four-year, Coed, Regionally Accredited, Southern Association of Colleges and Schools. Rural setting, Small town (2,500–9,999), Commuter campus. Academic Calendar: Semester.

Student Body: Full-Time Undergrads: 6,320. Men: 43%, Women: 57%. Total Undergrad Population: Native American or Native Alaskan: 0%. Asian American or Pacific Islander: 1%. African American: 16%. Latino: 1%. Caucasian: 79%. International: 3%. Out-of-State: 4%. Total all graduate and professional students: 573.

Academics: Full-Time Faculty: 1,518.

Admissions: Regular Application Deadline: 8/1. Priority Application Deadline: Unavailable. Early Decision Deadline: Unavailable. Transfer Priority Deadline: 7/1. Financial Aid Deadline: Unavailable. Total Number of Students Applied: Unavailable. Percent Admitted: 82%. Number Enrolled: 1,201. Test Scores (Middle 50%): SAT Critical Reading: Unavailable. SAT Math: Unavailable. SAT Writing: Unavailable. ACT Comp: 19–24. HS Rank of Entering Freshmen: Top 10%: 34%. Top 25%: 63%. Avg. HS GPA: Unavailable.

Cost: Tuition and Fees: In-State: $4,665. Out-of-State: $14,137. Room and Board: $4,410.

Inst. Aid: FT Undergrads Receiving Aid: Unavailable. Avg. Amount per Student: Unavailable.

UNIVERSITY OF TEXAS AT AUSTIN

Austin, TX
www.utexas.edu

General Info: Public, University, Four-year, Coed, Regionally Accredited, Southern Association of Colleges and Schools, College Board member. Commuter campus, Urban setting, Very large city (over 500,000). Academic Calendar: Semester.

Student Body: Full-Time Undergrads: 39,000. Men: 44.1%, Women: 48.3%. Part-Time Undergrads. Men: 3.9%, Women: 3.7%. Total Undergrad Population: Native American or Native Alaskan: 0%. Asian American or Pacific Islander: 17.4%. African American: 4.6%. Latino: 17.8%. Caucasian: 55.6%. International: 3.9%. Out-of-State: 6%. Living Off-Campus: 43.4%. % In Fraternities: 12.6%. % In Sororities: 9.6%. Total all graduate and professional students: 11,101.

Academics: Full-Time Faculty: 2,482.

Admissions: Regular Application Deadline: 2/1. Priority Application Deadline: Unavailable. Early Decision Deadline: Unavailable. Transfer Priority Deadline: Unavailable. Financial Aid Deadline: Unavailable. Total Number of Students Applied: Unavailable. Percent Admitted: 57%. Number Enrolled: 7,369. Test Scores (Middle 50%): SAT Critical Reading: 530–660. SAT Math: 570–690. SAT Writing: 520–640. ACT Comp: 23–29. HS Rank of Entering Freshmen: Top 10%: 68%. Top 25%: 92%. Avg. HS GPA: Unavailable.

Cost: Tuition and Fees: In-State: $7,630. Out-of-State: $20,364. Room and Board: $8,176.

Inst. Aid: FT Undergrads Receiving Aid: Unavailable. Avg. Amount per Student: Unavailable.

UNIVERSITY OF THE PACIFIC

Stockton, CA
admissions@pacific.edu; www.pacific.edu

General Info: Private, University, Four-year, Coed, Regionally Accredited, College Board member. Suburban setting, Large city (250,000–499,999), Residential campus. Academic Calendar: Semester.

Student Body: Full-Time Undergrads: 3,535. Men: 44%, Women: 56%. Total Undergrad Population: Native American or Native Alaskan: 1%. Asian American or Pacific Islander: 38%. African American: 2%. Latino: 8%. Caucasian: 33%. International: 4%. Out-of-State: 16%. Total all graduate and professional students: 584.

Academics: Full-Time Faculty: 426.

Admissions: Regular Application Deadline: 1/15. Priority Application Deadline: 1/15. Early Decision Deadline: Unavailable. Transfer Priority Deadline: 2/15. Financial Aid Deadline: Unavailable. Total Number of Students Applied: 5,893. Number Admitted: 3,483. Number Enrolled: 766. Test Scores (Middle 50%): SAT Critical Reading: 500–620. SAT Math: 540–670. SAT Writing: 500–610. ACT Comp: 22–27. HS Rank of Entering Freshmen: Top 10%: 41%. Top 25%: Unavailable. Avg. HS GPA: 3.47.

Cost: Tuition and Fees: In-State: $27,350. Out-of-State: $27,350. Room and Board: $8,700.

Inst. Aid: FT Undergrads Receiving Aid: Unavailable. Avg. Amount per Student: Unavailable.

Interested in Sports Management?

University of Massachusetts

Bowling Green

Ohio University

University of Florida

UNIVERSITY OF TULSA

Tulsa, OK
admission@utulsa.edu; www.utulsa.edu

General Info: Private, University, Four-year, Presbyterian Church (USA), Coed, Regionally Accredited, College Board member. Urban setting, Large city (250,000–499,999), Residential campus. Academic Calendar: Semester.

Student Body: Full-Time Undergrads: 2,882. Men: 51%, Women: 49%. Total Undergrad Population: Native American or Native Alaskan: 4%. Asian American or Pacific Islander: 3%. African American: 6%. Latino: 5%. Caucasian: 68%. International: 6%. Out-of-State: 45%. Total all graduate and professional students: 670.

Academics: Full-Time Faculty: 307.

Admissions: Regular Application Deadline: 6/1. Priority Application Deadline: 2/15. Early Decision Deadline: Unavailable. Financial Aid Deadline: Unavailable. Total Number of Students Applied: Unavailable. Percent Admitted: 75%. Number Enrolled: 660. Test Scores (Middle 50%): SAT Critical Reading: 540–700. SAT Math: 550–710. SAT Writing: Unavailable. ACT Comp: 23–30. HS Rank of Entering

Freshmen: Top 10%: 59%. Top 25%: 79%. Avg. HS GPA: Unavailable.

Cost: Tuition and Fees: In-State: $20,738. Out-of-State: $20,738. Room and Board: $7,052.

Inst. Aid: FT Undergrads Receiving Aid: Unavailable. Avg. Amount per Student: Unavailable.

UNIVERSITY OF UTAH

Salt Lake City, UT

admissions@sa.utah.edu; www.utah.edu

General Info: Public, University, Four-year, Coed, Regionally Accredited, Northwest Association of Schools and Colleges, College Board member. Urban setting, Large city (250,000–499,999), Commuter campus. Academic Calendar: Semester.

Student Body: Full-Time Undergrads: 22,661. Men: 55%, Women: 45%. Total Undergrad Population: Native American or Native Alaskan: 0%. Asian American or Pacific Islander: 6%. African American: 1%. Latino: 5%. Caucasian: 79%. International: 2%. Out-of-State: 17%. Total all graduate and professional students: 5,375.

Academics: Full-Time Faculty: 1,217.

Admissions: Regular Application Deadline: 4/1. Priority Application Deadline: 2/15. Early Decision Deadline: Unavailable. Transfer Priority Deadline: 2/15. Financial Aid Deadline: Unavailable. Total Number of Students Applied: Unavailable. Percent Admitted: 92%. Number Enrolled: 3,868. Test Scores (Middle 50%): SAT Critical Reading: 500–630. SAT Math: 500–630. SAT Writing: Unavailable. ACT Comp: 21–26. HS Rank of Entering Freshmen: Top 10%: 23%. Top 25%: 50%. Avg. HS GPA: Unavailable.

Cost: Tuition and Fees: In-State: $4,663. Out-of-State: $14,593. Room and Board: $5,831.

Inst. Aid: FT Undergrads Receiving Aid: Unavailable. Avg. Amount per Student: Unavailable.

UNIVERSITY OF VERMONT

Burlington, VT

admissions@uvm.edu; www.uvm.edu

General Info: Public, University, Four-year, Coed, Regionally Accredited, New England Association of Colleges and Schools, College Board member. Suburban setting, Large town (10,000–49,999), Residential campus. Academic Calendar: Semester.

Student Body: Full-Time Undergrads: 10,504. Men: 45%, Women: 55%. Part-Time Undergrads. Men: 39%, Women: 61%. Total Undergrad Population: Native American or Native Alaskan: 0%. Asian American or Pacific Islander: 2%. African American: 1%. Latino: 2%. Caucasian: 93%. International: 1%. Out-of-State: 74%. Living Off-Campus: 46%. % In Fraternities: 6%. % In Sororities: 5%. Total all graduate and professional students: 1,320.

Academics: Full-Time Faculty: 586.

Admissions: Regular Application Deadline: 1/15. Priority Application Deadline: Unavailable. Early Decision Deadline: Unavailable. Transfer Priority Deadline: 4/1. Financial Aid Deadline: Unavailable. Total Number of Students Applied: 18,814. Number Admitted: 13,079. Number Enrolled: 2,430. Number accepting place on waitlist: 1,261. Number of waitlisted students admitted: 5. Test Scores (Middle 50%): SAT Critical Reading: 540–630. SAT Math: 540–640. SAT Writing: 530–630. ACT Comp: 23–28. HS Rank of Entering Freshmen: Top 10%: 23%. Top 25%: 61%. Avg. HS GPA: Unavailable.

Cost: Tuition and Fees: In-State: $10,422. Out-of-State: $26,306. Room and Board: $8,024.

Inst. Aid: FT Undergrads Receiving Aid: 4,785. Avg. Amount per Student: $16,135. Freshmen Receiving Non-Need Scholarship or Grant: 89. Avg. Amount per Student: $1,961.

UNIVERSITY OF VIRGINIA

Charlottesville, VA

undergradadmission@virginia.edu; www.virginia.edu

General Info: Public, University, Four-year, Coed, Regionally Accredited, Southern Association of Colleges and Schools, College Board member. Suburban setting, Small city (50,000–249,999), Residential campus. Academic Calendar: Semester.

Student Body: Full-Time Undergrads: 14,676. Men: 44%, Women: 56%. Part-Time Undergrads. Men: 46%, Women: 54%. Total Undergrad Population: Native American or Native Alaskan: 0%. Asian American or Pacific Islander: 11%. African American: 8%. Latino: 4%. Caucasian: 64%. International: 5%. Out-of-State: 33%. Living Off-Campus: 57%. % In Fraternities: 30%. % In Sororities: 30%. Total all graduate and professional students: 7,693.

Academics: Full-Time Faculty: 1,253.

Admissions: Regular Application Deadline: 1/2. Priority Application Deadline: Unavailable. Early Decision Deadline: 11/1. Transfer Priority Deadline: Unavailable. Financial Aid Deadline: Unavailable. Total Number of Students Applied: 17,798. Number Admitted: 6,273. Number Enrolled: 3,246. Number accepting place on waitlist: 2,426. Number of waitlisted students admitted: 159. Test Scores (Middle 50%): SAT Critical Reading: 590–700. SAT Math: 610–720. SAT Writing: 600–710. ACT Comp: 26–31. HS Rank of Entering Freshmen: Top 10%: 87%. Top 25%: 96%. Avg. HS GPA: 4.05.

Cost: Tuition and Fees: In-State: $7,128. Out-of-State: $27,203. Room and Board: $7,820.

Inst. Aid: FT Undergrads Receiving Aid: 3,590. Avg. Amount per Student: $17,492. Freshmen Receiving Non-Need Scholarship or Grant: 120.

UNIVERSITY OF WASHINGTON

Seattle, WA
www.washington.edu

General Info: Public, University, Four-year, Coed, Northwest Association of Schools and Colleges, Regionally Accredited, College Board member. Urban setting, Very large city (over 500,000), Commuter campus. Academic Calendar: Quarter.

Student Body: Full-Time Undergrads: 27,836. Men: 47%, Women: 53%. Total Undergrad Population: Native American or Native Alaskan: 1%. Asian American or Pacific Islander: 29%. African American: 3%. Latino: 6%. Caucasian: 54%. International: 3%. Out-of-State: 18%. Total all graduate and professional students: 9,886.

Academics: Full-Time Faculty: 2,862.

Admissions: Regular Application Deadline: 1/15. Priority Application Deadline: Unavailable. Early Decision Deadline: Unavailable. Transfer Priority Deadline: Unavailable. Financial Aid Deadline: Unavailable. Total Number of Students Applied: Unavailable. Percent Admitted: 68%. Number Enrolled: 5,392. Test Scores (Middle 50%): SAT Critical Reading: 520–640. SAT Math: 550–670. SAT Writing: 510–630. ACT Comp: 23–28. HS Rank of Entering Freshmen: Top 10%: 66%. Top 25%: 86%. Avg. HS GPA: Unavailable.

Cost: Tuition and Fees: In-State: $5,985. Out-of-State: $21,283. Room and Board: $8,889.

Inst. Aid: FT Undergrads Receiving Aid: Unavailable. Avg. Amount per Student: Unavailable.

Want to Be a Nurse?

University of California–San Francisco

University of Pennsylvania

University of Washington

Cost: Tuition and Fees: In-State: $6,726. Out-of-State: $20,726. Room and Board: $6,920.

Inst. Aid: FT Undergrads Receiving Aid: Unavailable. Avg. Amount per Student: Unavailable.

UNIVERSITY OF WISCONSIN–MADISON

Madison, WI
onwisconsin@admissions.wisc.edu; www.wisc.edu

General Info: Public, University, Four-year, Coed, Regionally Accredited, North Central Association of Colleges and Schools, College Board member. Urban setting, Small city (50,000–249,999), Residential campus. Academic Calendar: Semester.

Student Body: Full-Time Undergrads: 28,459. Men: 46%, Women: 54%. Total Undergrad Population: Native American or Native Alaskan: 1%. Asian American or Pacific Islander: 6%. African American: 3%. Latino: 3%. Caucasian: 81%. International: 3%. Out-of-State: 39%. Total all graduate and professional students: 8,841.

Academics: Full-Time Faculty: 2,064.

Admissions: Regular Application Deadline: 2/1. Priority Application Deadline: Unavailable. Early Decision Deadline: Unavailable. Transfer Priority Deadline: Unavailable. Financial Aid Deadline: Unavailable. Total Number of Students Applied: Unavailable. Percent Admitted: 58%. Number Enrolled: 5,643. Test Scores (Middle 50%): SAT Critical Reading: 560–670. SAT Math: 610–710. SAT Writing: Unavailable. ACT Comp: 26–30. HS Rank of Entering Freshmen: Top 10%: 58%. Top 25%: 93%. Avg. HS GPA: Unavailable.

UNIVERSITY OF WISCONSIN–STEVENS POINT

Stevens Point, WI
admiss@uwsp.edu; www.uwsp.edu

General Info: Public, University, Four-year, Coed, Regionally Accredited, North Central Association of Colleges and Schools, College Board member. Rural setting, Large town (10,000–49,999), Residential campus. Academic Calendar: Semester.

Student Body: Full-Time Undergrads: 8,612. Men: 46%, Women: 54%. Total Undergrad Population: Native American or Native Alaskan: 1%. Asian American or Pacific Islander: 2%. African American: 1%. Latino: 2%. Caucasian: 93%. International: 2%. Out-of-State: 7%. Total all graduate and professional students: 230.

Academics: Full-Time Faculty: 357.

Admissions: Regular Application Deadline: 7/1. Priority Application Deadline: Unavailable. Early Decision Deadline: Unavailable. Transfer Priority Deadline: Unavailable. Financial Aid Deadline: 6/15. Total Number of Students Applied: Unavailable. Percent Admitted: 79%. Number Enrolled: 1,553. Test Scores (Middle 50%): SAT Critical Reading: Unavailable. SAT Math: Unavailable. SAT Writing: Unavailable. ACT Comp: 20–25. HS Rank of Entering Freshmen: Top 10%: 14%. Top 25%: 42%. Avg. HS GPA: Unavailable.

Cost: Tuition and Fees: In-State: $5,459. Out-of-State: $12,933. Room and Board: $4,542.

Inst. Aid: FT Undergrads Receiving Aid: Unavailable. Avg. Amount per Student: Unavailable.

Want to Be a Computer Programmer or Video Game Designer?

DigiPen Institute of Technology

Pepperdine University

Temple University

Western Michigan University

UNIVERSITY OF WYOMING

Laramie, WY

why-wyo@uwyo.edu; www.uwyo.edu

General Info: Public, University, Four-year, Coed, North Central Association of Colleges and Schools, Regionally Accredited, College Board member. Suburban setting, Large town (10,000–49,999), Residential campus. Academic Calendar: Semester.

Student Body: Full-Time Undergrads: 9,510. Men: 47%, Women: 53%. Total Undergrad Population: Native American or Native Alaskan: 1%. Asian American or Pacific Islander: 1%. African American: 1%. Latino: 4%. Caucasian: 82%. International: 1%. Out-of-State: 28%. Total all graduate and professional students: 3,383.

Academics: Full-Time Faculty: 692. With PhD: 80. Graduation Rates: 25.6% within 4 years. 55.6% within 6 years.

Admissions: Regular Application Deadline: 8/10. Priority Application Deadline: 3/1. Early Decision Deadline: Unavailable. Transfer Priority Deadline: 3/1. Financial Aid Deadline: Unavailable. Total Number of Students Applied: 3,366. Number Admitted: 3,220. Number Enrolled: Unavailable. Test Scores (Middle 50%): SAT Critical Reading: 480–610. SAT Math: 500–630. SAT Writing: Unavailable. ACT Comp: 21–26. HS Rank of Entering Freshmen: Top 10%: 20.4%. Top 25%: 49.5%. Avg. HS GPA: 3.46.

Cost: Tuition and Fees: In-State: $3,366. Out-of-State: $10,230. Room and Board: $7,284.

Inst. Aid: FT Undergrads Receiving Aid: 87. Avg. Amount per Student: Unavailable.

URSINUS COLLEGE

Collegeville, PA

admissions@ursinus.edu; www.ursinus.edu

General Info: Private, Liberal Arts College, Four-year, Coed, Regionally Accredited, College Board member. Suburban setting, Small town (2,500–9,999), Residential campus. Academic Calendar: Semester.

Student Body: Full-Time Undergrads: 1,564. Men: 47%, Women: 53%. Total Undergrad Population: Native American or Native Alaskan: 0%. Asian American or Pacific Islander: 4%. African American: 9%. Latino: 2%. Caucasian: 74%. International: 1%. Out-of-State: 39%.

Academics: Full-Time Faculty: 120.

Admissions: Regular Application Deadline: 2/15. Priority Application Deadline: Unavailable. Early Decision Deadline: 1/15. Transfer Priority Deadline: Unavailable. Financial Aid Deadline: 2/15. Total Number of Students Applied: Unavailable. Percent Admitted: 47%. Number Enrolled: 410. Test Scores (Middle 50%): SAT Critical Reading: 550–680. SAT Math: 540–660. SAT Writing: Unavailable. ACT Comp: 22–28. HS Rank of Entering Freshmen: Top 10%: 47%. Top 25%: 75%. Avg. HS GPA: Unavailable.

Cost: Tuition and Fees: In-State: $35,000. Out-of-State: $35,000. Room and Board: $8,000.

Inst. Aid: FT Undergrads Receiving Aid: Unavailable. Avg. Amount per Student: Unavailable.

VALDOSTA STATE UNIVERSITY

Valdosta, GA

admissions@valdosta.edu; www.valdosta.edu

General Info: Public, University, Four-year, Coed, Regionally Accredited, Southern Association of Colleges and Schools, College Board member. Suburban setting, Small city (50,000–249,999), Commuter campus. Academic Calendar: Semester.

Student Body: Full-Time Undergrads: 9,489. Men: 41%, Women: 59%. Total Undergrad Population: Native American or Native Alaskan: 0%. Asian American or Pacific Islander: 1%. African American: 27%. Latino: 2%. Caucasian: 66%. International: 1%. Out-of-State: 3%. Total all graduate and professional students: 1,399.

Academics: Full-Time Faculty: 435.

Admissions: Regular Application Deadline: 4/1. Priority Application Deadline: Unavailable. Early Decision Deadline: Unavailable. Financial Aid Deadline: Unavailable. Total Number of Students Applied: Unavailable. Percent Admitted: 61%. Number Enrolled: 1,744. Test Scores (Middle 50%): SAT Critical Reading: 480–560. SAT Math: 470–560. SAT Writing: Unavailable. ACT Comp: 20–23. HS Rank of Entering Freshmen: Top 10%: Unavailable. Top 25%: Unavailable. Avg. HS GPA: Unavailable.

Cost: Tuition and Fees: In-State: $3,490. Out-of-State: $11,172. Room and Board: $5,740.

Inst. Aid: FT Undergrads Receiving Aid: Unavailable. Avg. Amount per Student: Unavailable.

VALPARAISO UNIVERSITY

Valparaiso, IN

undergrad.admissions@valpo.edu; www.valpo.edu

General Info: Private, University, Four-year, Lutheran Church, Coed, Regionally Accredited, College Board member. Suburban setting, Large town (10,000–49,999), Residential campus. Academic Calendar: Semester.

Student Body: Full-Time Undergrads: 2,960. Men: 48%, Women: 52%. Total Undergrad Population: Native American or Native Alaskan: 0%. Asian American or Pacific Islander: 2%. African American: 5%. Latino: 5%. Caucasian: 82%. International: 4%. Out-of-State: 62%. Living Off-Campus: 35%. Total all graduate and professional students: 900.

Academics: Full-Time Faculty: 254.

Admissions: Regular Application Deadline: 8/15. Priority Application Deadline: Unavailable. Early Decision Deadline: 11/1. Transfer Priority Deadline: Unavailable. Financial Aid Deadline: Unavailable. Total Number of Students Applied: Unavailable. Percent Admitted: 89%. Number Enrolled: 760. Test Scores (Middle 50%): SAT Critical Reading: 500–620. SAT Math: 520–650. SAT Writing: 490–610. ACT Comp: 22–28. HS Rank of Entering Freshmen: Top 10%: 35%. Top 25%: 67%. Avg. HS GPA: 3.36.

Cost: Tuition and Fees: In-State: $26,070. Out-of-State: $26,070. Room and Board: $7,620.

Inst. Aid: FT Undergrads Receiving Aid: Unavailable. Avg. Amount per Student: Unavailable.

VANDERBILT UNIVERSITY

Nashville, TN

admissions@vanderbilt.edu; www.vanderbilt.edu

General Info: Coed, College Board member, College of Engineering, College of Music, Four-year, Liberal Arts College, Private, Regionally Accredited, Southern Association of Colleges and Schools, Teachers College/College of Education, University. Urban setting, Very large city (over 500,000), Residential campus. Academic Calendar: Semester.

Student Body: Full-Time Undergrads: 6,378. Men: 47%, Women: 53%. Total Undergrad Population: Native American or Native Alaskan: 0%. Asian American or Pacific Islander: 7%. African American: 9%. Latino: 6%. Caucasian: 63%. International: 3%. Out-of-State: 83%. Living Off-Campus: 16%. % In Fraternities: 35%. % In Sororities: 50%. Total all graduate and professional students: 5,315.

Academics: Full-Time Faculty: 785.

Admissions: Regular Application Deadline: 1/3. Priority Application Deadline: Unavailable. Early Decision Deadline: 11/1. Transfer Priority Deadline: Unavailable. Financial Aid Deadline: Unavailable. Total Number of Students Applied: Unavailable. Percent Admitted: 34%. Number Enrolled: 1,590. Test Scores (Middle 50%): SAT Critical Reading: 630–720. SAT Math: 650–740. SAT Writing: 630–710. ACT Comp: 28–32. HS Rank of Entering Freshmen: Top 10%: 77%. Top 25%: 93%. Avg. HS GPA: Unavailable.

Want to Be a Pharmacist?

Butler University

Northeastern University

University of Oklahoma

Cost: Tuition and Fees: In-State: $36,100. Out-of-State: $36,100. Room and Board: $12,028.

Inst. Aid: FT Undergrads Receiving Aid: Unavailable. Avg. Amount per Student: Unavailable.

VASSAR COLLEGE

Poughkeepsie, NY

admissons@vassar.edu; www.vassar.edu

General Info: Private, Liberal Arts College, Four-year, Coed, Regionally Accredited, College Board member. Suburban setting, Small city (50,000–249,999), Residential campus. Academic Calendar: Semester.

Student Body: Full-Time Undergrads: 2,423. Men: 38%, Women: 62%. Total Undergrad Population: Native American or Native Alaskan: 0%. Asian American or Pacific Islander: 10%. African American: 4%. Latino: 6%. Caucasian: 74%. International: 6%. Out-of-State: 75%. Total all graduate and professional students: 1.

Academics: Full-Time Faculty: 277.

Admissions: Regular Application Deadline: 1/1. Priority Application Deadline: Unavailable. Early Decision Deadline: 11/15. Transfer Priority Deadline: Unavailable. Financial Aid Deadline: 2/1. Total Number of Students Applied: Unavailable. Percent Admitted: 30%. Number Enrolled: 668. Test Scores (Middle 50%): SAT Critical Reading: 660–740. SAT Math: 640–720. SAT Writing: 650–740. ACT Comp: 29–31. HS Rank of Entering Freshmen: Top 10%: 67%. Top 25%: 94%. Avg. HS GPA: Unavailable.

Cost: Tuition and Fees: In-State: $36,030. Out-of-State: $36,030. Room and Board: $8,130.

Inst. Aid: FT Undergrads Receiving Aid: Unavailable. Avg. Amount per Student: Unavailable.

Want to Be a Doctor?

Harvard University

Johns Hopkins University

Washington University in St. Louis

VILLANOVA UNIVERSITY

Villanova, PA

gotovu@villanova.edu; www.villanova.edu

General Info: Private, University, Four-year, Roman Catholic Church, Coed, Regionally Accredited, College Board member. Suburban setting, Small town (2,500–9,999), Residential campus. Academic Calendar: Semester.

Student Body: Full-Time Undergrads: 7,254. Men: 51%, Women: 49%. Total Undergrad Population: Native American or Native Alaskan: 0%. Asian American or Pacific Islander: 8%. African American: 4%. Latino: 7%. Caucasian: 75%. International: 2%. Out-of-State: 78%. Total all graduate and professional students: 2,472.

Academics: Full-Time Faculty: 545.

Admissions: Regular Application Deadline: 1/7. Priority Application Deadline: Unavailable. Early Decision Deadline: Unavailable. Financial Aid Deadline: 2/7. Total Number of Students Applied: Unavailable. Percent Admitted: 43%. Number Enrolled: 1,634. Test Scores (Middle 50%): SAT Critical Reading: 570–670. SAT Math: 610–700. SAT Writing: 570–670. ACT Comp: 27–30. HS Rank of Entering Freshmen: Top 10%: 47%. Top 25%: 83%. Avg. HS GPA: Unavailable.

Cost: Tuition and Fees: In-State: $33,300. Out-of-State: $33,300. Room and Board: $9,560.

Inst. Aid: FT Undergrads Receiving Aid: Unavailable. Avg. Amount per Student: Unavailable.

VIRGINIA COMMONWEALTH UNIVERSITY

Richmond, VA

ugrad@vcu.edu; www.vcu.edu

General Info: Public, University, Four-year, Coed, Regionally Accredited, Southern Association of Colleges and Schools, College Board member. Urban setting, Small city (50,000–249,999), Commuter campus. Academic Calendar: Semester.

Student Body: Full-Time Undergrads: 21,260. Men: 42%, Women: 58%. Total Undergrad Population: Native American or Native Alaskan: 1%. Asian American or Pacific Islander: 12%. African American: 22%. Latino: 4%. Caucasian: 52%. International: 2%. Out-of-State: 10%. Total all graduate and professional students: 7,550.

Academics: Full-Time Faculty: 1,744.

Admissions: Regular Application Deadline: 2/1. Priority Application Deadline: Unavailable. Early Decision Deadline: Unavailable. Transfer Priority Deadline: 6/1. Financial Aid Deadline: Unavailable. Total Number of Students Applied: Unavailable. Percent Admitted: 66%. Number Enrolled: 3,499. Test Scores (Middle 50%): SAT Critical Reading: 480–580. SAT Math: 480–580. SAT Writing: 460–570. ACT Comp: 19–23. HS Rank of Entering Freshmen: Top 10%: 16%. Top 25%: 44%. Avg. HS GPA: Unavailable.

Cost: Tuition and Fees: In-State: $5,819. Out-of-State: $17,556. Room and Board: $7,536.

Inst. Aid: FT Undergrads Receiving Aid: Unavailable. Avg. Amount per Student: Unavailable.

VIRGINIA POLYTECHNIC INSTITUTE AND STATE UNIVERSITY

Blacksburg, VA

vtadmiss@vt.edu; www.vt.edu

General Info: Public, University, Four-year, Coed, Regionally Accredited, Southern Association of Colleges and Schools, College Board member. Rural setting, Large town (10,000–49,999), Residential campus. Academic Calendar: Semester.

Student Body: Full-Time Undergrads: 21,997. Men: 55%, Women: 45%. Total Undergrad Population: Native American or Native Alaskan: 0%. Asian American or Pacific Islander: 7%. African American: 3%. Latino: 2%. Caucasian: 67%. International: 2%. Out-of-State: 27%. Total all graduate and professional students: 6,111.

Academics: Full-Time Faculty: 1,304.

Admissions: Regular Application Deadline: 1/15. Priority Application Deadline: Unavailable. Early Decision Deadline: 11/1. Transfer Priority Deadline: Unavailable. Financial Aid Deadline: Unavailable. Total Number of Students Applied: Unavailable. Percent Admitted: 68%. Number Enrolled: 5,085. Test Scores (Middle 50%): SAT Critical Reading: 530–630. SAT Math: 570–660. SAT Writing: 530–620. ACT Comp: Unavailable. HS Rank of Entering Freshmen: Top 10%: 37%. Top 25%: 79%. Avg. HS GPA: Unavailable.

Cost: Tuition and Fees: In-State: $6,973. Out-of-State: $19,049. Room and Board: $4,956.

Inst. Aid: FT Undergrads Receiving Aid: Unavailable. Avg. Amount per Student: Unavailable.

WABASH COLLEGE

Crawfordsville, IN

admissions@wabash.edu; www.wabash.edu

General Info: Private, Liberal Arts College, Four-year, Men Only, Regionally Accredited, College Board member. Suburban setting, Large town (10,000–49,999), Residential campus. Academic Calendar: Semester.

Student Body: Full-Time Undergrads: 850. Men: 100%, Women: 0%. Total Undergrad Population: Native American or Native Alaskan: 0%. Asian American or Pacific Islander: 1%. African American: 5%. Latino: 6%. Caucasian: 80%. International: 6%. Out-of-State: 28%.

Academics: Full-Time Faculty: 90.

Admissions: Regular Application Deadline: 2/1. Priority Application Deadline: Unavailable. Early Decision Deadline: 11/15. Transfer Priority Deadline: 12/15. Financial Aid Deadline: 3/1. Total Number of Students Applied: Unavailable. Percent Admitted: 51%. Number Enrolled: 268. Test Scores (Middle 50%): SAT Critical Reading: 510–620. SAT Math: 560–650. SAT Writing: 500–610. ACT Comp: 22–28. HS Rank of Entering Freshmen: Top 10%: 39%. Top 25%: 73%. Avg. HS GPA: Unavailable.

Cost: Tuition and Fees: In-State: $26,350. Out-of-State: $26,350. Room and Board: $4,100.

Inst. Aid: FT Undergrads Receiving Aid: Unavailable. Avg. Amount per Student: Unavailable.

WAGNER COLLEGE

Staten Island, NY

adm@wagner.edu; www.wagner.edu

General Info: Private, Liberal Arts College, Four-year, Lutheran Church In America, Coed, Regionally Accredited, College Board member. Suburban setting, Very large city (over 500,000), Residential campus. Academic Calendar: Semester.

Student Body: Full-Time Undergrads: 1,962. Men: 34%, Women: 66%. Total Undergrad Population: Native American or Native Alaskan: 0%. Asian American or Pacific Islander: 2%. African American: 4%. Latino: 6%. Caucasian: 82%. International: 1%. Out-of-State: 65%. Total all graduate and professional students: 325.

Academics: Full-Time Faculty: 100.

Admissions: Regular Application Deadline: 2/15. Priority Application Deadline: Unavailable. Early Decision Deadline: 1/1. Financial Aid Deadline: Unavailable. Total Number of Students Applied: Unavailable. Percent Admitted: 61%. Number Enrolled: 579. Test Scores (Middle 50%): SAT Critical Reading: 530–630. SAT Math: 530–640. SAT Writing: Unavailable. ACT Comp: 23–27. HS Rank of Entering Freshmen: Top 10%: 17%. Top 25%: 64%. Avg. HS GPA: Unavailable.

Cost: Tuition and Fees: In-State: $27,300. Out-of-State: $27,300. Room and Board: $8,400.

Inst. Aid: FT Undergrads Receiving Aid: Unavailable. Avg. Amount per Student: Unavailable.

Want to Be a Veterinarian?

Cornell University

Michigan State University

University of Pennsylvania

WAKE FOREST UNIVERSITY

Winston-Salem, NC

admissions@wfu.edu; www.wfu.edu

General Info: Private, University, Four-year, Coed, Regionally Accredited, College Board member. Suburban setting, Small city (50,000–249,999), Residential campus. Academic Calendar: Semester.

Student Body: Full-Time Undergrads: 4,321. Men: 49%, Women: 51%. Total Undergrad Population: Native American or Native Alaskan: 1%. Asian American or Pacific Islander: 6%. African American: 7%. Latino: 2%. Caucasian: 84%. International: 1%. Out-of-State: 75%. Total all graduate and professional students: 2,376.

Academics: Full-Time Faculty: 1,226. With PhD: 341.

Admissions: Regular Application Deadline: 1/15. Priority Application Deadline: Unavailable. Early Decision Deadline: 11/15. Transfer Priority Deadline: Unavailable. Financial Aid Deadline: 3/1. Total Number of Students Applied: Unavailable. Percent Admitted: 43%. Number Enrolled: 1,121. Test Scores (Middle 50%): SAT Critical Reading: 620–700. SAT Math: 640–710. SAT Writing: Unavailable. ACT Comp: Unavailable. HS Rank of Entering Freshmen: Top 10%: 64%. Top 25%: 89%. Avg. HS GPA: Unavailable.

Cost: Tuition and Fees: In-State: $36,975. Out-of-State: $36,975. Room and Board: $9,945.

Inst. Aid: FT Undergrads Receiving Aid: Unavailable. Avg. Amount per Student: Unavailable.

WARREN WILSON COLLEGE

Asheville, NC

admit@warren-wilson.edu; www.warren-wilson.edu

General Info: Private, Liberal Arts College, Four-year, Presbyterian Church (USA), Coed, Regionally Accredited, College Board member. Rural setting, Small city (50,000–

249,999), Residential campus. Academic Calendar: Unavailable.

Student Body: Full-Time Undergrads: 841. Men: 38%, Women: 62%. Total Undergrad Population: Native American or Native Alaskan: 0%. Asian American or Pacific Islander: 0%. African American: 0%. Latino: 0%. Caucasian: 0%. International: 0%. Out-of-State: 82%. Total all graduate and professional students: 67.

Academics: Full-Time Faculty: 61.

Admissions: Regular Application Deadline: 3/15. Priority Application Deadline: 1/15. Early Decision Deadline: 11/15. Financial Aid Deadline: Unavailable. Total Number of Students Applied: Unavailable. Percent Admitted: 74%. Number Enrolled: Unavailable. Test Scores (Middle 50%): SAT Critical Reading: 550–670. SAT Math: 510–620. SAT Writing: 530–630. ACT Comp: 22–27. HS Rank of Entering Freshmen: Top 10%: Unavailable. Top 25%: Unavailable. Avg. HS GPA: Unavailable.

Cost: Tuition and Fees: In-State: $21,384. Out-of-State: $21,384. Room and Board: $6,700.

Inst. Aid: FT Undergrads Receiving Aid: Unavailable. Avg. Amount per Student: Unavailable.

Want to Be an Occupational Therapist?

Illinois College

Ithaca College

James Madison University

St. Vincent College

WASHINGTON AND LEE UNIVERSITY

Lexington, VA

admissions@wlu.edu; www.wlu.edu

General Info: Private, Liberal Arts College, University, Four-year, Coed, Regionally Accredited, College Board member. Rural setting, Small town (2,500–9,999), Residential campus. Academic Calendar: Unavailable.

Student Body: Full-Time Undergrads: 1,749. Men: 51%, Women: 49%. Total Undergrad Population: Native American or Native Alaskan: 0%. Asian American or Pacific Islander: 4%. African American: 5%. Latino: 2%. Caucasian: 84%. International: 4%. Out-of-State: 85%. Total all graduate and professional students: 5.

Academics: Full-Time Faculty: 215.

Admissions: Regular Application Deadline: 1/15. Priority Application Deadline: Unavailable. Early Decision Deadline: 11/15. Transfer Priority Deadline: Unavailable. Financial Aid Deadline: 2/1. Total Number of Students Applied: Unavailable. Percent Admitted: 27%. Number Enrolled: 465. Test Scores (Middle 50%): SAT Critical Reading: 650–740. SAT Math: 650–730. SAT Writing: Unavailable. ACT Comp: 28–31. HS Rank of Entering Freshmen: Top 10%: 76%. Top 25%: 96%. Avg. HS GPA: Unavailable.

Cost: Tuition and Fees: In-State: $34,650. Out-of-State: $34,650. Room and Board: $8,725.

Inst. Aid: FT Undergrads Receiving Aid: Unavailable. Avg. Amount per Student: Unavailable.

WASHINGTON STATE UNIVERSITY

Pullman, WA

admiss2@wsu.edu; www.wsu.edu

General Info: Public, University, Four-year, Coed, Regionally Accredited, Northwest Association of Schools and Colleges, College Board member. Rural setting, Large town (10,000–49,999), Residential campus. Academic Calendar: Semester.

Student Body: Full-Time Undergrads: 19,584. Men: 50%, Women: 50%. Total Undergrad Population: Native American or Native Alaskan: 1%. Asian American or Pacific Islander: 7%. African American: 2%. Latino: 4%. Caucasian: 81%. International: 1%. Out-of-State: 7%. Total all graduate and professional students: 3,219.

Academics: Full-Time Faculty: 1,057.

Admissions: Regular Application Deadline: Unavailable. Priority Application Deadline: 1/31. Early Decision Deadline: Unavailable. Financial Aid Deadline: Unavailable. Total Number of Students Applied: Unavailable. Percent Admitted: 74%. Number Enrolled: 3,089. Test Scores (Middle 50%): SAT Critical Reading: 490–600. SAT Math: 510–610. SAT Writing: Unavailable. ACT Comp: Unavailable. HS Rank of Entering Freshmen: Top 10%: 37%. Top 25%: 57%. Avg. HS GPA: Unavailable.

Cost: Tuition and Fees: In-State: $6,447. Out-of-State: $16,087. Room and Board: $6,890.

Inst. Aid: FT Undergrads Receiving Aid: Unavailable. Avg. Amount per Student: Unavailable.

WASHINGTON UNIVERSITY IN ST. LOUIS

St. Louis, MO
admissions@wustl.edu; www.wustl.edu

General Info: Private, University, Four-year, Coed, Regionally Accredited, College Board member. Suburban setting, Large city (250,000–499,999), Residential campus. Academic Calendar: Semester.

Student Body: Full-Time Undergrads: 7,386. Men: 51%, Women: 49%. Total Undergrad Population: Native American or Native Alaskan: 0%. Asian American or Pacific Islander: 14%. African American: 10%. Latino: 2%. Caucasian: 61%. International: 4%. Out-of-State: 91%. Total all graduate and professional students: 4,715.

Academics: Full-Time Faculty: 850.

Admissions: Regular Application Deadline: 1/15. Priority Application Deadline: Unavailable. Early Decision Deadline: 11/15. Transfer Priority Deadline: Unavailable. Financial Aid Deadline: 2/15. Total Number of Students Applied: Unavailable. Percent Admitted: 21%. Number Enrolled: 1,461. Test Scores (Middle 50%): SAT Critical Reading: 670–750. SAT Math: 700–780. SAT Writing: Unavailable. ACT Comp: 30–33. HS Rank of Entering Freshmen: Top 10%: 93%. Top 25%: 100%. Avg. HS GPA: Unavailable.

Cost: Tuition and Fees: In-State: $35,524. Out-of-State: $35,524. Room and Board: $11,252.

Inst. Aid: FT Undergrads Receiving Aid: Unavailable. Avg. Amount per Student: Unavailable.

WELLESLEY COLLEGE

Wellesley, MA
admission@wellesley.edu; www.wellesley.edu

General Info: College Board member, Four-year, Liberal Arts College, New England Association of Colleges and Schools, Private, Regionally Accredited, Women Only, One of the historical Seven Sister Schools. Large town (10,000–49,999), Residential campus, Suburban setting, 12 miles from Boston, MA; 40 miles from Providence, RI. Academic Calendar: Semester.

Student Body: Full-Time Undergrads: 2,318. Men: 0%, Women: 100%. Part-Time Undergrads. Men: 3%, Women: 3%. Total Undergrad Population: Native American or Native Alaskan: 1%. Asian American or Pacific Islander: 26%. African American: 6%. Latino: 7%. Caucasian: 43%. International: 8%. Out-of-State: 84%. Living Off-Campus: 80%.

Academics: Full-Time Faculty: 247. Percentage completing two or more majors: 40%. Graduation Rates: 85% within 4 years. 92% within 6 years.

Admissions: Regular Application Deadline: 1/15. Priority Application Deadline: Unavailable. Early Decision Deadline: 11/1. Fall Transfer Deadline: 3/1. Spring Transfer Deadline: 11/1. Transfer Priority Deadline: Unavailable. Financial Aid Deadline: 1/15. Total Number of Students Applied: 4,017. Number Admitted: 1,434. Number Enrolled: 590. Number accepting place on waitlist: 381. Number of waitlisted students admitted: 0. Number applied early decision: 206. Early decision admitted: 123. Test Scores (Middle 50%): SAT Critical Reading: 660–750. SAT Math: 640–730. SAT Writing: 660–730. ACT Comp: 29-32. HS Rank of Entering Freshmen: Top 10%: 78%. Top 25%: 95%. Avg. HS GPA: Unvailable.

Cost: Tuition and Fees: In-State: $36,404. Out-of-State: $36,404. Room and Board: $11,336.

Inst. Aid: FT Undergrads Receiving Aid: 59. Avg. Amount per Student: $31,530.

Graduates: No. of companies recruiting on campus: 300. Percentage of grads accepting a job at time of graduation: 63%. Alumni Giving %: 50%.

WESLEYAN UNIVERSITY

Middletown, CT
admissions@wesleyan.edu; www.wesleyan.edu

General Info: Private, Liberal Arts College, University, Four-year, Coed, Regionally Accredited, College Board member. Suburban setting, Large town (10,000–49,999), Residential campus. Academic Calendar: Semester.

Student Body: Full-Time Undergrads: 2,700. Men: 50%, Women: 50%. Total Undergrad Population: Native American or Native Alaskan: 0%. Asian American or Pacific Islander: 10%. African American: 6%. Latino: 10%. Caucasian: 63%. International: 6%. Out-of-State: 95%. Total all graduate and professional students: 407.

Academics: Full-Time Faculty: 365.

Admissions: Regular Application Deadline: 1/1. Priority Application Deadline: Unavailable. Early Decision Deadline: 11/15. Transfer Priority Deadline: Unavailable. Financial Aid Deadline: 2/15. Total Number of Students Applied: Unavailable. Percent Admitted: 28%. Number Enrolled: 720. Test Scores (Middle 50%): SAT Critical Reading: 640–750. SAT Math: 650–730. SAT Writing: 640–730. ACT Comp: 28–32. HS Rank of Entering Freshmen: Top 10%: 68%. Top 25%: 91%. Avg. HS GPA: Unavailable.

Cost: Tuition and Fees: In-State: $35,144. Out-of-State: $35,144. Room and Board: $9,540.

Inst. Aid: FT Undergrads Receiving Aid: Unavailable. Avg. Amount per Student: Unavailable.

WEST VIRGINIA UNIVERSITY

Morgantown, WV
go2wvu@mail.wvu.edu; www.wvu.edu

General Info: Coed, College Board member, Four-year, North Central Association of Colleges and Schools, Public, Regionally Accredited, University. Suburban setting, Small city (50,000–249,999), Residential campus. Academic Calendar: Semester.

Student Body: Full-Time Undergrads: 20,590. Men: 51%, Women: 42%. Part-Time Undergrads. Men: 2.9%, Women: 3.7%. Total Undergrad Population: Native American or Native Alaskan: 0.4%. Asian American or Pacific Islander: 1.9%. African American: 3.2%. Latino: 1.8%. Caucasian:

89.9%. International: 1.7%. Out-of-State: 50%. Total all graduate and professional students: 6,968.

Academics: Full-Time Faculty: 1,152. Graduation Rates: 31% within 4 years. 55% within 6 years.

Admissions: Regular Application Deadline: 8/1. Priority Application Deadline: 3/1. Early Decision Deadline: Unavailable. Transfer Priority Deadline: Unavailable. Financial Aid Deadline: 3/1. Total Number of Students Applied: 13,634. Number Admitted: 12,200. Number Enrolled: 4,731. Test Scores (Middle 50%): SAT Critical Reading: 470–560. SAT Math: 490–590. SAT Writing: Unavailable. ACT Comp: 21–26. HS Rank of Entering Freshmen: Top 10%: 18%. Top 25%: 43%. Avg. HS GPA: 3.3.

Cost: Tuition and Fees: In-State: $5,100. Out-of-State: $15,770. Room and Board: $7,434.

Inst. Aid: FT Undergrads Receiving Aid: 9,381. Avg. Amount per Student: $5,870. Freshmen Receiving Non-Need Scholarship or Grant: 920. Avg. Amount per Student: $2,101.

WESTERN KENTUCKY UNIVERSITY

Bowling Green, KY
admission@wku.edu; www.wku.edu

General Info: Public, University, Four-year, Coed, Southern Association of Colleges and Schools, Regionally Accredited. Suburban setting, Small city (50,000–249,999), Commuter campus. Academic Calendar: Semester.

Student Body: Full-Time Undergrads: 18,645. Men: 43%, Women: 57%. Total Undergrad Population: Native American or Native Alaskan: 0%. Asian American or Pacific Islander: 1%. African American: 13%. Latino: 2%. Caucasian: 80%. International: 2%. Out-of-State: 16%. Total all graduate and professional students: 2,597.

Academics: Full-Time Faculty: 694.

Admissions: Regular Application Deadline: 8/1. Priority Application Deadline: Unavailable. Early Decision Deadline: Unavailable. Transfer Priority Deadline: Unavailable. Financial Aid Deadline: Unavailable. Total Number of Students Applied: Unavailable. Percent Admitted: 91%. Number Enrolled: 2,870. Test Scores (Middle 50%): SAT Critical Reading: 440–550. SAT Math: 450–560. SAT Writing: Unavailable. ACT Comp: 18–24. HS Rank of Entering Freshmen: Top 10%: 15%. Top 25%: 36%. Avg. HS GPA: Unavailable.

Cost: Tuition and Fees: In-State: $5,952. Out-of-State: $14,400. Room and Board: $5,726.

Inst. Aid: FT Undergrads Receiving Aid: Unavailable. Avg. Amount per Student: Unavailable.

WESTERN WASHINGTON UNIVERSITY

Bellingham, WA
admit@wwu.edu; www.wwu.edu

General Info: Public, University, Four-year, Coed, Northwest Association of Schools and Colleges, Regionally Accredited, College Board member. Suburban setting, Small city (50,000–249,999), Residential campus. Academic Calendar: Quarter.

Student Body: Full-Time Undergrads: 12,838. Men: 48%, Women: 52%. Part-Time Undergrads. Men: 42%, Women: 58%. Total Undergrad Population: Native American or Native Alaskan: 2%. Asian American or Pacific Islander: 9%. African American: 3%. Latino: 4%. Caucasian: 77%. International: 0%. Out-of-State: 9%. Living Off-Campus: 70%. Total all graduate and professional students: 1,177.

Academics: Full-Time Faculty: 624. With PhD: 537. Graduation Rate: 64% within 6 years.

Admissions: Regular Application Deadline: 3/1. Priority Application Deadline: Unavailable. Early Decision Deadline: Unavailable. Financial Aid Deadline: Unavailable. Total Number of Students Applied: 8,850. Number Admitted: 6,447. Number Enrolled: Unavailable. Number accepting place on waitlist: 193. Number of waitlisted students admitted: 193. Test Scores (Middle 50%): SAT Critical Reading: 490–610. SAT Math: 500–610. SAT Writing: 480–590. ACT Comp: 21–26. HS Rank of Entering Freshmen: Top 10%: 26%. Top 25%: 60%. Avg. HS GPA: 3.5.

Cost: Tuition and Fees: In-State: $5,291. Out-of-State: $16,365. Room and Board: $7,090.

Inst. Aid: FT Undergrads Receiving Aid: Unavailable. Avg. Amount per Student: Unavailable.

Graduates: Alumni Giving %: 30%.

WESTMINSTER COLLEGE

Fulton, MO
admissions@westminster-mo.edu;
www.westminster-mo.edu

General Info: Private, Liberal Arts College, Four-year, Presbyterian Church (USA), Coed, Regionally Accredited, College Board member. Rural setting, Large town (10,000–49,999), Residential campus. Academic Calendar: Semester.

Student Body: Full-Time Undergrads: 936. Men: 57%, Women: 43%. Total Undergrad Population: Native American or Native Alaskan: 2%. Asian American or Pacific Islander: 1%. African American: 3%. Latino: 1%. Caucasian: 76%. International: 15%. Out-of-State: 22%.

Academics: Full-Time Faculty: 58.

Admissions: Regular Application Deadline: 2/1. Priority Application Deadline: Unavailable. Early Decision Deadline: Unavailable. Transfer Priority Deadline: Unavailable. Financial Aid Deadline: Unavailable. Total Number of Students Applied: Unavailable. Percent Admitted: 79%. Number Enrolled: 278. Test Scores (Middle 50%): SAT Critical Reading: 460–640. SAT Math: 490–640. SAT Writing: 470–640. ACT Comp: 22–27. HS Rank of Entering Freshmen: Top 10%: 30%. Top 25%: 57%. Avg. HS GPA: Unavailable.

Cost: Tuition and Fees: In-State: $16,650. Out-of-State: $16,650. Room and Board: $6,720.

Inst. Aid: FT Undergrads Receiving Aid: Unavailable. Avg. Amount per Student: Unavailable.

WHEATON COLLEGE

Norton, MA
admission@wheatoncollege.edu;
www.wheatoncollege.edu

General Info: Coed, College Board member, Four-year, Liberal Arts College, New England Association of Colleges and Schools, Private, Regionally Accredited. Suburban setting, Large town (10,000–49,999), Residential campus. Academic Calendar: Semester.

Student Body: Full-Time Undergrads: 2,550. Men: 40%, Women: 60%. Total Undergrad Population: Native American or Native Alaskan: 0%. Asian American or Pacific Islander: 3%. African American: 5%. Latino: 3%. Caucasian: 77%. International: 3%. Out-of-State: 65%.

Academics: Full-Time Faculty: 137. With PhD: 139. Percentage completing two or more majors: 13%. Graduation Rates: 74% within 4 years. 79% within 6 years.

Admissions: Regular Application Deadline: 1/15. Priority Application Deadline: Unavailable. Early Decision Deadline: 11/1. Transfer Priority Deadline: 4/1. Financial Aid Deadline: 2/1. Total Number of Students Applied: 3,833. Number Admitted: 1,411. Number Enrolled: 418. Number accepting place on waitlist: 283. Number of waitlisted students admitted: 16. Number applied early decision: 259. Early decision admitted: 193. Test Scores (Middle 50%): SAT Critical Reading: 580–670. SAT Math: 560–650. SAT Writing: Unavailable. ACT Comp: 25–28. HS Rank of Entering Freshmen: Top 10%: 44%. Top 25%: 70%. Avg. HS GPA: 3.5.

Cost: Tuition and Fees: In-State: $38,585. Out-of-State: $38,585. Room and Board: $9,150.

Inst. Aid: FT Undergrads Receiving Aid: 1,070. Avg. Amount per Student: $24,228. Freshmen Receiving Non-Need Scholarship or Grant: 70. Avg. Amount per Student: $11,609.

Graduates: No. of companies recruiting on campus: 22. Percentage of grads accepting a job at time of graduation: 20%. Alumni Giving %: 33.3%.

WHEATON COLLEGE

Wheaton, IL
admissions@wheaton.edu; www.wheaton.edu

General Info: Coed, College Board member, Four-year, Liberal Arts College, Nondenominational, North Central Association of Colleges and Schools, Private, Regionally Accredited. Suburban setting, Small city (50,000–249,999), Residential campus. Academic Calendar: Semester.

Student Body: Full-Time Undergrads: 2,400. Men: 42%, Women: 58%. Total Undergrad Population: Native American or Native Alaskan: 0.3%. Asian American or Pacific Islander: 7.1%. African American: 2.8%. Latino: 3.8%. Caucasian: 84.2%. International: 1.3%. Out-of-State: 80%. Total all graduate and professional students: 559.

Academics: Full-Time Faculty: 191. Percentage completing two or more majors: 13%. Graduation Rates: 77% within 4 years. 88% within 6 years.

Billionaire Colleges

Steve Ballmer (CEO of Microsoft)—Harvard University

Jeff Bezos (Founder of Amazon.com)—Princeton University

Michael Bloomberg (Founder of Bloomberg Financial Media)—Johns Hopkins University

Warren Buffet (Stock Market Investor)—University of Nebraska

Admissions: Regular Application Deadline: 1/10. Priority Application Deadline: 11/1. Early Decision Deadline: Unavailable. Fall Transfer Deadline: 3/1. Spring Transfer Deadline: 10/1. Transfer Priority Deadline: Unavailable. Financial Aid Deadline: Unavailable. Total Number of Students Applied: 2,336. Number Admitted: 1,295. Number Enrolled: 654. Number accepting place on waitlist: Unavailable. Number of waitlisted students admitted: Unavailable. Number applied early decision: Unavailable. Early decision admitted: Unavailable. Test Scores (Middle 50%): SAT Critical Reading: 630–720. SAT Math: 610–700. SAT Writing: 610–710. ACT Comp: 27–31. HS Rank of Entering Freshmen: Top 10%: 56%. Top 25%: 88%. Avg. HS GPA: 3.7.

Cost: Tuition and Fees: In-State: $23,730. Out-of-State: $23,730. Room and Board: $7,252.

Inst. Aid: FT Undergrads Receiving Aid: 1,515. Avg. Amount per Student: $20,591. Freshmen Receiving Non-Need Scholarship or Grant: 111. Avg. Amount per Student: $4,100.

Graduates: Percentage of grads accepting a job at time of graduation: 25%. Alumni Giving %: 34%.

WHITMAN COLLEGE

Walla Walla, WA
admission@whitman.edu; www.whitman.edu

General Info: Coed, College Board member, Four-year, Liberal Arts College, Private, Regionally Accredited, Western

Association of Schools and Colleges. Large town (10,000–49,999), Residential campus, Rural setting, 300 Annual Days of Sunshine. Academic Calendar: Semester.

Student Body: Full-Time Undergrads: 1,454. Men: 44%, Women: 52%. Part-Time Undergrads: Unavailable. Total Undergrad Population: Native American or Native Alaskan: 2%. Asian American or Pacific Islander: 9%. African American: 1%. Latino: 5%. Caucasian: 67%. International: 3%. Out-of-State: 65%. Living Off-Campus: 30%. % In Fraternities: 32%. % In Sororities: 28%. Total all graduate and professional students: Unavailable.

Academics: Full-Time Faculty: 119. With PhD: 115. Percentage completing two or more majors: Unavailable. Graduation Rates: 80% within 4 years. 88% within 6 years.

Admissions: Regular Application Deadline: 1/15. Priority Application Deadline: 11/15. Early Decision Deadline: 11/15. Fall Transfer Deadline: 3/1. Spring Transfer Deadline: 11/15. Transfer Priority Deadline: Unavailable. Financial Aid Deadline: 2/1. Total Number of Students Applied: 3,275. Number Admitted: 1,468. Number Enrolled: 438. Number accepting place on waitlist: 200. Number of waitlisted students admitted: Unavailable. Number applied early decision: 120. Early decision admitted: 90. Test Scores (Middle 50%): SAT Critical Reading: 630–730. SAT Math: 610–700. SAT Writing: 620–700. ACT Comp: 28–32. HS Rank of Entering Freshmen: Top 10%: 70%. Top 25%: 93%. Avg. HS GPA: 3.89.

Cost: Tuition and Fees: In-State: $35,192. Out-of-State: $35,192. Room and Board: $8,820.

Inst. Aid: FT Undergrads Receiving Aid: Unavailable. Avg. Amount per Student: Unavailable. No. of companies recruiting on campus: 30. Alumni Giving %: 52%.

Famous Community College Attendees

Tom Hanks—Chabot College

Clint Eastwood—Los Angeles City College

George Lucas—Modesto Junior College

Hilary Swank—Santa Monica College

Jackie Robinson—Pasadena City College

Billy Crystal—Nassau Community College

WILLAMETTE UNIVERSITY

Salem, OR

libarts@willamette.edu; www.willamette.edu

General Info: Private, Liberal Arts College, University, Four-year, United Methodist Church, Coed, Regionally Accredited, College Board member. Urban setting, Small city (50,000–249,999), Residential campus. Academic Calendar: Semester.

Student Body: Full-Time Undergrads: 1,943. Men: 45%, Women: 55%. Total Undergrad Population: Native American or Native Alaskan: 0%. Asian American or Pacific Islander: 6%. African American: 1%. Latino: 4%. Caucasian: 58%. International: 2%. Out-of-State: 67%. Living Off-Campus: 25%. Total all graduate and professional students: 632.

Academics: Full-Time Faculty: 200.

Admissions: Regular Application Deadline: 2/1. Priority Application Deadline: Unavailable. Early Decision Deadline: Unavailable. Transfer Priority Deadline: Unavailable. Financial Aid Deadline: 2/1. Total Number of Students Applied: 4,216. Number Admitted: 2,744. Number Enrolled: 503. Test Scores (Middle 50%): SAT Critical Reading: 570–670. SAT Math: 570–650. SAT Writing: Unavailable. ACT Comp: 25–29. HS Rank of Entering Freshmen: Top 10%: 49%. Top 25%: 73%. Avg. HS GPA: Unavailable.

Cost: Tuition and Fees: In-State: $33,750. Out-of-State: $33,750. Room and Board: $7,950.

Inst. Aid: FT Undergrads Receiving Aid: Unavailable. Avg. Amount per Student: Unavailable.

WILLIAMS COLLEGE

Williamstown, MA

admission@williams.edu; www.williams.edu

General Info: Private, Liberal Arts College, Four-year, Coed, Regionally Accredited, College Board member. Rural setting, Small town (2,500–9,999), Residential campus. Academic Calendar: 4-1-4.

Student Body: Full-Time Undergrads: 2,003. Men: 49%, Women: 51%. Total Undergrad Population: Native American or Native Alaskan: 0%. Asian American or Pacific Islander: 11%. African American: 10%. Latino: 8%. Caucasian: 64%. International: 7%. Out-of-State: 89%. Total all graduate and professional students: 46.

Academics: Full-Time Faculty: 268.

Admissions: Regular Application Deadline: 1/1. Priority Application Deadline: Unavailable. Early Decision Deadline: 11/10. Transfer Priority Deadline: Unavailable. Financial Aid Deadline: 2/15. Total Number of Students Applied: Unavailable. Percent Admitted: 17%. Number Enrolled: 534. Test Scores (Middle 50%): SAT Critical Reading: 660–760. SAT Math: 660–760. SAT Writing: Unavailable. ACT Comp: 29–33. HS Rank of Entering Freshmen: Top 10%: 90%. Top 25%: 95%. Avg. HS GPA: Unavailable.

Cost: Tuition and Fees: In-State: $33,700. Out-of-State: $33,700. Room and Board: $8,950.

Inst. Aid: FT Undergrads Receiving Aid: Unavailable. Avg. Amount per Student: Unavailable.

WITTENBERG UNIVERSITY

Springfield, OH

admission@wittenberg.edu; www.wittenberg.edu

General Info: Private, Liberal Arts College, Four-year, Evangelical Lutheran Church In America, Coed, Regionally Accredited, College Board member. Suburban setting, Small city (50,000–249,999), Residential campus. Academic Calendar: Semester.

Student Body: Full-Time Undergrads: 2,059. Men: 46%, Women: 54%. Total Undergrad Population: Native American or Native Alaskan: 0%. Asian American or Pacific Islander: 1%. African American: 5%. Latino: 1%. Caucasian: 76%. International: 2%. Out-of-State: 27%. Total all graduate and professional students: 30.

Academics: Full-Time Faculty: 148.

Admissions: Regular Application Deadline: 3/15. Priority Application Deadline: Unavailable. Early Decision Deadline: 11/15. Transfer Priority Deadline: 7/1. Financial Aid Deadline: Unavailable. Total Number of Students Applied: Unavailable. Percent Admitted: 82%. Number Enrolled: 500. Test Scores (Middle 50%): SAT Critical Reading: 520–650. SAT Math: 530–640. SAT Writing: Unavailable. ACT Comp: 21–24. HS Rank of Entering Freshmen: Top 10%: 27%. Top 25%: 56%. Avg. HS GPA: Unavailable.

Cost: Tuition and Fees: In-State: $29,280. Out-of-State: $29,280. Room and Board: $7,498.

Inst. Aid: FT Undergrads Receiving Aid: Unavailable. Avg. Amount per Student: Unavailable.

WOFFORD COLLEGE

Spartanburg, SC

admission@wofford.edu; www.wofford.edu

General Info: Private, Liberal Arts College, Four-year, United Methodist Church, Coed, Regionally Accredited, College Board member. Urban setting, Small city (50,000–249,999), Residential campus. Academic Calendar: 4-1-4.

Student Body: Full-Time Undergrads: Unavailable. Men: 49%, Women: 51%. Total Undergrad Population: Native American or Native Alaskan: 0%. Asian American or Pacific Islander: 3%. African American: 6%. Latino: 2%. Caucasian: 87%. International: 1%. Out-of-State: 43%.

Academics: Full-Time Faculty: 89.

Admissions: Regular Application Deadline: 2/1. Priority Application Deadline: Unavailable. Early Decision Deadline: 11/15. Transfer Priority Deadline: 2/1. Financial Aid Deadline: Unavailable. Total Number of Students Applied: Unavailable. Percent Admitted: 57%. Number Enrolled: 378. Test Scores (Middle 50%): SAT Critical Reading: 560–670. SAT Math: 590–680. SAT Writing: 530–660. ACT Comp: 22–27. HS Rank of Entering Freshmen: Top 10%: 58%. Top 25%: 83%. Avg. HS GPA: Unavailable.

Cost: Tuition and Fees: In-State: $26,110. Out-of-State: $26,110. Room and Board: $7,260.

Inst. Aid: FT Undergrads Receiving Aid: Unavailable. Avg. Amount per Student: Unavailable.

XAVIER UNIVERSITY

Cincinnati, OH

xuadmit@xavier.edu; www.xavier.edu

General Info: Private, University, Four-year, Roman Catholic Church, Society of Jesus (Jesuits), Coed, Regionally Accredited, College Board member. Urban setting, Large city (250,000–499,999), Residential campus. Academic Calendar: Semester.

Student Body: Full-Time Undergrads: 3,910. Men: 43%, Women: 57%. Total Undergrad Population: Native American or Native Alaskan: 1%. Asian American or Pacific Islander: 3%. African American: 11%. Latino: 4%. Caucasian: 81%. International: 1%. Out-of-State: 47%. Total all graduate and professional students: 2,756.

Academics: Full-Time Faculty: 294.

Admissions: Regular Application Deadline: 2/1. Priority Application Deadline: Unavailable. Early Decision Deadline: 12/1. Transfer Priority Deadline: 3/15. Financial Aid Deadline: Unavailable. Total Number of Students Applied: Unavailable. Percent Admitted: 72%. Number Enrolled: 813. Test Scores (Middle 50%): SAT Critical Reading: 530–640. SAT Math: 540–640. SAT Writing: 510–620. ACT Comp: 23–29. HS Rank of Entering Freshmen: Top 10%: 30%. Top 25%: 55%. Avg. HS GPA: Unavailable.

Cost: Tuition and Fees: In-State: $23,880. Out-of-State: $23,880. Room and Board: $8,640.

Inst. Aid: FT Undergrads Receiving Aid: Unavailable. Avg. Amount per Student: Unavailable.

Schools of Rock

Rivers Cuomo (Weezer)—Harvard University

Stephen Malkmus (Pavement)—University of Virginia

William Butler (The Arcade Fire)—Northwestern University

XAVIER UNIVERSITY OF LOUISIANA

New Orleans, LA
apply@xula.edu; www.xula.edu

General Info: Private, University, Four-year, Roman Catholic Church, Coed, Regionally Accredited, College Board member, Historically black. Urban setting, Very large city (over 500,000), Commuter campus. Academic Calendar: Semester.

Student Body: Full-Time Undergrads: 3,143. Men: 25%, Women: 75%. Total Undergrad Population: Native American or Native Alaskan: 0%. Asian American or Pacific Islander: 5%. African American: 87%. Latino: 1%. Caucasian: 1%. International: 1%. Out-of-State: 63%.

Academics: Full-Time Faculty: 241.

Admissions: Regular Application Deadline: 3/1. Priority Application Deadline: 11/1. Early Decision Deadline: 11/1. Transfer Priority Deadline: 6/1. Financial Aid Deadline: 1/1. Total Number of Students Applied: Unavailable. Percent Admitted: 83%. Test Scores (Middle 50%): SAT Critical Reading: 440–570. SAT Math: 430–540. SAT Writing: Unavailable. ACT Comp: 18–24. HS Rank of Entering Freshmen: Top 10%: Unavailable. Top 25%: Unavailable. Avg. HS GPA: Unavailable.

Cost: Tuition and Fees: In-State: $14,500. Out-of-State: $14,500. Room and Board: $6,800.

Inst. Aid: FT Undergrads Receiving Aid: Unavailable. Avg. Amount per Student: Unavailable.

YALE UNIVERSITY

New Haven, CT
undergraduate.admissions@yale.edu; www.yale.edu

General Info: Private, University, Four-year, Coed, Regionally Accredited, College Board member. Urban setting, Small city (50,000–249,999), Residential campus. Academic Calendar: Semester.

Student Body: Full-Time Undergrads: 5,333. Men: 50%, Women: 50%. Total Undergrad Population: Native American or Native Alaskan: 1%. Asian American or Pacific Islander: 15%. African American: 9%. Latino: 9%. Caucasian: 48%. International: 11%. Out-of-State: 93%. Living Off-Campus: 13%. Total all graduate and professional students: 6,083.

Academics: Full-Time Faculty: 1,577.

Admissions: Regular Application Deadline: 12/31. Priority Application Deadline: Unavailable. Early Decision Deadline: Unavailable. Transfer Priority Deadline: Unavailable. Financial Aid Deadline: 3/1. Total Number of Students Applied: 19,323. Number Admitted: 1,911. Number Enrolled: 1,320. Test Scores (Middle 50%): SAT Critical Reading: 700–790. SAT Math: 700–790. SAT Writing: 700–780. ACT Comp: 29-34. HS Rank of Entering Freshmen: Top 10%: 97%. Top 25%: 100%. Avg. HS GPA: Unavailable.

Cost: Tuition and Fees: In-State: $34,530. Out-of-State: $34,530. Room and Board: $10,470.

Inst. Aid: FT Undergrads Receiving Aid: 2,292. Avg. Amount per Student: $32,533.

Index of Schools by State

Alabama

Auburn University, Auburn
Birmingham-Southern College, Birmingham
Samford University, Birmingham
Tuskegee University, Tuskegee
University of Alabama, Tuscaloosa

Arkansas

Hendrix College, Conway
University of Arkansas, Fayetteville

Arizona

Arizona State University, Tempe
Northern Arizona University, Flagstaff
University of Arizona, Tuscon

California

Azusa Pacific University, Azusa
California Institute of Technology, Pasadena
California Polytechnic State University, San Luis Obispo
California State University–Chico, Chico
California State University–Long Beach, Long Beach
California State University–San Jose, San Jose
Claremont McKenna College, Claremont
Harvey Mudd College, Claremont
Loyola Marymount University, Los Angeles
Mills College, Oakland
Occidental College, Los Angeles
Pepperdine University, Malibu
Pitzer College, Claremont
Pomona College, Claremont
Saint Mary's College of California, Moraga
San Diego State University, San Diego
Santa Clara University, Santa Clara
Scripps College, Claremont
Stanford University, Stanford
University of California–Berkeley, Berkeley
University of California–Davis, Davis
University of California–Irvine, Irvine
University of California–Los Angeles, Los Angeles
University of California–San Diego, La Jolla
University of California–Santa Barbara, Santa Barbara
University of California–Santa Cruz, Santa Cruz
University of Redlands, Redlands
University of Southern California, Los Angeles
University of the Pacific, Stockton

Colorado

Adams State College, Alamosa
Colorado College, Colorado Springs
Colorado School of Mines, Golden
University of Colorado at Boulder, Boulder
University of Denver, Denver

Connecticut

Connecticut College, New London
Fairfield University, Fairfield
Quinnipiac University, Hamden
Trinity College, Hartford
United States Coast Guard Academy, New London
University of Connecticut, Storrs
Wesleyan University, Middletown
Yale University, New Haven

District of Columbia

American University, Washington
Catholic University of America, Washington
George Washington University, Washington
Georgetown University, Washington
Howard University, Washington

Delaware

University of Delaware, Newark

Florida

Eckerd College, St. Petersburg
Embry-Riddle Aeronautical University–Florida, Daytona Beach
Flagler College, St. Augustine

Georgia

Hawaii

Idaho

Illinois

Indiana

Iowa

Kansas

Kentucky

Louisiana

Maine

College of the Atlantic, Bar Harbor
University of Maine, Orono

Maryland

Goucher College, Baltimore
Johns Hopkins University, Baltimore
Loyola College in Maryland, Baltimore
Saint John's College, Annapolis
Saint Mary's College of Maryland, Saint Mary's City
Salisbury University, Salisbury
United States Naval Academy, Annapolis
University of Maryland–Baltimore County, Baltimore
University of Maryland, College Park

Massachusetts

Amherst College, Amherst
Babson College, Babson Park
Bentley College, Waltham
Boston College, Chestnut Hill
Boston University, Boston
Brandeis University, Waltham
Clark University, Worcester
College of the Holy Cross, Worcester
Emerson College, Boston
Franklin W. Olin College of Engineering, Needham
Hampshire College, Amherst
Harvard College, Cambridge
Massachusetts Institute of Technology, Cambridge
Merrimack College, North Andover
Mount Holyoke College, South Hadley
Northeastern University, Boston
School of the Museum of Fine Arts, Boston
Simmons College, Boston
Smith College, Northampton
Stonehill College, Easton
Tufts University, Medford
University of Massachusetts, Amherst
Wellesley College, Wellesley
Wheaton College, Norton
Williams College, Williamstown

Michigan

Albion College, Albion
Calvin College, Grand Rapids
Eastern Michigan University, Ypsilanti
Ferris State University, Big Rapids
Grand Valley State University, Allendale
Kalamazoo College, Kalamazoo
Kettering University, Flint
Michigan State University, East Lansing
Michigan Technological University, Houghton
University of Michigan, Ann Arbor

Minnesota

Carleton College, Northfield
Gustavus Adolphus College, St. Peter
Macalester College, St. Paul
St. Olaf College, Northfield
University of Minnesota–Twin Cities, Minneapolis/St. Paul

Mississippi

Millsaps College, Jackson

Missouri

College of the Ozarks, Point Lookout
Saint Louis University, St. Louis
Truman State University, Kirksville
University of Missouri, Columbia
University of Missouri, Rolla
Washington University in St. Louis, St. Louis
Westminster College, Fulton

Montana

Montana State University, Havre

Nebraska

Creighton University, Omaha
Hamilton College, Omaha
Hastings College, Hastings
University of Nebraska, Lincoln

Nevada

Deep Springs College, Dyer

University of Nevada, Las Vegas
University of Nevada, Reno

New Hampshire

Dartmouth College, Hanover
Saint Anselm College, Manchester
University of New Hampshire, Durham

New Jersey

College of New Jersey, Ewing
Drew University, Madison
Princeton University, Princeton
Rutgers, The State University of New Jersey, New Brunswick
Seton Hall University, South Orange

New Mexico

New Mexico Institute of Mining and Technology, Socorro
Saint John's College, Santa Fe
University of New Mexico, Albuquerque

New York

Adelphi University, Garden City
Alfred University, Alfred
Bard College, Annandale-on-Hudson
Barnard College, New York
Baruch College, New York
Canisius College, Buffalo
City University of New York–Brooklyn College, Brooklyn
City University of New York–John Jay College, New York
City University of New York–Lehman College, Bronx
City University of New York–Queens College, Flushing
Colgate University, Hamilton
Columbia University, New York
Cooper Union for the Advancement of Science and Art, New York
Cornell University, Ithaca
Culinary Institute of America, Hyde Park
Eugene Lang College–The New School for Liberal Arts, New York
Fashion Institute of Technology, New York
Fordham University, Bronx
Hamilton College, Clinton
Hobart and William Smith Colleges, Geneva
Hofstra University, Hempstead
Hunter College, New York
Iona College, New Rochelle
Ithaca College, Ithaca
Juilliard School, New York
Manhattanville College, Purchase
Marist College, Poughkeepsie
New School University, New York
New York School of Interior Design, New York
New York University, New York
Paul Smith's College, Paul Smiths
Rensselaer Polytechnic Institute, Troy
Rochester Institute of Technology, Rochester
Saint Lawrence University, Canton
Sarah Lawrence College, Bronxville
Skidmore College, Saratoga Springs
State University of New York at Albany, Albany
State University of New York at Binghamton, Binghamton
State University of New York–College of Environmental Science and Forestry, Syracuse
State University of New York at Geneseo, Geneseo
State University of New York at New Paltz, New Paltz
State University of New York at Purchase, Purchase
State University of New York at Stony Brook, Stony Brook
State University of New York at Buffalo, Buffalo
Syracuse University, Syracuse
Union College, Schenectady
United States Merchant Marine Academy, Kings Point
United States Military Academy, West Point
University of Rochester, Rochester
Vassar College, Poughkeepsie

Wagner College, Staten Island

North Carolina

Appalachian State University, Boone
Davidson College, Davidson
Duke University, Durham
East Carolina University, Greenville
Elon University, Elon
Guilford College, Greensboro
North Carolina School of the Arts, Winston-Salem
North Carolina State University, Raleigh
University of North Carolina at Chapel Hill, Chapel Hill
Wake Forest University, Winston-Salem
Warren Wilson College, Asheville

North Dakota

University of North Dakota, Grand Forks

Ohio

Bowling Green State University, Huron
Case Western Reserve University, Cleveland
Denison University, Granville
Kent State University, Kent
Kenyon College, Gambier
Miami University, Oxford
Oberlin College, Oberlin
Ohio State University, Columbus
Ohio University, Zanesville
University of Cincinnati, Cincinnati
University of Dayton, Dayton
Wittenberg University, Springfield
Xavier University, Cincinnati

Oklahoma

Oklahoma State University, Stillwater
Oral Roberts University, Tulsa
University of Oklahoma, Norman
University of Tulsa, Tulsa

Oregon

Lewis and Clark College, Portland
Oregon State University, Corvallis
Portland State University, Portland
Reed College, Portland
University of Oregon, Eugene
Willamette University, Salem

Pennsylvania

Allegheny College, Meadville
Bryn Mawr College, Bryn Mawr
Bucknell University, Lewisburg
Carnegie Mellon University, Pittsburgh
Chatham University, Pittsburgh
Delaware Valley College, Doylestown
Dickinson College, Carlisle
Drexel University, Philadelphia
Duquesne University, Pittsburgh
Franklin & Marshall College, Lancaster
Gettysburg College, Gettysburg
Grove City College, Grove City
Haverford College, Haverford
Indiana University of Pennsylvania, Indiana
Juniata College, Huntingdon
Lafayette College, Easton
Lehigh University, Bethlehem
Moravian College, Bethlehem
Muhlenberg College, Allentown
Penn State University at University Park, University Park
Susquehanna University, Selinsgrove
Swarthmore College, Swarthmore
Temple University, Philadelphia
University of Pennsylvania, Philadelphia
University of Pittsburgh, Pittsburgh
University of Scranton, Scranton
Ursinus College, Collegeville
Villanova University, Villanova

Rhode Island

Brown University, Providence
Bryant University, Smithfield
Johnson & Wales University, Providence
Providence College, Providence
Rhode Island School of Design, Providence
University of Rhode Island, Kingston

South Carolina

Clemson University, Clemson
College of Charleston, Charleston
Furman University, Greenville
The Citadel, the Military College of South Carolina, Charleston.
University of South Carolina at Columbia, Columbia
Wofford College, Spartanburg

South Dakota

University of South Dakota, Vermillion

Tennessee

Belmont University, Nashville
Fisk University, Nashville
Rhodes College, Memphis
Sewanee–The University of the South, Sewanee
University of Tennessee, Knoxville
University of Tennessee, Martin
Vanderbilt University, Nashville

Texas

Abilene Christian University, Abilene
Austin College, Sherman
Baylor University, Waco
Rice University, Houston
Southern Methodist University, Dallas
Southwestern University, Georgetown
Texas A&M University, College Station
Texas Christian University, Fort Worth
Texas Tech University, Lubbock
Trinity University, San Antonio
University of Dallas, Irving
University of Houston, Victoria
University of Texas at Austin, Austin

Utah

Brigham Young University, Provo
University of Utah, Salt Lake City
Westminster College, Fulton

Vermont

Bennington College, Bennington
Marlboro College, Marlboro
Middlebury College, Middlebury
Saint Michael's College, Colchester
University of Vermont, Burlington

Virginia

College of William and Mary, Williamsburg
George Mason University, Fairfax
Hampden-Sydney College, Hampden-Sydney
Hampton University, Hampton
Hollins University, Roanoke
James Madison University, Harrisonburg
Old Dominion University, Norfolk
Randolph-Macon College, Ashland
Saint Michael's College, Colchester
Sweet Briar College, Sweet Briar
University of Mary Washington, Fredericksburg
University of Richmond, Richmond
University of Virginia, Charlottesville
Virginia Commonwealth University, Richmond
Virginia Polytechnic Institute and State University, Blacksburg
Washington and Lee University, Lexington

Washington

Bastyr University, Kenmore
DigiPen Institute of Technology, Redmond
Evergreen State College, Olympia
Gonzaga University, Spokane
Pacific Lutheran University, Tacoma
Seattle University, Seattle
University of Puget Sound, Tacoma
University of Washington, Seattle
Washington State University, Pullman
Western Washington University, Bellingham
Whitman College, Walla Walla

West Virginia

West Virginia University, Morgantown

Wisconsin

Beloit College, Beloit
Marquette University, Milwaukee
Ripon College, Ripon
University of Wisconsin, Madison
University of Wisconsin, Stevens Point

Wyoming

University of Wyoming, Laramie

Index of Schools by Price

*$0–$5,000

Adams State College, Alamosa, CO

Appalachian State University, Boone, NC

Armstrong Atlantic State University, Savannah, GA

Baruch College, New York

Berea College, Berea, KY

Boise State University, Boise, ID

Bowling Green State University, Huron, OH

Brigham Young University, Provo, UT

California Polytechnic State University, San Luis Obispo, CA

California State University–Chico, Chico, CA

California State University–Long Branch, Long Branch, CA

City University of New York–Brooklyn College, Brooklyn, NY

City University of New York–John Jay College, New York, NY

City University of New York–Lehman College, Bronx, NY

City University of New York–Queens College, Flushing, NY

Cooper Union for the Advancement of Science and Art, New York, NY

Deep Springs College, Dyer, NV

East Carolina University, Greenville, NC

Emporia State University, Emporia, KS

Evergreen State College, Olympia, WA

Fashion Institute of Technology, New York, NY

Florida State University, Tallahassee, FL

Georgia Institute of Technology, Atlanta, GA

Hunter College, New York, NY

Louisiana State University and Agricultural and Mechanical College, Baton Rouge, LA

Montana State University, Havre, MT

New College of Florida, Sarasota, FL

New Mexico Institute of Mining and Technology, Socorro, NM

New School University, New York, NY

North Carolina School of the Arts, Winston-Salem, NC

Northern Arizona University, Flagstaff, AZ

Ohio University, Zanesville, OH

Oklahoma State University, Stillwater, OK

San Diego State University, San Diego, CA

State University of New York at Binghamton, Binghamton, NY

United States Naval Academy, Annapolis, MD

University of Arizona, Tucson, AZ

University of Arkansas, Fayetteville, AR

University of Florida, Gainesville, FL

University of Houston, Victoria, TX

University of Nevada, Las Vegas, NV

University of Nevada, Reno, NV

University of New Mexico, Albuquerque, NM

University of North Carolina at Chapel Hill, Chapel Hill, NC

University of South Florida, Tampa, FL

University of Tennessee, Martin, TN

University of Utah, Salt Lake City, UT

University of Wyoming, Laramie, WY

Valdosta State University, Valdosta, GA

*Annual tuition, not including room & board

$5,000–$10,000

Arizona State University, Tempe, AZ

Auburn University, Auburn, AL

Ball State University, Muncie, IN

California State University–San Jose, San Jose, CA

Clemson University, Clemson, SC

College of Charleston, Charleston, SC

College of William and Mary, Williamsburg, VA

Colorado School of Mines, Golden, CO

Eastern Kentucky University, Richmond, KY

Eastern Michigan University, Ypsilanti, MI

Ferris State University, Big Rapids, MI

George Mason University, Fairfax, VA

Grand Valley State University, Allendale, MI

Indiana University of Pennsylvania, Indiana, PA

Indiana University Bloomington, Bloomington, IN

Iowa State University, Ames, IA

James Madison University, Harrisonburg, VA

Kansas State University, Manhattan, KS

Kent State University, Kent, OH

Michigan State University, East Lansing, MI

Michigan Technological University, Houghton, MI

North Carolina State University, Raleigh, NC

Ohio State University, Columbus, OH

Old Dominion University, Norfolk, VA

Oregon State University, Corvallis, OR

Portland State University, Portland, OR

Purdue University, West Lafayette, IN

Rutgers, The State University of New Jersey, New Brunswick, NJ

Salisbury University, Salisbury, MD

State University of New York at Albany, NY

State University of New York College at Geneseo, NY

State University of New York at New Paltz, NY

State University of New York at Purchase, NY

State University of New York at Stony Brook, NY

State University of New York College at Buffalo, NY

State University of New York College of Environmental Science and Forestry, Syracuse, NY

Texas A&M University, College Station, TX

Texas Tech University, Lubbock, TX

The Citadel, the Military College of South Carolina, Charleston, NC

Truman State University, Kirksville, MO

University of Alabama, Tuscaloosa, AL

University of California–Berkeley, CA

University of California–Davis, CA

University of California–Irvine, CA

University of California–Los Angeles, CA

University of California–San Diego, La Jolla, CA

University of California–Santa Barbara, CA

University of California–Santa Cruz, CA

University of Cincinnati, Cincinnati, OH

University of Colorado at Boulder, CO

University of Connecticut, Storrs, CT

University of Delaware, Newark, DE

University of Georgia, Athens, GA

University of Hawaii at Manoa, Honolulu, HI

$10,000–$15,000

$15,000–$20,000

Abilene Christian University, Abilene, TX

Bastyr University, Kenmore, WA

Belmont University, Nashville, TN

College of the Ozarks, Point Lookout, MO

Culinary Institute of America, Hyde Park, NY

DigiPen Institute of Technology, Redmond, WA

Fisk University, Nashville, TN

Hastings College, Hastings, NE

Morehouse College, Atlanta, GA

New York School of Interior Design, New York, NY

Oral Roberts University, Tulsa, OK

Paul Smith's College, Paul Smiths, NY

Samford University, Birmingham, Al

Spelman College, Atlanta, GA

University of Indianapolis, Indianapolis, IN

Westminster College, Fulton, MO

$20,000–$25,000

Adelphi University, Garden City, NY

Alfred University, Alfred, NY

Austin College, Sherman, TX

Azusa Pacific University, Azusa, CA

Berry College, Mount Berry, GA

Birmingham-Southern College, Birmingham, AL

Bradley University, Peoria, IL

Calvin College, Grand Rapids, MI

Canisius College, Buffalo, NY

Centenary College of Louisiana, Shreveport, LA

Deleware Valley College, Doylestown, PA

DePaul University, Chicago, IL

Duquesne University, Pittsburgh, PA

Elon University, Elon, NC

Embry-Riddle Aeronautical University, Daytona Beach, FL

Goshen College, Goshen, IN

Guilford College, Greensboro, NC

Hanover College, Hanover, IN

Hendrix College, Conway, AR

Hollins University, Roanoke, VA

Iona College, New Rochelle, NY

Johnson & Wales University, Providence, RI

Kettering University, Flint, MI

Marist College, Poughkeepsie, NY

Millsaps College, Jackson, MS

Pacific Lutheran University, Tacoma, WA

Ripon College, Ripon, WI

Saint Anselm College, Manchester, NH

Seattle University, Seattle, WA

Texas Christian University, Fort Worth, TX

Trinity University, San Antonio, TX

University of Dallas, Irving, TX

University of Dayton, Dayton, OH

University of Tulsa, Tulsa, OK

Warren Wilson College, Asheville, NC

Wheaton College, Wheaton, IL

Xavier University, Cincinnati, OH

$25,000–$30,000

Agnes Scott College, Decatur, GA

Albion College, Albion, MI

Allegheny College, Meadville, PA

American University, Washington, DC

Baylor University, Waco, TX

Beloit College, Beloit, WI

Bryant University, Smithfield, RI

Butler University, Indianapolis, IN

Catholic University of America, Washington, DC

Centre College, Danville, KY

Chatham University, Pittsburgh, PA

Coe College, Cedar Rapids, IA

Cornell College, Mount Vernon, IA

Creighton University, Omaha, NE

DePauw University, Greencastle, IN

Drexel University, Philadelphia, PA

Emerson College, Boston, MA

Gonzaga University, Spokane, WA

Gustavus Adolphus College, St. Peter, MN

Hampden-Sydney College, Hampden-Sydney, VA

Hofstra University, Hempstead, NY

Illinois Institute of Technology, Chicago, IL

Ithaca College, Ithaca, NY

Juilliard School, New York, NY

Juniata College, Huntingdon, PA

Kalamazoo College, Kalamazoo, MI

Knox College, Galesburg, IL

Lewis & Clark College, Portland, OR

Loyola Marymount University, Los Angeles, CA

Loyola University New Orleans, LA

Marlboro College, Marlboro, VT

Marquette University, Milwaukee, WI

Mercer University, Macon, GA

Merrimack College, North Andover, MA

Moravian College, Bethlehem, PA

Quinnipiac University, Hamden, CT

Randolph-Macon College, Ashland, VA

Rice University, Houston, TX

Rochester Institute of Technology, Rochester, NY

Saint Anselm College, Manchester, NH

Saint Louis University, St. Louis, MO

Saint Mary's College of California, Moraga, CA

Savannah College of Art and Design, Savannah, GA

School of the Museum of Fine Arts, Boston, MA

Seton Hall University, South Orange, NJ

Simmons College, Boston, MA

Southwestern University, Georgetown, TX

Stetson University, DeLand, FL

Stonehill College, Easton, MA

Sweet Briar College, Sweet Briar, VA

University of Redlands, Redlands, CA

University of Scranton, Scranton, PA

University of the Pacific, Stockton, CA

Valparaiso University, Valparaiso, IN

Wabash College, Crawfordsville, IN

Wagner College, Staten Island, NY

Wittenberg University, Springfield, OH

Wofford College, Spartanburg, SC

$30,000–$35,000

Babson College, Babson Park, MA

Barnard College, New York, NY

Bentley College, Waltham, MA

Brown University, Providence, RI

California Institute of Technology, Pasadena, CA

Case Western Reserve University, Cleveland, OH

Claremont McKenna College, Claremont, CA

Clark University, Worcester, MA

College of the Atlantic, Bar Harbor, ME

Cornell University, Ithaca, NY

Dartmouth College, Hanover, NH

Davidson College, Davidson, NC

Denison University, Granville, OH

Drew University, Madison, NJ

Duke University, Durham, NC

Eckerd College, St. Petersburg, FL

Emory University, Atlanta, GA

Eugene Lang College–The New School for Liberal Arts, New York, NY

Fordham University, Bronx, NY

Franklin & Marshall College, Lancaster, PA

Franklin W. Olin College of Engineering, Needham, MA

Furman University, Greenville, SC

Georgetown University, Washington, DC

Goucher College, Baltimore, MD

Grinnell College, Grinnell, IA

Hamilton College, Omaha, NE

Harvard College, Cambridge, MA

Harvey Mudd College, Claremont, CA

Hobart and William Smith Colleges, Geneva, NY

Illinois Wesleyan University, Bloomington, IL

Lafayette College, Easton, PA

Lake Forest College, Lake Forest, IL

Loyola College in Maryland, Baltimore, MD

Manhattanville College, Purchase, NY

Massachusetts Institute of Technology, Cambridge, MA

Mills College, Oakland, CA

New York University, New York, NY

Northeastern University, Boston, MA

Pepperdine University, Malibu, CA

Pitzer College, Claremont, CA

Pomona College, Claremont, CA

Princeton University, Princeton, NJ

Providence College, Providence, RI

Rhode Island School of Design, Providence, RI

Rhodes College, Memphis, TN

Rollins College, Winter Park, FL

Rose-Hulman Institute of Technology, Terre Haute, IN

Saint Michael's College, Colchester, VT

Saint Olaf College, Northfield, MN

Santa Clara University, Santa Clara, CA

School of the Art Institute of Chicago, IL

Sewanee–The University of the South, Sewanee, TN

Skidmore College, Saratoga Springs, NY

Smith College, Northampton, MA

Southern Methodist University, Dallas, TX

Stanford University, Stanford, CA

Susquehanna University, Selinsgrove, PA

Swarthmore College, Swarthmore, PA
Syracuse University, Syracuse, NY
University of Chicago, IL
University of Denver, CO
University of Miami, Coral Gables, FL
University of Pennsylvania, Philadelphia, PA
University of Puget Sound, Tacoma, WA
University of Southern California, Los Angeles, CA
Ursinus College, Collegeville, PA
Villanova University, Villanova, PA
Washington and Lee University, Lexington, VA
Willamette University, Salem, OR
Williams College, Williamstown, MA
Yale University, New Haven, CT

$35,000+

Amherst College, Amherst, MA
Bard College, Annandale-on-Hudson, NY
Bates College, Lewiston, ME
Bennington College, Bennington, VT
Boston College, Chestnut Hill, MA
Boston University, Boston, MA
Bowdoin College, Brunswick, ME
Brandeis University, Waltham, MA
Bryn Mawr College, Bryn Mawr, PA
Bucknell University, Lewisburg, PA
Carleton College, Northfield, MI
Carnegie Mellon University, Pittsburgh, PA
Colby College, Waterville, ME
Colgate University, Hamilton, NY
College of the Holy Cross, Worcester, MA
Colorado College, Colorado Springs, CO
Columbia University, New York, NY
Connecticut College, New London, CT
Dickinson College, Carlisle, PA
Fairfield University, Fairfield, CT
George Washington University, Washington, DC
Gettysburg College, Gettysburg, PA
Hamilton College, Clinton, NY
Hampshire College, Amherst, MA
Haverford College, Haverford, PA
Johns Hopkins University, Baltimore, MD
Kenyon College, Gambier, OH
Lehigh University, Bethlehem, PA
Macalester College, St. Paul, MI
Middlebury College, Middlebury, VT
Mount Holyoke College, South Hadley, MA
Muhlenberg College, Allentown, PA
Northwestern University, Evanston, IL
Oberlin College, Oberlin, OH
Occidental College, Los Angeles, CA
Reed College, Portland, OR
Rensselaer Polytechnic Institute, Troy, NY
Saint John's College, Annapolis, MD
Saint John's College, Santa Fe, NM
Saint Lawrence University, Canton, NY
Sarah Lawrence College, Bronxville, NY
Scripps College, Claremont, CA
Trinity College, Hartford, CT
Tufts University, Medford, MA

Unavailable

[illegible]

United States Coast Guard Academy, New London, CT

United States Merchant Marine Academy, Kings Point, NY

United States Military Academy, West Point, NY

Tulane University, New Orleans, LA

Union College, Schenectady, NY

University of Notre Dame, Notre Dame, IN

University of Richmond, Richmond, VA

Vassar College, Poughkeepsie, NY

Villanova University, Villanova, PA

Virginia Military Institute, Lexington, VA

Wake Forest University, Winston-Salem, NC

Washington University in St. Louis, St. Louis, MO

Wellesley College, Wellesley, MA

Wesleyan University, Middletown, CT

[illegible]

Whitman College, Walla Walla, WA

10 Hot Green Careers

ENVIRONMENTAL CONSERVATION

WHY IT'S GREAT TO BE AN ENVIRONMENTAL CONSERVATIONIST

Conservationists are in the unique position literally to save the Earth. Whether they are working to save a natural habitat, a species, or our natural resources, they are the champions for those without a voice.

WHAT CONSERVATIONISTS ARE DOING TO PRESERVE AND IMPROVE OUR WORLD

If land developers had anything to say about it, you can be certain that just about every square inch of the United States would be covered in tract housing and shopping malls. Thankfully, that is not the case. Dedicated conservationists make sure that future generations will be able to enjoy the same natural beauty and diversity of species that are found on the earth today.

SKILLS TO BE A SUCCESSFUL CONSERVATIONIST

To be a successful conservationist, one must work well with people, have a solid foundation in research, and exhibit great patience—saving an ecosystem or a species does not happen overnight. The skills are similar for conservation directors.

CHALLENGES THAT CONSERVATIONISTS FACE

Especially when it comes to preserving land, conservationists can have a hard time convincing landowners or land operators that it is financially worthwhile to set aside property for conservation. In addition, land is being developed at ever-faster rates each year. Fund raising is a particular issue—conservation organizations are always trying to raise money to further the cause.

HOW CURRENT ENVIRONMENTAL ISSUES AFFECT THE JOB MARKET

Although conservation is more important than ever, the growth of this career is not expected to be overwhelming. Still, areas negatively impacted by erosion and drought are badly in need of conservationists. Also, as the country's ecological landscape changes, so will the need for specific types of conservationists.

WHERE THE JOBS ARE

Conservationists can be found in every state. The majority of conservationists work for the local, state, or federal government. The proliferation of nonprofit grassroots conservation organizations means that conservationists can also find work in this sector. Areas with large plots of undeveloped land or with large amounts of natural resources typically have a higher concentration of conservationist jobs. Conservation directors lead these organizations.

AREAS OF SPECIALTY

Specialty areas within the conservation field include wildlife conservation, soil conservation, water conservation, natural resource conservation, and forest conservation, among others.

EDUCATIONAL REQUIREMENTS

Entry-level conservation positions typically require a BS in a related science, such as agriculture, biology, ecology, environmental science, or natural resource management. Advanced degrees (MS or PhD) are required for top-level conservation positions with large conservation organizations. In some cases, conservation directors may not have a degree in an environmental field but rather in business administration, public policy, or communication.

TOP COLLEGES FOR PURSUING A CAREER AS A CONSERVATIONIST

- Cornell University
- University of Massachusetts, Department of Natural Resources Conservation
- Yale University, School of Forestry

COURSE WORK AND CLASSES TO HELP YOU BECOME A CONSERVATIONIST

Course work in any and all of the sciences, including biology, zoology, ecology, and physics, is instrumental in becoming a conservationist. Small grassroots organizations may only require employees to have a passion for the environment.

SALARY RANGE

According to the Bureau of Labor Statistics, conservationists, also known as conservation scientists, can earn anywhere from $24,000 to $80,000 per year. The salary for conservation directors may be higher, depending on the size and funding of the conservation organization.

FAMOUS CONSERVATIONISTS

- **John Muir**, a profound lover of nature and first president of the Sierra Club, was passionately dedicated to preserving and conserving the beautiful wilderness of the United States.
- Although **Theodore Roosevelt** is best known for being president of the United States, he was also a dedicated conservationist. He created the National Wildlife Refuge and was instrumental in establishing national parks, such as the Grand Canyon, in the American West.

WHERE TO LEARN MORE

U.S. Department of Agriculture, Natural Resources Conservation Service
Attn: Legislative and Public Affairs Division
P.O. Box 2890
Washington, DC 20013
www.nrcs.usda.gov

Society for Conservation Biology
4245 N. Fairfax Dr., Suite 400
Arlington, VA 22203
www.conbio.org

Sierra Club National Headquarters
85 2nd St., 2nd Floor
San Francisco, CA 94105
www.sierraclub.org

WORDS OF WISDOM

"Conservation biology is not a path to riches. The people who work in this field do it because they are passionate about it. I give three pieces of advice to students: one, follow your passion; two, don't worry about the money; and three, as you advance in your career, make sure you keep doing the things that you really care about."

—Liz Thompson, Conservation Director

"In general, the people who work in the environmental nonprofit community are very intelligent, tons of fun, extremely committed, and incredibly talented. Working with these other caring individuals is a pleasure."

—Joan Clayburgh, Director of the Sierra Nevada Alliance

Elizabeth Thompson, Conservation Biologist
Conservation Biology Partnership Director, University of Vermont
University of Maine—Orono, 1979
Major: Botany

How does your career have an impact on efforts to improve our environment?

I work regularly with landowners who have an influence on water quality, wildlife habitat, rare species, and significant natural communities. I influence how these people manage their land, and I also influence policy makers regarding these issues.

How do the environmental issues that our world is facing have an impact on your career?

Climate change affects everything. My work is in land conservation, and when we conserve land, we must think about how it will change as climate changes. Also, I work with water quality issues a lot on a day-to-day basis.

What was your first job after graduation?

I was a biologist at The Nature Conservancy. I conducted an ecological inventory of a spectacular nature reserve on the Maine coast. It was a dream job.

What criteria did you use when deciding which college(s) to apply to?

I considered the school's strengths in my area of interest, botany and ecology. I also considered the school's location, since I wanted to be away from urban areas.

Did you attend your first choice school?

Yes. I knew I wanted to go to UM—Orono because it had the rural setting and academic programs I was looking for.

Did you already have a career in mind when you applied to college?

Generally. I knew that I wanted to work in botany and field biology.

Did the school you attended have a significant impact on your career opportunities?

Yes. It was an excellent school, and I met many interesting people who were connected to my field of interest.

Knowing what you know now, which college would you apply to (and why)?

I would have applied to Yale School of Forestry, Cornell, and University of Michigan. These schools are also excellent in natural resources.

Which college or colleges are turning out the leaders in your profession today?

Yale School of Forestry, Cornell, University of Michigan, University of Wisconsin, University of Maine, and the University of Vermont graduate school (which is where I got my master's degree) are a few of them. There are others as well.

Did you have an "Aha!" moment when you realized what you wanted to do?

When the woods behind my house were cleared for a new development, my heart sank. These woods were my refuge—where I listened to birds, noticed wild plants, followed the stream, chased frogs, and enjoyed a peaceful solitude. Development was happening quickly all over my hometown, and so much was being lost every day. If there was one single event that shaped my career path, the loss of my personal place of refuge may have been it.

What were your majors in college?

Botany, plant and soil science.

Did you change your major? If so, why?

I changed my major once. I had a brief foray into agriculture, thinking that might be interesting. At that time, the teaching of agriculture was not very forward thinking, so I quickly got bored.

Which classes were most valuable in preparing you for your career or in helping you decide on your career?

I found plant ecology to be a very valuable class—it really helped me to decide that I was making the right career decision.

How did your professors have an impact on your career choice or preparation?

Good professors are everything. I had a course that was team-taught by five or six ecology professors. It was an incredible opportunity to get a variety of points of view and some excellent training. Several of these people influenced me. Mac Hunter, Bob Vadas, Ron Davis, Bucky Owen, Dick Homola, and Benedict Neubauer were all influential. Bob Vadas was perhaps the most influential. He was an algal ecologist and was simply passionate about his work. That was infectious.

Did you have a job and/or internship during college that influenced your career choice or career preparation in any way?

Nothing that significantly impacted my current career.

How important was your college experience in getting you to where you are today?

I would say that it was extremely important. The training was great, the influence of several inspired faculty members was great, and the contact the professors had with the conservation world were vital.

Do you have an advanced degree? Is one helpful or required in your field?

Yes, I have a master's of science degree in botany from the University of Vermont. I worked in the conservation biology field for two years before returning to graduate school and received my degree in 1984. Having an advanced degree is extremely helpful and pretty much required in my line of work.

What do you love most about your job?

One of my favorite things about being a conservationist is that I get to spend a lot of time in the woods!

What is the most difficult or challenging aspect of your job?

The paperwork and meetings.

What was the biggest obstacle you faced in getting to where you are in your career?

This may sound odd, but I had to fight against more responsibility. Many people want more responsibility; but for me, that meant more meetings and more paperwork, things that I don't really like. As a result, I demoted myself several times.

What skills are an absolute must for someone interested in pursuing your career?

Excellent observational skills, the ability to integrate many pieces of information to see the whole, an ability to work with a diverse range of people, good communication skills. Specifically, one needs to be a good naturalist, in many areas.

Whom do you admire most in your industry/field?

There's not one single person—there are many people I admire. Most of the people I admire most are not well known, because they prefer it that way.

What is one piece of advice you would give to someone who is interested in pursuing your career?

Get out in the woods every day. That's the best way to learn.

If you could do everything all over again, what would you do differently?

I would refuse to do any work that was not meaningful for me. That might have meant going broke more of the time, but it would have been worth it.

Do you have any additional comments you think might be helpful to someone hoping to pursue your career?

Conservation biology is not a path to riches. The people who work in this field do it because they are passionate about it. I give three pieces of advice to students: one, follow your passion; two, don't worry about the money; and three, as you advance in your career, make sure you keep doing the things that you really care about.

Joan Clayburgh, Conservation Director
Executive Director, Sierra Nevada Alliance
University of California—San Diego, 1985
Major: Communications

How does your career have an impact on efforts to improve our environment?

My career is very focused on improving the environment. The organization I direct works to protect and restore Sierra lands, water, wildlife, and rural communities. We do this by building the capacity of organizations and individuals working to protect the environment and by uniting efforts together to create regional change. We have created models for watershed stewardship, smart land use planning, and how to address climate change in our region. We are seeing results and making progress every month.

How do the environmental issues that our world is facing have an impact on your career?

Climate change and population growth are the greatest challenges the environment has ever faced. These two mega-issues impact every environmental issue. At the same time, these incredible threats present our environmental movement an opportunity to have everyone understand and embrace sustainability.

What was your first job after graduation?

I was a CALPIRG (California Public Interest Research Group) canvasser.

What criteria did you use when deciding which college(s) to apply to?

I wanted to attend a college that had a good communications department, affordable tuition, on-campus housing for freshmen, and a pleasant environment.

Did you attend your first choice school?

Yes.

Did you already have a career in mind when you applied to college?

When I applied to college, I thought that I wanted to pursue a career in journalism, although this wasn't the career path that I ultimately pursued.

Did the school you attended have a significant impact on your career op-portunities?

No.

Knowing what you know now, which college would you apply to (and why)?

I'd probably still go to UC—San Diego—but perhaps I would've considered applying to UC—Berkeley as well. Berkeley has a great rhetoric department, also.

Which college or colleges are turning out the leaders in your profession today?

You could name almost every college. People who are now noted for their work in environmental nonprofits attended a wide variety of colleges.

Did you have an "Aha!" moment when you realized what you wanted to do?

One day, someone asked me at a table on campus if I cared about the environment—and that started me volunteering on environmental campaigns. That led me to my career, and I've never looked back since.

What were your majors in college?

I was a communications major.

Which classes were most valuable in preparing you for your career or in helping you decide on your career?

My college classes taught me a larger worldview and how to be a critical thinker. However, volunteering for organizations was much more valuable in helping me decide on my career and preparing me for my specific career.

How did your professors have an impact on your career choice or preparation?

My professors didn't really have much of an impact on my career decisions.

Did you have a job and/or internship during college that influenced your career choice or preparation in any way?

Yes. I worked at a movie theater to pay the bills, but I completed a media internship with CALPIRG, volunteered at the campus radio station, and volunteered with local environmental campaigns on campus. My exposure (through CALPIRG) to politics, the media, and social change inspired me to pursue a career working with environmental nonprofits.

How important was your college experience in getting you to where you are today?

College helped me form a foundation from which I perceive the world, and it taught me to be a critical thinker. It provided me a foundation to understand international, national, state, and local politics. It provided me a greater understanding of human information processing and how communication shapes culture.

Do you have an advanced degree? Is one helpful or required in your field?

Having an advanced degree is somewhat helpful but not always required. I personally don't have one.

What do you love most about your job?

Making a positive difference in protecting the natural environment, which provides us a higher quality of life—and inspiration.

What is the most difficult or challenging aspect of your job?

Time management is the most challenging aspect of my job. There are more opportunities than actual resources in the nonprofit world. It is tempting to just work longer hours to get more done. However, to sustain a career for the long term, it is important to learn to say no, postpone activities, reduce the scope of projects, delegate, and add capacity. It is always tempting to work longer and longer hours to cover more opportunities.

What is the biggest misconception people have about what you do?

That somehow working for nonprofits is a sacrifice to my quality of life. People assume you don't get paid well and work in poor-quality conditions. But the reality is that the salaries are comfortable, the working conditions very pleasurable, and most importantly, the work is very satisfying. Working for environmental nonprofits is a privilege, not a sacrifice.

What was the biggest obstacle you faced in getting to where you are in your career?

Entry-level positions involving fund-raising can be challenging. I overcame this challeng by changing my attitude. I realized fund-raising was simply another means to share important issues with other people regarding how to make a difference. I changed my perception that fund-raising was asking for "favors" from people to fund-raising is providing people an opportunity to help an issue they care deeply about.

What skills are an absolute must for someone interested in pursuing your career?

You must love working with people, have a passion for the issues you work on, and be able to learn new information constantly in an ever-changing environment.

Whom do you admire most in your industry/field?

I really admire Cesar Chavez. He spoke up to highlight incredible environmental injustices at a time when you could get seriously injured for doing so. He empowered and organized millions of others to join him to create change. When he started organizing, he was up against incredible pressure to be quiet. When he died, he left behind strong organizing tools to create change and a public awareness that anyone from any economic level or race or gender or workforce can make a difference.

What is one piece of advice you would give to someone who is interested in pursuing your career?

Follow your heart. If you care about an issue, create a career around it. If you enjoy certain tactics more than others, focus on those tactics. We excel personally and professionally when we do what we love.

If you could do everything all over again, what would you do differently?

I would have learned to balance my recreation and personal life with my career more quickly. I was a workaholic for a number of years when I first started. This took a physical toll on me. Now I do the same work and balance that with my family, recreation, and personal life outside of work. Consequently, my balanced life allows me to do my work more effectively when I'm there.

Do you have any additional comments you think might be helpful to someone hoping to pursue your career?

In general, the people who work in the environmental nonprofit community are very intelligent, tons of fun, extremely committed, and incredibly talented. Working with these other caring individuals is a pleasure.

ENVIRONMENTAL DESIGN

WHY IT'S GREAT TO BE AN ENVIRONMENTAL DESIGNER

First, some clarification: the *environmental* in the career title doesn't immediately pertain to "ecologically sound." Instead, *environmental* means, literally, the existing three-dimensional environment in which the design is completed. With the world as their backdrop, these designers, in diverse disciplines including graphic, architectural, landscape, and industrial design, have limitless opportunities to express their visions.

WHAT ENVIRONMENTAL DESIGNERS ARE DOING TO PRESERVE AND IMPROVE OUR WORLD

Since we're talking about design that isn't just found on a computer desktop or a piece of paper, it is important that these environmental designers respect the environment. As often as possible, these professionals aim to use environmentally friendly and/or recycled materials, nontoxic supplies, and sustainable practices.

SKILLS TO BE A SUCCESSFUL ENVIRONMENTAL DESIGNER

A career in design requires vision and a great deal of creativity. These skills, balanced with attention to detail and time management, are essential to success. In addition, strong interpersonal and communication skills are a must.

CHALLENGES THAT ENVIRONMENTAL DESIGNERS FACE

Environmental designers have to bring together their own vision and the vision of their clients. In addition, clients sometimes have to be educated on the feasibility of using recycled or sustainable materials.

HOW CURRENT ENVIRONMENTAL ISSUES AFFECT THE JOB MARKET

The consumer affects the work of an environmental designer more than the global environement. As consumers become more aware of environmental stewardship, they look more for environmental designers who respect the environment. Leadership in Energy and Environmental Design (LEED) accreditation is an increasingly important distinction for these designers to have.

WHERE THE JOBS ARE

Environmental designers can find work virtually anywhere in the United States, although large cities might offer more opportunities. Some designers prefer to work independently, but some choose to work for large or national firms, which can attract large projects and contracts.

AREAS OF SPECIALTY

The general term *environmental designer* applies to several different design specialties, including graphic, architectural, landscape, and industrial design.

EDUCATIONAL REQUIREMENTS

Almost any specialty of environmental design requires a minimum of a bachelor's or associate's degree. More specialized environmental designers, such as landscape architects, may need a master's degree. Almost all environmental design positions require licensure at the state level. In addition, as mentioned above, LEED accreditation is increasingly important.

TOP COLLEGES FOR PURSUING A CAREER AS AN ENVIRONMENTAL DESIGNER

- Harvard University
- Parsons School of Design
- University of Georgia—Athens, School of Environmental Design

COURSE WORK AND CLASSES TO HELP YOU BECOME AN ENVIRONMENTAL DESIGNER

Regardless of specialization, courses in design, mathematics, and even business are helpful.

SALARY RANGE

Among environmental design careers, there is a wide range of salaries. According to the Bureau of Labor Statistics, salaries can start as low as $24,000 for entry-level graphic designers and range as high as $95,000 for an experienced landscape architect.

FAMOUS ENVIRONMENTAL DESIGNERS

- **Frederick Law Olmsted**, although deceased for more than a century, is eternally famous for Central Park, located in Manhattan in New York City. He is also known as the father of the landscape architecture profession in the United States.
- **Thomas D. Church** is famous for establishing the "California garden," which is suited to its particular climate and known for its use of native plants.

WHERE TO LEARN MORE

Society for Environmental Graphic Design
1000 Vermont Ave., Suite 400
Washington, DC 20005
www.segd.org

U.S. Green Building Council (LEED accreditation)
1800 Massachusetts Avenue N.W., Suite 300
Washington, DC 20036
www.usgbc.org

American Society of Landscape Architects
636 Eye St. N.W.
Washington, DC 20001
www.asla.org

WORDS OF WISDOM

"I think working in environmental design takes a little bit of idealism, because we're all just trying to make the built world a better place—make it work better, be better used, better appreciated, better protected."

—Suzanne Pritchard, Landscape Architect and LEED-Accredited Professional

"The only way you can be truly successful and excel in a fast-paced career is to love what you do. If you don't, the rewards don't outweigh the sacrifice."

—Nate Burns, Landscape Architect

L. Suzanne Pritchard, Landscape Architect
Landscape Architect and LEED AP (accredited professional)
Duke University, 2000
Majors: Biology and Visual Arts

How does your career have an impact on efforts to improve our environment?

Landscape architects analyze, plan, design, manage, and protect the natural and built environments. The work we do directly impacts the environment and how people use it. If we do our job well and adhere to high principles and standards of sustainability, we can improve the environment.

How do the environmental issues that our world is facing have an impact on your career?

There is a growing movement for green design within the United States and around the world, and landscape architects are at the forefront of this movement. As people become more concerned about these issues, there is also a growing demand for landscape architects who have training in the principles of green design.

What was your first job after graduation?

I was an associate at a landscape architecture firm.

What criteria did you use when deciding which college(s) to apply to?

I was looking for a challenging school with lots of opportunities within a semi-close proximity to my hometown. Ultimately, I attended a great school that was about a three-hour drive away.

Did you attend your first choice school?

Yes, both for undergraduate and graduate school.

Did you already have a career in mind when you applied to college?

Yes, when I began my first semester in college, I thought that I wanted to go into the field of biochemistry. I had spent several summers at various college-preparatory programs in science, and I had always really enjoyed both biology and chemistry in high school. During my first semester of college, I was taking a sculpture course, a biodesign course, and a chemistry course. One day, I realized that I hated the chemistry class and loved the sculpture and biodesign classes.

Did the school you attended have an impact on your career opportunities?

Yes and no. For my undergraduate years, I attended a school that did not offer a professional degree in landscape architecture, something that is basically mandatory to become a landscape architect at this point in time. I still took courses related to landscape architecture (as it's really a broad field that draws on knowledge from many disciplines—art, art history, design, ecology, geology, hydrology) at Duke. But I knew to become a landscape architect, I would need to get a professional degree at another school.

Knowing what you know now, which college would you apply to (and why)?

I don't have any regrets about attending Duke, and my parents basically covered the costs of my undergraduate education. But if I had known how much my student loan payments for graduate school were going to be and I had known that I wanted to be a landscape architect, I would have gone to a school like North Carolina State or the University of Georgia. They are both great schools (semi-close to my hometown), and they both have excellent undergraduate programs in landscape architecture. When I was graduating from high school, however, I could not have made that decision, and I'm glad that I went to a college that offered a great, broadly based liberal arts education. Duke challenged me, and through its facilities, I was able to figure out what kind of career I wanted.

Which college or colleges are turning out the leaders in your profession today?

I'm not as familiar with undergraduate programs, but if you look at the top firms, their employees are coming from the University of Pennsylvania, Harvard, and the University of Georgia.

Did you have an "Aha!" moment when you realized what you wanted to do?

Yes. When I had returned from Christmas break my freshman year of college, I was reading *The New Yorker* in the commons room of the dorm, waiting on another friend to return. In the back of the magazine, I saw an ad for Harvard's Graduate School of Design Program in Landscape Architecture. Suddenly it all clicked. I found a career that would combine my interests, creative drive, and scientific predisposition. As I learned more about landscape architecture, this "Aha!" moment was only confirmed.

What were your majors in college?

Biology and visual arts.

Did you change your major? If so, why?

I didn't change my major, but I did add the major of visual arts. I thought the combination of biology and visual arts would allow me to take classes that best prepared me for graduate work in landscape architecture.

Which classes were most valuable in preparing you for your career or in helping you decide on your career?

Biodesign, physics, ecology, population biology, geology, hydrology, environmental geology, botany, sculpture, art history, drawing, and architectural theory.

How did your professors have an impact on your career choice or preparation?

The professors in Duke's art department were enormously encouraging. They pointed me in directions of study and introduced me to other like-minded students. The art department even awarded me a grant to study Japanese gardens in Japan the summer before graduate school.

Did you have a job and/or internship during college that influenced your career choice or career preparation in any way?

I had several jobs but none that really significantly influenced my ultimate career choice. I worked in the library as a special searcher, the pottery studio as an assistant, the local Whole Foods grocery as a cashier, a café as a barista and manager, and the vascular herbarium as a curatorial assistant.

How important was your college experience in getting you to where you are today?

My education at Duke was amazing and world expanding. Duke taught me a lot; I think the things I learned there have enabled me to be a better scholar, graduate student, and landscape architect.

Do you have an advanced degree? Is one helpful or required in your field?

I have a master's in landscape architecture. It is required if you did not receive a bachelor's degree in landscape architecture.

What do you love most about your job?

The variety of projects I work on. One day I may be working on a high-end residential garden, the next day a LEED-certified bank, the next day a master plan for a Boy Scout camp, the next day a mixed-use community plan, the next day making renderings for a public park, etc.

What is the most difficult or challenging aspect of your job?

Dealing with architects or others who feel that landscape architects should only deal with a site by planting its perimeter. Sometimes there is a real lack of collaboration among the disciplines; much better projects could be realized if architects, engineers, and developers came to us much earlier in a project's history to help plan the site.

What is the biggest misconception people have about what you do?

People ask me questions about lawn and plant maintenance. As a landscape architect, I only do drawings. I don't install any plant material or build any structures. I have knowledge about optimal conditions for plants, but I can't help people fix diseased plants. People assume that landscape architects only work on a very small scale and that our only tool is planting. We deal with all scales of design—from the small garden to planning a region—and we have many tools in our palette: plantings, earthworks, hardscape and structures, lighting, circulation, programs, etc.

What was the biggest obstacle you faced in getting to where you are in your career?

Getting through studio in graduate school was very difficult. I think that every student of landscape architecture faces some type of studio experience where you learn to design by solving some type of real-world problem. You work very hard on a project, you're completely sleep deprived, you pour your heart and soul into your own creative solution to a design problem. Then you go to a "jury" (professionals in your field), you present your work to the jury, and they proceed to criticize your project, point out the flaws, and applaud the triumphs (if they see any).

You really have to learn to accept blatant criticism and advice. It builds your character. I think I've repressed many of my jury experiences from school. It's not that I did that badly, it's just that the experiences are so stressful. It's hard. The only way to get through them is to work hard, be confident in your work, present your work well (I spent a lot of time practicing presentations because I would get so nervous), and then gracefully respond to the jury's questions and comments.

What skills are an absolute must for someone interested in pursuing your career?

I think that landscape architecture is one of the most broadly based fields out there. You have to know about psychology, real estate, design, art history, biology, geology, hydrology, and horticulture. It really requires someone to be curious about everything in life.

Whom do you admire most in your industry/field?

Right now, I'm at the point where I'm starting to think about my future in terms of raising a family. I admire women in my field who can balance raising a baby or children and still have time to meet the demands of this career.

What is one piece of advice you would give to someone who is interested in pursuing your career?

Learn everything and go everywhere.

If you could do everything all over again, what would you do differently?

I'm not sure. One of my options was to go for a dual degree—both a master's in architecture and landscape architecture. I would do that now if I were back in school again.

Do you have any additional comments you think might be helpful to someone hoping to pursue your career?

I think working in environmental design takes a little bit of idealism, because we're all just trying to make the built world a better place—make it work better, be better used, better appreciated, better protected.

Nathaniel Burns, Landscape Architect/Planner
Senior Staff Landscape Architect, Langan Engineering and Environmental Services
Delaware Valley College, 1999
Major: Ornamental Horticulture and Environmental Design

How does your career have an impact on efforts to improve our environment?

Any decision I make can have either positive or negative impacts on the environment. The work I do physically exists and comprises the natural environment. Because of this, the ways I envision the solution to any given problem either benefit or have a negative impact on its surroundings.

How do the environmental issues that our world is facing have an impact on your career?

Any changes to the environment alter the way it currently acts and my understanding of it. This can keep me from making the right decisions and could have potentially dangerous consequences.

What was your first job after graduation?

I was a restoration specialist.

What criteria did you use when deciding which college(s) to apply to?

I chose to attend both graduate and undergraduate programs based on the small class sizes and their hands-on approaches.

Did you attend your first choice school?

Yes.

Did you already have a career in mind when you applied to college?

Yes. The availability of the landscape architecture major, combined with a pragmatic approach to learning and small class size, was the reason I chose to attend Delaware Valley College. I knew I wanted to be a landscape architect.

Did the school you attended have a significant impact on your career op-portunities?

Yes, the specific study areas and focus of each program provided me guidance in narrowing my interest. Additionally, specific niche skills I developed allowed me to be more competitive as a prospect for potential employers.

Knowing what you know now, which college would you apply to (and why)?

The only consideration I would make to changing schools would be based on a specific program's professional accreditation status. My undergrad program was unaccredited, and this posed some additional hurdles for me to pass while obtaining my professional license.

Which college or colleges are turning out the leaders in your profession today?

Locally, Penn State University, Rutgers, and Temple University. It's hard to say on a national scene, since this field tends to be very regionalized. UMass, West Virginia University, and University of Wisconsin all have good national programs. I'm sure I am missing some others, though. Penn State is usually top five.

Did you have an "Aha!" moment when you realized what you wanted to do?

Not really.

What were your majors in college?

Ornamental horticulture and environmental design.

Did you change your major?

No, I did not change my major.

Which classes were most valuable in preparing you for your career or in helping you decide on your career?

Design studios focused on hand drafting were the basis of our program. Spending almost all of our time working by hand allowed us to understand the process involved in design, without being bogged down in CAD.

How did your professors have an impact on your career choice or preparation?

My main design professor focused on ecological restoration and really helped me to understand its importance in the overall field of landscape architecture.

How important was your college experience in getting you to where you are today?

It provided me with the tools I needed to pursue my career. It also provided me with some of the initial contacts to get started.

Do you have an advanced degree? Is one helpful/required in your field?

Yes, I have an advanced degree. For an entry-level position, a bachelor's is fine, but for advanced levels of employment, an advanced degree is preferred. Also, depending on your type of undergraduate degree, you may be required to obtain an advanced degree to attain licensure.

What do you love most about your job?

The variety of things I can work on.

What is the most difficult or challenging aspect of your job?

Since landscape architecture is a deadline-driven field, you are often given short notice to finish large amounts of work. This often means long days and late nights to get the job done. To be successful and maintain a high level of work quality under these circumstances, you need to be dedicated to your job and the product you produce.

What is the biggest misconception people have about what you do?

Many people have a very romantic idea of what a landscape architect actually does, but in most cases, the daily practice is much more utilitarian.

What was the biggest obstacle you faced in getting to where you are in your career?

Obtaining my professional licensure while maintaining a more than full-time career was a challenge. It required a great deal of dedication to put forth the time to learn the materials required within a busy schedule.

What skills are an absolute must for someone interested in pursuing your career?

Determination—that's pretty much it. Great verbal and written communication skills are also very helpful.

Whom do you admire most in your industry/field?

Fredrick Law Olmstead—he is one of the people who really helped to shape what our field is today. Additionally, many of the great public spaces in the United States are a direct result of his influence.

What is one piece of advice you would give to someone who is interested in pursuing your career?

Don't forget that design begins with drawing. You also really need to be committed and love what you do.

If you could do everything all over again, what would you do differently?

Nothing really. If I would have done anything differently, I wouldn't be where I am today.

Do you have any additional comments you think might be helpful to someone hoping to pursue your career?

The only way you can be truly successful and excel in a fast-paced career is to love what you do. If you don't, the rewards don't outweigh the sacrifice.

ENVIRONMENTAL ENGINEERING

WHY IT'S GREAT TO BE AN ENVIROMENTAL ENGINEER

Environmental engineers have the opportunity to combine two passions—the environment and science—to develop practical solutions to serious problems, such as carbon-based energy, pollution, and overpopulation, which affect everyone on the planet. This branch of engineering focuses on environmental protection, hazardous waste, and global warming. Environmental engineers also design municipal waste systems and industrial water treatment plants and plan the use of land in environmentally sustainable ways.

WHAT ENVIRONMENTAL ENGINEERS ARE DOING TO PRESERVE AND IMPROVE OUR WORLD

Environmental engineers are not about problems; they are about solutions. They also focus on mitigating problems before they even occur. So whether they are preventing the spread of hazardous materials into our soil or finding innovative ways to recycle different materials, environmental engineers are on the forefront of the movement to save the earth. Conducting soil suitability tests, designing wind farms, or developing a new system for air pollution control are just some of the projects undertaken by environmental engineers.

SKILLS TO BE A SUCCESSFUL ENVIRONMENTAL ENGINEER

Environmental engineers must be creative in their critical thinking skills. Attention to detail, strong math skills, and a scientific mind are also very important. Still, engineering does not happen in a vacuum. Strong written and verbal communication skills are very important.

CHALLENGES THAT ENVIRONMENTAL ENGINEERS FACE

Especially when required to prevent problems before they occur, environmental engineers face unique creative and design challenges. In addition, even with the most meticulous planning, the earth and its systems can be unpredictable.

HOW CURRENT ENVIRONMENTAL ISSUES AFFECT THE JOB MARKET

The current state of the environment almost guarantees that environmental engineers will have no trouble finding employment. Serious issues, such as pollution, conservation, and global warming, all present challenges for environmental engineers to solve.

WHERE THE JOBS ARE

Because local, state, and federal governments as well as various industries are all under pressure to minimize negative environmental impact, the solutions provided by environmental engineers are greatly in demand throughout the United States and the rest of the world. While most environmental engineers work in the government sector, some work as independent consultants. Environmental engineers are also employed by private research firms, testing laboratories, corporations, and private businesses.

AREAS OF SPECIALTY

There are almost no limits to how specialized an environmental engineer can be. Some common areas of specialty are air and water pollution, waste disposal, recycling, and industrial hygiene.

EDUCATIONAL REQUIREMENTS

A bachelor's degree in an engineering specialty (in some cases, simply science or mathematics) is a prerequisite for almost any entry-level employment. Higher-level positions (faculty or research positions) usually require a graduate degree in engineering or a related field. Engineers who offer their services to the public must be licensed. License requirements include a degree from an engineering program, four years of work experience, and passing a licensing exam.

TOP COLLEGES FOR PURSUING A CAREER AS AN ENVIRONMENTAL ENGINEER

- Stanford University
- University of California—Berkeley
- University of Michigan—Ann Arbor

COURSE WORK AND CLASSES TO HELP YOU BECOME AN ENVIRONMENTAL ENGINEER

Coursework in mathematics, environmental science, and engineering are all vitally important to becoming an environmental engineer.

SALARY RANGE

According to the Bureau of Labor Statistics, an environmental engineer can earn anywhere from $43,000 to $106,000, depending on experience and other factors.

FAMOUS ENVIRONMENTAL ENGINEERS

- **Ellen Swallow Richards** was the first woman admitted to the Massachusetts Institute of Technology (MIT) and is credited with being the first female environmental engineer.
- **Kevin Olmstead** is probably more famous for winning the highest payoff ever ($2,180,000) on a TV game show than for being an accomplished environmental engineer.

WHERE TO LEARN MORE

American Society of Civil Engineers
1801 Alexander Bell Dr.
Reston, VA 20191
www.asce.org

American Academy of Environmental Engineers
130 Holiday Court, Suite 100
Annapolis, MD 21401
www.aaee.net

WORDS OF WISDOM

"A degree in environmental engineering will give you a diverse range of career options—from industry and government to nonprofit organizations and academia. It's a wide-open field, and with growing global awareness of environmental problems, good environmental engineers will always be in demand. It's a career that will give you many opportunities for making a difference."

—Jill Houlihan, Environmental Engineer

"Don't be afraid to try new things. Don't be afraid to try and fail or make mistakes as long as you learn from the experience. Find something that you are passionate about and are excited about when you get up in the morning."

—Marleen Troy, Environmental Engineer

Marleen A. Troy, PhD, PE, Environmental Engineer

Chair and Associate Professor of Environmental Engineering, Department of Environmental Engineering and Earth Sciences (EEES), Wilkes University

Drexel University, 1980

Major: Biological Science

How does your career have an impact on efforts to improve our environment?

By increasing public awareness and finding solutions for many of today's environmental problems.

How do environmental issues that our world is facing have an impact on your career?

When I was in school, we concentrated on learning "end-of-pipe" technologies (i.e., learning how to treat the air or water pollution that came out of a pipe). Now we are aware that there is a better approach than the pipe—what can we do or how can we operate or manufacture to get rid of that pipe? Green engineering—designing, building, and operating green buildings; promoting pollution prevention; energy efficiency; and sustainability—are all important concepts for our future. Global climate change and our efforts to mitigate the actions that are contributing to it will also continue to be a central issue for environmental engineers.

What was your first job after graduation?

I was a project engineer with an environmental services contractor.

What criteria did you use when deciding which college(s) to apply to?

I was looking for a school that had a good reputation in the major I was interested in (as an undergraduate, this was biology), had good facilities, and was within a four-hour drive of my home.

Did you attend your first choice school?

Yes, Drexel University was my first choice school.

Did you already have a career in mind when you applied to college?

Yes. I knew I wanted to pursue a career in the applied science field—I was initially interested in being a marine biology researcher. Ultimately, I pursued a career that is a hybrid of my biology and engineering background.

Did the school you attended have a significant impact on your career op-portunities?

Yes, I attended a school that had an undergraduate co-op program that allowed me to gain valuable experience and that introduced me to new career opportunities that I was not initially aware of.

Knowing what you know now, which college would you apply to (and why)?

I would still apply to a school with a co-op program; however, I would pursue a different major.

Which college or colleges, are turning out the leaders in your profession today?

There are many excellent schools for the environmental engineering field. I would recommend Wilkes University and Drexel University for the undergraduate degree and Drexel University for graduate degrees.

Did you have an "Aha!" moment when you realized what you wanted to do?

As an undergraduate, I was able to work as a technician on several environmental research projects. I was given considerable responsibility and enjoyed the work immensely. For one of the projects, I assisted in the analysis of salt marsh water samples that required collection and analysis of these samples during off-peak times. I remember being out in the marsh in the middle of the night under a beautiful starlit sky—collecting the samples, taking instrument readings, getting bitten alive by insects—and enjoying every minute of the experience.

What were your majors in college?

As an undergraduate student, I majored in biological science. I went on to receive an MS in microbiology and an MSCE and PhD in civil engineering.

Did you change your major? If so, why?

I did change my major, and there were a number of reasons I did so. It was primarily due to the lack of a good job market when I graduated with my master's degree and having no desire to stay on for a PhD in microbiology. I became aware of and was interested in the opportunities that an engineering degree would afford me. I was also able to get a laboratory technician position at a university that allowed me to take the required undergraduate engineering courses that enabled me be admitted to the graduate engineering program.

Which classes were most valuable in preparing you for your career or in helping you decide on your career?

I found all of my classes beneficial. However, in graduate school, I took a series of classes in the new field of hazardous waste management that encouraged me to combine my biology/microbiology and engineering backgrounds to specialize in the bioremediation of hazardous waste sites.

How did your professors have an impact on your career choice or preparation?

They all did. I was very fortunate. They were all encouraging and supportive. I appreciated the opportunity as an undergraduate to be involved in research projects and perform field research.

Did you have a job and/or internship during college that influenced your career choice or career preparation in any way?

I went through the co-op program at Drexel University. I had valuable co-op experience with the Philadelphia Water Department at their water and wastewater treatment facilities. I was able to gain a lot of valuable hands-on experience that complemented what I was learning in the classroom. I also found that I liked the type of work I was doing.

How important was your college experience in getting you to where you are today?

My college experience was valuable, but my industry experience (seven years as an engineer with environmental contractors and consultants) allowed me to gain an important perspective on how to apply what I learned, manage projects, work on teams, and interact with clients and regulatory agencies.

Do you have an advanced degree? Is one helpful/required in your field?

Yes. I have an MS in microbiology and an MSCE and a PhD in civil engineering. You can get a good job with a BS degree. However, the environmental engineering field is constantly changing, and an advanced degree will be very beneficial to your knowledge base and will enhance your career opportunities.

What do you love most about your job?

I like the multidisciplinary nature of the environmental engineering field. It is also a chance to make a difference. When I was in industry, I was fortunate to be a part of projects that were able to be taken to completion (the remediation of contaminated sites). In academia, I enjoy being a part of the process of getting students excited about the future.

What is the most difficult or challenging aspect of your job?

Finding time to keep current with new trends and technologies.

What is the biggest misconception people have about what you do?

I find that on occasion, there is a misconception or a lack of understanding and familiarity with what an environmental engineer is and does. They know about civil, chemical, and mechanical engineers but not environmental engineers. I sometimes get referred to as an "environmentalist" or "tree-hugger." In my opinion, there is nothing wrong with these labels, but they are not an accurate representation of what an environmental engineer is and what we do.

What was the biggest obstacle you faced in getting to where you are in your career?

Getting downsized as a result of a change in the business direction and operations of my last employer. I was able to overcome this by being able to apply the skill sets that I had developed over the years in a different setting.

What skills are an absolute must for someone interested in pursuing your career?

It would be very beneficial to have good analytical and organizational skills, be comfortable being a team player, have good communication skills (oral and written), and have a sense of humor.

Whom do you admire most in your industry/field?

I admire those individuals who have increased our awareness about important environmental issues and are also offering solutions for these problems. Examples would include Rachel Carson, Wangari Maathai, Paul Hawken, and Ray Anderson.

What is one piece of advice you would give to someone who is interested in pursuing your career?

Talk to someone who is doing the type of work you would like to do. Shadow them if you can for a day. Check out the websites of some of the professional organizations (American Academy of Environmental Engineers, American Society of Civil Engineers). Find out what you are passionate about. Find out what you don't like to do. (Do you like fieldwork? Do you hate being in the office?)

If you could do everything all over again, what would you do differently?

I probably would have pursued engineering or architecture initially. I also would have obtained more training/education in business operations.

Do you have any additional comments you think might be helpful to someone hoping to pursue your career?

Don't be afraid to try new things. Don't be afraid to try and fail or make mistakes as long as you learn from the experience. Find something that you are passionate about and are excited about when you get up in the morning.

Jane Houlihan, Environmental Engineer
Vice President for Research, Environmental Working Group
Georgia Institute of Technology, 1987
Major: Civil Engineering

How does your career have an impact on efforts to improve our environment?

It's what I work on all day long. We conduct research to achieve policies that strengthen public health and environmental protections, and our work has helped drive important changes. We are currently working very hard in support of a bill called the Kids Safe Chemical Act that would be the first major reform of our country's 30-year-old toxics law and would for the first time require chemicals to be proven safe for children and other vulnerable populations before they're sold.

How do the environmental issues that our world is facing have an impact on your career?

I am with an organization that works to clean up the environment. I choose research projects that I hope will help solve pressing environmental issues.

What was your first job after graduation?

After graduation, I became an engineer at an environmental consulting firm.

What criteria did you use when deciding which college(s) to apply to?

I looked at published ratings in college guides for engineering programs.

Did you attend your first choice school?

Yes. I was sure of my decision to attend Georgia Institute of Technology.

Did you already have a career in mind when you applied to college?

Yes, but it wasn't related to the career I eventually pursued. I began as a piano performance major, but I'd always loved math and science, and I knew that I could keep music in my life even if it weren't my career. I changed my major to engineering.

Did the school you attended have a significant impact on your career op-portunities?

I switched schools when I changed my major to attend a school with a strong engineering program. But I would say that it did not have a significant impact. What I've observed is that a great school can open doors that would otherwise be closed, but strong grades or experience (and a great cover letter and solid references) can open those doors as well.

Knowing what you know now, which college would you apply to (and why)?

Georgia Tech would still be my top choice, because their blend of the practical and theoretical makes for an easy transition into the real world. I would also consider schools with diverse strengths, like Stanford or the University of Michigan, for example, where strong liberal arts and science/engineering programs give students maximum flexibility.

Which college or colleges are turning out the leaders in your profession today?

Many, but based on recent graduates and faculty I'm familiar with, I'd note in particular the Universities of Illinois, Michigan, and Texas; Stanford; UC Berkeley; and Virginia Tech. And my alma mater, Georgia Tech.

Did you have an "Aha!" moment when you realized what you wanted to do?

I knew I wanted to major in a field that would combine my passion for the environment with my interest in science and problem solving. My "Aha!" moment came when I was trying to figure out what major to declare at Georgia Tech. Reading the detailed curricula for various science and engineering programs, I had a revelation that engineers use science to solve problems in the world, and that civil/environmental engineering would be the perfect fit for my technical skills and my goal to do work that helps protect the environment.

What were your majors in college?

Piano performance, biology, and civil engineering (with a focus on environmental engineering).

Did you change your major? If so, why?

I did change my major. When I looked across my range of interests—everything from music and writing to science, math, the environment, and public policy—I decided that a degree focused on science and math would give me the greatest flexibility for future career paths. I've found ways to keep my other interests in my life, even though they're not part of my official career.

Which classes were most valuable in preparing you for your career or in helping you decide on your career?

I came out of my bachelor's and master's programs with a strong theoretical background in fluid mechanics, chemistry, and materials that has served me well over the years. But other classes that were immediately useful in my career were surprising to me. They included electives I chose that were very practical, like a course that taught us how to comply with EPA regulations in planning Superfund site cleanups; how to design a port (where we solved problems in moving massive amounts of materials and organizing complicated systems with many moving parts); and a class that focused on pulling as much technical information as possible about soils, geology, hydrology, and topography from simple aerial photographs of sites.

I'd also advise any engineering student to focus on building technical writing skills as much as possible. Take writing classes. You can't overestimate how much of your job success will hinge on your skill as a writer, to document what you've done and convince others that your conclusions and recommendations are the right ones. Expect to spend at least half your time as an engineer writing. Learning to do it clearly and effectively while you're in school is a great investment.

How did your professors have an impact on your career choice or preparation?

My professors have played a big role in my career choices. I solicited advice from them on the best companies to work for and the strongest graduate programs to attend. I'd advise any engineering student to do the same. In my department at Georgia Tech, many professors had on-the-ground knowledge of the job market from their own consulting practices and from following the career paths of their graduates. My professors have also been invaluable as references when I've applied for jobs.

Did you have a job and/or internship during college that influenced your career choice or career preparation in any way?

I interned at the Department of Transportation, conducting environmental surveys in advance of proposed construction of new roads and running chemical analyses of stream water in the state lab. It really helped me to gain an understanding of how to look for a workplace filled with talented, goal-oriented, productive people. The perspective that even a little bit of relevant job experience provides is unbeatable. My current job involves hiring newly graduating engineers. I look for students with some job experience, because I've found that what students do in their summers gives clues about their interests, motivation, and the energy and enthusiasm they will bring to a job.

How important was your college experience in getting you to where you are today?

My engineering education included training in a diverse range of sciences. I currently work in the field of environmental and public health research and advocacy, where I do work to advance health and environmental safeguards against industrial chemical pollution. The technical expertise I gained in college is invaluable in my work as an environmental advocate—it allows me to design and conduct analyses and then make arguments that are based on data and facts. It allows me to find gaps in the technical arguments made by "the other side" in debates about environmental cleanups and health standards. I use the knowledge I gained in college every day.

Do you have an advanced degree? Is one helpful or required in your field?

I have a master's degree in civil engineering from Georgia Tech that I received in 1988, and I also completed a postgraduate research fellowship a few years after my master's. It's not required, but it's helpful. A master's degree is the working degree for engineers.

What do you love most about your job?

I love doing work that helps people and protects the environment. I love the diversity in my work—all the jobs I've held over the years have included the practical application of science and math, fun and challenging problem solving, and many opportunities to communicate what is important to me through both writing and public speaking. I also enjoy the people I work with. Despite its reputation, engineering is a very social occupation with a lot of teamwork and opportunities to learn from (and teach) others.

What is the most difficult or challenging aspect of your job?

Most engineers evolve in their careers from doing detailed technical work to managing others who are doing the detailed technical work, and then to overseeing complex projects, departments, or even companies. I've worked hard to add management and communication skills to my repertoire over the years, the things that engineers aren't usually taught in school.

What is the biggest misconception people have about what you do?

I'm an environmental engineer actively involved in environmental advocacy. Our research faces initial skepticism from some people that comes from general impressions about the environmental movement and a misconception that environmentalists can't "do" science. Because of this misconception, our science has to be rock solid.

What was the biggest obstacle you faced in getting to where you are in your career?

I haven't faced big obstacles in my career. But I would advise new engineers to keep building new skills and to make connections with a diverse range of groups and people—these things turn into opportunities.

What skills are an absolute must for someone interested in pursuing your career?

Writing, writing, writing. Public speaking. Project management. Having a team player attitude. An ability and willingness to document your work thoroughly and clearly. Creativity that lets you blow through or go around barriers to solving problems.

Whom do you admire most in your industry/field?

I admire environmental engineers who do research designed to improve people's lives. Think about it: environmental engineers learn how to make water safe to drink, how to reduce and manage waste, how to clean up industrial pollution, and increasingly, how to design in ways that are sustainable. We have tools that are increasingly in demand by companies and governments in many parts of the world.

What is one piece of advice you would give to someone who is interested in pursuing your career?

Do something in your work that you are excited about.

If you could do everything all over again, what would you do differently?

I'd do it all again.

Do you have any additional comments you think might be helpful to someone hoping to pursue your career?

A degree in environmental engineering will give you a diverse range of career options—from industry and government to nonprofit organizations and academia. It's a wide open field, and with growing global awareness of environmental problems, good environmental engineers will always be in demand. It's a career that will give you many opportunities for making a difference.

ENVIRONMENTAL SCIENCE

WHY IT'S GREAT TO BE AN ENVIRONMENTAL SCIENTIST

Environmental scientists are especially keen to conserve our environment. By studying the relationship that people and other living creatures have with the environments in which they live, environmental scientists have an in-depth perspective on what we can all do to help improve and preserve our natural environment.

WHAT ENVIRONMENTAL SCIENTISTS ARE DOING TO PRESERVE AND IMPROVE OUR WORLD

The nature (no pun intended) of being an environmental scientist is to preserve earth's natural resources and populations. These scientists' research and inventions help minimize the effects of pollution of soil, air, and water and make sure that future generations aren't left picking up the pieces. Whether they are studying the effects of pollution on marine life, the changing temperatures of the Arctic waters, or how pesticides affect soil nutrition, environmental scientists have the earth's future in their hands.

SKILLS TO BE A SUCCESSFUL ENVIRONMENTAL SCIENTIST

To be a successful environmental scientist, one must have a passion for the environment. It's not just about hard science and lab research; this work has very real-life applications, so a global interest is key. At the same time, the ability to balance this passion with objectivity, logic, and reason is crucial.

CHALLENGES THAT ENVIRONMENTAL SCIENTISTS FACE

The proliferation of negative environmental issues, such as pollution, the depletion of the ozone layer, and overstressed landfills, means that environmental scientists are under pressure to perform. In addition, when undoing the damage done by generations before, they must also present preventative measures for the future.

HOW CURRENT ENVIRONMENTAL ISSUES AFFECT THE JOB MARKET

Because there are so many pressing environmental issues at hand, environmental scientists will have no trouble finding work. The strong focus on pollution means that scientists might find themselves occasionally working with hazardous materials.

WHERE THE JOBS ARE

Many environmental scientists work for state or local government or in academia, where they conduct their own research while also teaching future generations of environmental scientists. Many environmental scientists work as consultants with businesses and government agencies to ensure they are in compliance with existing environmental policies. A large percentage of jobs are found in the nonprofit environmental sector.

AREAS OF SPECIALTY

There are seemingly limitless areas of specialties for environmental scientists. Some include environmental ecology, environmental chemistry, environmental biology, or forestry science.

EDUCATIONAL REQUIREMENTS

In almost all cases, a bachelor's degree in environmental science or a general science (biology, chemistry, physics, earth science) is enough to garner an entry-level job as an environmental scientist. Those who have not specifically pursued environmental science find it easy to apply the science they have studied to the environment. Upper-level and applied research jobs increasingly require a master's degree in environmental science or in another field of science.

TOP COLLEGES FOR PURSUING A CAREER AS AN ENVIRONMENTAL SCIENTIST

- State University of New York, College of Environmental Science and Forestry
- Rutgers, the State University of New Jersey
- Lewis University

COURSE WORK AND CLASSES TO HELP YOU BECOME AN ENVIRONMENTAL SCIENTIST

Environmental scientists need a strong foundation in the traditional sciences (biology, chemistry, physics, earth science) but also in social sciences. Increasingly, courses in ecology, conservation, and environmental law are important to environmental scientists.

SALARY RANGE

According to the Bureau of Labor Statistics, an environmental scientist can earn anywhere from \$34,000 to \$94,000, depending on experience and other factors.

FAMOUS ENVIRONMENTAL SCIENTISTS

- **Jane Goodall** first started studying chimpanzees in Africa back in 1960. In the last 40-plus years, she has continued to study, write about, and protect chimpanzees and their natural habitats.
- **Aldo Leopold** graduated from Yale Forest School in 1909 and went on to become the founder of the wilderness system in the United States.

WHERE TO LEARN MORE

The National Association of Environmental Professionals
389 Main St., Suite 202
Malden, MA 02148
www.naep.org

Union of Concerned Scientists
2 Brattle Square
Cambridge, MA 02238
www.ucsusa.org

WORDS OF WISDOM

"The key thing for any career choice (including environmental science) is to be sure that it is of interest to you and is fun."

—Virginia Dale, Environmental Scientist

"Follow your passion when deciding on a career."

—Doug Frank, Environmental Scientist

Douglas Frank, Plant/Ecosystem Ecologist
Professor of Biology, Syracuse University
University of Illinois, 1973
Major: Ecology, Ethology, and Evolution

How does your career have an impact on efforts to improve our environment?

I think that the primary influence I have had on improving the environment is through teaching. This impact, I believe, is geometrical, as students that I have hopefully educated about environmental issues educate their friends, and in turn, those individuals educate others, and so on.

My research specifically has been used to develop national park policy and is part of a body of scientific knowledge that has informed other environmental policy makers about the environmental and anthropogenic forces that control terrestrial ecosystems.

How do the environmental issues that our world is facing have an impact on your career?

It has influenced the types of questions that I am seeking to answer with my research. Among these are how management and climate affect terrestrial ecosystem processes and what factors influence soil carbon retention among the different types of North American ecosystems (e.g., desert, grassland, forest, tundra).

What was your first job after graduation?

I was a naturalist for the National Park Service.

What criteria did you use when deciding which college(s) to apply to?

I was undecided about what I wanted to major in, so general strength of academics and breadth of programs and course work mattered to me.

Did you attend your first choice school?

No. My first choice school was Washington University. Although I had been accepted at a number of more expensive, smaller private schools, my decision to go to the University of Illinois was largely based on finances.

Did you already have a career in mind when you applied to college?

No. I knew that I liked biology, in general, but I also had an interest in architecture.

Did the school you attended have an impact on your career opportunities?

Yes. Some early classes in biology, particularly an honors ecology seminar and a course in invertebrate biology, really turned me on to biology. In my junior year, I did some independent research in aquatic ecology that ultimately got me interested in ecology, even though my path would eventually lead me to studying terrestrial ecology. I found that I received a strong foundation in biology. University of Illinois had a good reputation, so when I applied to graduate programs, I benefited from having graduated from the University of Illinois.

Knowing what you know now, which college would you apply to (and why)?

I think that there would be a lot of options to consider. The important features of a school would be good academics, serious students, a wide range in types of biology classes offered, and a program that provides the option to conduct supervised, independent research.

Which college or colleges, are turning out the leaders in your profession today?

Normally, the professor whose lab someone trains in as a graduate student is considered more important than the undergraduate institution, when considering where leading environmental scientists are coming from. There are dozens of labs across the United States and the world that are producing the next generation of leading environmental scientists.

Did you have an "Aha!" moment when you realized what you wanted to do?

Yes. It was on a summer canoe trip in Quetico Provincial Park in Ontario. I was standing out on a rocky point that jutted out into a lake. It was a beautiful morning, and I was listening to loons call from opposite ends of the lake. It was at that point that I realized that I wanted to become a field biologist.

What were your majors in college?

Ecology, ethology, and evolution (one major).

Did you change your major? If so, why?

I did not change my major, but I remained undecided as long as I could so I could weigh my options carefully.

Which classes were most valuable in preparing you for your career or in helping you decide on your career?

The most valuable "class" was an independent research project. This experience made me realize I was interested in research.

How did your professors have an impact on your career choice or preparation?

A number of my professors had an impact on me. Most important were the professors of the relatively small upper-division biology courses that I took and the advisor of my independent research.

Did you have a job and/or internship during college that influenced your career choice or preparation in any way?

Well, I worked at the university bookstore and quickly realized that I was not interested in retail!

How important was your college experience in getting you to where you are today?

I simply would not have received the necessary training if I had not attended the right college.

Do you have an advanced degree? Is one helpful/required in your field?

Yes. I earned a PhD from Syracuse University in 1990. It is a requirement for the type of work I do.

What do you love most about your job?

Pretty much everything. I enjoy teaching undergraduate and graduate students in the classroom, field, and laboratory. I enjoy performing my own research, which includes a diversity of tasks, including the creative part of designing experiments to investigate a question of interest; conducting the experiment, which normally occurs in the field in my case; analyzing the data; writing up the results for publication; and presenting the findings at scientific conferences.

What is the most difficult or challenging aspect of your job?

Probably finding sufficient time for my family and time-demanding job.

What is the biggest misconception people have about what you do?

Probably the fact that science is an incredibly exciting endeavor.

What was the biggest obstacle you faced in getting to where you are in your career?

I really didn't consider it an obstacle, because I was enjoying myself so much, but someone interested in being a college professor has to recognize the years of extra schooling it will take, usually four to six years after receiving a bachelor's degree.

What skills are an absolute must for someone interested in pursuing your career?

Perseverance.

Whom do you admire most in your industry/field?

There are many environmental scientists that I have come to admire for their contributions to science and society.

What is one piece of advice you would give to someone who is interested in pursuing your career?

Conduct some independent research as an undergraduate to see if you would be interested in a career in science.

If you could do everything all over again, what would you do differently?

Certainly there were individual decisions that in retrospect were misjudgments, which is true for anyone. But the major decisions of what schools to go to and what to major in worked out pretty well for me.

Do you have any additional comments you think might be helpful to someone hoping to pursue your career?

Follow your passion when deciding on a career.

Virginia Dale, Environmental Scientist
Corporate Fellow, Oak Ridge National Laboratory
University of Tennessee, 1974
Major: Mathematics

How does your career have an impact on efforts to improve our environment?

Environmental scientists influence how natural resources are managed and help emphasize the need to take the long view relative to our environmental stewardship responsibilities.

My work has influenced decisions made about resource management at the international, national, state, and local levels. It has also had an influence on the development of new fields of study within ecology and new ways to think about how resources are managed.

How do environmental issues that our world is facing have an impact on your career?

Funding usually follows the concerns of the public. Before the concern is generally recognized, it is difficult to obtain research support for what scientists perceive as a new field of concern. In actuality however, the research on a topic usually precedes its being recognized by the public (e.g., research on climate change has been occurring for decades, and now climate change seems to be finally accepted as a reality). What this means is that those of us who are on the cutting edge on new scientific investigations must write many proposals and work hard to obtain research funding.

What was your first job after graduation?

I was a research assistant at Oak Ridge National Laboratory.

What criteria did you use when deciding which college(s) to apply to?

The only criterion I used was finding a school that would accept me. Unfortunately, I let my parents' and friends' opinions have a larger influence than my own perspectives. As a result, I ended up at a junior college that proved to be not suitable for me at all. After one year at the junior college, I transferred to a university. But when I felt my interest in school was lagging, I dropped out for two semesters. When I returned to college, I was paying for it myself. The University of Tennessee (UT) was the only school I could afford to attend (my residency was in that state). I found UT had a great diversity of classes and professors who were highly engaged in learning and teaching. On this second round at college, I was going to school because it was my deliberate choice. I also wanted to be sure that I spent my money wisely. My college and class selection then reflected my desire to make a difference in the world, enjoy my work, and achieve balance in my life.

Did you attend your first choice school?

Yes, I attended my first choice, but I transferred after one year.

Did you already have a career in mind when you applied to college?

I had no specific career ideas, but I did know that I was interested in mathematics.

Did the school you attended have an impact on your career opportunities?

The junior college that I first attended had a large impact, because it was immediately clear that I was not challenged there and that they did not have many courses in my main area of interest (mathematics). I transferred to a university after my first year, and the university from which I ultimately graduated had a large impact on my career opportunities. Professors at that university were interested in developing a graduate program in a field of great interest to me. They asked me to stay on at the university to attend graduate school and be the first graduate student in that new program.

Knowing what you know now, which college would you apply to (and why)?

If I knew my career interest, then I would probably apply to a small college that has a focus on that topic. If I did not know my career interest, then I would likely select a university that would allow me flexibility in exploring fields of interests.

Which college or colleges are turning out the leaders in your profession today?

There are lots of small colleges and large universities turning out leaders in the field of environmental sciences. The diversity of colleges producing leaders relates to the diversity of backgrounds of environmental scientists. The background of leading environmental scientists includes ecology, soil science, chemistry, physics, geology, forestry, agriculture, botany, zoology, microbiology, and hydrology.

The field of ecology is very diverse, and there are so many excellent institutions. When I look at lists online and in books of colleges that offer classes in ecology and environmental science, I find that many excellent schools are not included. The best advice I can give is to talk with many recent graduates and people who are doing work that seems of interest and ask them about their experience at particular schools. Visiting the colleges and meeting the professors is very helpful as well. Summer jobs during high school can make this decision clearer.

Did you have an "Aha!" moment when you realized what you wanted to do?

When taking a required science class at the university, I heard the words *mathematical ecology* and became entranced. I walked out of that classroom and asked a math professor what this field was. That question resulted in me being the only student in a class called mathematical ecology. Using mathematical tools to understand ecological relationships was immediately appealing and eventually became the focus of my career.

What was your major in college?

I started in mathematics but switched to a joint major in math/sociology/political science.

Did you change your major? If so, why?

As I became uninterested in school, I realized that I could graduate earlier with a different major and subsequently had a joint major approved in math/sociology/political science. However, I soon realized that the problem was not my field of study but rather my lack of interest in school. Therefore, I dropped out of college for two semesters and when I returned took up my math major once again.

Which classes were most valuable in preparing you for your career or in helping you decide on your career?

An introductory philosophy course introduced me to logic. A political science class in public administration helped me understand how organizations work (and don't work).

All of my math classes demonstrated the value of carefully documenting each step and not skipping steps. In other words, they demonstrated the approach of a careful researcher.

My first ecology class introduced me to a whole new field of study and got me tremendously interested in the fun of learning about the interconnections of life.

How did your professors have an impact on your career choice or preparation?

My most influential and helpful professors were those who took the time to help me with individual instruction. The professor with whom I took the class in mathematical ecology had a big effect on my career. Also, the professor who taught my first ecology class had a big impact, for he introduced me to the interesting entanglements of ecology.

Did you have a job and/or internship during college that influenced your career choice or career preparation?

I had a summer job at a hospital where I passed instruments in the operating room. That job introduced me to the strong hierarchy of the workplace. I remember that no one ever asked me if I wanted to be a doctor, but lots of people asked if I wanted to a nurse. Also, I enjoyed reading the medical textbooks but was discouraged from doing so. These experiences influenced my rebellious nature to seek for something more.

During college, I also worked in the bookstore and then was a waitress, but gave up that relatively lucrative occupation to grade math papers (for 50 cents per hour). The change from being a waitress to grading papers was a career decision, for it let me get to know my professors better and made sure that I knew the subject matter.

How important was your college experience in getting you to where you are today?

I was not very interested in school or in a career until after starting college. I felt that I was doing what other people expected of me. It was in college that I found my own path and interests.

Do you have an advanced degree? Is one helpful or required in your field?

I obtained an MS in mathematics with a minor in ecology from the University of Tennessee in 1975. My PhD in mathematical ecology (a special program that I developed with the approval of the graduate school) is from the University of Washington in 1980. This degree is both helpful and needed at my level of work. It lets me be a principal investigator on proposals and gives me instant recognition as being an expert in my field.

What do you love most about your job?

Getting to learn new things and figuring out how the pieces fit together to instigate change.

What is the most difficult or challenging aspect of your job?

There is always too much to do in my job, so I must constantly set my own priorities. I love the challenges of science, and my favorite quote is: "Basic research is what I do when I don't know what I am doing." (Wernher von Braun)

What is the biggest misconception people have about what you do?

People confuse being an environmental scientist with being an environmental activist.

What was the biggest obstacle you faced in getting to where you are in your career?

Maintaining a positive balance in my personal life and career. I am still working on this. I think about this need for balance a lot and deliberately do things to seek that balance. For example, when I am I not traveling, I never work in the evenings and almost always have dinner with my family. Instead, I often get up early and work when my family is sleeping.

What skills are an absolute must for someone interested in pursuing your career?

Having in-depth skills in one area is essential for environmental scientists, but the choice of that field of specialization may differ from person to person. My in-depth skill is mathematical ecology, but other environmental scientists have strong skills in all kinds of other subdisciplines in ecology.

Whom do you admire most in your industry/field?

My friend and colleague Monica Turner, for she is at the top of her field, is raising two well-rounded children, and does a good job of maintaining her balance among career, family, and community interests.

What is one piece of advice you would give to someone who is interested in pursuing your career?

Be persistent.

If you could do everything all over again, what would you do differently?

I would have focused more on my college choice and possible career interests when I was in high school and while selecting a college.

Do you have any additional comments you think might be helpful to someone hoping to pursue your career?

The key thing for any career choice is to be sure that it is of interest to you and is fun.

GEOTHERMAL DEVELOPMENT

WHY IT'S GREAT TO BE A GEOTHERMAL DEVELOPER

Renewable energy sources seem to be gaining in popularity by the day. As more people realize that fossil fuel and other nonrenewable resources are only getting more harmful, more limited, and more expensive, it's just a matter of time before the whole world looks at geothermal energy.

WHAT GEOTHERMAL DEVELOPERS ARE DOING TO PRESERVE AND IMPROVE OUR WORLD

Geothermal energy is produced naturally by hot water reserves beneath the earth's surface. Hot water reservoirs can provide heat to residential and commercial properties, but very hot (225 to 600 degrees Fahrenheit, according to TechValleyCareers.org) water reservoirs can produce enough energy to run an electricity turbine. This use of a natural, renewable resource minimizes pollution and ozone damage.

SKILLS TO BE A SUCCESSFUL GEOTHERMAL DEVELOPER

Geothermal developers must be experts in existing technology but also must forge ahead with new advances so that the industry does not face the slump it did in the 1990s. In addition to having strong math and science skills, geothermal developers must be adept with computers (for modeling purposes) and machinery (used in geothermal energy plants).

CHALLENGES THAT GEOTHERMAL DEVELOPERS FACE

If drilling into the center of the earth to tap geothermal energy sources was easy, it would have been done a long time ago. In fact, drilling isn't that easy. And even when the technology is available, drilling a massive hole isn't done without research and impact studies by environmental scientists and other geology professionals. Also, while this is a growing field, it is still somewhat nascent, and only a limited number of jobs are available.

HOW CURRENT ENVIRONMENTAL ISSUES AFFECT THE JOB MARKET

As the costs and negative effects of traditional, nonrenewable energy sources increase, citizens and companies alike are pursuing renewable energy sources, such as geothermal energy. The increased demand for geothermal energy means that the job market for developers is on the rise.

WHERE THE JOBS ARE

Geothermal developers are especially in demand where there are large underground hot water reservoirs—typically in less developed areas of the western and middle United States. However, the future of geothermal energy lies in tapping reservoirs deep beneath the earth's surface, which means that everywhere in the country could be developed for geothermal use. According to the Geothermal Energy Association, most geothermal employees are concentrated in one of ten companies, and most geothermal firms tend to be very small. About one in four geothermal employees is an independent contractor.

AREAS OF SPECIALTY

The process of tapping geothermal energy means that developers can be focused on the geology of the land being accessed or on the engineering aspects of creating a pathway to the reservoirs.

EDUCATIONAL REQUIREMENTS

Although a bachelor's degree is essential for most entry-level geothermal jobs, an advanced degree, such as a master's or PhD, is required for most mid- to high-level jobs. Years of on-the-job experience can supplant the need for an advanced degree.

TOP COLLEGES FOR PURSUING A CAREER AS A GEOTHERMAL DEVELOPER

- Stanford University
- Southern Methodist University (SMU)
- Massachusetts Institute of Technology (MIT)

COURSE WORK AND CLASSES TO HELP YOU BECOME A GEOTHERMAL DEVELOPER

Geothermal developers need to have a broad exposure to many fields. This includes geology, geophysics, geochemistry, and engineering.

SALARY RANGE

There are no national statistics on salary ranges, but geothermal developers with both high levels of education and experience can earn over $100,000.

FAMOUS GEOTHERMAL DEVELOPERS

- Frenchman **Francois de Larderel** so impressed Leopold II, the Grand Duke of Tuscany, that the town of Montecerboli was renamed Larderello in honor of the man whose innovations led to the world's first demonstration of geothermal energy in 1904.
- **The Geysers** in California is famous for being the first commercial geothermal energy plant in the United States. The Geysers, which opened in 1960, is still in operation today.

WHERE TO LEARN MORE

Geothermal Energy Association
209 Pennsylvania Ave. S.E.
Washington, DC 20003
www.geo-energy.org

International Geothermal Association
c/o Samorka
Sudurlandsbraut 48
108 Reykjavik
Iceland
http://iga.igg.cnr.it/index.php

U.S. Department of Energy
1000 Independence Ave. S.W.
Washington, DC 20585
www.energy.gov

WORDS OF WISDOM

"It is more important to know about the earth, geology, and geography than to know about renewable energy from a business standpoint if you want to do research or exploration."

—Maria Richards, Geothermal Researcher

"Study hard, be tenacious, gain new experiences, and keep learning!"

—Curt Robinson,
Geothermal Resources Director

Maria Richards, Geothermal Researcher
Southern Methodist University (SMU) Geothermal Lab Coordinator
Michigan State University, 1986
Major: Physical Geography

How does your career have an impact on efforts to improve our environment?

Geothermal energy is able to produce electricity without all the fossil fuel contamination of the air and damage to the earth. Also, geothermal heat pumps are able to reduce the need for electricity by using the ground temperature to heat or cool a building.

How do the environmental issues that our world is facing have an impact on your career?

There are more people interested in geothermal since it is a clean technology.

What was your first job after graduation?

I worked with the Student Conservation Association.

What criteria did you use when deciding which college(s) to apply to?

Experience of faculty, size of school, reputation.

Did you attend your first choice school?

Yes.

Did you already have a career in mind when you applied to college?

Yes, but it changed over the years.

Did the school you attended have a significant impact on your career op-portunities?

Yes, it opened up new opportunities for travel, and it broadened my skill base, giving me greater opportunities to sell myself to employers.

Knowing what you know now, which college would you apply to (and why)?

I would choose Michigan State again for my undergraduate degree, since it has strong programs with the advantages of a large school, but the geography program is small within it. If I lived in the South, I would have considered the University of Tennessee. It's a growing program with dynamic faculty.

Which college or colleges, are turning out the leaders in your profession today?

Michigan State University, University of Tennessee—Knoxville, University of Wisconsin, and University of Texas—Austin.

Did you have an "Aha!" moment when you realized what you wanted to do?

Not really. Just more finding out that geography had many more aspects to it than just maps and traveling. That part was exciting since it allowed me to use my outdoor interest in a professional way.

What were your majors in college?

I started with biochemical engineering, then math education, and finally geography.

Did you change your major? If so, why?

I did change majors. I was going to be a math teacher but decided I didn't like the slow pace of classrooms.

Which classes were most valuable in preparing you for your career or in helping you decide on your career?

Math, environmental studies, and all of my geography classes.

How did your professors have an impact on your career choice or preparation?

At Michigan State, Professor Duke Winters is the reason I really went on to get a master's degree. He also taught geomorphology, which was by far my favorite class and one of the hardest.

Did you have a job and/or internship during college?

I worked at the Michigan Department of Natural Resources and on campus in the cafeterias.

Did any of them influence your ultimate career choice or career preparation in any way?

It was very helpful to have done fieldwork with the Michigan Department of Natural Resources and to learn computer programs. My DNR position is still very helpful to me today. It is very helpful to remember what it's like to be a student worker since I have student employees working on geothermal projects in the lab.

How important was your college experience in getting you to where you are today?

Without college my career would not be possible. I learned about the earth, resources, computers, writing skills, research, how to give speeches, etc.

Do you have an advanced degree? Is one helpful or required in your field?

I have a master's of science in physical geography from the University of Tennessee—Knoxville. With a strong undergraduate degree, a person could get into the field, but to be a researcher or leader, they need to have at least a master's degree.

What do you love most about your job?

The variability.

What is the most difficult or challenging aspect of your job?

Timelines, and the need to keep writing proposals to support research.

What is the biggest misconception people have about what you do?

They don't usually know what geothermal is, so just the topic sounds "really scientific" to them.

What was the biggest obstacle you faced in getting to where you are in your career?

Being confident in myself. As a geographer, you need to be able to sell yourself, since most companies are not looking for a geographer. I used networking to get positions.

What skills are an absolute must for someone interested in pursuing your career?

Computer skills, math skills, and a willingness to work with the public are important.

Whom do you admire most in your industry/field?

Dave Blackwell: He has spent 40 years working on geothermal development, and even after all this time, he still has much enthusiasm and interest in the field. He genuinely cares about the profession and about the future of the geothermal industry.

What is one piece of advice you would give to someone who is interested in pursuing your career?

Geothermal research, like most research, has different aspects to it. Find the one that is of interest to you, not just what is popular. Also, be creative and flexible in the job because it changes with each new grant contract.

If you could do everything all over again, what would you do differently?

I would travel more in my 30s because the older you get, the harder it is to get away from work and your responsibilities.

Do you have any additional comments you think might be helpful to someone hoping to pursue your career?

It is more important to know about the earth, geology, and geography than to know about renewable energy from a business standpoint if you want to do research or exploration.

Curt Robinson, Educator
Executive Director, Geothermal Resources Council
University of California—Davis, 1974
Major: Geography and History

How does your career have an impact on efforts to improve our environment?

Geothermal energy is a clean, constant, and renewable form of energy. It is indigenous and readily available here in the United States. Having a diverse energy portfolio is part of the solution to our dependence on fossil fuels.

How do the environmental issues that our world is facing have an impact on your career?

The growing awareness of global climate change and the probable causes suggest that a diversified and renewable energy portfolio is one of the most important issues facing humans today. Because energy drives economies and probably contributes to global climate change, geothermal energy is becoming recognized as an important source of power.

What was your first job after graduation?

I was an accountant/auditor for ITT.

What criteria did you use when deciding which college(s) to apply to?

Location and breadth of programs.

Did you attend your first choice school?

Yes, I wanted to attend the University of California.

Did you already have a career in mind when you applied to college?

Yes, I thought that I wanted to become an attorney—until other opportunities opened up.

Did the school you attended have a significant impact on your career op-portunities?

Yes, I ended up taking classes in the humanities, classics, art, etc. These classes, and more importantly, these professors shaped my thinking and critical reasoning abilities. I had great opportunities at this university. I was elected to student government, was editor-in-chief of the daily newspaper, and served as a grader my senior year. Each experience had a profound impact upon me.

Knowing what you know now, which college would you apply to (and why)?

I would probably do the same, although I probably would have taken some classes at UC—Berkeley and perhaps participated in the study abroad program.

Which college or colleges are turning out the leaders in your profession today?

Stanford, MIT, University of Nevada—Reno, and Southern Methodist University.

Did you have an "Aha!" moment when you realized what you wanted to do?

No, I'd worked in higher education and government and had served on several boards, and this opportunity presented itself, synthesizing my experience and education.

What was your major in college?

History, with a minor in art history.

Did you change your major? If so, why?

No, I really loved history. It provided a context for exploring science and the world of ideas. However, in graduate school, I changed my emphasis from history to geography.

Which classes were most valuable in preparing you for your career or in helping you decide on your career?

Classes that encouraged critical thinking—rhetoric and art history. Critical thinking has proved to be a far better resource than rote memorization and passing tests.

How did your professors have an impact on your career choice or preparation?

Both the rhetorician and art historian who taught me were instrumental in encouraging critical thinking.

Did you have a job and/or internship during college that influenced your ultimate career choice or career preparation in any way?

Yes, I was editor-in-chief of my college daily newspaper; I also worked as a grader for an upper-division class. I have always gravitated to public education and public service.

How important was your college experience in getting you to where you are today?

I studied at a land-grant university, where public service is emphasized. The university was large enough to enable a broad array of educational experiences.

Do you have an advanced degree? Is one helpful or required in your field?

At UC—Davis, I received MA and PhD degrees in geography. Geography is a great discipline because it blends environmental science with human activity on this planet. It is especially meaningful today. It is absolutely helpful to have a degree in this field because it is so tied to the earth and environmental sciences.

What do you love most about your job?

The variety, and contributing to the greater public good. Geothermal energy is part of the solution to the United States' energy needs. It is also part of the solution for other countries' energy needs for their developing economies.

What is the most difficult or challenging aspect of your job?

This is a multifaceted job with many dimensions. It requires a jack-of-all-trades to be successful. You have to have management experience, government experience, a background in the earth sciences, writing and publishing experience, etc.

What is the biggest misconception people have about what you do?

Geothermal energy is fairly abstract in comparison to other renewables. Also, I head up an educational and scientific organization—not a lobbying group.

What was the biggest obstacle you faced in getting to where you are in your career?

Not sure, although it takes time to develop the variety of skills and breadth of experience that this job requires. I had a diverse and multifaceted career in higher education and government, which helped me to develop the skills necessary to be successful.

What skills are an absolute must for someone interested in pursuing your career?

It is critical to have interest and experience in science and public policy.

Whom do you admire most in your industry/field?

There are many people I admire.

What is one piece of advice you would give to someone who is interested in pursuing your career?

Develop broad interests beyond your major. Read.

If you could do everything all over again, what would you do differently?

Take more geography and geology classes, and I would study more science.

Do you have any additional comments you think might be helpful to someone hoping to pursue your career?

Study hard, be tenacious, gain new experiences, and keep learning!

GREEN INTERIOR DESIGN

WHY IT'S GREAT TO BE A GREEN INTERIOR DESIGNER

Like traditional interior designers, green practitioners of this profession work with colors, fabrics, textures, lighting, and furniture to create a space that meets both the functional and aesthetic needs of the client. However, green interior designers have the added benefit of knowing their designs promote environmental sustainability.

WHAT GREEN INTERIOR DESIGNERS ARE DOING TO PRESERVE AND IMPROVE OUR WORLD

Gone are the days when homeowners lacquered their homes with lead paint and filled their living rooms with toxin-emitting furniture made from virgin materials. Green interior designers, especially those accredited with Leadership in Energy and Environmental Design (LEED) by the U.S. Green Building Council, are more attuned to environmental sustainability and eco-friendly practices.

SKILLS TO BE A SUCCESSFUL GREEN INTERIOR DESIGNER

Green interior designers have to have the same creative design vision as traditional interior designers. They also need to have strong listening skills (helpful when working with clients) and the ability to manage their time and their client's money. In addition, when working with architects, they must be able to read blueprints and be up-to-date on building codes and other environmental policies.

CHALLENGES THAT GREEN INTERIOR DESIGNERS FACE

Although the products available are better than ever, there is still a challenge in making environmentally friendly products as good as their nongreen counterparts. For example, nontoxic paints might not have the same durability as traditional paints. In addition, environmentally friendly products tend to be more expensive, which can cause difficulties when staying within a strict budget.

HOW CURRENT ENVIRONMENTAL ISSUES AFFECT THE JOB MARKET

Although the environment is no doubt an important concern for everyone, not all clients have sustainability on the top of their list of priorities when remodeling or planning a space. Still, in the best interest of a client's health, green designers have a responsibility to create a toxin-free space and to use recyclable or sustainable materials whenever possible.

WHERE THE JOBS ARE

The field of interior design offers a lot of employment variety. Some designers choose to work freelance, some establish their own firms, and others work for large design firms. Jobs are found throughout the country, although large cities are likely to be home to large design firms.

AREAS OF SPECIALTY

Green interior designers may choose to specialize in residential interior design or commercial/industrial interior design. Some interior designers work specifically in health care settings. Other specializations may include home offices, elder design, or even something as specific as home theaters.

EDUCATIONAL REQUIREMENTS

According to the *Occupational Outlook Handbook*, there are 145 accredited interior design bachelor's programs in the United States. Although in some cases an associate's degree or certification is enough to earn an entry-level position, most jobs require a bachelor's degree. After graduation, hopefuls must complete a one- to three-year apprenticeship and, depending on the state, then become licensed. Professional associations, accreditations, and other certifications all bolster a designer's employability.

TOP COLLEGES FOR PURSUING A CAREER AS A GREEN INTERIOR DESIGNER

- Carnegie Mellon
- Boston Architectural College (BAC)
- New York School of Interior Design

COURSE WORK AND CLASSES TO HELP YOU BECOME A GREEN INTERIOR DESIGNER

Standard interior design courses, including computer-aided design (CAD), are plenty to get someone started. However, those who want to distinguish themselves as green should look into courses on sustainability and renewable resources, and they should pursue LEED accreditation.

SALARY RANGE

According to the Bureau of Labor Statistics, interior designers can earn anywhere from $24,000 to $78,000 or more. Those with LEED accreditation or other specialization can earn more for their services.

FAMOUS GREEN INTERIOR DESIGNERS

- *House Beautiful* magazine recently named **Jessica Helgerson** one of the top 25 young designers in the United States. Not only that, her firm's website features extensive information on green design and materials.
- **Bridget Dunn** was just a student at Florida State University when her design won the prestigious "Best of Competition" acknowledgment from the International Interior Design Association's annual sustainable design contest.

WHERE TO LEARN MORE

American Society of Interior Designers
608 Massachusetts Ave. N.E.
Washington, DC 20002
www.asid.org

The Interior Design Society
3910 Tinsley Dr., Suite 101
High Point, NC 27265
www.interiordesignsociety.org

International Interior Design Association (IIDA)
222 Merchandise Mart Plaza, Suite 567
Chicago, IL 60654
www.iida.org

U.S. Green Building Council (LEED accreditation)
1800 Massachusetts Ave. N.W., Suite 300
Washington, DC 20036
www.usgbc.org

WORDS OF WISDOM

"The home is a mirror of self and should be a nurturing, loving environment, so everyone should cultivate a healthy lifestyle—body, mind, and spirit—in order to live our greatest and highest potential. Cultivate self-honor, respect, gratitude, humility…and a good sense of humor!"

—Cheryl Terrace, Green Interior Designer

"There is a true need for more people who are willing to dedicate their lives to this, the ultimate cause. It's also a field where one person can make an immediate and positive impact."

—Elizabeth Gruben,
Green Building Consultant

Elizabeth Gruben, Green Building Consultant
Project Consultant
The Art Institute Online, 2007
Major: Interior Design

How does your career have an impact on efforts to improve our environment?

It's green building consulting. Buildings have a large impact on the environment. We can actually repair most of the damage we have done over the last 100 years or so—simply by building smarter and consuming less.

How do the environmental issues that our world is facing have an impact on your career?

All of us that provide green building consulting (at least that I know) would love to work ourselves out of a job. Unfortunately, that will probably not happen in my lifetime.

What was your first job after graduation?

I was a green building consultant.

What criteria did you use when deciding which college(s) to apply to?

I needed an intense program that would provide the opportunity to work on several diverse projects and work with architects who were knowledgeable and interested in green building.

Did you attend your first choice school?

Yes.

Did you already have a career in mind when you applied to college?

Yes.

Did the school you attended have a significant impact on your career op-portunities?

Yes. Because it was so intense and there was more focus than usual on the structural aspects of interior design, it helped tremendously in attaining this position.

Knowing what you know now, which college would you apply to (and why)?

The very same one. I got the education I needed and wanted along with the convenience of online courses.

Which college or colleges are turning out the leaders in your profession today?

My profession is a new one, but I think University of Virginia (UVA) might be one and Carnegie Mellon, as well as Boston Architectural College (BAC).

Did you have an "Aha!" moment when you realized what you wanted to do?

Yes. I was attending an American Society of Interior Designers (ASID) meeting where there was a panel discussion on Leadership in Energy and Environmental Design (LEED), and I realized that I wanted to help to educate builders and architects in green building to help with the climate change crisis.

What were your majors in college?

Media arts and animation (BFA), interior design (BFA), interior design (BS).

Did you change your major? If so, why?

Yes. I was originally in a BFA program for media arts and animation. I later realized that I wanted to move into architecture, so I changed after the first two years. Then, I changed to a BS so that I would get more science of building (physics, structural design).

Which classes were most valuable in preparing you for your career or in helping you decide on your career?

LEED commercial interiors, green building, geometry, physics.

Did any of your professors have an impact on your career choice or preparation?

They all did. Most of them were at least interested, and many knew quite a bit about green building. They allowed me to make every project center around sustainable design.

Did you have a job and/or internship during college that influenced your career choice or career preparation in any way?

The job I have now was actually an internship that was supposed to be temporary but turned into a "real" job when my internship was completed.

How important was your college experience in getting you to where you are today?

It helped, but also designing my own green home (completion targeted for spring '08) was important. I also have been an involved environmentalist.

Do you have an advanced degree? Is one helpful or required in your field?

I am currently working on an MFA in interior architecture from The Academy of Art University and a graduate certificate in sustainable design from Boston Architectural College. Absolutely, it is helpful. It is not required, but most of us who don't have one yet are working on one. I expect that my graduate certificate in sustainable building will help more than the master's degree.

What do you love most about your job?

Helping clients change the world in a positive way.

What is the most difficult or challenging aspect of your job?

Greening specs for large commercial projects. It's very tedious and time-consuming but quite important.

What is the biggest misconception people have about what you do?

Not sure. Maybe that it's not as complicated as it is.

What was the biggest obstacle you faced in getting to where you are in your career?

Knowing where to start or who to call. I made a lucky guess, and my timing just happened to be right.

What skills are an absolute must for someone interested in pursuing your career?

Understanding how buildings are put together and all the ways that it can adversely impact the planet if done carelessly.

Whom do you admire most in your industry/field?

My immediate supervisor and the owner of our firm. They are two women who have been pioneers in the business of green building consulting before it was the trending topic. They continue to learn more and are generous with their time and knowledge.

What is one piece of advice you would give to someone who is interested in pursuing your career?

Learn all you can about buildings and green materials and ways that building systems can work together for higher performance and low environmental impact.

If you could do everything all over again, what would you do differently?

Not a thing.

Do you have any additional comments you think might be helpful to someone hoping to pursue your career?

You don't have to have an interior design degree, but anything that helps you understand the built environment is a must. There are also peripheral jobs in the industry. There is a true need for more people who are willing to dedicate their lives to this, the ultimate cause. It's also a career where one person can make an immediate and positive impact.

Cheryl Terrace, Interior Designer
President and Founder, Vital Design Ltd.
New York School of Interior Design (NYSID), 1998
Major: Design

How does your career have an impact on efforts to improve our environment?

I founded Vital Design Ltd. as an alternative to regular design practices in 1997—before all the green buzz. Vital is all about healthy client and planet choices, doing things more mindfully, and giving back—with fair trade, working with the right people and elements—sort of like the organic food movement for the home.

How do the environmental issues that our world is currently facing have an impact on your career?

I have always been an environmentalist. I have not eaten meat in over 25 years, do yoga daily, and have always considered the environment in my day-to-day choices—be it recycling, not buying plastic packaging, whatever. Everything that everyone luckily is now talking about has been a norm for me. I am thrilled that eco-awareness has exploded and that people now consider how simple, mundane choices, from the food they eat to what they drive, make a huge impact on one another and the world. Again, just how everything is interconnected. I am so happy to get off the soapbox! Actually, I have been off for a long time—it was too exhausting trying to change the world!

What was your first job after graduation?

I was a salesperson at Domain.

What criteria did you use when deciding which college(s) to apply to?

Location (NYC) and student-to-faculty ratio.

Did you attend your first choice school?

Yes, NYSID is the premier place to study interior design, with its great location, superb facilities, distinguished faculty, as well as its challenging and comprehensive curriculum that gives emphasis to both residential and contract design.

Did you already have a career in mind when you applied to college?

Not the first time. I went to Kean University for psychology and then (after a marriage) NYSID.

Did the school you attended have a significant impact on your career op-portunities?

NYSID's focus is solely interior design. Unfortunately, at the time, there were no "green-eco-environmental" studies available; now more schools are incorporating those studies into their curriculums—which I think is terrific and necessary.

Knowing what you know now, which college would you apply to (and why)?

Perhaps going back in time, the Rhode Island School of Design—it's a very hip school doing some progressive thinking. I would have fit in perfectly there.

Which college or colleges are turning out the leaders in your profession today?

In the world of design, it is more about application than school necessarily—and a good internship or learning by working with an established designer/decorator.

Did you have an "Aha!" moment when you realized what you wanted to do?

After renovating a house for myself (and my husband at the time), I realized I was really good at all the details and design decisions. It was after my divorce and soul-searching that I got a chance to ask myself, "What do you want to be when you grow up?" I enrolled in a few classes and VOILA! I realized now that this is what I am supposed to be doing! I loved every minute of school and could very well be a perpetual student.

What was your major in college?

At NYSID, the curriculum for a degree in design means there is only one major, although there are many courses.

Did you change your major?

No, because I went to a school that is specifically focused on interior design.

Which classes were most valuable in preparing you for your career or in helping you decide on your career?

A design degree exposes one to the artistic and varied elements of design, art, drawing, drafting, furniture history (which is called "historical styles" and which I referred to as "hysterical styles" because it is a very condensed timeline of the history of furniture). I loved the architectural courses and more of the abstract-thinking professors. They made me realize it was okay not be part of the mainstream thinkers, which being one of the first greenies, I certainly wasn't!

How did your professors have an impact on your career choice or preparation?

An art instructor named Bill Engel was incredibly inspirational. He exposed us to thinking outside the box. He understood me, and I will never forget the day he took me to the library and showed me architectural books by Zaha Hadid and Frank Gehry that blew my mind (in a good way).

Did you have a job and/or internship during college that influenced your career choice or career preparation in any way?

I had many. Since I was paying for school myself, I gained credits by doing all the extracurricular activities that I could. I bartended at events, was a tour guide at new buildings, and did anything to help with the cost. It also exposed me to wonderful designers and gave me the chance to see some great places behind the scenes.

I also worked with Larry Laslo for seven years and learned tremendously from that experience. Larry Laslo had just completed Takashimaya on Fifth Avenue, and it is still one of the most beautiful department stores in the United States. He has very high-profile clientele, and I worked as his right-hand person and saw every aspect of the design machine. That gave me invaluable experience.

I learned very high-end design from Larry and also how to deal with very demanding clients. He is not particularly an environmentalist, so we would have fun "discussions" on that front. When I incorporated Vital Design Ltd., I was still working with Larry, and it was not a conflict because his clients were not the types of people (way back in 1997) who would care so much about the eco-friendly aspects of things—it just wasn't the vogue.

How important was your college experience in getting you to where you are today?

Design school does not prepare you to deal with clients (one of the most important aspects of the business) or how to run a business—believe it or not! That is why it is so important to learn from someone and why some of the bigger-name design folks have/had a parent in the business.

Do you have an advanced degree? Is one helpful/required in your field?

No. It is not required—some of the top designers are decorators without any design schooling. Just right place, right time (along with hard work, people skills, knowing the right people, etc.). I believe that the "school of experience" is most important.

What do you love most about your job?

The freedom of time and quality of life I am able to have by making my own schedule. Dealing with wonderful people who are so appreciative of what I do for them—which is create a beautiful and healthy home environment for themselves and their loved ones.

What is the most difficult or challenging aspect of your job?

Paperwork, bookkeeping, and the million details involved in the simplest of design decisions. Also time frame (lead times) to get items and everything done.

What is the biggest misconception people have about what you do?

How glamorous they think it is! They have little idea of all the behind-the-scenes details it takes. Along with all the things that go wrong. Miscommunications, so many people involved who have their own agenda and egos—also, construction sites can be dangerous and dirty! Also, I am schlepping stuff all the time. I refer to myself as "sherpa design" when I am toting stone, carpeting, fabrics—you name it!

What was the biggest obstacle you faced in getting to where you are in your career?

Being one of the first green designers when no one knew or understood what green meant! I used to have people think I designed green (as in the color) interiors! And trying to explain what healthy design is to the uninitiated can be challenging because it is so complex.

I refer to what I do as "thoughtful design." It is something that I believe in as the only way to do things—I look at things a little more in-depth in terms of how the health of the client is affected by what I specify, as well as the health of the planet. Luckily, the rest of the world has caught on. Thank you, Al Gore!

What skills are an absolute must for someone interested in pursuing your career?

Yoga (kidding, but I do believe that my dedicated yoga practice helps me deal with all of the crazy aspects of the job—demands, personalities, and challenges of this business) and good communication skills. Regarding the eco aspect (which is the future after all), a respect and understanding of how everything is interconnected in nature (and with one another). Good basic design knowledge is also helpful!

Whom do you admire most in your industry/field?

I think Axel Vervoordt is brilliant because of the way he puts a space together—it truly is timeless, not trendy, which ultimately is the most environmentally friendly way to design.

What is one piece of advice you would give to someone who is interested in pursuing your career?

Have patience, do it because you love it, learn all that you can from many sources—art, fashion, culture. Our homes should not be isolated environments but nurturing and loving havens.

If you could do everything all over again, what would you do differently?

I see that every decision brings you to where you are now, which is the place you are supposed to be. In New York, so many people rush around to get nowhere and lose the present moment, which is called life. So this is a difficult question for me—the "should have, would have, could have" place goes against my belief system.

Do you have any additional comments you think might be helpful to someone hoping to pursue your career?

What I do has become so much more than just designing a beautiful space for a person to live in. I have become (like it or not) somewhat of a healthy lifestyle guru. Home is a mirror of self and should be a nurturing, loving environment, so everyone should cultivate a healthy lifestyle—body, mind, and spirit—in order to live our greatest and highest potential (if you could put this into words without sounding trite). Cultivate self-honor, respect, gratitude, humility…and a good sense of humor!

HYDROLOGY

WHY IT'S GREAT TO BE A HYDROLOGIST

We all take for granted that when we turn on the tap, fresh, drinkable water will be there. However, it's hydrologists we have to thank for getting it there. Hydrologists study the earth's water—both on the surface and underground. They study how and where water flows and aim to minimize the spread of pollution and minimize damage caused by floods and other water-related disasters.

WHAT HYDROLOGISTS ARE DOING TO PRESERVE AND IMPROVE OUR WORLD

Although oil receives the most media attention in discussions about limited resources, it's really water that we cannot live without. By studying water's movements, its cycles, and its travels through the earth, hydrologists are working to preserve this precious resource for future generations.

SKILLS TO BE A SUCCESSFUL HYDROLOGIST

Because so much of hydrology relies on computer-generated models, it is essential for hydrologists to have excellent computer skills. Hydrologists also use several sensitive pieces of equipment, so they must be able to learn how to use these tools accurately. In addition, hydrologists must be able to work well in teams and be able to convey their thoughts in writing.

CHALLENGES THAT HYDROLOGISTS FACE

Hydrologists who are completing hands-on work in the field (typically entry-level hydrologists) must be able to meet the sometimes challenging physical demands of the work. In addition, as technology improves rapidly, hydrologists must be able to adapt to new equipment and be able to incorporate new technology into their practice.

HOW CURRENT ENVIRONMENTAL ISSUES AFFECT THE JOB MARKET

By studying how pollutants make their way through the ground into our water supplies, hydrologists can develop ways to prevent this from happening. In addition, as hydrologists understand how water (contaminated or otherwise) can travel globally through currents or precipitation, they can find ways to contain pollution and conserve this precious resource as best as possible.

WHERE THE JOBS ARE

Hydrologists can be found throughout the United States. Most hydrologists work as consultants for various water and other environmental firms. In 2006, 28 percent of the nation's hydrologists were employed by the federal government. Another 21 percent worked for state governments. Only a very small number of hydrologists are self-employed.

AREAS OF SPECIALTY

Typically, hydrologists fall into two areas of specialty: underground water or surface water. However, some hydrologists focus on both areas in their careers.

EDUCATIONAL REQUIREMENTS

You typically need at least a master's degree to pursue a career in hydrology. That said, water treatment facilities typically hire people who have a bachelor's in a hydrology-related field.

TOP COLLEGES FOR PURSUING A CAREER AS A HYDROLOGIST

- Princeton University
- Washington State University
- University of Arizona

COURSE WORK AND CLASSES TO HELP YOU BECOME A HYDROLOGIST

In addition to hydrology courses, geography courses, mathematics courses, and environmental science courses are all important areas of study for would-be hydrologists.

SALARY RANGE

According to the *Occupational Outlook Handbook*, hydrologists can earn anywhere from $42,000 to $98,000 or more, depending on experience and location.

FAMOUS HYDROLOGISTS

- **Edmund Halley**, an English scholar born in the 17th century and most famous for his namesake comet, is also known for developing the theory of the hydrological cycle.
- **Dr. Lorenzo Richards** developed an important equation for "unsteady unsaturated subsurface flow in a porous medium." Known as the Richards equation, it is still revered in the hydrology community.

WHERE TO LEARN MORE

American Institute of Hydrology
300 Village Green Circle, Suite 201
Smyrna, GA 30080
www.aihydro.org

The International Association for Environmental Hydrology
2607 Hopeton Dr.
San Antonio, TX 78230
www.hydroweb.com

National Association of Environmental Professionals
389 Main St., Suite 202
Malden, MA 02148
www.naep.org

WORDS OF WISDOM

"Identify people who share your interest and communicate with them. This includes acquaintances, colleagues, and older (more experienced) people, such as counselors and university professors (possible mentors)."

—Thomas Croley, Research Hydrologist

"Water is an important issue and is only becoming more important. There are so many aspects to hydrology, from surface water to groundwater and chemistry, biology, geology, geography, etc., that you can incorporate the science or math you love into helping with water issues."

—Erin Blankert, Hydrologist

Erin Blankert, Hydrologist
Hydrologist, U.S. Geological Survey
University of Miami, 2001
Majors: Environmental Science; Conservation and Management; Environmental Sciences and Policy

How does your career have an impact on efforts to improve our environment?

Though most of what I do now is related to the human aspect of water science, maintaining proper water balances is essential to maintaining ecology. We're helping the environment by trying to correct water flows, improving water quality, reducing aquifer contamination, etc.

How do the environmental issues that our world is facing have an impact on your career?

We as hydrologists are impacting the serious water issue that our world is currently facing. Water is precious and necessary, and we cannot live without it. Hydrologists are trying to maintain water supplies and provide clean, drinkable water to people, as well as decontaminate soils and water sources for plants, animals, and humans alike.

What was your first job after graduation?

Student hydrologist for the U.S. Geological Survey.

What criteria did you use when deciding which college(s) to apply to?

I think the most important criteria were if I could afford to go to a specific college, if I liked the location of the school, and if the school had a program with a degree in which I was interested.

Did you attend your first choice school?

Yes, I did.

Did you already have a career in mind when you applied to college?

I didn't have a specific career in mind, but I have always known I wanted to do something working with the environment.

Did the school you attended have a significant impact on your career op-portunities?

Both my undergraduate and graduate schools are located in places with major water issues, so the schools definitely had an impact in choosing a career in water science. I went straight from my undergraduate to my graduate school, which afforded me so many opportunities, from working closely with professors to working outside in the field with government offices.

Knowing what you know now, which college would you apply to (and why)?

My situation was unique. I had tuition remission to the University of Miami, so I wasn't about to pass up a free education at a great school. I think it depends on where one wants to live. I love the desert Southwest, so schools in the Southwest would be my first choices.

Which college or colleges are turning out the leaders in your profession today?

I went to the University of Arizona for a number of years, and they have a great hydrology program, as well as programs in watershed management and soil, water, and environmental science. One doesn't have to major in hydrology to be a hydrologist. A lot of great hydrologists are also coming out of the Colorado schools.

Did you have an "Aha!" moment when you realized what you wanted to do?

I didn't have an "Aha!" moment as much as a moment where I thought water science is fascinating and there is so much to it!

What were your majors in college?

My undergraduate major was environmental science: conservation and management. My graduate major was environmental sciences and policy.

Did you change your major? If so, why?

I never changed my major.

Which classes were most valuable in preparing you for your career or in helping you decide on your career?

I think it depends on which aspects of water science you like the most. Math classes are a must, but the most helpful science courses were hydrology, water quality, soil-related classes, and watershed management classes.

How did your professors have an impact on your career choice or preparation?

No one professor influenced me the most.

Did you have a job and/or internship during college that influenced your career choice or career preparation in any way?

As an undergraduate, I interned with a wildlife crew for the Forest Service in Arizona, but as a graduate student, I was a teaching assistant for six years. I also began my U.S. Geological Survey work as a student employee. Working for the U.S. Geological Survey as a student and then transitioning to full-time work was the ultimate career preparation.

How important was your college experience in getting you to where you are today?

While college courses do an excellent job preparing you for your field, nothing truly prepares you for a career like working in your field. I'd suggest an internship or being a student employee in your field.

Do you have an advanced degree? Is one helpful or required in your field?

Yes, I have an MS, and I worked on a PhD degree for four years before I decided to leave the program and work full-time. Having an advanced degree is very helpful. You are much more likely to be taken seriously with an advanced degree, though it is not always required.

What do you love most about your job?

Apart from the fun work, I love the people with whom I work.

What is the most difficult or challenging aspect of your job?

Water is such a major issue in the desert Southwest right now, so there is a constant stream of data to gather and analyze.

What is the biggest misconception people have about what you do?

Because I work for the federal government, a lot of people think we are trying to take away their water, which is not the case. We get branded as the bad guys because we work for the government.

What was the biggest obstacle you faced in getting to where you are in your career?

I think it would be finding the right job. Job searches don't always yield the jobs you want! A professor sent me an email about an opening for a student employee position for the U.S. Geological Survey in a water science capacity, so I followed through with that. Professors and organizations can be great places to find job information.

What skills are an absolute must for someone interested in pursuing your career?

Skills in hydrology are difficult to obtain without prior work in hydrology, so I would take hydrology labs and do an internship or be a student employee to get the training in the equipment you would need. Knowing how to use GPS, GIS, hydrology software, and equipment used for either surface water measurements or groundwater measurements is difficult without training.

Whom do you admire most in your industry/field?

I think everyone is on an equal playing field. We're all working for the same goal.

What is one piece of advice you would give to someone who is interested in pursuing your career?

Talk to several different people in several different locations who work in water science to get to know what they do and how the location affects their work. Water-related issues in a very wet area like Miami are very different from those in a very dry area like Arizona. You will learn different things and techniques depending on where you are.

If you could do everything all over again, what would you do differently?

I would have started looking for a water-related career after my master's degree and asked professors for good places to look for those careers.

Do you have any additional comments you think might be helpful to someone hoping to pursue your career?

Water is an important issue and is only becoming more important. There are so many aspects to hydrology, from surface water to groundwater and chemistry, biology, geology, geography, etc., that you can incorporate the science or math you love into helping with water issues.

Thomas E. Croley II, Hydrologist
Research Hydrologist, Great Lakes Environmental Research Laboratory
Ohio State University, 1969
Major: Civil Engineering

How does your career have an impact on efforts to improve our environment?

Forecasting of both watershed runoff and water quality helps improve our environment.

How do the environmental issues that our world is facing have an impact on your career?

They shape the issues I am facing in my career. I respond somewhat to funding opportunities in emerging issues, and I have done much of my work recently as part of a team addressing these issues.

What was your first job after graduation?

Assistant professor/research engineer.

What criteria did you use when deciding which college(s) to apply to?

Expense; status of engineering programs.

Did you attend your first choice school?

Yes, I was fortunate to have the opportunity to do so.

Did you already have a career in mind when you applied to college?

I knew that I wanted to be an engineer but was unsure of what kind. After two years as a pre-engineering candidate, I chose civil engineering.

Did the school you attended have a significant impact on your career op-portunities?

Yes. OSU requires two years in general courses and offers survey courses to help you choose your branch of engineering. The people there helped me to develop a passion for hydrology and an interest in research.

Knowing what you know now, which college would you apply to (and why)?

A large university with a large student body that is renowned for the subject of interest to me.

Which college or colleges are turning out the leaders in your profession today?

There are many: Ohio State, Michigan State, Colorado State, University of Arizona, Princeton, Washington State, to name but a few.

Did you have an "Aha!" moment when you realized what you wanted to do?

Yes, I realized I wanted to work outside and chose civil engineering because I thought it would allow me to do so. However, I ended up at a university teaching and doing research because by then, those were my interests. Finally, I switched to pure research when I learned how much I loved that. (I guess those were not actually "Aha!" moments, as it took a little time each time to make the decisions.)

What was your major in college?

Civil engineering.

Which classes were most valuable in preparing you for your career or in helping you decide on your career?

Survey courses were most valuable, as they give you a little idea of what the different disciplines are like as well as the kinds of work there are to do in each. Also, counselors can be very helpful; it's useful to have someone knowledgeable who is interested in helping you decide.

How did your professors have an impact on your career choice or preparation?

My hydraulics/hydrology professor took an interest in me, probably because I worked so hard in his class. He encouraged me to continue for advanced degrees and helped me find support.

Did you have a job and/or internship during college that influenced your ultimate career choice or career preparation in any way?

I had a number of odd jobs as an undergraduate: waiter, inspector, low-skill carpenter, and so forth. As a graduate, I found teaching and research assistantships to support myself and pay tuition. I found out that I wanted to do more than menial labor and later became very interested in the projects at hand (during the assistantships).

How important was your college experience in getting you to where you are today?

My career was only possible by going to a good school and working hard. College taught me most of what I needed to know to get started on my career. My college experience taught me analytical skills and communication skills I still use every day to do my work.

Do you have an advanced degree? Is one helpful or required in your field?

Yes. I have an MCE and a PhD. It is required in my field.

What do you love most about your job?

I get the most satisfaction in problem solving or figuring out how things work and how to model them on the computer. I also enjoy publishing my results.

What is the most difficult or challenging aspect of your job?

For me, social networking is the most challenging aspect of my job.

What is the biggest misconception people have about what you do?

Many people simply are not educated as to what a hydrologist does, particularly a research hydrologist.

What was the biggest obstacle you faced in getting to where you are in your career?

Being too focused on only one discipline. I learned to work with people of other disciplines to solve a problem with each of us bringing our own special skill sets to bear.

What skills are an absolute must for someone interested in pursuing your career?

You should be skilled in mathematics, writing and other communication skills, and working as part a team.

Whom do you admire most in your industry/field?

Dr. Vincent Ricca, who was my advisor, boss, and mentor while I was at OSU.

What is one piece of advice you would give to someone who is interested in pursuing your career?

Go to a good school and work hard.

If you could do everything all over again, what would you do differently?

Look at more career choices.

Do you have any additional comments you think might be helpful to someone hoping to pursue your career?

Identify people who share your interest and communicate with them. This includes acquaintances, colleagues, and older (more experienced) people, such as counselors and university professors (possible mentors).

ORGANIC AGRICULTURE

WHY IT'S GREAT TO BE AN ORGANIC FARMER

It's easy to romanticize life on a farm. While those Americana stereotypes are not always true, organic farming does allow farmers to be hands-on with their products from beginning to end, knowing that the end result is something that is delicious, healthy, and good for the environment.

WHAT ORGANIC FARMERS ARE DOING TO PRESERVE AND IMPROVE OUR WORLD

According to the Organic Trade Organization, organic foods are produced "without the use of antibiotics, synthetic hormones, genetic engineering and other excluded practices, sewage sludge, or irradiation." Knowing that sewage sludge is being kept out of your food, and thus out of your body, is comforting enough, but by upholding these high standards, organic farmers are ensuring the health of future generations.

SKILLS TO BE A SUCCESSFUL ORGANIC FARMER

It also takes a strong business sense to be a successful organic farmer, as the ability to identify markets and adapt to varying consumer supply and demand is crucial. Organic farming is typically done on a small scale, not on large farm "factories." As a result, the work is very labor-intensive and hands-on. An organic farmer must be physically strong (unless laborers are hired) and have the fortitude to ride the highs and lows of a career in agriculture.

CHALLENGES IN BEING AN ORGANIC FARMER

As with all farming, it is labor-intensive, and to a large extent, farmers are at the mercy of weather conditions (e.g., drought, temperature, wind) and market prices. In addition, organic products certified as such by the U.S. Department of Agriculture (USDA) must meet rigorous standards from planting to processing.

HOW CURRENT ENVIRONMENTAL ISSUES AFFECT THE JOB MARKET

As consumers become more aware of the harmful health effects of some traditional farming practices (e.g., chemical pesticide use), they are looking for more healthy alternatives. This growth in demand benefits organic farmers, who find larger markets for their organic products.

WHERE THE JOBS ARE

The states with the largest number of farms are Texas, Iowa, Missouri, Kentucky, and Tennessee, although there are lots of farms in California, Nebraska, and Kansas as well. There are organic farms in every state, but as one would expect, they are located in rural areas well outside large cities.

AREAS OF SPECIALTY

Organic farming is a broad category, and most organic farmers specialize in a particular product, for example, salad greens or dates. Most organic farmers typically focus on either produce (plants, vegetables, etc.), livestock (goats, cows, etc.), or fish.

EDUCATIONAL REQUIREMENTS

Not all farmers have been to college; farms can stay in the hands of a single family for generations. However, organic farmers increasingly have a bachelor's degree in an agriculture-related field, such as dairy science, agricultural economics, or crop and fruit science.

TOP COLLEGES FOR PURSUING A CAREER AS AN ORGANIC FARMER

- Cornell University
- Texas A&M, College of Agriculture and Life Sciences
- University of California—Davis, Sustainable Agriculture Research and Education Program

COURSE WORK AND CLASSES TO HELP YOU BECOME AN ORGANIC FARMER

In addition to agricultural course work, would-be organic farmers should complete classes in business management as well as vehicle repair. Organic farmers may have to manage their own finances and repair their own farming equipment.

SALARY RANGE

Because the prices of agricultural products can vary widely year to year, the annual salary for an organic farmer can vary widely as well. The U.S. Department of Agriculture stated that in 2005, the average farm business income for farm operator households was $15,603. This does not take into account grants and subsidies provided to farmers.

FAMOUS ORGANIC FARMERS

- All the farmers at **Point Reyes Farmers Market**, north of San Francisco, got their 15 minutes of fame when Prince Charles and Duchess Camilla Parker Bowles visited this all-local organic market in late 2005.
- Writer **Wendell Berry** is well known for his novels, poems, and essays, but he is also a renowned farmer in Port Royal, Kentucky.

WHERE TO LEARN MORE

U.S. Department of Agriculture
1400 Independence Ave. S.W.
Washington, DC 20250
www.usda.gov

Organic Trade Organization
PO Box 547
Greenfield, MA 01302
www.ota.com

WORDS OF WISDOM

"Keep in shape and eat healthy. Always keep your eyes and ears open. And always be open to learning something new."

—Tena Bellovich, Organic Farmer

"There are opportunities right now in sustainable agriculture unprecedented in the span of my 30-year career. It is rewarding work—it's as intellectual as you want to make it or as physical as your body can take. Farmers are consistently on the top of survey lists of people to be trusted and looked on as pillars of their communities."

—Don Kretschmann, Organic Farmer

Don Kretschmann, Organic Farmer
Owner, Kretschmann Farm
College: St. Vincent College, University of Vienna (Austria), 1971
Major: Psychology

How does your career have an impact on efforts to improve our environment?

Farmers are the first environmentalists. Though public efforts at conservation come and go, efforts by farmers on particular pieces of land go on for generations. Environmentalism is really looking at the big picture for the long range. The best of farming is falling in love with a particular piece of the earth and always trying to leave it for the next generation to enjoy.

How do environmental issues that our world is facing have an impact on your career?

Both consumers and farmers are waking up to the responsibility we have to conserve the natural world we have inherited. There are those not directly involved in farming, for example, large corporations who supply farmers with industrial inputs, who are largely responsible for practices that deleteriously impact the environment through farming. This is creating an opportunity for conservation-minded farmers to become educators, innovators, and political activists. Because consumers are more numerous and are demanding responsibility, this is creating a tremendous opportunity in sustainable agricultural production.

What was your first job after graduation?

I was a painter.

What criteria did you use when deciding which college(s) to apply to?

I wanted a school with a good science department and a rural environment.

Did you attend your first choice school?

No, my first choice was Notre Dame, but I didn't enroll there because it offered only a partial scholarship.

Did you already have a career in mind when you applied to college?

Yes, nuclear or theoretical physics.

Did the school you attended have an impact on your career opportunities?

Not really.

Knowing what you know now, which college would you apply to (and why)?

Perhaps Cornell—it has a reputation in fruit/vegetable agriculture, and I admire its longstanding commitment to sustainable agriculture. Also, it is located in a similar geographical region as mine, so its agriculture is likely to be similarly oriented.

Which college or colleges are turning out the leaders in your profession today?

Cornell, the University of Maine, the University of Vermont, University of California—Davis, University of California—Santa Cruz, Iowa State University, North Carolina State.

Did you have an "Aha!" moment when you realized what you wanted to do?

I was introduced to the wider food movements by students from all over the world in Vienna, Austria, and exposed to widely different foods, agriculture, and cuisines traveling in Europe, Asia, and Mexico. The closest to an "Aha!" moment was tasting the first batch of apple cider produced on the spot at a custom press from apples we had ourselves gathered. It was both "aha" and "mmm." Also, being encouraged by a former truck farmer and greenhouse grower and being successful making money our first year growing produce. We've never had a losing year and never one that wasn't better than the year before. "Aha!"

What were your majors in college?

Physics, mathematics, and psychology.

Did you change your major? If so, why?

Yes, I did change my major during college. Vietnam brought the decision to a head. I realized a theoretical physicist would likely have his life's work used for dubious purposes. Moral reasons brought me to organic and sustainable agriculture as something I would never regret. I would always be working for something people truly need, and I would be able to direct my efforts at every stage—no compromises.

Which classes were most valuable in preparing you for your career or in helping you decide on your career?

Mathematics, philosophy, art, chemistry, and biology.

How did your professors have an impact on your career choice or preparation?

Many of my professors impacted me in different ways. Perhaps the most influential was Dr. Dzombak, an organic chemistry professor, whose class on the liberal arts I attended. This was where I began to develop into more like a Renaissance man with many interests and passions, taking pleasure and satisfaction in a wide variety of pursuits.

Did you have a job and/or internship during college that influenced your career choice or career preparation in any way?

All of my work experiences had an influence on me. I worked in steel mills, I worked for the Deutsche Bundesbahn (railroad), and I worked as a self-employed gardener. In the steel mills, I saw many unfulfilled people working to a fraction of their capacity, fearful to change. As a foreigner working in Germany, I learned to never see language as a barrier to either work or friendship. Being self-employed at what I liked doing was invaluable. The subsequent lifelong responsibilities, rewards, and creativity involved in farming were all started with that small ad placed in a local paper almost 40 years ago.

How important was your college experience in getting you to where you are today?

It helped in that the experience exposed me to things that were not part of my previous world—in other words, sustainable and organic agriculture. It didn't specifically help me gain expertise in that area, but did give me the general tools to explore. But then, at that time, there was little known and certainly no courses of study in organic agriculture. I believe that nearly everyone benefits from a time of personal exploration and expansion of one's mental horizons, which college affords.

Do you have an advanced degree? Is one helpful or required in your field?

I don't have an advanced degree. On the academic side, I'm not sure advanced degrees are required as such, but it might be helpful to fill in some gaps that might exist because one's undergraduate degree didn't provide sufficient training. Further study or training might be helpful in certain areas as one's career develops—a course or two. I might suggest some courses: accounting/bookkeeping, agronomy/soil science, information technology, basic income tax preparation, marketing, even management. My own informal education filled in a lot of this via reading, short courses, workshops, soliciting help from others in the appropriate fields, and having worked part-time in income tax preparation. Advanced degrees are mostly via the School of Hard Knocks. (Tuition is a bit steep.)

What do you love most about your job?

Being able to experience the natural world directly almost each and every day. To be working at that very nexus where mineral elements are being brought to life is exciting and rewarding. Providing the best food for people and taking care of the earth in the process is profoundly fulfilling Also, the feeling of using all of one's talents.

What is the most difficult or challenging aspect of your job?

Accepting the cards I'm dealt and responding in the best way. For example, dealing with the vagaries of the weather, the soils, and terrain I'm given; training the largely inexperienced help. Making all the puzzle pieces fit and changing hats so often is challenging. It's also very challenging to be that person on whose desk the buck always stops.

What is the biggest misconception people have about what you do?

That farming is for unintelligent people who can't do anything else. It's actually one of the most demanding tasks and requires a variety of skills seldom required in any other profession.

What was the biggest obstacle you faced in getting to where you are in your career?

Shyness in asking for compensation commensurate with the quality of the products I raise.

I overcame this by developing more self-confidence and listening to my wife, who consistently says, "Raise prices." I've also been persistent in working toward what I've always believed in.

What skills are an absolute must for someone interested in pursuing your career?

Physical stamina, determination, common sense, and a penchant for organization.

Whom do you admire most in your industry/field?

J. I. Rodale—he saw the big picture two generations before anyone had an inkling. Joel Salatin—creativity and holistic thinking. Wes Jackson—pioneer. There are many people I admire in this field. These are just a few.

What is one piece of advice you would give to someone who is interested in pursuing your career?

Follow your dreams. Learn all you can from others, but don't wait too long to try it out for real. Start small, then move in the direction where you see opportunities. No two farms are alike, and I'm constantly amazed at the variety of different ways farms can make it. Don't borrow too much. Always make a profit; we're not in this to lose money.

If you could do everything all over again, what would you do differently?

Certainly today, I would visit many organic/sustainable farms and work on one or more.

Do you have any additional comments you think might be helpful to someone hoping to pursue your career?

There are opportunities right now in sustainable agriculture unprecedented in the span of my 30-year career. It is rewarding work—it's as intellectual as you want to make it or as physical as your body can take. Farmers are consistently on the top of survey lists of people to be trusted and looked on as pillars of their communities. Successes are readily apparent and not dependent on others declaring them so. It's not a flash in the pan and will take a lifetime to get there, but it's something no one can take away with a pink slip. It's rewarding on so many levels. The sky's the limit. It's a profession like no other!

Tena Bellovich, Organic Farmer, Faculty at University of Missouri—Kansas City
Owner/Operator of Shroomheads
University of Missouri, 1981
Majors: Psychology and Math

How does your career have an impact on efforts to improve our environment?

Organics is the future. With produce and mushrooms, you can create a symbiotic relationship that can be almost self-sustaining. Mushrooms live off of dead plants and other agricultural wastes.

How do the environmental issues that our world is facing have an impact on your career?

Well, for one, the global warming issue is controversial, but when you are a farmer, you can see how the climate is changing. Warm winters mean that larvae survive in the soil that would normally be killed. Warm winters also mean more rain than snow. Snow is the best water source for spring planting. As snow melts, it adds moisture to the soil a little bit at a time. That way, the moisture can be absorbed by the soil and not just become runoff. A warm winter isn't a blessing to a farmer.

What was your first job after graduation?

I was an unloader for UPS.

What criteria did you use when deciding which college(s) to apply to?

Curriculum and cost.

Did you attend your first choice school?

Yes. It was a junior college. Almost like an extension of high school.

Did you already have a career in mind when you applied to college?

Yes. I wanted to be an artist. However, I've changed careers about five times in my life.

Did the school you attended have an impact on your career opportunities?

Yes, it did. I gave up art as a career because an instructor gave me a B when I really deserved an A. But he gave me a B because he wanted to see me put in more effort. I also took a lot of general studies courses, which opened up my eyes to other subjects that I really excelled in.

Knowing what you know now, which college would you apply to (and why)?

Kansas State University or University of Missouri—Columbia. These two colleges have wonderful research and outreach programs for the students as well as the community.

Which college or colleges are turning out the leaders in your profession today?

University of Missouri—Rolla.

Did you have an "Aha!" moment when you realized what you wanted to do?

The "Aha!" moment came when I moved to an apartment complex with a large wooded area behind it. I would walk the trails and take my dogs and let them run in the woods. I started mushroom hunting like I did when I was a kid. Then I started studying mushrooms. This led to growing them, and that led to growing produce. I finally found the perfect piece of land to do my farming in conjunction with my mushrooms. I even have a few rescue animals on the side.

What were your majors in college?

Art, psychology, engineering, math, physics, and geology.

Did you change your major? If so, why?

I changed my major many times. I liked everything—math, physics, geology, computers, art, music, environmental science, agriculture…I still do. I don't ever want to not be in school.

Which classes were most valuable in preparing you for your career or in helping you decide on your career?

Math, geology, biology, chemistry, and environmental engineering.

How did your professors have an impact on your career choice or preparation?

Quite a few had an impact. Most of my professors were good old farm boys before going off to college or war. They always had farm stories to tell.

Did you have a job and/or internship during college that influenced your career choice or career preparation in any way?

All of them had an influence. I was a math tutor, a supplemental instructor for math, a software engineer, and an IT specialist for a Mac and PC lab at Longview Community College and at UM—Kansas City. Education is something that you use every day, whether you are aware of it or not. A day doesn't go by that I don't stop and think about something crucial that a professor had included in a lecture.

How important was your college experience in getting you to where you are today?

Very important. I know a little bit about everything. Because of my education, there isn't a doubt in my mind that there isn't anything I can't do. I use almost every bit of my education every day. I couldn't measure out a fence without math. Without physics, I wouldn't know how much force I would need to pump water from a pond. Or if I wanted to drip irrigate, how high would I have to place the water source? What diameter of hose would I need? Without geology and environmental science, I wouldn't know about water tables and how to read geographic maps. The list is endless.

Do you have an advanced degree? Is one helpful or required in your field?

I'm working on a degree in mathematics and engineering. An advanced degree is very helpful, but it is not required for organic farming.

What do you love most about your job?

Being my own boss! Being outside and one with nature. Doing a hard day's work and actually seeing the rewards when you harvest. This is another endless list.

What is the most difficult or challenging aspect of your job?

Heavy lifting. I am not a big woman, so I realized my limitations immediately. There are just some things I absolutely can't do alone.

What is the biggest misconception people have about what you do?

People think you walk out your back door into a lovely tropical garden and just start picking produce and mushrooms. They don't realize what goes into actually getting to the point where you can start to harvest. So many people offer to help pick when the crops are ready, but very few offer to plant, weed, and water during the summer months. They find out that even the picking isn't as easy as they thought. When you are organic, you do a lot of things just by sweat equity.

What was the biggest obstacle you faced in getting to where you are in your career?

Dealing with local farmers markets. Everyone wants to tell you what you should be growing and how you should grow it. You have to be at the market between 6:00 A.M. and 8:00 A.M. and stay until 12:30 P.M. or 1:00 P.M. after being up all night picking and preparing your products. AND you have to PAY someone else to use their market. There aren't many jobs that will tell you when you will be there, when you can go home, and what you can sell and then ask you to pay them a big chunk of your profits, whether you made anything or not. You try to find places where you can set up and sell for free. You have to do your own advertising, but it's worth it. And you can pass the savings on to your customers.

What skills are an absolute must for someone interested in pursuing your career?

Reading! You have to be able to research what you are growing. That takes a lot of research.

Whom do you admire most in your industry/field?

I admire anyone that tries to do organic gardening. To be truly organic is a lot of back-breaking work.

What is one piece of advice you would give to someone who is interested in pursuing your career?

Do internships, visit your local organic farmer, go to farmers markets and talk to the vendors. Most farmers just love to tell you how they grew what they are selling.

If you could do everything all over again, what would you do differently?

I would have taken more classes in plant biology while I was at a university that offered them.

Do you have any additional comments you think might be helpful to someone hoping to pursue your career?

Keep in shape and eat healthy. Always keep your eyes and ears open. And always be open to learning something new.

SOLAR ENERGY ENGINEERING

WHY IT'S GREAT TO BE A SOLAR ENERGY ENGINEER

Solar energy engineers take the world's largest free source of energy—solar energy—and convert it into power for our homes, offices, and other buildings. Not only do we get power (electricity) from the sun, but low-temperature solar collectors gather heat energy to heat water or even buildings.

WHAT SOLAR ENERGY ENGINEERS ARE DOING TO PRESERVE AND IMPROVE OUR WORLD

By harnessing the clean and seemingly limitless power of the sun, solar energy engineers help reduce our reliance on nonrenewable energy sources, such as coal. At a minimum, the use of solar power offsets the use of fossil fuels for electricity.

SKILLS TO BE A SUCCESSFUL SOLAR ENERGY ENGINEER

Solar energy engineers, like any engineers, must have strong critical thinking and logical reasoning skills. Some solar energy engineers double as project managers, so they must know how to manage personnel and keep projects on schedule and budget.

CHALLENGES THAT SOLAR ENERGY ENGINEERS FACE

Although solar energy has gained popularity in recent times, this technology is still a mystery to many people. Educating the public about how solar energy works and its benefits is one challenge faced by the entire industry. Also, as solar technology changes, engineers must stay on top of new developments and, again, translate these to the general public.

HOW CURRENT ENVIRONMENTAL ISSUES AFFECT THE JOB MARKET

There is almost no question that the United States cannot keep relying entirely on nonrenewable energy sources. For this reason, alternative energy careers are growing quickly. Solar energy, unlike wind or geothermal energy, can be harnessed just about anywhere in the United States. The solar energy industry is expected to grow rapidly as interest in renewable energy sources becomes more mainstream.

WHERE THE JOBS ARE

Although foreign markets, such as Germany and Japan, are willing consumers and active manufacturers of solar energy technology, the United States is home to an impressive 31 photovoltaic manufacturing companies and 25 solar thermal collector manufacturing companies, according to the American Solar Energy Society's report on renewable energy jobs. Within the United States, Michigan, Pennsylvania, and Illinois all have solar collectors, and western states, such as California and Nevada, are also home to large solar plants. Many jobs can be found with the state and federal governments, but independent solar energy firms also employ a large number of engineers.

AREAS OF SPECIALTY

Engineers may focus on three main types of solar energy systems: photovoltaic cells (converting sunlight to energy), concentrating solar power technologies (reflecting the sun's heat to an electric generator), and low-temperature solar collectors (using the sun's heat to heat water or buildings).

EDUCATIONAL REQUIREMENTS

An entry-level career in solar engineering may only require a bachelor's in engineering, but more often, an advanced degree in renewable energy or solar energy engineering is required.

TOP COLLEGES FOR PURSUING A CAREER AS A SOLAR ENERGY ENGINEER

- Massachusetts Institute of Technology (MIT)
- California Institute of Technology (CIT)
- University of Minnesota

COURSE WORK AND CLASSES TO HELP YOU BECOME A SOLAR ENERGY ENGINEER

Courses in electrical engineering, math, science, and renewable energy are all essential for a successful career in solar energy engineering.

SALARY RANGE

There is no national information about the salary ranges for solar energy engineers. However, based on figures for jobs in the more general renewable energy field, solar energy engineers may earn anywhere from $35,000 to $120,000. Starting salaries typically top out at $60,000.

FAMOUS SOLAR ENERGY ENGINEERS

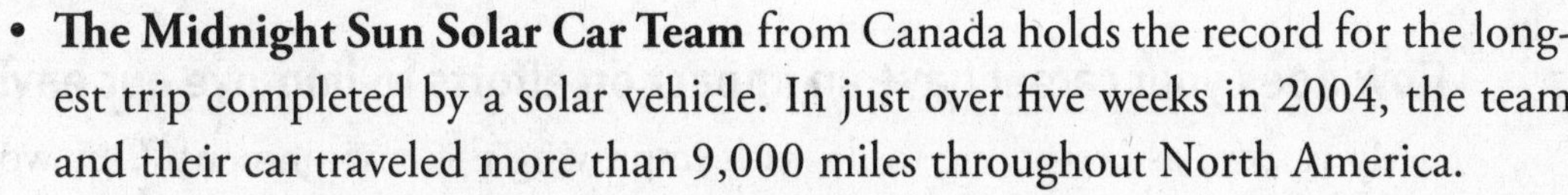

- **The Midnight Sun Solar Car Team** from Canada holds the record for the longest trip completed by a solar vehicle. In just over five weeks in 2004, the team and their car traveled more than 9,000 miles throughout North America.
- Although **Rudolf Diesel** is more famous for his diesel engine, he did experiment with solar-powered heat engines as early as the 1800s.

WHERE TO LEARN MORE

American Solar Energy Society
2400 Central Ave., Suite A
Boulder, CO 80301
www.ases.org

Solar Energy Industries Association
805 15th St. N.W., Suite 510
Washington, DC 20005
www.seia.org

U.S. Department of Energy
1000 Independence Ave. S.W.
Washington, DC 20585
www.energy.gov

WORDS OF WISDOM

"Solar jobs are out there. The solar industry is hiring across the board for all types of majors."

—Logan Boutilier, Solar Systems Engineer

"I think the most important thing is to pursue what you have a passion in and learn as much about it as you can. It's also important to stay flexible and allow the twists and turns of your career to benefit yourself and society."

—Chuck Kutscher,
Group Manager/Principal Engineer

Chuck Kutscher, Engineer/Manager
Group Manager/Principal Engineer, National Renewable Energy Laboratory
SUNY—Albany, 1972
Major: Physics

How does your career have an impact on efforts to improve our environment?

My career has everything to do with improving the environment. Our work on solar and geothermal energy, as well as the work of my colleagues on wind and biofuels, will help reduce greenhouse gases and air pollution.

How do the environmental issues that our world is facing have an impact on your career?

The current interest among the states in reducing greenhouse gas emissions is spurring a great deal of activity in the renewable energy industry. Similarly, interest in Congress is leading to more funding for our laboratory.

What was your first job after graduation?

I was a computer programmer at Sperry Rand.

What criteria did you use when deciding which college(s) to apply to?

I was interested in majoring in physics and wanted to attend a college where I could take advantage of a New York State Regents scholarship.

Did you attend your first choice school?

No. I wanted to attend the University of Michigan, but they did not accept many non-Michigan residents.

Did you already have a career in mind when you applied to college?

Sort of. I had physics in mind, and my career has always been close to physics.

Did the school you attended have a significant impact on your career op-portunities?

My master's degree in nuclear engineering at the University of Illinois opened a lot of doors back in 1975, because Illinois had an excellent reputation in this field.

Knowing what you know now, which college would you apply to (and why)?

My undergraduate school did not have an engineering program. In retrospect, it would have been better to go to a school where I would have been able to take some engineering classes. It's a good idea to maintain your options.

Which college or colleges are turning out the leaders in your profession today?

There are many schools that have top-notch engineering departments, including many state schools. Getting an excellent fundamental engineering education is more important than specializing in solar energy in school. But a few schools, like the University of Wisconsin and the University of Minnesota, do a good job of solar energy education and research.

Did you have an "Aha!" moment when you realized what you wanted to do?

I became interested in solar energy in the late 1970s when I saw the logic of utilizing solar energy in buildings. In the late 1990s, when I was elected to a two-year term as chair of the American Solar Energy Society, I began to study broader issues and became convinced that climate change was the greatest challenge we face. That has motivated my work ever since.

What were your majors in college?

BS in physics, MS in nuclear engineering, and PhD in mechanical engineering.

Did you change your major? If so, why?

Yes, in graduate school. I originally went to graduate school to get a PhD in physics. I decided my graduate physics classes were more theoretical than I liked, and it was fairly easy for physics students to switch to nuclear engineering, so I got my master's in that. Later, after working for many years in the areas of heat transfer and fluid dynamics, I decided to get my PhD in the broader field of mechanical engineering.

Which classes were most valuable in preparing you for your career or in helping you decide on your career?

My heat transfer class had the greatest impact on my career.

How did your professors have an impact on your career choice or preparation?

When I was getting my master's in nuclear engineering, I took a heat transfer class from an excellent professor, and that started my interest in that subject.

Did you have a job and/or internship during college that influenced your career choice or preparation in any way?

I worked as a lifeguard during the summers in college, but it didn't have an impact on my career choices. It's probably best to spend at least a summer working in your field of interest to get a sense of what it's like.

How important was your college experience in getting you to where you are today?

I am fortunate to work in a job where I regularly use my college training in science and engineering. But I have also learned a lot on the job.

Do you have an advanced degree? Is one helpful or required in your field?

I have an MS in nuclear engineering and a PhD in mechanical engineering. I work at a national laboratory. At my lab, a master's degree is definitely preferable to a bachelor's degree because of the additional math and engineering knowledge it provides. A PhD is even better, but is not essential.

What do you love most about your job?

I love many things about my job. The two biggest things are that I believe in our mission to improve our environment, and I work with many very bright and dedicated colleagues.

What is the most difficult or challenging aspect of your job?

As in any job, there is more paperwork than we would like. Also, our funds come from Congress, so we don't have complete freedom to choose which projects are the most important.

What is the biggest misconception people have about what you do?

Some people feel that solar energy is too intermittent or too expensive compared to fossil fuels like coal and oil. But costs have come way down in recent years, and it is important to factor in the costs of environmental damage resulting from the burning of fossil fuels. As we get serious about addressing climate change, renewable sources will become more recognized as mainstream energy sources, and we are already starting to see this happen.

What was the biggest obstacle you faced in getting to where you are in your career?

In getting my degree in physics, I did not take any undergraduate courses in fundamental engineering. This was a problem when I later started working as an engineer. As a result, I decided to pursue a professional engineering license. This involved passing first the Fundamentals of Engineering exam and later the Professional Engineering exam. I took review courses and studied hard for both of those exams.

What skills are an absolute must for someone interested in pursuing your career?

You need to have a love of math, science, and engineering and good fundamental courses in these subjects if you want to do science and engineering work in renewable energy. But the renewable energy field also needs economists, systems analysts, technical communicators, marketing, and many other skills.

Whom do you admire most in your industry/field?

Although he does not work directly in my field, I most admire Dr. James Hansen, director of the Goddard Institute for Space Studies. For four decades, he has done outstanding research on climate change. But just as importantly, he has had the courage to speak out and educate all of us about the seriousness of addressing the climate change crisis.

What is one piece of advice you would give to someone who is interested in pursuing your career?

Focus in school on learning the fundamentals, read the renewable energy literature, and try to get a summer internship working in the field. Look for opportunities and stay flexible.

If you could do everything all over again, what would you do differently?

I would probably go to an undergraduate school that would allow me to take engineering courses. However, my undergraduate education in physics helped nurture my inquisitive attitude, which I believe has helped me be creative in my engineering work.

Do you have any additional comments you think might be helpful to someone hoping to pursue your career?

I think the most important thing is to pursue what you have a passion in and learn as much about it as you can. It's also important to stay flexible and allow the twists and turns of your career to benefit yourself and society.

Logan Boutilier, Solar Systems Engineer
Design Engineer, Borrego Solar
University of California—San Diego, 2006
Major: Mechanical Engineering

How does your career have an impact on efforts to improve our environment?

We are providing solutions for homeowners and business owners to produce green power and help alleviate our dependence on fossil fuels. Our industry is full of opportunities to educate people about the threat of global warming and the future of our planet.

How do the environmental issues that our world is facing have an impact on your career?

The more educated people become about global warming and the feasibility of solar helping alleviate some of the side effects, the more our industry will grow. Actually, our industry depends on them [world environmental issues]. Legislation concerning the environment, specifically the effects of using fossil fuels, affects how affordable solar is for homeowners and business owners.

What was your first job after graduation?

My first job was in general contracting.

What criteria did you use when deciding which college(s) to apply to?

I looked at location, as I wanted to go to a school that was close to home; academic rankings; and whether or not they had a reputable baseball team.

Did you attend your first choice school?

No. I wanted to go to Dartmouth.

Did you already have a career in mind when you applied to college?

Not 100 percent. I did know that I wanted to be an engineer, but I originally went in to college as an electrical engineering major. I switched when I found out more information about the two majors (electrical and mechanical).

Did the school you attended have an impact on your career opportunities?

Yes, UC—San Diego provided me with different options in the field of engineering. I am only now two years out of college, but the reputation that UCSD has and is gaining in the work world helped in securing a job.

Knowing what you know now, which college would you apply to (and why)?

I cannot say any particular school. It would probably be a school that provides more real-world skills with practical applications, like California Polytechnic University—San Luis Obispo. UCSD is a very research-focused university that teaches students how to perform research but sometimes overshadows the need for practical knowledge.

Which college or colleges are turning out the leaders in your profession today?

Any technical school (MIT, Michigan Tech, Cal Tech, California Polytechnic University—San Luis Obispo, etc.). The technical schools seem to equip young engineers with the proper tools to understand the issues the solar industry currently has.

Did you have an "Aha!" moment when you realized what you wanted to do?

Not really. I've always had an innate knowledge of the way things work and how to fit stuff together and an inclination to protect the environment and conserve our natural resources.

What were your majors in college?

Electrical engineering and mechanical engineering.

Did you change your major? If so, why?

Yes. I spoke with a friend who was a PhD candidate in electrical engineering (my previous major) while we analyzed a broken VCR. He pointed out the differences between the mechanical side and the electrical side. I realized that I enjoyed the mechanical components much more than electrical, so I switched.

Which classes were most valuable in preparing you for your career or in helping you decide on your career?

Introduction to mechanical design (electrical components and drafting), structural design, physics (mechanics and electromagnetism), electrical circuits, and mechanics of materials.

How did your professors have an impact on your career choice or preparation?

They did not have a significant impact.

Did you have a job and/or internship during college that influenced your career choice or career preparation in any way?

I did not have a job or an internship that pertained to my major while I was in college.

How important was your college experience in getting you to where you are today?

College educated me in a wide spectrum of engineering principles. Solar, for example, requires knowledge of structural, mechanical, and electrical principles. All of these fields are part of a degree in mechanical engineering. The biggest thing that college taught me was how to teach myself and where to find information.

Do you have an advanced degree? Is one helpful or required in your field?

No, I attained a BS. It is not required and is only minimally helpful. Practical, real-world experience would be more valuable.

What do you love most about your job?

We are bringing solar energy to people and helping solve the world's energy problems. The combination of providing green energy solutions to people while doing something that I love has to be my favorite thing.

What is the most difficult or challenging aspect of your job?

Each job is different. There is no cookie-cutter job where if you've done one, you've done them all. Each day and each project provide a new challenge.

What is the biggest misconception people have about what you do?

I don't know what conceptions people have of my current position. The industry is approaching a very professional level and is becoming more popular and, therefore, is still free of stereotypical conceptions. A few years from now, this will change. If there had to be one thing, I would say the concept that this industry is full of hippies who wear sandals all the time and grow long hair. This, like any other stereotype, is based on a slice of the truth.

What was the biggest obstacle you faced in getting to where you are in your career?

Finding a job in the green sector at the college that I was at. I did some research myself and believed that it was important that I find something that I loved to do. Sticking to what I love to do has been a key to my success. I looked for a job that would just fit what I wanted to do with my career. Nothing popped up at career fairs or the career services department on campus. By doing some research myself after working at my first job for a year, I found the company that I am at now. The industry will become more and more popular, which will allow us to advertise more and recruit heavily from college campuses. I'll be proud of the day when Borrego has a booth on campus and I can tell the young engineers about a future in solar.

What skills are an absolute must for someone interested in pursuing your career?

A technical knowledge of electronics, mechanics, and structural principles is important. Imagination and being able to visualize things in your mind is very important as well.

Whom do you admire most in your industry/field?

Because solar is a relatively new industry, at least large scale, there are not many role models as of yet. However, John Wiles out of Sandia National Laboratories in New Mexico has been and is continuing to develop standards for the solar electric industry. He is paving the way for safety, quality, and ultimately more efficient systems for the future. The steps he is taking now are ensuring that people trust the quality of work coming out of the solar industry. In certain aspects, I admire Al Gore for his work to educate people about global warming.

What is one piece of advice you would give to someone who is interested in pursuing your career?

Ask questions and pursue your curiosities. My grandpa bought me an erector set when I was ten years old. Playing with this toy provided me irreplaceable experience in dealing with small-scale structures, electronics, and mechanics. In addition, seek excellence and the highest quality in all things that you do. A great mentor of mine used the phrase "class and professionalism at all times." I live by this daily.

If you could do everything all over again, what would you do differently?

I would have joined a club or organization on campus that either supported solar power or was involved in green causes. Solar is a very political field and understanding why you do what you do is greater motivation to provide quality results in your career.

Joining an organization on campus would have provided me with companions with similar interests.

Do you have any additional comments you think might be helpful to someone hoping to pursue your career?

Solar jobs are out there. The solar industry is hiring across the board for all types of majors. If you have any feeling to join the industry, don't hesitate to act.

TRANSPORTATION SYSTEMS PLANNING

WHY IT'S GREAT TO BE A TRANSPORTATION SYSTEMS PLANNER

No one likes to sit in traffic, especially transportation systems planners. That's because they actually have the ability to do something about it. By planning roadways, train routes, and bus systems, transportation systems planners can have a direct effect on how 300 million Americans get around.

WHAT TRANSPORTATION SYSTEMS PLANNERS ARE DOING TO PRESERVE AND IMPROVE OUR WORLD

Cars get us where were need to go, but they are also a major source of pollution. Transportation systems planners help troubleshoot and problem solve transportation issues so that more efficient, and often more environmentally friendly, methods are available for widespread use. By ensuring that efficient roads and fast, relatively inexpensive public transportation are available, these planners are reducing the consumption of fossil fuels and the resulting pollution.

SKILLS TO BE A SUCCESSFUL TRANSPORTATION SYSTEMS PLANNER

Critical thinking skills and the keen ability to correlate large amounts of information (demographic, scientific, etc.) are crucial. Communication skills are also extremely important to this career.

CHALLENGES THAT TRANSPORTATION SYSTEMS PLANNERS FACE

Except for those in newly developed areas, most transportation systems are long established. Working within the parameters of existing road, rail, and water systems can present a challenge. However, the nature of the job is problem solving, so these are not insurmountable challenges. Transportation systems planners must also be able to help create a consensus among all interested parties.

HOW CURRENT ENVIRONMENTAL ISSUES AFFECT THE JOB MARKET

Air pollution and skyrocketing gas prices are excellent motivators for governments to find transportation solutions. Improving public transportation is of particular interest in terms of the environment, as it minimizes pollution from single-rider vehicles.

WHERE THE JOBS ARE

The overwhelming majority of jobs is found with the local, state, and federal governments. Because transportation planning falls under the general heading of urban planning, most jobs are found in cities and bustling suburbs. Rural and sparsely populated areas do not present the same need for planners, but as communities grow and merge, transportation planners become essential.

AREAS OF SPECIALTY

Transportation systems planners can often be grouped according to the type of transportation. For example, you could have highway planners, waterway planners, or railway planners.

EDUCATIONAL REQUIREMENTS

The number of schools and universities that offer a major in urban planning is somewhat limited (15 total in 2007, according to the *Occupational Outlook Handbook*). In addition, some jobs require a master's degree. Entry into a master's degree program generally requires a bachelor's in urban planning, geography, environmental design, or another related field.

TOP COLLEGES FOR PURSUING A CAREER AS A TRANSPORTATION SYSTEMS PLANNER

- University of Illinois—Chicago
- University of California—Berkeley
- University of California—San Diego

COURSE WORK AND CLASSES TO HELP YOU BECOME A TRANSPORTATION SYSTEMS PLANNER

Because transportation systems planners work in real-life settings, course work in urban planning, urban development, mathematics, statistics, and transportation is essential.

SALARY RANGE

According to Bureau of Labor statistics, planners (not necessarily transportation planners) can expect to earn from $30,000 to about $80,000, depending on experience and location. This salary range is more or less in line with that of transportation systems planners.

FAMOUS TRANSPORTATION SYSTEMS PLANNERS

- **The Wheelmen of America** were avid fans of the novelty of bicycle riding back in the 1800s. Their desire for better roads for riding led to the Good Roads movement, which eventually led to the creation of state highways.
- Born and raised in New York City, **Harland Bartholomew** was no stranger to public transportation systems. It took many years to conceive of, design, and construct a rapid transit system in Washington, D.C., but thanks to Mr. Bartholomew, it came to fruition.

WHERE TO LEARN MORE

Institute of Transportation Engineers
1099 14th St. N.W., Suite 300 W.
Washington, DC 20005
www.ite.org

U.S. Department of Transportation
1200 New Jersey Ave. S.E.
Washington, DC 20590
www.dot.gov

WORDS OF WISDOM

"In my case, the work experience I received while going to school was just as valuable (maybe more) than the class work to my career."

—Craig O'Riley, Transportation Planner

"Urban planning is such a varied and exciting field. I think anyone with an interest could apply just about any skill set and make a valuable contribution. Urban planning is the perfect combination of political science, architecture, economics, land use law, environmental science, and design. There is a little bit of something for everyone, and the field is wide open with countless opportunities."

—Megan James, Transportation Planner

Megan James, Planner

Transportation Planner, Utah Department of Transportation

Boston University, 2000

Major: Art History

How does your career have an impact on efforts to improve our environment?

We are constantly thinking about how we can improve air quality through transportation planning and how we can mitigate other environmental impacts. It is a huge part of the job and getting bigger all the time.

How do the environmental issues that our world is facing have an impact on your career?

Departments of Transportation (DOTs) around the nation are hiring environmental experts to help with transportation planning and urban planning in general.

What was your first job after graduation?

I worked in planning for the Utah Department of Transportation (UDOT).

What criteria did you use when deciding which college(s) to apply to?

I wanted to go someplace far from home and experience life away from home and family.

Did you attend your first choice school?

My first choice was anything in New England, and I chose Boston University because they offered me the most financial support of all the schools to which I applied. I also applied to Boston College and Trinity College.

Did you already have a career in mind when you applied to college?

No. I wanted to travel and see the world, so art history seemed the best choice for those particular goals at the time. I didn't even know that urban planning was a possible option. I ultimately chose urban planning as a graduate degree and a career choice a few years later.

Did the school you attended have a significant impact on your career op-portunities?

No, not really.

Knowing what you know now, which college would you apply to (and why)?

I am glad I chose to study in Boston, because I had a great experience living there for four years. I am also glad I chose to study urban planning in Utah, because that is where I chose to live and where I wanted to find a job.

Which college or colleges are turning out the leaders in your profession today?

You can go to just about any program/school and be a leader in the profession today. It's more about experience and also motivation.

Did you have an "Aha!" moment when you realized what you wanted to do?

My "Aha!" moment happened about four years after I finished college. I had been looking at graduate programs in a variety of fields for a long time and couldn't decide on one. When I started reading up on urban planning, I realized that it combined all of my interests and it was the perfect choice for me. I haven't ever regretted that decision, and I'm glad I took my time and made the right choice for me.

What were your majors in college?

International relations, geography, art history, Russian.

Did you change your major? If so, why?

I changed my major a few times. During college, there wasn't one major that captured all of my interests.

Which classes were most valuable in preparing you for your career or in helping you decide on your career?

Classes in urban demographics, economic development, and urban transportation were very helpful.

How did your professors have an impact on your career choice or preparation?

My professors didn't have much of an impact on me.

Did you have a job and/or internship during college that influenced your career choice or career preparation in any way?

Not related to urban planning. I mostly worked in art galleries.

How important was your college experience in getting you to where you are today?

It helped me learn more about myself, my interests, and the world around me. However, I don't think my particular choice of major had any impact on my current career choice.

Do you have an advanced degree? Is one helpful or required in your field?

I have an MA in urban planning. Having an advanced degree could be helpful, but it's definitely not required. A lot of people with BA degrees do very well.

What do you love most about your job?

The ability to be creative. I get to see a challenge/problem and think of creative solutions.

What is the most difficult or challenging aspect of your job?

Working to bring various groups/individuals together in agreement about a particular issue/plan.

What is the biggest misconception people have about what you do?

People usually don't have any idea what a planner does.

What was the biggest obstacle you faced in getting to where you are in your career?

Deciding what career to choose. I took my time and waited to apply to graduate school until I felt sure about the program and direction.

What skills are an absolute must for someone interested in pursuing your career?

There is opportunity for just about any skill set in this field: engineer, planner, demographer, statistician, economist, designer, mapper.

Whom do you admire most in your industry/field?

Those who are willing to be creative and see solutions to problems that haven't been tried yet. There is so much opportunity to try new things and really have an impact on the world around you.

What is one piece of advice you would give to someone who is interested in pursuing your career?

Do it! No matter what your specific interests are, they can be applied to urban planning in some way.

If you could do everything all over again, what would you do differently?

Pay more attention in my demographics classes, and I would have taken GIS courses as well.

Do you have any additional comments you think might be helpful to someone hoping to pursue your career?

Urban planning is such a varied and exciting field. I think anyone with an interest could apply just about any skill set and make a valuable contribution. Urban planning is the perfect combination of political science, architecture, economics, land use law, environmental science, and design. There is a little bit of something for everyone, and the field is wide open with countless opportunities.

Craig O'Riley, Planner
Transportation Planner, Iowa Department of Transportation
Iowa State University, 1974
Major: Agricultural Economics

How does your career have an impact on efforts to improve our environment?

Transportation planning sets the stage to move people and goods through investments that strengthen our economic vitality. These investments enhance our ability to compete economically, provide mobility and accessibility for everyone, and enhance our natural resources.

How do the environmental issues that our world is facing have an impact on your career?

New federal legislation requires us to look for ways to protect and enhance the environment, improve quality of life, and promote energy conservation in the transportation-planning process.

What was your first job after graduation?

I was a research assistant with the Department of Economics at Iowa State University.

What criteria did you use when deciding which college(s) to apply to?

The criteria included staying close to home and looking at state colleges with a business program.

Did you attend your first choice school?

My first choice was Iowa State University, but I attended a community college for two years for the core courses and to save on costs.

Did you already have a career in mind when you applied to college?

Yes, I was planning on a business career with an emphasis on accounting, due to my math skills.

Did the school you attended have a significant impact on your career op-portunities?

Yes, I got a job doing agricultural transportation research and became very interested in transportation. As a result, I took several transportation classes. The class work and the practical job experience opened the door for me to work in the transportation arena.

Knowing what you know now, which college would you apply to (and why)?

I would still take the same route. It prepared me for a career in transportation that I have thoroughly enjoyed for 30 years.

Which college or colleges are turning out the leaders in your profession today?

University of Illinois—Chicago, University of California—Berkley, Iowa State University, University of Iowa. In my opinion, there are a number of colleges where you can get a good foundation for your career. What you do with it depends more on your motivation and passion.

Did you have an "Aha!" moment when you realized what you wanted to do?

Yes, my "Aha!" moment came from my job experience working on transportation in the Economics Department. I enjoyed the work we were doing and the group of people.

What were your majors in college?

Industrial administration (currently business administration) and agricultural economics.

Did you change your major? If so, why?

No, but I did pursue a master's degree in agricultural economics.

Which classes were most valuable in preparing you for your career or in helping you decide on your career?

The classes most valuable to me included basic economics, agricultural marketing, statistics, and transportation. These classes gave me a firm foundation for my job at the Iowa Department of Transportation.

How did your professors have an impact on your career choice or preparation?

My major professor, Dr. C. Phillip Baumel, had a big impact on me. Dr. Baumel lead the transportation research group that I was part of. He was an excellent teacher and serious about what he was doing, yet had fun doing it. He really enjoyed what he was doing, and it showed in the way people responded who worked with him.

Did you have a job and/or internship during college that influenced your career choice or career preparation in any way?

I had a job working with a group doing research on agricultural transportation. My transportation research experience helped me obtain a job with the Iowa Department of Transportation.

How important was your college experience in getting you to where you are today?

The research job I had while going to school gave me an opportunity to apply what I learned in class, making the class work come to life.

Do you have an advanced degree? Is one helpful or required in your field?

I have a master's degree in agricultural economics from Iowa State University. While an advanced degree is not required in my field, it helps with the technical skills needed to analyze more detailed and complex transportation problems.

What do you love most about your job?

I love the variety of transportation issues that we get to address and the people that I work with. Transportation is a lifeline of our economy and is constantly changing.

What is the most difficult or challenging aspect of your job?

The most difficult aspect includes communication with a wide variety of people.

What is the biggest misconception people have about what you do?

People don't understand what transportation planning involves: the relationship among planning, programming, and project implementation and the various data that must be analyzed to adequately plan for transportation improvements.

What was the biggest obstacle you faced in getting to where you are in your career?

Getting people to understand the value of planning. I overcame this by consistently producing quality products in a timely fashion and networking with others.

What skills are an absolute must for someone interested in pursuing your career?

The skills include understanding economics, being able to perform technical analyses, and having the ability to communicate with a variety of people.

Whom do you admire most in your industry/field?

There are three people whom I have admired in transportation—Dr. C. Phillip Baumel, Dr. Ben Allen, and Dr. Dave Forkenbrock. These individuals are truly dedicated to their professions, have fun with what they do, and relate well to various people.

What is one piece of advice you would give to someone who is interested in pursuing your career?

It is important to get a solid foundation in transportation economics and analytical techniques and to get some practical experience before graduation.

If you could do everything all over again, what would you do differently?

I would not change anything except working more on communication skills. I did not realize that my job in transportation would involve a significant level of communication with a wide variety of people.

Do you have any additional comments you think might be helpful to someone hoping to pursue your career?

In my case, the work experience I received while going to school was just as valuable (maybe more) than the class work to my career.

GREEN ORGANIZATIONS

To help get you thinking green, following are some organizations that are focused on addressing environmental issues. Interested in volunteering or learning more? Check out their websites for additional information.

ORGANIZATION	WEBSITE	FOCUS
Commission for Environmental Cooperation (CEC)	www.cec.org	As NAFTA did with economic issues, the CEC helps Canada, the United States, and Mexico coordinate their environmental efforts.
Conservation International	*www.conservation.org*	This organization, founded more than two decades ago, focuses on the conservation of wildlife and nature for future generations.
Co-op America	*www.coopamerica.org*	Co-op America focuses on creating economic strength through environmental sustainability.
Earth First!	*www.earthfirst.org*	Known for being radical, this organization prefers to focus on its actions speaking louder than its words.
Earth Island Institute	*www.earthisland.org*	This nonprofit focuses on conservation, preservation, and restoration of nature and the environment.
EnvironmentalCareer.com	*www.environmentalcareer.com*	This site helps people find green-collar jobs in the United States.
Environmental Careers Organization	*www.eco.org*	This nonprofit organization develops professionals in the environmental field through paid internships.
Environmental Investigation Agency	*www.eia-international.org*	Since 1984, this small but effective organization has gone undercover to expose crimes against nature and the environment.
Environmental Protection Agency	*www.epa.gov*	This government agency is responsible for enforcing U.S. federal environmental law, and the site is a source of information on environmental issues in the United States.
Focus the Nation	*www.focusthenation.org*	On January 31, 2008, Focus the Nation planned simultaneous symposia on global warming at more than 1,000 educational institutions.
Friends of the Earth (FOE)	*www.foe.org*	Part of FOE International, this group is a network of grassroots efforts around the United States.
Global Green USA	*www.globalgreen.org*	This is the American affiliate of Green Cross International, which focuses on climate change, water preservation and conservation, and the elimination of weapons of mass destruction.

ORGANIZATION	WEBSITE	FOCUS
Green People	*www.greenpeople.org*	This is the largest directory of environmentally friendly products and services available.
Greenpeace	*www.greenpeace.org*	Funded entirely by individual citizens, this organization fights to protect animals and their environments around the world.
John Muir Project	*www.johnmuirproject.org*	This nonprofit project aims to keep nationally owned forests beyond the use of commercial foresters.
National Geographic Society	*www.nationalgeographic.com*	Although best known for its magazine, the society focuses on exploration, education, and conservation.
National Resources Defense Council	*www.nrdc.org*	This organization focuses on using legal means to protect and preserve the environment.
The Nature Conservancy	*www.nature.org*	The Nature Conservancy protects land around the world to preserve natural diversity.
Network for New Energy Choices	*www.newenergychoices.org*	Created by a nonprofit agency in 2006, this site promotes alternative energy sources and maintains a National Energy Resource Database.
Scientific Committee on Problems of the Environment (SCOPE)	*www.icsu-scope.org*	SCOPE is a network of scientists and institutions that combine their knowledge to aid the decision-making process about environmental solutions.
Seacology	*www.seacology.org*	This nonprofit focuses entirely on the delicate and endangered environments of islands around the world.
Sierra Club	*www.sierraclub.org*	Founded in 1892, this club has chapters all over the world dedicated to every type of environmental issue.
Worldwatch Institute	*www.worldwatch.org*	Through publications and global partnerships, this organization keeps sustainability and how to achieve it at the forefront.

GREEN GLOSSARY

Following are some of the terms and buzzwords you'll often hear being used when green issues are being discussed. Use this list to help you think—and talk—like a green expert.

80 PLUS ROGRAM:
Electric utility–funded incentive program to integrate more energy-efficient power supplies into desktop computers and servers; power supplies in computers and servers must be 80 percent or more energy efficient.

ALTERNATIVE ENERGY:
Energy, such as solar, wind, geothermal, or nuclear energy, that can substitute or supplement traditional fossil-fuel sources, such as coal, oil, or natural gas.

AMERICAN COLLEGE AND UNIVERSITY PRESIDENTS CLIMATE COMMITMENT (ACUPCC):
Agreement signed by various college and university presidents to implement methods to achieve carbon neutrality, reduce greenhouse gases, and publicize their results by releasing them to the Association for the Advancement of Sustainability in Higher Education (AASHE).

ANTHROPOGENIC EMISSIONS:
Result of human activity, such as using fossil fuels, that unnaturally releases carbon dioxide emissions into the atmosphere.

BIOGENIC EMISSIONS:
Result of natural biological processes, such as the decomposition or combustion of vegetative matter, these are part of a closed carbon loop; they are balanced by the natural uptake of carbon dioxide by growing vegetation, resulting in carbon net-zero contribution.

BIODIESEL:
Biodegradable, nontoxic biofuel in usable diesel form, standardized as methyl ester, that is made from vegetable oils or animal fats.

BIOFUEL:
Fuel, such as wood or ethanol, that comes from from biomass.

BIOMASS:
Organic matter, such as plant matter, that can be transformed into fuel; potential energy source.

CARBON FOOTPRINT:
Measure of the impact of human activities on the environment in terms of the amount of greenhouse gases produced, measured in units of carbon dioxide; ecological footprint.

CARBON OFFSETS:
The elimination of carbon emissions through alternative projects, such as the generation of solar or wind energy or reforestation.

CARBON-NEUTRAL:
Releasing no carbon dioxide into the atmosphere or absorbing carbon dioxide to result in a carbon net-zero footprint; often achieved through carbon offsets.

CARBON ZERO:
No carbon is released into the environment.

CARBON NET ZERO:
Any carbon released into the environment is counteracted such that no carbon is in the environment after a technology or activity's implementation; net amount of carbon is zero.

CERTIFIED ORGANIC:
This standard clarifies the percentage of organic food in a product: "100 percent organic" means made entirely with certified organic ingredients and methods, "organic" means 95 percent organic ingredients, and "made with organic ingredients" means products containing at least 70 percent organic ingredients.

COMPACT FLUORESCENT LIGHTBULB (CFL):
Uses less energy and has a longer life than an incandescent lamp; an electrical current passes through a gas-filled tube that causes it to emanate ultraviolet light, which excites a white phosphor coating on the inside of the tube, emanating visible light.

COGENERATION:
Using a heat engine or power station to produce both electricity and heat at the same time (combined heat and power, or CHP); a thermodynamically efficient use of fuel.

COMPOST:
Mixture of decaying organic substances, such as dead leaves or manure, used to fertilize soil.

CONVENTIONAL POWER:
Combustion of fossil fuels, such as coal, natural gas, and oil, and the nuclear fission of uranium that releases greenhouse gases and air pollution.

ENERGY STAR:
U.S. government rating program to promote energy-efficient products by requiring that appliances achieve 80 percent or greater efficiency using the standards supplied by the 80 Plus Program.

ENVIRONMENTAL STEWARDSHIP:
Ethic in which citizens interact with organizations and communities to take care of the earth's natural resources, such as air, land, water, and biodiversity, thus ensuring long-term sustainability; includes recycling, conservation, regeneration, and restoration.

ENVIRONMENTAL PROTECTION AGENCY (EPA):
U.S. government agency created to protect human health and safeguard the natural environment: air, water, and land.

FAIR TRADE:
Trade that satisfies certain criteria along the supply chain, usually including fair payment for producers and social and environmental considerations, or that conforms to a fair-trade agreement.

FAST FOOD:
Food, such as hamburgers, pizza, or fried chicken, that is prepared in quantity by a standardized method and can be dispensed quickly and inexpensively.

GEOTHERMAL ENERGY:
Energy obtained from the earth's core by drawing out the planet's internal heat.

GLOBAL ELECTRIC MOTORCARS (GEM):
Producer of speed-limited, battery-powered electric vehicles, termed Neighborhood Electric Vehicles (NEV).

GRAY WATER:
Dirty water, such as that from sinks, showers, bathtubs, and washing machines, that can be recycled, such as for use in flushing toilets.

GREEN:
Environmentally sound or beneficial; term for a social and political movement that espouses global environmental protection, bioregionalism, social responsibility, and nonviolence.

GREEN POWER:
Electricity produced from solar, wind, geothermal, biogas, biomass, and small, low-impact hydroelectric sources.

GREEN POWER PARTNER:
Initiative begun by the U.S. Environmental Protection Agency to encourage companies to use green power.

HYBRID VEHICLE:
Vehicle with more than one power source, such as an electric motor and internal combustion engine or an electric motor with battery and fuel cells for energy storage; plug-in hybrid electric vehicles (PHEV) are a subset that uses both fossil fuels and electricity for power and can be recharged.

INCANDESCENT LAMP:
Produces light through the transition of electrons from one energy level to another as an electrical current passes through and heats up a thin filament until it produces light; operating principle is similar to that of blackbody radiation.

LEADERSHIP IN ENERGY AND ENVIRONMENTAL DESIGN (LEED):
LEED's Green Building Rating System is a suite of standards for environmentally sustainable construction; it addresses six areas—sustainable sites, water efficiency, energy and atmosphere, materials and resources, indoor environmental quality, and innovation and design—Certification levels—certified silver (lowest) to gold to platinum (highest)—are based upon a score ranging from 26 to 69.

NONRENEWABLE:
Of or relating to an energy source, such as oil or natural gas, or a natural resource, such as metallic ore, that is not replaceable after it has been used.

NUCLEAR ENERGY:
Energy discharged by reactions within atomic nuclei; usually from nuclear fission, which presents an environmental problem with long-term radioactive waste storage.

ORGANIC:
Noting or pertaining to a class of chemical compounds that formerly comprised only those existing in or derived from plants or animals; containing carbon; characteristic of, pertaining to, or derived from living organisms.

PHOTOVOLTAIC (PV):
Capable of producing a voltage, usually through photoemission, when exposed to radiant energy, especially light.

POSTCONSUMER WASTE:
Waste type produced by the end-user of a material; result of use that does not involve the production of another product; essentially, garbage that individuals routinely discard.

PRECONSUMER WASTE:
Manufacturing scrap, such as trimmings from paper production and defective aluminum cans; recycling of preconsumer waste back into the manufacturing process is not recycling in the traditional sense.

RECYCLEMANIA:
Competition among over 200 college and university recycling programs in the United States to see which institution can collect the largest amount of recyclables per student, collect the largest amount of total recyclables, generate the least amount of trash per student, or have the highest recycling rate.

RENEWABLE:
Relating to or being a commodity or resource, such as solar energy or firewood, that is inexhaustible or replaceable by new growth.

RENEWABLE ENERGY:
Fuel sources that restore themselves quickly and do not diminish, such as sun, wind, moving water, organic plant and waste material (biomass), and the earth's heat (geothermal).

SOLAR ENERGY:
Energy obtained from the sun in the form of solar radiation.

SLOW FOOD:
Any dish or meal cooked with care and attention to detail, often according to traditional recipes and using few or no modern appliances like microwaves.

SUSTAINABILITY:
Ability to be continued with minimal long-term effect on the environment.

TALLOIRES DECLARATION:
Declaration for sustainability signed by presidents of institutions of higher learning around the world that commits their institutions to being world leaders in developing, creating, supporting, and maintaining environmental sustainability (begun by Jean Mayer, president of Tufts University, at a convention in Talloires, France).

WIND POWER:
Power obtained from wind used to produce electricity or mechanical power; wind energy.

Plus 25 More Career Possibilities! Arts and Humanities

ADVERTISING AND PUBLIC RELATIONS

WHY CHOOSE TO WORK IN ADVERTISING OR PUBLIC RELATIONS?

Advertising and public relations (PR) professionals are creative and have excellent communication skills. People in advertising are hired by companies to create campaigns or advertisements to promote their products or services in order to increase sales. People in PR generally work behind the scenes to track public opinion and affect in a positive way how the public views a certain product, idea, service, person, or organization.

WHERE THE JOBS ARE

A full-service advertising agency will create advertisements, and that includes writing ad copy, creating the art, and then placing the ad on TV, in magazines, or another form of media. However, most firms specialize in one area or part of the process, such as outdoor advertising or selling advertising space on TV or in newspapers. People in PR can work for a firm with a variety of clients, or they can work for one organization to handle all of its PR. Clients of PR agencies can include large corporations, nonprofits, politicians, or any organization or person with a public image. The advertising and PR industries are concentrated in New York and California, but they are also located in larger cities throughout the country. Advertising and PR is considered a “glamour” industry and has always attracted a large number of qualified job seekers, making it a very competitive field. However, the industry is expected to grow considerably due to the expanding economy. The growth of the Internet as a media source will also increase opportunities in both fields.

AREAS OF SPECIALTY

There are many different types of jobs in the advertising industry. Some are creative, such as art directors or copy writers, and others more managerial, such as account managers and media planners. People in public relations can specialize in a certain industry, such as real estate or technology, or in a specific type of PR, such as crisis management.

EDUCATIONAL REQUIREMENTS

Most people who work in advertising or PR have a bachelor's degree, sometimes in communications, advertising, or journalism, but a broad liberal arts background is also considered helpful. The Public Relations Society of America offers a voluntary accreditation certificate that involves work experience and passing an exam.

SALARY RANGE

Salaries for both industries vary widely depending on the job performed and level of experience. In 2004, nonsupervisory workers in advertising and public relations averaged $633 a week.

Pros: Creative and varied work

Cons: Long hours, competitive industry

FAMOUS FIGURES IN ADVERTISING AND PUBLIC RELATIONS

- **Leo Burnett**, advertising executive who created the Jolly Green Giant, the Pillsbury Doughboy, and Tony the Tiger.
- **Volney B. Palmer**, who opened the first American advertising agency in Philadelphia in 1841.
- **Ivy Lee**, credited with developing the modern press release, a main tool of the PR industry.

WHERE TO LEARN MORE

American Association of Advertising Agencies
405 Lexington Avenue
New York, NY 10174
(212) 682-2500; fax: (212) 682-8391
www.aaaa.org

Public Relations Society of America, Inc.
33 Maiden Lane
New York, NY 10038
www.prsa.org

American Advertising Federation
1101 Vermont Avenue N.W., Suite 500
Washington, DC 20005
www.aaf.org

Advertising Age
www.adage.com

PRWeek
www.prweek.com/us

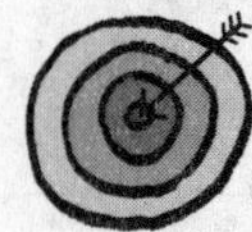

WORDS OF WISDOM

"Figuring out solutions and never saying 'no' or "that's impossible" really pushes you to get solutions that might not be immediately evident."

—Paul Sutton, Senior Integrated Producer

"While public relations is behind the scenes, we are responsible for managing a myriad of activities that affect a company and client, and you must have the fortitude to direct people effectively as well as ask for what you need to accomplish your objectives."

—Gary McCormick, Director of Public Relations

Carol Mangis, Online and Magazine Editor
Senior Editor, Ziff Davis Media
CUNY—Hunter College, 1997
Major: English Language Arts/Psychology (double)

What was your first job after graduation?

Assistant account executive at an advertising agency.

What criteria did you use when deciding which colleges to apply to?

I looked for a strong undergraduate business program and a college located in a city.

What was your first choice school?

Wharton Business School at University of Pennsylvania.

What career did you have in mind when you applied to college?

Marketing.

Did the school you attended have a significant impact on your career opportunities?

It gave me a good marketing background, but it had no significant impact on career choice.

Can you please describe the "Aha!" moment when you realized what you wanted to do?

When I was on an interview at an advertising agency and the interviewer described the role of account management, it reflected all of my business interests.

Which classes were most valuable in preparing you for your career or in helping you decide on your career?

Consumer behavior, international business.

How did your professors impact your career choice or preparation?

I had one course where the professor arranged for us to work with a client and do a project that made for a real-world experience.

Did you have a job and/or internship during college that influenced your career choice or career preparation in any way?

I interned as a pollster for President Carter. It taught me how numbers and analysis can tell a story.

Do you have an advanced degree? Is one helpful or required in your field?

I have an undergraduate degree in marketing and business administration. A graduate degree is not required but may be helpful.

What do you love most about your job?

The constant interaction with interesting, smart, creative people.

What is the most difficult or challenging aspect of your job?

Balancing the strong personalities of a diverse workforce.

What is the biggest misconception people have about what you do?

That I am always calm.

What was the biggest obstacle you faced in getting to where you are in your career?

Balancing the demands of work, life, and family; I have to prioritize and multitask.

What skills are an absolute must for someone interested in pursuing your career?

Organization, insight, strong interpersonal skills, creativity, and humanity are essential.

Whom do you admire most in your industry or field? Why?

I admire Donny Deutsch, a smart businessman who approaches the agency like a brand.

What is one piece of advice you would give to someone who is interested in pursuing your career?

Start reading the trade magazines and business publications to get a flavor of the business.

If you could do everything all over again, what would you do differently?

In my early years, I would not sweat the small stuff.

Can you please add any additional comments you think might be helpful to someone hoping to pursue your career?

Meet with as many people as you can. You become conversant in how the business works.

Eric Webber, Public Relations
Vice President/Communications Director, GSD&M
University of Texas—Austin, 1983
Major: Advertising

What was your first job after graduation?

Political campaign worker.

What criteria did you use when deciding which colleges to apply to?

Location, social life, academic reputation.

What career did you have in mind when you applied to college?

Journalism.

How did the school you attended impact on your career choice and opportunities?

University of Texas—Austin (UT) has one of the better advertising schools in the country. Once I got into it, I changed my career choice, and it opened a number of doors for me.

Which college or colleges are turning out the leaders in your profession today?

University of Texas—Austin, University of California—Los Angeles, New York University, Virginia Commonwealth University.

Can you please describe the "Aha!" moment when you realized what you wanted to do?

Somewhere in the middle of the first group project I did during an advertising campaigns class.

Did you change your major? If so, why?

Yes. The first major was more or less a placeholder.

Can you please list your majors?

English, advertising.

Which classes were most valuable in preparing you for your career or in helping you decide on your career?

Introduction to Advertising, Advertising Campaigns, PR Practice, and several writing classes.

How did your professors impact your career choice or preparation?

I had a few who took a very personal interest in their students and several who had real-world experience to add to their academic credentials.

Did you have a job and/or internship during college that influenced your career choice or career preparation in any way?

I interned at the agency for which I now work and learned more there in a year than in five years of college.

Do you have an advanced degree? Is one helpful or required in your field?

No, and I don't think one is necessary.

What do you love most about your job?

I work with some of the smartest, most innovative thinkers I know of. I like the fast pace and the constantly shifting landscape.

What is the most difficult or challenging aspect of your job?

Money could be better. Egos are big. Arrogance is a factor as well.

What is the biggest misconception people have about what you do?

That it's easy.

What was the biggest obstacle you faced in getting to where you are in your career?

I left the ad business for several years. Getting back in isn't always easy for people. I overcame it mostly by luck and by finding an agency that could see the value in a diverse résumé.

What skills are an absolute must for someone interested in pursuing your career?

The ability to absorb and comprehend great amounts of information, and then distill that down to its essence.

Whom do you admire most in your industry or field? Why?

Roy Spence, founder and president of GSD&M because he's a maverick. Martin Sorrel, head of WPP, because he's so smart.

What is one piece of advice you would give to someone who is interested in pursuing your career?

Never take a job for money—if you love what you do, everything else is trivial.

If you could do everything all over again, what would you do differently?

Start my own agency earlier.

Paul Sutton, Advertising
Senior Integrated Producer, Crispin Porter + Bogusky
Boston College, 2003
Major: Communications

What was your first job after graduation?

Junior producer at Arnold Worldwide.

What criteria did you use when deciding which colleges to apply to?

I wanted to find a school that would offer me a lot of internships in the communication field; this pushed me to look at schools in metropolitan areas rather than smaller, rural schools.

What career did you have in mind when you applied to college?

I had an interest in advertising during high school, so I knew that was a field I would ultimately like to go into. The creative path (e.g., art director or copywriter) was what first grabbed my attention. However, I wasn't familiar enough with the inner workings of an ad agency to be able to commit to one occupation over another so early on.

How did the school you attended impact on your career choice and opportunities?

Going to school in Boston gave me a lot of internship opportunities that wouldn't have been matched by a smaller city. By working at several internships, I was better able to discover the occupation that best fit my own abilities. Also, I was able to arrange one-on-one interviews with people in different positions at each company to get a more in-depth feel of what their job entailed.

Do you now wish you had attended a different school? Which one and why?

Attending a college in New York City would have provided the greatest number of internship opportunities in my field. After several semesters bugging human relations (HR) representatives at agencies, I was accepted to an internship in Boston that led to other great opportunities. It took more work to discover options in Boston than it would of in New York, but that extra effort also galvanized my commitment to that career path.

Which college or colleges are turning out the leaders in your profession today?

Advertising draws people from different places, and many people at the agency are quite successful despite not having a four-year degree. However, students from art and design schools tend to quickly jump into the pace of an agency, and those are the résumés I most look forward to seeing.

Can you please describe the "Aha!" moment when you realized what you wanted to do?

Reading the book *Tibor Kalman, Perverse Optimist* really got me interested in advertising. He led an amazing life: he attended (for one year) New York University (NYU), lived in Cuba, created art that you can view in the Museum of Modern Art (MOMA), created album covers for The Talking Heads, and later devoted much of his time to social campaigns including AIDS and the death penalty. Seeing such an array of possibilities that marketing could lead to got me going down this path.

Which classes were most valuable in preparing you for your career or in helping you decide on your career?

Advertising classes were extremely helpful and practical. In Advanced Advertising we prepared a full campaign to compete against other schools, and Ad Copy and Design helped me develop my presentation and portfolio skills. Also, some classes that weren't directly related to advertising were extremely helpful in building skills I find myself using every day, such as debate theory and computer science courses.

How did your professors impact your career choice or preparation?

My professors would set me up with people who were already in the industry and arrange interviews to learn more about the options out there.

Did you have a job and/or internship during college that influenced your career choice or career preparation in any way?

Getting an internship at Arnold Worldwide was not only difficult to get, but it was also unpaid. In the short term, it was hard to justify taking this when there were other internships available that paid. However, it really opened doors for me and was ultimately the first job offer I received.

Do you have an advanced degree? Is one helpful or required in your field?

I just hold a bachelor's degree. There are programs out there at ad schools that offer portfolio development for people who want to become art directors or copywriters. Some examples of these are The Creative Circus, Miami Ad School, and Virginia Commonwealth University. They are very good programs for people who want to pursue a creative field but don't yet feel like they've developed their skills enough.

What do you love most about your job?

The independence to do projects as I think they should be done.

What is the most difficult or challenging aspect of your job?

The workload is pretty heavy, so it requires you to constantly be prioritizing and communicating so that nothing falls through the cracks.

What is the biggest misconception people have about what you do?

Being a producer is not just a matter of managing a schedule and budget but is also a very creative job as well. Figuring out solutions and never saying "no" or "that's impossible" really push you to get solutions that may not be immediately evident.

What was the biggest obstacle you faced in getting to where you are in your career?

Getting the initial job at an ad agency was particularly difficult, especially because the job market was in a downturn. I stayed in touch with all of the contacts I had met at various internships in Boston until one of them had a position.

What skills are an absolute must for someone interested in pursuing your career?

People interested in becoming producers should have a strong interest in a particular medium (Internet, TV, radio, or art buying) and also be extremely communicative.

What is one piece of advice you would give to someone who is interested in pursuing your career?

Persistence pays off, and don't be afraid to call up people you may have a loose connection to or spoke to a while back. Some agencies are always hiring, just waiting for the right candidate to drop in.

Can you please add any additional comments you think might be helpful to someone hoping to pursue your career?

Before any interview, learn as much as you can about the company you want to work for. Know who the partners are, what kind of projects they've done in the past, how big they are, and what their history is. Going into an interview where you already know the basics saves you from asking basic questions and also impresses the interviewer that you took effort.

Gary McCormick, Public Relations

Director of Public Relations, Scripps Networks, DIY, and Fine Living TV Networks

Colorado State University, 1977

Majors: Technical Journalism, Public Relations Concentration; Sociology, Research Methods

What was your first job after graduation?

Director of public relations, Colorado Women's College.

What criteria did you use when deciding which colleges to apply to?

I looked principally at larger in-state schools that had advertising and graphic design curricula.

What was your first choice school?

I had scholarships to Stanford and Northwestern, either of which would have been my pick. However, for monetary reasons, I couldn't afford to go to school out of state.

What career did you have in mind when you applied to college?

I originally intended to major in graphic design and advertising.

How did the school you attended impact on your career choice and opportunities?

When I took my initial classes in design, I was introduced to its uses in PR and advertising. I became interested in the public relations profession and pursued course work in it as well.

Do you now wish you had attended a different school? Which one and why?

While another school may have given me a better foundation in my field, it was still an emerging career as a major for most schools in 1977 and principally resided in the schools of journalism. I may have ended up majoring in journalism or a completely different area had I attended another school.

Which college or colleges are turning out the leaders in your profession today?

There are many colleges that have great programs for PR. While there are many good programs today that can prepare a student, some of those that are turning out leaders in recent years include University of Maryland, University of South Carolina, University of Florida, Brigham Young University, Illinois State University, Ball State University, and Syracuse University.

Can you please describe the "Aha!" moment when you realized what you wanted to do?

I started working at a local radio station when I was 15 year old and still in high school. During college I worked at a newspaper as the production manager. I knew that I wanted something to do with advertising and media from an early age, but it wasn't fully defined until I actually began working after college. I think that we each have mentors who influence our lives and opportunities that present themselves that help to define our "Aha!" moments more than we do for ourselves.

Did you change your major? If so, why?

I had never declared a major in my freshman year, but I did change the course work I was taking to investigate public relations more fully. That course work led me to declare my major and seek acceptance into the program at the end of my sophomore year.

Can you please list your majors?

Technical journalism, public relations concentration; and sociology, research methods.

Which classes were most valuable in preparing you for your career or in helping you decide on your career?

I think that the sociology research course work laid the foundation for my understanding of human behavior that impacted my work in PR the most. I focused on research-based social science to understand the communication process and circles of influence that can drive effective PR. I also believe that both creative writing and journalism courses are a strong foundation for success.

How did your professors impact your career choice or preparation?

My journalism professors did more to discourage my career choice in PR than to encourage it. On the other hand, the sociology professors were enthusiastic about the application of social science to this new field and inspired my continuing interest in applying social science to the PR communication process. Rather than a strictly journalism and writing tactical approach, I instead looked at behavioral change and circles of influence long before it became an industry standard approach.

Did you have a job and/or internship during college that influenced your career choice or career preparation in any way?

Working in media (radio and newspaper) provided a strong basis for understanding news value, how the business of media works, and the best ways to approach reporters and editors with a story. There is a long-standing animosity between journalists and PR professionals that can be diminished to a large extent by having "walked in their shoes," such that they realize you understand and respect their job.

Do you have an advanced degree? Is one helpful or required in your field?

I do not have an advanced degree, but I believe that lifelong learning is required for PR. Whether it is combined to gain an advanced degree or not, the successful PR professional must continue to stay knowledgeable about the business environment, technology, and whatever innovations or developments are occurring that impact your client or company. In recent years there is a growing interest in combining a PR degree and an MBA to provide the credibility and skills necessary to guide and direct business in its communication needs.

What do you love most about your job?

Being on the inside and helping to shape and determine the direction of a client or company. I find it exciting to know the inner workings and motivations that drive a company or client and to help them determine the strategy that can help to achieve their goals. I have always been very goal-oriented, and this has worked to maximize my own personality and drive by combining my interests and skills in a profession that utilizes them to their fullest.

What is the most difficult or challenging aspect of your job?

Getting clients and management to understand that you can't control what is written or said about you in the press. You can present the facts and try to position the information in the best possible light, but at the end of the day, the reporter or writer can say and do what they want with the information. Given that the media is a business that must attract viewers and readers, it is often the controversy, bad news, or conflict that rises to the surface to keep up ratings and subscriptions. I tell everyone I work with that you pay for advertising (because you get to write and design your message exactly the way you want it), you pray for good PR (because you can't promise anything).

What is the biggest misconception people have about what you do?

They believe that we spin or change information to cover up bad behavior or performance. In fact, PR professionals only have their own credibility on which to stake their careers. Without that, you'll have a short-lived life as a PR professional.

What skills are an absolute must for someone interested in pursuing your career?

A strong PR person needs an ability to write well, to develop strong presentation and persuasion skills, and to gain an understanding of business.

What is one piece of advice you would give to someone who is interested in pursuing your career?

Network early; it's the basis of our profession. Find mentors in the industry, become involved in the Public Relations Student Society of America, do as many internships as possible, and read business and trade journals for contacts and style.

If you could do everything all over again, what would you do differently?

I would take additional business courses in order to better understand the motivation of company exectutives and improve communication with them.

Can you please add any additional comments you think might be helpful to someone hoping to pursue your career?

Public relations, in many aspects, requires many of the skills necessary to be successful in sales. Many times a professional has to pick up the phone and call someone to ask for something. Individuals who are not comfortable in this role should consider whether this is the right career path for them. While public relations is behind the scenes, we are responsible for managing a myriad of activities that affect a company and client, and you must have the fortitude to direct people effectively as well as ask for what you need to accomplish your objectives.

Jeff Cannon, Advertising/Public Relations
President, The Cannon Group
Syracuse University, 1985
Majors: Accounting and Business Law

What was your first job after graduation?

Burson-Marsteller—public relations.

What criteria did you use when deciding which undergraduate colleges to apply to?

It was partially about academics but also about the social fabric of the school. Not in terms of who threw the best party, but who had a mix of students, disciplines, and organizations I thought I would fit in and learn from. College is not just about academics. It is about learning how to network, socialize and most important, to explore and try to find out what you want to do.

What was your first choice school?

I wanted a cosmopolitan flavor, but I didn't want to be in the city. Pennsylvania State University and University of California—Los Angeles (UCLA) were my two top choices.

What career did you have in mind when you applied to college?

I had no idea as to what I wanted to do. I started with marine biology, then switched to business when I learned what the biologist's lifestyle was like. Without knowing what I wanted to do, I took the two most difficult majors—CPA accounting and business law—but quickly learned I did not want to do either. It was in networking and during an internship that I decided on my career.

How did the school you attended impact on your career choice and opportunities?

Syracuse impacted it greatly. Not only for the academics, but for the social factors and my ability to learn about different disciplines, different areas of work and play. It enabled me to try new things and find out what was most appealing to me.

Do you now wish you had attended a different school? Which one and why?

I may have wanted UCLA. Syracuse has some terrible winters, and UCLA provides an amazing campus and education.

Which college or colleges are turning out the leaders in your profession today?

It's less the college and more the student and what they do with the educational opportunities available. From what I've seen, Syracuse does an incredible job, along with New York University and Pennsylvania State University. Also, we've seen some great candidates out of Temple.

Can you please describe the "Aha!" moment when you realized what you wanted to do?

It started during junior year, when I decided I didn't want to be an accountant or a lawyer. I took an internship between the summer of my junior and senior years with Burson-Marsteller. That was the year I figured it out.

Did you change your major? If so, why?

I kept my major, thinking the business background would come in handy at some time. Now that I'm running my own business, it continues to help me.

Which classes were most valuable in preparing you for your career or in helping you decide on your career?

From philosophy to art to accounting—they have all provided me with a rounded education, which is what I feel is most important in my field.

How did your professors impact your career choice or preparation?

The majority of professors did little to impact my career choice. However, one of my law professors had a profound impact. Not only in career choice but in deciding what it was I wanted to do.

Do you have an advanced degree? Is one helpful or required in your field?

I made a decision several years out of school to learn from doing rather than returning to school. I'm still not sure if it was the best route, but it worked for me.

What do you love most about your job?

It has to be working with great people, developing new ideas, and most of all, playing in a creative field.

What is the most difficult or challenging aspect of your job?

Finding the mix between the business aspect of this career and the creative aspect. Making sure we turn out great creative ideas but also maintaining profitability.

What is the biggest misconception people have about what you do?

That it's all fun and games, cocktail parties, and networking events. It is long hours and a lot of hard work.

What was the biggest obstacle you faced in getting to where you are in your career?

I'm not a natural-born networker. I am a more private person. So learning the value of contacts and working on becoming a better networker was crucial.

What skills are an absolute must for someone interested in pursuing your career?

Discipline and focus are the most important. Writing is critical. Networking is essential.

Whom do you admire most in your industry or field? Why?

I admire the ad people from the 1960s who turned out great ideas and great work. They took the time to learn about their clients and their clients' products. They really understood the products they were marketing, rather than just forcing campaigns.

What is one piece of advice you would give to someone who is interested in pursuing your career?

Make sure you want to do it. Make sure that it is what you enjoy. Because it does take up most of your waking hours. Also, make sure you want to do the work, and not just have the glory—because that doesn't come until much later.

If you could do everything all over again, what would you do differently?

Nothing at all. Life is an adventure. Life is about trying new things. I have delved into several fields, from producing films to writing books. Each of them has been a benefit to what I am doing now.

Can you please add any additional comments you think might be helpful to someone hoping to pursue your career?

Life is a process. Make sure you enjoy what you are doing. If you do not know what you want to do, try different things. Explore. Find out what you enjoy and then pursue that. But most important, be passionate about what you do.

ARCHITECTURE

WHY CHOOSE TO BECOME AN ARCHITECT?

Architects are creative, have a good design sense, and strong visual skills. Architects design buildings of every type, including homes, schools, offices, and shopping malls. They take into consideration the requirements of the people who will use the building, the clients' budgets, and the needs of the surrounding community. Architects can be involved in every phase of the building process, from initial ideas through final construction.

WHERE THE JOBS ARE

A majority of architects work for architecture firms, and about a quarter are self-employed. Architecture jobs are closely tied to the construction industry: the more building that is taking place, the more architects will be needed. Although job prospects for architects in general may be good, employment opportunities may not be strong across the board, but rather in certain specific areas. As the population ages, there will be a strong demand for architects to design retirement communities, hospitals, and nursing homes. There will also be a need for architects to design schools and other institutional or public buildings. Some architecture firms have begun to outsource drafting and other chores usually performed by entry-level employees or interns, which means that new hires may face more competition.

AREAS OF SPECIALTY

Architects can specialize in a type of building (homes or hospitals, for example) or a phase of the building process, such as predesign or construction management.

EDUCATIONAL REQUIREMENTS

Architects must be licensed before they can practice. Licensing requires a professional architecture degree, on-the-job experience, and a passing grade on the Architect Registration Examination. There are three types of professional degrees. A five-year bachelor of architecture is meant for those entering university-level studies from high school or those without previous architectural experience. There is also a two-year master of architecture program for students with a preprofessional undergraduate degree in architecture or a related area, and finally, a three- or four-year master of architecture program for those with a degree in an area other than architecture.

SALARY RANGE

The median salary for architects in 2004 was $60,300.

Pros: Creative work, satisfaction in seeing something you designed be built

Cons: Often, many people to please before a final design can be executed

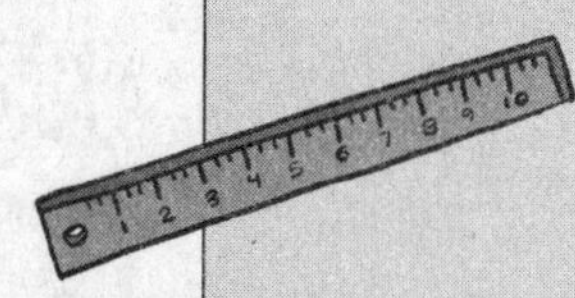

FAMOUS ARCHITECTS

- **Frank Lloyd Wright**, who designed homes to fit into their natural environment
- **Julia Morgan**, who designed Hearst Castle in San Simeon, California
- **Louis Sullivan**, who is considered to be the father of the modern skyscraper

WHERE TO LEARN MORE

The American Institute of Architects

1735 New York Avenue N.W.

Washington, DC 20006

(800) AIA-3837 or (202) 626-7300;
fax: (202) 626-7547

Email: *infocentral@aia.org*

www.aia.org

Intern Development Program

National Council of Architectural Registration Boards

801 K Street N.W., Suite 1100K

Washington, DC 20006-1310

www.ncarb.org

WORDS OF WISDOM

"Many people think architecture is exotic, exciting and filled with creative, red wine-filled napkin sketches of genius. The reality is that requires a good deal of preparation and steady technical progress."

—-Craig Dykers, Principal Architect

"Get involved with your student organization of the American Institute of Architects. This is a great avenue to expand your exposure to the profession and a wonderful opportunity to advocate for your peers and to network with firms and architects in your area. It is also a great way to get involved with and give back to your community."

—John Padilla, Principal Architect

Craig Dykers, Architect
Principal Architect and Cofounder, Snøhetta
University of Texas—Austin, 1985
Major: Architecture

What was your first job after graduation?

Coy Howard & Company.

What criteria did you use when deciding which colleges to apply to?

Breadth of disciplines available, close proximity, and cost were important considerations for me in choosing a school.

What career did you have in mind when you applied to college?

I was interested in clothing design and business as I entered university. I was primarily interested in designing women's clothing, in particular.

How did the school you attended impact on your career choice and opportunities?

Access to alternative sources of information was very good at my university. The library was exceptional! Also, the link between the university and the surrounding city was important to me. I felt I needed to be connected to the world beyond the walls of academia. This has varying degrees of importance, but in architecture, I find that notion valuable.

Do you now wish you had attended a different school? Which one and why?

I don't have any regrets. If I were considering alternatives, they would have included a school that had a more direct link with the fine arts, such as the California College of the Arts.

Which college or colleges are turning out the leaders in your profession today?

I'm not certain. I have seen very good applicants from the Massachusetts Institute of Technology (MIT) in New England. There is always someone who studied at the Architectural Association (AA) School of Architecture in London.

Can you please describe the "Aha!" moment when you realized what you wanted to do?

My first project in architecture school led me to be completely immersed in creating things; it was a simple sculpture that involved rolling a marble along a construction for as long a time as possible without stopping. Afterward, a second wind came when exploring the work of Coy Howard, who came to my studio. Attending a lecture by the artist and architect Siah Armajiani and seeing a film of a lecture by Robert Smithson made a considerable impact. All of this was sustained by the understanding that space, the definition of space, the creation of objects, and human interaction allow for an infinite variety in defining presence and time.

Did you change your major? If so, why?

My course of study changed many times. However, in retrospect, all of these changes were linked to an understanding of the human condition, its form and its relation to life and the objects humans interact with.

Which classes were most valuable in preparing you for your career or in helping you decide on your career?

Although the curriculum was obviously essential, I found attending calendar lectures, especially those outside of my field of study, to be valuable. The literature and art departments often had a strong lecture series. Also, the access to museums on campus was valuable, the ability to see and experience authentic works rather than simply seeing a picture or hearing someone else talk about them was important in creating a view of my own studies. One of the classes I seem to think of often was my freshman English class. My grasp of language and the recognition of the importance of language have remained important to me in my understanding of my professional life. A few design classes allowed me to see the value of design in direct relation to life and human nature.

How did your professors impact your career choice or preparation?

Some professors nearly chased me out of school due to their exceptional inability to describe their curriculum in a way that made it connect to the world around me. I simply felt they were quoting sources without providing useful examples. I would have rather read the book myself alone on my sofa. Other professors remain in my mind to this day, as if I can still hear their voices as I consider my own work, some 20 years later. These professors did not simply teach, they brought knowledge to life. They instilled in me the notion that action has consequence beyond what is often intended.

Did you have a job and/or internship during college that influenced your career choice or career preparation in any way?

I worked several jobs of various types in order to pay for my schooling. I was an editorial illustrator, an assistant in an architecture office, a highway maintenance worker, and a street performer. I felt that having this broad range of interests helped inform my thoughts of architecture beyond what I would find simply working in an architecture office.

Do you have an advanced degree? Is one helpful or required in your field?

I do not have an advanced degree and do not think it is useful unless you have a very specific interest that requires singular focus.

What do you love most about your job?

Each day is a new exploration. This should not imply that each day is pleasant; the climb is filled with considerable pitfalls. Each day brings a new insight into human interaction and culture; this is a wide spectrum, ranging from the difficult and evil to the joyful and unexpected.

What is the most difficult or challenging aspect of your job?

Perhaps the biggest challenge includes ensuring that all the various people working toward the same goal are able to speak and understand the same language, even if everyone is speaking the same dialect. The second biggest challenge is keeping the office functioning.

What is the biggest misconception people have about what you do?

Many people think architecture is exotic, exciting, and filled with creative, red wine–filled napkin sketches of genius. The reality is that it requires a good deal of preparation and steady technical progress.

What was the biggest obstacle you faced in getting to where you are in your career?

Architecture is a profession that requires a good deal of professional or personal connections. If you come from a background that is outside of this exposure, then it often requires more work to bypass the nepotism that is so often the norm. My particular background, as a military child, meant that I traveled considerably and never had the possibility to connect to a place or group of people. My personal method of dealing with this was to allow it to become a strength. I have been on the fringe all my life, and it is this "otherness" that has allowed me to enter the center.

What skills are an absolute must for someone interested in pursuing your career?

It is important to have the capacity to speak well, to understand language in both its verbal and graphic forms, to have good hand-eye coordination, to judge dimensional differences, and to enjoy struggle.

Whom do you admire most in your industry or field? Why?

I admire Sverre Fehn, John Lautner, the Aga Khan, and a number of lesser-known architects who are doing great work.

What is one piece of advice you would give to someone who is interested in pursuing your career?

Despite the enormous importance of architecture, it is always important to remember that it is merely a reflection of life.

If you could do everything all over again, what would you do differently?

I would like to have spent more time learning music and learning to play an instrument.

Carl Krebs, Architect
Partner, Davis Brody Bond
Harvard, 1981
Majors: History and Science

What was your first job after graduation?

Paralegal.

What criteria did you use when deciding which colleges to apply to?

Academic excellence across a wide range of fields, as I had not decided on a career.

What was your first choice school?

Harvard University.

What career did you have in mind when you applied to college?

International relations or possibly law.

How did the school you attended impact on your career choice and opportunities?

It encouraged me to value the importance of learning for its own sake andnot to fixate on professional education as the purpose of college. As a result, I gradually evolved toward an interest in architecture, which allowed me to continue to explore ideas that are of sustaining interest and satisfaction.

Which college or colleges are turning out the leaders in your profession today?

It's not easy to answer, as very few colleges offer undergraduate professional programs in architecture. Most of the best schools are limited to graduate master's programs. Of the graduate schools, Harvard, Columbia, and Yale are well regarded. However, the best students and professionals come out of these schools with diverse undergraduate backgrounds. In general, I found the best students usually had an undergraduate liberal arts background as opposed to an undergraduate architectural degree.

Can you please describe the "Aha!" moment when you realized what you wanted to do?

Third grade, watching a filmstrip about what an architect does. I decided that was what I wanted to do.

Which classes were most valuable in preparing you for your career or in helping you decide on your career?

Seminar courses revolving around small group discussion in which you needed to present and defend ideas.

Did you have a job and/or internship during college that influenced your career choice or career preparation in any way?

No. However, after college, I took a weekend course in architectural design at a local school to explore my interests further. This program was not available at Harvard.

Do you have an advanced degree? Is one helpful or required in your field?

Yes, an M.Arch. A professional degree is required, either a five-year bachelor's (B.Arch) or a master's degree. The latter seems to be becoming the standard.

What do you love most about your job?

Its creative aspects as well as the ability to contribute to society with built projects that influence and affect daily life.

What is the most difficult or challenging aspect of your job?

Managing public constituencies and multiheaded clients.

What is the biggest misconception people have about what you do?

That you need to be good in mathematics (though it doesn't hurt).

What was the biggest obstacle you faced in getting to where you are in your career?

Getting my first job.

What skills are an absolute must for someone interested in pursuing your career?

Drive and internal motivation, strong visual aptitude, and interest and good communication skills.

Whom do you admire most in your industry or field? Why?

I admire my senior colleague and partner, who was a professor of mine in graduate school and has devoted a significant part of his practice to exposing good design and architecture to underserved urban communities.

What is one piece of advice you would give to someone who is interested in pursuing your career?

Do what motivates and compels you, not what is safely employable or highly compensated. Your work and career define so much of your life that it is a tragedy to look back with regret on a chance you didn't take.

If you could do everything all over again, what would you do differently?

Not much. I would have traveled more as a student and studied abroad (which was not an option for Harvard in 1980 but is now).

John A. Padilla, Architect
Owner-Principal, Padilla & Associates Architects
University of Houston
Major: Architecture

What was your first choice school?

The University of Texas—Austin (UT).

What career did you have in mind when you applied to college?

I've always wanted to be an architect.

How did the school you attended impact on your career choice and opportunities?

The University of Houston (UH), being located in Houston, gave me the opportunity to work as well as go to school.

Do you now wish you had attended a different school? Which one and why?

At times I regret not taking advantage of an opportunity that presented itself to me to attend University of Pennsylvania, but all things considered, UH was the right choice.

Which college or colleges are turning out the leaders in your profession today?

There are many excellent schools and colleges of architecture across the country, and each has their own strong points (design, sustainability, construction, etc.), so to single out a specific school would not be fair. The education at architecture school provides the ability to pursue a career in architecture as well as many other alternative careers. The individual is a critical thinker, solution-oriented, and can be an asset to any employer.

Can you please describe the "Aha!" moment when you realized what you wanted to do?

It was the summer before my freshman year in high school, and I saw some of my friends drafting work they had created in their high school drafting shop class. It caught my eye, my attention, and my heart, and I've been hooked ever since.

Which classes were most valuable in preparing you for your career or in helping you decide on your career?

All my architectural classes were of value in preparing me for my career.

How did your professors impact your career choice or preparation?

As with anything, there were good and bad professors. Some were doing it because it was a job, but others were doing it because they loved architecture and were dedicated to sharing that love for their profession with their students.

Did you have a job and/or internship during college that influenced your career choice or career preparation in any way?

I have been working for architects and engineers since I was a senior in high school; I was hooked early on and have not regretted the choice.

Do you have an advanced degree? Is one helpful or required in your field?

No.

What do you love most about your job?

The ability to see the end product of the client's design in my head and then being able to translate that to paper and see it being built, and the client then moving in and occupying the space we designed together.

What is the most difficult or challenging aspect of your job?

The business side of architecture, which was not taught in college.

What is the biggest misconception people have about what you do?

That all architects are wealthy and drive expensive sports cars!

What was the biggest obstacle you faced in getting to where you are in your career?

Being from a family of six kids and from the barrio of San Antonio, Texas, with no one in the business who could show me the way or maybe provide me a break. I had to do it all on my own and be committed to this dream of mine. With the love and moral support of my family and their example of honesty and dedication, I was able to get to where I am now.

What skills are an absolute must for someone interested in pursuing your career?

Dedication and commitment to a dream. It's a lot of work but well worth the effort.

Whom do you admire most in your industry or field? Why?

I admire my colleagues who are members of the American Institute of Architects (AIA) and who not only practice but advocate for their fellow architects across the country.

What is one piece of advice you would give to someone who is interested in pursuing your career?

Keep your eye on the target and stay focused. It's a long haul, and there are times when you might want to give up. But stay the course and reap the benefits that await you at the end of the line.

If you could do everything all over again, what would you do differently?

I would take more business classes to be smarter about how to run a business.

Can you please add any additional comments you think might be helpful to someone hoping to pursue your career?

Get involved with your student organization of the American Institute of Architects. This is a great avenue to expand your exposure to the profession and a wonderful opportunity to advocate for your peers and to network with firms and architects in your area. It is also a great way to get involved with and give back to your community.

Walter Schacht, Architect
Principal Architect, Schacht Aslani Architects
Connecticut College, 1978
Major: Architectural Studies

What was your first job after graduation?

Woodworker.

What criteria did you use when deciding which undergraduate colleges to apply to?

I was interested in attending a small, liberal arts college that offered me the opportunity to engage in a dialog with teachers and students.

What was your first choice school?

Tufts University.

What career did you have in mind when you applied to college?

Political science, with an interest in pursuing a career in government.

How did the school you attended impact on your career choice and opportunities?

My studies in political science and philosophy and my participation in the political process during the 1972 presidential election brought me to the realization that I was interested in a career that would allow me to see the results of my efforts in concrete, tangible things. As a result, my long-term interest in design and construction resurfaced, and I changed direction part way through my junior year.

Do you now wish you had attended a different school? Which one and why?

I am happy that I attended Connecticut College. It was the right place for me to be and I made lifelong friends.

Which college or colleges are turning out the leaders in your profession today?

The list of colleges that are turning out professional leaders is too long to list. Prospective architecture students who are choosing an undergraduate school should remember they are likely to pursue a master of architecture degree. A strong liberal arts background in verbal and graphic communications that promotes an understanding of history, philosophy, psychology, and the arts is the key to a good undergraduate education for architecture.

Can you please describe the "Aha!" moment when you realized what you wanted to do?

I was working as a carpenter, during a two-year period when I took time off from my college education, when I realized that I could combine my love of building and my passion for community by becoming an architect.

Did you change your major? If so, why?

I changed my major from political science to architectural studies because I felt that a career in architecture would allow me to see the tangible results of my efforts as well as contribute to the social and cultural development of my community.

Which classes were most valuable in preparing you for your career or in helping you decide on your career?

Visual arts, art history, world history, language arts, psychology, and philosophy.

Do you have an advanced degree? Is one helpful or required in your field?

I have a master of architecture (M.Arch.) degree from University of Washington. The M. Arch. is a professional degree and is an important credential in obtaining a license to practice architecture. Although a master's degree is not absolutely required to practice in the field, it is the preferred educational path for most prospective architects.

What do you love most about your job?

I love the variety of things that I do as part of my work, from conceptualizing and drawing design ideas, to working hands-on with groups of people, to being on the job site of one of our construction projects. In the end, we get to see the vision we develop with our clients realized in our built work. It is very fulfilling.

What is the most difficult or challenging aspect of your job?

Realizing the client's program within the client's budget is the most challenging aspect of architecture. It takes creativity and discipline to design a project that fits the client's pocketbook.

What is the biggest misconception people have about what you do?

People think that architects spend most of their time drawing design ideas. Actually, that is only a percentage of what occupies our time. Communications, management, and strategic thinking are required to create an environment for design. Administration is required to handle the construction phase. Design is the central focus of all of our efforts, but a great deal of time must be invested to allow the design to become a reality.

What was the biggest obstacle you faced in getting to where you are in your career?

The biggest obstacle I faced was my tendency to explore design alternatives without being able to decide which option to pursue. It took years of practice for me to develop an intuitive sense of which ideas would make good buildings so that I could move on from developing many ideas to executing the best one.

What skills are an absolute must for someone interested in pursuing your career?

An architect must be skilled in verbal and graphic communications, understand how to relate to people, have a strong sense for the cultural and physical factors that influence design, and have strong management skills. Most importantly, an architect must be a strategic thinker. There are many issues involved in the design of a building. It takes a strategic approach to order them so that a great building can be achieved.

Whom do you admire most in your industry or field? Why?

I appreciate the ideas and skills of a lot of different architects. For me, the architects who take a wide range of issues into consideration and develop designs that fit the individual circumstances of their environments are the most admirable.

What is one piece of advice you would give to someone who is interested in pursuing your career?

I would advise prospective architects to expand their horizons and develop sensitivity for the cultural issues that influence design. Travel is a great way to see architecture and to develop sensitivity for how buildings relate to their places.

If you could do everything all over again, what would you do differently?

I would have started developing my graphic communications skills much earlier in my life—starting in middle school. It took me a long time to develop a drawing style that allowed me to explore my design ideas effectively.

Can you please add any additional comments you think might be helpful to someone hoping to pursue your career?

Architecture is a field that demands that you love the work and aren't afraid to put in the effort required to realize a great idea in built form. It's not the most remunerative of the professions, but it is one of the most rewarding in terms of seeing the fruits of your labors.

Prescott Reavis, Architect
Project Coordinator/Internship Coordinator, Anshen + Allen
Howard University, 1996
Major: Architecture

What was your first job after graduation?

Intern at HLM Design, Portland, Oregon.

What criteria did you use when deciding which undergraduate colleges to apply to?

An outstanding reputation; location; the ability to have outside learning experiences and meet diverse people; a place of higher learning more concerned with your ability to think than your race, religion, or socioeconomic background.

What was your first choice school?

Howard University.

What career did you have in mind when you applied to college?

Computer science engineering.

How did the school you attended impact on your career choice and opportunities?

I believe Howard was the perfect school for me. I had professors who had their own firms or were major contributors to the firm they worked for. They provided an extremely realistic viewpoint about the profession, the rewards, and the pitfalls.

Which college or colleges are turning out the leaders in your profession today?

A leader to me is someone who provides opportunities, visions, and contributions to improve the quality of life for those who do not have the ability or the wherewithal to speak on the inequalities of life and environment. University of Cincinnati, Howard University, Ball State University, California College of the Arts, University of Texas—Austin, Cal Poly, and all the Ivies. The Ivy League schools don't meet my criteria, but the mainstream world and media believe they are changing the world in a positive way. But I believe most of them never spend the time to really understand the issues of the average person.

Can you please describe the "Aha!" moment when you realized what you wanted to do?

When I worked at my first internship for Ernest Davis and saw how much positive impact he had on his community.

Did you change your major? If so, why?

Yes. I was bored with computer science engineering.

Which classes were most valuable in preparing you for your career or in helping you decide on your career?

All my classes outside of the school of architecture (I minored in education) really allowed me to understand that we were not being prepared to design buildings or plan communities, but we were being taught a process of how to solve problems and communicate on multiple levels.

How did your professors impact your career choice or preparation?

My professors were a strong influence on my career choice. My third-year professor had the greatest impact on me because he prepared us to be true professionals from the first day of class. He educated us on the way we should present our work, how to eloquently discuss our process, and how our thinking related directly to the clients' and/or users' needs. He also encouraged us to pursue our own unique approach, but at the same time, he always made us aware of what our weaknesses were and how to improve them. He also introduced our class to laboratory and hospital design, which are the sectors where I have worked since I graduated.

Did you have a job and/or internship during college that influenced your career choice or career preparation in any way?

Yes. I interned for Ernest Davis my second and third years, and he was always impressing on me to work hard and to think more about the idea and who will really be using the facility. He owned his own firm, was a county legislator, and owned over ten buildings. He was a pillar in his community and always would help those who could not afford his services. Most importantly, he was a great mentor.

Do you have an advanced degree? Is one helpful or required in your field?

No, I think a master's degree does really nothing for you in architecture unless you want a straight-line path as a lead designer. If you want to be more of an overall architect and work on every phase, the only things that matter are your work ethic, your ability to communicate at multiple levels, and being a strong team leader.

What do you love most about your job?

The project types I work on (medical and university buildings), my current coworkers, and the ability to shape and mentor the ideas of students on what architecture is about and should be about.

What is the most difficult or challenging aspect of your job?

Helping the client and users understand what we really do and the value we bring to the overall team, and the demanding deadlines and lack of concern by many people in the profession to the ownership of their work.

What is the biggest misconception people have about what you do?

I draw pretty pictures all day, I wear a bow tie, and there are no really great minority architects.

What was the biggest obstacle you faced in getting to where you are in your career?

My race is still a big issue. When I was interviewing for jobs when I graduated from Howard, I went to Bellingham, Washington, to interview for a position. When one of the principals came out to meet me for the interview, he was like, "Oh, you are Prescott." Then he called the other principal over, and he did the same thing. And I could see in their eyes they never expected to see a black person, let alone a young black man with dreadlocks. Today, after ten years of experience, I see in many of our clients' eyes when they first meet me that they don't believe I can do the work because of my race.

How did you overcome it?

I work hard and show them I understand the issues and I am here to produce a high-quality project for them, and I have a team-player attitude.

What skills are an absolute must for someone interested in pursuing your career?

The ability to work with and within a team, to take ownership of your work, and to listen and observe.

Whom do you admire most in your industry or field?

I admire Jack Travis, Allison Williams, Ernest Davis, and Santiago Caltrava. All four of these architects have been unwavering about their ideas, heritage, and belief that they are here to improve the world for all communities. They see solutions most cannot understand, but when a project is complete, the simplicity and elegance of their contribution to the community is seen and understood by all. They also are concerned about the next generation of architects and support and mentor many established and budding architects.

What is one piece of advice you would give to someone who is interested in pursuing your career?

Do it because you enjoy it. If you don't, leave and go do what you enjoy.

If you could do everything all over again, what would you do differently?

Travel more while in school.

CRIMINAL JUSTICE

WHY CHOOSE A CAREER IN CRIMINAL JUSTICE?

People who work in criminal justice have good analytical skills, an attention to detail, and a desire to protect individuals and society as a whole. Criminal justice is a wide field that fundamentally involves investigating, pursuing, and arresting those who threaten to or actually do commit crimes.

WHERE THE JOBS ARE

Most people who work in criminal justice are employed by the government. Local governments hire their own police forces, and the federal government's Department of Justice (DOJ) oversees such agencies as the Drug Enforcement Agency (DEA) and the Federal Bureau of Investigation (FBI). Private investigators provide their services to the general public for a fee. They are often hired by lawyers to gather evidence for lawsuits or criminal investigations and generally work on a per-project basis. Because of attractive benefits and challenging careers, there is a lot of competition for jobs with the federal government. Although it will still remain a competitive industry, demand for private detectives is expected to rise, in part due to increasing Internet crime, lawsuits, and the fact that employee background checks are becoming more commonplace.

AREAS OF SPECIALTY

People who work in criminal justice tend to specialize in investigating specific types of crimes, including homicide or narcotics. Private investigators also generally concentrate their practices on a few areas of investigation, including insurance investigations, background checks, or missing persons.

EDUCATIONAL REQUIREMENTS

Most jobs in criminal justice require at least a bachelor's degree; one exception, however, is the police officer, a job that often only requires an associate's degree. Jobs with the federal government frequently have stricter educational requirements, which vary by division and job. FBI agents, for example, must either have a law degree or a bachelor's degree in either accounting, electrical engineering, or information technology; fluency in a foreign language; or three years of related full-time work experience. There are no educational requirements for becoming a private investigator; however, many do have bachelor's degrees. In most states, investigators must be licensed, but licensing requirements vary from state to state.

SALARY RANGE

Salaries vary depending on the specific job and experience level. Criminal investigators working for the federal government earned an average annual salary of $79,100. Median annual earnings of salaried private investigators were $32,110; those who own their own firms could potentially earn more.

Pros: Challenging work, the satisfaction that comes from protecting people and their property

Cons: Sometimes long and irregular hours, dangerous work

FAMOUS FIGURES IN CRIMINAL JUSTICE

- **William J. Flynn**, former head of the Secret Service, became the first director of the FBI in 1919.
- **Elliot Ness**, U.S. Treasury agent who helped send mobster Al Capone to prison; the movie, television series, and book *The Untouchables* are based on his exploits.

WHERE TO LEARN MORE

National Association of Legal Investigators
908 21st Street
Sacramento, CA 95814-3118
(800) 266-6254
www.nalionline.org

U.S. Department of Justice
950 Pennsylvania Avenue NW
Washington, DC 20530-0001
(202) 514-2000
www.usdoj.gov

Central Intelligence Agency
Office of Public Affairs
Washington, DC 20505
(703) 482-0623; fax: (703) 482-1739
www.cia.gov

WORDS OF WISDOM

"When I solved my first case. It was a burglary that the police couldn't solve so the victim came to me. I proved it was an inside job, and that it was actually committed by one of the victim's very good friends."

—Frank Ritter, Private Investigator

"It takes special skills and professional discipline to establish strong human relationships that result in high-value intelligence from clandestine sources."

—Melvin Leon Gamble,
National Clandestine Officer

Francis "Frank" D. Ritter, Private Investigator
Owner, Backtrack Unlimited Co.
St. Edwards University (Austin, Texas), 1968
Major: History

What was your first job after graduation?

Director of personnel.

What criteria did you use when deciding which undergraduate colleges to apply to?

I wanted a Catholic college with a great reputation.

What was your first choice school?

University of Notre Dame was my first choice, but I couldn't afford it. I then discovered that the faculties at Notre Dame and St. Edwards University (SEU) interchanged. Hence, I was able to get a Notre Dame education at an SEU price.

What career did you have in mind when you applied to college?

I had a vague idea about becoming a lawyer.

How did the school you attended impact on your career choice and opportunities?

I had to declare my major within the first seven days of school. I didn't know what I wanted to declare, so I asked my counselor what would give me the broadest possible education. Without hesitation he told me to major in history. He was absolutely correct. Studying history taught me how to investigate, only now I don't go back into history quite as far.

Which college or colleges are turning out the leaders in your profession today?

Virtually none. Colleges are teaching the wrong subjects to turn out investigators. The vast majority of criminal justice courses are designed and taught by either current or ex–law enforcement, who don't have the vaguest idea of what it takes to be an investigator or to do a terrific investigation. However, some colleges down in Florida learned that a very large percentage of criminal justice students do not want to be street cops (which is what most criminal justice courses are aimed at). City College in Florida is the leader in this area and even offers both AA and BA degrees in investigation. Their students are getting jobs in this field the easiest. Hopefully, they will become the industry leaders down the line, but all of this is so new. It is too early to tell, but there is no reason they shouldn't fulfill the leadership roles.

Can you please describe the "Aha!" moment when you realized what you wanted to do?

When I solved my first case. It was a burglary that the police couldn't solve, so the victim came to me. I proved it was an inside job and that it was actually committed by one of the victim's very good friends.

Which classes were most valuable in preparing you for your career or in helping you decide on your career?

Every class that taught me how to think, how to research, and how to write. Any decent investigator can teach the basics of investigation, but we can't teach a person how to think logically or how to write a decent report or how to understand what they are reading. These are things that they must bring to the table when they interview for a job.

How did your professors impact your career choice or preparation?

They demanded that I learn and use the language properly; they taught me how to think in logic classes; they taught me how to investigate the past, which is exactly what I do now.

Do you have an advanced degree? Is one helpful or required in your field?

An advanced degree is not required and not particularly helpful, except that it shows that the degree holder can stick with a project and see it to completion. It also implies a certain level of intelligence, but along with intelligence, investigators need a fair amount of "street smarts." I know two investigators who have PhDs, and a few have master's degrees, but for the most part they rarely go beyond a bachelor's degree. Like me, they get their education at seminars. I spend about 50 hours a year in learning seminars.

What do you love most about your job?

The challenges. I specialize in catastrophic plaintiff personal injury. Because the injuries are so horrific, the dollar amounts tend to be quite high and the fight very demanding. There can be no mistakes. It will be me, the attorney, and the expert the attorney hires standing up against major corporations and governments. We rarely ever lose, and that is a terrific feeling.

What is the most difficult or challenging aspect of your job?

Getting it right. Knowing that because of the seriousness of the injury, whole families are devastated, and it is just the team I am on standing between them and disaster. A case is like a game of chess, a couple of wrong moves and the game is lost. The stakes are way too high for careless and incompetent investigations.

What is the biggest misconception people have about what you do?

TV and the movies are a big source of misinformation. We don't break laws. We don't function in any "gray" legal area. I haven't carried a gun in over ten years. We also don't have friends on the police department who think we are great and give us tons of information illegally. Private investigation is a very professional and extremely broad field, and most folks have no concept of what we do. In California, the licensing test failure rate for ex–law enforcement is 50 to 80 percent the first time through, and 30 to 50 percent the second time through because they think that because they were cops they can be private investigators (PIs). Big mistake.

What was the biggest obstacle you faced in getting to where you are in your career?

There are states in which no licensing is required. In Colorado, the retired FBI agent association fights licensing and testing because they are "FBI and know how to investigate." In the United States, there are somewhere in the neighborhood of 50,000 to 70,000 active PIs, and sadly, most of them do not have the vaguest idea of what they are doing. Incompetence abounds. Because of this, many attorneys have a bad taste in their mouths formed by terrible investigations. My first obstacle was convincing people that I actually did know what I was doing. I overcame the obstacle by learning my craft. I am a certified legal investigator (CLI) and a certified international investigator (CII). It is very difficult to earn a CLI certification, and right now there are only 107 of us in the entire nation.

What skills are an absolute must for someone interested in pursuing your career?

Reading, writing, and thinking. Also, one must not be afraid of or be put off by details. Investigation is a world of details. I have written reports in excess of 100 pages many times. I determined a long time ago that if a person could understand what they read, could write a decent description of something, I could teach them how to investigate. But I added one other thing: I will only hire folks who somehow dabble in the arts. I don't care if the person is the meanest football player on the line, I want to know if he sits in the john at three in the morning and writes poetry. I don't care which form of the arts, but that shows me they have patience (which is a required personality trait) and are not afraid of, and may actually enjoy, details.

Whom do you admire most in your industry or field? Why?

I admire my fellow CLIs because I trust them to truly know their business. I can safely refer a case or client to them and know the job will be done properly, in a timely way, and professionally.

What is one piece of advice you would give to someone who is interested in pursuing your career?

Understand what you are getting into, and then truly learn your profession. Strive to be the very best investigator out there.

If you could do everything all over again, what would you do differently?

I would have gone straight into investigation instead of wasting time in the securities industry, where I was in personnel and portfolio management. For the most part, it was wasted years as far as a profession for me was concerned.

Can you please add any additional comments you think might be helpful to someone hoping to pursue your career?

Take the basic courses like English and history; take logic courses—any courses that make you think, not memorize, but actually think. Once you get out into the working world, look for good schools that teach investigation, not criminal justice. There are a few colleges and even fewer private investigative schools that teach what you need. Do something in the arts. Teach yourself to enjoy details because the difference between a really good investigation and a truly great investigation lies in the case's nuances—the tiny details.

Melvin Leon Gamble, National Clandestine Officer
Chief of Clandestine Service Hiring Division,
Central Intelligence Agency
Howard University, 1972
Majors: History; International Public Administration

What was your first job after graduation?

Central Intelligence Agency (CIA).

What criteria did you use when deciding which colleges to apply to?

Where I would be most challenged and receive the best education. I was also looking for diversity since I was the first Afro-American to graduate from my high school.

What was your first choice school?

Howard University (my parents wanted me to attend Yale University or Harvard University).

What career did you have in mind when you applied to college?

I wanted to be a lawyer, then become a U.S. senator.

How did the school you attended impact on your career choice and opportunities?

I was waiting to enter law school when I was persuaded to apply and work full-time at the CIA.

Do you now wish you had attended a different school? Which one and why?

No. Howard University was challenging and a great social experience for me.

Which college or colleges are turning out the leaders in your profession today?

There are a wide variety of colleges. Things have changed a great deal from the early days of my career, when many of the applicants came from Ivy League colleges. We recruit from a wide variety of universities and colleges from across the country. We need such a variety of skill sets to help complete our mission.

Can you please describe the "Aha!" moment when you realized what you wanted to do?

Initially, I was uncertain that I wanted to be an operations officer (or "spy"), but after serving overseas and working against the Russians and other targets, I realized that I had made the right decision.

Which classes were most valuable in preparing you for your career or in helping you decide on your career?

History, prelaw courses, public administration, international relations.

How did your professors impact your career choice or preparation?

Strongly. I had excellent professors for history and international relations who challenged conventional thinking and the students.

Did you have a job and/or internship during college that influenced your career choice or career preparation in any way?

I worked as a summer employee at the CIA. We offer many student work opportunities in the form of undergraduate student internships or co-ops, and graduate studies programs.

Do you have an advanced degree? Is one helpful or required in your field?

Yes, I have an advanced degree, but it is not required. It does help broaden your perspective on issues, however.

What do you love most about your job?

Clandestine officers—also called operations officers—serve on the front lines of the human intelligence collection business by clandestinely recruiting and handling sources of foreign intelligence; we call them "assets." It takes special skills and professional discipline to establish strong human relationships that result in high-value intelligence from clandestine sources. I love recruiting and handling assets and the planning of operations. Operations officers must be able to deal with fast-moving, ambiguous, and unstructured situations. This requires physical and psychological health, energy, intuition, and street sense.

What is the most difficult or challenging aspect of your job?

The most difficult aspect is planning and implementing successful operations against difficult targets.

What is the biggest misconception people have about what you do?

That we work without oversight or restrictions—not true. Our job is to protect American lives as well as carry out the orders of the president of the United States.

What was the biggest obstacle you faced in getting to where you are in your career?

Initially, it was discrimination—it was a different era in America in the early 1970s. But many good officers wanted me to succeed and I overcame the obstacles with persistence, a strong belief that I had the abilities to be successful, and some great mentors.

What skills are an absolute must for someone interested in pursuing your career?

The ability to think on your feet, good interpersonal skills, good communication skills (writing and speaking), and a sense of humor.

Whom do you admire most in your industry or field? Why?

I admire former Director of Central Intelligence (DCI) George Tenet and the other officers who remain undercover.

What is one piece of advice you would give to someone who is interested in pursuing your career?

Join with an open mind, be flexible, and maintain a can-do attitude.

If you could do everything all over again, what would you do differently?

I would learn more foreign languages.

Meredith DeKalb, Forensic Investigator
Document Examiner
(currently self-employed but previously worked at the FBI)
Colorado State University, 1992
Major: Social Science

What was your first job after graduation?

Intern for Senator Wayne Allard.

What criteria did you use when deciding which undergraduate colleges to apply to?

I wanted a big school in Colorado.

What career did you have in mind when you applied to college?

Musician.

How did the school you attended impact on your career choice and opportunities?

I interviewed on campus for Senator Allard and was rejected for the internship in Washington, D.C. Fortunately, I followed up with them and worked in the local office in Ft. Collins, Colorado. When the internship became available after graduation, I was first in line. This decision brought me to Washington, D.C., where I obtained a master's in forensic science, and brought me to the FBI.

Which college or colleges are turning out the leaders in your profession today?

There is no particular school, however, the leading forensic science programs are at George Washington University in Washington, D.C., University of Birmingham, and John Jay College of Criminal Justice in New York.

Can you please describe the "Aha!" moment when you realized what you wanted to do?

I was in my master's program and took one forensic science class as an elective. I was hooked!

Which classes were most valuable in preparing you for your career or in helping you decide on your career?

Psychology, social science, and logic.

How did your professors impact your career choice or preparation?

My counselor told me not to worry too much about my major (I switched to social science from political science), just get the degree and move forward.

Do you have an advanced degree? Is one helpful or required in your field?

Yes. It is beneficial to have an advanced science degree.

What do you love most about your job?

I get to work on interesting cases and my work is different every day.

What is the most difficult or challenging aspect of your job?

Keeping up-to-date with current technology, which can affect my examinations of the evidence.

What is the biggest misconception people have about what you do?

That it is just like CSI on the TV shows.

What was the biggest obstacle you faced in getting to where you are in your career?

There are no obstacles, just opportunities. Keep trying different things until you know exactly what you want to do. I worked on several internships at once, made no money, and just kept pressing forward.

What skills are an absolute must for someone interested in pursuing your career?

Attention to detail, ability to pass a background check and a drug test. You must have a good work ethic and be able to approach problems with logic.

Whom do you admire most in your industry or field? Why?

I admire my coworkers at the FBI. They teach me things every day.

What is one piece of advice you would give to someone who is interested in pursuing your career?

Take internships, talk to people in your field, apply for the lowest job just to get your foot in the door.

James M. Cawley, Secret Service Agent
Special Agent in Charge, United States Secret Service
Bucknell University, 1982
Major: Economics

What was your first job after graduation?

Chemical Bank (Security/Fraud Department).

What criteria did you use when deciding which colleges to apply to?

When deciding what college I wanted to attend, I considered the following criteria: academic reputation, size of the college, location, and the baseball program.

What was your first choice school?

Bucknell University (BU) was my first choice.

What career did you have in mind when you applied to college?

I did not have a specific career in mind when I first applied to college.

How did the school you attended impact on your career choice and opportunities?

I believe BU's reputation as one of the premier schools in the area enhanced the level of opportunity, but that had little to do with my ultimate decision to pursue a career in law enforcement.

Which college or colleges are turning out the leaders in your profession today?

Our profession truly features a wide range of backgrounds with regard to our organization's leaders.

Can you please describe the "Aha!" moment when you realized what you wanted to do?

My "Aha!" moment came when I spent several months in my first nine-to-five job at the bank, coupled with a career-counseling session with my mentor—my father.

Which classes were most valuable in preparing you for your career or in helping you decide on your career?

The most valuable classes that prepared me for my career in federal law enforcement were political geography, economics, and organic chemistry.

How did your professors impact your career choice or preparation?

Several professors encouraged critical thinking and some posed extremely challenging and interactive sessions.

Do you have an advanced degree? Is one helpful or required in your field?

I do not have an advanced degree; however, I feel that even though it is not required, it is always helpful eventually.

What do you love most about your job?

The wide range of challenges, extensive travel, and the unpredictability of the mission, as well as the critical nature of what we do as an agency.

What is the most difficult or challenging aspect of your job?

The most difficult aspect of my job is balancing family life, travel time, and the day-to-day challenges of my position.

What is the biggest misconception people have about what you do?

The biggest misconception the public has of the U.S. Secret Service is that it is a secret agency.

What was the biggest obstacle you faced in getting to where you are in your career?

The biggest obstacle I faced was spending such a large percentage of time on shift work and traveling while on protective assignments.

What skills are an absolute must for someone interested in pursuing your career?

Common sense skills, a solid background, good physical fitness, and a college degree would be beneficial to anyone pursuing a career with the U.S. Secret Service.

Whom do you admire most in your industry or field? Why?

In the field of law enforcement, I feel that the most complex position, as well as the most critical, is that of the police commissioner of New York City. I think that Ray Kelly is doing an outstanding job in that position.

What is one piece of advice you would give to someone who is interested in pursuing your career?

My advice to the students would be to always be careful what you do in high school and in college so that nothing negatively impacts a career you would like to pursue in the future.

Casey McEnry, DEA Special Agent
Criminal Investigator, Drug Enforcement Administration (DEA)
California State University—Sacramento, 1993
Major: Criminal Justice

What was your first job after graduation?

Probation counselor.

What criteria did you use when deciding which colleges to apply to?

Proximity to home and majors offered.

What career did you have in mind when you applied to college?

Counselor.

How did the school you attended impact on your career choice and opportunities?

Sacramento State University offered many criminal justice classes, and at the time I attended, their program was ranked third in the state of California.

Which college or colleges are turning out the leaders in your profession today?

Today it's University of California—Berkeley, among other colleges.

Can you please describe the "Aha!" moment when you realized what you wanted to do?

In one of my introductory criminal justice classes taught by a retired FBI agent, I heard about conducting criminal investigations, and I knew that was what I wanted to do for my career.

Did you change your major? If so, why?

I changed from psychology to criminal justice because I wanted to pursue a career in the criminal justice field.

Which classes were most valuable in preparing you for your career or in helping you decide on your career?

Introductory criminal justice classes.

How did your professors impact your career choice or preparation?

By speaking about their life experiences in the field of criminal justice.

Do you have an advanced degree? Is one helpful or required in your field?

I do not have an advanced degree nor is one required in my field.

What do you love most about your job?

Every day is different. Some days are office days, other days are in the field, and sometimes you're in court.

What is the most difficult or challenging aspect of your job?

It can be difficult with long work hours that are not consistent.

What is the biggest misconception people have about what you do?

That I live this undercover life. I still function normally like everyone else.

What was the biggest obstacle you faced in getting to where you are in your career?

Balancing a demanding career and a personal life can be challenging. Finding the middle of the road, setting limitations, and having a good support system helps.

What skills are an absolute must for someone interested in pursuing your career?

Writing skills are a must, and verbal communication skills are equally important.

Whom do you admire most in your industry or field? Why?

I admire our deputy administrator, Michele M. Leonhart. She started out as a street agent, has risen through the ranks, and is the number two person in charge at the DEA.

What is one piece of advice you would give to someone who is interested in pursuing your career?

Be persistent and don't get discouraged; when the time and career is right, you will know.

If you could do everything all over again, what would you do differently?

Apply to the DEA earlier! I waited almost two years after graduation.

Can you please add any additional comments you think might be helpful to someone hoping to pursue your career?

Be flexible, eager, and willing to do what it takes to succeed in the beginning. A career in law enforcement can be very demanding and extremely rewarding.

CULINARY ARTS

WHY CHOOSE A CAREER IN THE CULINARY ARTS?

People who work in the restaurant industry are creative, love cooking, and love food and wine. Chefs and restaurateurs conceive menus and individual dishes in addition to actually preparing food. They also run the kitchen, which means they order food supplies and manage staff.

WHERE THE JOBS ARE

Most chefs work in restaurants and hotels of varying sizes and types across the country. Personal chefs, however, cook meals for customers in their own homes. Some chefs also work as teachers and research chefs, which means they test recipes and experiment with new products and equipment. A combination of increased leisure time and families with two incomes (allowing for more disposable income as well as less time to cook) has been increasing the number and popularity of restaurants. However, careers in the culinary arts are very popular, and competition for jobs at well-known restaurants will continue to be intense.

AREAS OF SPECIALTY

Established chefs generally specialize in a type or style of food, such as French, Italian, or fusion.

EDUCATIONAL REQUIREMENTS

Becoming a chef in a fine restaurant takes years of training and experience. Some chefs attend culinary school or degree programs in hospitality or culinary arts. In addition, some programs require an apprenticeship at a restaurant. People who own their own restaurants often have a degree in business or hospitality.

SALARY RANGE

Chefs' salaries vary greatly depending on the type of restaurant, the amount of experience, and their location; however, their median hourly earnings in the year 2007 were $14.75.

Pros: Creative work

Cons: Long, irregular hours; low pay, especially when starting out

FAMOUS CHEFS

- **Julia Child**, credited with popularizing French cooking in America.
- **James Beard**, considered the father of American gastronomy.
- **Georges Auguste Escoffier**, who updated and popularized traditional French cooking.

WHERE TO LEARN MORE

National Restaurant Association

1200 17th Street N.W.

Washington, DC 20036-3097

(202) 331-5900 or (800) 424-5156;
fax: (202) 331-2429

www.restaurant.org

American Culinary Federation

180 Center Place Way

St. Augustine, FL 32095

(800) 624-9458 or (904) 824-4468;
fax: (904) 825-4758

www.acfchefs.org

International Council on Hotel, Restaurant, and Institutional Education

2613 N. Parham Road, 2nd Floor

Richmond, VA 23294

(804) 346-4800; fax: (804) 346-5009

www.chrie.org

American Personal & Private Chef Association

4572 Delaware Street

San Diego, CA 92116

(800) 644-8389

Email: *info@personalchef.com*

www.personalchef.com

Food & Wine Magazine

www.foodandwine.com

Gourmet Magazine

www.epicurious.com/gourmet/

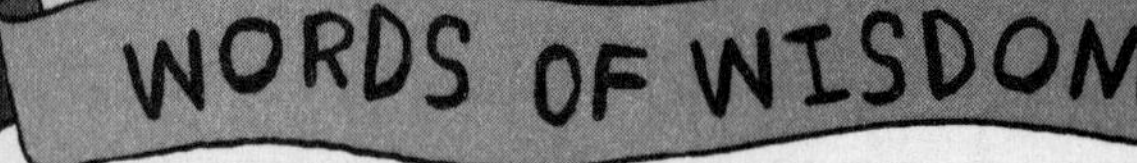

"I find that regardless of your educational foundation, the restaurant industry crosses so many components of our society and business environment that something yoou have learned will be valuable to you."

—Edward Tinsley III, Restaurant Owner

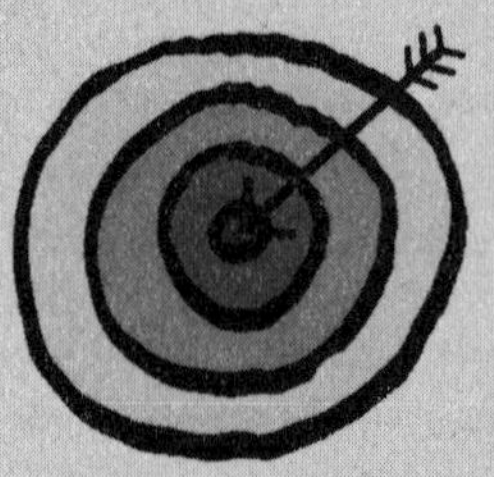

"It is not only just cooking any longer; it is all the other factors that are necessary to succeed. Trying to find out what the public wants and to be able to give it to them, as they have become more demanding."

—Bert Cutino, Restraunteur/
Property Developer/Chef

Lon Symensma, Chef
Chef de Cuisine, Buddakan New York City
Culinary Institute of America, 1999
Major: Culinary Arts

What was your first job after graduation?

La Bastide Saint Antoine, France.

What criteria did you use when deciding which undergraduate colleges to apply to?

I wanted to attend the best school there was in the country.

What was your first choice school?

The Culinary Institute of America.

What career did you have in mind when you applied to college?

Culinary arts.

How did the school you attended impact on your career choice and opportunities?

It opened the door to many of the top restaurants.

Do you now wish you had attended a different school? Which one and why?

Absolutely not!

Which college or colleges are turning out the leaders in your profession today?

The Culinary Institute of America and Johnson and Wales.

Can you please describe the "Aha!" moment when you realized what you wanted to do?

When I flipped my first burger at a diner at age 15.

Which classes were most valuable in preparing you for your career or in helping you decide on your career?

Gastronomy and charcuterie.

How did your professors impact your career choice or preparation?

They would share stories of their own personal experiences in the field.

Did you have a job and/or internship during college that influenced your career choice or career preparation in any way?

I did an externship for Chef Donald Miller at the University of Notre Dame.

Do you have an advanced degree? Is one helpful or required in your field?

No, to be a chef, it is not necessary.

What do you love most about your job?

I like to see other people enjoying the dishes I make for them.

What is the most difficult or challenging aspect of your job?

Constantly inspiring and motivating the people who work for me in the restaurant.

What is the biggest misconception people have about what you do?

Many people feel that being a chef is cool and glamorous and may not realize the hard work and dedication involved.

What was the biggest obstacle you faced in getting to where you are in your career?

This is a career that requires many years of long hours and financial strain, but once you develop a reputation for yourself, opportunities seem endless.

What skills are an absolute must for someone interested in pursuing your career?

Organization, discipline, and creativity.

Whom do you admire most in your industry or field? Why?

I admire Daniel Boulud because he is the most dedicated chef in the field.

What is one piece of advice you would give to someone who is interested in pursuing your career?

Don't be in a rush to become too big too fast.

If you could do everything all over again, what would you do differently?

I would have spent more than only one year living and working in Europe.

Can you please add any additional comments you think might be helpful to someone hoping to pursue your career?

Figure out what your goals are and work hard to make your dreams come true.

Anne-Marie Abrigo, Personal Chef
Chef/Owner, Saving You Thyme
San Jose State University, 1989
Major: Business Administration

What was your first job after graduation?

Technical support at Intuit.

What criteria did you use when deciding which undergraduate colleges to apply to?

Did it have the program that fit my needs, location, cost.

What career did you have in mind when you applied to college?

I am what you call a Silicon Valley refugee. I was in the dot.com world and it went bust. So I went looking for a new career where I could do something that I loved to do. I found the personal chef career field, which fit my needs and wants. I decided to go back to school to learn about the cooking industry. I did not want to start without understanding the industry.

Which college or colleges are turning out the leaders in your profession today?

If you are looking for a leading school for culinary arts in the United States, I would say Culinary Institute of America (CIA) based in New York. There are many, many good schools for learning the art of cooking. It just depends on what you can afford.

Can you please describe the "Aha!" moment when you realized what you wanted to do?

At the time, I was recovering from surgery and I was downsized again from another dot.com company. The longer I stayed away from the high-tech industry, the more I did not want to return. So I started thinking about a second career. I wanted to do something that I would love and get paid for it. I started surfing the Web and looking for opportunities connected with cooking food. I knew that I did not want to work in a restaurant (that is for the young, and I was 38 when I went back to school). I found a site called PersonalChef.com, and it described a career that seemed to fit what I was looking for. I thought to myself, wow, this is a career I can do. I can make a living in the cooking field and not be working crazy hours at low pay. I would be my own boss!

Which classes were most valuable in preparing you for your career or in helping you decide on your career?

Any class that exposes you to the real world of your chosen career, that helps you run a business successfully, and that helps you develop people skills.

Did you have a job and/or internship during college that influenced your career choice or career preparation in any way?

I was in an internship program that showed me what goes on in a commercial kitchen, both good and bad.

What do you love most about your job?

I am doing what I love to do and getting paid to do it.

What is the most difficult or challenging aspect of your job?

Because I am the sole proprietor of my business, I have all the job titles: CEO, CFO, marketing and sales, accountant, chef, and dishwasher. The most challenging part of my job is to network and find clients and jobs.

What is the biggest misconception people have about what you do?

Most people have no idea how hard it is to plan and execute a party event. They are surprised at the number of chef hours needed (I charge by the hour, plus the food for events). The hours include menu design, travel, shopping, prep time, cooking, and cleanup. Some clients have the tendency to compare my price per meal with going out for a meal, and they think that the price per meal is too high. But they are forgetting that they are paying for the personalized and customized service.

What was the biggest obstacle you faced in getting to where you are in your career?

Finding the career (goal) and then planning the steps needed to get to that goal. Believing that I could achieve that goal.

What skills are an absolute must for someone interested in pursuing your career?

A passion for cooking, business mindedness (the bottom line is to make money), people skills, multitasking skills.

Whom do you admire most in your industry or field? Why?

I admire my mentor Chef John Britto. He learned to be a chef in the Navy. He was able to attain the rank of E-9 after only 16 years. He was the first to do that. After retiring from the military, he began his second career as a chef instructor. He spent the next 20 years developing the program and teaching students how to cook. He has retired from that career and is now in his third career as a culinary consultant and loving every minute of that new career. I admire him because he has shown me that it is never too late to start a new career.

What is one piece of advice you would give to someone who is interested in pursuing your career?

Stay focused, find a mentor, and become the expert in your chosen field. Also, understand the industry as a whole, not just your career field. You never know where opportunities will come from.

If you could do everything all over again, what would you do differently?

I would have skipped my first career in high tech and started younger in the food industry.

Edward R. Tinsley III, Restaurant Owner
CEO, Tinsley Hospitality Group, LLC
University of Texas—Austin
Major: Accounting

What was your first job after graduation?

Lawyer.

What criteria did you use when deciding which colleges to apply to?

Good football team; no sandstorms; lakes; good looking girls; oh yeah, a good business school.

What career did you have in mind when you applied to college?

Accounting and law.

How did the school you attended impact on your career choice and opportunities?

Good education and great contacts and relationships.

Do you now wish you had attended a different school? Which one and why?

No, never.

Can you please describe the "Aha!" moment when you realized what you wanted to do?

Briefing a case for a trial that I had, and I was worrying more about my client's fate than mine, with little appreciation from the client for doing so.

Which classes were most valuable in preparing you for your career or in helping you decide on your career?

Accounting, statistics, and virtually all my law school classes.

How did your professors impact your career choice or preparation?

None. My father was an independent businessperson whom I respected tremendously, and he gave me the confidence to pursue my dream.

Do you have an advanced degree? Is one helpful or required in your field?

Yes, and I think it's helpful.

What do you love most about your job?

Service and interaction with people, knowing when a job is getting done right, and seeing the rewards happen before your eyes with satisfied guests and employees.

What is the most difficult or challenging aspect of your job?

Recruitment and retention of a quality and enthusiastic workforce.

What is the biggest misconception people have about what you do?

There is a lack of respect and opportunity for our restaurant industry.

What was the biggest obstacle you faced in getting to where you are in your career?

Challenges would be a better way to describe it, not obstacles. It's difficult balancing something I love doing with personal and family time.

What skills are an absolute must for someone interested in pursuing your career?

People skills and a good work ethic.

What is one piece of advice you would give to someone who is interested in pursuing your career?

You must enjoy people, be ready for changes, and accept that better ideas usually come from others. Do what you love, and love what you do.

Can you please add any additional comments you think might be helpful to someone hoping to pursue your career?

I find that regardless of your educational foundation, the restaurant industry crosses so many components of our society and business environments that something you have learned will be valuable to you. I am constantly amazed at how many great and successful restaurant operators and owners I meet come from such varied backgrounds, educationally, culturally, and geographically. The diversity is wonderful, and the opportunities to grow and learn from other operators never, ever ceases.

Montgomery Knott, Restaurant Owner
Director, Monkey Town
Hampshire College, 1991
Majors: Political Theory and Anthropology

What was your first job after graduation?

Clerk, Texas House of Representatives.

What criteria did you use when deciding which colleges to apply to?

Good campus and faculty, interesting curriculum, independent study.

What was your first choice school?

Princeton University.

What career did you have in mind when you applied to college?

None, but maybe writing.

How did the school you attended impact on your career choice and opportunities?

I studied broadly. My skills are broad and my career is flexible and ever changing.

Do you now wish you had attended a different school? Which one and why?

No regrets; I'm quite happy.

Which college or colleges are turning out the leaders in your profession today?

Brown University and Rhode Island School of Design (RISD). Can't escape them.

Can you please describe the "Aha!" moment when you realized what you wanted to do?

I'm still awaiting this. There are so many options.

Which classes were most valuable in preparing you for your career or in helping you decide on your career?

Many of my off-campus classes at Smith College and Amherst College. These were the most grounded in creative focus and theoretical stimulation.

How did your professors impact your career choice or preparation?

My advisor/professor had a great impact. He did not direct me to do anything in particular, but he encouraged me to study widely.

Did you have a job and/or internship during college that influenced your career choice or career preparation in any way?

No, though I had plenty of jobs that made me know what I didn't want to do.

Do you have an advanced degree? Is one helpful or required in your field?

No, I don't, and I'm not sure it would be helpful.

What do you love most about your job?

The people I meet and that I'm the boss.

What is the most difficult or challenging aspect of your job?

I'm the boss. My job is among the most difficult imaginable: long-hour workweeks, sub-minimum wage.

What is the biggest misconception people have about what you do?

That it makes money and that it is glamorous.

What was the biggest obstacle you faced in getting to where you are in your career?

I have faced few obstacles beyond owning one's own business, specifically a restaurant business, and that is one giant obstacle.

What skills are an absolute must for someone interested in pursuing your career?

Stamina and access to large amounts of capital.

Whom do you admire most in your industry or field? Why?

There is really nobody on earth who does what I do. I am a restaurateur, a cultural programmer, a bookkeeper, and a menu consultant.

What is one piece of advice you would give to someone who is interested in pursuing your career?

It is impossible to do without a giant amount of capital. Triple the cost of everything when raising capital.

If you could do everything all over again, what would you do differently?

Raise more capital and hire better chefs.

Bert Cutino, Restaurateur/Property Developer/Chef
General Partner, Cannery Row Company; Cofounder, COO, The Sardine Factory Restaurant
Monterey Peninsula College, 1962
Major: Business Administration

What was your first job after graduation?

Managing a restaurant.

What criteria did you use when deciding which colleges to apply to?

Unfortunately, due to finances and to be able to still help my family, I went to the local college.

What career did you have in mind when you applied to college?

I thought that I would either be in the restaurant business or the real estate business, although I also thought I would be a teacher like my late brother, Pete, who was a famous water polo coach, and my sisters, who also went into teaching. It was sort of automatic that I would think about going into the education field.

How did the school you attended impact on your career choice and opportunities?

There was not a school that really impacted my career choice and my opportunities. Much later I would have to say I was thinking about going to San Francisco State University (hospitality program) once I made up my mind that I wanted to be in the hospitality industry.

Do you now wish you had attended a different school? Which one and why?

Knowing what I know now, in that I moved more into the culinary arts, I would have loved to have gone to the Culinary Institute of America in Hyde Park, New York, and really gone through a formal culinary school instead of the three-year apprenticeship program of the American Culinary Federation that I did in the early stages of my career. I would have to say that Cornell University is somewhere I would have loved to go, too.

Which college or colleges are turning out the leaders in your profession today?

A lot of the culinary schools that we have are really doing a terrific job. Cornell University, which I believe is top-notch for the hospitality industry, has certainly turned out some people in leadership roles who have also gone on to culinary school. I know they have made a difference.

Can you please describe the "Aha!" moment when you realized what you wanted to do?

I guess that would have to be when I was nine years old and I knew I wanted to be in business. I wanted to be independent. I wanted to have my own bike and eventually my own car, my own house, and my own business, and I achieved all those things that I wanted to do. I just needed a vehicle to get there, so to speak, and I found it in the hospitality industry.

Which classes were most valuable in preparing you for your career or in helping you decide on your career?

Business law was a tremendous help, as well as accounting. You have to know the numbers, and especially in my industry, numbers are everything. It really came easy to me, and I was at one point doing accounting for five restaurants at night while I was going to college. I was learning about the numbers and how important they were.

How did your professors impact your career choice or preparation?

A couple of professors did impact my career choice, as far as understanding the restaurant business. In fact, the professor that I enjoyed the most eventually became the president of the school. He had been in the workforce and understood what business was all about. He was not just someone who went through a school program and then came out and became a teacher.

Did you have a job and/or internship during college that influenced your career choice or career preparation in any way?

I was in an externship and a job from day one. All through high school, if I was not commercial fishing with my father, I was working as a busboy or washing dishes, and I was doing internships with the school with the job-training program. I guess that working in the hospitality industry influenced me the most, and that was eventually where I wanted to be.

Do you have an advanced degree? Is one helpful or required in your field?

No, I do not have a formal advanced degree, but I had a determination to succeed. My advanced degree is all the time I took in the last 40 years learning the business and being exposed to it through seminars, correspondence courses, conferences, and conventions.

What do you love most about your job?

The action, as it is ever changing. It is always stimulating. If I want to work the front of my restaurant, greeting people, etc., I enjoy that as much as working in the kitchen with my chefs, creating a dish.

What is the most difficult or challenging aspect of your job?

Dealing with a lot of the changes that have happened through the years in the hospitality industry. It is not only just cooking any longer; it is all the other factors that are necessary to succeed. Trying to find out what the public wants and to be able to give it to them, as they have become more demanding. Dealing with costs of things we used to take for granted, such as the cooking gas and electricity.

What is the biggest misconception people have about what you do?

We make it look easy; we make it like it is a party every night—that the business is so great and it is nothing but profit, profit, profit. However, people don't realize there is a lot more that goes into it.

What was the biggest obstacle you faced in getting to where you are in your career?

The biggest obstacle I had was financial. I didn't have any money, and we went into business on a shoestring, taking the initiative to live on very little to be able to put more into the business. Hard work and dedication helped us to achieve what we wanted. If you want to make it, you can; you just have to put that extra effort into it.

What skills are an absolute must for someone interested in pursuing your career?

You have to have the knowledge of the business. You have to learn the numbers and have business acumen. You have to learn marketing and human relations, as you deal on a daily basis with people from all walks of life and ethnic groups. If you want to be a skilled chef, you have to have the training, the education, and the experience.

Whom do you admire most in your industry or field? Why?

I admire Ferdinand Metz, who was the president of the Culinary Institute of America. He went through the programs of culinary education, applied himself, took risks, and became very successful, very innovative, and actually was a tremendous influence on many culinary professionals in this country. As far as the industry goes, a fellow by the name of Jerry Burns is very inspirational; he owned the famous 21 Club in New York. He recently passed away at 97, but he was always there reaching out to people as they came to his restaurant. Dave Thomas, who was an orphan, started Wendy's restaurants. And Warren Leruth, who was a chef's chef and a genius.

What is one piece of advice you would give to someone who is interested in pursuing your career?

They have to have the passion and the love for the industry. It is not the easiest industry in the world because of the long hours. You have to be willing to put the industry first. Of course, your family should always be first, but in some cases, you sacrifice a little in that respect. I know I had that situation with my sons growing up, but fortunately, it is not the quantity of time you spend with your family, but the quality of time.

If you could do everything all over again, what would you do differently?

I would do a lot of the same things, but I might have gone further with my education if I had the money to go to school. I would take a little more time off than I did. I could have, but I was too much of a workaholic, as they say. Otherwise, as far as the success of the restaurant, the hotels, and the properties, I would not change anything for the world.

Can you please add any additional comments you think might be helpful to someone hoping to pursue your career?

Stay focused on what they want to do when they are in the middle of it and strive to succeed even more. Don't be afraid of yourself. Don't believe in failure; try to believe in success. Look at the positive side of things before you look at the negative side of things. The positive side always has to outweigh the negatives. If it doesn't, then you have a problem.

Keep in mind the importance of family, friends, and customers. I believe your customers are the kings and queens who walk through the doors, and they are the ones who are paying the bills and making you a success. They need to be made to feel terrific when they come to your place, and make them feel better than they feel at home, which is why they are out dining.

Personalization is so important. Always look at your fellow employees with respect. You may work with a diverse ethnic group, and this gives everyone an opportunity to interact. I believe if more people did that, it would be a better world. Be able to reflect and pass on your knowledge to those who don't have it. Don't be afraid to express your talent; it is important. Show me what you can do. I have even gotten ideas from a dishwasher and a menu item from a pantry person who is a natural. He became one of my sous chefs over the years and went on to own his own restaurant. He has even retired before I have, as I don't believe in retirement. The industry keeps me going because I love it.

FILM

WHY CHOOSE A CAREER IN FILM?

Most people whoe choose a career in film work in editing. Film and video editors take raw footage and work with directors and producers to convey the mood and set the pace of the story being told. They can also fix mistakes made by the director, camera operator, or actors.

WHERE THE JOBS ARE

Editors work in television, in film, on commercials, and on instructional or promotional videos. They can be employed directly by the television or film studios, but many editors choose to work freelance, taking jobs on different projects as they become available. Most editors work in either Los Angeles or New York, which are the centers of the television and film industry. As with most careers in the film and television industry, there is a lot of competition for jobs. Many people make connections at film school or start working as interns to get their foot in the door.

EDUCATIONAL REQUIREMENTS

Most film and video editors have a bachelor's degree in film studies or a related field, where they learn basic film editing skills. An advanced degree from a film school is not a requirement; however, many in the industry find one helpful, especially if their undergraduate degree was in something other than film.

SALARY RANGE

The median salary for film and video editors in 2004 was $43,590.

Pros: Creative and varied work

Cons: Tight deadlines; sometimes have to take conflicting direction from different people

FAMOUS EDITORS

- **Edwin Porter** is considered the father of film editing.
- **Verna Fields** is a successful film editor who is credited with saving the film *Jaws* when the mechanical shark repeatedly malfunctioned.

WHERE TO LEARN MORE

American Cinema Editors

100 Universal City Plaza, Building 2352, Room 202

Universal City, CA 91608

(818) 777-2900; fax: (818) 733-5023

www.ace-filmeditors.org

Motion Picture Association of America

15503 Ventura Boulevard

Encino, CA 91436

(818) 995-6600; fax: (818) 382-1795

www.mpaa.org

American Film Institute

2021 N. Western Avenue

Los Angeles, CA 90027-1657

(323) 856-7600; fax: (323) 467-4578

www.afi.com

WORDS OF WISDOM

"The combination of creativity with technical execution is what really keeps me interested. Not only am I required to tell a story in a clear and interesting way, but I have to figure out how to solve any number of technical or creative problems, which keeps me on my toes."

—Vince Anido, Film and Television Editor

"I think being a good editor is 30 percent technical, 30 percent artistic, and 40 percent diplomatic. You have to know your craft and your software, but more important is the ability to articulate your opinions to others, even sometimes articulating for others what they are thinking when they can't find a way to articulate it themselves.""

—Jeff Turboff, Video Editor

Vince Anido, Editor
Film and Television Editor, Self-Employed
University of Southern California, 2002
Majors: Cinema; Television Critical Studies

What was your first job after graduation?

The Stonecutter, an independent feature film.

What criteria did you use when deciding which undergraduate colleges to apply to?

The most important aspect was, of course, a good program for studying film and television, but there were a number of other deciding factors. Location was important to me. Because success in this field relies so heavily on connections, I wanted it to be close to somewhere I would like to live. I also knew I wanted to go to a school that not only would have great peers in the program with me but one that had significant connections and respect in the industry. It also was important to me to find a school that appreciated a balance between scholastic work and a social life.

What career did you have in mind when you applied to college?

I knew I wanted to work in the film and television industry, but I wasn't sure which position would fit me best. There are so many career paths available it was very overwhelming at first.

How did the school you attended impact on your career choice and opportunities?

The wide breadth of topics that the program exposed me to allowed me to get a feel for what interested me most and led me on my way to becoming an editor. The school then goes beyond simple introductions and allows you to deeply explore various job functions that can either cement your decision or allow you to discover that another path might be better for you.

Do you now wish you had attended a different school? Which one and why?

No. I couldn't imagine going to a school that was better suited to me than the University of Southern California (USC).

Which college or colleges are turning out the leaders in your profession today?

University of Southern California and New York University are always thrown around a lot, but going to another school doesn't necessarily prevent anyone from succeeding in this field.

Can you please describe the "Aha!" moment when you realized what you wanted to do?

I was working on a short film with a group sophomore year, and everyone was burnt out after the shoot so no one wanted to edit it. I put a pot of coffee on and started. Within five minutes of sitting down, I knew I was going to really enjoy editing.

Which classes were most valuable in preparing you for your career or in helping you decide on your career?

There were a couple of senior classes that I would consider invaluable to my understanding of the medium itself. I had a fabulous film theory professor who played a large role in teaching me to deconstruct why good movies were good movies, rather than simply identify them.

How did your professors impact your career choice or preparation?

While I would consider every one of the professors I had as good, there were a couple of exceptional people that went above and beyond to prepare me for my career. My writing professor taught me a number of strategies for promoting myself, which was one of the great things about the professors USC has assembled: so many of them are willing to personally help students succeed and constantly go out of their way to help that happen.

Did you have a job and/or internship during college that influenced your career choice or career preparation in any way?

I was an intern for *The Real World—New Orleans* in their story department when I met an editor who allowed me to spend an hour before work and an hour afterwards on his editing system helping him, watching him, and editing my own sequence. This was my first exposure to a nonlinear editing system, and it was invaluable when it came time to get my first job.

Do you have an advanced degree? Is one helpful or required in your field?

I do not, and on the creative side of the film and TV business there is very little to be gained by getting one because so much can be learned on the job. If I did not have a major in the field, having a graduate degree might be an okay investment.

What do you love most about your job?

The combination of creativity with technical execution is what really keeps me interested. Not only am I required to tell a story in a clear and interesting way, but I have to constantly figure out how to solve any number of technical or creative problems, which keeps me on my toes.

What is the most difficult or challenging aspect of your job?

As crazy as it sounds, it's the politics. As an editor, I constantly have to take notes from a number of different producers that often conflict with each other. Learning to understand everyone's ideas and address everyone's concerns while making the best show possible is the high-wire act that no one tells you about when you become an editor.

What is the biggest misconception people have about what you do?

At parties I often have to distill my job description down to "I cut out the bad parts," which isn't at all what I do. I look at my job as writing with words that have already been written. The script is really just a guide after the show is shot and really has little value beyond that. The real story lies within all the footage and must be assembled in a way that works best for what actually happened—not what was supposed to happen. Oh yeah, editors are often thought of as quirky, caffeine-addicted insomniacs. There might be a little of those traits in some of us, so I'll just leave that there.

What was the biggest obstacle you faced in getting to where you are in your career?

Getting started is extremely difficult. It often requires working for free, taking two jobs at once, and putting in a lot of time. So it's extremely important to have confidence in yourself and to also have a good support system to keep you on track and in focus. I started working professionally while I was still in college, which allowed me to get entry level experience right along with my college degree. So when I graduated I was able to begin earning an income, which made life significantly easier.

What skills are an absolute must for someone interested in pursuing your career?

Without a doubt, drive is the most important quality. There is a lot of uncertainty and instability involved with the industry, and getting back up and going after what you want is the only way to succeed. Drive also comes across in a desire to go beyond what is necessary and asked of you, and it is often very well rewarded.

Whom do you admire most in your industry or field? Why?

I've had the privilege of speaking with editor John Wright on a number of occasions, and I really admire the path he's taken in his career. When you get to that highest level of this business, it can be difficult to continually excel, and I often look to his career when contemplating decisions about my own.

What is one piece of advice you would give to someone who is interested in pursuing your career?

You must understand that working in the film or television industry rarely will give you a steady job so that you can have a five-to ten-year path to follow to success—especially if you choose to work in production. Since most of the work is freelance, I constantly change jobs, usually every three to nine months. After a job finishes, I look for a new one. Be aware of this when choosing this path. I've seen so many people fall out and change careers because they were unable to cope with the unsteadiness of work, especially during the first few years. Plan on having weeks, or even months, without work.

But I love changing jobs regularly. Each new job is a new challenge, and it makes me feel as though I'm constantly learning new things. Plan financially for the breaks, and you won't have any issues. Anticipate your out-dates and start hustling for work before that date, which will keep your breaks to a minimum. Don't be afraid to call old contacts for work, and when all else fails, use the time off for that side project you've been putting off for "when you have time." The key to success is never to stop believing you can make it, working hard when you have the work, and enjoying the time off when you have that too. The next sprint to a deadline is around the corner.

If you could do everything all over again, what would you do differently?

I have been very happy with the way everything has panned out so far in my career. The only thing I wish is that I could have learned everything I have just a bit sooner so I could have capitalized more on some opportunities that I failed to see when they were available.

Can you please add any additional comments you think might be helpful to someone hoping to pursue your career?

Work hard, put in extra time, own up to your mistakes, and do what's needed to fix them, and someone will take notice.

Jeff Turboff, Editor
Video Editor, Freelance, but currently working full-time at ABC News
University of Texas—Austin, 1993
Major: Radio-TV-Film

What was your first job after graduation?

Studio manager/assistant to head of sales at a TV commercial production company.

What criteria did you use when deciding which undergraduate colleges to apply to?

I only wanted to attend the University of Texas—Austin (UT).

What career did you have in mind when you applied to college?

I was completely undecided, and at my father's suggestion, I entered college as a business major.

How did the school you attended impact on your career choice and opportunities?

Because I attended UT, I ended up in New York because my first job was offered to me by an alumnus of the school. As he was vacating his entry-level job to move up in the company, he wanted to hire someone from his alma mater to fill his shoes.

Do you now wish you had attended a different school? Which one and why?

I think I may have had a much different kind of career if I had attended University of Southern California (USC) or University of California—Los Angeles (UCLA), which are better at filtering their graduates into the ranks of Hollywood's workers. UT had a decent program, and my main teacher had worked in Hollywood, but I was really unprepared coming out of college. Austin is a long way, geographically and physically, from New York and Hollywood and from the way the industry operates on either coast. Austin has become something of a "third coast," but it's still a very long way from rivaling either New York City or Hollywood.

Which college or colleges are turning out the leaders in your profession today?

As far as I know, it's still University of Southern California, University of California—Los Angeles, and New York University, but I'm not very well informed on this subject.

Can you please describe the "Aha!" moment when you realized what you wanted to do?

I had a few "Aha!" moments. One was during high school, when my parents told me I could go to Houston's High School for the Performing and Visual Arts. I was going to be attending as a student in the media studies program, which felt natural and right, like I had found my calling. But then I got in trouble with my parents, who decided to send me to military school instead. I pretty much forgot all about media studies until my roommate in college told me that a radio-TV-film major was easy. I switched majors my second semester and again things felt like I had found the right track. Once I got into the working world in New York City, I got to see the pieces of commercials go from separate, unrelated shots to first rough cut to fine cut to final cut to final cut with color correct and sound mix, and the more I saw that process unfold, the more I was drawn to editing.

Did you change your major? If so, why?

I was a business major for one semester and hated macroeconomics so much I rarely attended class. Also, the people I met in business school were generally not very creative, open-minded, artistic people. I was a misfit in business school. Everyone else was very buttoned up, which I was definitely not.

Which classes were most valuable in preparing you for your career or in helping you decide on your career?

My multicamera TV production class actually was the biggest editing challenge in college and really gave me a great sense of what can be done in editing, got me jazzed about the editing process, and gave me an initial sense of editing prowess. Also, TV criticism and analysis with Horace Newcomb was a great class and possibly did as much for my understanding of the medium as the production courses.

How did your professors impact your career choice or preparation?

I was disappointed that my TV production professor, while truly a guru with a deep and wide understanding of the medium, was never a mentor and supporter for me personally. In fact, I suspect he didn't like me. Or if he did, he concealed it well.

Do you have an advanced degree? Is one helpful or required in your field?

I don't have an advanced degree, and it's not at all necessary. What's more important is ability, experience, contacts, reputation, ability to get along with others, willingness to work hard and work long hours, and as an editor, a willingness to be an unsung hero to everyone except your producer or director. Editing is not the field for you if you want to be in the limelight.

What do you love most about your job?

I love finding the best way, the right way, to tell a story. For most every moment in a piece, there is a best choice, and finding that choice—the one that will move the story forward with clarity and intention, without any wasted motion—is the joy of editing.

What is the most difficult or challenging aspect of your job?

The same things I love about editing are also the most challenging. That, and in the news environment, there is absolutely never a situation in which missing a deadline is ever acceptable.

What is the biggest misconception people have about what you do?

People think that editing is just taking away what doesn't work. But what's really happening is that a piece is built from the ground up.

What was the biggest obstacle you faced in getting to where you are in your career?

My own business naiveté and youthful sense of entitlement hurt my career more than anything else. Taking martial arts classes helped me to learn to be less self-centered and more realistic.

What skills are an absolute must for someone interested in pursuing your career?

I think being a good editor is 30 percent technical, 30 percent artistic, and 40 percent diplomatic. You do have to know your craft and your software, but more important is the ability to articulate your opinions to others, even sometimes articulating for others what they are thinking when they can't find a way to articulate it themselves. Diplomacy is a very important skill in the edit room, so it is important to learn to negotiate your opinions with the opinions of others.

Whom do you admire most in your industry or field? Why?

I'm not sure. It's hard to know when you're watching an edited piece how much was the editor's input.

What is one piece of advice you would give to someone who is interested in pursuing your career?

Learn your craft, study the masterworks, and then put it into practice, especially by making your own films.

If you could do everything all over again, what would you do differently?

I wouldn't have partied as much in college, and I would've gone on to grad school. Even though it's not necessary for career success, I took ten years between graduating from high school and graduating from college. I wasn't ready for the working world until then, but at least I could've accumulated more knowledge and experience in that time, rather than wandering aimlessly.

Can you please add any additional comments you think might be helpful to someone hoping to pursue your career?

I encourage you to go out and make your film, don't wait to make the perfect film, just make a film—this month! It's incredible what you can do with $20 and an idea. I've seen it over and over and over again. Join forces with others who are interested in doing the same and make a club. Critique each other's work and get better at it. Check out Group 101 films, or Quick Flicks, or any of a number of other groups that are now doing this sort of thing. Grab your camera and get out there and make your first film. Stop thinking about it and do it.

William Simonett, Editor
Film Editor, Loft54
Mississippi State University, 1977
Major: Business

What was your first job after graduation?

Camera sales.

What criteria did you use when deciding which undergraduate colleges to apply to?

Cost and location.

What was your first choice school?

Not going to college or school!

What career did you have in mind when you applied to college?

Photography.

How did the school you attended impact on your career choice and opportunities?

It opened up other doors and opportunities.

Which college or colleges are turning out the leaders in your profession today?

University of Southern California, University of California—Los Angeles, New York University.

Can you please describe the "Aha!" moment when you realized what you wanted to do?

I took a film class in graduate school at Ohio University.

Which classes were most valuable in preparing you for your career or in helping you decide on your career?

The editing classes.

How did your professors impact your career choice or preparation?

They encouraged experimentation.

Did you have a job and/or internship during college that influenced your career choice or career preparation in any way?

Yes, I had a teaching fellowship.

Do you have an advanced degree? Is one helpful or required in your field?

Yes, I have one. Yes, it has been helpful, but not necessary.

What do you love most about your job?

The creativity.

What is the most difficult or challenging aspect of your job?

Satisfying clients.

What is the biggest misconception people have about what you do?

That it's easy.

What was the biggest obstacle you faced in getting to where you are in your career?

Patience and creativity—don't give up.

What skills are an absolute must for someone interested in pursuing your career?

Patience and creativity.

Whom do you admire most in your industry or field? Why?

I admire feature film editors who seem to be the most creative.

What is one piece of advice you would give to someone who is interested in pursuing your career?

Don't expect instant success.

If you could do everything all over again, what would you do differently?

Move to New York City or Los Angeles earlier in my career.

Can you please add any additional comments you think might be helpful to someone hoping to pursue your career?

Get as much real-world experience as possible. Do as many internships as you can, even if they don't pay!

Chris Murrin, Editor
Film Editor, Freelance, but mostly for 20th Century Fox
Columbia University, 1994
Major: Film Studies

What was your first job after graduation?

Graduate school.

What criteria did you use when deciding which undergraduate colleges to apply to?

Location, emphasis on academic life over athletics, prestige, variety of course work available, size and condition of campus.

What was your first choice school?

Princeton University, but I wasn't accepted.

What career did you have in mind when you applied to college?

I wanted to be a physicist.

How did the school you attended impact on your career choice and opportunities?

The course work in physics was very difficult, and living in the city expanded my outlook, opening me to new career ideas. Thus, I had to rethink my career path.

Do you now wish you had attended a different school? Which one and why?

Absolutely not.

Which college or colleges are turning out the leaders in your profession today?

Leaders in my profession come from absolutely anywhere, but if forced to pick for filmmaking overall, I would say Columbia University (CU), University of Southern California, FSU, UT—Austin, UCLA, and New York University are good choices.

Can you please describe the "Aha!" moment when you realized what you wanted to do?

After cycling through a few majors, I realized I needed to focus my studies. I sat one afternoon trying to decide how I would spend the rest of my college experience, if not my life. I knew that to be happy in life, I would need to be happy at my job, so I tried to think of what has always made me happy. Since childhood, I'd always been happiest when seeing movies. I knew that a career in film of some sort would be best for me. However, the career choices within the world of filmmaking are many. In its undergraduate course of film studies, Columbia University offers one production class. My teacher for that class was James Mangold (later the director of *Heavy*, *Cop Land*, *Identity*, *Walk the Line*, and many other films). Part of the introduction to the course involved learning the basics of tape-to-tape editing. To that end, James gave us footage from his short film, *Vincent,* to use for practice. Literally, the first time I sat down at the machine and made a single edit, it felt as if I'd been struck by lightning. Editing would be my primary career. It also didn't hurt that I heard a fellow student behind me say, "Nice cut."

Did you change your major? If so, why?

I began as a physics major. What I found, though, was that while I loved some aspects of physics, there were other aspects that were vitally important to its study that just didn't capture my imagination the way the study of mechanics had in high school. However, science and mathematics had always been my strongest suits, so I then decided to try mathematics. A poor showing and some lack of interest in calculus quickly showed me that mathematics would not work for me. I decided to go into film, but at that time, Columbia had no undergraduate film program so I became an English major because the English department had close ties to the film department, and I would then be allowed to take film classes. However, at the end of my second semester, the undergraduate film program opened up.

Which classes were most valuable in preparing you for your career or in helping you decide on your career?

The video production class with James Mangold and the various courses in the language of cinema taken with Stefan Sharff and James Schamus.

How did your professors impact your career choice or preparation?

As an editor, you must have an understanding of every aspect of filmmaking. Learning the semiotics of film enhanced my ability to tell the director's story effectively.

Did you have a job and/or internship during college that influenced your career choice or career preparation in any way?

I regret that I did not do as much internship work as I could have. Were I to change one aspect of my college experience, it would be to do far more intern work. That said, I did work on the sets of many graduate student films during college and began working professionally, starting with an internship at a local production company, while still in graduate school.

Do you have an advanced degree? Is one helpful or required in your field?

I have a master of fine arts degree from Florida State University (FSU). In my field, no education of any kind is "required." However, the experience I gained in both undergraduate and graduate school has been priceless in my career.

What do you love most about your job?

I liken editing to putting together a puzzle when you have four times as many pieces as you need and no idea what the final image is supposed to be. That aspect, the problem solving and piecing together of footage to tell just the right story or create the perfect moment, that's what excites me about editing.

What is the most difficult or challenging aspect of your job?

Film is a collaborative medium by its very nature. You have to work well with others in order to have a career in this field. Oftentimes while editing, you spend full days or even weeks with a single person sitting a couple of feet away. Sometimes either personalities or creative ideas clash. During those times, editing can be an excruciating process.

What is the biggest misconception people have about what you do?

People oftentimes think that because I've worked in sports a great deal, that I mainly edit highlights. I've never edited a highlight in my career. For editing in general, though, a common misconception is that the real storytelling is already done by the time the editor gets involved: the writer, directors, and actors do the storytelling, and the editor merely assembles the footage in the right order. Nothing could be farther from the truth. Every single person who works on a film is to some degree involved in the storytelling, editors included. The choices an editor makes affect the flow of information, the mood, the pacing, the performances, etc. found in a film. The editing room is where a director/producer and editor take the raw materials provided by a shoot and fine-tune them into the final product you see on screen.

What was the biggest obstacle you faced in getting to where you are in your career?

My biggest obstacle was and still is shyness. This field requires a certain amount of networking ability and skill in self-promotion, which I greatly lack. I have yet to overcome this issue.

What skills are an absolute must for someone interested in pursuing your career?

To be an editor you must have communication skills, as you are essentially translating the instructions and notes you are given into a film. You must also have problem-solving capabilities, as you will often find that the shot you need doesn't exist, and you will have to work around that problem. Finally, you must have the confidence to speak your opinion but be able to sublimate your ego and not take it personally when your suggestions and/or opinions are not followed.

Whom do you admire most in your industry or field? Why?

There are so many, but the editors I admire most are Paul Barnes, Thelma Schoonmaker, and Michael Kahn. They have an ability to create moments and thereby enhance the films on which they work.

What is one piece of advice you would give to someone who is interested in pursuing your career?

Learn every aspect of filmmaking as well as you possibly can because, as an editor, it is your job to look for both the best and worst moments the crew has provided you. Without a deep knowledge of the entire filmmaking process, you won't know what you're looking for.

If you could do everything all over again, what would you do differently?

I would seek out every internship I possibly could.

Can you please add any additional comments you think might be helpful to someone hoping to pursue your career?

The question I'm most often asked by those interested in becoming an editor is, "What system should I learn?" My answer: any hammer can drive a nail. The system is a tool. It is far more important to learn how to edit—how to spot the good and poor moments, how to manipulate footage, where to look for "missing" shots, etc.—than it is to learn any specific system.

Michael Klein, Editor
Television Videotape Editor, CBS-Paramount
California State University—Long Beach, 1989
Major: Radio-TV-Film

What was your first job after graduation?

City of Long Beach TV.

What criteria did you use when deciding which undergraduate colleges to apply to?

Industry reputation, facilities, and campus culture.

What was your first choice school?

University of California—Los Angeles (UCLA), but they were only accepting 23 out of 400 applicants.

What career did you have in mind when you applied to college?

Television director.

How did the school you attended impact on your career choice and opportunities?

California State University—Long Beach (CSULB) had little effect on my career choice, and I wish they had more of an influence on me. I wish I would have paid more attention to the film world and made more connections with those students because that would have opened more doors for me to pursue a film career. I learned later in life that the two paths rarely cross, and to this day I have no connections to the film world (including made-for-TV film opportunities).

Do you now wish you had attended a different school? Which one and why?

UCLA and University of Southern California (USC) have really penetrated Hollywood. Students from these schools have more opportunities open up for them in the internship world. Additionally, the connections you make in college seem to continue to build for years in the postcollegiate world. For instance, if you make a film with ten other students and any one of those students hits it big, they tend to bring their fellow filmmakers along for the ride. It also doesn't hurt to have Lucas and Spielberg donating millions to their facilities. It should be noted that Steven Spielberg eventually graduated from CSULB and to this day is more associated with USC—go figure.

Which college or colleges are turning out the leaders in your profession today?

University of California—Los Angeles, University of Southern California, New York University, and Loyola Marymount University.

Can you please describe the "Aha!" moment when you realized what you wanted to do?

I was hired by my neighbor to put her brother's photos and audio diary together to tell the story of his climb of Mt. Kilimanjaro. After listening to 18 hours of tape, I realized that the man who went up the mountain was a different man than came down the mountain. He seemed to really be moved by his experience. So I made a 90-minute epic to document his time up there. We had the premiere at my parent's house, and we invited his whole family over to watch. The brother was so moved by the experience that he began weeping halfway through, and at the end I received a standing ovation and my parents gave me a mock Oscar. But my "Aha!" moment came when I realized that if I can make a grown man cry, I am destined to be an editor.

Which classes were most valuable in preparing you for your career or in helping you decide on your career?

The most valuable class I took was the course on producing. I learned volumes about the business side of show business. We did an exercise where we had to go to a Hollywood script store and buy a finished film script. Then with it, we had to create a budget and shooting schedule to make the film. I use what I learned from that experience every day. I did start a minor in business, which I still feel was vital to my success. Understanding corporate culture and working in a team environment are critical to understanding how to survive in show business.

How did your professors impact your career choice or preparation?

One professor forced us to choose a profession, and for the rest of that course he talked to us as if we were that professional, and he pressured us to make the kinds of real-life decisions someone in that career would have to make. I chose to be a director and decided to take over the whole production, and I bulldozed over everyone who worked under me. In doing so I created one of the lousiest and most horrific films any of us have ever witnessed. I learned volumes making that lousy film. I had another professor who showed a new movie every week and had someone who worked on that movie talk about their experience afterward. That, too, was a real education in filmmaking.

Did you have a job and/or internship during college that influenced your career choice or career preparation in any way?

I had several internships, and they were vital to the collegiate experience and to starting a career in this field. My advice is to make all of your mistakes and connections during this time because once you are hired, it is assumed that you have gotten all of that out of your system.

Do you have an advanced degree? Is one helpful or required in your field?

No, it is not required unless, I guess, you are teaching in this field.

What do you love most about your job?

Editing is a very powerful craft. It is the purest act of storytelling. A movie isn't a movie until it is edited. The editor will always have the final rewrite of the script. The editor is the one who fixes all of the acting mistakes, the camera mistakes, the directing mistakes. There is no better place to train to be a director than from an editor's point of view. I love that what I do is seen by millions of viewers every day. With that comes the responsibility to do your best every day. Millions of viewers are depending on me to entertain them and keep them interested in the story I am telling. They watch to take their mind off of their own troubles, and I feel an accountability to really craft the few minutes I have with them every day.

What is the most difficult or challenging aspect of your job?

It is a constant struggle to balance quality with the looming on-air deadline. The producers want it now, and I want it as best as it can be. It's a real battle to cram as much visual candy into the story before the show ends up with a black hole where your video was supposed to be.

What is the biggest misconception people have about what you do?

My job is not glamorous and celebrities are mostly just regular people.

What was the biggest obstacle you faced in getting to where you are in your career?

The biggest obstacle I have in my career is accepting that the TV show is not my TV show. I work under supervisors, directors, producers, executive producers, all of whom are slaves to Neilson ratings tracked closely by TV stations and network executives who report to a board of directors who report to shareholders. Every decision I make has to please everyone, and that is a challenging place to be. I think the best way to overcome this obstacle is to simply let go of the fact that it is not your show! However, "letting go" to me translates to not caring, and that is something that is impossible for me to do. So one must balance obedience with creativity; and mastering that is the key to success.

What skills are an absolute must for someone interested in pursuing your career?

Business and management skills are critical to effective communication in this business. You need to be able to communicate effectively to your subordinates, peers, and management. There's no better place to learn those skills than in the business career track.

Whom do you admire most in your industry or field? Why?

I admire Mark Cuban, owner of the Dallas Mavericks and HDNet. Here is a man that marches to the beat of his own drum. He took his dot-com fortune and became a maverick himself. He started the nation's first all high-definition (HD) television network and has programmed it to target the people who were first adopters of HD television. Now HDNet is bigger than ever and is the de facto standard in this arena. Many people considered him too ahead of his time. He ignored them, and it has paid off in spades.

What is one piece of advice you would give to someone who is interested in pursuing your career?

As an intern be the absolute best in the most menial, bottom-of-the-barrel tasks. Be the best car washer, food delivery person, courier, secretary, tape eraser, librarian you can be. Outshine all of the other interns. Do it with enthusiasm and with a smile—like you have been waiting your whole life to get that cup of coffee. Believe me, you will get noticed and you will move up. Those are the people I will be working for someday. Enthusiasm is the fuel for what drives this industry. The best executive producers I have worked with are the ones with the most enthusiasm.

If you could do everything all over again, what would you do differently?

I would do better in high school to make sure I got into UCLA. I would also take the SAT more seriously. Once in UCLA I would pursue an editing/directing career in film. I also would make more of an effort to make friends in college and stay in touch for years afterward.

Can you please add any additional comments you think might be helpful to someone hoping to pursue your career?

Remember that when someone says "you'll never make it in this town" that they are full of it. And possibly the best advice I ever received: choose wisely to whom you donate your time. People who promise the world in exchange for free work probably will never deliver on that promise.

FINANCE, BANKING, AND TRADING

WHY CHOOSE TO WORK IN THE FINANCIAL WORLD?

People who work in the financial world have an interest in mathematics and in investing. They also need to have good interpersonal skills because in many jobs they are required to recruit new clients and/or work closely with them.

- **Personal financial advisors** work with clients to decide how best to invest their money, while considering their financial goals.
- **Financial analysts** look at the performance of a company and its industry to advise a business on how to invest its money. They also gather and present information for financial reports.
- **Investment bankers** advise companies on merging with or acquiring other businesses, selling their stock to the public, or issuing bonds to raise money.
- **Traders** buy and sell securities (the broad term for tradable financial assets, such as stocks, bonds, and currencies) for institutions.

WHERE THE JOBS ARE

- **Financial analysts** work directly for the businesses they serve or for banks or financial advisory companies that provide services for other companies.
- **Personal financial** analysts generally work for a firm that provides its services to the public; they can also work for themselves.
- **Traders** work for banks, institutions, or businesses, investing their money and hoping to make a profit, or they can work for brokerage houses that provide services to the general public.
- **Investment bankers** work for large banks or companies, such as Goldman Sachs or Merrill Lynch, or smaller "boutique" firms that specialize in a few services.

EDUCATIONAL REQUIREMENTS

To work in the finance industry, a bachelor's degree is an almost unstated minimum requirement. In addition, a license is required to trade securities or recommend investments. There are various licenses, but the most common for brokers is the Series 7, which requires a passing score on an exam administered by the National Association of Securities Dealers (NASD). Financial analysts and advisors are not required to be licensed or certified. However, a financial analyst can become a chartered financial analyst (CFA). To qualify, analysts must have a bachelor's degree and at least three years of relevant work experience. They also must pass a series of three yearly essay exams. Personal financial advisors can become certified financial planners (CFPs). To earn this designation, issued by the Certified Financial Planner Board of Standards (CFPBOS), advisors must have relevant work experience, meet certain education requirements, pass an exam, and follow an enforceable code of ethics.

SALARY RANGE

Jobs in the financial industry are some of the highest paying of any career. In addition to high salaries, employees can receive bonuses that are often more than their yearly salaries, as well as earn commissions.

Pros: High pay

Cons: Long hours, high stress

FAMOUS FINANCIERS

- **J. P. Morgan**, steel magnate and banker, was one of the wealthiest men of his time.
- **Warren Buffett** is the legendary investor and CEO of Berkshire Hathaway.
- **Jim Cramer**, former hedge fund manager, hosts a TV investment show.

WHERE TO LEARN MORE

Association for Financial Professionals
7315 Wisconsin Avenue, Suite 600
West Bethesda, MD 20814
Phone: (301) 907-2862; fax: (301) 907-2864
www.afponline.org

The Financial Planning Association
4100 E. Mississippi Avenue, Suite 400
Denver, CO 80246
(800) 322-4237 or (303) 759-0749
www.fpanet.org

The Wall Street Journal
www.wallstreetjournal.com

Bloomberg.com
www.bloomberg.com

WORDS OF WISDOM

"The most challenging aspect of my job is staying current and up to date with the reading required to be on top of all the financial publications. There is so much information out there."

—Amy Hoffman, Certified Financial Planner

"My financial planning and analysis (FP&A) team likes to joke that we're 'data consolidators.' The amount of work that goes into compiling and forecasting numbers is tremendous. Also, people think corporate finance jobs have short hours. I have been putting in plenty of 80 hour weeks."

—Daniel Semo, Finance Analyst

Sumeet Wadhera, Investment Banker
Director, Deutsche Bank
St. Lawrence University, 1994
Majors: Mathematics and Economics

What was your first job after graduation?

Financial analyst, General Electric.

What criteria did you use when deciding which colleges to apply to?

Reputation and availability of financial aid.

What was your first choice school?

Brown University.

What career did you have in mind when you applied to college?

I was unsure.

Do you now wish you had attended a different school? Which one and why?

No.

Which college or colleges are turning out the leaders in your profession today?

The Ivy League schools.

Can you please describe the "Aha!" moment when you realized what you wanted to do?

I fell into my career, since I was still undecided in my senior year.

Did you change your major? If so, why?

Yes. Decided not to be a chemical engineer and decided I liked being more of a generalist.

Which classes were most valuable in preparing you for your career or in helping you decide on your career?

Several mathematics and economics classes, which I enjoyed, and the organic chemistry class (which I hated).

How did your professors impact your career choice or preparation?

My professors were extremely flexible and allowed me to shape my curriculum in an effort to help determine what I enjoyed most.

Do you have an advanced degree? Is one helpful or required in your field?

Yes, I have an MBA. It is helpful, though not required.

What do you love most about your job?

The challenge and the learning.

What is the most difficult or challenging aspect of your job?

The long hours.

What was the biggest obstacle you faced in getting to where you are in your career?

Being a foreign resident. To a large extent, I overcame it through luck.

What skills are an absolute must for someone interested in pursuing your career?

Different kinds of people have been successful in my space: they are typically driven, analytical, client-oriented, and comfortable with uncertainty.

Whom do you admire most in your industry or field? Why?

No one person. I do admire innovative people and those willing to take risks.

What is one piece of advice you would give to someone who is interested in pursuing your career?

Be flexible in pursuing opportunities that present themselves because they morph over time.

If you could do everything all over again, what would you do differently?

Pursue different opportunities earlier in my career.

What was your first job after graduation?

Training program, Mellon Bank.

What criteria did you use when deciding which undergraduate colleges to apply to?

Reputation, feel, location, friends who attended.

Bernard J. Picchi, Financial Analyst—Energy
Senior Managing Director, Wall Street Access
Georgetown University, 1971
Major: Foreign Service (International Affairs)

What was your first choice school?

The one I attended—Georgetown University (GU).

What career did you have in mind when you applied to college?

Law.

How did the school you attended impact on your career choice and opportunities?

Hugely. My background in international affairs is enormously helpful to me as an energy analyst.

Do you now wish you had attended a different school? Which one and why?

Perhaps: overseas school (Oxford University, London School of Economics) or small, excellent liberal arts school (St. John of Annapolis, Bowdoin College, Hamilton College).

Which college or colleges are turning out the leaders in your profession today?

Columbia University, Stanford University, Yale University, Brown University, New York University, Georgetown University.

Can you please describe the "Aha!" moment when you realized what you wanted to do?

Easy: the first hour I spent as an intern in the investment research department of Mellon Bank! Like being struck by lightning. I was 21!

Did you change your major? If so, why?

Yes—I didn't want to do mathematics or chemistry!

Can you please list your majors?

English then international affairs (actually tougher than English).

Which classes were most valuable in preparing you for your career or in helping you decide on your career?

Economics, English composition, constitutional law.

Do you have an advanced degree? Is one helpful or required in your field?

No, I have a chartered financial analyst (CFA) degree. I enrolled in business school and thought it was a huge waste of time!

What do you love most about your job?

It keeps me thinking all the time!

What is the most difficult or challenging aspect of your job?

Marketing; talking to people who really don't want to hear me.

What is the biggest misconception people have about what you do?

That I can predict the price of oil.

What was the biggest obstacle you faced in getting to where you are in your career?

I was not a natural speaker; it took a lot to make calls to people.

What skills are an absolute must for someone interested in pursuing your career?

Analytical mind, organizational skills, inordinate curiosity about how things really work.

Whom do you admire most in your industry or field?

I admire Warren Buffett, of course, because he really does follow the Golden Rule and lets it guide everything he does in business. Also, he's just brilliant.

What is one piece of advice you would give to someone who is interested in pursuing your career?

Travel and read extensively; learn one or two foreign languages.

If you could do everything all over again, what would you do differently?

Live overseas for a major portion of my young adulthood.

Amy Hoffman, Certified Financial Planner
Director, Client Services and Financial Planning, Advisors Financial, Inc.
The University of Akron, 1994
Major: Finance

What was your first job after graduation?

Planning analyst.

What criteria did you use when deciding which colleges to apply to?

I attended a private Catholic high school. While filling out my college applications, I quickly learned that there were no funds for college. Since I had to finance my own education, I decided to stay close to home. I attended the University of Akron (UA), just a few miles down the road from my parent's home.

What was your first choice school?

I did visit and tour other schools. However, when I realized how expensive they were, I couldn't justify the cost since I was undecided about a major.

What career did you have in mind when you applied to college?

At the time, my dream was to be an archeologist. But I knew that I would not be able to get this background at UA. I did take some anthropology and ancient civilization classes as electives.

How did the school you attended impact on your career choice and opportunities?

I guess you could say UA limited me in that I was not able to study archeology. But archeology was a dream. I also knew that I wanted to have a family and a more stable life than running around playing Indiana Jones.

Do you now wish you had attended a different school? Which one and why?

I don't have any regrets regarding college. I feel that I got a good education at an excellent value.

Which college or colleges are turning out the leaders in your profession today?

There are a few schools that have a financial planning program: Texas Tech University, Virginia Polytechnic Institute and State University, Kansas State University.

Can you please describe the "Aha!" moment when you realized what you wanted to do?

I think that this came much later, after I was already working in the financial planning profession. One day, my grandmother said to me that no one in our family has ever enjoyed their work. She was pleased that I was happy with what I was doing.

Did you change your major? If so, why?

When I finally declared my major, it was mathematics. I switched about a year later because I was having trouble in calculus and did not enjoy studying Spanish to fulfill the liberal arts language requirement. I switched to the school of business so that I would not have to take a language. I was on the fence about majoring in accounting versus finance. After five years of school, I had enough credits to get my degree with a major in finance. I was ready to graduate and just wanted to be done.

Which classes were most valuable in preparing you for your career or in helping you decide on your career?

The classes that prepared me the most for my career were my debate class and college prep English courses in high school. Those classes taught me the basics about writing, research, and communicating that are the foundation of everything I do today. I also had two upper-level business classes that involved case analysis that furthered my researching skills.

How did your professors impact your career choice or preparation?

I really did not have any strong relationships with my professors. UA is the third largest school in the state of Ohio. I did not have much one-on-one with professors.

Did you have a job and/or internship during college that influenced your career choice or career preparation in any way?

When I entered the business school at UA, there was a very organized and structured internship program for accounting students. There was nothing equivalent for finance majors. I realized that if I wanted to start exploring finance opportunities, then I was going to have to create my own career experience. I got in touch with a local Paine Webber broker and told him that I wanted to come work for him a couple of days a week to see what it was like to work in his office and learn about his business. I worked for him without pay for a year.

When I graduated, I told him that I would stay on until I found a full-time job. He offered me an $18,000 salary to come to work for him. I did not accept the job. Shortly after that, I received a call from a local Akron financial planning firm that had received my résumé from the UA Career Center. They were interested in me because of my internship experience at Paine Webber. I started this job in June 1994 at a starting salary of $20,000.

Do you have an advanced degree? Is one helpful or required in your field?

After college I enrolled in the self-study program. I studied and passed Introduction to Financial Planning and Retirement, on my own. For Investments, Tax, and Estate Planning, I received classroom instruction. I took a Dalton review course before sitting for the CFP exam. I received the CFP designation September 2000.

What do you love most about your job?

I have two passions. I love working and talking with clients. It gives me great satisfaction to know that I am impacting the life goals of people every day. In addition, I also love the high I get from writing a financial plan. I have enjoyed writing since high school. Digging into a financial plan, learning about a new family, and analyzing the last 20 to 40 years of their financial life is a fascinating process.

What is the most difficult or challenging aspect of your job?

The most challenging aspect of my job is staying current and up-to-date with the reading required to be on top of all the financial publications. There is so much information out there.

What is the biggest misconception people have about what you do?

I don't think that the public understands the nature of financial planning. Much of what we do is to educate. Many people do not understand money. These days, many people don't even know how to balance their checkbook. We provide financial guidance and knowledge that people deserve.

What was the biggest obstacle you faced in getting to where you are in your career?

I am a bad test taker, so my biggest obstacle was passing the CFP exam. I triumphed by being stubborn. I kept sitting for the exam until I finally passed.

What skills are an absolute must for someone interested in pursuing your career?

Being detail-oriented is one of the most important skills. When dealing with other people's money, you can't afford to let things fall through the cracks. You have to be organized and learn to anticipate the requests of supervisors and clients. Following through on the promises you make and the obligations that you take on will make you worth your weight in gold.

What is one piece of advice you would give to someone who is interested in pursuing your career?

I would tell anyone entering a professional field to learn how to communicate. By this, I mean learn how to write and speak correctly. Image is important. Professional dress and manners do make a difference during an interview and in the workplace. Business writing involves using complete sentences and correct punctuation and spelling. The workplace and clients will not tolerate slang or inappropriate behavior. To be treated like an adult, then one must accept responsibility for their actions and act like an adult.

If you could do everything all over again, what would you do differently?

I don't like having regrets. I am pleased with how things have worked out so far. I wouldn't change a thing.

Can you please add any additional comments you think might be helpful to someone hoping to pursue your career?

I was asked this question in an interview a few years ago. I have the same answer now as I did then: if you are sitting for the CFP exam, take a review course. Find a mentor and check in with him or her regularly. Attend the Financial Planning Association's residency program.

Neil Hirsch, Trader
Valhalla Capital Advisors
Washington University, 1988
Major: Business

What was your first job after graduation?

Working at Loews Corporation.

What criteria did you use when deciding which undergraduate colleges to apply to?

I wanted to go to school in the Midwest, where my father grew up.

What career did you have in mind when you applied to college?

I always wanted to be a trader.

How did the school you attended impact on your career choice and opportunities?

There really weren't many trading opportunities in St. Louis, so school didn't help me there.

Do you now wish you had attended a different school? Which one and why?

I wish I had gone to Princeton University; I would have made a lot of helpful connections.

Can you please describe the "Aha!" moment when you realized what you wanted to do?

I started trading stocks in high school, and I've been hooked ever since.

Which classes were most valuable in preparing you for your career or in helping you decide on your career?

Finance and sociology.

Did you have a job and/or internship during college that influenced your career choice or career preparation in any way?

I was an intern at Solomon Brothers. Their trading environment is legendary.

Do you have an advanced degree? Is one helpful or required in your field?

I have an MBA; it is helpful but not critical.

What do you love most about your job?

I love the flexibility and freedom to do what I want.

What is the most difficult or challenging aspect of your job?

There's a lot of pressure to make money.

What is the biggest misconception people have about what you do?

That it's not a creative environment.

What was the biggest obstacle you faced in getting to where you are in your career?

Consistency in making money; you need to be disciplined and develop a winning formula.

What skills are an absolute must for someone interested in pursuing your career?

Mathematics and analytics.

Whom do you admire most in your industry or field? Why?

I admire Warren Buffett because he's a very long-term investor.

What is one piece of advice you would give to someone who is interested in pursuing your career?

Study history.

What was your first job after graduation?

Financial management program at General Electric (GE).

Daniel Semo, Finance
Analyst, Financial Management Program, General Electric
University of Wisconsin—Madison, 2006
Majors: Finance, Investments, Banking

What criteria did you use when deciding which colleges to apply to?

I applied to a lot of colleges (12 to be exact). I looked for schools with strong liberal arts programs that also had business schools. I wanted a school in a city, but it had to have a campus.

What was your first choice school?

University of Pennsylvania (UP) was my top choice school. My father is a Wharton graduate.

What career did you have in mind when you applied to college?

I've always wanted to start my own company or be CEO of a Global 10!

How did the school you attended impact on your career choice and opportunities?

The business school at the University of Wisconsin—Madison (UW—Madison) gave me a strong background in business and its great on-campus recruiting gave me plenty of choices for jobs. UW—Madison has an unbelievable selection of classes, and when I found myself always eyeing the business classes, I decided to apply to the business school. The core business courses allowed me to survey options in business, and I found myself drawn to my accounting and finance classes. Ultimately, I decided to go with finance. As graduation was approaching, many great companies came to campus, and I was fortunate enough to have options upon graduation.

Do you now wish you had attended a different school? Which one and why?

That's hard to answer. I certainly would have liked to go to a more prestigious school. When I went to UW—Madison, I went knowing that I would transfer after one year. But after my first semester, I was having so much fun I didn't want to leave. I will say that the class size was cause for concern—as were the multiple-choice exams.

Which college or colleges are turning out the leaders in your profession today?

University of Wisconsin—Madison and Harvard University currently have the most fortune 500 CEOs. I mean top schools turn out top people. As a percentage of graduates, the Ivy League is probably still doing the best.

Can you please describe the "Aha!" moment when you realized what you wanted to do?

I think that came when I was five years old. I would walk around events shaking adults' hands with my right hand and slipping them my dad's business card with my left.

Did you change your major? If so, why?

I was accounting and management and ended up being finance. I met with a teacher, and she asked me why I chose those majors. I told her I liked accounting. She asked if I wanted to be an accountant. I said, "No!" She asked why I chose it again, and I said I wanted a strong financial background. She said go for finance, and I said, "Good point!"

Which classes were most valuable in preparing you for your career or in helping you decide on your career?

My certificate (our minor) was in integrated liberal studies. It was basically cannon philosophy. The assignments in the class were very thought provoking and taught me a lot about how to think.

Did you have a job and/or internship during college that influenced your career choice or career preparation in any way?

Not really. My internship was in retail management store-side with Target. Now I work in a cube doing finance.

Do you have an advanced degree? Is one helpful or required in your field?

No, no advanced degree—yet. If I stay with GE, it is not required, but I will probably get one. Every parent I grew up knowing had at least one higher education degree post-college.

What do you love most about your job?

The people and how much I'm learning. They give you an unbelievable amount of responsibility the first day you start. (Numbers that I put together get reported to corporate, and within my first three months, I was pitching to officers of GE Corp.)

What is the most difficult or challenging aspect of your job?

Prioritizing! Everything is urgent and everything needs to be accurate. To say that it's multitasking is an understatement.

What is the biggest misconception people have about what you do?

My financial planning and analysis (FP&A) team likes to joke that we're "data consolidators." The amount of work that goes into compiling and forecasting numbers is tremendous. Also, people think corporate finance jobs have short hours. I have been putting in plenty of 80-hour weeks.

What skills are an absolute must for someone interested in pursuing your career?

Being personable, a team player, detail-oriented but able to see the big picture, a multitasker. Being good with Excel is helpful, but we can teach people Excel. It is often one's personality and ability to work with others that differentiates.

Whom do you admire most in your industry or field? Why?

I have a few favorite CEOs. I'd say Warren Buffett, Steve Jobs, and the Google guys are at the top of my list. Warren because he's damn good and still lives in the same home he's been in for some 40 years. He has remembered where he came from and has not lost sight of where he's going. Steve because he thinks for himself and follows his gut instinct (Apple does not heavily rely on market research like other companies do). Not to mention that he was ousted from the company he founded only to go start Pixar, and then came back and saved his company from going under—not too shabby. And the Google guys because they are trendsetters. They do things their own way. They keep people guessing and are always one step ahead of the pack.

What is one piece of advice you would give to someone who is interested in pursuing your career?

Be yourself and don't be afraid to break trends. Just because it's the way things are done today doesn't mean it's right.

If you could do everything all over again, what would you do differently?

Get into my top choice college.

JOURNALISM

WHY CHOOSE TO BECOME A JOURNALIST?

Journalists have an intellectual curiosity and good communication skills, both oral and written. Journalists gather information from various sources and report their findings in print, on television, on the radio, or on the Web. Most journalists present their stories in an objective way, meaning without including their own opinions; others state their own opinions or perspectives.

WHERE THE JOBS ARE

Journalists can work for a variety of news outlets: newspapers and magazines or television and radio (and their corresponding websites), or online. A journalist can also work as a freelancer for different organizations, getting paid only for work that is published. Most journalists begin their careers in small towns or cities and advance to larger markets as they gain experience. The competition for journalism jobs will continue to be intense as the number of traditional media outlets decreases. One area of growth is in the online market, both for established newspapers and magazines and those that appear only on the Web.

AREAS OF SPECIALTY

Journalists can specialize in one subject area, such as sports or politics. They can also be responsible for performing different tasks, including reporter, editor, correspondent, or features writer.

EDUCATIONAL REQUIREMENTS

Most journalists have at least a bachelor's degree in journalism or communications. Advanced degrees from journalism schools are also common but rarely required.

SALARY RANGE

Journalists' salaries vary widely depending on their experience, location, and the type of work they do. However, the median salary in 2004 for reporters and correspondents was $31,320.

Pros: Challenging work that changes on a daily basis, the opportunity for millions of people to be exposed to your work

Cons: May have to relocate to find jobs, nonstandard work hours, tight deadlines

FAMOUS JOURNALISTS

- **Carl Bernstein** and **Bob Woodward**, *Washington Post* reporters, covered the Watergate scandal that led to the impeachment of President Nixon.
- **Edward R. Murrow** is considered the father of modern journalism; his reports contributed to the downfall of Senator Joseph McCarthy.
- **Nellie Bly** was an undercover reporter who exposed the insane asylum system in New York in 1887.

WHERE TO LEARN MORE

Society of Professional Journalists
Eugene S. Pulliam National Journalism Center
3909 N. Meridian Street
Indianapolis, IN 46208
(317) 927-8000; fax: (317) 920-4789
www.spj.org

The Project for Excellence in Journalism
1615 L Street N.W. 700
Washington, DC 20036
(202) 419-3650; fax: (202) 419-3699
Email: *Mail@journalism.org*
www.journalism.org

WORDS OF WISDOM

"Even though I wasn't thinking as an undergrad about going into journalism, I got a job at the school newspaper because I was a good editor. That was a good experience. I highly recommend internships and other part-time jobs during college in fields a student is considering."

—Susan Albright, Editorial Writer

"Strive to uphold and improve the reputation for the publication for which one works, make the ultimate difference, cross train for extra insight and perspective, and give reasons for people to relate to the content: how does it affect their lives and why is the article's matter important for them to know."

—Steve Palisin, Newspaper Writer

Sidmel Estes-Sumpter, Television Journalist
Executive Producer and Company President, BreakThrough Inc.
Northwestern University, 1976
Major: Broadcast Journalism

What was your first job after graduation?

Television reporter.

What criteria did you use when deciding which undergraduate colleges to apply to?

Whether the school offered a journalism major and its national ranking.

What career did you have in mind when you applied to college?

Journalist.

How did the school you attended impact on your career choice and opportunities?

This is what I have always wanted to do since I was in the sixth grade. The major at Northwestern University gave me the tools to compete in a very competitive industry.

Which college or colleges are turning out the leaders in your profession today?

Northwestern University, Columbia University, University of Missouri.

Can you please describe the "Aha!" moment when you realized what you wanted to do?

I was watching television news during the civil rights era, and all the people anchoring the news were white. And they were not telling all of the story because the people in my community who were protesting had a different point of view. That's when I knew that I wanted to be part of the message that was being told about my community.

Which classes were most valuable in preparing you for your career or in helping you decide on your career?

My hands-on experience working for a Chicago newspaper and the television newsroom we created in the downtown classroom.

How did your professors impact your career choice or preparation?

I am still in contact with a couple of my professors, and they have always been encouraging me to do my thing and to represent them well. They have not been disappointed.

Did you have a job and/or internship during college that influenced your career choice or career preparation in any way?

I worked for two Chicago newspapers and did public relations (PR) for a health facility. That's when I knew I did not want to do PR.

Do you have an advanced degree? Is one helpful or required in your field?

Yes. It is somewhat helpful because our program allows people to gain more experience working with the equipment and covering stories, and that ultimately improves your performance in the workplace.

What do you love most about your job?

I love being in control of my own fate now as the owner of my own company. But when I was in the newsroom, I loved being one of the first people to know when news breaks around the world. I also love telling stories that can affect change in our society.

What is the most difficult or challenging aspect of your job?

As an executive producer, I am a manager, and the people issues I had to deal with were the most difficult part of the job. I don't like being a babysitter.

What is the biggest misconception people have about what you do?

They think that I make a lot of money, and that it is a very glamorous profession.

What was the biggest obstacle you faced in getting to where you are in your career?

I faced discrimination on several different levels: as a woman, as an African American, and as an overweight woman in a profession that is critical of appearances. I overcame those obstacles by performance—by simply being the best.

What skills are an absolute must for someone interested in pursuing your career?

Now students must be able to master the technology that is used to convey these various messages. The student must be able to communicate that message in a clear and engaging manner, and that is difficult to do in a society that operates in high speed.

Whom do you admire most in your industry or field? Why?

Not many people now because the industry has changed so much. But I admire people like Ed Bradley, Bryan Monroe, Robin Roberts, and Gerald Boyd because they were able to succeed in the face of overwhelming odds.

What is one piece of advice you would give to someone who is interested in pursuing your career?

Never give up and never compromise your value system. There will be a lot of pressure to change you, but you must be true to yourself.

If you could do everything all over again, what would you do differently?

I would have prepared more to make my transition from the newsroom into entrepreneurship. In every major corporation, in the end, everyone has to leave. I did not see my departure from the company coming so soon. But it was not my timetable that was at work. So I am in the process of reinventing myself to continue to do quality journalism as well as operate a profitable business.

Susan Albright, Editorial Writer
Editor of the Editorial Pages, *Star Tribune* (Minneapolis)
Kent State University, 1969
Major: English

What was your first job after graduation?

Youth librarian, Cleveland Public Library.

What criteria did you use when deciding which undergraduate colleges to apply to?

I didn't give it as much thought as young people do today; I wanted a large university with a wide selection of courses and majors. I also had very little money and thought a state university would be the best way to get a college education.

What career did you have in mind when you applied to college?

I was undecided, though I was especially interested in English, social sciences, and music. I wanted to try a wide variety of courses before deciding.

How did the school you attended impact on your career choice and opportunities?

It gave me a solid liberal arts education, useful in any field. Oddly enough, I didn't choose to get into journalism until three years after I finished my undergraduate degree. My major was English. Kent State University (KSU) actually has a fine journalism department, so if I'd known what I wanted to do while there I could have benefited from it. Instead, I got a more general liberal arts degree and focused on literature. I later went on to get a master's degree in journalism at Syracuse University (SU).

Do you now wish you had attended a different school? Which one and why?

I personally would have been better off at a smaller liberal arts school, I think. Coming as I did from a small high school and town, the large university was a bit overwhelming. But it all worked out! I got a solid liberal arts education and fine-tuned the professional part later.

Which college or colleges are turning out the leaders in your profession today?

Many are good, including my alma maters. I'd mention Northwestern University and the University of Missouri as two top ones. Also, at the graduate level, Columbia University.

Can you please describe the "Aha!" moment when you realized what you wanted to do?

It was more of a slow dawning than an "Aha!" It was when I realized that my personality was not really suited for specialization, as in, say, getting a doctorate in William Blake studies and becoming an English professor. I wanted to learn a little about a lot of things, not a lot about one thing, if you will. I wanted more breadth and to be out in the world more. So journalism turned out to be a good fit.

Did you change your major? If so, why?

I considered all kinds of fields, eventually getting practically a double major in English and music. Neither became my profession, but I use the knowledge from both all the time in my work and in life.

Which classes were most valuable in preparing you for your career or in helping you decide on your career?

Since I got into journalism only at the master's level, I'd have to say that the English classes I took while I was an English major were the most helpful in developing me as a writer. Also, I had a part-time job at the *Daily Kent Stater*, the school newspaper, which was helpful. I found it difficult to decide on a career because I was interested in so many things. Of course, those wide interests are what ultimately made journalism a good fit for me.

How did your professors impact your career choice or preparation?

They encouraged me, but I didn't know that I would enter this field until after I graduated—several years after, actually.

Did you have a job and/or internship during college that influenced your career choice or career preparation in any way?

Even though I wasn't thinking as an undergraduate about going into journalism, I got a job at the school newspaper because I was a good editor. That was a good experience. I highly recommend internships and other part-time jobs during college in fields a student is considering.

Do you have an advanced degree? Is one helpful or required in your field?

I do. As I mentioned above, it was through SU's master's program in journalism (public communications) that I actually got into this field. SU had a program through which a person with a bachelor's degree in a variety of fields could enter journalism. But a master's degree is not necessary to succeed in journalism. I think an undergraduate major or minor is helpful, as is working on the school newspaper and getting summer internships at publications; in fact, such jobs are not only excellent in giving you an idea of what the work would be like, they are great for producing writing that will help you get the real job after college. Those who are hiring in journalism like to see completed internships, and they like to have writing samples that were published as well.

What do you love most about your job?

As an editorial writer and editor, I am able to write about all sorts of fascinating things that go on in the world—everything from the Iraq war to whether the Twins should get a new stadium. I feel part of the larger world and as an opinion writer, feel that I can make a difference through my work. I also like the collegiality of an editorial department.

What is the most difficult or challenging aspect of your job?

Keeping up with local, national, and international current events and researching public-policy issues to the point where I feel comfortable that we're writing authoritatively and knowledgeably about those issues.

What is the biggest misconception people have about what you do?

Many think that opinion writers, whether editorialists or columnists, simply write what they're thinking off the top of their heads, not realizing how much research, interviewing, and study we do.

What was the biggest obstacle you faced in getting to where you are in your career?

Probably shyness. Journalism requires people to intrude into people's lives, to ask questions that are sometimes uncomfortable, to meet many people, etc. I overcame it by doing what I needed to do whether it was difficult or not—and sure enough, it got easier the more times I did it.

What skills are an absolute must for someone interested in pursuing your career?

Writing, critical thinking, interviewing, researching.

Whom do you admire most in your industry or field? Why?

I can't think of just one I'd single out overall. There are many, many dedicated people in journalism. Today, however, I'll mention John Burns, chief of the Baghdad Bureau of the *New York Times*. He's done terrific work during the war, and for decades before, all over the world. He is thoughtful, a solid reporter, courageous, and careful in his analysis.

What is one piece of advice you would give to someone who is interested in pursuing your career?

Develop your intellectual curiosity.

If you could do everything all over again, what would you do differently?

I'd have taken more risks early in my career, trying more aspects of journalism than the ones I did.

Can you please add any additional comments you think might be helpful to someone hoping to pursue your career?

Don't worry if you don't know just exactly what you want to do in the field. Start with something that interests you and see where it takes you. You can always move around within a newspaper staff or even between media. Above all, don't settle for just a job! Go for meaningful work that truly interests you and pour your energies into it.

Steve Palisin, Newspaper Writer
Features Staff Writer, *Sun News* (Myrtle Beach, South Carolina)
Cleveland State University, 1990
Major: Communications

What was your first job after graduation?

Copy editor.

What criteria did you use when deciding which undergraduate colleges to apply to?

I wanted to stay at home and not have to live in a dorm. And I didn't want to give up my lucrative paper-route delivery job, which paid handsomely.

What career did you have in mind when you applied to college?

Radio.

How did the school you attended impact on your career choice and opportunities?

Having professors in real-life careers teaching us aspects of the business, such as public relations, TV, and newspapers.

Do you now wish you had attended a different school? Which one and why?

No. School doesn't give real-life experience. It teaches the process of how to learn, how to have antennae piqued.

Which college or colleges are turning out the leaders in your profession today?

There's a varied assortment. Also, I don't understand the prudence of master's degrees in journalism, etc. Getting a job in this field is the graduate school, as my first boss taught me.

Can you please describe the "Aha!" moment when you realized what you wanted to do?

Working for the main college student newspaper, I could express myself so much better than by voice or in person. Thomas Jefferson was a quiet man, but he was loud and unmatched with his pen, and ditto for James Madison—the standard for me.

Did you change your major? If so, why?

No, just a switch under the all-encompassing, vague "communications" umbrella.

Which classes were most valuable in preparing you for your career or in helping you decide on your career?

PR, philosophy, voice and diction, and news writing—all avenues to develop how to rationalize and express one's self.

How did your professors impact your career choice or preparation?

Slightly. The ones who have worked and now work in the field impressed me most.

Did you have a job and/or internship during college that influenced your career choice or career preparation in any way?

Yes, I interned outside of college in my senior year, covering all kinds of things, even council meetings, for the local weekly chain, Sun Newspapers, in Greater Cleveland. It was terrific, invaluable experience not gained through sitting in a class. The variety of subject fare gave me quite the taste of all a newspaper tackles in words.

Do you have an advanced degree? Is one helpful or required in your field?

No and no.

What do you love most about your job?

Helping give readers new pages and insight every day in the ever-changing daily encyclopedia we call a newspaper.

What is the most difficult or challenging aspect of your job?

Keeping the resolve, creativity, and wherewithal to find another way to find answers or info when a barrier is encountered, whether someone with details is not available or someone refuses to help.

What is the biggest misconception people have about what you do?

That we have poor judgment or bias, stereotypes that certain news entities held in high regard without accountability uphold blindly, and that subjects think we write stories for them.

What was the biggest obstacle you faced in getting to where you are in your career?

Finding a quality publication that truly wants to make a difference for its readers and community and does not talk down to them and realizes the three markets it serves: readers, advertisers, and employees. In amassing experience, I've gotten to be a writer, copy editor, page designer, business editor, city editor, features editor, and features writer. Having worked on copy and city desks and keeping up my writing and later going back to writing, I gained an extra perspective as to what is expected of the writer, and of things copy and city desks should not have to waste precious time on in cleaning up copy.

What skills are an absolute must for someone interested in pursuing your career?

Engendering trust and respect in the market or beat covered and never forgetting that we are the face of our employer in the field. Also, remember: we write for and serve the readers, not the subjects we cover.

Whom do you admire most in your industry or field? Why?

I admire travel and food editor, Janet Podolak, of the *News-Herald* in Willoughby, Ohio, outside Cleveland. She turned me on to feature writing full-time, allowing me to realize that features are a reason people want to read a paper, for a diversion from all the hard news rammed downed people's throats on TV, radio, etc. The travel writing I did under her guide let me think outside the box and made me more aware of all environs in painting that picture for readers. She pointed out the simple, basic ways to resonate with readers.

What is one piece of advice you would give to someone who is interested in pursuing your career?

Figure out how to concisely engage the reader to keep that person's attention to finish out every story, and realize if we're asking for his or her time to read our news, make it worth the time and make the person wiser for that privilege granted to us.

If you could do everything all over again, what would you do differently?

I would be more flexible to move out of town or state to get bigger jumps into the business; it's a big world out there.

Can you please add any additional comments you think might be helpful to someone hoping to pursue your career?

Strive to uphold and improve the reputation for the publication for which one works, make the ultimate difference, cross train for extra insight and perspective, and give reasons for people to relate to the content: how does it affect their lives and why is the article's matter important for them to know?

Diane Goldie, Newspaper Editor
Assistant Managing Editor for Crossmedia, *Newsday* (New York)
Fordham University, 1977
Major: Communications

What was your first job after graduation?

Reporter at the *Hudson Dispatch* in New Jersey.

What criteria did you use when deciding which undergraduate colleges to apply to?

A good communications program.

What career did you have in mind when you applied to college?

Journalist or lawyer.

How did the school you attended impact on your career choice and opportunities?

The contacts I made—students and professors—nudged me down my career path.

Do you now wish you had attended a different school? Which one and why?

Perhaps. I was not that savvy about targeting schools and I did not have sophisticated guidance from high school staff, family, or friends at that time. I'm not sure what other schools I might have pursued, but I wish I had better guidance.

Which college or colleges are turning out the leaders in your profession today?

I am not plugged in to hiring at that level for most of our positions. Most of the people we hire have several years of professional experience. Other than the obvious universities—Columbia, Northwestern, Syracuse—our staffers come from a variety of schools.

Can you please describe the "Aha!" moment when you realized what you wanted to do?

When I began working at the *Hudson Dispatch* newspaper as a reporter, I just fell in love with the profession.

Did you change your major? If so, why?

Yes. From English to communications because I didn't want to teach and thought communications would provide me with the skills and background to actually get a job in journalism or PR.

Which classes were most valuable in preparing you for your career or in helping you decide on your career?

Reporting, writing, internships, and a variety of journalism classes.

How did your professors impact your career choice or preparation?

By discussing their experiences and setting up internships.

Did you have a job and/or internship during college that influenced your career choice or career preparation in any way?

My job as a part-time reporter/clerk at the *Riverdale Press* made me want to be a journalist. Working as a PR intern assistant in the corporate communications department at W.R. Grace & Co. made me realize I did not want to go into this field. I was more interested in hearing about the past experiences of the ex-journalists who were working in PR.

Do you have an advanced degree? Is one helpful or required in your field?

Yes, a master's in journalism from Columbia University. It is not required, but I found it helpful. I worked at newspapers for three years before I attended grad school, which I believe helped me focus on what skills I wanted to improve. I also was fairly skilled at the basics so I could concentrate on bolstering more sophisticated skills and techniques. I believe some of the skills and instincts that make a top-notch journalist really cannot be taught. Some students who were obviously smart and good learners did not have the demeanor, instincts, or drive to become journalists. So it is by no means important to have an advanced degree in this field. If you go to a prestigious school, it can add a bit of sparkle to your résumé and you do make some contacts that may be valuable down the road.

What do you love most about your job?

I think journalists perform an important role in society, informing the public about what is going on in the world and, at times, impacting what happens to people and their communities. I like learning about different subjects and relating those stories to the public. Working on daily newspapers for 20-plus years and, in the last 6 years, the Web, I've always enjoyed the immediacy and fast pace of the work. When I was a reporter, I loved covering a beat and meeting different people. I liked writing my own pieces and editing others' stories. As an editor, I enjoy helping to shape an entire newspaper and website. To raise the quality of staffers' work and see the overall products grow and improve. With technology and the industry changing so quickly, I am challenged with integrating our print and online products.

What is the most difficult or challenging aspect of your job?

Integrating our print and online products. Keeping up with the lightning-fast changes in the industry and convincing a newsroom filled with many unwilling journalists to participate in the salvation of their profession. While it is exciting to be at the forefront of these changes, the Web staffers often feel isolated, dismissed, and sometimes disliked by print employees. The atmosphere is improving, but there is still a level of suspicion and hostility to be overcome.

What is the biggest misconception people have about what you do?

I believe a majority of the public dislikes and distrusts journalists. The boom in gossip/celebrity journalism has cheapened the profession a bit, and some people may not take us so seriously. Others think that we're all a bunch of unpatriotic liberals who want to topple the government. That we pursue our own agendas and are biased.

What was the biggest obstacle you faced in getting to where you are in your career?

There was some sexism when I began more than 20 years ago.

What skills are an absolute must for someone interested in pursuing your career?

I believe most good journalists have a natural curiosity about people, places, things, events, and generally what's going on in the world. They must be good listeners, storytellers, and writers. Have a good command of language. They must work well under pressure, meet deadlines, juggle many tasks at once, and be flexible and thick-skinned.

What is one piece of advice you would give to someone who is interested in pursuing your career?

If you have a particular area you want to pursue in journalism, regularly read publications and writers who produce top-notch work. Line up internships at the best publications where you can learn from professionals. Be willing to work hard and long hours that often spill into nights, weekends, and holidays. If you want to be a reporter, you should be willing to leave the office to go out and meet people. Too many young reporters conduct interviews solely through emails or just over the phone. Have a good attitude. I'd rather deal with a less talented staffer who is a team player and behaves professionally than a hotshot who constantly complains, doesn't meet deadlines, and is generally difficult. Don't burn bridges. If you leave a job or have differences with colleagues, don't leave on horrible terms or totally trash staffers. It's a small, often insular profession, and word gets around.

If you could do everything all over again, what would you do differently?

Be more ambitious and maybe a tad more savvy and political about getting ahead.

Can you please add any additional comments you think might be helpful to someone hoping to pursue your career?

Journalism often involves working long hours for little pay and often little recognition, so you really have to love it. But I think it is one of the most interesting and rewarding professions there is.

John Foren, Newspaper Editor
Local News Editor, *Flint Journal* (Michigan)
Michigan State University; Henry Ford Community, 1983
Major: Journalism

What was your first job after graduation?

Reporter, the *Dearborn Heights Leader,* Dearborn Heights, Michigan.

What criteria did you use when deciding which undergraduate colleges to apply to?

Which schools had the most prominent journalism programs in Michigan.

What career did you have in mind when you applied to college?

Journalism.

How did the school you attended impact on your career choice and opportunities?

Being on the school newspaper at Michigan State University (MSU) more than anything convinced me that this was the career for me.

Can you please describe the "Aha!" moment when you realized what you wanted to do?

I'd say it was simply being in the newsroom at the *State News* at MSU and feeling so comfortable, as if I never wanted to leave. I loved the feel of the place and the attitudes of everyone there.

Which classes were most valuable in preparing you for your career or in helping you decide on your career?

I'd say basic news reporting classes plus journalism law (which especially helped when I became an editor).

How did your professors impact your career choice or preparation?

Not a great deal. I had one professor who really encouraged me in journalism, but I can't say my professors had a big impact.

Did you have a job and/or internship during college that influenced your career choice or career preparation in any way?

I was an intern at the weekly paper in my hometown of Dearborn. It was a starting job but at least convinced me I could find work.

Do you have an advanced degree? Is one helpful or required in your field?

No. It's helpful but not required. Real-life experience tops everything else in journalism.

What do you love most about your job?

The freedom and interesting things we deal with every day.

What is the most difficult or challenging aspect of your job?

Doing your job in public, which means leaving yourself open to heavy scrutiny.

What is the biggest misconception people have about what you do?

That journalists lie or purposely stretch the truth in order to sell papers.

What was the biggest obstacle you faced in getting to where you are in your career?

My biggest obstacle was just overcoming the fact that other people had better internships at big papers or had more sterling college careers, or whatever. You have to overcome the feeling that you can't stand out in a very competitive field.

What skills are an absolute must for someone interested in pursuing your career?

Basic understanding of English and writing. You also have to be curious and open to new experiences. And the best reporters and editors are driven.

Whom do you admire most in your industry or field? Why?

I admire the retired Ben Bradlee of the *Washington Post* because he epitomizes a strong editor and leader.

What is one piece of advice you would give to someone who is interested in pursuing your career?

Get on your school newspaper, freelance for your community newspaper, and keep reading and learning how the professionals do it.

If you could do everything all over again, what would you do differently?

Pursue a stronger internship in college and travel out of state to do it.

Can you please add any additional comments you think might be helpful to someone hoping to pursue your career?

Unlike some careers, I think to pursue journalism you really have to love it. You have to feel it in your bones. I think most people in the business had a feeling at the start that this was where we belonged, as if you're part of some special clique. Having that feeling negates the long hours, low pay, etc.

LANGUAGES

WHY CHOOSE A CAREER IN LANGUAGES?

In many ways, interpreters and translators help bridge the gaps in communication across cultures, which is crucial as the world become increasingly more interconnected. But the career goes beyond simple translation from one language to another; it helps facilitate the free exchange of ideas, needs, and concepts and goes a long way to promote patience, understanding, and open-mindedness among people across the globe. In sum, it is a very rewarding and rapidly growing career path with lots of opportunities.

Professionals in this field have the opportunity to work with and serve a diverse range of people and needs in a variety of settings, from global corporations and government institutions to schools, hospitals, the legal system, and beyond. Although there is a great deal of overlap in the career demands of both interpreters and translators, and many experienced professionals perform the job functions of both, the main difference is that interpreters generally deal with the spoken language and translators deal with the written language. However, one thing is true for both—they are wonderful and fulfilling careers for those who love languages and want to help people from different countries and cultures to connect.

WHERE THE JOBS ARE

Although job prospects for interpreters and translators vary by area of specialty, these fields are experiencing rapid growth across the board, and qualified individuals will find a wealth of opportunities in a variety of settings and locales. Urban areas and large metropolitan cities, where immigrant populations grow fastest, including New York, Los Angeles, and Washington, D.C., are offering the greatest employment opportunities. However, job growth in rural settings and small communities is healthy as well.

AREAS OF SPECIALTY

Interpreters convert one spoken language, known as the source language, into another, the target language.

- Simultaneous interpretation requires interpreters to listen and speak (or sign) at the same time. In simultaneous interpretation, the interpreter begins to convey a sentence while the speaker is still talking.
- Consecutive interpretation begins only after the speaker has verbalized a group of words or sentences. Consecutive interpreters often take notes while listening to the speakers, so they must develop some type of note-taking or shorthand system. This form of interpretation is used most often for person-to-person communication, during which the interpreter is positioned near both parties.

Translators convert written materials from one language into another. Assignments may vary in length, writing style, and subject matter.

Areas of speciality include judiciary translators, literary translators, localization translators, and medical translators.

EDUCATIONAL REQUIREMENTS

Although the educational backgrounds of interpreters and translators can vary significantly, most have a bachelor's degree, and many professionals have advanced degrees, which are becoming increasingly more necessary for career advancement. Interpreters and translators must be fluent in at least two languages. Many also complete job-specific training programs, and in some career settings, demonstrating specific job-related proficiency is essential.

Formal programs in interpreting and translation are available at colleges nationwide and through nonuniversity training programs, conferences, and courses. Real-world experience is an essential part of a successful career in either interpreting or translation. It may include spending time abroad, engaging in direct contact with foreign cultures, and reading extensively on a variety of subjects in English and at least one other language. Professionals need a solid grasp of the languages to be translated, a thorough understanding of technical concepts and vocabulary, and a high degree of knowledge about the intended target audience.

SALARY RANGE

The median salary for interpreters and translators in 2006 was $17 an hour. The middle 50 percent earned between $12.94 and $22.60. The lowest 10 percent earned less than $9.88, and the highest 10 percent earned more than $30.91.

Earnings vary greatly in this field, depending on languages spoken, subject matter, skill, experience, education, certification, and type of employer. Individuals classified as language specialists for the federal government earned an average of $76,287 annually in 2007. Some highly skilled interpreters and translators—for example, high-level conference interpreters—working full-time can earn more than $100,000 annually.

For those who are not salaried, earnings may fluctuate, depending on the availability of work. Freelance interpreters usually earn an hourly rate, whereas freelance translators typically earn a rate per word or per hour.

FAMOUS INTERPRETERS AND TRANSLATORS

- The first interpreters probably worked in Egypt around 3000 B.C.; the ancient Egyptians had a hieroglyphic signifying interpreter. Since then, interpreters have played indispensable roles whenever two cultures have interacted, whether through conquest, trade, or a quest for mutual understanding.
- By one count, **Sir Richard Francis Burton** (1821–1890) spoke 29 European, Asian, and African languages. He is well known for his translations of *The Thousand and One Nights* from the Persian and the *Kama Sutra* from the Sanskrit, among his many international exploits.

WHERE TO LEARN MORE

American Translators Association
225 Reinekers Lane, Suite 590,
Alexandria, VA 22314
www.atanet.org

American Literary Translators Association
University of Texas—Dallas
P.O. Box 830688, Mail Station JO51
Richardson, TX 75083
www.utdallas.edu/alta

The National Association of Judiciary Interpreters and Translators
603 Stewart Street, Suite 610
Seattle, WA 98101
www.najit.org

National Council on Interpreting in Health Care
270 W. Lawrence Street
Albany, NY 12208
www.ncihc.org

Registry of Interpreters for the Deaf
333 Commerce Street
Alexandria, VA 22314
www.rid.org

U.S. Department of State, Office of Language Services
2401 E. Street N.W., SA-1, Room H1400
Washington, DC 20520
www.state.gov

WORDS OF WISDOM

"Do what you love and enjoy, dedicate yourself to excellence, and you will be rewarded with a fulfilling career."

—Sean Maroney, Translator and Journalist

"Remember that learning is a lifelong process."

—Ryan Quesada, Translator

Peter Galante, Education/Translation
Chief Operating Officer
Hofstra University, 1997
Major: Economics

What was your first job after graduation?

I was a teacher in Japan, which laid the foundation for fluenty in Japanese

What criteria did you use when deciding which colleges to apply to?

Class size was the main criteria.

What was your first choice school?

SUNY—Oswego was my first choice school.

What career did you have in mind when you applied to college?

I wanted to become a lawyer.

How did the school you attended have an impact on your career choice and opportunities?

At Hofstra I met teachers that helped me think outside the box, and encouraged me to set out and see the world.

Do you now wish you had attended a different school? Which one and why?

I would attend the same school. I'm happy with my decision.

Which college or colleges are turning out the leaders in your profession today?

Middlebury College has been turning out leaders in the linguistic field.

Which classes were most valuable in preparing you for your career or in helping you decide on your career?

Economics, English Grammar, Creative Writing and Japanese.

How did your professors impact your career choice or preparation?

My economics professor provided me life lessons and insight into analytical approaches for solving problems, and my Japanese professor provided me with encouragement to go to Japan, which was a wonderful experience.

Did you have a job and/or internship during college that influenced your ultimate career choice or career preparation in any way?

No.

Can you please describe the "Aha!" moment when you realized what you wanted to do?

When I heard a translation of something that didn't accurately convey what was intended, and the listening party missed an important opportunity I knew that translating was something I wanted to do for a living.

Did you change your major? If so, why?

I didn't change my major, but I was influenced to maor in Economics by an amazing professor.

How important was your college experience in getting you to where you are today?

The college expierience was extremely important in shaping my analytical proble solving skills and preparing me for the business world.

Do you have an advanced degree? Is one helpful or required in your field?

Yes, I do, and while it is not a requirement in my line of work it is an asset.

What do you love most about your job?

I love the positive responses I get from customers and clients.

What is the most difficult or challenging aspect of your job?

Finding ways to continue being innovative is a challenge.

What is the biggest misconception people have about what you do?

That it is a simple job that anyone can do.

What was the biggest obstacle you faced in getting to where you are in your career?

Building my own network from scratch. I had some failures along the way, but I always learned from them. The people you surround yourself with have a lot to do with how far you can go.

What skills are an absolute must for someone interested in pursuing your career?

Having an excellent command of English is essential.

Whom do you admire most in your industry or field?

James Curtis Hepburn, who compiled a Japanese-English dictionary and a revised Romanization system.

What is one piece of advice you would give to someone who is interested in pursuing your career?

Master the complexities and intricacies of the English language.

If you could do everything all over again, what would you do differently?

I wouldn't change a thing.

Maite Lamberri, Translator
Spanish Translator/Instructor
University of Valladolid, 1994
Major: English Studies

What was your first job after graduation?

I taught English in Spain.

What criteria did you use when deciding which colleges to apply to?

I wanted a school that was close to my house.

What was your first choice school?

The school I attended was my first choice.

What career did you have in mind when you applied to college?

I wanted to pursue a career in English philology.

How did the school you attended have an impact on your career choice and opportunities?

It provided me with a wonderful education and helped me to define my career focus and recognize available opportunities.

Do you now wish you had attended a different school? Which one and why?

I would have spent more time in a foreign college.

Which college or colleges are turning out the leaders in your profession today?

I don't know.

Which classes were most valuable in preparing you for your career or in helping you decide on your career?

All of my classes were valuable in my development.

How did your professors impact your career choice or preparation?

Mrs. Fernandez, a professor of mine, helped me obtain a scholarship to spend my second year of my master's studies in Canada.

Did you have a job and/or internship during college that influenced your ultimate career choice or career preparation in any way?

None that influenced my career.

Can you please describe the "Aha!" moment when you realized what you wanted to do?

I don't think I had a moment like that.

Did you change your major? If so, why?

I didn't change my major.

How important was your college experience in getting you to where you are today?

I'd say that the mix of course work and real-world experience I got while in college helped me to get where I am today.

Do you have an advanced degree? Is one helpful or required in your field?

Yes, I have one, and it is a requirement in my field.

What do you love most about your job?

I can't really define any specific things that I love about my job.

What is the most difficult or challenging aspect of your job?

Working with a diverse group of students, each with his or her own set of needs, can be a challenge.

What is the biggest misconception people have about what you do?

That it is an easy job that anyone can do, even without training.

What was the biggest obstacle you faced in getting to where you are in your career?

As a translator, dealing with a wide array of cultural differences can be an obstacle.

What skills are an absolute must for someone interested in pursuing your career?

Patience is the most valuable skill to have.

Whom do you admire most in your industry or field?

I have admiration and respect for anyone working in this challenging field.

What is one piece of advice you would give to someone who is interested in pursuing your career?

Perseverance and hard work.

If you could do everything all over again, what would you do differently?

Study harder and spend more time traveling.

Do you have any additional comments you think might be helpful to someone hoping to pursue your career?

Learn more than two languages.

Ryan Quesada, Translator
Senior Translator, TransLang Services Inc.
University of Michigan, 1998
Major: Spanish Language

What was your first job after graduation?

I was an English teacher for an adult literacy program.

What criteria did you use when deciding which colleges to apply to?

I wanted a school with an excellent academic reputation that was relatively close to my home.

What was your first choice school?

I can't remember thinking about attending a school other than Michigan University.

What career did you have in mind when you applied to college?

I considered being a Spanish teacher, but I feel that my current position as a translator is a good one for me.

How did the school you attended have an impact on your career choice and opportunities?

Michigan University is wonderful in the sense that it has the power to inspire young adults and expose them to a world of career possibilities. My college experience really helped me to grow and better understand the world.

Do you now wish you had attended a different school? Which one and why?

I never doubted my college choice.

Which college or colleges are turning out the leaders in your profession today?

I'm not sure. I do know that the University of Michigan is turning out great professionals.

Which classes were most valuable in preparing you for your career or in helping you decide on your career?

All of my language classes helped me to prepare career-wise.

How did your professors impact your career choice or preparation?

I was lucky to have some wonderful and caring teachers. Beyond the course basics, they were able to inspire confidence in me, that I would be able to find success in anything I chose to do.

Did you have a job and/or internship during college that influenced your ultimate career choice or career preparation in any way?

I didn't, but I strongly recommend to students that they seek an internship, so they are able to decide if they're making the right career choices while in school.

Can you please describe the "Aha!" moment when you realized what you wanted to do?

When we had mock teaching sessions in school. I knew I wanted to spread my love of languages to others and help to promote communication between people who speak different languages.

Did you change your major? If so, why?

I didn't.

How important was your college experience in getting you to where you are today?

It provided me with an excellent education and the confidence to go out in the world and find success in exactly what I wanted to do.

Do you have an advanced degree? Is one helpful or required in your field?

I have a master's degree, and it is extremely helpful to have one.

What do you love most about your job?

Helping bridge the gaps of communication between people who speak different languages.

What is the most difficult or challenging aspect of your job?

Working with people who are frustrated or impatient due to limited language understanding can be a real challenge. It takes a great deal of professionalism.

What is the biggest misconception people have about what you do?

That anyone with a basic understanding of language can do this job. It takes professionalism, experience, and language mastery to really excel.

What was the biggest obstacle you faced in getting to where you are in your career?

Dealing with the everyday challenges of the job, but I always persevered.

What skills are an absolute must for someone interested in pursuing your career?

A real love for what you do is key.

Whom do you admire most in your industry or field?

Anyone with the necessary experience, sensitivity, and patience to really help people and make a difference.

What is one piece of advice you would give to someone who is interested in pursuing your career?

Remember that learning is a lifelong process.

If you could do everything all over again, what would you do differently?

Nothing.

Do you have any additional comments you think might be helpful to someone hoping to pursue your career?

Do what you love, don't forget why you started doing it in the first place, and you will find success.

Sean Maroney, Translator and Journalist
International Broadcaster
University of North Carolina—Chapel Hill, 2006
Majors: Spanish; Journalism and Mass Communication

What was your first job after graduation?

A freelance translator and international broadcaster with Voice of America.

What criteria did you use when deciding which colleges to apply to?

Strength of academic program, campus atmosphere, proximity to North Carolina, and financial aid.

What was your first choice school?

I didn't have a first choice. I applied to five schools: UNC—Chapel Hill, North Carolina State University, Wake Forest, Elon University, and Duke University.

What career did you have in mind when you applied to college?

I wanted to be a lawyer.

How did the school you attended have an impact on your career choice and opportunities?

My college experience really helped me to figure out the direction I wanted my career to take.

Do you now wish you had attended a different school? Which one and why?

I would still go to UNC—Chapel Hill. I really appreciated the networking opportunities I had, the strength of their academic program, the study-abroad opportunities, the campus atmosphere, and the 2005 NCAA men's college basketball national championship.

Which college or colleges are turning out the leaders in your profession today?

UNC—Chapel Hill, Northwestern, Arizona State University.

Which classes were most valuable in preparing you for your career or in helping you decide on your career?

Voice and diction classes, language classes, and my study abroad experience in Mexico.

How did your professors impact your career choice or preparation?

Betsy Sandlin, my Spanish professor, inspired and encouraged me tremendously.

Did you have a job and/or internship during college that influenced your ultimate career choice or career preparation in any way?

My work experience as a Spanish-to-English translator during college was invaluable.

Can you please describe the "Aha!" moment when you realized what you wanted to do?

It happened when I realized that I could make a positive impact by helping people who speak different languages share their stories with others.

Did you change your major? If so, why?

No, I didn't.

How important was your college experience in getting you to where you are today?

It provided me with the skills and real-world experience I needed to hit the ground running on day one.

Do you have an advanced degree? Is one helpful or required in your field?

I don't, and it's not a requirement, but it's helpful to have one.

What do you love most about your job?

I love how I am constantly required to learn something new.

What is the most difficult or challenging aspect of your job?

It is challenging to communicate effectively with the individuals I work with.

What is the biggest misconception people have about what you do?

That this job doesn't require a great deal of seasoning and talent—it does!

What was the biggest obstacle you faced in getting to where you are in your career?

My young age. It forced me to work harder than everyone else.

What skills are an absolute must for someone interested in pursuing your career?

Good language, grammar, writing, and communication skills.

Whom do you admire most in your industry or field?

I admire people who are dedicated to their craft and who commit themselves to making a difference and helping people.

What is one piece of advice you would give to someone who is interested in pursuing your career?

Do what you love and enjoy, dedicate yourself to excellence, and you will be rewarded with a fulfilling career.

If you could do everything all over again, what would you do differently?

I also would have learned Arabic in college.

Do you have any additional comments you think might be helpful to someone hoping to pursue your career?

Get an internship that will let you do as much as possible.

Milagros Lupiz, Translator
Language Learning Coordinator, TransLang Services Inc.
Saint John's University, 2005
Major: Education

What was your first job after graduation?

Administrative coordinator at TransLang Services.

What criteria did you use when deciding which colleges to apply to?

I was looking for an affordable school with a good academic reputation.

What was your first choice school?

I wanted to go to Saint John's University.

What career did you have in mind when you applied to college?

I had a few ideas, either in education or possibly in social work.

How did the school you attended have an impact on your career choice and opportunities?

College helped me to define my career goals and make a plan to achieve them.

Do you now wish you had attended a different school? Which one and why?

If I'd had all the money in the world I might have considered other schools, but I'm happy with my choice and proud of my accomplishments.

Which college or colleges are turning out the leaders in your profession today?

I think the individual is just as important as the school. You'll find great leaders coming from schools all over the country.

Which classes were most valuable in preparing you for your career or in helping you decide on your career?

My education and language courses were very valuable to me and my career.

How did your professors impact your career choice or preparation?

They helped to educate me and helped me grow as a person. They showed me that I was making the right career choices and that I would be great in this field.

Did you have a job and/or internship during college that influenced your ultimate career choice or career preparation in any way?

I worked as a summer intern at a day care for special needs children, and it really helped me grow as an adult and work towards addressing the needs of others, which is crucial in this field.

Can you please describe the "Aha!" moment when you realized what you wanted to do?

When I started working in this field, I knew that I had made the right choice.

Did you change your major? If so, why?

I didn't change.

How important was your college experience in getting you to where you are today?

It was very important—I don't think I'd be where I am today without it.

Do you have an advanced degree? Is one helpful or required in your field?

I'm currently working on an advanced degree, and I recommend everyone in this field get one.

What do you love most about your job?

Helping people is the best part for me.

What is the most difficult or challenging aspect of your job?

You work with all sorts of people and personalities in this field, with very different needs. You want to help everyone with everything, but it can be tough.

What is the biggest misconception people have about what you do?

That it is just translating sentences from one language to the other. It can be so much more than that.

What was the biggest obstacle you faced in getting to where you are in your career?

Working on my advanced degree while having a job. It takes real dedication to do both together.

What skills are an absolute must for someone interested in pursuing your career?

Patience, understanding, and an open mind are very necessary.

Whom do you admire most in your industry or field?

I admire all of my coworkers. They are very dedicated individuals, and they inspire me.

What is one piece of advice you would give to someone who is interested in pursuing your career?

Try it while in school so that you can decide if it's right for you.

If you could do everything all over again, what would you do differently?

I'd try and save up more money for undergraduate and graduate school.

Do you have any additional comments you think might be helpful to someone hoping to pursue your career?

Remember that you're in it to help people and that this is the main goal of the job.

LAW

WHY CHOOSE TO BECOME A LAWYER?

Lawyers have good reasoning and analytical skills and are detail-oriented. Lawyers fill two main roles, one is to advocate for their clients by gathering and presenting evidence and arguing to defend them in court. The other is to act as advisors by counseling their clients as to their legal rights and responsibilities in both business and personal situations.

WHERE THE JOBS ARE

Lawyers can work with a group of other lawyers in a law firm, by themselves in private practice, for an organization or business as in-house counsel, or for non-profit agencies. Lawyers are also employed by the government as state attorneys general, prosecutors, and public defenders. Lawyers who work for the federal government investigate cases for the U.S. Department of Justice and other agencies. Much of what a lawyer does depends on his or her specialty. Trial lawyers, for example, represent their clients in court, but still spend a majority of their time outside of the courtroom doing such things as gathering evidence, researching cases, and interviewing witnesses. Because of the large number of law school graduates and the popularity of the field of law in general, competition for jobs, especially at prestigious firms, will continue to be very aggressive.

AREAS OF SPECIALTY

There are two broad categories of law: civil and criminal. In criminal cases, lawyers defend clients who are accused of crimes, and district attorneys, who are lawyers representing the state, prosecute them. Civil law resolves disputes in which no crime has been committed but where one party feels it has been wronged by the other, as in contract disputes, divorces, or personal injury cases. Most lawyers specialize in a specific area of law, such as bankruptcy, divorce, environmental law, or intellectual property.

EDUCATIONAL REQUIREMENTS

To practice law, students need seven years of post–high school training. This includes four years of college and three years of law school (in a few states, students can substitute work experience for law school). In addition, lawyers need to be licensed by the state where they plan to practice, a process that involves passing a written exam to prove their legal knowledge and in some states, another exam covering ethics.

SALARY RANGE

Lawyers' salaries vary widely depending on the type of law they practice, years of experience, and the setting in which they work. Partners in law firms, for example, share in the profits of the firm, while associates work for a set salary. However, the median salary for all lawyers in 2004 was $94,930.

Pros: Intellectually challenging work, the opportunity to affect the lives of others, high pay

Cons: Long hours, stressful work

FAMOUS LAWYERS

- **Thurgood Marshall**, first African American to serve on the Supreme Court, was instrumental in ending legal segregation in the United States.
- **Clarence Darrow**, civil liberties lawyer, is best known for defending a teacher of evolution in what is often called the Scopes Monkey Trial.
- **Sandra Day O'Connor** was the first woman nominated to the Supreme Court.

WHERE TO LEARN MORE

American Bar Association
321 N. Clark Street
Chicago, IL 60610
(312) 988-5000 or (800) 285-2221
www.abanet.org

The American Lawyer
www.americanlawyer.com

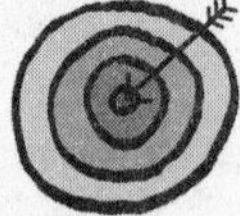

WORDS OF WISDOM

Work as hard as you possibly can. Your time in school is an invaluable chance to learn and explore that will not be repeated. Your efforts will determine the opportunities that are available to you later."

—Dave Johnson, Patent Attorney

"Many people believe all lawyers are rich and make a lot of money right out of law school, but it is not entirely true. While some people are able to get high paying jobs out of law school, many people do not and have to work long and hard before they get high paying salaries."

—Gary Garson, Corporate Lawyer

William Sloan Coats, Trial Lawyer
Executive Partner, White & Case
University of San Francisco, 1972
Majors: Psychology; Premed

What was your first job after graduation?

U.S. Army.

What criteria did you use when deciding which undergraduate colleges to apply to?

A combination of geography, school size and class size, and liberal arts orientation.

What was your first choice school?

University of San Francisco (USF).

What career did you have in mind when you applied to college?

History professor.

How did the school you attended impact on your career choice and opportunities?

It allowed a breadth of classes and provided a classic liberal arts education. I took a chemistry class and enjoyed it and changed my career orientation to premed.

Do you now wish you had attended a different school? Which one and why?

No. My finalists were Columbia University (CU) and USF, but after visiting CU in the 1960s, it did not seem a very pleasant physical environment. It is now much improved—my oldest daughter went there and my youngest daughter also went to USF.

Which college or colleges are turning out the leaders in your profession today?

Many; choice of undergraduate institution has little influence on a legal career. Choice of law school is significant.

Can you please describe the "Aha!" moment when you realized what you wanted to do?

Somewhat hard to describe, as it happened when I was finishing graduate school, teaching undergraduates, and comparing my options and lifestyle with friends who had attended law school. Being a lawyer seemed to be, and turned out to be, fun.

Did you change your major? If so, why?

Many times. Whatever my favorite class was in a given semester influenced me to try something else as a major. College was fun. I decided to be a premed, and psychology was the most flexible major for going to med school at USF.

Can you please list your majors?

History, chemistry, biology, psychology.

Which classes were most valuable in preparing you for your career or in helping you decide on your career?

Chemistry, statistics, philosophy, and English were most helpful.

How did your professors impact your career choice or preparation?

I felt that the size of USF allowed me to interact with teachers, and I enjoyed that personal level of interaction. I found many good role models.

Do you have an advanced degree? Is one helpful or required in your field?

Yes, and it is required to practice law. I also went to graduate school but did not finish.

What do you love most about your job?

I get to deal with problems on the edge of the law and new technologies. It is a job of ever-changing issues and complexities, so I am always challenged and always learning. It is fun.

What is the most difficult or challenging aspect of your job?

Long hours and hard work.

What is the biggest misconception people have about what you do?

People underestimate by far the sheer amount of boring detail work that is required to try complex cases. The trial/courtroom part is fun, but that is a very small percentage of what I get to do. Preparation and practice take up far more of my time.

What was the biggest obstacle you faced in getting to where you are in your career?

The stress of it all. Being a trial lawyer is a stressful lifestyle that frequently requires sacrificing personal interests. If you do not enjoy being a trial lawyer, you should do something else. I like what I do, and I use family as a balance to work. I try never to work at home.

What skills are an absolute must for someone interested in pursuing your career?

Good writing skills and ability to do careful, detailed work. For someone who wants to litigate technology cases, a background and interest in technology and the ability to convey complex technologies simply to others.

Whom do you admire most in your industry or field? Why?

I admire Jack Brown, Woody Woodland, Sandy Shapiro, Antonin Scalia, all masters of careful and thoughtful legal analysis.

What is one piece of advice you would give to someone who is interested in pursuing your career?

Determination and hard work are the keys to success as a lawyer.

If you could do everything all over again, what would you do differently?

I would have finished my master's degree even though I had decided to go to law school. It would have involved minimal effort, but instead I just dropped out and started working to save for law school.

Can you please add any additional comments you think might be helpful to someone hoping to pursue your career?

It's fun but stressful.

Dave Johnson, Patent Attorney
Owner of Patent Law Firm
Columbia University, 1983
Major: English Literature

What was your first job after graduation?

Administrative assistant.

What criteria did you use when deciding which colleges to apply to?

Location and engineering school ranking.

What was your first choice school?

California State Technical University (Cal Tech).

What career did you have in mind when you applied to college?

Computer architect.

How did the school you attended impact on your career choice and opportunities?

It didn't have much impact on my career choice, but a degree from a recognized college has always been helpful in terms of opportunities.

Which college or colleges are turning out the leaders in your profession today?

Stanford University, Penn State University, University of California.

Can you please describe the "Aha!" moment when you realized what you wanted to do?

I took an intellectual property law class in law school.

Did you change your major? If so, why?

Yes. The engineering program was dull and not engaging, and my liberal arts friends were having a more rewarding experience.

Can you please list your majors?

Originally, computer science, switched to English literature.

Which classes were most valuable in preparing you for your career or in helping you decide on your career?

Intellectual property class in law school, computer and electrical engineering classes in graduate school.

How did your professors impact your career choice or preparation?

Some teachers keep time and resources available to support self-directed explorations by motivated students. They are the ones who change lives.

Did you have a job and/or internship during college that influenced your career choice or career preparation in any way?

No, but experience from internships in graduate school has been very helpful.

Do you have an advanced degree? Is one helpful or required in your field?

A Juris Doctorate (JD) is necessary for a patent attorney.

What do you love most about your job?

Working on the cutting edges of technology.

What is the most difficult or challenging aspect of your job?

Writing legal documents that must withstand attacks by very smart and motivated people for the next 20 years.

What is the biggest misconception people have about what you do?

I don't think people have any conception at all about what a patent attorney does.

What was the biggest obstacle you faced in getting to where you are in your career?

Succeeding in law school.

What skills are an absolute must for someone interested in pursuing your career?

An ability to communicate and a willingness to work 60–80 hours per week for at least the first several years.

Whom do you admire most in your industry or field? Why?

Inventors who follow through with their ideas, because they create the new technologies that enrich our lives. Attorneys who defend companies against bogus patent complaints, because they protect the integrity of the patent system.

What is one piece of advice you would give to someone who is interested in pursuing your career?

Work as hard as you possibly can. Your time in school is an invaluable chance to learn and explore that will not be repeated. Your efforts now will determine the opportunities that are available to you later.

If you could do everything all over again, what would you do differently?

Work harder as an undergraduate.

Can you please add any additional comments you think might be helpful to someone hoping to pursue your career?

Take advantage of extracurricular activities, school competitions, the chance to audit other classes, etc., in order to explore other areas that may be interesting to you.

Gary W. Garson, Corporate Lawyer
General Counsel, Loews Corporation
CUNY—Queens College, 1967
Major: Economics

What was your first job after graduation?

Corporate lawyer, associate.

What criteria did you use when deciding which undergraduate colleges to apply to?

Reputation and tuition.

What was your first choice school?

Queens College, City University of New York.

What career did you have in mind when you applied to college?

Law.

How did the school you attended impact on your career choice and opportunities?

It didn't have an impact.

Which classes were most valuable in preparing you for your career or in helping you decide on your career?

Economics, political science.

Do you have an advanced degree? Is one helpful or required in your field?

Yes, and a law degree is required.

What do you love most about your job?

Variety, responsibility, work environment.

What is the most difficult or challenging aspect of your job?

Ever-changing laws and business.

What is the biggest misconception people have about what you do?

People don't understand the nature of the law and business conditions.

What skills are an absolute must for someone interested in pursuing your career?

Analytical and writing skills; communication generally.

What is one piece of advice you would give to someone who is interested in pursuing your career?

Get good training at a corporate law firm.

Keathan B. Frink, Attorney
Law Office of Keathan B. Frink, P.A.
Florida State University, 1997
Major: Criminal Justice

What was your first job after graduation?

Office of the Public Defender.

What criteria did you use when deciding which colleges to apply to?

Location and reputation.

What career did you have in mind when you applied to college?

Lawyer.

How did the school you attended impact on your career choice and opportunities?

I participated in a program for freshmen and sophomores that introduced us to law school by offering mock law school classes at the law school.

Which college or colleges are turning out the leaders in your profession today?

I think the leaders in my profession come from many different schools.

Which classes were most valuable in preparing you for your career or in helping you decide on your career?

Accounting, philosophy of the arts, creative writing, race and racism, African American literature.

Do you have an advanced degree? Is one helpful or required in your field?

Yes. You have to have a Juris Doctorate (JD) in order to practice law.

What do you love most about your job?

The ability to impact the lives of my clients and possibly change the law in this country.

What is the most difficult or challenging aspect of your job?

Dealing with unreasonable opposing counsel and clients.

What is the biggest misconception people have about what you do?

Many people believe all lawyers are rich and make a lot of money right out of law school, but it is not entirely true. While some people are able to get high paying jobs out of law school, many people do not and have to work long and hard before they get high paying salaries.

What was the biggest obstacle you faced in getting to where you are in your career?

Law school was very difficult because I didn't get the grades I was used to getting in undergraduate. I found activities such as Trial Team that I excelled at and helped demonstrate the skills I possessed outside of the classroom.

What skills are an absolute must for someone interested in pursuing your career?

Self-confidence, determination, and poise.

What is one piece of advice you would give to someone who is interested in pursuing your career?

Law school is a difficult and humbling experience. One must have the self-confidence and determination to get through it; so believe in yourself.

John Maggio,Attorney
Associate, Condon & Forsyth, LLP
SUNY—Binghamton, 1993
Major: Philosophy/Law and Society

What was your first job after graduation?

Law school.

What criteria did you use when deciding which undergraduate colleges to apply to?

U.S. News rankings, extracurricular activities, internships, classes and courses offered.

What was your first choice school?

Cornell University.

What career did you have in mind when you applied to college?

Attorney.

Can you please describe the "Aha!" moment when you realized what you wanted to do?

I wanted to be an attorney since I was seven years old.

Did you change your major? If so, why?

Yes, I planned on majoring in political science, but I did not like the faculty bias, so I majored in philosophy, which I knew little about before college.

Which classes were most valuable in preparing you for your career or in helping you decide on your career?

Philosophy of law.

How did your professors impact your career choice or preparation?

They gave me exposure to a variety of legal ideas and different sides of an argument.

Do you have an advanced degree? Is one helpful or required in your field?

Yes, a Juris Doctorate (JD) is required.

What do you love most about your job?

I enjoy practicing law.

What is the most difficult or challenging aspect of your job?

Obtaining new clients.

What is the biggest misconception people have about what you do?

People think lawyers are in court every day.

What was the biggest obstacle you faced in getting to where you are in your career?

Mediocre grades; I relied on experiences, past jobs, and law school internships.

What skills are an absolute must for someone interested in pursuing your career?

Good speaking ability.

Whom do you admire most in your industry or field? Why?

I admire Supreme Court Justice John Roberts, particularly for what he did early in his career; he has amazing accomplishments for such a short career.

What is one piece of advice you would give to someone who is interested in pursuing your career?

Take advantage of what law school has to offer.

If you could do everything all over again, what would you do differently?

Study harder in law school.

LIBRARY SCIENCE

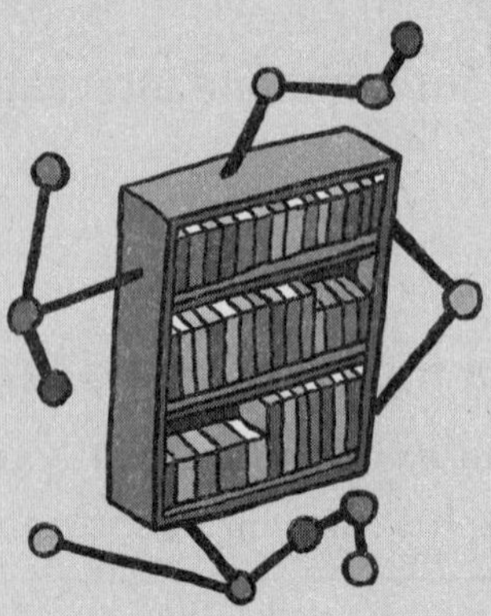

WHY CHOOSE A CAREER IN LIBRARY SCIENCE?

Library science is a broad field with many wonderful career opportunities. Librarians work in diverse public, institutional, and academic settings. The changes wrought by information technologies have transformed the field in recent years. Librarians are among the most tech-savvy professionals, with access to some of the most extensive databases in the world. Librarians may produce websites or deploy search engines that bring specialized information and research services to a variety of clients. Librarians who aid those in the corporate world generally work with large, networked office systems. Yet librarians also serve as visionaries who have tailored personal computers for their own specific needs, and they are likely inventing some of the applications we will use in managing the information of tomorrow.

WHERE THE JOBS ARE

The current job market in library science is robust. Typically, graduates can expect to find employment within six months of commencement, as the American Library Association reports that more than one-quarter of professionals currently employed as librarians are expected to retire by 2009. Librarians are in demand in the medical and legal fields and are employed by legislative bodies at all levels of government. They are present in academic settings from grammar school to university and can expect to find work with a variety of special interest groups, including environmental activists, religious organizations, and technology researchers.

AREAS OF SPECIALTY

Librarians may be as specialized in their knowledge as the data they help to manage. Career options range from being a K–12 or academic librarian to overseeing collections of medical or legal documents. Government entities often maintain their own libraries of documents pertaining to their areas of influence and expertise. Other career possibilities include information consulting, systems management, patent research, and the archiving of rare books or other historical documents. Possibilities outside common library settings include roles as content managers, information brokers, or database administrators.

EDUCATIONAL REQUIREMENTS

A master's of library science (MLS) degree prepares students for work in the field. The graduate program typically takes two years to complete, though some students may take longer, depending upon their circumstances and the program of choice. Undergraduate degrees in information sciences with a minor in languages are common, though not required. Technology skills are in high demand. Candidates who bring diversity, energy, and job skills outside the normal purview of library science are highly desirable.

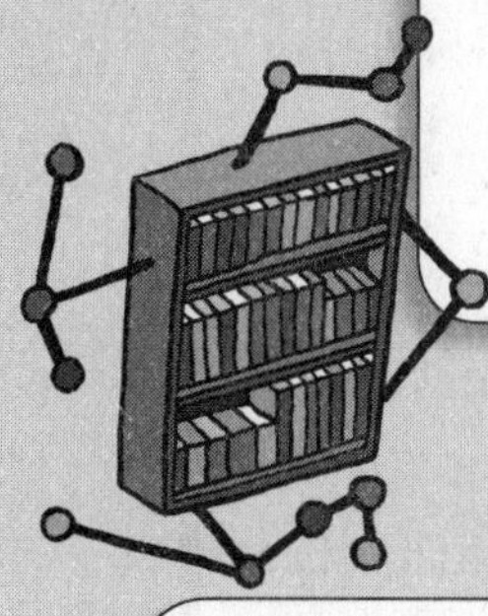

SALARY RANGE

Starting salaries for librarians range from about $30,000–$60,000 a year. Many employees receive excellent benefits, including paid vacation, sick leave, and health and dental insurance, plus retirement plans. In recent years, the federal government has earmarked funds to be used to recruit and train the next generation of librarians.

FAMOUS LIBRARY SCIENCE PROFESSIONALS

- **Laura Bush**, wife of the 43rd president of the United States, George W. Bush, was a librarian and holds a master's degree in library science.
- Author **Beverly Cleary** worked as a librarian and earned her degree from the University of Washington.

WHERE TO LEARN MORE

American Library Association
www.ala.org

Library and Information Sciences Career Information
www.becomealibrarian.org

WORDS OF WISDOM

"Learn to enjoy the outside-the-library aspects of the job as much as the inside-the-library aspects. Professional development is extremely important to career advancement and satisfaction."

—Dennis Harper, Academic Law Librarian

"One great thing about librarianship is that you can come at it from any direction—it really doesn't matter what career you had before or what you studied as an undergraduate. In fact, having knowledge or experience of another field is often an asset. It's a really versatile field with a great outlook."

—Siobhan McKiernan, Librarian

Dennis Harper, Academic Law Librarian
Serials Librarian
Cornell University, 2003
Major: Psychology

What was your first job after graduation?

Law librarian.

What criteria did you use when deciding which colleges to apply to?

Academic reputation, location, size, breadth of course offerings.

What was your first choice school?

Cornell University.

What career did you have in mind when you applied to college?

I had some vague ideas but not one that I ultimately pursued.

How did the school you attended have an impact on your career choice and opportunities?

Only in that it was prestigious enough to help me get into a good graduate school.

Do you now wish you had attended a different school? Which one and why?

No, I have no regrets about my attendance.

Which college or colleges are turning out the leaders in your profession today?

None has cornered the market, though there is a slight bias for those who've attended schools in the Northeast (especially private liberal arts schools or large research universities).

Which classes were most valuable in preparing you for your career or in helping you decide on your career?

My legal research classes while at law school were the most helpful. Many of my undergraduate psychology courses familiarized students with the research process, though, and were also very helpful.

How did your professors impact your career choice or preparation?

Some unintentionally dissuaded me from pursuing career choices they had made. Others were helpful in writing me letters of recommendation.

Did you have a job and/or internship during college that influenced your ultimate career choice or career preparation in any way?

I worked in an academic music library, which helped me realize how much I enjoy libraries.

Can you please describe the "Aha!" moment when you realized what you wanted to do?

I didn't have one; the experience was gradual for me.

Did you change your major? If so, why?

I changed to psychology from undecided. I no longer thought my vague original career intention was optimal and enjoyed the idea of studying psychology for the next few years.

How important was your college experience in getting you to where you are today?

I could have easily ended up where I am today with a variety of college experiences, though mine prepared me as well as any would.

Do you have an advanced degree? Is one helpful or required in your field?

Yes. An MLIS is required for any librarian, and a JD is strongly encouraged for law librarians (especially academic law librarians). Most academic librarians in general are expected to hold a second advanced degree in addition to their MLS/MLIS.

What do you love most about your job?

Working in an academic setting.

What is the most difficult or challenging aspect of your job?

Always learning something new.

What is the biggest misconception people have about what you do?

To the extent anyone would bother to imagine what I do, I would bet they would be unable to imagine the variety of different tasks involved.

What was the biggest obstacle you faced in getting to where you are in your career?

Law school is extremely trying. Having an optimistic outlook was very helpful.

What skills are an absolute must for someone interested in pursuing your career?

Too many others in my career seem to have gotten there with no skills, but I would say that patience and professionalism are extremely helpful.

Whom do you admire most in your industry or field?

Academic law library directors, for their ability to please the 20 librarians under them and the 20 administrators/faculty above them at the same time.

What is one piece of advice you would give to someone who is interested in pursuing your career?

I would suggest researching it heavily by talking to actual librarians in the specialty in which the advisee is interested. I would also suggest immersing oneself in the career 100 percent as soon as one is able to commit to it, as the earliest start and display of enthusiasm impresses the most.

If you could do everything all over again, what would you do differently?

I would have planned better financially so I could have attained my MLIS quicker. This would have allowed me to start working even faster.

Do you have any additional comments you think might be helpful to someone hoping to pursue your career?

Learn to enjoy the outside-the-library aspects of the job as much as the inside-the-library aspects. Professional development is extremely important to career advancement and satisfaction.

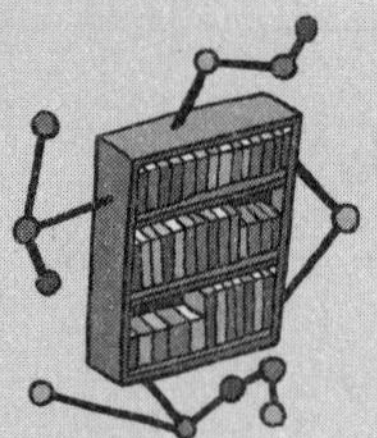

Sandy Bochese, Librarian
School Library Media Specialist
Seton Hall University, 1978
Major: Education

What was your first job after graduation?

I was a middle school English teacher.

What criteria did you use when deciding which colleges to apply to?

I was interested in a college that had a strong teacher education program and was close enough to commute to and from my home.

What was your first choice school?

Seton Hall was my first choice.

What career did you have in mind when you applied to college?

I applied to college to pursue a career in education.

How did the school you attended have an impact on your career choice and opportunities?

Seton Hall absolutely had a significant impact on my career opportunities. We were required to complete a field experience each semester, so I was observing in a variety of classes beginning in my freshman year. I was able to see teachers in both middle and high school and in suburban and urban districts. This exposure opened my eyes to the differences, similarities, and challenges of these different environments.

Do you now wish you had attended a different school? Which one and why?

Given the same financial constraints, I would probably apply to the same school.

Which college or colleges are turning out the leaders in your profession today?

A number of the New Jersey state colleges, such as Montclair State University, are currently offering a program that leads to the school library media specialist certification. I believe that each state has different programs and requirements leading to certification as a school librarian/media specialist, so college students should consult with their advisors about specific requirements.

Which classes were most valuable in preparing you for your career or in helping you decide on your career?

All of the field experience components of my education classes provided me with valuable insight into the actual day-in and day-out processes of teaching. I began my teaching career well aware of the amount of energy and time that are required to be a successful teacher.

How did your professors impact your career choice or preparation?

I believe that one professor, Dr. Rosemary Skeele, had a huge impact on my career choice as a school library media specialist. She was, and currently is, the director of the Seton Hall University graduate program, which prepares candidates for the school library media specialist certification. She was always helpful and approachable and shared her practical advice on how we could make the transition from teaching to serving as school library media specialists.

Did you have a job and/or internship during college that influenced your ultimate career choice or career preparation in any way?

During my undergraduate years, I had a number of jobs. I was a domestic, a restaurant hostess, and a clerk in the physical plant office on the Seton Hall campus. As a graduate student, I was hired to be a graduate assistant to tutor undergraduates in one-on-one and small-group sessions. This job paid for most of my graduate courses, so I was able to finish a 36-credit graduate program in three semesters. I had no social life, but I was motivated to finish the program as quickly as possible and get on with my career. My various jobs reinforced for me the notion that I really wanted to work with students and not in the corporate world.

Can you please describe the "Aha!" moment when you realized what you wanted to do?

My "Aha!" moment came after my second year of teaching English. I was "RIF-ed" (reduction in force) from a high school English job and found very few openings for English teachers in my area. I went back to my advisor at Seton Hall for some suggestions on how to retool my career, and she told me about the master's in education program that led to the school library media specialist certification. It seemed like a perfect route to remaining in education while capitalizing on my love of books and reading. I did not want to pursue a master's in library science, as I felt that my calling was to work in a school environment rather than public library.

Did you change your major? If so, why?

No, I was confident in my decision.

How important was your college experience in getting you to where you are today?

My college experience offered me the chance to learn the skills necessary to operate a school library media center and to make the transition from classroom teacher to school librarian.

Do you have an advanced degree? Is one helpful or required in your field?

Yes, I have one. In New Jersey, school library media specialists must have a master's degree.

What do you love most about your job?

I love interacting on a daily basis with the students and the faculty. I guess you could say I am a "people person." That is one of the reasons I went into teaching in the first place.

What is the most difficult or challenging aspect of your job?

The most challenging aspect of my current job is that I only have the benefit of support staff two days a week. My job involves a lot of clerical tasks, and I am often bogged down with those tasks (covering and shelving books, etc.) instead of working on tasks that involve interacting with the students. In my previous job in a high school library in another district, I had the benefit of two full-time assistants every day. Their help with the clerical tasks freed me to interact more with the students and staff.

What is the biggest misconception people have about what you do?

Outside of the school environment, people think that all I do is "SHHH…" the kids! Unless you have experience in a school environment, you are not aware of the multitude of tasks we are expected to accomplish on a daily basis. The role of the school library media specialist is vastly different from that of the public librarian—not better or worse, just different.

What was the biggest obstacle you faced in getting to where you are in your career?

I think that the biggest obstacle was obtaining my master's degree. At first, it seemed daunting. I overcame this obstacle by accepting a position as a graduate assistant and basically giving up my own personal life for about a year while I completed the 36-credit program.

What skills are an absolute must for someone interested in pursuing your career?

School library media specialists must enjoy working with children, appreciate interacting with colleagues, and work to remain current with the advancing technologies that we have available to us.

Whom do you admire most in your industry or field?

I admire all the other school library media specialists who work with very limited budgets and in less than ideal circumstances. Every district allots different amounts of money and places different priorities on the school library media center, so the facility can be expansive or neglected, depending on the philosophy of the administration. These library media specialists often work with very few resources yet still strive to provide their students with quality programs and materials.

What is one piece of advice you would give to someone who is interested in pursuing your career?

Be sure that you enjoy teaching, because most of what you will do revolves around the students.

If you could do everything all over again, what would you do differently?

The only change I might have made was to perhaps begin my master's degree immediately after receiving my undergraduate degree so that I could have spread out the course work over a longer period of time.

Do you have any additional comments you think might be helpful to someone hoping to pursue your career?

Right now, the job market for school library media specialists in New Jersey is excellent, so it is certainly worth considering.

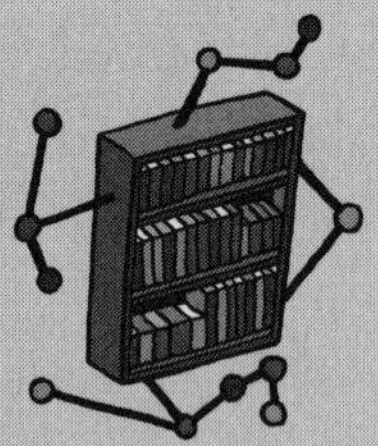

Siobhan McKiernan, Librarian
Clinical Librarian
Eugene Lang College, New School for Social Research, 2000
Major: Creative Writing

What was your first job after graduation?

I was an editorial assistant.

What criteria did you use when deciding which colleges to apply to?

Location was a big factor for me—I was also interested in a strong writing program and small classes.

What was your first choice school?

The New School was my first choice.

What career did you have in mind when you applied to college?

I didn't really have a specific career in mind.

How did the school you attended have an impact on your career choice and opportunities?

It didn't really have a huge impact. My interest in writing led me to work in publishing, but I'm not sure that my specific school contributed to that choice.

Do you now wish you had attended a different school? Which one and why?

My college had a strong writing program but limited choices in other areas; I would probably go to a larger school with a broader range of course options, like NYU (which was my second choice).

Which college or colleges are turning out the leaders in your profession today?

Librarianship requires a master's in library and information science (LIS), but it draws people from all fields of study and a variety of backgrounds. There are very few undergrad programs in LIS.

Which classes were most valuable in preparing you for your career or in helping you decide on your career?

None, in all honesty.

How did your professors impact your career choice or preparation?

They didn't really have a big impact on me.

Did you have a job and/or internship during college that influenced your ultimate career choice or career preparation in any way?

I had several work-study jobs and worked in the HR department of a publishing company during my senior year. The publishing job helped me get into editing—even though it was in a different department, it was helpful to have experience in publishing.

Can you please describe the "Aha!" moment when you realized what you wanted to do?

I didn't have one. I had volunteered in the library in high school and had always thought about librarianship as a career option.

Did you change your major? If so, why?

No, I didn't.

How important was your college experience in getting you to where you are today?

My college experience was mostly helpful in getting me into publishing—having a strong background in writing was definitely a plus when I wanted to become an editor. Ultimately, though, work experience and graduate education have been the most important factors in establishing and advancing my career.

Do you have an advanced degree? Is one helpful or required in your field?

Yes, I have a master's in library and information science from Louisiana State University. Nearly all librarian positions require an MLIS degree from a program accredited by the American Library Association. The major exception is school library media specialist/school librarian jobs—requirements for these vary by state.

What do you love most about your job?

I really enjoy helping patrons with their reference questions, particularly when they are surprised by what's out there and what I am able to find for them—it's very gratifying to help people connect with the information they need.

What is the most difficult or challenging aspect of your job?

Librarianship is very much about customer service, and with that comes all the challenges of interacting with people all day. It can be challenging to help a patron who is especially frustrated or can't get what he or she wants right away.

What is the biggest misconception people have about what you do?

That I get to read all day! Most librarians I know do love books, but our jobs are busy and demanding—there is always work to do. Also, the profession is more and more about technology and less about managing collections of just books.

What was the biggest obstacle you faced in getting to where you are in your career?

Moving from my previous field (publishing) to librarianship was a major challenge—I didn't have any real work experience in a library when I started graduate school. I decided that I was willing to start pretty low on the totem pole; I took a part-time job as an assistant in the library where I am now a librarian.

What skills are an absolute must for someone interested in pursuing your career?

Although not all library jobs involve interaction with the public, it's important to have a service-oriented mind-set and be really interested in helping people. Communication, organizational, and problem-solving skills are also very important.

Whom do you admire most in your industry or field?

Librarians are generally pretty low-profile, but I have been really amazed and impressed by the professional community's response to the aftermath of the hurricane here in New Orleans. All kinds of libraries were affected, and librarians locally and nationally have done so much in terms of outreach, collaboration, and volunteering to help us get back on our feet. It's inspiring and makes me proud to be part of this profession.

What is one piece of advice you would give to someone who is interested in pursuing your career?

Work experience is crucial in finding a good job after library school—although it's said that there is an abundance of jobs, employers are reluctant to hire a full-time librarian who has little or no actual library experience. In contrast, it's easy to find part-time library work while you are in school; libraries love to hire grad students because they know you have an investment and a long-term interest in the work.

If you could do everything all over again, what would you do differently?

I don't know that I would do anything differently. I've been lucky to have a great education and work with a lot of wonderful people.

Do you have any additional comments you think might be helpful to someone hoping to pursue your career?

One great thing about librarianship is that you can come at it from any direction. It really doesn't matter what career you had before or what you studied as an undergraduate. In fact, having knowledge or experience of another field is often an asset. It's a really versatile field with a great outlook.

Sue Maberry, Librarian
Director of Library and Instructional Technology
California State University—San Jose, 1992
Major: Library Science

What was your first job after graduation?

Newspaper librarian at the *Daily News*.

What criteria did you use when deciding which colleges to apply to?

Reputation, majors offered, and location.

What was your first choice school?

Cal State—San Jose.

What career did you have in mind when you applied to college?

I wanted to become a social worker.

How did the school you attended have an impact on your career choice and opportunities?

I first attended Cal Poly Pomona, which I hated. I later returned to school and went to Pitzer for my BA, which was prestigious but didn't ultimately have a significant impact. Cal State—San Jose didn't have a huge impact, except that it offered an MLS.

Do you now wish you had attended a different school? Which one and why?

I think my choices were fine. UCLA for graduate school would have been more prestigious, but that wasn't an option for an older, working person.

Which college or colleges are turning out the leaders in your profession today?

It's less about the school and more about the person and their interests and abilities.

Which classes were most valuable in preparing you for your career or in helping you decide on your career?

All my classes were beneficial in some way.

How did your professors impact your career choice or preparation?

I sought out professionals to advise me about what the daily routine of the job would be like.

Did you have a job and/or internship during college that influenced your ultimate career choice or career preparation in any way?

No.

Can you please describe the "Aha!" moment when you realized what you wanted to do?

After I had worked for many years, I realized that to go further, I needed an advanced degree. I thought long and hard about my strengths and interests and came up with the idea to become a librarian.

Did you change your major? If so, why?

Yes. As an undergrad, I realized I would never be happy as a social worker.

How important was your college experience in getting you to where you are today?

It was very important. You can't get far without college.

Do you have an advanced degree? Is one helpful or required in your field?

Yes. The MLS degree was an absolute requirement for the job. It provided theoretical perspectives that I couldn't have gotten any other way.

What do you love most about your job?

Autonomy, variety, being around intelligent people, and getting to learn new things.

What is the most difficult or challenging aspect of your job?

Since librarianship is female dominated, people sometimes underrate the skills necessary. One example: although many librarians are as "techie" as staff in IS departments, they are often paid less and overlooked for promotions.

What is the biggest misconception people have about what you do?

That I sit around and read all day.

What was the biggest obstacle you faced in getting to where you are in your career?

I didn't have enough money to be able to just go to school without working. It took me 21 years to get a BA. I had to start and stop a lot.

What skills are an absolute must for someone interested in pursuing your career?

Interest in technology and teaching, good collaborative and service skills.

Whom do you admire most in your industry or field?

Tim Berners-Lee. He invented the World Wide Web, and he didn't take a dime for it. He gave it away to serve higher purposes.

What is one piece of advice you would give to someone who is interested in pursuing your career?

Go for it. Librarians are the future.

If you could do everything all over again, what would you do differently?

I would have figured out what I wanted to do earlier and started earlier. But the path you take is the one you take.

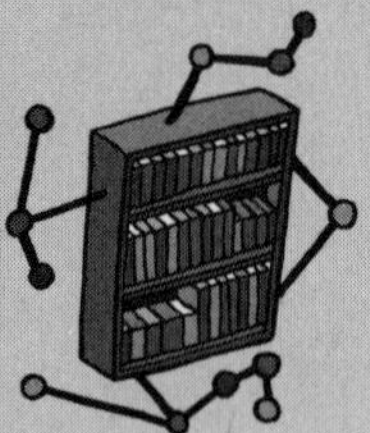

Tinsley E. Silcox, Librarian
Director of Public Services
University of Tennessee—Knoxville, 1987
Major: Library and Information Science

What was your first job after graduation?

I was an assistant professor and reference bibliographer for the humanities at the University of Mississippi.

What criteria did you use when deciding which colleges to apply to?

Reputation of the graduate program and its faculty; location.

What was your first choice school?

University of Tennessee—Knoxville was my first choice.

What career did you have in mind when you applied to college?

I knew that I wanted a career in library and information science.

How did the school you attended have an impact on your career choice and opportunities?

My course work prepared me well for a position in which I was interested, and former instructors provided references.

Do you now wish you had attended a different school? Which one and why?

I would still apply to and attend the master's in library science program at UTK. They continue to offer competent faculty and relevant course offerings.

Which college or colleges are turning out the leaders in your profession today?

University of Tennessee—Knoxville, Indiana University, University of Alabama, University of Arizona, etc. There is a complete listing of schools with ALA-accredited degree programs at the American Library Association website.

Which classes were most valuable in preparing you for your career or in helping you decide on your career?

Course work in reference, academic libraries, library administration, and management.

How did your professors impact your career choice or preparation?

My professor of reference had a big impact on my path to subject discipline reference work. He also encouraged me to pursue the management track.

Did you have a job and/or internship during college that influenced your ultimate career choice or career preparation in any way?

While in the MLIS program, I worked full-time as the circulation assistant in the music library. This led me to make the career choice I did, because I found it so rewarding.

Can you please describe the "Aha!" moment when you realized what you wanted to do?

I was working as a technical processing assistant in a university music library when I realized that combining my music degree with a degree in library science would offer me the opportunity to have the best of both worlds in my work life.

Did you change your major? If so, why?

No.

How important was your college experience in getting you to where you are today?

The technical expertise to perform my first job out of grad school could only have come from a program such as the one in which I was enrolled.

Do you have an advanced degree? Is one helpful or required in your field?

Yes I do, and for this field it is a requirement.

What do you love most about your job?

It is different every day. There are always new challenges and opportunities, especially in helping students.

What is the most difficult or challenging aspect of your job?

Managing a large professional staff with sometimes competing agendas.

What is the biggest misconception people have about what you do?

That I get to sit around and read books all the time!

What was the biggest obstacle you faced in getting to where you are in your career?

Getting managerial experience. I overcame this by working in the trenches and building a progressively more challenging managerial base.

What skills are an absolute must for someone interested in pursuing your career?

Thinking on your feet, flexibility, analytical skills, people skills/customer service ethic.

Whom do you admire most in your industry or field?

Anyone who has risen to the rank of dean or university librarian because it takes tough-mindedness, wit, tenacity, and integrity.

What is one piece of advice you would give to someone who is interested in pursuing your career?

When you take your first professional position, make sure it is one in which you can test the waters, have permission to fail, permission to grow, and with managers who are interested in your success.

If you could do everything all over again, what would you do differently?

I would have gotten involved much sooner with national organizations such as ALA, including serving on national-level committees and other groups.

Do you have any additional comments you think might be helpful to someone hoping to pursue your career?

Librarianship, and especially academic librarianship and library management, is a rewarding career. It is an opportunity to work with students, faculty, and colleagues in an environment of research and study.

PERFORMING ARTS

WHY CHOOSE A CAREER IN THE PERFORMING ARTS?

People in the performing arts are passionate about their talent and enjoy performing in front of and entertaining others. Performers use their voice, body, and/or a musical instrument to express themselves.

WHERE THE JOBS ARE

Performing artists work alone or as part of a group, in television, film, theatre, and in various regional and traveling companies. The performing arts industry is highly concentrated in New York and Los Angeles, but opportunities exist in most major cities as well. The performing arts are among the most competitive and difficult ways to make a living and require a combination of skill, talent, drive, and luck to succeed. Many people take other jobs or teach as a way to earn money while they pursue their art. However, there are many performers who are not household names but who still manage to support themselves through their art.

AREAS OF SPECIALTY

People in the performing arts generally choose one main area of performance, such as acting, singing, dancing, or music performance. They also often have a specialty within their chosen field, such as classical music, modern dance, or opera.

EDUCATIONAL REQUIREMENTS

Most careers in the performing arts require a high degree of training. That training can take place in conservatories, specialized schools, or in the various performing arts departments at many colleges and universities. There are no formal educational requirements for a career in the performing arts; however, many earn a bachelor's degree as a way to both improve their skills and to earn a living while they pursue their art. Teachers of the performing arts generally need a master's degree to qualify for most positions and a PhD to teach at the college level.

SALARY RANGE

Salaries in the performing arts vary more than in almost any other profession, and it is rare for performers to work in one job for any extended period of time. Some performers struggle to support themselves, and a very few earn high salaries. Many performers join unions that set specific minimum salaries for various jobs. For example, actors with speaking parts on television or in movies earned a daily rate of $715 in 2005. Very few actors are considered stars who command enormous salaries; out of almost 100,000 members of the Screen Actors Guild, only about 50 would fall into this category.

Pros: Creative work, the satisfaction of entertaining others

Cons: Uncertain income, the stress of auditioning and performing

FAMOUS FIRSTS

The first ballet was performed in 1489.

The first commercial theater opened in London in 1576.

The first opera, *Daphne,* was performed in 1598.

WHERE TO LEARN MORE

National Association of Schools of Music
11250 Roger Bacon Drive, Suite 21
Reston, VA 20190
http://nasm.arts-accredit.org

National Association of Schools of Dance
11250 Roger Bacon Drive, Suite 21
Reston, VA 20190
http://nasd.arts-accredit.org

National Association of Schools of Theater
1250 Roger Bacon Drive, Suite 21
Reston, VA 20190
http://nast.arts-accredit.org

Screen Actors Guild
5757 Wilshire Boulevard
Los Angeles, CA 90036-3600
(323) 954-1600
www.sag.com

Back Stage
www.backstage.com

The Hollywood Reporter
www.hollywoodreporter.com

Variety
www.variety.com

WORDS OF WISDOM

"It is amazing how many people assume the arts aren't a career—that they are a diversion. Of course, that is because those not in the arts utilize the arts as their diversion. I think many people fail to recognize the energy, skill level, time, and discipline that must go into creating the arts they so enjoy in their leisure."

—Norah Long, Actor/Singer

"Go wherever you can and don't get too discouraged. Everyone feels that at some point in time. Listen to yourself and you'll find out if it's not what you want—it's never too late to try something new."

—Mary Bacon, Actress

Norah Long, Actor/Singer
Guthrie Theater, Florida Stage, Theatre de la Jeune Lune, Arvada Center (Denver), Minnesota Orchestra, many others
North Central Bible College, 1991
Major: Music Performance (Voice/Piano)

What was your first job after graduation?

Soprano, the Dale Warland Singers.

What criteria did you use when deciding which undergraduate colleges to apply to?

Strength of their music programs, personal faith, familiarity, community.

What was your first choice school?

North Central Bible College.

What career did you have in mind when you applied to college?

Music.

How did the school you attended impact on your career choice and opportunities?

I found the preconceptions based on the religious affiliation of the school elicited questions, and its lack of name recognition kept it from specifically aiding me; otherwise, it has made little difference.

Do you now wish you had attended a different school? Which one and why?

Perhaps, yes. On one hand, my experience shaped me in a way that led me to where I am today, and I am successful and content in my profession. On the other hand, to have attended a more "prestigious" school may have afforded me a faster track to where I am now, which could have afforded me an opportunity to have worked on a much broader scope by my same age. Ultimately, I think to look back and make wishes such as this is a less than helpful approach; we each make our decisions based on where we are in life at the moment, and we can never know what gifts and tools we may have lost if a different choice had been made.

Which college or colleges are turning out the leaders in your profession today?

The Juilliard School, Yale University, Cincinnati Conservatory.

Can you please describe the "Aha!" moment when you realized what you wanted to do?

I was quite young—fifth grade—when I participated in my first theater performance. There was never a question after that.

Which classes were most valuable in preparing you for your career or in helping you decide on your career?

Private lessons, music theory, and most importantly, experience.

How did your professors impact your career choice or preparation?

Their connections with professional organizations led me to pursue the specific earliest jobs I had after college; and in general, having leaders challenge, encourage, and direct me kept me focused and motivated.

Did you have a job and/or internship during college that influenced your career choice or career preparation in any way?

No. Except that having jobs outside my field of interest (as a way to pay my school bills) helped to reaffirm that I did not want to do those other things.

Do you have an advanced degree? Is one helpful or required in your field?

I do not. I have found that continued education in the performing arts is most helpful for those people who wish to teach. Of course, many performers have acquired master's degree; but in general, continued private lessons in voice and coaching, and the lessons learned in the actual process of working are as great an asset, in my opinion, as a higher degree.

What do you love most about your job?

I like to say it's like getting paid to go on recess. Yes, it requires a great amount of commitment, responsibility, and focus, but if you are doing something you truly enjoy (whatever that is), nothing can be more exhilarating than getting to do it for your "real job." I love the variety, the energy, the social aspect, the creativity. It is a job for extroverts.

What is the most difficult or challenging aspect of your job?

Being a performing artist requires that you have a very different schedule than the rest of the world. In a way, you become isolated, except for your performing community. It can be rather difficult to maintain a social life outside of work when you are working when others are socializing. I also cannot leave out the constant "starting over." For those who need to have a long-term plan for their lives, the arts may not be the right field; you must have a particular disposition to not be distressed by having to look for a new job so often.

What is the biggest misconception people have about what you do?

It is amazing how many people assume the arts aren't a career—that they are a diversion. Of course, this is because those not in the arts utilize the arts as their diversion. I think many people fail to recognize the energy, skill level, time, and discipline that must go into creating the arts they so enjoy in their leisure.

What was the biggest obstacle you faced in getting to where you are in your career?

I suppose it was a combination of the competition and having to acquire name recognition. When you have to seek a new job every few months (or if you aren't working, audition as often as possible to find a job), having a body of work under your belt serves to give you credibility and visibility, so that the next hiring agent sees you as an asset and not just a talent. It is amazing how many talented people audition alongside you for each job, and the ones who tend to get hired are the ones who are known. So if level of visibility is the obstacle, the way to overcome it is to persevere and work when you can, and when you do, make sure you are the kind of person others will want to work with again.

What skills are an absolute must for someone interested in pursuing your career?

Listening, being flexible, people skills, perseverance, a strong work ethic. And of course, talent.

Whom do you admire most in your industry or field? Why?

It's difficult for me to answer this question with recognizable names because I'm not inclined to simply list those who I think are the biggest talents. I admire those (performers and directors alike) who are genuinely nice—who put aside competition and a quest for personal gain in lieu of a generous and honest nature. I think most people who truly achieve and maintain success in my field embody these qualities, and without them, a long career is rare. I want to encourage developing performers to remember this because there can be a misconception that, when you are talented or "the star," it's okay to be a diva; even more, being difficult or outlandish embodies star quality more than being humble. In fact, while divas tend to command attention, it doesn't tend to be positive attention, and in my opinion, those performers who are most admirable are the ones who are, first and foremost, admirable as people.

What is one piece of advice you would give to someone who is interested in pursuing your career?

Have fun. And don't let people dissuade you from pursuing the arts as a career if it is what you love; if it doesn't work out, so be it. You can always change careers if you need to, but you will know you tried.

If you could do everything all over again, what would you do differently?

I'd not let fear of failure or the unknown keep me from trying more things. Everyone fails sometimes. The regret will only come in not knowing whether you could have if only you would have tried.

Can you please add any additional comments you think might be helpful to someone hoping to pursue your career?

Two things. (1) Auditions are unavoidable. And they never stop. Learn to love them somehow—approach them not as a moment when someone has power to reject or accept you, but rather as a moment for you to practice and hone what you have been working on. No one gets every job they audition for. (2) In the same vein, since your tool in this craft is yourself, do not neglect to develop that self into someone you are wholly proud of. I firmly believe that a sense of personal stability, awareness, and health equips us in this line of work to have the most successful work life as well.

Vikki Jones, Opera Singer
Catholic University of America, 1994
Major: Vocal Performance

What was your first job after graduation?

Teacher's aide.

What criteria did you use when deciding which undergraduate colleges to apply to?

I used the guidance of my music teachers.

What was your first choice school?

My first choice was the Catholic University of America (CUA).

What career did you have in mind when you applied to college?

I wanted a solo career in music.

How did the school you attended impact on your career choice and opportunities?

CUA impacted my choice because of the constant exposure they gave me to other performers in the same field, but my own desire to sing afforded me the opportunities I was given to perform.

Do you now wish you had attended a different school? Which one and why?

I wish I had attended the Juilliard School of Music because I feel I could have benefited from the intensity of a conservatory setting.

Which college or colleges are turning out the leaders in your profession today?

The Juilliard School of Music is constantly turning out leaders in my profession.

Can you please describe the "Aha!" moment when you realized what you wanted to do?

The "Aha!" moment for me was when I was singing with the Baltimore Symphony Chorus and Marietta Simpson was the soloist. It was then that I knew I wanted to be like her, in front of the orchestra, not behind!

Which classes were most valuable in preparing you for your career or in helping you decide on your career?

My voice lessons were most valuable particularly my first year because my teacher would have all of her students perform for one another.

How did your professors impact your career choice or preparation?

My professors impacted me by teaching me how to take apart a piece of music, and with that I was able to perform to the best of my ability and enjoy it!

Do you have an advanced degree? Is one helpful or required in your field?

Upon graduation I did audition for a master's degree and was accepted; however, I declined. My mother died of lung cancer when I was just 14 years old, and even though half of my tuition was covered with scholarships, the financial strain on my father would have been too great. I also felt that although there appeared to be more performance opportunities on the graduate level, there were no guarantees and I simply couldn't risk it financially, especially when tuition was approximately $22,000 a year.

What do you love most about your job?

The best part of my job is being on stage and working with other performers.

What is the most difficult or challenging aspect of your job?

The most difficult part of my job is the effort it takes to get gigs.

What is the biggest misconception people have about what you do?

I think the biggest misconception is that it's easy and all glamour and glitz.

What was the biggest obstacle you faced in getting to where you are in your career?

The biggest obstacle was and continues to be the financial hardships that a career in performance can entail.

What skills are an absolute must for someone interested in pursuing your career?

The absolute skills are a sound vocal technique, music ability, and language skills.

Whom do you admire most in your industry or field? Why?

The person I admire most till this day is Leontyne Price. She was so consistent in every one of her performances, and her technique was astounding and the length of her career was amazing!

What is one piece of advice you would give to someone who is interested in pursuing your career?

No matter what, don't give up.

If you could do everything all over again, what would you do differently?

I would have applied to conservatories and would have pursued studying abroad.

J. Hammons, Teacher, Dancer, Director
Head of Dance Program, Lusher High School
University of Southern Mississippi, 1988
Major: Psychology

What was your first job after graduation?

Dancer.

What criteria did you use when deciding which colleges to apply to?

Price, scholarships; it had an honors college.

What was your first choice school?

Boston University.

What career did you have in mind when you applied to college?

Therapist/psychology.

How did the school you attended impact on your career choice and opportunities?

I had no idea when I entered that there was even such a thing as a career in dance—it just so happened that the school I attended had a great dance teacher.

Which college or colleges are turning out the leaders in your profession today?

Ohio State University, State University of New York—Purchase, Arizona State University, The Juilliard School, University of Washington—Seattle, University of Utah.

Can you please describe the "Aha!" moment when you realized what you wanted to do?

When I attended a summer dance festival and discovered I could compete with other dancers around the country.

Did you change your major? If so, why?

I added a dance major for a while but dropped it because it would have taken another year to get the one class I needed.

Which classes were most valuable in preparing you for your career or in helping you decide on your career?

Dance improvisation, dance technique, dance composition.

How did your professors impact your career choice or preparation?

One professor in particular was the sole reason I became a professional dancer.

Do you have an advanced degree? Is one helpful or required in your field?

Yes, two of them, and they are required.

What do you love most about your job?

When I teach, I enjoy making a difference in kids' lives. When I perform, I am contributing to our culture.

What is the most difficult or challenging aspect of your job?

The bureaucracy and the lack of money.

What is the biggest misconception people have about what you do?

It's an isolated experience; that it doesn't have anything to do with anything else.

What was the biggest obstacle you faced in getting to where you are in your career?

Too few positions available for talent pool.

What skills are an absolute must for someone interested in pursuing your career?

Core talent, adaptability, patience, and unfortunately, political savvy.

Whom do you admire most in your industry or field? Why?

I admire David Dorfman, who has always had just the right blend of artistic talent, social skills, and sense of play.

What is one piece of advice you would give to someone who is interested in pursuing your career?

If it's not your driving passion, don't bother; if it is your driving passion, don't give up.

If you could do everything all over again, what would you do differently?

Get more peripheral skill sets—pilates or any other body work training.

Can you please add any additional comments you think might be helpful to someone hoping to pursue your career?

For a professional dance career, go to as many workshops as you can—get a variety of training—get seen.

Christopher Chaffee, Music Professor, Flutist, Music and Arts Critic
Assistant Professor of Music, Wright State University
University of Rochester Eastman School of Music, 1995
Major: Flute Performance

What was your first job after graduation?

Graduate school and freelance performing.

What criteria did you use when deciding which undergraduate colleges to apply to?

National and international reputation, personality and ability of music faculty, especially in my major, academic reputation and elite standards, urban setting, educational opportunity.

What career did you have in mind when you applied to college?

Orchestral musician.

How did the school you attended impact on your career choice and opportunities?

University of Rochester Eastman School of Music (URESM) opened my mind to a broad future, including music careers outside of the traditional mold. The faculty and students shared a passion for music that I have never encountered anywhere else.

Which college or colleges are turning out the leaders in your profession today?

Great musicians will thrive nearly anywhere, especially with quality mentoring and experience, so the "brand name" schools, while vital, are not the only choice these days. Career success is not guaranteed if you attend an elite institution. However, it is worth trying your best to earn a place at one of the top schools for the student experience and the daily exposure to outstanding music making. Schools have peaks and low points, but in the long term, if a school has earned a reputation over several decades (e.g., University of Rochester Eastman School of Music, The Juilliard School, University of Michigan, etc.), there will always be a recognized value to the degree. Do not ignore the value of a great education elsewhere. Talent, charisma, and discipline combined with good training are keys. The name of the school does not get you a job by itself.

Can you please describe the "Aha!" moment when you realized what you wanted to do?

My "Aha!" moment happened before college study. I was considering two paths: music or liberal arts/literature. When I was still a junior in high school, I had the privilege of playing under a famous conductor. In the postconcert trance, hours after, when my feet were still not touching the ground, I realized that playing music was first and foremost.

Which classes were most valuable in preparing you for your career or in helping you decide on your career?

At URESM, I was constantly playing in school ensembles, recitals, new music concerts, and more. For a career in performing music, this was ideal. Academic classes were equally important, especially my "writing about music" course.

How did your professors impact your career choice or preparation?

In some cases, it was an abstract idea: maintain high standards, work hard, and believe in great art. In others, it was practical, including a "business of music" course that helped me market myself as a teacher and performer once I left the school.

Did you have a job and/or internship during college that influenced your career choice or career preparation in any way?

I had many part-time jobs as an undergraduate, most having nothing to do with music, but by my senior year, I landed occasional playing jobs and participated in a chamber music festival apprenticeship that helped me realize the value of building audiences and community outreach.

Do you have an advanced degree? Is one helpful or required in your field?

Yes. I have a master's (MM) and doctorate (DMA). The latter is essential for college teaching.

What do you love most about your job?

I live with music every single day: teaching, playing, or writing.

What is the most difficult or challenging aspect of your job?

Teaching, on any level, requires tremendous attention to detail, passion, and patience. There are days of frustration: Are you working hard enough? Are your students equal to the challenge?

What is the biggest misconception people have about what you do?

University professors do more than teach. My job is equal parts teaching, research, and service to both the university and the community. On paper, it looks like I work only a few hours a week. This is simply not true. As a music professor, I also have to maintain the highest standards as a performer, so the countless hours of practice and preparation often go unnoticed.

What was the biggest obstacle you faced in getting to where you are in your career?

Simple: music is competitive. I had to endure many auditions and interviews with no instant success. Perseverance is key. I never stopped dreaming and working hard.

What skills are an absolute must for someone interested in pursuing your career?

Highly polished performance skills, charisma in the classroom and in private teaching studio, ability to work well with others, imagination, patience, organization.

Whom do you admire most in your industry or field? Why?

I have many idols: Leon Bottstein, Tom Waits, James Galway, Jim Harrison, etc. I admire anyone with absolute dedication to their art and a broad mind that accepts many worldviews and ideas.

What is one piece of advice you would give to someone who is interested in pursuing your career?

Practice, practice, practice. Read, read, read. Walk in the woods as needed.

Can you please add any additional comments you think might be helpful to someone hoping to pursue your career?

Have faith. Never give up. For every hour you work, someone else is doing two. Keep up.

Mary Bacon, Actress
Carnegie-Mellon School of Drama, 1995
Major: Acting

What was your first job after graduation?

TheatreworksUSA.

What criteria did you use when deciding which colleges to apply to?

I was looking for good conservatory programs—well known for excellence in drama. Carnegie Mellon University (CMU) has a great history and well-known alumni.

What was your first choice school?

CMU. I was attracted to a BFA inside a larger university, rather than an isolated conservatory.

What career did you have in mind when you applied to college?

I first went to Whittier College without one, I but transferred to CMU when I heard about conservatory training and understood that there was a more detailed way to go about working as a professional actress.

How did the school you attended impact on your career choice and opportunities?

The training steered me to New York rather than Los Angeles, though that was an individual choice as well. At the time, my boyfriend, a young director, was in New York; and most of my friends had gone off to New York, so I went too.

Do you now wish you had attended a different school? Which one and why?

I work with a lot of actors from the New York University graduate program. They seemed a little better prepared for the business end of working in New York theater, but I have plenty of colleagues from CMU who are doing very well without having spent their schooling in the city.

Which college or colleges are turning out the leaders in your profession today?

Carnegie-Mellon School of Drama, New York University Tisch School of the Arts, The Juilliard School, Yale University, North Carolina School of the Arts, Rutgers University MFA in drama, University of California—San Diego, University of Washington, etc.

Can you please describe the "Aha!" moment when you realized what you wanted to do?

I just remember realizing I could actually go to school to study acting and theatre 24/7, and that was radical to me.

Did you change your major? If so, why?

I was an English major at Whittier College, and I wanted to be a writer and pursue journalism like my parents. But I changed because I kept getting drawn into the theater and because I got a lot of support in it.

Can you please list your majors?

English, journalism (communications), then BFA in Acting.

Which classes were most valuable in preparing you for your career or in helping you decide on your career?

Definitely English classes, history, philosophy, bioethics—anything that helped me to think for myself and to understand or expand my worldview a bit.

How did your professors impact your career choice or preparation?

My professors helped me learn to act and to use what worked for me. They were not as helpful in terms of how to get acting work, and I took it for granted that we were to figure that out on our own. They, of course, let us all know how difficult it is, a very unstable field.

Did you have a job and/or internship during college that influenced your career choice or career preparation in any way?

Summer theater, interning at bigger theaters, where one could meet and get to know or be mentored by older actors. I worked with Northwestern University's Cherubs Program and have met and worked with many, many people who were involved in it. Also, Perry Mansfield Performing Arts Camp has come back into my life, which also helped me professionally, as they are now implementing a professional workshop before the camp begins.

Do you have an advanced degree? Is one helpful or required in your field?

I do not. I think the MFA helps for acting work if you went to a certain school where the faculty and students work a lot outside—that is, its name is well regarded—but other than that, it would only be necessary to teach. And many actors do end up teaching. I don't think not having an MFA has really hindered me in terms of getting acting jobs.

What do you love most about your job?

The variety—the people! The people I meet and work with (so many people in a given year!), and I get to work in so many places and meet so many different folks—it's a very social business, and it's the best part of it. And getting to crawl inside another's shoes.

What is the most difficult or challenging aspect of your job?

Getting through the times of unemployment, and every year there is a guaranteed amount of unemployment just by the virtue of not being able to audition for all things at one time. And every job comes to an end. And one has got to get used to that, expect it, and not be unnecessarily thrown by it. Unemployment for an actor hopefully means "between engagements," and when one is working, it is all-consuming: in theater six days a week and all weekend, so having spurts of downtime are important. But never comfortable—even Dustin Hoffman complains about never working again.

What is the biggest misconception people have about what you do?

People think it pays better than it does. People think we work normal workday hours, and we don't. People think one is either a huge household name or trying to make it, and most of my colleagues are just regular working actors and have been for years. People confuse celebrity with working actors.

What was the biggest obstacle you faced in getting to where you are in your career?

Not sure I have overcome it, but for me probably trust in myself. That something better is coming around the corner. And fear of people—casting people—and learning what I can't control, what someone else thinks of me. And working on what I can, my work, the audition, and showing myself the best way I can. And knowing I don't need or want every job.

What skills are an absolute must for someone interested in pursuing your career?

I think talent, but there are people who work a lot without a lot of talent. Ability to muster up energy to keep working when a job isn't in front of you.

Whom do you admire most in your industry or field? Why?

I admire Meryl Streep. She never stops working; her performances are finely detailed, observant, and she seems ageless because of this. I really think she is about the acting—breathing a full person to life. She keeps challenging herself, and she always looks beautiful because I think she finds humanity beautiful. She never seems to be dishonestly presenting herself to impress. I don't think she leaves anyone unaffected ever by her work.

What is one piece of advice you would give to someone who is interested in pursuing your career?

Keep alive. Watch the better actors, learn all you can, try it out, and be of service and give back what you get. No matter what you do, try to leave the profession a little better than what you found. Have dignity.

If you could do everything all over again, what would you do differently?

I might have gone to school in New York. I would have taken more musical theater courses, to better equip myself and because I enjoy it a lot.

Can you please add any additional comments you think might be helpful to someone hoping to pursue your career?

There are a million ways to go about working in the field, but if you must have celebrity, you may not need to study acting to do that. Go wherever you can and don't get too discouraged. Everyone feels that at some point in time. Listen to yourself and you'll find out if it's not what you want—it's never too late to try something new. Or have a grand time in this field. There are grand times to be had!

POLITICS AND PUBLIC SERVICE

WHY CHOOSE A CAREER IN POLITICS OR PUBLIC SERVICE?

People who work in politics and public service want to be involved in their communities and make a difference in the lives of the people they serve. Politicians are elected government employees who decide on issues that affect their constituents. Beyond elected officials, the field of politics and public service is a wide one and includes government workers and civil servants, who are appointed to their positions and are involved in the proper functioning of government agencies, and positions in a variety of other nongovernmental, private sector organizations. People who work in the field of public policy use elements of economics, philosophy, and political science to evaluate and create government programs and policies.

WHERE THE JOBS ARE

Washington, D.C., is the center of political activity in the United States, but people who work on policy issues or for local governments are also employed in every state capital and in every community. People who work in politics and public service can also work for state, local, and the federal government, think tanks (organizations that conduct research and analysis on policy issues), nonprofit organizations, political action committees (PACs), advocacy organizations, and lobbyists. Elected officials also hire entire staffs to help them do their jobs, including campaign workers, aides, and policy analysts. Politicians also hire political consultants to advise them on how to run their campaigns.

AREAS OF SPECIALTY

People who work in politics or public service can specialize in a specific area or issue they want to affect, such as education, poverty, or housing, or a specific activity, such as voter turnout or campaigns.

EDUCATIONAL REQUIREMENTS

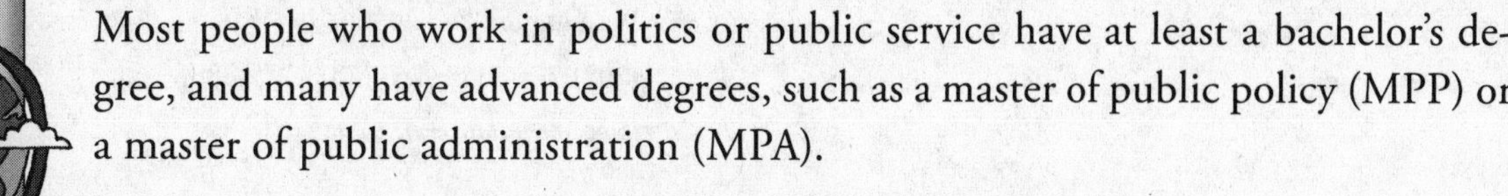

Most people who work in politics or public service have at least a bachelor's degree, and many have advanced degrees, such as a master of public policy (MPP) or a master of public administration (MPA).

SALARY RANGE

Salaries vary as widely as the jobs. While politicians do not generally get rich from their salaries, government workers in general have attractive compensation packages, including generous benefits and vacation time.

Pros: The ability to make changes that can help others

Cons: Lack of privacy for elected officials; job security often depends on the candidates in power

POLITICAL TRIVIA

- In 1872, **Victoria Woodhull** was the first woman nominated for president.
- **Dwight D. Eisenhower** held the first presidential news conference filmed for TV in 1955.
- **John F. Kennedy's** book, *Profiles in Courage,* was awarded the Pulitzer Prize before he became president.

WHERE TO LEARN MORE

American Political Science Association

1527 New Hampshire Avenue N.W.

Washington, DC 20036-1206

www.apsanet.org

National Association of Schools of Public Affairs and Administration

1120 G Street N.W., Suite 730

Washington, DC 20005

www.naspaa.org

American Society for Public Administration

1301 Pennsylvania Avenue N.W., Suite 840

Washington, DC 20004

(202) 393-7878; fax: (202) 638-4952

Email: *info@aspanet.org*

www.aspanet.org

Partnership for Public Service

1725 Eye Street N.W., Suite 900

Washington, DC 20006

(202) 775-9111; fax: (202) 775-8885

www.ourpublicservice.org/

WORDS OF WISDOM

"You really need an ability to be strategic—to be able to figure out the easiest and most effective way to get things done with the least amount of work."

—David Rosenfield, Political Organizer

"Public service is the best thing we can do for each other. Whether you end up an elected U.S. senator or a PTA president, our communities work by virtue of the fact that we care enough to work together for the betterment of the world. Speak up for the people who can't."

—Sally J. Clark, City Council Member

David Rosenfeld, Political Organizer
National Program Director, The Student Public Interest Research Groups (Student PIRGs)
Rutgers University, 1995
Major: Political Science

What was your first job after graduation?

Campus organizer.

What criteria did you use when deciding which colleges to apply to?

My mother is a high school teacher at a public high school. My family is very pro public schools, and we didn't have a ton of money, so I knew I wanted to go to a public university with a good academic reputation and a wide selection of classes and programs. I also wanted to go to a pretty big school with lots of different kinds of people and also to stay close to my family. Rutgers University (RU) fit the bill for all of this, plus it's less than an hour from New York City, which was a bonus.

What career did you have in mind when you applied to college?

Something in the teaching profession, either at the high school or college level.

How did the school you attended impact on your career choice and opportunities?

RU had an amazing array of extracurricular activities, including a lot of political organizations and a good group of professors who encouraged getting involved and connecting the classroom experience with my activities.

Which college or colleges are turning out the leaders in your profession today?

University of Wisconsin—Madison, University of Oregon, University of California—Santa Cruz, University of Illinois, University of North Carolina—Chapel Hill, Yale University, Dartmouth, and the Claremont Colleges have given us some great people. But great leaders are coming from schools all over the country.

Can you please describe the "Aha!" moment when you realized what you wanted to do?

I was in my sophomore year at RU and helping to run a major nonpartisan voter registration campaign for the 1992 presidential election. We were working day and night to build a huge coalition of student organizations and coordinating voter registration activities. In just four days, we registered 6,000 new student voters, a record at the time. It was the first time I really got a taste of people power, at what the world might look like. At the same time, I was in a lot of introductory political science classes and learning about the formation of our democracy and the various individuals who championed pushing truly participatory democracy—and the people who have resisted those efforts. I'd say that whole semester was one big "Aha!" moment that still hasn't left me.

Which classes were most valuable in preparing you for your career or in helping you decide on your career?

My political science and history classes had an impact by putting my real-world activities into a historical and meaningful context. In particular, my classes about the formation of American democracy and the various thinkers behind it (going way back into Europe), about the American labor movement, the late 19th-century farmers alliance/populism movements, urban political machines, and the civil rights movements. That particular context helped validate my sense that the best way to make an impact was to be a grassroots organizer and that such a path was noble, rich with history, and filled with as much, if not more, craftsmanship as other, more well-known "good guy" career paths.

How did your professors impact your career choice or preparation?

They helped by being good at their jobs. They were knowledgeable and passionate about their subject areas, encouraging of my out-of-the-classroom work, willing to engage with students on topics, and willing to give hard feedback on our attempts to make sense of what we were learning.

Did you have a job and/or internship during college that influenced your career choice or career preparation in any way?

Hands down, my activities with the New Jersey Public Interest Research Group (NJPIRG) Student Chapters shaped and prepared me for my career choice. NJPIRG—like all of the student PIRGs—has an incredible volunteer and internship program at RU. I took on a lot of responsibility with NJPIRG during school. Besides the 1992 voter registration campaign I mentioned before, I also coordinated projects to mobilize the student body around endangered species and toxic waste issues and ran a campaign to connect the various Rutgers campuses with bike lanes. I also became an officer with NJPIRG—it is a student directed and funded organization—and so I helped design a lot of our statewide programs, approved the organizational budget, did staff reviews, and helped train younger leaders to run their own projects. I did a lot of this as a volunteer, but an awful lot of it I did through the internship program, and actually earned course credit towards my graduation.

By the time I graduated college, I had a bunch of amazing skills. I knew how to do very basic grassroots organizing, like recruiting volunteers, petitioning, fund-raising, and public speaking. But I also knew how to design big campaigns from scratch, develop a strategy, choose tactics, and manage the whole thing from start to finish. And I knew how to manage an organization, with everything that comes along with that.

Do you have an advanced degree? Is one helpful or required in your field?

No, and I do not think an advanced degree is needed for my line of work—and for many lines of work for that matter. This is not a popular idea right now, what with so many people saying you need a master's or law degree to take on any responsibility in the public interest movement. But based on my observation of the education levels of the people who run the PIRGs—both on the grassroots organizing and the policy sides—it seems like the only thing you need to do well and take on more leadership is smarts, attention to detail, willingness to work really hard, and lots of experience (i.e., making lots of mistakes). Message to undergraduates: you don't need to wait until you're 25 years old and out of graduate school to get experience; I was running a statewide organization by the time I was 25.

What do you love most about your job?

It's righteous: I tackle society's biggest challenges every day. It's smart: I think what I'm doing is strategic and effective; therefore, I believe we're winning.

What is the most difficult or challenging aspect of your job?

Our corporate-influenced culture has stripped people of a sense of the power of the collective and our ability to make a difference by working together. That makes everything we try to do much more difficult.

What is the biggest misconception people have about what you do?

That I'm some adobe-hut-living, Mother Theresa–like martyr.

What was the biggest obstacle you faced in getting to where you are in your career?

I like to talk a lot, and I can be a terrible listener. In organizing, that's the kiss of death because you can only motivate people to do the right thing if you understand where they are coming from and engage them personally. My mentors were great by zeroing in on that weakness and getting me to stop talking and to ask more questions. Once I started asking more questions, things really took off.

What skills are an absolute must for someone interested in pursuing your career?

You really need an ability to be strategic—to be able to figure out the easiest and most effective way to get things done with the least amount of work. The second most important skill is to be a good listener. It also helps to embrace a work ethic that goes beyond what most of society considers normal. Long hours, weekends, and being "on call" most of the time. You also need gumption—willingness to go far, far outside of your comfort zone at the drop of a dime, over and over again.

Whom do you admire most in your industry or field? Why?

I admire a lot of past organizers: Bob Moses, John L. Lewis, Cesar Chavez, in particular, for the organizations they built in the civil rights and labor movements. I admire a lot of the people I work with in the PIRGs who I think are some of the sharpest and creative organizers out there today.

What is one piece of advice you would give to someone who is interested in pursuing your career?

The world needs you.

If you could do everything all over again, what would you do differently?

Nothing. Don't ever look back.

Doug Whitworth, Local Government Auditor

Auditor II, Staff Auditor, Office of the City Auditor, City of Austin, Texas

Southwestern University, 1999

Major: Communications

What was your first job after graduation?

Business analyst.

What criteria did you use when deciding which undergraduate colleges to apply to?

Academic rigor, prestige, proximity to Austin.

What was your first choice school?

Rice University for undergraduate, Princeton University for graduate school.

What career did you have in mind when you applied to college?

Dentistry—can you believe it?

How did the school you attended impact on your career choice and opportunities?

It allowed me to see that a solid liberal arts program allows a whole host of career opportunities.

Do you now wish you had attended a different school? Which one and why?

I wish I had applied to the Ivy Leagues, but I was afraid of moving out of state and shouldering college loans.

Which college or colleges are turning out the leaders in your profession today?

The Lyndon B. Johnson School of Public Affairs, The Kennedy School of Public Affairs, and the Woodrow Wilson School of Public Affairs.

Did you change your major? If so, why?

I was unsure of a career path and spent several years in the military in different cities around the world. A master of public affairs allowed me to pool my experiences and package the practical with the academic.

Can you please list your majors?

Chemical engineering, chemistry, liberal arts, Middle Eastern studies, communications.

Which classes were most valuable in preparing you for your career or in rhelping you decide on your career?

Public financial management, public administration, and the Policy Research Project.

How did your professors impact your career choice or preparation?

They helped guide me in my understanding of governmental processes and procedures, as well as quantitative and qualitative analysis.

Did you have a job and/or internship during college that influenced your career choice or career preparation in any way?

I worked for the Office of the City Auditor between my first and second years of graduate school.

Do you have an advanced degree? Is one helpful or required in your field?

Yes, I have an MPA from the Lyndon B. Johnson School of Public Affairs, and it is very helpful though not required in my field.

What do you love most about your job?

I love working in public service in a city that I thoroughly enjoy—particularly when I get to speak on camera to elected officials.

What is the most difficult or challenging aspect of your job?

Writing about issues that I care about passionately in a dispassionate, balanced, and professional way.

What is the biggest misconception people have about what you do?

That auditors only do mathematics.

What was the biggest obstacle you faced in getting to where you are in your career?

I thought that I would not be able to ever work in the public sector and earn enough money to raise a family, but luckily I found a profession that has allowed me to do that.

What skills are an absolute must for someone interested in pursuing your career?

Critical thinking, solid writing, and public speaking skills.

Whom do you admire most in your industry or field? Why?

I admire Mark Funkhouser—he understands the way that professional public servants, academics, and politicians interact to create good government.

What is one piece of advice you would give to someone who is interested in pursuing your career?

Find a good graduate school for public affairs and choose an area of specialization early.

If you could do everything all over again, what would you do differently?

I would not have spent five years in the military but would have traveled instead.

Michael Wenger, Public Policy Executive
Acting Vice President for Communications, Joint Center for Political and Economic Studies
CUNY—Queens, 1965
Majors: Political Science; Education

What was your first job after graduation?

Social studies teacher, junior high school.

What criteria did you use when deciding which undergraduate colleges to apply to?

Cost, courses offered.

What was your first choice school?

Cornell University.

What career did you have in mind when you applied to college?

Civil engineering.

How did the school you attended impact on your career choice and opportunities?

I attended Cornell University for two years as a civil engineering student. My transfer to Queens College of the City University of New York (QCCUNY), largely for financial reasons, led me to change my career choice to education.

Do you now wish you had attended a different school? Which one and why?

No. I enjoyed my experience at Cornell University, but QCCUNY provided me with an excellent education at minimal cost and set me on a life course that I have found extremely fulfilling.

Can you please describe the "Aha!" moment when you realized what you wanted to do?

An education professor I had at QCCUNY inspired me to pursue efforts to address social justice issues. At first, I chose to do that as a public school teacher, but I quickly decided I would prefer to be involved in community-based and political activities.

Did you change your major? If so, why?

Yes. I lost interest in civil engineering and was inspired by a professor at QCCUNY.

Which classes were most valuable in preparing you for your career or in helping you decide on your career?

An introductory course in education and a course on the sociology of race.

Did you have a job and/or internship during college that influenced your career choice or career preparation in any way?

I did an internship in a settlement house on the Lower East Side of New York that helped to solidify my interest in social justice activities.

Do you have an advanced degree? Is one helpful or required in your field?

No, but it would have been helpful.

What do you love most about your job?

The subject matter and the sense that I am making a difference in the lives of some people.

What is the most difficult or challenging aspect of your job?

Management issues, because I don't particularly enjoy management functions.

What was the biggest obstacle you faced in getting to where you are in your career?

Simply finding my niche—what I enjoyed, found fulfilling, and did well—was probably the biggest obstacle. I overcame it by continuing to search until I found it.

What skills are an absolute must for someone interested in pursuing your career?

Excellent communication, both written and oral, is vital, as are good people skills.

Whom do you admire most in your industry or field? Why?

Two people whom I greatly admire are historian John Hope Franklin and former Mississippi governor, William Winter. Dr. Franklin, who is still going strong at this writing at the age of 93, has written the most significant history of our nation, *From Slavery to Freedom*, and continues to eloquently speak out about issues of race. Governor Winter, who is also still going strong at this writing at the age of 83, has been a courageous leader on racial justice under extremely trying circumstances throughout his adult life. Dr. Franklin chaired President Clinton's Advisory Board on Race, and Governor Winter was a member of the seven-person board.

What is one piece of advice you would give to someone who is interested in pursuing your career?

Be prepared. Success is a combination of luck and skill. If you happen to be fortunate enough to get an opportunity at a fulfilling position, you have to be prepared to take advantage of the opportunity.

Sally J. Clark, Elected Official
City Councilmember, City of Seattle
University of Washington, 1990
Majors: Spanish; Political Science

What was your first job after graduation?

Writer/editor/barista.

What criteria did you use when deciding which colleges to apply to?

Status of school, presence of quality biology program, and location.

What was your first choice school?

University of California—San Diego.

What career did you have in mind when you applied to college?

Marine biologist.

How did the school you attended impact your career choice and opportunities?

Science classes were great but very difficult; I pursued journalism instead.

Do you now wish you had attended a different school? Which one and why?

No. I made great friends. I would enjoy the experience of a small liberal arts college, but in addition to my big college experience.

Which college or colleges are turning out the leaders in your profession today?

The University of Wisconsin.

Which classes were most valuable in preparing you for your career or in helping you decide on your career?

I obtained an MPA, which helped with public sector work, but my most helpful classes were the journalism ones where I learned to read, write, listen, and ask.

How did your professors impact your career choice or preparation?

The professors who demanded high-quality work and treated you like an adult were the best trainers.

Did you have a job and/or internship during college that influenced your career choice or career preparation in any way?

I had two internships with newspapers, one as a political reporter in the state capitol.

Do you have an advanced degree? Is one helpful or required in your field?

I have an MPA, and it is helpful.

What do you love most about your job?

It's something different every day, and it's easy to feel important.

What is the most difficult or challenging aspect of your job?

Keeping from feeling too important, keeping perspective.

What is the biggest misconception people have about what you do?

That I know the answers.

What was the biggest obstacle you faced in getting to where you are in your career?

Self-confidence. Don't overthink; just do it and prepare really well.

What skills are an absolute must for someone interested in pursuing your career?

Effective communication and conflict resolution skills.

What is one piece of advice you would give to someone who is interested in pursuing your career?

Watch, listen, research, be ready.

If you could do everything all over again, what would you do differently?

I'd go into the Coast Guard. Well, first I would learn how to swim.

Can you please add any additional comments you think might be helpful to someone hoping to pursue your career?

Public service is the best thing we can do for each other. Whether you end up an elected U.S. senator or a PTA president, our communities work by virtue of the fact that we care enough to work together for the betterment of our world. Speak up for the people who can't.

Nancy Chan, Public Policy Research Analyst
Research Associate, The Urban Institute
Massachusetts Institute of Technology, 1996
Major: Electrical Engineering

What was your first job after graduation?

Strategy management consultant.

What criteria did you use when deciding which undergraduate colleges to apply to?

I wanted to major in engineering, and I wanted to go to the top engineering school, which was Massachusetts Institute of Technology (MIT). I also applied there because two of my cousins attended. In addition, I applied to Rice University and Cornell University because I had cousins who attended those schools as well, and they both have strong engineering programs. Finally, I applied to a "safety school," McGill University, because I lived in Montreal and it was very inexpensive to go there.

What career did you have in mind when you applied to college?

I wanted to be an electrical engineer (EE).

How did the school you attended impact on your career choice and opportunities?

In terms of career choice, I realized while I was at MIT that I just wasn't cut out to be an engineer. I saw how intellectually curious my classmates were about technology and realized that I was unlike them. I had chosen the major simply because (1) I felt it to be a challenge since there are so few women who are EEs, and I am a woman (one of my classmates had told me that I couldn't make it as an EE); (2) I was pressured by my parents to be an engineer, lawyer, or doctor (typical amongst Asians); (3) I was really good at mathematics and physics. Even though upon graduation I had decided not to pursue a career in engineering, MIT had opened many doors for me. For one, having a degree in EE from MIT is a credential that says I am smart, analytical, and can conquer almost any intellectual challenge. As such, it has been relatively easy to move from one type of job to another, even if the positions are not technical in nature.

Do you now wish you had attended a different school? Which one and why?

Sometimes I do wish I had attended Stanford University (SU). It is an excellent school in many areas, including engineering, and I find that graduates tend to be more well-rounded and happy coming out of there. So many people I know who graduated from MIT led very anxiety-ridden, sleep-deprived lives, whereas SU grads tend to look back on their time in college quite fondly. The California weather doesn't hurt, either.

Which college or colleges are turning out the leaders in your profession today?

In terms of public policy analysis, I would not say that Massachusetts Institute of Technology is turning out leaders. I would say that the Ivy League colleges or liberal arts colleges are turning out public policy analysts.

Can you please describe the "Aha!" moment when you realized what you wanted to do?

I actually have been trying to figure out what I want to do for the past 13 years. I have conducted over 70 informational interviews with people in various professions, including law, business, technology, theology, social work, library sciences, and public policy. Through this process, I found that I would like to use my analytical skills to help alleviate poverty in tangible ways. I wanted to bridge policy, practice, and research. However, this was all still quite vague. Finally, I happened upon a panel discussion that my think tank coordinated, regarding the interaction between nonprofits and the government. One of the panelists mentioned how he was frustrated about the huge disconnect between academic social science research and grassroots social entrepreneurs/small nonprofits. Most research tends to be on large-scale government programs. I heard him articulate this problem, and I realized immediately that I wanted to be part of the solution. So now I know that I want to conduct research on grassroots social entrepreneurs and extract best practices that can be used by practitioners to revitalize inner-city neighborhoods and communities. These findings could also inform academic research. I see this as linking practice to research and back to practice. (However, my current research position is not in grassroots research.)

Which classes were most valuable in preparing you for your career or in helping you decide on your career?

None of my classes at MIT were specifically related to what I do now. However, I have to say that MIT has generally trained me to be extremely analytical in all that I do, to resist rote learning by asking questions about why things are the way that they are and not accepting them at face value, to challenge assumptions and venture outside of the box, and not to take no as an answer.

How did your professors impact your career choice or preparation?

My academic advisor was wonderfully supportive in general, but since I did not choose engineering as a career, he was not able to help career-wise. I had another professor at the Sloan School of Management who has been a terrific sounding board regarding empirical social science research and thoughts about business school. I've kept in touch with both through the years.

Did you have a job and/or internship during college that influenced your career choice or career preparation in any way?

I had several research positions working for professors at MIT. I also had a summer internship at Texas Instruments. All of these experiences helped me to realize that engineering is not a good fit for me. It was more through a volunteer experience with a nonprofit working with inner-city kids in Cambridge, Massachusetts, that helped shape my passions today.

Do you have an advanced degree? Is one helpful or required in your field?

Yes—master's in public policy. I think that one is required to advance in my field. A PhD would also be useful.

What do you love most about your job?

It is intellectually stimulating and I am constantly exposed to new ideas.

What is the most difficult or challenging aspect of your job?

Sometimes I feel disconnected from the real world. Working at a think tank often seems very ivory-towerish. I ask: Does this research actually help anyone? If I want to help inner-city kids improve their education, is my time better spent doing research or in direct service work (e.g., tutoring)?

What is the biggest misconception people have about what you do?

People think that I just sit around and think all day since I work at a think tank (non-profit research organization). Most people just don't have any idea what a think tank is.

What was the biggest obstacle you faced in getting to where you are in your career?

I had very little background in politics/policy, as most of my previous work experience and education was in technology, business, and theology. I had to play catch-up by doing a lot of background reading, keeping up with current events, and attending seminars/crash courses on politics and policy.

What skills are an absolute must for someone interested in pursuing your career?

Good quantitative skills (econometrics, statistics), no fear of numbers, analytical skills, writing skills, communication skills, willingness to market your research.

What is one piece of advice you would give to someone who is interested in pursuing your career?

It's important to network. I think this is true across all careers, but particularly in policy jobs because they are so competitive. If you are taking classes, be sure to talk to your professors. Do informational interviews with everyone. Be willing to take internships for little or no pay just to get your foot in the door. Also, I think that having actual and constant contact with people in poverty is important to inform how we analyze policy. Otherwise, poverty can become a faceless concept, and we lose sight of whom we are trying to serve. Being in direct contact with the underserved helps to keep us grounded.

If you could do everything all over again, what would you do differently?

I might have gotten a joint MBA-MPP degree. I think that the MPP encompasses the heart of public service. I learned all about policy and was given tools to analyze it. But I think that an MBA is a bit more of a "practical" degree—an MBA gives you skills to help you get in and run an organization. In contrast, an MPP may help you to analyze the impacts of that organization. I've heard that an MBA is the head, and an MPP is the heart.

Can you please add any additional comments you think might be helpful to someone hoping to pursue your career?

I think having a genuine passion to help improve people's lives and promote the public good is important to enter into this field.

PSYCHOLOGY

WHY CHOOSE A CAREER IN PSYCHOLOGY?

Psychologists study the human mind and behavior. They are empathetic and like working with people and helping them solve their problems. Psychologists who practice in the health care field can work in hospitals, clinics, schools, or in private practice. In most states, psychologists are not allowed to prescribe medication, but they often work with physicians to choose appropriate medications for their clients. Some psychologists also research the physical, cognitive, emotional, or social aspects of human behavior. Others work in government agencies, businesses, or nonprofits to train, research, or advocate for psychology as a profession.

WHERE THE JOBS ARE

About 40 percent of psychologists are self-employed, meaning they work in private practice. A majority of psychologists are clinical psychologists, who treat mentally or emotionally disturbed clients or help people recover from traumatic events, such as divorce or the death of a loved one.

Clinical psychologists also work in rehabilitation settings, helping clients recover from physical illnesses, such as strokes or spinal cord injuries. Psychologists also work in schools, where they work with teachers, parents, and the school staff on a variety of student issues, including behavior problems and substance abuse. Industrial-organizational psychologists work to improve the quality of life and productivity in workplace settings.

Other psychologists make careers out of conducting research, often at universities, or studying areas of human development or the ways that people interact with each other or their environment. Demand for trained psychologists is expected to grow in the coming years, mostly in schools, hospitals, social service agencies, mental health centers, substance abuse treatment clinics, and consulting firms.

AREAS OF SPECIALTY

Experimental or research, clinical, social, developmental, industrial-organizational, and school psychologist.

EDUCATIONAL REQUIREMENTS

Most specialists, including clinical and counseling psychologists, must have a doctoral degree. Graduate programs in psychology are extremely competitive. School psychologists need an educational specialist degree, and industrial-organizational psychologists need a master's degree. Psychologists in private practice or who treat patients in any way are required to be certified or licensed in every state.

SALARY RANGE

The median annual earnings (wage and salary) of clinical, counseling, and school psychologists in 2004 were $54,950. The median salary for industrial-organizational psychologists was $71,400.

Pros: Rewarding work, interacting with people in a positive way

Cons: Treating emotionally disturbed patients

FAMOUS PSYCHOLOGISTS

- **B. F. Skinner** pioneered experimental psychology.
- **Sigmund Freud**, psychologist, is best known for his theories about the unconscious mind.

WHERE TO LEARN MORE

American Psychological Association
750 1st Street N.E.
Washington, DC 20002-4242
(800) 374-2721 or (202) 336-5500
www.apa.org/students

American Counseling Association
5999 Stevenson Avenue
Alexandria, VA 22304-3300
(800) 347-6647; fax: (800) 473-2329
www.counseling.org

WORDS OF WISDOM

"For the field in general, I guess I would say that you should have a genuine interest in both the science and the practice of human behavior at work."

—Eric Heggestad,
Industrial-Organizational Psychologist

"I admire those who do research and find ways to validate the profession and those who are high profile and make it clear money can be made in this profession and you can still help people (many think these are mutually exclusive)."

—Martha McIntosh,
Licensed Professional Counselor

Paul Clavelle, Clinical Psychologist
Chief, Employee Assistance Program
Saint Michael's College (Winooski Park, Vermont), 1970
Major: English

What was your first job after graduation?

Psychologist, U.S. Army.

What criteria did you use when deciding which colleges to apply to?

I had a scholarship that was only good for Catholic school, and I wanted a hometown school to minimize expenses.

What career did you have in mind when you applied to college?

The priesthood.

Can you please describe the "Aha!" moment when you realized what you wanted to do?

I can't say I had one. It was more of a gradual dawning that psychology appealed to me. Reading Freud and Jung was certainly a major factor.

Did you change your major? If so, why?

As an undergraduate, I started in philosophy (since I was planning on studying for the Catholic priesthood). I switched to English when I decided I would not become a priest. I would have changed to psychology, but the college I was attending did not have a psychology major, so I took all the psychology courses I could and indulged my interest in literature as I completed my last two years of college.

Do you have an advanced degree? Is one helpful or required in your field?

A PhD is required in Maryland to be a licensed psychologist.

What do you love most about your job?

Working with people.

What is the most difficult or challenging aspect of your job?

I am currently a manager, and juggling all the personnel, budgetary, and other details of the job is demanding. I often say, "Being a clinical psychologist is a piece of cake for me compared to being a manager." I still try to spend at least 25 percent of my time doing clinical work.

What is the biggest misconception people have about what you do?

That psychologists primarily give advice.

What was the biggest obstacle you faced in getting to where you are in your career?

One of my undergraduate English professors actually discouraged me from going into psychology. It made me feel like maybe I didn't have what it takes. I'm glad I went against his advice.

What skills are an absolute must for someone interested in pursuing your career?

The ability to listen nonjudgmentally; wisdom to know when to act and when to let the client carry the direction of counseling.

Whom do you admire most in your industry or field? Why?

I admire Freud, for his insight and courage in pursuing his ideas despite opposition and misunderstanding; and Carl Rogers, for his humanistic approach to helping people; and many others.

What is one piece of advice you would give to someone who is interested in pursuing your career?

Learn to listen and to respect the client's personal internal process.

Eric Heggestad, Industrial-Organizational Psychologist

Assistant Professor of Psychology,
University of North Carolina—Charlotte

St. Olaf College, 1993

Major: Psychology

What was your first job after graduation?

Personnel research scientist for the U.S. Air Force.

What criteria did you use when deciding which colleges to apply to?

I was looking for a smaller liberal arts school. I was also looking for a school relatively close to where I grew up.

What career did you have in mind when you applied to college?

I thought I was going to be a physics major, but I also had ideas about psychology. Both of these interests were based on high school classes I had taken.

How did the school you attended impact on your career choice and opportunities?

Immensely. I knew that I wanted to go to graduate school in psychology. In the spring semester of my junior year, one of my professors handed me a sheet about a summer research program at the University of Minnesota (UM). I applied and was accepted. The people I worked with that summer took me as a graduate student a year later, and they became my PhD advisors. Another key factor in my college experience is that my professors really helped me develop a passion for psychological research, and they did a great job of helping me to develop skills that I would need in graduate school.

Can you please describe the "Aha!" moment when you realized what you wanted to do ?

As a freshman I was a physics major. I decided to start as a physics major right away because the path to the major took a long time and you really had to start first semester freshman year. About two-thirds of the way through the semester, I realized that I didn't want to be a physicist—the experiments just weren't as cool as they were in high school. So I became a psychology major. It was in the introductory class that I realized that psychology was, in fact, a science and not just counseling. I was hooked. I could study a topic that interested me (psychology) and still be a scientist. I didn't realize that I wanted to specialize in industrial-organizational (I/O) psychology until I was in graduate school.

Which classes were most valuable in preparing you for your career or in helping you decide on your career?

Undergraduate: statistics, research methods, social psychology seminar, independent study. Graduate: regression, psychometrics, human abilities, work motivation.

How did your professors impact your career choice or preparation?

My undergraduate professors really helped me get the experiences I needed to get into and be successful in graduate school.

Did you have a job and/or internship during college that influenced your career choice or career preparation in any way?

I did a summer research program at UM. It was called the Undergraduate Research Opportunities Program. It was fantastic. The goal was to show us what it was like to be a graduate student—and it did. I am pretty sure that I would not have ended up in graduate school at UM had I not taken part in this program.

Do you have an advanced degree? Is one helpful or required in your field?

Yes. There are several career paths you can take in I/O psychology. There is rather little that you can do in this field without a graduate degree. There are some jobs that you can do with a master's degree; these fall on the practice side of our field. To be a faculty member you really need a PhD. About 70 percent of the people with PhDs actually work outside of academics. They typically work for a company or for a consulting firm.

What do you love most about your job?

Working with the graduate students.

What is the most difficult or challenging aspect of your job?

Time management—balancing teaching and research takes a lot of time, and both are very important.

What is the biggest misconception people have about what you do?

Many people, including my mom, believe that my job is teaching. People don't really realize that teaching is only about 50 percent of my job and that I am required to do research and publish.

What was the biggest obstacle you faced in getting to where you are in your career?

Making it through graduate school. I overcame it with a lot of effort and hard work.

What skills are an absolute must for someone interested in pursuing your career?

Intelligence, motivation, interest, perseverance, creativity.

Whom do you admire most in your industry or field? Why?

I admire Dr. Paul Sackett. He has an amazing way of understanding difficult problems in our field. He really sees the core of the issue and can often explain it in a rather simple and elegant manner. He has also been prolific in his research.

What is one piece of advice you would give to someone who is interested in pursuing your career?

For the field in general, I guess I would say that you should have a genuine interest in both the science and the practice of human behavior at work. For the job of professor, I would say that you have to have a passion for the science of I/O psychology.

If you could do everything all over again, what would you do differently?

Really, I don't think anything. Seriously!

Arthur Owen Linskey, Psychologist
Clinical Director, Center for Advancement and Personal Actualization
University of North Carolina—Chapel Hill, 1957
Major: Educational Psychology

What was your first job after graduation?

Middle school counselor.

What criteria did you use when deciding which colleges to apply to?

My first college, Saint Mary's Seminary and University, was chosen for me. I was on a priesthood career track within the Diocese of Hartford. There, I earned a bachelor's degree, first in philosophy, then in theology. About 18 months before ordination to the priesthood, I left Saint Mary's, worked at several common labor jobs for ten months, took the Graduate Record Examination at Columbia University, and was admitted to the University of Notre Dame (UND). UND was my "halfway house," where I learned to adjust to the secular world gradually. After two years, I took a year off and learned some educational psychology. I had bonded with a highly experienced teacher who steered me to the Department of Educational Psychology at University of North Carolina—Chapel Hill.

What career did you have in mind when you applied to college?

For Catholics during my time, the seminary offered higher education. My grandparents barely learned to read and write. My parents fought their way up to the ninth grade. But my mother's brother became a Franciscan and earned eight years of university education. He was tough as nails but kind and caring; he was my model.

Which college or colleges are turning out the leaders in your profession today?

Harvard University publishes the *Harvard Mental Health Letter*, involving university students in community education and promoting leadership behavior in their psychology students.

Can you please describe the "Aha!" moment when you realized what you wanted to do?

As I watched Dr. Carl Rogers demonstrate active listening and saying only, "Uhuh," and displaying genuineness and unconditional positive regard.

Which classes were most valuable in preparing you for your career or in helping you decide on your career?

Psychological assessment, psychotherapy, career guidance and counseling, personality theory and assessment, abnormal psychology, occupational and industrial psychology, group dynamics, sociology of child development, attachment behavior, open and closed minds (Milton Rokeach), self-actualization (Abraham Maslow).

How did your professors impact your career choice or preparation?

By modeling caring, altruism, genuineness, open-mindedness, curiosity, loving mental and behavioral health, and the ideas and practices that empower the individual.

Did you have a job and/or internship during college that influenced your career choice or career preparation in any way?

I interned at the UNC Testing Center in Chapel Hill and became enamored of Dr. Edward Strong's early work in assessing values, interests, and aptitudes (VIA) to empower adolescents and young adults in choosing their career paths.

Do you have an advanced degree? Is one helpful or required in your field?

A PhD in psychology is required to be a licensed psychologist in Texas.

What skills are an absolute must for someone interested in pursuing your career?

Altruism, balanced with caring for self.

What is one piece of advice you would give to someone who is interested in pursuing your career?

Complete a self-assessment with the Strong Interest Inventory, the Campbell Assessment of Interests and Skills, the Armed Services Vocational Aptitude Battery (ASVAB), or the Differential Aptitudes Tests (DAT).

If you could do everything all over again, what would you do differently?

I would accept my limits and not aspire to empower everybody.

Martha McIntosh, Licensed Professional Counselor
Professional Projects Coordinator, American Counseling Association
The Catholic University of America, 1990
Major: Psychology

What was your first job after graduation?

Mental health therapist in community mental health center.

What criteria did you use when deciding which colleges to apply to?

That it had an easy transition from master's degree program to doctorate degree program, and location.

What was your first choice school?

University of Maryland—College Park (UMCP).

What career did you have in mind when you applied to college?

I wanted to be a counselor in private practice.

How did the school you attended impact on your career choice and opportunities?

Since I had to find my own internship, I started with the telephone book and found the community mental health centers (local government) as the most willing to accept and supervise students. Since they needed staff for programs for the chronically mentally ill, I ended up working with this population for a significant period of time and found my first job with a large county in Virginia. Luckily, my contacts in the county eventually led me to join a group private practice and allowed me to explore other career paths in the county government.

Do you now wish you had attended a different school? Which one and why?

I don't think the school or its status in the professional community made much difference. However, I believe the difference came from the major (psychology) versus something else (social work, counseling, education, mental health). If I were to do it over again, I probably would have worked harder to get into the counseling program at UMCP, or I would have decided to get an MBA instead.

Which college or colleges are turning out the leaders in your profession today?

Since my most recent focus has been with private practice, the college doesn't really matter—it's whether you can run a successful business or not and what kind of work you are doing (your niche). Clients very rarely ask where you went to school; the high-profile counselors have found a higher-paying niche or are academics doing research and publishing.

Did you change your major? If so, why?

I started with political science because I thought about going to law school but found the senior students too unwelcoming. I then moved into physical education/teaching and found teaching to be too limiting. After a stint of doing retail management, I went back to school in counseling.

Which classes were most valuable in preparing you for your career or in helping you decide on your career?

Actually, it wasn't the classes but the people in the classes that made the difference. I didn't care for too many of my professors, as they didn't reflect real-world attitudes about the profession—too lofty, not pragmatic. So my colleagues had more of an impact—watching what they did, what happened to them as a result of their choices, etc.

Did you have a job and/or internship during college that influenced your career choice or career preparation in any way?

I was directed toward working with the chronically mentally ill, as that was where the need existed. Eventually, the community mental health center transitioned to some solution-focused programs, and so I broadened my skill set to include these techniques. Moving to private practice let me use any technique/skill to get the results clients wanted.

Do you have an advanced degree? Is one helpful or required in your field?

I have a master's degree, and it is required for licensure.

What do you love most about your job?

My current job allows me to use my experience as a counselor in a way that is different than working with clients. It is more about becoming aware of issues that affect the profession.

What is the most difficult or challenging aspect of your job?

Although I no longer work with a client population, I still have group dynamics to contend with in a work environment. It is no different in an association.

What is the biggest misconception people have about what you do?

The biggest misconception is that a counselor has the answer and should provide direction, and it is just the opposite. Clients know the answer and need support in taking the necessary action to get different results.

What was the biggest obstacle you faced in getting to where you are in your career?

My two big obstacles were a lack of business acumen and knowledge of technology. Neither of these is emphasized in the profession; they're just starting to become a focus of attention.

What skills are an absolute must for someone interested in pursuing your career?

Know your career options and/or progression. The other is to get adequate supervision your entire professional career. Client results (or lack thereof) can't provide you with an accurate measure of your skill.

Whom do you admire most in your industry or field? Why?

I admire those who do research and find ways to validate the profession and those who are high profile and make it clear money can be made in this profession and you can still help people (many think these are mutually exclusive).

What is one piece of advice you would give to someone who is interested in pursuing your career?

Before pursuing any career, I would suggest trying some kind of national service first—Peace Corps, Conservation Corps, military. And then maybe take on a number of different work experiences that require similar skill sets and populations to see if you really want to do this or have a passion for it. Take your time picking any career.

If you could do everything all over again, what would you do differently?

If I had chosen some type of national service prior to going to college, my college education would have been more diverse (a skill set that could be generalized to any career path). I still would have chosen to work for an organization that was fairly large so there would be a variety of work experiences available, and then I would have worked hard to find a passion versus just a job/career.

What was your first job after graduation?

Social worker for the Department of Social Work, New York City.

What criteria did you use when deciding which colleges to apply to?

There was no contest: I was told a city college or no college, and I had good enough grades at the time to get into City College of New York.

What career did you have in mind when you applied to college?

Psychologist.

How did the school you attended impact on your career choice and opportunities?

It connected me to people who were instrumental in helping me decide a career path and got me into grad school.

Do you now wish you had attended a different school? Which one and why?

Yes and no. The school I went to had a world-renowned psychology department, and I made great connections that got me into grad school. Only status concerns would have had me go to Cornell University if I had the money and guts to do it myself at the time.

Can you please describe the "Aha!" moment when you realized what you wanted to do?

In high school I knew I was good with and interested in people.

Which classes were most valuable in preparing you for your career or in helping you decide on your career?

Clearly those courses relating to clinical and developmental psychology. However, I found a great author was often a better psychologist than a professional in the field.

How did your professors impact your career choice or preparation?

There are always those who have a mentor-like influence in one's life. I was fortunate enough to have a few such professors who guided and protected me.

Do you have an advanced degree? Is one helpful or required in your field?

Yes, and it is mandatory.

What do you love most about your job?

Interacting with and being helpful to people. Letting people allow for and accept their humanness.

What is the most difficult or challenging aspect of your job?

Treating severely disturbed people who may be suicidal and those that are otherwise self-sabotaging.

What is the biggest misconception people have about what you do?

That I have all the answers and that my life must be or should be perfect.

What was the biggest obstacle you faced in getting to where you are in your career?

Moving from a paid position in a hospital to full-time private practice. By allowing myself to take a major salary cut, I was able to transition. Also, allowing that there are many useful theories and techniques, and there is not a one that fits all ways of helping people.

What skills are an absolute must for someone interested in pursuing your career?

The capacity to be genuine, warm, and empathic.

Whom do you admire most in your industry or field? Why?

I admire many people in the field. Those who are authentic and honest about their own struggles are the most admirable to me: Harold Serles, Irvin Yalom, M. Brewster Smith, Carl Rogers, Edgar Levenson, and Bertam Schaffner are a few that come to mind.

What is one piece of advice you would give to someone who is interested in pursuing your career?

Be open, compassionate, and patient.

If you could do everything all over again, what would you do differently?

I doubt anything. Besides, as John Lennon said, "life is what happens while you are planning something else." It is all a series of events. If you take out a piece, the whole changes.

PUBLISHING

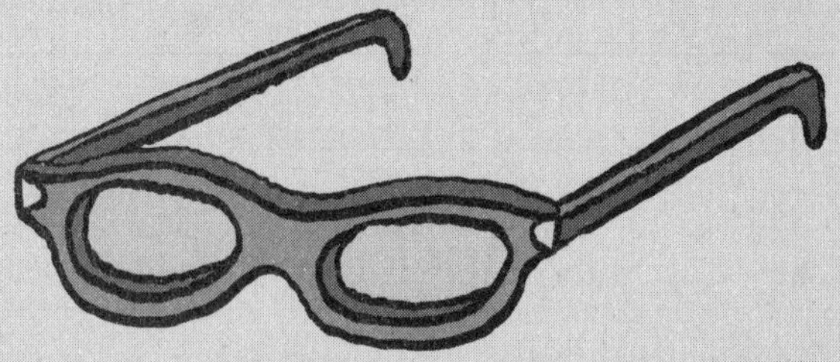

WHY CHOOSE A CAREER IN PUBLISHING

Publishing professionals have excellent communications skills, are analytical thinkers, and enjoy reading and writing. Editors assign stories to writers, acquire manuscripts, and work with authors to review, rewrite, and edit their work to ensure it suits the needs of their publication.

WHERE THE JOBS ARE

Most of the publishing industry is located in New York. Jobs at local magazines, trade journals, university presses, and smaller publishing houses, however, are available throughout the country. The publishing industry as a whole has been shrinking; magazine and book publishers have merged to create fewer opportunities in general. Areas that will experience growth are textbook publishing (due to the growing student population), the Internet, and custom publishers, which produce newsletters and magazines to a client's specifications and that are generally used for promotions or advertising.

AREAS OF SPECIALTY

A large percentage of new graduates search for editorial jobs. Editors can specialize in a stage of the editing process, such as acquisitions or development; a subject matter or genre, such as poetry, science, fiction, or history; and/or in a specific medium, such as magazines, books, or the Web. (Newspaper editors, while sometimes performing the same tasks, are generally considered journalists because they also often decide the placement and relevance of news stories.)

EDUCATIONAL REQUIREMENTS

Publishing Professionals need at least a bachelor's degree, usually in journalism, communications, or English, and some have advanced degrees. Postcollege publishing programs, which generally last one summer, are a good way to network and learn basic skills.

SALARY RANGE

The median salary for publishing professionals in 2006 was $43,890

Pros: Intellectually stimulating and creative work

Cons: Tight deadlines (especially for magazine editors), long hours, and relatively low pay

FAMOUS EDITORS

- **Maxwell Perkins** was editor of such novelists as Ernest Hemingway and F. Scott Fitzgerald.
- **Sarah Hale** was a magazine editor who persuaded Abraham Lincoln to declare Thanksgiving a national holiday.
- **Anna Wintour** was longtime editor-in-chief of *Vogue Magazine*.

WHERE TO LEARN MORE

Magazine Publishers of America
810 Seventh Avenue, 24th Floor
New York, NY 10019
(212) 872-3700
Email: *mpa@magazine.org*
www.magazine.org

Association of American Publishers
71 Fifth Avenue, 2nd Floor
New York, NY 10003
(212) 255-0200; fax: (212) 255-7007
www.publishers.org

Publishers Weekly
www.publishersweekly.com

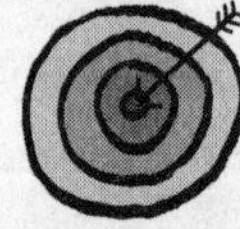

WORDS OF WISDOM

"Get in the door somewhere. I started with an internship at a publishing house and later as an editorial assistant at a magazine."

—-Sarah Richardson, Magazine Editor

"I love editing. It's a puzzle to piece together a story in a way that is interesting and readable and compelling. It also feels like polishing a sculpture. It's a very tactile thing. I also enjoy working with writers, and with my coworkers on the magazine—I'm a team player who loves that interaction."

—Michele Kort, Magazine Editor

Carol Mangis, Online and Magazine Editor
Senior Editor, Ziff Davis Media
Hunter College, CUNY, 1997
Major: English Language Arts/Psychology (double)
First job after graduation: copy editor at PC Magazine

What was your first job after graduation?

Editorial assistant at an academic publisher.

What criteria did you use when deciding which undergraduate colleges to apply to?

I looked for a good school that I could afford.

What was your first choice school?

University of California—Los Angeles (UCLA).

What career did you have in mind when you applied to college?

I did not have a career goal at that time.

How did the school you attended impact on your career choice and opportunities?

I pursued my interests, and that background has helped put a lot of the research I cover into perspective.

Can you please describe the "Aha!" moment when you realized what you wanted to do?

I did not have an "Aha!" moment, but I did discover that I enjoyed reading popular articles and books about science.

Which classes were most valuable in preparing you for your career or in helping you decide on your career?

Intellectual history and history of science courses.

How did your professors impact your career choice or preparation?

They piqued my interest in the role the past plays in shaping the present and future.

Do you have an advanced degree? Is one helpful or required in your field?

No, I don't, but I suspect an advanced degree may help someone get in the door these days. It is not required.

What do you love most about your job?

I am exposed to and can follow a variety of ideas that influence the course of history—as well as research that puts the past in a new light.

What is the most difficult or challenging aspect of your job?

Deciding which of the many interesting stories out there is the best story to cover in the magazine.

What is the biggest misconception people have about what you do?

They think I have specialized training in science. I do not.

What was the biggest obstacle you faced in getting to where you are in your career?

I had a lot of anxiety about my own abilities. It took a long time for me to recognize and accept my strengths and focus less on my weaknesses.

What skills are an absolute must for someone interested in pursuing your career?

Curiosity and skepticism are essential. An attention to detail is also crucial, and of course, a commitment to writing clearly about complex ideas.

Whom do you admire most in your industry or field? Why?

I admire Sharon Begley of the *Wall Street Journal,* who is an interesting model of someone who keeps growing and applies the wealth of her experience to a diverse set of topics.

What is one piece of advice you would give to someone who is interested in pursuing your career?

Get in the door somewhere. I started with an internship at a publishing house and later as an editorial assistant at a magazine.

If you could do everything all over again, what would you do differently?

Get a better foundation in statistics in order to analyze and critique research results.

Can you please add any additional comments you think might be helpful to someone hoping to pursue your career?

Most readers have a superficial acquaintance with the process of science, so keep in mind the big picture of the story you want to tell. Whether you are pitching, writing, or editing a story, figure out which elements and details are most compelling and essential and which aren't. Keep in the mind the questions that are driving the research; that usually establishes the human interest to move a story along.

Carol Mangis, Online and Magazine Editor
Senior Editor, Ziff Davis Media
CUNY—Hunter College; 1997
Majors: English Language Arts and Psychology

What was your first job after graduation

Copy editor at *PC Magazine.*

What criteria did you use when deciding which colleges to apply to?

My interests and cost.

What was your first choice school?

Hunter College.

What career did you have in mind when you applied to college?

Therapist.

How did the school you attended impact on your career choice and opportunities?

I took a number of English and writing classes; my experience was so positive that I decided to double major and look for a publishing job when I graduated.

Which college or colleges are turning out the leaders in your profession today?

Columbia University, New York University, Northwestern University, Syracuse University, University of Maryland, University of California—Berkeley.

Can you please describe the "Aha!" moment when you realized what you wanted to do?

A short story I wrote was accepted into my school's literary magazine, and I realized I was a good writer and others saw it too. I wanted to use that skill in my professional life.

Did you change your major? If so, why?

I didn't change it; I added another major to psychology.

Which classes were most valuable in preparing you for your career or in helping you decide on your career?

Creative writing workshops.

How did your professors impact your career choice or preparation?

One professor in particular was very positive about my writing and language abilities early on; he was the first person to encourage me in that area. Another professor, who taught several creative writing workshops I participated in, encouraged me to volunteer for my school's literary magazine as an editor, which was when I began to discover I had a knack for that kind of work.

Do you have an advanced degree? Is one helpful or required in your field?

I don't. It's not required, but I'm sure it would be helpful.

What do you love most about your job?

No one day is exactly like any other; there are always new things to learn. I often get to meet very interesting, bright people who are tops in their fields.

What is the most difficult or challenging aspect of your job?

Right now, the kind of publication I work for is financially challenged; we're understaffed.

What is the biggest misconception people have about what you do?

I work for a technical magazine, so people assume I'm technical myself. Not so much.

What was the biggest obstacle you faced in getting to where you are in your career?

I earned my BA while working full-time. I had to be patient and take it one semester at a time so as not to be overwhelmed. It took a long time but was very worthwhile.

What skills are an absolute must for someone interested in pursuing your career?

Grammar, writing, editing.

Whom do you admire most in your industry or field? Why?

I admire Peter Rojas, cofounder of Engadget—he has vision, intelligence, and strong knowledge in his field and has parlayed that into the most successful and well-respected gadget blog.

What is one piece of advice you would give to someone who is interested in pursuing your career?

Everyone will tell you how competitive this field is, but don't be discouraged by that if you really want to be an editor or writer. You'll find a way.

If you could do everything all over again, what would you do differently?

I'd probably not work at a technology publication; after several years it's difficult to switch to a different topic, and it's not my number one choice.

Can you please add any additional comments you think might be helpful to someone hoping to pursue your career?

Know as much as you can about any publication you apply to. Be willing to start in an assistant job or a tangential job (such as copy editor).

Michele Kort, Magazine Editor
Senior Editor, *Ms. Magazine*
University of California—Los Angeles, 1971
Major: Art History

What was your first job after graduation?

Receptionist for music publishers (but that was before going back to graduate school for an MBA in arts management at University of California—Los Angeles (UCLA); my first job after that was as director of the Womanspace Gallery at the Woman's Building).

What criteria did you use when deciding which undergraduate colleges to apply to?

I was actually looking for an exciting, progressive school at first—Brandeis University or University of California—Santa Cruz (UCSC). Then I decided a private school such as Brandeis University was too expensive.

What was your first choice school?

I wanted to go to UCSC and didn't get accepted—it had only recently opened and was very competitive. UCLA was second on my list. I had always wanted to go there when I was younger, as I loved the sports program, especially basketball!

What career did you have in mind when you applied to college?

I wanted to be a psychologist but after taking a year's worth of psychology courses, decided it was too behaviorist for me—I was more interested in the humanistic side.

How did the school you attended impact on your career choice and opportunities?

I discovered art history at UCLA, had some fabulous teachers, and so I switched majors. I had no idea what career that would lead me to, however. Then the Arts Management program came into being at UCLA's graduate school of management, and I was drawn to that. But ultimately, I fell into journalism—it really had very little to do with my college education.

Which college or colleges are turning out the leaders in your profession today?

University of Southern California (USC) has a very good journalism program; I'm not really familiar with other journalism schools, although we had a good intern from Syracuse.

Can you please describe the "Aha!" moment when you realized what you wanted to do?

My "Aha!" moment was when I got a job at The Grantsmanship Center as an assistant editor—although I had no journalism experience (I did have grantsmanship experience at that point)—and quickly realized how much I enjoyed being a journalist.

Did you change your major? If so, why?

As I said above, I changed from psychology to art history, and then studied arts management in graduate school.

Which classes were most valuable in preparing you for your career or in helping you decide on your career?

The composition class I took from Mrs. Walker in high school was most helpful in learning how to write. I also learned quite a lot from doing a master's thesis in arts management.

How did your professors impact your career choice or preparation?

Many professors inspired me, but not in terms of career choice. I loved learning art history from Jean Weisz and Susan Downey. In graduate school, Samuel Culbert really taught us how to demand the learning experience that we wanted, and that was quite valuable.

Did you have a job and/or internship during college that influenced your career choice or career preparation in any way?

I did internships at the Pasadena Museum of Modern Art and at the Whitney Museum. The former taught me how to "fake it 'til you make it" when I had to get the director's support for a grant proposal (I felt—and was!—very young at the time). The latter taught me that if you're an administrator, you have no one but yourself to blame if a task you assign isn't done.

What do you love most about your job?

I love editing. It's a puzzle to piece together a story in a way that is interesting and readable and compelling. It also feels like polishing a sculpture. It's a very tactile thing. I also enjoy working with writers and with my coworkers on the magazine—I'm a team player who loves that interaction.

What is the most difficult or challenging aspect of your job?

Balancing the needs of everyone on the team.

What is the biggest misconception people have about what you do?

I think the biggest misconception about editing is that it's just some sort of grammar check, rather than a reconceptualization of a story. And I think that many people think that writing is a skill anyone can master. Also, just because people can write in one medium doesn't mean they can write in another.

What was the biggest obstacle you faced in getting to where you are in your career?

I would say it's all about self-confidence, believing in yourself; faking it until you make it.

What skills are an absolute must for someone interested in pursuing your career?

Writing and editing skills, obviously, but I think people skills help quite a lot as well. You have to work with your magazine team, but you also have to dance carefully with the egos of writers.

Whom do you admire most in your industry or field? Why?

David Remnick of *The New Yorker,* Adam Moss of *New York Magazine* Martha Nelson of The People Group of magazines, Joan Didion.

What is one piece of advice you would give to someone who is interested in pursuing your career?

Learn as much as you can about an area that interests you and then you'll be the go-to person in that field.

If you could do everything all over again, what would you do differently?

Maybe I would have found my ambition a little earlier. Maybe I would have studied journalism. But I'm mostly happy that things worked out the way they did.

Can you please add any additional comments you think might be helpful to someone hoping to pursue your career?

Read!!!!! Read a lot of good magazines, begin to analyze why you like certain stories or writers. Feel the rhythm of good writing. Explore topics that interest you. Pitch stories to local papers or magazines to build up your clips. Read friends' writing and edit it. Join a writers' group (also helps hone editing skills).

Nick Gillespie, Magazine Editor
Editor-in-Chief, *Reason Magazine*
BA, Rutgers College/Rutgers University, 1985;
MA, Temple University, 1990; PhD, SUNY—Buffalo, 1996
Majors: English and Psychology (double major)

What was your first job after graduation?

Gas station attendant.

What criteria did you use when deciding which undergraduate colleges to apply to?

I applied to three universities: Rutgers College (where my older siblings had gone), Boston University (because my high school guidance office had a scholarship flyer from there), and the College of William and Mary (because I liked colonial American history).

What was your first choice school?

Rutgers College.

What career did you have in mind when you applied to college?

None really. Maybe becoming a psychologist.

How did the school you attended impact on your career choice and opportunities?

Significantly. Rutgers had an excellent and large daily newspaper, which I started writing for in my freshman year, eventually becoming a paid editor of the weekly arts and entertainment section. My English classes also helped intensify my interest in literature and writing.

Do you now wish you had attended a different school? Which one and why?

No. I came from a family that, prior to my generation, had zero experience with higher education (in fact, my father did not even graduate from high school). As a massive research school with a top-flight, if largely disconnected faculty, Rutgers allowed me opportunities to find myself in ways that I didn't fully appreciate at the time. I squeezed just about every drop out of my undergraduate years, both in educational and social terms.

Which college or colleges are turning out the leaders in your profession today?

None in particular. Opinion journalism is very individualized, and I can't say that particular schools routinely turn out good reporters, writers, and editors. Undergraduate journalism programs do seem to have a negative effect on many people if the students don't have an area of interest in which they gain specific knowledge or expertise.

Can you please describe the "Aha!" moment when you realized what you wanted to do?

I am still waiting for that.

Did you change your major? If so, why?

I double majored in psychology and English. I was originally a psychology major, and then realized I was taking a ton of literature classes and was on track to fulfill the requirements of that as a major too.

How did your professors impact your career choice or preparation?

I had one English professor, William Vesterman, who more than any single instructor taught me how to do close reading, which turned out to be a hugely useful skill.

Did you have a job and/or internship during college that influenced your career choice or career preparation in any way?

I wrote a lot for the *Daily Targum* and eventually was elected to a paying position there as an arts and entertainment editor and writer. That made journalism—and arts criticism—seem like a viable career path to me.

Do you have an advanced degree? Is one helpful or required in your field?

I have a master's in English with a concentration in creative writing from Temple University (1990) and an MA and PhD in English from the State University of New York at Buffalo (1996). After I graduated from college, I worked as a journalist for three years. I worked for some small papers in New Jersey, and then I wrote and edited for a series of teen, music, and movie magazines in Manhattan. It was fun but eventually got boring, and I decided to go to graduate school so I could focus on fiction writing and studying literature. I don't think an advanced degree is necessary in my field, but it is essential that one learn a body of knowledge and a mode of analysis. It really grounds you and sets you off from run-of-the-mill counterparts.

What do you love most about your job?

Participating in debates about politics, culture, and ideas—about the world we've inherited and the world we're making. I also really like it when either I or someone on my staff brings a story to light that has been neglected or misunderstood by other media outlets.

What is the most difficult or challenging aspect of your job?

Managing a staff. There's nothing in writing and editing that prepares you for that. It's a completely different set of skills.

What is the biggest misconception people have about what you do?

That it is glamorous on some level. And that "thinkers" shouldn't do much reporting. The best writing and thinking comes from intense engagement with reality in all its messy complexity.

What was the biggest obstacle you faced in getting to where you are in your career?

The biggest obstacle was getting my original job at *Reason* as an assistant editor back in 1993. I was in graduate school working on my doctoral dissertation when the magazine, which I had read since I was in high school, advertised an opening. I was one of about 70 applicants, I think, but I got the job. More than that, the big obstacle to any career is conceptualizing the life you want to live and then going out and making it happen. I noted above that my first job after college was working in a gas station, which I did for about six months. In the long run, it turned out to be useful not to rush into one thing or another but to take time and figure out what sorts of things I wanted to do.

What skills are an absolute must for someone interested in pursuing your career?

In terms of skills, good reading and writing skills. You need to be able to critically evaluate all sorts of information even when you're not expert in a field. The ability to take criticism and be coachable is huge—to learn from failure and success alike and realize that it will be a long time, maybe never, before you master something. Beyond skills per se, it really helps to have curiosity about the world and your own preconceptions. You need to bust myths—your own myths first and foremost. Also, determination and doggedness. No one will miss you if you stop writing and engaging them.

Whom do you admire most in your industry or field? Why?

As editor-in-chief of a magazine, I admire folks who have launched publications that became central to their time and place. I was lucky enough to work with Louis Rossetto, the cofounder of *Wired Magazine*, on a redesign of *Reason* in 2001 (he had been a reader of *Reason* since it started in 1968). With *Wired*, Louis and his partner, Jane Metcalfe, did more than chronicle the rise of digital culture—they helped conceptualize it and make it happen. They created a publication that not only rewrote the style book but served as a virtual community for cyberspace and a host of related technologies that inform how we live.

What is one piece of advice you would give to someone who is interested in pursuing your career?

Don't go into writing at any level if it fills you with anxiety, paralysis, and dread. You will make yourself and everyone around you miserable. Nothing is worth that sort of feeling. But it's amazing how many people refuse to admit they hate writing.

If you could do everything all over again, what would you do differently?

I would have written more fiction and long-form nonfiction when I was younger.

Can you please add any additional comments you think might be helpful to someone hoping to pursue your career?

In journalism—certainly magazine journalism—there is no right path to a fulfilling career. You need to have the energy and passion to create that path. You need to create an individual identity and voice and perspective while also excelling at the norms of the field (you need to be trustworthy, diligent, timely, etc.). Always place the story first and make it clear to your readers why they should care about your particular topic. If you can't explain that, you haven't thought things through enough to be writing on the topic.

Yungpa Cho, Online Editor
Editorial Program Manager, Microsoft
University of California—Berkeley, 1992
Major: English

What what your first job after graduation?

Hotel front desk clerk.

What criteria did you use when deciding which colleges to apply to?

I took into account location, reputation, and character of the school.

What was your first choice school?

Of the colleges I applied to, University of California—Berkeley was my first choice.

What career did you have in mind when you applied to college?

I thought I would go into something related to content or language, possibly publishing.

How did the school you attended impact on your career choice and opportunities?

Berkeley has a strong English department, and because the classes were so good there, I ended up majoring in English and subsequently choosing a career in that field. In general, going to a school with a good reputation opened up more opportunities when it came to finding jobs.

Do you now wish you had attended a different school? Which one and why?

I'm happy I attended the university I did. However, I wish I had taken the time to apply to some of the private universities I was interested in, Princeton University, for example. I was interested in living on the East Coast, and I knew these schools had good English programs.

Which college or colleges are turning out the leaders in your profession today?

Any school with a good liberal arts reputation can turn out leaders in my profession.

Can you please describe the "Aha!" moment when you realized what you wanted to do?

There was no "Aha!" moment for me. Some of it was trial and error. Ultimately, this career was a good fit for my background, interests, and the opportunities available in the area I live.

Which classes were most valuable in preparing you for your career or in helping you decide on your career?

All of my classes were equally important in preparing for and deciding on my career. As a collective whole, the success and enjoyment of these classes affected my career choices.

How did your professors impact your career choice or preparation?

Good professors are an integral part of learning and enjoyment of classes.

Did you have a job and/or internship during college that influenced your career choice or career preparation in any way?

No, and this is my biggest regret about college—that I did not have an internship during school. I had other part-time jobs, but not related to my career. As a result, when I graduated, I had a difficult time breaking into my career field.

Do you have an advanced degree? Is one helpful or required in your field?

I have one, but for my career, it's really not necessary.

What do you love most about your job?

I enjoy improving and shaping content into its final stages.

What is the most difficult or challenging aspect of your job?

When I was a writer, it was sometimes hard not to take criticism personally. Writing can be personal, but when you write for business purposes, you have to be more objective.

What is the biggest misconception people have about what you do?

People always think I do technical writing because I work in Silicon Valley. But in reality, there are many other kinds of writing: marketing collateral, website copy, news articles, etc.

What was the biggest obstacle you faced in getting to where you are in your career?

The biggest obstacle I faced was getting my first job in the field without related professional experience. For a while, I worked as an administrative assistant. I finally started a technical writing certificate at a nearby junior college. I don't know if it was having that on my résumé, or because the job market for content positions was booming at the time, but that's when I got my first writing job.

What skills are an absolute must for someone interested in pursuing your career?

Solid writing skills, knowledge of the industry you're working for, whether it's health care, hi-tech, publishing, retail, etc., and of course, communication skills, which are important in any career.

Whom do you admire most in your industry or field? Why?

I respect the founder of Microsoft, Bill Gates. He is a technically brilliant man but also a great speaker and good leader.

What is one piece of advice you would give to someone who is interested in pursuing your career?

It can be hard to get your first break without job experience. An internship in college is invaluable in helping you land your first career job.

If you could do everything all over again, what would you do differently?

I would have taken on an internship during college. I don't think I would have stopped working to get my master's. I might have tried to do it while working. Some companies will pay for your education while you're working.

Can you please add any additional comments you think might be helpful to someone hoping to pursue your career?

Technical skills, like HTML, are helpful. Also, all writers and editors should be familiar with a basic style guide, such as Associated Press Style. I would also recommend searching for jobs on the Internet and seeing what kind of skills they look for. If you find a lot of jobs want you to know a program like Dreamweaver, you could learn that on your own and add it to your résumé.

SPECIAL EDUCATION

WHY CHOOSE A CAREER IN SPECIAL EDUCATION?

People who work in special education (now also called instructional support services) enjoy the challenge of working with people with disabilities and the opportunity to establish meaningful relationships with them. They come to know the person on a one-to-one basis and develop specific programs for that person. The career is very rewarding because the educator can see firsthand the progress made by each person they help.

In special education, all aspects of the person's development are taken into account, such as academic ability, physical ability, and social-emotional maturity. A key aspect of special education is the ability to meet the individual needs of every person and for this to be done in the least restrictive and most beneficial environment that is conducive to the person's learning style.

WHERE THE JOBS ARE

The majority of jobs are in teaching. Most work is in general education classrooms in public and private educational institutions. Special educators instruct at the elementary, middle, and secondary school level, although some work with infants and toddlers.

Some general education classrooms include supplementary services, such as collaborative team teaching. In collaborative team teaching, special education teachers and general education teachers work together to adapt curriculum materials and teaching techniques to meet the needs of students with disabilities. They coordinate the work of teachers and related personnel, such as therapists and social workers, to meet the individualized needs of the student within inclusive special education programs.

Many educators also work in state-supported or state-operated nonpublic institutions for people who are blind, deaf, or gifted or for those who have mental health or specific physical or developmental disabilities. A smaller number work in social assistance agencies, residential facilities, or hospital environments.

AREAS OF SPECIALTY

The field of special education branches out into many different areas. Some areas of specialty include autistic spectrum disorders, blindness, deafness, hearing impairment, visual impairment, emotional disturbance, learning disability, mental retardation, orthopedic impairment, and speech or language impairment.

Another type of special education teacher is a resource room teacher. A resource room is a pullout or "resource" classroom, where the student with the special need goes leaving the regular classroom to attend smaller, more intensive instructional sessions. Where a special education teacher may teach only one subject, a resource room teacher must help the student with all subject classes and preparation for all standardized tests as well. Study skills are taught using resources such as computers and textbooks. Resource room teachers stay in contact with general education teachers so that the progress of the student can be monitored regularly.

EDUCATIONAL REQUIREMENTS

Many states offer alternative licensure programs to attract college graduates who do not have training in education, but traditional licensing requires the completion of a special education teacher training program and at least a bachelor's degree, and many states require a master's degree. Excellent job prospects are expected due to the rising enrollment of special education students and a shortage of qualified teachers.

Special education teachers may also earn advanced degrees and become instructors in colleges that prepare others to teach special education.

SALARY RANGE

The median salary for special education teachers in 2006 was $48,330. The middle 50 percent earned between $38,910 and $62,640. The lowest 10 percent earned less than $32,760, and the highest 10 percent earned more than $78,020.

FAMOUS SPECIAL EDUCATION TEACHER

- **Anne Sullivan**, after regaining her eyesight from a series of operations and graduating as class valedictorian in 1886 from the Perkins Institute for the Blind, began teaching Helen Keller. Sullivan first taught lessons in obedience, followed by the manual and Braille alphabets. All were amazed at Anne's ability to reach Helen and Helen's ability to grasp concepts deaf and blind students before her had not learned.

WHERE TO LEARN MORE

Council for Exceptional Children
1110 North Glebe Road, Suite 300
Arlington, VA 22201
(888) 232-7733
www.cec.sped.org

Learning Disabilities Association of America
4156 Library Road
Pittsburgh, PA 15234
(412) 341-1515
www.ldanatl.org

National Center for Learning Disabilities
381 Park Avenue. S., Suite 1401
New York, NY 10016
(212) 545-7510
www.ncld.org

National Center for Special Education Personnel & Related Service Providers at the National Association of State Directors of Special Education
1800 Diagonal Road, Suite 320
Alexandria, VA 22314
(866) 232-6631
www.personnelcenter.org

WORDS OF WISDOM

"Hard work and dedication during the lengthy education process will eventually pay off with a rewarding career with many opportunities in a variety of work settings."

—Dr. Eileen Chu, School Psychologist

Make sure that you love children and will always be able to encourage them in positive ways!

—Joyce Jacknick, Special Education Teacher

Joyce Jacknick, Special Education Teacher
SUNY—New Paltz, 1974
Majors: Speech and Hearing; Elementary Education; Special Education

What was your first job after graduation?

Itinerant teacher of speech improvement.

What criteria did you use when deciding which colleges to apply to?

I knew that I wanted to become a teacher, so a college that had a quality teacher education program was important. I first attended Herbert H. Lehman College, which is part of the City University of New York (CUNY). After attending there for two years, I transferred to SUNY—New Paltz.

Did you attend your first choice school?

Yes. I don't seem to remember the pressure that high school students experience today in applying and being accepted to schools of their choice, but maybe that's because I didn't put that pressure on myself. I just wanted to go to a school that had a program I was interested in and where some of my friends were going.

What career did you have in mind when you applied to college?

I originally thought that I wanted to be a speech/language pathologist, so I pursued my undergraduate degree in that major. After I graduated, I thought about getting my master's in speech/language pathology but felt that it might be too limiting. I decided instead to pursue a master's in special education.

How did the school you attended have an impact on your career choice and opportunities?

SUNY—New Paltz had been a "teachers' college" prior to my attendance there. It offered an excellent teacher training program. It also had top-notch professors in speech pathology and audiology.

Which college or colleges are turning out the leaders in your profession today?

The Bank Street School of Education comes to mind, but there are a multitude of excellent universities that provide teacher education programs. I think it would be a good idea to carefully select a graduate school based on a specific area that one might be interested in.

Which classes were most valuable in preparing you for your career or in helping you decide on your career?

One class in particular still stands out in my mind. It was a graduate class called Language and Cognition, taught by a professor who was exciting and motivating. Classes that offered practical experience were the most meaningful and made me realize that this career was the right one for me.

How did your professors impact your career choice or preparation?

I was impacted most by professors who were extremely knowledgeable in their field and who brought the material across in exciting, motivating, and even humorous ways. They were the ones who had the most impact and encouraged the most learning.

Did you have a job and/or internship during college that influenced your ultimate career choice or career preparation in any way?

I had a part-time job when I went to Lehman College, but it was unrelated to my career. It was a clerical position at the New York Telephone Company.

Can you please describe the "Aha!" moment when you realized what you wanted to do?

I didn't really have one. My parents always encouraged teaching as a field that I should pursue.

Did you change your major? If so, why?

No, I didn't change my major.

How important was your college experience in getting you to where you are today?

Teachers obviously must have a student teaching course/internship as part of their college experience, so that was the most important aspect of my college experience.

Do you have an advanced degree? Is one helpful or required in your field?

Yes, I have a master's degree. In the two states that I have taught in, New York and Connecticut, a master's degree is required.

What do you love most about your job?

The children! I often say that if I could just teach the children and remove some of the extraneous duties that come with teaching, I would be even happier.

What is the most difficult or challenging aspect of your job?

Finding the best ways to teach students with special needs can be quite challenging. No two students are alike, and a multitude of creative methods are necessary to promote learning. Dealing with a student's negative behavior can be difficult as well. Special education requires a great deal of paperwork, including keeping data on students, writing reports, IEPs, etc.—this is not my favorite part of the job!

What is the biggest misconception people have about what you do?

Many people think that teachers have it really easy because they work from 9:00 A.M. to 3:00 P.M., have so many days off during the year, and don't work in the summer—wrong! They don't see the intensity and demands of the job on a day-to-day basis, including the huge responsibility of ensuring that children learn. This is especially true for special education students, who often struggle yet are expected to meet the same standards as typical students. Teachers are often at school before and after the regular school hours, and they have homework, too, just like their students! Having time off helps teachers to renew and revitalize, making them better teachers.

What was the biggest obstacle you faced in getting to where you are in your career?

I must admit that I didn't face any obstacles getting to where I am in my career today.

What skills are an absolute must for someone interested in pursuing your career?

In addition to a sound foundation in child development, people skills are critical in this field for dealing with students, administrators, teachers, and parents.

Whom do you admire most in your industry or field?

Maria Montessori was someone who influenced my teaching style. Multisensory, hands-on learning experiences are essential for learning and also provide a fun environment in which young children truly learn. Jean Piaget influenced my understanding of child development. Currently, there is a great deal of ongoing research in the study of autism. I admire those who are pursuing this research in the hope of unlocking autism's mysteries.

What is one piece of advice you would give to someone who is interested in pursuing your career?

Make sure that you love children and will always be able to encourage them in positive ways!

If you could do everything all over again, what would you do differently?

I probably would have liked to pursue an advanced degree in child psychology.

Gloria Marsilia, High School Teacher
Special Education English Teacher
CUNY—Queens College, 1988
Major: Special Education

What was your first job after graduation?

A teacher.

What criteria did you use when deciding which colleges to apply to?

Subject area, including what programs the colleges were offering; convenience, such as how close the school was to my home; and tuition.

What was your first choice school?

Queens College, which I was fortunate enough to attend.

What career did you have in mind when you applied to college?

I didn't have one.

How did the school you attended have an impact on your career choice and opportunities?

It is where I decided that I wanted to become a teacher!

Do you now wish you had attended a different school? Which one and why?

No, I would do everything the same way.

Which college or colleges are turning out the leaders in your profession today?

Queens College—they worked me to death, but I learned so much; the professors were superb!

Which classes were most valuable in preparing you for your career or in helping you decide on your career?

The classes in which you went to different schools to do your practicum were the most valuable. These classes enabled you to really participate in a classroom setting and gain knowledge and experience in what being a teacher is really all about.

How did your professors impact your career choice or preparation?

There were quite a few unique, independent-minded professors whom I'll always remember. One boosted my self-esteem and confidence and opened my eyes to the real world.

Did you have a job and/or internship during college that influenced your ultimate career choice or career preparation in any way?

Yes. I did some student teaching at a high school in a self-contained class. I also was a teacher's assistant working with physically handicapped high school students. I also did volunteer work at the U.S. Department of Veterans Affairs at St. Albans Primary and Extended Care Center. They prepared me for the real world and to be able to take on real-life experiences and to have realistic expectations about teaching and the education system.

Can you please describe the "Aha!" moment when you realized what you wanted to do?

I already had my bachelor's degree but was working in a department store. My colleague was attending school to become a teacher; she told me that the board of education was looking for special education teachers. On a whim, I went to them, took a test, and decided to become a teacher!

Did you change your major? If so, why?

Yes, I did. I had a BA in psychology and wanted to advance and get a master's in psychology, but the classes were too hard.

How important was your college experience in getting you to where you are today?

Student teaching was the best and most necessary preparation for a teaching career. Also, in college you meet all types of people, and it is where I learned to have much tolerance and respect for others.

Do you have an advanced degree? Is one helpful or required in your field?

Yes, it is required in teaching, and it is helpful because having one gives you an increase in salary.

What do you love most about your job?

The students, of course! I also like having the summers off (if you choose), and the school hours are accommodating.

What is the most difficult or challenging aspect of your job?

Dealing with the bureaucracy of the administration. Because of budget cuts, it appears that sometimes we teachers are becoming more than just teachers; we are performing duties of secretaries, psychologists, etc. and are handling work that others should be doing.

What is the biggest misconception people have about what you do?

They think that teachers have it made because of our hours and that we have summers off—but they have never worked in a classroom with special needs students!

What was the biggest obstacle you faced in getting to where you are in your career?

The biggest obstacle that I faced was going to college for my master's while raising a family. You must have perseverance and determination! Never give up!

What skills are an absolute must for someone interested in pursuing your career?

Patience, tolerance, resilience.

Whom do you admire most in your industry or field?

Myself—because I worked hard to get to where I am!

What is one piece of advice you would give to someone who is interested in pursuing your career?

You might have your days when you are frustrated and want to give up, whether it is in class or student teaching, but don't!

If you could do everything all over again, what would you do differently?

I would go for a master's and PhD in psychology.

Frank Ierardo, High School Teacher
Resource Room Teacher
CUNY—Queens College, 1977
Major: Physical Education

What was your first job after graduation?

Physical education teacher.

What criteria did you use when deciding which colleges to apply to?

The criteria I used when deciding what colleges to apply to were tuition costs and distance of the school from my home.

What was your first choice school?

I first went to Queensborough Community College and then transferred to Queens College.

What career did you have in mind when you applied to college?

I initially wanted to be an accountant, but I discovered that I didn't like accounting; I found the workload to be difficult and tedious. I am a people person and was very involved in athletics, so I decided that becoming a physical education teacher would be a perfect fit.

How did the school you attended have an impact on your career choice and opportunities?

Queens College showed me exactly what I would be doing on the actual job because in the courses I took, I worked with high school students who came to the school and participated in various athletic programs. It was one of the foremost physical education programs in the country at the time, and getting a degree from there was very difficult. The school helped me prepare academically for the tests that were given by the NYC Board of Education to get my teaching license.

Do you now wish you had attended a different school? Which one and why?

I would have applied to a college in upstate New York, like SUNY—Cortland, because its physical education program was considered the best at that time. I think if I had a degree from there, it might have opened more doors for me because it was a well-respected state school that had a high-quality program.

Which college or colleges are turning out the leaders in your profession today?

Columbia University, New York University, Queens College, and Penn State—University Park.

Which classes were most valuable in preparing you for your career or in helping you decide on your career?

Student management classes, psychology, and student teaching—where I actually worked and dealt with students in an everyday environment in a NYC public school. I also got to work with exceptional and professional supervisors and teachers.

How did your professors impact your career choice or preparation?

One professor in particular stands out. He said to always treat an individual in the manner that you would like to be treated yourself. He also stated that being honest, fair, respectful, and positive will bring out the best in the students. This has helped create significant relationships with the majority of students that I work with. Because of this teaching philosophy, I have created meaningful relationships with my students that have lasted over the course of my entire career. Some of my former students still contact me and visit me, and I get the privilege of seeing what an impact I have had on their lives and how they have impacted on mine as well.

Did you have a job and/or internship during college that influenced your ultimate career choice or career preparation in any way?

During my college career, I worked at a YWHA for two years, running a physical education program for seven to ten-year-olds in the community. For one term, I also fulfilled a college requirement for student teaching in a NYC public school in both physical and special education. Clearly, having all these jobs prepared me to deal with the multipersonalities that one faces every day in a classroom setting. It also helped me to deal with administrators, supervisors, and other teachers and most importantly, the bureaucracy within the school system.

Can you please describe the "Aha!" moment when you realized what you wanted to do?

It was when I was working with an emotionally handicapped individual whom everyone had given up on. I was able to work with him through the sports program at Queens College on a continual basis. Through this time, I also helped him with his academic deficits, and he realized that controlling and dealing with his handicap was possible. When this was accomplished, he was able to concentrate and perform better in his everyday activities and had improvement in his academic as well as his social skills. I found this to be very rewarding, which made me think about pursuing a master's in special education.

Did you change your major? If so, why?

Yes. I changed my major from physical education to special education. I did so because of the experience I had working with an emotionally handicapped individual.

How important was your college experience in getting you to where you are today?

Without my college experience, I would have never known that I wanted to go into special education. The rewards one gets in seeing an individual develop and succeed and knowing that you were a part of this process is very fulfilling.

Do you have an advanced degree? Is one helpful or required in your field?

Yes. A master's in special education. An advanced degree is both helpful and required in becoming a NYC public school teacher. Having a master's in a specific area prepares you to understand and deal with the situations that you might face on the job. Having one also qualifies you to receive a higher salary, gives you more prestige, and provides you with a better chance of a school hiring you quickly.

What do you love most about your job?

Seeing students develop as individuals, creating their own methods for coping with academic situations like preparing for exams, but dealing maturely with real-world situations also, such as preparing for job interviews, handling interpersonal relationships, and overall, just becoming well-rounded, viable members of society. Another thing I enjoy is helping the students with their personal problems that arise throughout the school year; it is almost like being a second parent or mentor to an individual.

What is the most difficult or challenging aspect of your job?

To create a relationship that is educational, professional, and respectful yet making the student feel that you are paying specific attention to his/her needs. This is very difficult because a majority of these students have emotional problems that impede their academic abilities as well as their social relationships with authority figures.

What is the biggest misconception people have about what you do?

That it is an easy job! In fact, it is one of the most difficult jobs in the world because we are working with the future of this country and what we do will impact their relationships, their community, and their ultimate goals in life. One very important misconception is that once you leave the building, the job is over, but in fact, there is a tremendous amount of preparation writing lesson plans, preparing methods of how you will present material to students, etc. In working with special education students, preparation of their IEPs and general paperwork take time as well. Working with special education students can sometimes take its toll on a teacher because you become emotionally involved in the student's development, and if you have a bad day, you might take that issue home with you.

What was the biggest obstacle you faced in getting to where you are in your career?

The biggest obstacle was getting into a decent public high school that had modern equipment, new textbooks, and principal/supervisors who really assist the teachers. When you start out in your first school, it can be intimidating because you do not know your colleagues or the students and are not prepared for what might arise. In the NYC public school system, you either sink or swim. Since it is such an overwhelming job when you first begin, dealing with the students is not easy, but dealing with the administration can be just as overwhelming. You watch what other, more tenured teachers do and then find your own teaching method that works for you and build upon that to establish yourself as a hardworking, caring teacher.

What skills are an absolute must for someone interested in pursuing your career?

Patience, determination, love of learning, creativity, accepting that you will only make a moderate salary, love of children, ability to listen, ability to multitask continuously throughout the class period, and putting up with a multitude of different personalities in each and every class. Another important aspect of this job is to accept the student as he/she is and to nurture positive aspects that the student has or can develop to make him/her a better person. In this way, they will build confidence in their abilities academically as well as socially.

Whom do you admire most in your industry or field?

The people that I most admire are the students themselves. Some fail continuously but are willing to stay an extra year to two years to complete the program and get a high school diploma. Today's students face many outside pressures that hinder their ability to concentrate on getting a degree. I admire the students who overcome these obstacles and eventually reach their goals.

What is one piece of advice you would give to someone who is interested in pursuing your career?

You have to be a realistic, caring, patient, hardworking individual who must love kids for who they are and work with the student on an individual basis, not trying to change who they are but trying to make them better so they can be better prepared for the outside world. Before someone enters this field, they must spend some time in the actual setting that they will be working in for at least a six-month period to get a real feel for what the job will be like.

If you could do everything all over again, what would you do differently?

I still would have become a teacher, but I would have pursued an alternate career working at the board of education to try and make realistic changes and develop programs that would be able to reach all the different types of students that special education teachers work with. I would have liked to implement programs that students would be interested in and would want to learn from and to develop vocational programs that are currently lacking in the public school system.

Do you have any additional comments you think might be helpful to someone hoping to pursue your career?

A person pursuing a career in special education must understand themselves and human nature very well in order to deal with the special needs and complex personalities of these students. They must also understand that they could be working in a bureaucracy that does not see them as individuals but only as part of a whole. Teaching is really an individual, complex process that takes a lifetime to master.

Eileen Chu, Psychologist
Licensed Psychologist
New York University, 1996
Major: Counseling/School Psychology

What was your first job after graduation?

A school psychologist.

What criteria did you use when deciding which colleges to apply to?

The three most important criteria that I used when choosing a college were its program descriptions, the college's reputation, and the location of the school.

What was your first choice school?

Columbia University.

What career did you have in mind when you applied to college?

I knew that I wanted to pursue a career in psychology.

How did the school you attended have an impact on your career choice and opportunities?

The school's reputation and program content have provided many opportunities for employment in a variety of settings.

Do you now wish you had attended a different school? Which one and why?

Even knowing what I know now, I would still apply to the same college that I applied to. Despite the exorbitant tuition costs, the school is still extremely popular and well recognized.

Which college or colleges are turning out the leaders in your profession today?

Columbia University, University of Maryland, and University of Southern California.

Which classes were most valuable in preparing you for your career or in helping you decide on your career?

Introduction to psychology, child development, tests and measurements, counseling theory and practice, and clinical psychology.

How did your professors impact your career choice or preparation?

My professors did not have a real impact on my career decisions.

Did you have a job and/or internship during college that influenced your ultimate career choice or career preparation in any way?

Yes. At New York University, I was a graduate assistant and a counseling extern at the New York University Counseling Center and at the New York University Mental Health Clinic. I was also a psychology intern at the New York State Office of Mental Health at Creedmoor Psychiatric Center. My internships provided much real-life exposure to the field and also provided me with future job opportunities in hospital settings.

Can you please describe the "Aha!" moment when you realized what you wanted to do?

I didn't have quite an "Aha!" moment, but I did have my career goals established during my junior high school years.

Did you change your major? If so, why?

No, I didn't change my major. I was confident in my decision.

How important was your college experience in getting you to where you are today?

My college experience helped to provide the foundation for my training in the career of psychology. However, the practical aspects of my career were learned through my internships and practicum.

Do you have an advanced degree? Is one helpful or required in your field?

Yes, I have a PhD. An advanced degree is advantageous and is increasingly becoming more necessary given the competition within the field.

What do you love most about your job?

I love assessing the needs of the students, providing intervention, and helping students get the services they need. Another significant part of my job deals with the students' parents—educating them about their child's needs and abilities and how they themselves can assist their child at home.

What is the most difficult or challenging aspect of your job?

The most difficult and challenging aspects of being a school psychologist are dealing with bureaucratic agencies, trying to work successfully with parents who are uninvolved in their child's life and/or uncooperative, and following through on service recommendations and keeping up with a student's progress.

What is the biggest misconception people have about what you do?

That psychologists are judgmental and analyze everything that you say!

What was the biggest obstacle you faced in getting to where you are in your career?

Being a woman and a minority, the biggest obstacles I faced in my career were bias and discrimination. Hard work and perseverance were a big help.

What skills are an absolute must for someone interested in pursuing your career?

First off, you have to be a people person and be able to deal with their mental and emotional problems with compassion but also with rationality. Another skill you need to have is to communicate effectively to the student, his/her parents, his/her teachers, and your administrators. Lastly, you must be able to analyze information in a clear manner and have excellent writing skills when writing reports.

Whom do you admire most in your industry or field?

The people I admire in this industry are the ones who make incisive assessments of an individual's needs and abilities. The psychologists who take initiative and implement supportive services that promote growth and development for their patients.

What is one piece of advice you would give to someone who is interested in pursuing your career?

Hard work and dedication during the lengthy and sometimes grueling education process will pay off with a rewarding career and an opportunity to work in a multitude of settings with a variety of people.

If you could do everything all over again, what would you do differently?

Nothing.

Do you have any additional comments you think might be helpful to someone hoping to pursue your career?

Psychology is not a career goal for anyone who is seeking to make a lot of money. It is a career that you must really love and have a real passion for.

Laura M. Giglio, High School Teacher
Special Education Social Studies Teacher
Hofstra University, 1993
Majors: History; Secondary Education

What was your first job after graduation?

I worked in insurance sales.

What criteria did you use when deciding which colleges to apply to?

I looked at many private schools that were close to home. I wanted schools that received high-quality reviews and that would accept my GPA and SAT score.

What was your first choice school?

Hofstra University, the school I attended.

What career did you have in mind when you applied to college?

I had lots of ideas about what I wanted to do when I first applied to college, but I didn't pursue them.

How did the school you attended have an impact on your career choice and opportunities?

Because it had a reputation for being a credible and good school, it opened the door to more interviews for me than for other students who attended community or city colleges.

Do you now wish you had attended a different school? Which one and why?

Even knowing what I know now, I would still apply to the same school. I enjoyed Hofstra University because it was a great learning environment that employed excellent professors who were always helpful, was set on a beautiful campus, and offered lots of resources available to all students.

Which college or colleges are turning out the leaders in your profession today?

Columbia University, New York University, Queens College (CUNY), Adelphi University, and Hofstra University.

Which classes were most valuable in preparing you for your career or in helping you decide on your career?

History, sociology, and psychology.

How did your professors impact your career choice or preparation?

One history professor I had in my freshman year of college made history so interesting, I just wanted to learn as much as I could! I took all the classes she taught. What I realized from her was that I wanted to be able to teach and inspire others the same way that she taught and inspired me.

Did you have a job and/or internship during college that influenced your ultimate career choice or career preparation in any way?

I had an internship and was able to student teach in my senior year of college. During the summers, I always worked in a business setting (e.g., tax department of a corporation, secretary for a computer firm, and researcher for a TV production company). Although these jobs did not have much to do with teaching, each job I had gave me experience cooperating and dealing with people in a work environment.

Can you please describe the "Aha!" moment when you realized what you wanted to do?

I didn't really have an "Aha!" moment.

Did you change your major? If so, why?

Yes. I was a business major with hopes of becoming a corporate lawyer. But I could not handle the math classes and foreign language requirements for the major.

How important was your college experience in getting you to where you are today?

Simply, I learned what I was good and not good at doing. I had wonderful teachers who took an interest in my success and who inspired me to try and push through obstacles that were in my way.

Do you have an advanced degree? Is one helpful or required in your field?

Yes, I have two master's degrees. Yes, one master's degree is required for teaching. I went for a second one for advancement within my career.

What do you love most about your job?

Working with students and helping them become successful!

What is the most difficult or challenging aspect of your job?

A lack of resources, a lack of support from the administration, and unfortunately, sometimes a lack of parental involvement in the students' lives.

What is the biggest misconception people have about what you do?

That because you work from 8:00 A.M. to 3:00 P.M. and you get lots of holidays and summers off, the job is easy. This is not true!

What was the biggest obstacle you faced in getting to where you are in your career?

The biggest obstacle I faced was getting a job when I first got out of college. Persistence was key! Looking everywhere, filling out hundreds of applications (if that's what it takes), and just making the most of your resources that are available to you.

What skills are an absolute must for someone interested in pursuing your career?

You must love children/teenagers (or whichever age group you decide to teach.) You need to be patient, hardworking, and understanding of the needs of others. Also, you have to be prepared to handle a lot of paperwork!

Whom do you admire most in your industry or field?

Dr. Jack Zevin, a Queens College professor. He worked in an urban setting for many years and never gave up his passion for inspiring students.

What is one piece of advice you would give to someone who is interested in pursuing your career?

It is never an easy job, so do not go into this field thinking that it will be! But with a good work ethic, it will pay off when you see your students succeed.

If you could do everything all over again, what would you do differently?

Nothing!

Do you have any additional comments you think might be helpful to someone hoping to pursue your career?

If you don't like student teaching (which you will have to do as an internship), do not go into teaching—do not have the false idea that it gets better!

SPORTS MANAGEMENT

WHY CHOOSE A CAREER IN SPORTS MANAGEMENT?

If you have a strong interest in sports, as either a participant or a spectator, sports management may be the career for you. If you're analytical, competitive, creative, and enjoy networking and negotiating, the multibillion-dollar sports industry offers a wide range of employment opportunities at all levels of competition. From high-profile major league and international contests to local professional and amateur events, sports management professionals promote and manage athletes, teams, sports facilities, and sports-related businesses and organizations.

Sports management professionals carry a variety of job titles. Program director in community sports programs, marketing and promotions director, academic services for student athletics, corporate sales director, director of ticketing and finance, sporting goods sales representative, intramural director of campus recreation, facilities coordinator, athletic director, compliance director, athletic business manager, golf pro, and fitness manager are all within the field of sports management.

WHERE THE JOBS ARE

When you hear sports management, you might think of Tom Cruise's character in *Jerry Maguire*. Today, sports management job opportunities offer more options than becoming an agent for a professional athlete, and they are available nationwide, not just in big cities like New York and Los Angeles. College campuses around the country offer jobs in sports marketing and promotions, sports information, academic student services, and development within intercollegiate sports. Other sports management opportunities can be found in sports marketing agencies, equipment manufacturers, public relations firms, convention and tourism offices, sports facilities, sports organizations (like the NBA or NASCAR), and even at your local parks and recreation office.

AREAS OF SPECIALTY

Sports management professionals can choose to specialize in a wide variety of areas, including facilities management, promotions, community relations, college athletics, and more. Some professionals focus their careers on a specific sport, while others may specialize after pursuing advanced graduate education in disciplines such as law, accounting, or business management.

EDUCATIONAL REQUIREMENTS

Most people in sports management have a bachelor's degree. Some recommended courses of study are marketing, accounting, business management, and business law. Many top sports executives, agents, and marketers have graduate degrees in business management or law. If you want to specialize in sports information, consider majoring in journalism and then working in the media before you pursue a career in sports management. No licensing or certification is required to work in the field.

SALARY RANGE

Salaries in sports management careers vary widely, depending on your experience, level of education, location, and specific job. Beginning salaries in educational institutions and minor league professional sports may be in the $25,000–$35,000 range. Professional teams and management firms typically pay highly competitive salaries. Rapid advancement is the norm in sports management, and jobs at the director level and higher generally pay $75,000 and can go way beyond. Some jobs pay a base salary plus commissions.

In addition, sports management jobs are known to offer many benefits, including the opportunity to work with people who share your love of sports and a reputation for excellent health and wellness benefits.

FAMOUS SPORTS MANAGEMENT PROFESSIONALS

- **George Steinbrenner** is a billionaire businessman and principal owner of the New York Yankees. In 2005, the Yankees were established as the first professional sports franchise to be conservatively estimated as being worth over $1 billion. Under Steinbrenner's stewardship, the Yankees have won ten pennants and six World Series titles.
- **Gloria Connors** put a tennis racket in son Jimmy's hand when he turned 2 and taught him how to play the game. She worked as Jimmy's manager throughout his professional tennis career, negotiating even his shoe contracts.
- **Don King,** boxing promoter, is known for his vertical hairstyle and flashy style.

WHERE TO LEARN MORE

North American Society for Sport Management (NASSM)

www.nassm.com

National Sports Marketing Network (NSMN)

www.sportsmarketingnetwork.com

ExSport II: The Expert Answer to Your Sport Career

http://personal.bgsu.edu/~jparks/ExSport/index.html

SportsLinksCentral.com

www.sportslinkscentral.com/professional_associations.htm

WORDS OF WISDOM

"If you make it, there is a lot of money to be made, but the majority of agents barely make ends meet and are chasing the dream. As long as you understand that coming into it, you'll be fine."

—Terry Bross, VP Baseball Operations

"Try to get experience as soon as possible through internships, connecting with athletes in college, and informational interviews with alumni."

—Kristen Kuliga, Sports Attorney and Agent

Terry Bross, Sports Management
VP Baseball Operations, Gaylord Sports Management
Saint John's University, 1988
Major: Computer Science

What criteria did you use when deciding which colleges to apply to?

I went to school on an athletic scholarship, so I evaluated both the sports and academic programs to find a good fit.

What was your first choice school?

Saint John's University. They had good programs at the Division 1 level for both baseball and basketball.

What career did you have in mind when you applied to college?

I wanted to become a professional basketball player, but I ended up playing professional baseball with the NY Mets.

How did the school you attended have an impact on your career choice and opportunities?

Going to Saint John's was very important because at the time it was ranked number one in the country, and I got to play in the final four in 1985. Being on that stage prepared me to understand sports as a business and how big college programs and professional sports work.

Do you now wish you had attended a different school? Which one and why?

No, I'm happy with my decision.

Which classes were most valuable in preparing you for your career or in helping you decide on your career?

Math—it teaches very good reasoning and logic skills.

What do you love most about your job?

I love the challenges and having a chance to secure someone's future for them. I enjoy protecting athletes from the pitfalls that are out there and helping them avoid some of the ones I fell into.

What is the most difficult or challenging aspect of your job?

Getting clients to learn from my mistakes and not make their own.

What is the biggest misconception people have about what you do?

People think that everyone is making lots of money and all we do is hang out and golf or go out to dinner with celebrity clients.

What was the biggest obstacle you faced in getting to where you are in your career?

Inexperience and fierce competition are the biggest obstacles. I worked not only harder and longer but smarter than others. People can feel your integrity if you are honest in all dealings—it shows through in the long run.

What skills are an absolute must for someone interested in pursuing your career?

You must be able to sell! Being a sports agent is 70 percent sales and 30 percent service. You must be selling all the time.

What is one piece of advice you would give to someone who is interested in pursuing your career?

Take the time to build your career properly. It will take most people without relationships in professional sports a minimum of ten years to build a feasible business.

If you could do everything all over again, what would you do differently?

I would work harder on my education and get a master's degree or higher. I would also attend more sales seminars and really learn the art of selling before I got into the business. The best advice I can give is learn to sell insurance or cars after you have a master's degree or, better yet, a law degree. Then you will be ready for this industry.

Joseph Groch, Sports Management
Director of Golf, The Glades Country Club
Saint Joseph University, 1980
Major: Accounting

What criteria did you use when deciding which colleges to apply to?

I was looking for a private liberal arts school. I wanted a school with a good reputation, one that felt right.

What was your first choice school?

Saint Joseph's University was the right choice for me.

What career did you have in mind when you applied to college?

I wanted to be a lawyer. The lawyers I talked to regarding an undergraduate degree recommended that I study accounting. And as I started studying business and accounting, I started to really enjoy business.

How did the school you attended have an impact on your career choice and opportunities?

My college experience was invaluable because I not only received practical business knowledge, I also developed the ability to think critically and conceptually and to solve problems creatively. My extracurricular activities helped me develop my leadership and public speaking skills.

Do you now wish you had attended a different school? Which one and why?

I would still go to Saint Joe's. At a classical liberal arts school, I believe I not only received a good education for my career but also for life.

Which college or colleges are turning out the leaders in your profession today?

Penn State and many of the colleges with a Golf Professional Management program.

Which classes were most valuable in preparing you for your career or in helping you decide on your career?

The diversity of my entire education, including my business and liberal arts classes, allowed me to stay open to all possibilities.

Did you have a job and/or internship during college that influenced your ultimate career choice or career preparation in any way?

Caddying at a country club helped prepare me to work in that environment.

Can you please describe the "Aha!" moment when you realized what you wanted to do?

After I sold the computer company I owned, I started playing golf again. My wife suggested that I look into a career as a golf professional. After I picked myself up off the floor, I said, "Aha!"

What do you love most about your job?

I love the diversity of roles I play: teacher, business manager, accomplished player, psychologist, rules official, marketing manager, master of ceremonies, operations manager, golf equipment specialist, merchandiser, policy advisor—the list goes on and on.

What is the biggest misconception people have about what you do?

That all I do is teach and play golf.

What skills are an absolute must for someone interested in pursuing your career?

The ability to communicate, work well with people, and assume a leadership role.

What is one piece of advice you would give to someone who is interested in pursuing your career?

Develop your business skills by working in a non-golf-related field to enhance your own knowledge in the "real" world and also to learn how to deal and communicate with non-golf-related professionals on their terms.

Do you have any additional comments you think might be helpful to someone hoping to pursue your career?

Love the work, love the play, love the members, love the game, love the challenges—because in the end, it's all just golf.

Nancy Lough, Sports Management
Associate Professor, Sport Education Leadership,
University of Nevada—Las Vegas
College: Adams State College, 1986
Major: Sports Management

What criteria did you use when deciding which colleges to apply to?

I wanted a school with strong sports and education programs.

What was your first choice school?

My first choice was Adams.

What career did you have in mind when you applied to college?

I had always been successful as an athlete and hoped to one day succeed as a coach. I did become a high school coach, then a college coach, and I followed up my coaching experience with a career in higher education preparing future coaches and athletic administrators.

How did the school you attended have an impact on your career choice and opportunities?

The cross-country program at Adams State has long been a powerhouse. As I began my career, having experience as an athlete there and having the endorsement of my former coach opened several doors for me. I was well prepared because my coach also had a doctoral degree and was one of my primary faculty members in the core discipline. The coach I had while an athlete at Adams State College had a tremendous influence on my desire to be a coach. He was an inspiration to all and as successful as a coach can possibly be. He was a real role model, both as a coach and as an educator.

Do you now wish you had attended a different school? Which one and why?

I highly recommend small colleges like Adams State College to students coming from small towns or small high schools. I know I would have been overwhelmed at a large university. For graduate work, the bigger universities that support research and are classified as research-intensive universities tend to provide the best programs at the higher levels.

Which college or colleges are turning out the leaders in your profession today?

For sport management faculty, the schools that have strong reputations for preparing leaders include Ohio State, Florida State, Texas, University of Northern Colorado, and the University of New Mexico. As a professor at UN—Las Vegas, I primarily prepare sports leaders such as high school and college athletic administrators.

Which classes were most valuable in preparing you for your career or in helping you decide on your career?

Sports marketing was my favorite class. I teach it today and also conduct sports marketing research.

How did your professors impact your career choice or preparation?

Dr. Joe I. Vigil was a big influence during my undergraduate preparation at Adams State College. He was also my coach and integrated an intellectual approach to our preparation and training for competition. Dr. David Stotlar was my advisor in my doctoral program, and to this day, he is an inspiration. He is one of the most highly regarded leaders in sports marketing/management education.

Did you have a job and/or internship during college that influenced your ultimate career choice or career preparation in any way?

As an undergraduate student, I had a work-study job as part of my athletic scholarship. During my master's degree, my graduate assistantship entailed coaching the women's cross-country and track teams. During my doctoral work, I spent a year working as an athletic administrator at the University of Northern Colorado.

Can you please describe the "Aha!" moment when you realized what you wanted to do?

My "Aha!" moment came one summer while I was giving a coaching clinic. The keynote speaker attended my session and stayed afterward to ask me what I planned to do next after coaching. He suggested that I consider pursuing a doctoral degree and becoming a faculty member. I realized then that my long-term career would be preparing future sports leaders to lead, instead of training athletes.

Working as a graduate assistant at Stephen F. Austin State University served as preparation to become a college coach. Working as an athletic administrator helped me to realize that I enjoyed teaching future leaders more than conducting the day-to-day operations of an athletic department.

Do you have an advanced degree? Is one helpful or required in your field?

I have both a master's degree and a doctorate. Typically, a master's degree is required to work in athletic administration or as a college coach. A doctorate is required to be a faculty member at a top college or university.

What do you love most about your job?

I love the intellectual stimulation and challenge. I enjoy students who prompt my thinking and come up with great questions; good research starts with great questions.

What is the biggest misconception people have about what you do?

Most people think my job is the same as a public school teacher. There is very little understanding that teaching is only one of three areas in which university professors are evaluated. Research is often given the most weight at top universities, which means there is pressure to conduct quality studies, get them published in top-tier journals, present your research at national and international conferences, and seek grant money for future research.

What was the biggest obstacle you faced in getting to where you are in your career?

Being a woman in sports presents many obstacles. Primarily, men feel sports are their entitlement and often feel that women don't belong in the sports industry. I have always had to prove myself as competent, qualified, and better than the competition because of my gender.

In order to overcome this, I selected paths that were true to my passion. As the first researcher to study corporate sponsorship of women's sports, I opened others' eyes to new possibilities. As an educator, I regularly challenge conventional notions of gender bias and discrimination that continue to exist in the sport industry. Awareness is the first step; after that, empowerment through knowledge is the key. Being an advocate for equity in women's sports is such a big part of who I am that no obstacle can stop me in my pursuit.

What skills are an absolute must for someone interested in pursuing your career?

Communication skills are critical: speaking in front of all types of people; writing in a publishable form; and listening to students, colleagues, and what the research is saying.

Whom do you admire most in your industry or field?

Billie Jean King for her leadership and continued advocacy for women's sports, Dr. Donna Lopiano for leadership of the Women's Sports Foundation, Dr. Donna Pastore for her contributions to the field of sports management, and Dr. David Stotlar for his leadership in sports marketing.

What is one piece of advice you would give to someone who is interested in pursuing your career?

Make sure you have done extensive study into what the career involves and how higher education works. The business of sports is growing increasingly sophisticated, and therefore those who prepare the sports leaders of tomorrow need to be a step ahead. Read the research, get to know who the top scholars are, and talk with people to hear their perspectives on what this career involves. The field of sports management is more than games and fun.

If you could do everything all over again, what would you do differently?

There's nothing I would change. My experience has made me the person I am today. I'm still young with a long career ahead of me, and the next phase may be a new adventure that I'm not even aware of yet. Life is both a journey and an adventure. If you choose sports or the careers I've had, you need to be aware that moving to new states and new cities becomes necessary for career advancement. The chances of staying in one place for your entire career are increasingly slim, so embrace the adventure and have fun!

Do you have any additional comments you think might be helpful to someone hoping to pursue your career?

One career often leads to another. Follow your passion, and you will be amazed where it will take you!

Kristen Kuliga, Sports Attorney and Agent
President, K Sports & Entertainment LLC
University of Massachusetts—Amherst
Majors: Economics; Political Science

What criteria did you use when deciding which colleges to apply to?

I looked at both academics and sports programs.

What was your first choice school?

The school I attended, UMass.

What career did you have in mind when you applied to college?

Something in politics or law. But I took a sports law class, and my professor became a mentor to me. She encouraged me to apply to law school and to pursue the sports law field.

How did the school you attended have an impact on your career choice and opportunities?

I was exposed to students in the sports management major, and it opened up a whole new area of business to me, which I didn't really know about before.

Do you now wish you had attended a different school? Which one and why?

I would pursue the same school but possibly major in sports management, since that is the field I work in. UMass has one of the top sports management programs in the country.

Which college or colleges are turning out the leaders in your profession today?

UMass, Tulane Law, and Marquette Law.

Which classes were most valuable in preparing you for your career or in helping you decide on your career?

Sports law and writing courses.

Did you have a job and/or internship during college that influenced your ultimate career choice or career preparation in any way?

I interned at a sports management firm, which helped me to decide that this was the career path for me.

Can you please describe the "Aha!" moment when you realized what you wanted to do?

After interning at a sports management firm, I knew this was what I wanted to do.

Do you have an advanced degree? Is one helpful or required in your field?

Yes, I have a law degree. It's very helpful in the agent side of the business.

What do you love most about your job?

Connecting with people and negotiating deals.

What is the most difficult or challenging aspect of your job?

Recruiting college players.

What is the biggest misconception people have about what you do?

That it is glamorous and cool to hang with the athletes.

What was the biggest obstacle you faced in getting to where you are in your career?

Building a client base of NFL clients was the biggest obstacle, but I continued to work hard and didn't settle for no as an answer.

What skills are an absolute must for someone interested in pursuing your career?

Good negotiating and selling skills.

Whom do you admire most in your industry or field?

Gary Wichard, who has been in the business for 25 years. He has built a great client base of quality guys both on and off the field. He recruits only a few players each year, so his clients get personal attention.

Do you have any additional comments you think might be helpful to someone hoping to pursue your career?

Try to get experience as soon as possible through internships, connecting with athletes in college, and informational interviews with alumni.

Scott Cohen, Sports Management
Director of Pro Personnel, Philadelphia Eagles
Dickinson College, 1991
Major: Economics

What criteria did you use when deciding which colleges to apply to?

I was mainly looking at smaller liberal arts colleges where I could play both football and baseball. The quality of academics was a big factor as well.

What was your first choice school?

Dickinson was my first choice.

What career did you have in mind when you applied to college?

I knew I wanted to work in sports.

How did the school you attended have an impact on your career choice and opportunities?

The Washington Redskins held their training camp at Dickinson College, and I was able to procure an internship with them following my sophomore year. I then did internships with the Redskins the next three summers, and that eventually led to my first job with the team and my career in sports management.

Obviously, having the opportunity to intern with the Redskins would have been a lot less likely had I not attended Dickinson. From an educational standpoint, it was helpful to be successful in a difficult academic environment while playing two sports. That gave me the confidence that I could succeed in the scouting profession.

Do you now wish you had attended a different school? Which one and why?

I wouldn't change a thing since my career, my wife, and many great memories were the result of going to Dickinson.

Did you have a job and/or internship during college that influenced your ultimate career choice or career preparation in any way?

In addition to the three summers of interning for the Redskins, I also had an internship with the Dickinson College Athletic Department.

Can you please describe the "Aha!" moment when you realized what you wanted to do?

In my second summer internship with the Redskins, the person running training camp became ill and had to leave for two weeks, leaving me in charge. As a junior in college, I was able to keep the camp running smoothly. It made a positive impression on Charley Casserly and Joe Gibbs, which helped lead the way into an eventual job with the Redskins.

Do you have an advanced degree? Is one helpful or required in your field?

Yes, I have a master's in sports management from University of Massachusetts—Amherst. It's helpful to have an advanced degree in sports management but not necessarily required.

What do you love most about your job?

I love when something I've done leads to the success of our team. I also love being able to come to work every day doing something that I enjoy.

What is the biggest misconception people have about what you do?

People think that all we do is watch football and that it's an easy job. They don't understand the number of hours we put into it and the experience that's necessary to be very good at it.

What was the biggest obstacle you faced in getting to where you are in your career?

The biggest obstacle was getting hired in the first place. After being told numerous times that there would not be a job for me, I kept working harder and finding new ways to make myself invaluable.

What skills are an absolute must for someone interested in pursuing your career?

Having a good memory and being open-minded, organized, detail oriented, and able to communicate well are skills necessary for player personnel.

Whom do you admire most in your industry or field?

Guys like Bill Polian and Charley Casserly who reached the top of the field from starting at the bottom, working their way up, and doing so with the core values that I try to emulate.

What is one piece of advice you would give to someone who is interested in pursuing your career?

Try to get an internship while in college; make an impression and prove yourself invaluable without being overbearing.

Plus 25 More Career Possibilities!
Science

COMPUTER PROGRAMMING AND SOFTWARE ENGINEERING

WHY CHOOSE COMPUTER PROGRAMMING OR SOFTWARE ENGINEERING?

Computer programmers write instructions, or lines of code, in a programming language that tell a computer what to do—which information to use, how to process it, and what equipment to use. Programmers also test and update programs that are already written. Software engineers use the principles of computer science to create software and systems that allow computers to perform many applications. They are often the ones who tell the programmers what type of programs to write.

WHERE THE JOBS ARE

Because computers are so prevalent, programmers and engineers are employed in virtually every industry. Because not all companies need a full-time programmer, many are temporary workers or consultants. One of the fastest growing segments of the industry is software development, and programmers who work to create packaged software, including games and educational and financial planning software, are likely to have the best job opportunities. As computer networking (including the Internet) continues to grow, the demand for software engineers will grow along with it. In fact, software engineering is expected to be one of the fastest-growing occupations.

AREAS OF SPECIALTY

Computer programmers and engineers often work in two main categories: (1) applications, which execute a specific task and (2) systems, which work with computer systems software, such as operating systems.

EDUCATIONAL REQUIREMENTS

Computer programmers often have a bachelor's degree, but many two-year colleges offer certificates that would qualify applicants for some entry-level jobs. With growing competition for jobs, however, having a bachelor's degree will be a distinct advantage. Programmers can distinguish themselves in the job market by getting certified in various programming languages. Software engineers are expected to have a bachelor's degree, usually in computer science, and they often are required to have a master's degree.

SALARY RANGE

The median salary in 2004 for computer programmers was $62,890 and $74,980 for software engineers.

Pros: The satisfaction that comes with problem solving, constantly learning new technologies

Cons: Long hours, strict deadlines

FAMOUS COMPUTER PROGRAMMERS

- **Bill Gates**, founder of Microsoft.
- **Ada Byron**, writer of the first computer program; her holographic image is on the Microsoft authenticity seal.
- **Linus Torvalds**, creator of the Linux operating system.

WHERE TO LEARN MORE

AeA, Advancing the Business of Technology
601 Pennsylvania Avenue N.W.
Suite 600, North Building
Washington, DC 20004
(202) 682-9110; fax: (202) 682-9111
www.aeanet.org

IEEE Computer Society
1730 Massachusetts Avenue N.W
Washington, DC 20036-1992
(202) 371-0101; fax: (202) 728-9614
www.computer.org

Dr. Dobb's Portal
www.ddj.com

WORDS OF WISDOM

I found that to make strides in my career I just had to volunteer to take responsibility for tasks outside of my area. Those who are willing to step up and take responsibility are normally recognized and will rise up quickly."

—Chris Bream, Video Game Programmer

"Be able to constantly adapt. Technology is always changing so you have to be prepared to change as well.""

—Susan Land, Software Engineer/ Production Planner

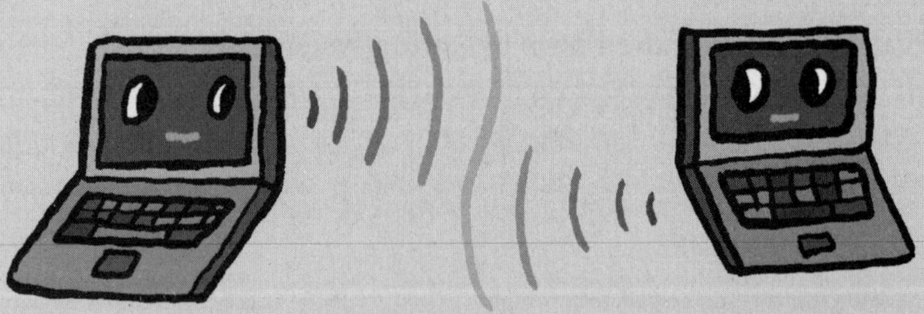

Chris Bream, Video Game Programmer
Technical Director, Terminal Reality
University of North Texas, 2000
Major: Computer Science

What was your first job after graduation?

Associate programmer at Terminal Reality.

What criteria did you use when deciding which undergraduate colleges to apply to?

I evaluated the quality of the computer science programs. Location also factored in (I lived in the Dallas/Fort Worth area at the time).

What was your first choice school?

My decision came down to either Carnegie-Mellon University or University of North Texas (UNT).

What career did you have in mind when you applied to college?

Video game programmer.

How did the school you attended impact on your career choice and opportunities?

Because UNT was one of the few schools with a video game class at the time, it was one of the few schools to provide contact with people within the video game industry. I was able to meet people who worked in the industry and secure job opportunities through these contacts.

Do you now wish you had attended a different school? Which one and why?

No. I believe UNT provided me with a unique opportunity to learn about and get involved in the game industry. My education at UNT is a big part of the reason I have my job today.

Which college or colleges are turning out the leaders in your profession today?

Many of my colleagues are from UNT, so that school is still turning out leaders in this profession. Other local universities are now providing a video game industry education, including Southern Methodist University (SMU) and University of Texas—Dallas (UTD). There are also national schools that specialize in a video game education such as DigiPen and Full Sail. I still believe a strong traditional computer science background with a passion for video games (and the motivation to work on your own video game projects outside school) is the best bet to gain the skills required for the industry.

Can you please describe the "Aha!" moment when you realized what you wanted to do?

I determined that computer programming was what I wanted to do when I took a programming class in high school. I really enjoyed programming, and it seemed really intuitive to me. Along with my passion for video games, this career seemed like a perfect match for me.

Which classes were most valuable in preparing you for your career or in helping you decide on your career?

It's hard to choose a single computer science class since a strong background in computer science is so important. Any classes that concentrate on algorithms and data structures are important. Linear algebra and a strong mathematics background are also very valuable.

How did your professors impact your career choice or preparation?

My video game professor, Dr. Ian Parberry, gave me a chance to exercise my passion for video games in challenging class projects. Through these class projects, I gained skills and confidence in my ability to be a video game programmer.

Did you have a job and/or internship during college that influenced your career choice or career preparation in any way?

Yes. I took an internship at Terminal Reality in my final semester of college and stayed on after I graduated.

Do you have an advanced degree? Is one helpful or required in your field?

I have a BS in Computer science. While any advanced education can be helpful, especially to gain specialized knowledge (e.g., computer networking), I don't believe they are essential. In the video game industry, you are constantly learning new technologies that aren't part of the curriculum in school (it's too hard for schools to stay up with the cutting-edge trends). You need to have a strong background and the ability to continue learning independent of school to survive in this industry.

What do you love most about your job?

I make video games! I love the casual atmosphere of the video game industry. It's a very young industry and demands innovation not only in technology but in business methodologies. There is a focus on obtaining and keeping talented employees, which in turn means companies try hard to make sure you love what you are doing.

What is the most difficult or challenging aspect of your job?

Keeping up with the latest trends and remaining competitive. You simply can't stop learning and improving or you'll be left behind. This requires lots of motivation because you must actively work to find the latest information and consume it (and many times it's not as easy as going to the bookstore).

What is the biggest misconception people have about what you do?

That it's all play and no work. Or that it's not a serious job. There's a ton of work in the video game industry. There are so many people out there who want to get into this industry and are willing to work 12-hour days for a job. Those people are the competition. That means you have to constantly demonstrate your worth. While work can be lots of fun, that doesn't mean it isn't taken seriously.

What was the biggest obstacle you faced in getting to where you are in your career?

Because the video game industry is such a young industry, there aren't proven tracks for getting places. I found that to make strides in my career I just had to volunteer to take responsibility for tasks outside of my area. Those who are willing to step up and take responsibility are normally recognized and will rise up quickly. If you don't realize this early in your career, you can waste lots of time idling in one place. Once you understand this "secret," you can go anywhere you want as long as you are willing to work for it.

What skills are an absolute must for someone interested in pursuing your career?

Self-motivated, passionate about video games, passionate about improving yourself and learning. After that, strong mathematics and computer skills are a must for programming.

Whom do you admire most in your industry or field? Why?

That's a tough question. I know so many talented individuals in this industry. I certainly admire all the people I work with at Terminal Reality, including Mark Randel, the company founder and a technical genius. I admire Shigeru Miyamoto for his game design brilliance; he's the best there is when it comes to game design and understanding game psychology. I've admired John Carmack's programming abilities ever since I first played Doom.

What is one piece of advice you would give to someone who is interested in pursuing your career?

Take your fate into your own hands. If you want to make video games, start making video games—research on the Internet, read books, start writing your own video game code. Don't wait for someone else to give you the opportunity. Start proving yourself now. If you have access to a computer and the Internet, there's no reason you can't get started writing video game code right now. Do it and then show video game companies what you've got.

If you could do everything all over again, what would you do differently?

I don't have any regrets about the choices I've made, but if I could live life over and over again, I'd do it differently every time. As far as my career and school choices, I believe they've been good choices. I suppose I would have taken more psychology or management classes in school if I could have. I've found I have a good understanding of computers but a poor understanding of people (though that's changing). From the company perspective, people are more important than computers when it comes to making great video games.

Can you please add any additional comments you think might be helpful to someone hoping to pursue your career?

If you love video games and want to work in video games, it's up to you to make it happen. This industry recognizes self-motivated people with a passion for video games. If you can muster up the determination to start learning and working on video games in your spare time, you are bound to crack into the industry.

Susan K. Land, Software Engineer/Production Planner
Program Manager/Technical Fellow, Northrop Grumman
University of Georgia, 1984
Major: Education

What criteria did you use when deciding which colleges to apply to?

I went to the nearest large state school.

What career did you have in mind when you applied to college?

I was premed.

How did the school you attended impact on your career choice and opportunities?

It was too large, had limited counseling, and a terrible Computer Science Department.

Can you please describe the "Aha!" moment when you realized what you wanted to do?

While I was in college, I had a job in the Department of Genetics and I fell into working on their computer systems. I was the only individual who understood their mainframes.

Did you change your major? If so, why?

Yes, started out honors premed. One of my first courses at Georgia was an honors course in chemistry and then in physics; these had over 200 students, taught by assistants. No tutoring or outside assistance was available. I did not do well. I changed my major to education, and I basically slept the rest of the way through college.

Which classes were most valuable in preparing you for your career or in helping you decide on your career?

Basic programming and software engineering and English 101, 102.

What do you love most about your job?

The ability to provide management oversight for multiple projects at once; this is challenging. I also get to affect positive software process change.

What is the most difficult or challenging aspect of your job?

Working with integrated teams spread across a wide geographic area.

What is the biggest misconception people have about what you do?

That software engineering is not engineering (this is changing).

What was the biggest obstacle you faced in getting to where you are in your career?

Starting out in the early 1980s, I had to overcome the gender bias, being the only woman in the laboratory. I am still the only woman, but now I lead the project; people are gender blind if you can do the work.

What skills are an absolute must for someone interested in pursuing your career?

Being able to motivate and lead teams and being technically savvy.

Whom do you admire most in your industry or field? Why?

I admire Robert (Bob) Colwell, who led Pentium development teams at Intel. He never sacrificed his principles or lost his sense of humor. I admire Ann Q. Gates, who worked in the industry for years, then in her 40s went back and got her PhD, and now teaches full-time. Alan Clements has written some of the leading architecture books of our time, yet has dedicated his career to leading student competitions and to furthering computer science excellence. James W. Moore continues to push forward the standardization of software engineering and establishment of software engineering as a legitimate engineering profession.

What is one piece of advice you would give to someone who is interested in pursuing your career?

Be able to constantly adapt. Technology is always changing so you have to be prepared to change as well. Be able to move around; do not get stuck in a dead-end job. Legacy technology is a career killer.

Can you please add any additional comments you think might be helpful to someone hoping to pursue your career?

Find your own way. You cannot mimic someone else's career path. What works for one person will not work for another. The most successful people often travel the most nontraditional paths toward success.

Donna Kocak, Software Engineer

Technology Development Manager and Lead Software Engineer, Advanced Technologies Group, Inc.

University of Central Florida, 1989

Majors: Computer Science (Computer Vision specialization) and Business

What was your first job after graduation?

Software engineer at Harbor Branch Oceanographic Institution.

What criteria did you use when deciding which colleges to apply to?

Location, program quality, cost.

What was your first choice school?

University of Central Florida (UCF).

What career did you have in mind when you applied to college?

Computer scientist (not sure of field of specialty).

How did the school you attended impact on your career choice and opportunities?

UCF had a very good computer science program. Two professors steered my choice of specialty in computer vision and graphics. Just as I began my master's studies, I worked as an intern at the Naval Training Systems Center (NTSC), which was located in the research park next to the university. This steered my career choice toward the oceanography field. Rather than continue with military applications at NTSC, I switched to marine science and engineering applications.

Do you now wish you had attended a different school? Which one and why?

No, UCF offered me many good opportunities and continues to have a very good reputation for quality in the computer science field.

Which college or colleges are turning out the leaders in your profession today?

Carnegie-Melon University (CMU), Massachusetts Institute of Technology (MIT), to name two.

Can you please describe the "Aha!" moment when you realized what you wanted to do?

In high school I took a beginner's programming class and although the teacher was trying to discourage us from entering the computer science field, I still became interested. However, the "Aha!" moment was probably when my father encouraged me to get into a field that paid well. "If I was going to work for a living, I might as well do something that is rewarding (financially)," is what he used to tell me.

Did you change your major? If so, why?

I did not change while attending college during my first two degrees: BS and MS in computer science. However, I have recently gone back to school for an Executive MBA degree. I intend this to add tremendously to my skill set and core competence, complementing my technical expertise. When working for small businesses, it is vital to wear multiple hats.

Which classes were most valuable in preparing you for your career or in helping you decide on your career?

Mathematics and science courses.

How did your professors impact your career choice or preparation?

Other than my high school teacher, who actually discouraged me from choosing this career path, most of my professors encouraged me, particularly since there were not many women in the field at the time.

Did you have a job and/or internship during college that influenced your career choice or career preparation in any way?

I had an internship at NTSC that influenced my choice of entering the oceanographic field.

Do you have an advanced degree? Is one helpful or required in your field?

I have a master of science in computer science. An advanced degree is not required in my field, but it is certainly helpful.

What do you love most about your job?

Working with cutting-edge technologies, travel opportunities, challenges.

What is the most difficult or challenging aspect of your job?

Working on research and development projects that push the limits of available technology. It is important to constantly upgrade your skills and knowledge through journals, classes, etc.

What is the biggest misconception people have about what you do?

You have to be a genius to do it. (Not!)

What was the biggest obstacle you faced in getting to where you are in your career?

The biggest obstacle by far is having the perseverance to stick tough times out.

What skills are an absolute must for someone interested in pursuing your career?

Good computer and mathematics skills.

What is one piece of advice you would give to someone who is interested in pursuing your career?

Go for it and stick with it!

Can you please add any additional comments you think might be helpful to someone hoping to pursue your career?

Pursuing a career in computer science or engineering is a great choice. These fields relate to everything in our society. You can use your skills in any field, whether it be oceanography, aerospace, sports and entertainment, medical, etc.

Dennis J. Frailey, Software Engineering Fellow
Principal Fellow, Raytheon
University of Notre Dame; Purdue University, 1966
Major: Mathematics

What was your first job after graduation?

Assistant professor of computer science.

What criteria did you use when deciding which colleges to apply to?

Academic quality and availability of well-rounded education (I turned down Massachusetts Institute of Technology (MIT) because they didn't have many sports teams).

What was your first choice school?

University of Notre Dame.

What career did you have in mind when you applied to college?

Physics or mathematics researcher/professor.

How did the school you attended impact on your career choice and opportunities?

I learned about computers and decided to go into that field. I also got a very solid and well-rounded education, so I was able to get into all the graduate schools I applied to. I took advantage of the opportunity to take a lot of electives outside of my major.

Which college or colleges are turning out the leaders in your profession today?

There are so many that I don't think it's right to single out a few of them. Too many people think all the leaders come from a small set of schools, but that is not so. I think it is most important to pick a school that fits you as an individual. In general, I prefer medium-sized schools to larger ones, but not too small.

Can you please describe the "Aha!" moment when you realized what you wanted to do?

When I first started programming a computer at a summer job when I was a senior in high school and realized that I really enjoyed computers.

Did you change your major? If so, why?

I started in physics and then changed to mathematics because I liked mathematics better. Later, for graduate school, I switched to computer science, again because I enjoyed it more. The bottom line was always to do what I liked to do rather than what might have the best career potential. I later found that this is important because when times get tough, it is easier to pull through in something you love to do.

Which classes were most valuable in preparing you for your career or in helping you decide on your career?

Work experience in summer employment was much more valuable than any class, but if I had to pick some I'd pick some special topics classes in computing that I took during a time when computer science did not exist as a major.

How did your professors impact your career choice or preparation?

Most of them opposed my desire to go into computer science, but that was because they were not really up with the times. One professor, Alan Brady, convinced me that computer science was a viable degree field. He was on the math faculty and kind of a rebel. There were other professors whom I greatly admired, but I felt that few of them had any genuine understanding of careers outside of academia.

Did you have a job and/or internship during college that influenced your career choice or career preparation in any way?

Absolutely. I had a summer job at Ford Motor Company that had me developing software. I loved developing software, and this more than any other factor influenced my career choice and preparation.

Do you have an advanced degree? Is one helpful or required in your field?

I have an M.S. and a Ph.D. Both have been valuable for different reasons. The MS took me deeper into the subject. The PhD gave me the "union card" to be able to teach at respectable universities, and the doctor title has occasional value for getting the attention of people or being accepted in certain circles.

What do you love most about your job?

The fact that using computers is what I do most of the day, even though I no longer program them.

What is the most difficult or challenging aspect of your job?

Dealing with difficult people or people in positions of power who don't know how to do their jobs well and impose stupid things on people who work for them.

What is the biggest misconception people have about what you do?

People think being in the field of software engineering means mostly programming. In fact, for a truly professional organization, programming is a very small and relatively unimportant part of the whole thing.

What was the biggest obstacle you faced in getting to where you are in your career?

The biggest obstacle was not being recognized for what I could do by those in power. Much of this was bias by people who did not understand what I did and assumed it did not take much capability. I overcame this by performing above and beyond the call of duty, doing a lot of outside-the-job professional activities (so that in the long run I became known and respected outside of my company), publishing papers, and also by being patient. I waited 17 years for one key promotion, for example.

What skills are an absolute must for someone interested in pursuing your career?

Strong mathematical skills (for reasoning skill, thinking skill); excellent ability to read and write and present (communication); broad understanding of computing and of how to do trade-offs of different technical approaches, options, languages, methods, etc.

Whom do you admire most in your industry or field? Why?

I admire a great many people who make important contributions every day but are seldom recognized by the world at large. These are the people who make the world run. These are the engineers, technicians, etc., who do the actual work and solve the real problems as opposed to the ones who pontificate.

What is one piece of advice you would give to someone who is interested in pursuing your career?

Remember that computers have relevance only when they solve a problem in some other field, so find something you love besides computing and learn about it and how computers can be used to improve it.

If you could do everything all over again, what would you do differently?

I have learned and grown from everything I've done, and I cannot think of anything I would do differently except for a few times I made stupid remarks that, in retrospect, were embarrassing. So perhaps I should say that I would have spoken less and listened more.

Can you please add any additional comments you think might be helpful to someone hoping to pursue your career?

Do what you love, and love something outside of computing so you'll have an application in which to use your computing skills.

Ben Andersen, Film Production Technician,

Technical Director, Pixar Animation Studios

Simon's Rock College of Bard (1999–2001),
State University of New York—Oneonta (2001–2002),
University of Massachusetts—Amherst (2003)

Majors: Math; Computer Science

What was your first job after graduation?

I have been at Pixar Animation Studios since I left the University of Massachusetts—Amherst.

What criteria did you use when deciding which undergraduate colleges to apply to?

My first college was Simon's Rock College of Bard (SRC), and it was the only college I had applied to at the time. The majority of students who attend SRC would otherwise be juniors in high school; we were all 16 years old. Students who attend SRC choose to leave high school for many reasons. In my case, the high school curriculum was not engaging enough for me, and so I had difficulty maintaining focus in class. I saw SRC as an opportunity to advance my own life and to escape some of the unfortunate situations that are commonplace in public high schools. At SRC, I was able to develop my education and my sense of self in a way that was not possible at my high school.

I left SRC after four semesters because it is a liberal arts school, and developing a technical education would have been extremely difficult. I applied to only State University of New York (SUNY)—Oneonta before leaving SRC because I had met and interviewed with Sven Anderson, the head of Oneonta's graphics program, a year earlier. I bought the sales pitch and transferred so I could learn from him. The college was close to home and relatively cheap as well.

After a year, I was able to get a job at a computer graphics company called Kleiser-Walczak Construction Company (KWCC) in northwest Massachusetts. I transferred to UMass—Amherst to pursue a more rigorous computer science base and so I could commute to KWCC twice a week. I was accepted for an internship at Pixar Animation Studios after one semester, and I have been here since.

What career did you have in mind when you applied to college?

I grew up with computers all my life. With two working parents and living out in the middle of the woods, I developed a fairly advanced knowledge of computers, as not many other social activities were available to me. I went into college thinking that I would want to be a computer programmer of some sort.

How did the school you attended impact on your career choice and opportunities?

I give credit to SRC as having the biggest impact on my choice of career. SRC has extremely small class sizes (I had one class that only had three students in it), and so the personal attention I received really allowed me to explore areas about which I felt passionate. Honestly, SRC was the best thing that has ever happened to me, in terms of finding myself. I transferred to SUNY—Oneonta and UMass—Amherst specifically to study graphics, so attending those schools simply reinforced my desire to work in computer graphics.

Do you now wish you had attended a different school? Which one and why?

I am very satisfied with the way my life has turned out so I do not wish that I had attended any different schools. Despite not having attended any schools with a top-notch computer graphics program, I was able to learn to use the necessary tools and grasp the necessary concepts to succeed in this field. It was just the right amount of input that I needed to push myself to take charge of my own education.

Which college or colleges are turning out the leaders in your profession today?

Pixar seems to recruit lots of people from Texas A&M University, University of California—Berkeley, Ringling School of Art and Design, and Savannah College of Art and Design (SCAD). Really any school that has strong computer science and art programs are leaders.

Can you please describe the "Aha!" moment when you realized what you wanted to do?

I never really felt that "Aha!" feeling. Lots of people ask me, "How did you know what you wanted to do?" And my answer is really that I didn't. I knew that doing computer graphics would be fun for me and that I needed to choose something. I took the computer graphics ball and just ran with it. I feel that I should add that I hold the belief that most people don't really know what they want to do for the rest of their life when they're in college but that most people don't choose a direction soon enough. It's okay not to know, but everyone should choose something they might like and do their best with that until something better comes along. Spreading yourself out into too many general fields will be worse than choosing something that might not be perfect and changing majors if needed.

Did you change your major? If so, why?

I started out as simply computer science but later added the double major for computer art as well.

Which classes were most valuable in preparing you for your career or in helping you decide on your career?

I feel that the function of college was not necessarily to teach me how to do my work directly, but rather, to teach me to teach myself. There were a few classes that were project based, instead of homework-based, in which I could really explore my passions. The project-based nature of my favorite classes taught me that I am responsible for my own success. If I was going to succeed in these classes and learn something from them, that burden was mine alone to bear.

How did your professors impact your career choice or preparation?

One professor suggested that I look into computer graphics as a real career. Until then it had almost seemed like a "fake" job or a job that can't simply be trained; a job that requires so much luck that it seems firmly outside of the realm of my possibilities—like being a movie star or a film director. My first graphics professor made computer graphics a real option for me.

Did you have a job and/or internship during college that influenced your career choice or career preparation in any way?

I worked for a company called RadioWoodstock.com doing Web design work. The company flopped, but I was able to take a project and really make it my own there. I had an opportunity to develop my artistic and technical abilities, which was something I really loved to do. Even though doing technical work for Pixar is different, it still provides an opportunity to be both technical and artistic.

Do you have an advanced degree? Is one helpful or required in your field?

I do not have an advanced degree. For my current set of responsibilities, it would not be that helpful and is not required, obviously. If I were to move into a more technical direction, such as tools development, then an advanced degree would certainly be helpful and may be required.

What do you love most about your job?

I love the freedom to explore my own solutions to problems. I will be given a few shots at the beginning of the week, which are expected at the end of the week. I can then spend the rest of the week however I want to, really, as long as my shots are ready on time. Most of the time, this means that I spend a few days developing a technique, then the rest of the week implementing it. Not having someone breathing down my neck all the time about progress really improves my job satisfaction.

What is the most difficult or challenging aspect of your job?

The most difficult aspect of working for Pixar is making sure that I have a life outside of Pixar. It is very hard to leave on time when my projects aren't finished yet.

What is the biggest misconception people have about what you do?

The biggest misconception about my job is that it is all fun and games. Pixar requires long days (8 to 14 hours) of very high levels of concentration. If one is not extremely careful, burnout is a very real possibility and happens to lots of people in this field sooner or later. This is especially true for smaller studios where there isn't such a clear division of labor and each artist is responsible for many different, smaller aspects of the project. Unpaid overtime is almost to be expected at these smaller studios, and if one is not careful, real health risks can result.

What was the biggest obstacle you faced in getting to where you are in your career?

The biggest obstacle I faced was coming to the realization that my education was my own responsibility and that I wouldn't necessarily be able to rely on my professors to teach me everything I needed to learn to get a job in the industry. The obstacle that I needed to overcome was finding the resources necessary to learn all the material, some of which was outside of my immediate college network. I overcame this obstacle by networking with some people who were working in the industry. I met them in a public Internet relay chat (IRC) channel called #maya. I went there looking for help with homework, and eventually one of them hired me as an intern to KWCC, working on Mystique for X2. I can say with certainty that if I had not gone seeking their help, I would not be at Pixar.

What skills are an absolute must for someone interested in pursuing your career?

Someone interested in the technical aspect of computer graphics must have a keen eye for detail, be moderately to very technically minded, and above all, must have a personal need to be successful and do the best job possible. There is too much competition for these jobs to get by with a second-rate job.

Whom do you admire most in your industry or field? Why?

Of all the computer graphic artists, Kevin Noone has been the biggest inspiration and best mentor to me. Ever since first meeting him, he has guided me with an extremely patient, knowledgeable, and supportive manner. Kevin Noone has been able to master so many aspects of computer graphics and always wants to learn more, and I aspire to be like him.

What is one piece of advice you would give to someone who is interested in pursuing your career?

Three things go into getting a job in computer graphics: timing, networking, and skill. Having your application received closer to the time when a company has an opening is important. The application will be fresher in the recruiter's mind when they're thinking of the applicants for the job. So apply often and whenever you hear of a job opening that sounds good. Don't be too disappointed with initial rejections!

Networking is very important. If you know someone who can give you an inside recommendation, your application will be remembered much more so than someone without any inside friends. This means hanging out in chat channels (I mentioned #maya

CYBERSECURITY

WHY CHOOSE A CAREER IN CYBERSECURITY?

In recent years, computers have become an integral part of everyday life, existing in our homes, work, schools, and nearly everywhere else. Almost all types of information, both public and private, from widespread to highly classified, now exist in digital form, and a society in which electronic documents and folders replace paper and hard-copy files is not far off. With all of this vital information at stake, what could be more important than making sure it is safe and secure?

The explosive growth of computers in society has created demand for highly qualified, technically savvy cybersecurity professionals who can ensure that our digital world isn't improperly exposed or threatened. Cybersecurity professionals work to maintain information security across computers, systems, and networks. It is a challenging yet rewarding field for anyone who's passionate about computers and technology. It's a rapidly evolving field as well—technology changes so fast that cybersecurity professionals must stay on top of all the latest innovations in hardware and software and a step ahead of all potential cyber-threats. As a result, cybersecurity professionals are at the cutting edge of technological progress.

Highly qualified cybersecurity professionals can enjoy a rewarding career in a variety of settings: private practice and major corporations, key government agencies and institutions, and wherever computer networks exist, including schools, hospitals, libraries, and beyond. Cybersecurity is a relatively new, exciting, and rapidly growing field, and as such its career opportunities will continue to expand and evolve over time. From firewalls and cryptography to antivirus software, systems access control, and data protection, professionals in this field have the opportunity to work with a diverse clientele and be responsible for preventing dangers that could cause catastrophic damage.

WHERE THE JOBS ARE

Rapid technological growth across all facets of society has led to an increased demand for cybersecurity specialists. Businesses, institutions, and government continue to invest heavily in cybersecurity to protect vital computer networks, information, and electronic infrastructures from attack. The information security field is expected to generate many new jobs over the next decade, as firms across all industries place a high priority on safeguarding data and systems. As a result, qualified individuals will be able to find jobs across the nation in virtually every type of work environment.

However, employment of cybersecurity professionals may be tempered somewhat by offshore outsourcing, as potential clients transfer work to countries with lower prevailing wages and highly skilled workforces. However, this trend holds more for other types of technology professions, such as systems administrators, and for services that can be provided remotely. The outlook and opportunities available to cybersecurity professionals within the United States are expected to remain robust.

AREAS OF SPECIALTY

Areas of specialization within the field of cybersecurity continue to expand and evolve with advances in technology. From securing operating systems, security architecture, and risk evaluation, assessment, and management to information and data security and coding, the field is constantly changing. Perhaps the only constant in this field is that a successful professional must be a veritable jack-of-all-trades, highly knowledgeable of all emerging technological innovation and able to handle all current and emerging potential cyber-threats.

Cybersecurity professionals can specialize in specific work environments, and the options are endless, from banks and insurance companies to government agencies, hospitals, schools, and beyond—wherever computers exist, the need for individuals to protect them will continue to grow.

EDUCATIONAL REQUIREMENTS

Due to the wide range of skills required, potential employers generally hire individuals with at least a bachelor's degree in a related technological discipline, and advanced degrees are preferred. Extensive computer experience and advanced certifications are highly valued in this field. Certification training programs, offered by a variety of vendors and product manufacturers, may help some people to qualify for entry-level positions. Since advancements in this field rapidly change the nature of the work, qualified professionals must commit to staying on top of all technological innovations over the course of their careers.

Successful cybersecurity professionals often have strong problem-solving, analytical, and communication skills, because troubleshooting and helping others are vital parts of the job. The constant interaction with other computer personnel, customers, and employees requires the ability to communicate effectively on paper, via email, over the phone, and in person.

SALARY RANGE

The median salary for cybersecurity professionals in 2006 was $82,000. The middle 50 percent earned between $71,000 and $93,000.

Earnings vary greatly in this field, depending on experience, qualifications, and type of employer. For example, individuals working in the private sector whose clients include major global corporations can easily earn a six-figure annual salary and beyond.

FAMOUS CYBERSECURITY PROFESSIONALS

Cybersecurity professionals often prefer to keep their accomplishments low profile. However, a look at one of the most destructive cybersecurity events of the past decade highlights the importance of their work: the Sasser worm of 2004, created by a German high school student, was responsible for causing tens of millions of dollars in damage and disrupted satellite communications and computer network systems across the globe.

WHERE TO LEARN MORE

The League of Professional System Administrators

15000 Commerce Parkway, Suite C

Mount Laurel, NJ 08054

www.lopsa.org

National Workforce Center for Emerging Technologies

3000 Landerholm Circle S.E.

Bellevue, WA 98007

www.nwcet.org

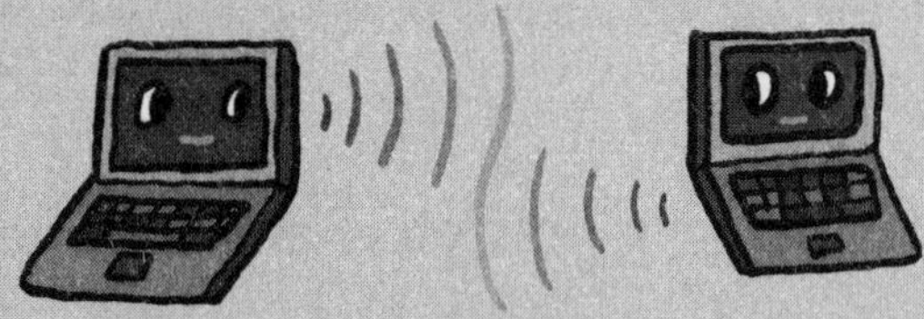

WORDS OF WISDOM

"Don't do this if you aren't interested in learning new things constantly. You need to have the motivation to seek out new knowledge, and if you slack off in the personal development area even for a bit, whole new areas of security can pass you by and you will be struggling to keep up."

—Kevin Stadmeyer,
Information Security Consultant

"Stay interested in current events. Read blogs and security books. Try to make it a hobby. If that is fun for you, then this is a great line of work. If that seems like a chore, you're probably cut out for something different."

—Joshua Stabiner, Senior Security Auditor

Kevin Stadmeyer, Information Security Consultant
Security Consultant, Trustwave
Rochester Institute of Technology, 2004
Major: Information Technology

What was your first job after graduation?

I was a security consultant.

What criteria did you use when deciding which colleges to apply to?

Majors offered, school ranking for my major, size of school, and geographic location.

What was your first choice school?

Rochester Institute of Technology (RIT) was my first choice school.

What career did you have in mind when you applied to college?

I knew I wanted a career in information technology.

How did the school you attended have an impact on your career choice and opportunities?

It opened up a lot of great career opportunities for me.

Do you now wish you had attended a different school? Which one and why?

I'm happy with the school I attended, but maybe I would've considered going to a more "fun" school with more social possibilities.

Which college or colleges are turning out the leaders in your profession today?

RIT is still pretty top-notch, along with the normal ones like Carnegie Mellon, MIT, Cal Tech, and Stanford.

Which classes were most valuable in preparing you for your career or in helping you decide on your career?

Intro to networking, computer forensics, and networking security.

How did your professors impact your career choice or preparation?

I had a number of outstanding professors who really knew a lot about information security, and their enthusiasm for the subject helped me realize that I had made the right choice.

Did you have a job and/or internship during college that influenced your ultimate career choice or career preparation in any way?

I had a rather terrible co-op for Pratt and Whitney doing database programming. The work was so bad and mind numbing that I decided that I could never do it for a living, and I had to go into security.

Can you please describe the "Aha!" moment when you realized what you wanted to do?

My moment came when I realized that people got paid to break into computers and it was a legitimate career.

Did you change your major? If so, why?

No, I didn't change my major.

How important was your college experience in getting you to where you are today?

The classes themselves were not particularly applicable, mostly because of how fast security changes. But having the degree with a concentration in security helped get my foot in the door for my first security job.

Do you have an advanced degree? Is one helpful or required in your field?

No, I don't. It's definitely not required. There is a definite attitude that the best learning experiences are available outside of the classroom. This is partially because schools are afraid to teach the hard-core security concepts lest they be sued (RIT requires you to take an ethics course first) and also because the field is changing so rapidly, any course materials are quickly outdated.

What do you love most about your job?

Being able to work from home. Stealing money and information from companies with their blessing (sadly I do not get to keep it).

What is the most difficult or challenging aspect of your job?

It is difficult to stay focused sometimes when working from home, and every so often, you get a very advanced project that requires everything you have to do properly—but I consider this a positive.

What is the biggest misconception people have about what you do?

That information security professionals are just antisocial hackers who sit in their basements with the lights off hacking 24/7. I'm sure some people are like that, but the fact is that this is a customer-oriented field. You won't be successful if you can't give a CTO or CEO a 50,000-foot view of their problems and do so clearly. You need to be professional to be taken seriously.

What was the biggest obstacle you faced in getting to where you are in your career?

The biggest difficulty was getting the first job in security. But I overcame this through hard work, constantly applying as well as becoming involved in open source community security projects and always learning as much as I could on my own.

What skills are an absolute must for someone interested in pursuing your career?

Solid understanding of very advanced computer concepts in a variety of fields, everything from network protocols to binary file formats to just about every computer language in use today.

Whom do you admire most in your industry or field?

This is a tough question. I suppose I most admire a couple of people, Brian Holyfield and Carey Nairn. They were two of my managers at my first job and have subsequently gone on to start their own business, Gotham Digital Security, in the info security field. I can really say that 90 percent of what I know about the security field I owe to those two (as well as several other old and current coworkers). In this field, you really need to network nonstop and constantly talk to your friends and coworkers to find out the latest exploit or the latest technique making the rounds.

What is one piece of advice you would give to someone who is interested in pursuing your career?

Don't do this if you aren't interested in learning new things constantly. You need to have the motivation to seek out new knowledge, and if you slack off in the personal development area even for a bit, whole new areas of security can pass you by and you will be struggling to keep up.

If you could do everything all over again, what would you do differently?

Nothing.

Do you have any additional comments you think might be helpful to someone hoping to pursue your career?

I think info sec is the best possible career for someone just out of college. The possibilities are limitless. Not once since I started (three long years, ha!) has the possibility entered my mind that I would have trouble finding a new job—or keeping my current one, for that matter. I also believe it would be very easy to switch jobs if I felt it was time for that, although I love my current company. The caveat is that getting that initial job can be very difficult, but once you are in and become well known, the possibilities are endless.

David Whitehead, Cybersecurity, Analyst
IT Analyst
Swarthmore College, 2003
Major: Engineering

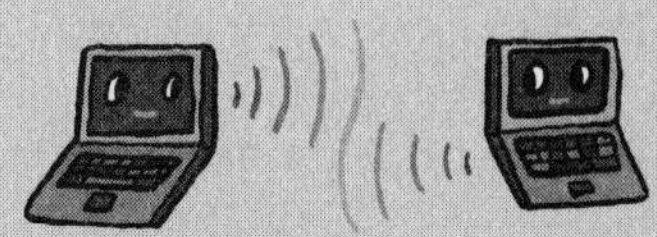

What was your first job after graduation?

I was a Web developer.

What criteria did you use when deciding which colleges to apply to?

I wanted a liberal arts education with an engineering program incorporated into it.

What was your first choice school?

Swarthmore was my first choice.

What career did you have in mind when you applied to college?

I wanted to be either a computer or electrical engineer.

How did the school you attended have an impact on your career choice and opportunities?

I definitely think it gave me an analytical background, which helped open up a broad choice of career possibilities.

Do you now wish you had attended a different school? Which one and why?

No, I'm happy with my decision.

Which college or colleges are turning out the leaders in your profession today?

I'm honestly not sure. I'd assume that any college with a strong engineering focus is turning out competent professionals.

Which classes were most valuable in preparing you for your career or in helping you decide on your career?

Computer science is key.

How did your professors impact your career choice or preparation?

All of my engineering, math, and computer science professors helped to provide me with a solid knowledge base, which has helped me advance in my career path.

Did you have a job and/or internship during college that influenced your ultimate career choice or career preparation in any way?

I was a summer intern for the Howard Hughes Medical Research Society and focused on researching and building electrical circuit devices for a wide range of products. I was also a technical support associate for their IT department. These experiences helped shape my analytical problem solving and thinking and gave me hands-on, real-world experience.

Can you please describe the "Aha!" moment when you realized what you wanted to do?

I didn't really have one. I always loved computers and have been working with them ever since I got my first 486 machine back in the 90s.

Did you change your major? If so, why?

No, I never changed my major.

How important was your college experience in getting you to where you are today?

I don't think I could have gotten to where I am today without a college education.

Do you have an advanced degree? Is one helpful or required in your field?

I don't have an advanced degree. It is certainly very helpful to have. However, certifications and experience tend to be more relevant in this field.

What do you love most about your job?

Being able to interact with a broad range of people and solve their technological problems.

What is the most difficult or challenging aspect of your job?

Keeping up with the changing technological world and dealing with a wide range of diverse problems.

What is the biggest misconception people have about what you do?

That all we do is fix computers. Obviously we do far more than that, from ensuring network and user security to dealing with a wide range of software and hardware issues.

What was the biggest obstacle you faced in getting to where you are in your career?

Finding a place where the job market in my field was booming. You must be one of the best in your field and be able to network with career contacts. It is essential that you stand out from the crowd. I looked in an area of the country I knew was hiring in my field, and I found an alumnus from my college that knew the quality of student that came out of the school. Alumni can open many doors, and I had a demonstrated knowledge and desire to work in IT.

What skills are an absolute must for someone interested in pursuing your career?

Being able to think on your feet and not give up when a problem you have never seen before comes your way. There are many ways to solve IT problems. Some are more elegant than others. Nothing is impossible. Be able to think outside the box and be able to have great interpersonal skills.

Whom do you admire most in your industry or field?

Sergey Brin and Larry Page (Google founders). What I see them doing in the world today and what they've accomplished is absolutely incredible.

If you could do everything all over again, what would you do differently?

I would certainly be more proactive than I was in searching for jobs in general, and I would pursue specific certifications in my field.

Brian Holyfield, Security Consultant
Cofounder, Gotham Digital Science
University of Florida, 1999
Major: Accounting

What was your first job after graduation?

I was an IT risk consultant.

What criteria did you use when deciding which colleges to apply to?

Growing up in south Florida, I always wanted to go to the University of Florida (UF). My decision was finalized when I went up to visit my sister when I was in high school.

What was your first choice school?

The University of Florida.

What career did you have in mind when you applied to college?

I majored in accounting. This was not only my father's profession, but I also took an aptitude test that recommended this as a top career choice for me. Additionally, the accounting school at UF is a top-ranked program. I was always good at math so I figured, why not.

How did the school you attended have an impact on your career choice and opportunities?

Not only was the program I was in nationally recognized, but the sheer size of UF makes it a very attractive recruiting ground for just about every large employer. As such, there were no shortage of companies to interview with.

Do you now wish you had attended a different school? Which one and why?

If anything, I would have probably majored in computer science instead of accounting. This is an area I'm much more interested in and passionate about.

Which college or colleges are turning out the leaders in your profession today?

I don't think there's any one school. However, there are a handful that have always been well known for their computer science programs, and security is no exception—MIT, Carnegie Mellon, Stanford, and UC—Berkeley are high on the list.

Which classes were most valuable in preparing you for your career or in helping you decide on your career?

When I entered the program at UF, they had just recently started an IT systems audit specialization, which I decided to pursue (as opposed to financial audit or tax). All of the IT-related classes I took were extremely relevant, especially the programming classes.

How did your professors impact your career choice or preparation?

They didn't really have an impact on me.

Did you have a job and/or internship during college that influenced your ultimate career choice or career preparation in any way?

I did an internship at Ernst & Young before I graduated. It provided me with valuable work experience.

Can you please describe the "Aha!" moment when you realized what you wanted to do?

I have always been very passionate about computers since I was a child. In retrospect, I have no idea why I didn't major in computer science to begin with. I think I was more focused on a career choice that would be financially lucrative instead of one that I was passionate about.

Did you change your major? If so, why?

I didn't change, but I procrastinated on choosing a specific major until I was forced to do so, at which point I chose accounting. I think at the time I was pretty sure I wanted to do something in the general business realm.

How important was your college experience in getting you to where you are today?

College is critical, not just for the information you learn but more for teaching you *how* to learn. A college degree proves that you're teachable, even if your major is unrelated to your profession.

Do you have an advanced degree? Is one helpful or required in your field?

Yes, I have a master's degree. Although it isn't required in my line of work, I think it adds some extra credibility when people know you have an advanced degree. However, I don't think that the additional knowledge gained from having one helps much, at least not in my case. The main reason for this is that things move so quickly in the IT world. A lot of the technology I work with today didn't exist ten years ago.

What do you love most about your job?

It's fun, and I'm passionate about it. This is the most important thing about what I do. If you find something you're passionate about, success will follow. Never pick a career for monetary reasons; you'll wind up being miserable.

What is the most difficult or challenging aspect of your job?

Currently, I also have to help run the company in addition to serving clients, so time management is my biggest challenge.

What is the biggest misconception people have about what you do?

That we are all a bunch of geeks who spend all day locked in a basement.

What was the biggest obstacle you faced in getting to where you are in your career?

Always having to stay ahead of the curve and continually learn new things. I think this is a challenge in any IT-related field but even more so in security. IT security is a constant cat-and-mouse game between the good guys and the bad guys. The environment we work in, by definition, is in a constant state of flux. It helps to learn as much as you can on your own time in order to keep up in such a constantly evolving field.

What skills are an absolute must for someone interested in pursuing your career?

The desire to constantly learn new things. In order to succeed in this field, you need to be willing to spend personal time advancing your skills.

Whom do you admire most in your industry or field?

I have always admired all of the early dot-com founders. They were all able to become extremely successful by doing what they love most and are passionate about. Most of them didn't start off with the objective of making billions—that was merely a side effect.

What is one piece of advice you would give to someone who is interested in pursuing your career?

In this field, it is extremely important to be well-rounded. A lot of great technical people have very poor soft skills (presentation style, public speaking, writing, etc.). Soft skills are just as important as technical skills if you want to get ahead in the business world.

If you could do everything all over again, what would you do differently?

I should have stopped day-trading in 1999.

Joshua Stabiner, Ethical Hacker and Penetration Tester
Senior Security Auditor
Dartmouth College, 2003
Major: Computer Science

What was your first job after graduation?

I was a researcher for Institute for Security Technology Solutions.

What criteria did you use when deciding which colleges to apply to?

Reputation, quality of life, and area.

What was your first choice school?

Dartmouth was my first choice.

What career did you have in mind when you applied to college?

I didn't have one in mind.

How did the school you attended have an impact on your career choice and opportunities?

Specifically, my professors and graduate advisor were extremely helpful in allowing me to clarify and pursue my career options and path.

Do you now wish you had attended a different school? Which one and why?

No, nothing could have beat my college experience.

Which college or colleges are turning out the leaders in your profession today?

Dartmouth, Carnegie Mellon, Syracuse, NYU, and University of Illinois—Urbana.

Which classes were most valuable in preparing you for your career or in helping you decide on your career?

Security seminar, operating systems, theory of computation, and algorithms were very valuable.

How did your professors impact your career choice or preparation?

One of my professors, who later became my advisor, got me very interested in security. He would meet with me outside of class, help me with independent research, and guide me to work with students that had similar interests.

Did you have a job and/or internship during college that influenced your ultimate career choice or career preparation in any way?

I was a system administration intern for Manhattan Psychiatric Center and a programming intern for BlackRock. I learned from these experiences that I didn't want to be a programmer (I previously thought I would).

Can you please describe the "Aha!" moment when you realized what you wanted to do?

After working on my master's for two years trying to help fix things, I realized it might be fun to work at a place that simply tried to break things.

Did you change your major? If so, why?

No, I didn't change.

How important was your college experience in getting you to where you are today?

I would say that it was an extremely important and invaluable experience.

Do you have an advanced degree? Is one helpful or required in your field?

Yes, I have an MS, also from Dartmouth college. Without a doubt, it's a helpful thing to have.

What do you love most about your job?

Everything. I work with smart people on interesting assignments and get to live in a city that I love. What's not to like?

What is the most difficult or challenging aspect of your job?

Working on poorly (or non-) documented, brand-new technologies.

What is the biggest misconception people have about what you do?

People think hacking is movielike. You type a few commands, and poof, you're in the network. In reality, there's a lot of strategy planning, experimenting, and research. The typical movie scene may take a hacker a week or more to execute.

What skills are an absolute must for someone interested in pursuing your career?

Ability to learn quickly and adapt to changing systems. If you were the type of kid who used to take things apart just to see how they worked, then this is a fun career.

Whom do you admire most in your industry or field?

My advisor from Dartmouth.

What is one piece of advice you would give to someone who is interested in pursuing your career?

Stay interested in current events. Read blogs and security books. Try to make it a hobby. If that is fun for you, then this is a great line of work. If that seems like a chore, you're probably cut out for something different.

If you could do everything all over again, what would you do differently?

Nothing. I am really happy where I am today.

David Chong, Cybersecurity
Network IT Administrator
New York University, 2006
Major: Information Systems Management

What was your first job after graduation?

The same as my current position.

What criteria did you use when deciding which colleges to apply to?

A school that had a strong program in information systems management.

What was your first choice school?

NYU was my first choice.

What career did you have in mind when you applied to college?

I knew I wanted to work in computer technology, and college helped me to refine my career focus.

How did the school you attended have an impact on your career choice and opportunities?

It educated me as to the various career paths and possibilities that exist in this field and helped me make an informed decision about the path that was best for me.

Do you now wish you had attended a different school? Which one and why?

I would still attend NYU. It was a great experience for me.

Which college or colleges are turning out the leaders in your profession today?

I'm certain that NYU is among the top colleges for turning out leaders in my field.

Which classes were most valuable in preparing you for your career or in helping you decide on your career?

My bridging and routing classes and my Windows networking classes were very valuable.

How did your professors impact your career choice or preparation?

My professors didn't have much of an impact.

Did you have a job and/or internship during college that influenced your ultimate career choice or career preparation in any way?

I didn't have a job or internship during college.

Can you please describe the "Aha!" moment when you realized what you wanted to do?

I didn't have such a moment.

Did you change your major? If so, why?

I never changed my major.

How important was your college experience in getting you to where you are today?

College prepared me for my field with a strong knowledge foundation, but field experience is crucial.

Do you have an advanced degree? Is one helpful or required in your field?

I don't have an advanced degree, but having one in my field is very helpful.

What do you love most about your job?

I love being able to help people.

What is the most difficult or challenging aspect of your job?

Keeping up with all the advances in technology can be a challenge.

What is the biggest misconception people have about what you do?

That current technology is always easy and trouble-free. This is far from the truth.

What was the biggest obstacle you faced in getting to where you are in your career?

Staying updated and current in such a rapidly changing field. It requires constant effort and hard work.

What skills are an absolute must for someone interested in pursuing your career?

Knowing how to deal with diverse issues and people is key.

What is one piece of advice you would give to someone who is interested in pursuing your career?

Learn all you can and continue learning throughout your career.

If you could do everything all over again, what would you do differently?

I wouldn't do anything differently.

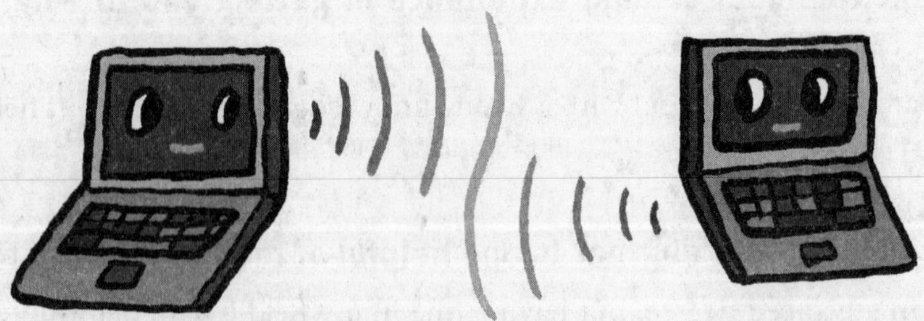

MEDICINE

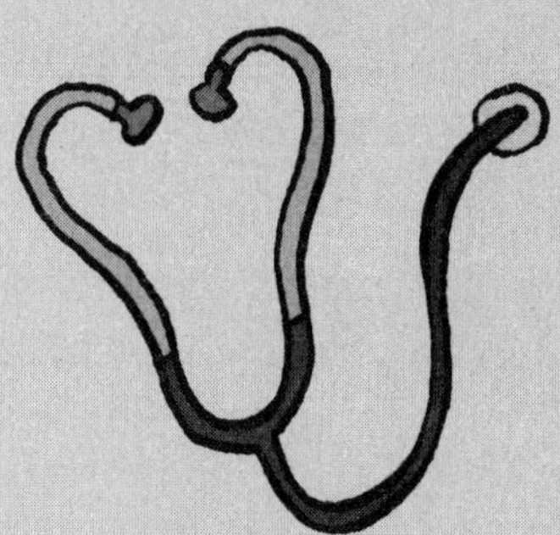

WHY CHOOSE A CAREER IN MEDICINE?

Students who go into medicine have an interest in science and a desire to help people. Physicians and surgeons diagnose and treat injuries, illnesses, and diseases. They examine patients and take their medical histories; order, perform, and analyze the results of diagnostic tests; and counsel patients on general lifestyle and health issues.

WHERE THE JOBS ARE

Many physicians work in private practice, either alone or as part of a group of doctors providing similar or complementary services. They also work in hospitals and clinics. The job market for trained physicians and surgeons is expected to be excellent in coming years, especially in rural or low-income areas. One of the main reasons for the increase in demand is the increasing population in general. The growing aging population, in particular, will require the services of more and more physicians.

AREAS OF SPECIALTY

A huge variety of specialties exists within the field of medicine. Some of the larger specialties include anesthesiology, family and general medicine, general internal medicine, general pediatrics, obstetrics and gynecology, psychiatry, and surgery.

EDUCATIONAL REQUIREMENTS

The number of years of schooling required to become a doctor is among the highest of any career. In addition to a bachelor's degree, there are four years of medical school, and then an internship and residency training, which can last from three to eight years, depending on the area of specialty. Some medical schools offer a combined undergraduate and graduate degree program, which lasts six years instead of eight. In addition to their years of schooling, doctors must also pass a licensing exam in order to practice medicine.

SALARY RANGE

Physicians and surgeons are among the highest paid careers. Depending on the specialty, the median total compensation in 2004 ranged from $132,953 to $259,948 for physicians in practice for less than two years (according to the Medical Group Management Association, "Physician Compensation and Production Report," 2005).

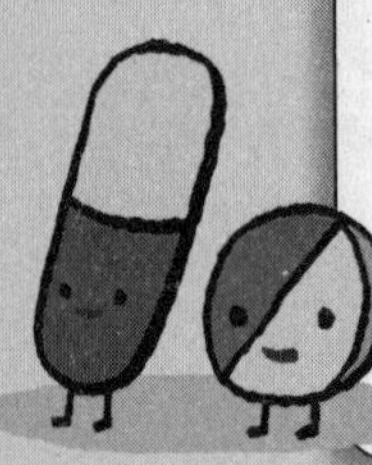

Pros: The ability to heal people or save their lives, high salary

Cons: Long hours, some doctors are on-call nights and weekends,stress of being responsible for someone's health

FAMOUS PHYSICIANS

- **Hippocrates**, ancient Greek physician, was the first to describe many diseases.
- **Elizabeth Blackwell**, in 1849, was the first American woman to receive a medical degree.
- **Orvan Walter** Hess designed the first fetal heart monitor and successfully treated the first patient with penicillin.

WHERE TO LEARN MORE

American Medical Association
515 N. State Street
Chicago, IL 60610
(800) 621-8335
www.ama-assn.org

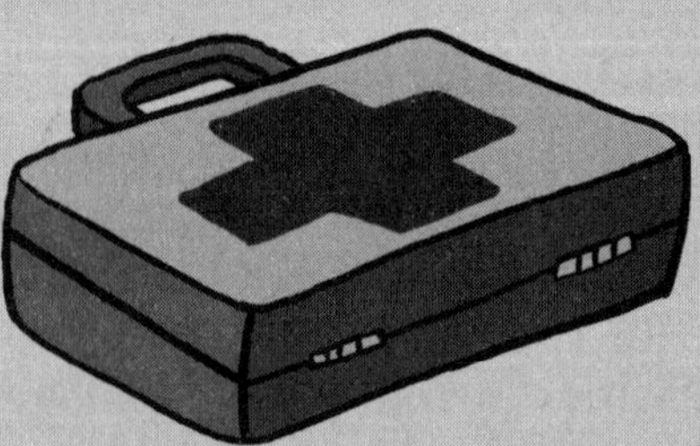

WORDS OF WISDOM

"I admire the people in medicine who have stuck with it and given good service to their patients. Many people don't see the compassion in physicians that used to be there. I still see many dedicated doctors."

—James Pollock, Physician/ Pediatrician/Allergist

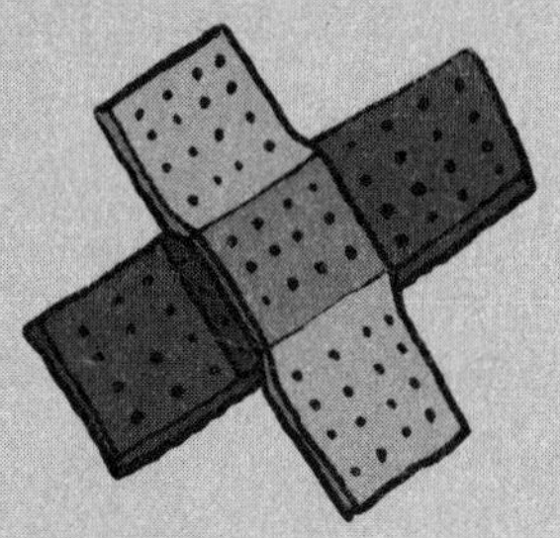

"Very few disciplines give you the chance to save a life, and there is no greater reward than doing just that. I love having a large fund of medical knowledge that grows on a daily basis. There isn't a day that passes that I don't learn something, and the constant pursuit of knowledge is an aspect of my profession I love."

—Michael Tocci, ER Physician

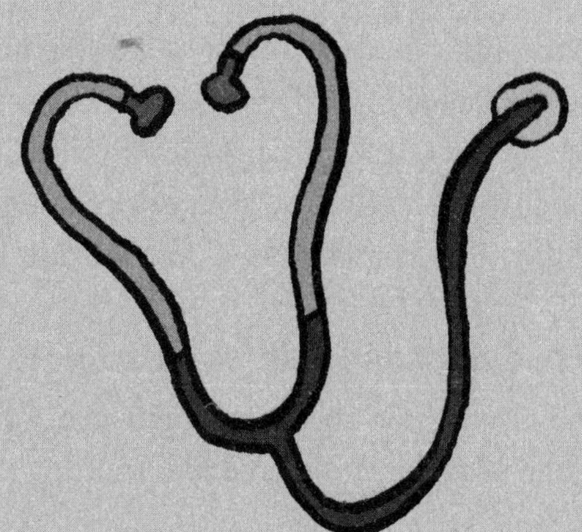

James D. Pollock, Physician
Pediatrician, Allergist,
Private Practice
Marquette University, 1964
Majors: Philosophy; Chemistry

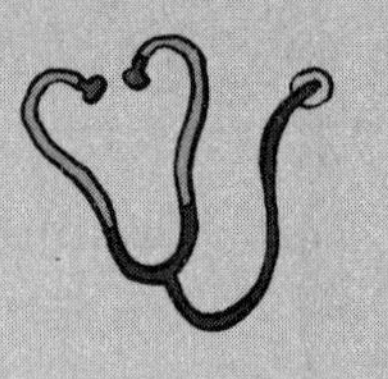

What was your first job after graduation?

Medical school.

What criteria did you use when deciding which undergraduate colleges to apply to?

I was raised Catholic and looked mainly at Catholic schools. I considered Gonzaga University and University of Notre Dame. At that time it was much easier getting into schools, and so that was not as much of a consideration. If I were choosing a school now, I would look at the ones that gave me the best chance of succeeding at what I wanted to do next. Ultimately, I stayed home and went to Marquette University (MU) for financial reasons—lack of money and a good part-time job.

What was your first choice school?

I would have gone to Gonzaga University.

What career did you have in mind when you applied to college?

Engineering (my dad was an engineer), but I decided on medicine.

How did the school you attended impact on your career choice and opportunities?

Back in my day, I don't think it made as much of a difference as it does today. I went to Marquette School of Medicine, possibly for financial reasons, but also because it was available. I was able to have a very good internship, excellent pediatric training at Children's Memorial Hospital in Chicago, and a very good fellowship at National Jewish Hospital in Denver. Today there is much more competition for the good programs.

Do you now wish you had attended a different school? Which one and why?

I was happy with my medical school choice, ultimately, but feel if I could have worked it out, I should have gone away for undergraduate training—for the experience of being away.

Which college or colleges are turning out the leaders in your profession today?

They come from all over. Schools in Boston (Massachusetts General), New York (Columbia University), but also Seattle (University of Washington). There is not one specific place.

Can you please describe the "Aha!" moment when you realized what you wanted to do?

The "Aha!" moment came sometime in my senior year of high school. I always thought I'd be an engineer—I had the aptitude and liked mathematics and science. I began to think about what I really wanted and thought that being a doctor was a better choice.

Did you change your major? If so, why?

I originally thought I'd go through engineering and then medicine. I found that the courses for premed did not fit well with engineering and switched to science with philosophy. Much of what I did was dictated by the premed course load. I ended up with a double major—philosophy and chemistry.

Which classes were most valuable in preparing you for your career or in helping you decide on your career?

The career choice was made in high school. I liked mathematics and science. In college, my career choice dictated what courses I took.

How did your professors impact your career choice or preparation?

I knew I wanted to go into medicine, so there was no impact on my career path. In medical school I did not like surgery and had very good pediatric professors who turned me toward this field. I really liked pediatric pulmonology, and with a history of asthma, chose to go into allergy/asthma next.

Do you have an advanced degree? Is one helpful or required in your field?

Following my medical degree, pediatric residency, then allergy fellowship are all needed for what I now do.

What do you love most about your job?

Interacting with patients.

What is the most difficult or challenging aspect of your job?

Keeping up with the developments in the profession.

What is the biggest misconception people have about what you do?

People don't see the behind-the-scenes preparation and the concern about making errors.

What was the biggest obstacle you faced in getting to where you are in your career?

Once the decision was made to pursue medicine, the path was straight. The hardest obstacle was choosing to leave a disastrous partnership situation and moving cities. My family (wife) still questions that decision.

What skills are an absolute must for someone interested in pursuing your career?

Obviously, you must be smart enough to do the work. I never thought medicine was a long grind because I always liked what I was doing. If you don't have a passion for medicine, don't do it. There are a lot of easier ways to make a living.

Whom do you admire most in your industry or field? Why?

I admire the people in medicine who have stuck with it and given good service to their patients. Many people don't see the compassion in physicians that used to be there. I still see many dedicated doctors.

What is one piece of advice you would give to someone who is interested in pursuing your career?

You won't get rich, but you'll have a full life if you like it. If you don't like it, do something else. But in medicine there are so many choices, including some where you will never see a patient.

If you could do everything all over again, what would you do differently?

I might have stayed in Denver, rather than moving to Chicago. I might have chosen emergency medicine, which I think fits my personality better. Many of my doctor friends also think we should have made a fortune in real estate. The other thing would be to do more charity work, which many physicians do rather than retire.

Can you please add any additional comments you think might be helpful to someone hoping to pursue your career?

Most of the people I know in medicine are happy, though we all complain. My advice would be to go work in a hospital or clinic to see if you have a desire to do this.

Michael J. Tocci, ER Physician

Emergency Medicine Resident, University of Connecticut Health Center/Hartford Hospital

Saint Joseph's University, 2001

Major: Biology

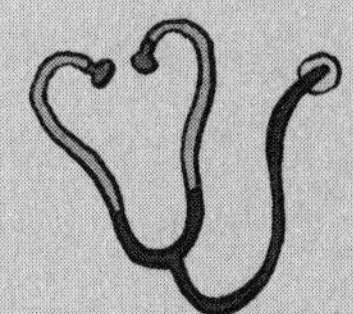

What was your first job after graduation?

Emergency medicine resident.

What criteria did you use when deciding which colleges to apply to?

The major factors I used to decide on college were the curriculum for my major, cost of the school, location, and scholarship offered. I wanted a curriculum that was rigorous enough to obtain a good grounding in my major since I knew that I wanted to go on to medical school. I am originally from Philadelphia, and I wanted to stay there for college to be close to my friends and family. This combination of the major's curriculum, school location, and the scholarship I was offered ultimately led me to my college.

What career did you have in mind when you applied to college?

I wanted to be a physician. I initially had the thought of this during middle school and definitively decided upon it midway through high school.

Do you now wish you had attended a different school? Which one and why?

Not at all. I was very happy with my college experience.

Which college or colleges are turning out the leaders in your profession today?

Leaders in my field have their origins throughout the country. I have colleagues from small local colleges as well as Ivy League schools. There is no one powerhouse school or group of schools that graduates more future physicians than others.

Can you please describe the "Aha!" moment when you realized what you wanted to do?

During college, when I was volunteering as a patient care assistant at a local children's hospital, I saw the physicians in action, the host of pathology encountered, and the breadth of knowledge they possessed. I knew that this was what I wanted for myself.

Which classes were most valuable in preparing you for your career or in helping you decide on your career?

The premed courses that were absolutely vital for me were anatomy, systemic physiology, histology, and microbiology. I also minored in psychology, and my courses in neurobiology and "Drugs, the Brain, and Human Behavior" were also valuable. The most memorable course I had in college was medical ethics. I still keep in contact with my professor from this course; he served as a mentor during college and the medical school application process.

How did your professors impact your career choice or preparation?

My biology professors were all supportive of my pursuit of a career in medicine, and several wrote me letters of recommendation during the application process. My medical ethics professor by far had the most influence on me. Having practiced medicine himself, he provided a perspective that was truly unique regarding the field of medicine and engendered in me a true regard for the practice of medicine. I owe a lot to him for the person I have become.

Did you have a job and/or internship during college that influenced your career choice or career preparation in any way?

I did volunteer work as a patient care assistant at a local children's hospital, specifically in the emergency department, where I assisted in the triage of patients and spent time with the families of children. It was this inside perspective that drew me toward the field of emergency medicine. The model for what a physician should be in my mind was represented by the physicians I saw there.

Do you have an advanced degree? Is one helpful or required in your field?

I have an MD, which I obtained at Jefferson Medical College. Either an MD or a DO degree is required for practice in my field.

What do you love most about your job?

The ability to truly make a difference in the lives of people. Very few disciplines give you the chance to save a life, and there is no greater reward than doing just that. I love having a large fund of medical knowledge that grows on a daily basis. There isn't a day that passes that I don't learn something, and that constant pursuit of knowledge is an aspect of my profession that I love.

What is the most difficult or challenging aspect of your job?

By far, the delivery of bad news to families is the most difficult aspect of my profession and possibly the hardest thing to do in my life. This is even more difficult when a patient dies in the emergency department or comes in from home after being found unresponsive by family members. There are times I've had to explain to parents that their child has died. Even though families are thankful for your kindness and honesty, I still find that it is never easy to express this news; but I am proud to bear this responsibility as a physician.

What is the biggest misconception people have about what you do?

The general public seems to believe that an ER physician is on-call at all hours and essentially lives in the hospital. In reality, I work shifts that are usually eight or nine hours. When I leave work, work doesn't follow me home. We do not take calls or have to answer pagers in the middle of the night. We do work overnight shifts, but when we aren't working in the hospital, our free time is completely our own.

What was the biggest obstacle you faced in getting to where you are in your career? How did you overcome it?

The hardest thing for me to rationalize was the amount of debt that I was building as a medical student. I didn't have any debt from college, but my medical school loans grew to over $100,000. The thought of this during college was something that I wasn't sure I'd be willing to endure. Ultimately though, after talking with my mentor, I realized that it was a small thing to overcome in the greater scheme of things. In reality, most students in medical school are there on loans and graduate in debt.

What skills are an absolute must for someone interested in pursuing your career?

Intelligence, an extensive fund of knowledge, critical thinking skills, split decision-making ability, procedural adeptness, instant rapport development, adaptability to the spectrum of patient presentation, and the capability to function as a united force along with colleagues in all medical disciplines. An outgoing personality is extremely beneficial in this field.

Whom do you admire most in your industry or field? Why?

I admire Dr. Joao Delgado, one of the attending physicians who works at my hospital. In my mind he possesses the qualities of the ideal physician: extremely intelligent with a wealth of knowledge that he readily applies to his practice, an incredible amount of patience, always maintains his composure regardless of the situation, and dedication to the resident education.

What is one piece of advice you would give to someone who is interested in pursuing your career?

Spend time in an emergency department in some capacity to see firsthand how the department works, whether as a volunteer or shadowing a physician. Talk with people in the field to get their perspective while also seeing it for yourself.

If you could do everything all over again, what would you do differently?

If everything I have done in my life has led me to where I am today, then I wouldn't change a thing.

Can you please add any additional comments you think might be helpful to someone hoping to pursue your career?

If you have the desire, then pursue your dreams regardless of the obstacles or what other people may say. I am incredibly happy to be where I am, and I owe it all to believing in myself and driving toward my goals. Seek a mentor in the field to get perspective from someone who is doing what you hope to be doing in the future. Above all, if you have the passion and dedication, you can achieve anything.

George F. Sheldon, Surgeon
Professor of Surgery and Social Medicine, Chair Emeritus, University of North Carolina—Chapel Hill
Kansas University, 1957
Majors: History; Premed

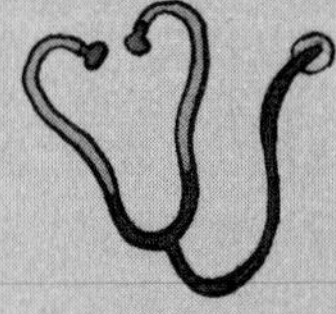

What was your first job after graduation?

United States Public Health Service—Coast Guard.

What criteria did you use when deciding which colleges to apply to?

I wanted to go to a state university with a medical school. Also, my father and two brothers attended Kansas University.

What career did you have in mind when you applied to college?

Medicine and surgery.

How did the school you attended impact on your career choice and opportunities?

Kansas University (KU) provided a broad liberal arts education, an emphasis on humanities for those contemplating medical school, and an excellent faculty.

Which college or colleges are turning out the leaders in your profession today?

The most important education is the last one. If one concludes at the bachelor of arts level then that should be the best and most prestigious school. In medicine, the last education experience is the residency and fellowship. For those, I did residency at the University of California—San Francisco and fellowship at the Harvard affiliate, Peter Bent Brigham Hospital.

Can you please describe the "Aha!" moment when you realized what you wanted to do?

My family had a lot of doctors. There was no single moment.

Which classes were most valuable in preparing you for your career or in helping you decide on your career?

My undergraduate influence was in history; medical school, it was all of the professors; and in residency, it was the general and trauma surgeons.

How did your professors impact your career choice or preparation?

The general surgeons in vascular and trauma were the most influential.

Do you have an advanced degree? Is one helpful or required in your field?

An MD is needed to practice medicine and surgery. Residency is required for practice in most states, and fellowship provides special skills.

What do you love most about your job?

It is wonderful to help people through an illness. Surgery has the instant gratification of seeing results almost immediately. Even relatively minor operations that have been done thousands of times still have to be done correctly and compulsively for each patient. Surgery is an athletic event—you may be recognized for your career of good results, but today's work also has to be successful.

What is the most difficult or challenging aspect of your job?

Keeping current with the evolving, enormous volume of medical information. Keeping up with new technology. Communication with patients is increasingly complicated. Dealing with the bureaucracy of medicine. The "gotcha" problems with medical malpractice. The continued reduction in reimbursement as other expenses increase.

What are the biggest misconceptions people have about what you do?

There is a basic misconception about the generic expectations of doctors. While there is a common basic education in the four-year run-up to an MD degree, most residency and fellowship time are five years or more. The residency and fellowship are the educational forums in which the special skills are obtained. Doctors are not interchangeable, except for some very basic skills. A urologist and a cardiologist, for example, can't provide similar services.

What was the biggest obstacle you faced in getting to where you are in your career?

The very demanding education of many years. It's very hard on family, but we seemed to make it.

What skills are an absolute must for someone interested in pursuing your career?

Strong work ethic, compulsiveness, integrity and honesty, attention to detail, good communication skills, leadership.

What is one piece of advice you would give to someone who is interested in pursuing your career?

Don't let anyone talk you out of it.

Can you please add any additional comments you think might be helpful to someone hoping to pursue your career?

Discuss your career choice with a number of people in the field and evaluate their responses carefully. Some will disparage other fields, which may seem impolite and may be that, but it may mean that they like what they do and can't imagine anyone not wanting to do their specialty. Take some of the available aptitude tests, which will help you focus. Be aware that at the age that people decide to go into medicine, they are at a critical decision-making point in their lives—often getting married, having parents die, etc. It is quite appropriate to view this educational experience as a preparation, but also as a chance to see a field that you may not have considered initially. The 20's are a time when you should be entitled to chart a new direction.

David Ross, Emergency Physician
Front Range Emergency Specialists, PC
University of Washington, 1978
Major: Nutritional Science

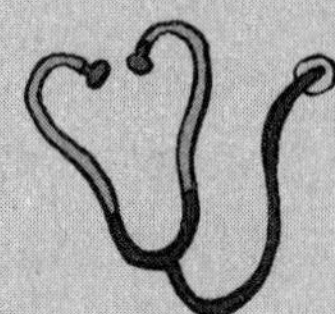

What was your first job after graduation?

Osteopathic medical school.

What criteria did you use when deciding which colleges to apply to?

I wanted a four-year college close to home that was affordable. I won a near complete scholarship to a Washington state school.

What career did you have in mind when you applied to college?

Medical school.

How did the school you attended impact on your career choice and opportunities?

Actually, the University of Washington (UW) did not help me much to achieve my goals. It is a very large school and as such, it takes a lot of self-direction to survive, especially as a premed.

Do you now wish you had attended a different school? Which one and why?

Yes. None in particular, but a decent, smaller, and affordable state school would have been better for me.

Which college or colleges are turning out the leaders in your profession today?

From an undergraduate perspective, I don't know. There are so many large and smaller schools that are good, yet distinct from each other. I believe it is really what feels right to the student that matters most.

Can you please describe the "Aha!" moment when you realized what you wanted to do?

I really enjoyed my chemistry class in high school. I liked the sciences, but I wanted to work with people, so medicine just popped into my head at that time, and I did not waiver much.

Which classes were most valuable in preparing you for your career or in helping you decide on your career?

I liked all of my nutrition classes. They were somewhat helpful in preparing me. Classes like inorganic chemistry, organic chemistry, and physics were necessary to apply to med schools, but only minimally helpful in medical school. Biology, biochemistry, and physiology were probably most helpful.

How did your professors impact your career choice or preparation?

At the UW, they really had no impact. I did consider a graduate degree in nutrition because some of the professors were inspiring, but I always hoped to go to medical school.

Did you have a job and/or internship during college that influenced your career choice or career preparation in any way?

Yes. I worked in the Department of Epidemiology at the UW School of Public Health. That was very useful and inspiring. I also worked in several areas at Harborview Hospital in Seattle, a major teaching hospital at the UW School of Medicine. That was very inspiring.

What do you love most about your job?

Being an emergency physician is excellent, as it offers the opportunity to impact patients' lives in some of their most critical times. The career also offers a lot of other nonclinical options if one chooses to take advantage of them.

What is the most difficult or challenging aspect of your job?

Difficult hours. We work all times of the day and night, along with weekends and very often holidays.

What is the biggest misconception people have about what you do?

That it is constant excitement and that we are making huge differences every ten minutes of every day. It is obviously not that fast paced at all (I wish it were sometimes). Nevertheless, it has its times when we can help people.

What was the biggest obstacle you faced in getting to where you are in your career?

I was not the most natural science student. I am probably more of a liberal arts type of student. So I had to work very hard in my classes—harder than some others that I was contemporary with. Also, the cost of medical school was a difficult proposition.

What skills are an absolute must for someone interested in pursuing your career?

Perseverance and strong, consistent goals.

Whom do you admire most in your industry or field? Why?

It's really very difficult to list just one person. There are so many great pioneers and researchers, yet some of the individual, everyday doctors I know are outstanding. What I admire most about physicians is the extreme high quality of the young people I know who want to get into it. In almost every case I think, "Wow, medicine would so benefit by having these young students in the profession. We would be lucky to have them." It says a lot for the profession as a whole that such high-quality people are very motivated to be a part of it.

What is one piece of advice you would give to someone who is interested in pursuing your career?

Try to identify your overall goals early and persevere. It is generally a lot easier to get medical school out of the way when you are younger and do not have a family. Not that it can't be done by older, second-career people with families, it just takes that much more perseverance and financial sacrifice.

If you could do everything all over again, what would you do differently?

Tried to get even better grades as an undergraduate so that I would not have had to sweat the application process as much as I did. Otherwise, I would not change anything.

Can you please add any additional comments you think might be helpful to someone hoping to pursue your career?

Good luck in whatever career you choose. I hope you are able to find one in which you generally are excited and look forward to going to work most days.

Marin Granholm, Family Physician
Staff Physician, Yukon-Kuskokwim Health Corporation
University of Utah, 1996
Major: Psychology

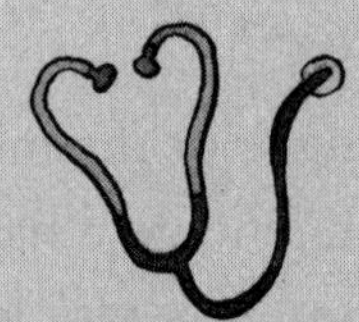

What was your first job after graduation?

Staff physician.

What criteria did you use when deciding which colleges to apply to?

I decided early on my state school, primarily for financial reasons.

What career did you have in mind when you applied to college?

I started school as an English major; I was considering becoming an English professor.

How did the school you attended impact on your career choice and opportunities?

At the University of Utah, I had a number of experiences that helped to define my career interests: I changed my major to psychology after enjoying several electives; I became involved in the Bennion Volunteer Center, in AIDS education, and Navajo cross-cultural education; I took a volunteer research position in a neuropsychology laboratory and found I enjoyed anatomy and physiology. All these experiences helped solidify my decision to attend medical school.

Do you now wish you had attended a different school? Which one and why?

I have friends who attended Ivy League schools, and I wonder how the experience would have been. I recognize now that compared to medical school, the cost of undergraduate education is relatively small.

Which college or colleges are turning out the leaders in your profession today?

I think one of the wonderful things about medicine is that it takes all kinds. Great doctors come from many places.

Can you please describe the "Aha!" moment when you realized what you wanted to do?

It was at a book fair in Denver, after the experiences listed above, when I met a favorite author and he suggested medicine.

Did you change your major? If so, why?

I changed from English to psychology because I didn't enjoy deconstructionism, which was the movement in English at the time, and also because I found I enjoyed psychology a great deal. I became premed later, but graduated as a psychology major.

Which classes were most valuable in preparing you for your career or in helping you decide on your career?

I think anatomy and physiology were what helped me decide; I think the psychology courses have been surprisingly useful in "real life."

How did your professors impact your career choice or preparation?

I had outstanding anatomy and organic chemistry professors. My chemistry professor encouraged me to study chemistry, which I considered at length before settling on medicine.

Did you have a job and/or internship during college that influenced your career choice or career preparation in any way?

I had several jobs that ended up being important, both volunteer and paid. I worked several years in a neuropsychology laboratory (studying brain function by running rats through mazes), and one summer performing an organic chemistry synthesis project. I also volunteered for a number of AIDS education and service organizations.

Do you have an advanced degree? Is one helpful or required in your field?

Yes, advanced degrees are required to practice medicine. I have an MD (Doctor of Medicine), but DOs (Doctors of Osteopathy) are also physicians in the United States. NDs are doctors of naturopathy, and PAs and NPs are physician assistants and nurse practitioners, respectively, who aid physicians in their work.

What do you love most about your job?

I love being able to serve people by putting all of my skills to use: problem-solving, communication, and procedural/technical. I love having a healing relationship with families and being a teacher and advocate for my community.

What is the most difficult or challenging aspect of your job?

A fact of life about where I live (rural Alaska) is that sometimes we do not have the resources to do some of the interventions we would be able to do in a larger city.

What is the biggest misconception people have about what you do?

In the lower 48, I find there is sometimes a misconception about what family doctors do. Where I am, we have to do everything. I work in the hospital, deliver babies, and take care of people in the emergency room (ER).

What was the biggest obstacle you faced in getting to where you are in your career?

During the first year of medical school, I had to adjust my expectations. I overcame this by talking through it with my colleagues, who were all going through the same thing.

What skills are an absolute must for someone interested in pursuing your career?

I think dedication and empathy are most important. Most of medicine is not that difficult; there is just a lot to learn (and keep learning). A lot of the time, when there is no treatment you can offer, the best thing you can do is be supportive.

Whom do you admire most in your industry or field? Why?

The Alaska Family Medicine Residency director, Dr. Harold Johnston, had the vision to recognize he could better serve Alaska by founding a training program than by practicing in rural Alaska himself. That vision is proving correct.

What is one piece of advice you would give to someone who is interested in pursuing your career?

I would not be afraid to go into rural practice, into work that you think may be too challenging. It is also the most rewarding.

Can you please add any additional comments you think might be helpful to someone hoping to pursue your career?

Shadow a doctor in your community. Don't be afraid to voice or pursue your interest in the arts. Be proud of your goal to become a family doctor, and don't forget it.

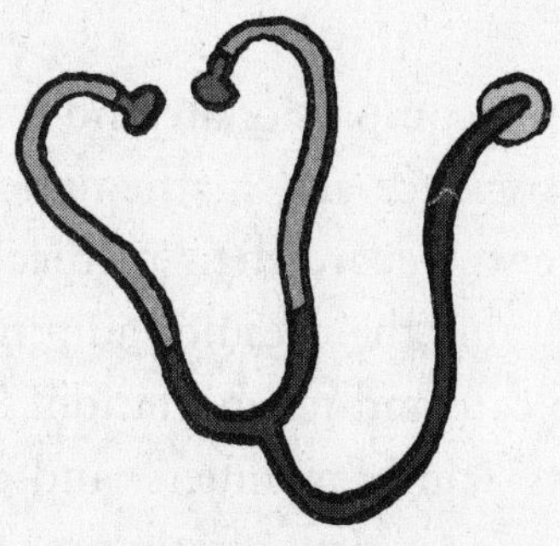

NURSING

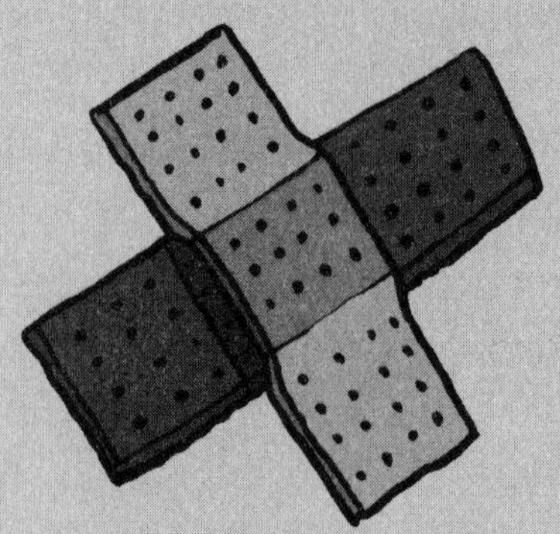

WHY CHOOSE A CAREER IN NURSING?

Nursing is a career for people who are compassionate and want to care for others. It also requires a good grasp of science and mathematics. The basic job of a nurse is to treat and educate patients, record their medical histories, assist in performing diagnostic tests and analyzing their results, administer treatment and medications, and provide follow-up care and rehabilitation. Nurses also provide information and support to patients' family members, and depending on their area of specialty, they can provide a wide variety of other services.

WHERE THE JOBS ARE

Most nurses work in hospitals, but others work in doctors' offices, nursing homes, or home health care facilities. As the number of medical procedures performed outside of hospitals, increases—in doctors' offices and medical clinics, for example, there will be a greater demand for nurses in these nonhospital settings. In many parts of the country there is, and will continue to be, a severe shortage of registered nurses. Because of this shortage, many employers are offering attractive incentives to prospective nurses, including higher pay and flexible hours. Nursing is one of the most in-demand careers in the country.

AREAS OF SPECIALTY

A huge variety of specialties is found within the nursing profession. Nurses can choose to specialize in treating a specific age group or illness type. They can also specialize in a combination of the two; in pediatric oncology, for example, nurses work with children who have cancer.

EDUCATIONAL REQUIREMENTS

To become a nurse, students must graduate from an approved nursing program and pass an examination to get a nursing license. The three main educational paths to becoming a nurse are a four-year BSN degree, an associate's degree in nursing, or a diploma. While entry-level positions as staff nurses are available to nurses with both associate's degrees and diplomas, there are many more professional opportunities for nurses with BSN or master's degrees.

SALARY RANGE

Median annual earnings of registered nurses was $52,330 in 2004. The middle 50 percent earned between $43,370 and $63,360. The lowest 10 percent earned less than $37,300, and the highest 10 percent earned more than $74,760.

Pros: Rewarding work, flexible schedule

Cons: Stressful environment; sometimes irregular work schedule, especially for non-senior positions

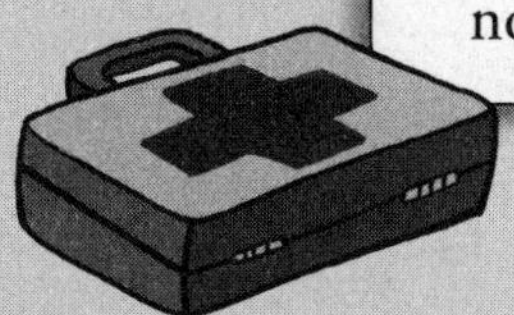

FAMOUS NURSES

- **Florence Nightingale** is considered the founder of modern nursing.
- **Clara Barton** created the American Red Cross.

WHERE TO LEARN MORE

National League for Nursing
61 Broadway
New York, NY 10006
(212) 363-5555
www.nln.org

American Nurses Association
8515 Georgia Avenue, Suite 400
Silver Spring, MD 20910
(301) 628-5000; fax: (301) 628-5001
http://nursingworld.org

American Association of the College of Nursing
One Dupont Circle N.W., Suite 530
Washington, DC 20036
(202) 463-6930; fax: (202) 785-8320
www.aacn.nche.edu

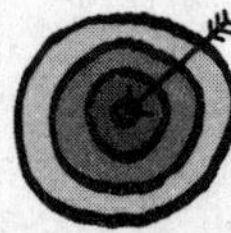

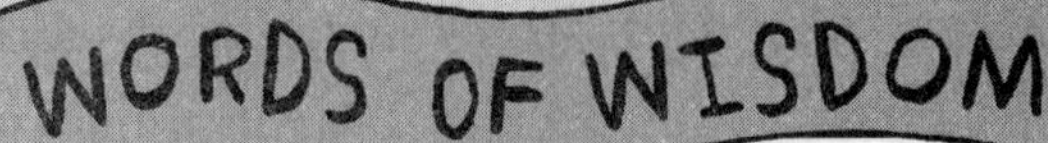

"Listen to patients and families, read all that you can on your area of interest, and trust your judgment and education to guide you."

—Megan Brunson, Registered Nurse

"A career in nursing requires a commitment to improving yourself every day and a dedication to follow through on doing what you say you'll do."

—Dennis Sherrod, Nurse Educator

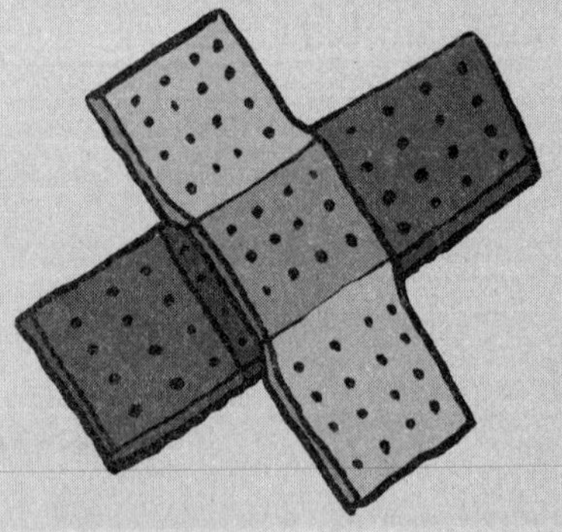

Dorene Albright, Registered Nurse,
Regional Director of Operations, RehabCare Group
Bradley University, 1976
Major: Nursing

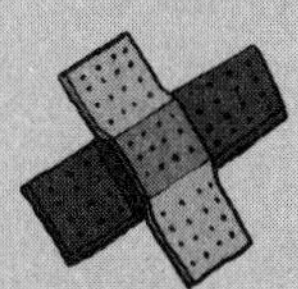

What was your first job after graduation?

Staff nurse.

What criteria did you use when deciding which colleges to apply to?

I was looking for a college that offered a bachelor's degree in nursing.

How did the school you attended impact on your career choice and opportunities?

At the time, there were not many nurses at the bedside with bachelor's degrees, which gave me many opportunities for advancement.

Can you please describe the "Aha!" moment when you realized what you wanted to do?

Nursing was always a calling for me!

Which classes were most valuable in preparing you for your career or in helping you decide on your career?

Sciences, but most valuable were the clinical experiences I received in health care settings. They gave me a broad perspective of what I could do as a nurse.

Did you have a job and/or internship during college that influenced your career choice or career preparation in any way?

I worked as a nursing assistant in a nursing facility and hospital.

Do you have an advanced degree? Is one helpful or required in your field?

I have a master's degree in nursing. Advanced practice degrees in nursing are helpful if you want more career choices.

What do you love most about your job?

Affecting the health of people in a positive way.

What is the most difficult or challenging aspect of your job?

Regulatory issues we must deal with.

What is the biggest misconception people have about what you do?

That nurses are just handmaids to physicians.

What was the biggest obstacle you faced in getting to where you are in your career?

In my case, it was financial. But I was able to work in the field and get scholarships.

What skills are an absolute must for someone interested in pursuing your career?

You must be adept at mathematics and sciences.

Whom do you admire most in your industry or field? Why?

I admire nurses who provide direct patient care. They really make the most personal influence in people's lives. It is hard work, both physically and mentally.

What is one piece of advice you would give to someone who is interested in pursuing your career?

Get your bachelor's degree, at least.

Can you please add any additional comments you think might be helpful to someone hoping to pursue your career?

Nursing has offered me many opportunities to work in a variety of settings. Often, people only think of nurses who work in hospitals and nursing homes. Nurses work in all aspects of health care. It is a very rewarding career—financially rewarding as well.

Megan Brunson, Registered Nurse
Saint Joseph Hospital, Atlanta, Georgia
Valparaiso University, 1997
Major: Nursing

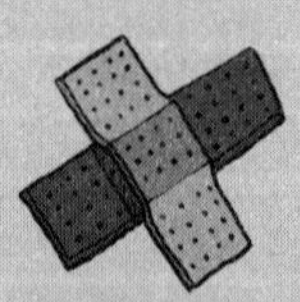

What was your first job after graduation?

Nurse.

What criteria did you use when deciding which colleges to apply to?

I wanted a small, private school.

What was your first choice school?

Saint Mary's College, Indiana.

What career did you have in mind when you applied to college?

Nursing.

How did the school you attended impact on your career choice and opportunities?

A smaller school allowed me to get a nursing degree without competing with other students. I was accepted into the program as a freshman and started nursing classes as a freshman, along with my basic classes. I did not have to have a certain grade point average (GPA) in order to apply the end of my sophomore year.

Can you please describe the "Aha!" moment when you realized what you wanted to do?

I was volunteering as a candy striper in an emergency room and saw the nursing staff save the life of an elderly women. I knew at that moment I would pursue the skills needed to change lives.

Which classes were most valuable in preparing you for your career or in helping you decide on your career?

Microbiology, anatomy and physiology, and leadership clinical my senior year.

How did your professors impact your career choice or preparation?

I was kicked out of nursing school my senior year for a conflict of interest related to an ROTC scholarship I had received. I was told by the dean of nursing that I was "to never practice nursing." I transferred schools and was even more determined after someone so horrible told me I could not ever be a nurse.

Did you have a job and/or internship during college that influenced your career choice or career preparation in any way?

I worked at Eckerd Drug as a pharmacy tech for eight years through high school and college. I learned a lot about medicine, side effects, personal attention to the sick, and the battles people face.

Do you have an advanced degree? Is one helpful or required in your field?

No.

What do you love most about your job?

I love the challenge that post–open heart surgery and critical care provide, with the second-to-second decision making. Not one patient is the same. I thrive on being an independent thinker and melding all body systems to save a life or respect it at the end of life.

What is the most difficult or challenging aspect of your job?

As a charge nurse of a 24-bed cardiovascular intensive care unit (CVICU), I find it difficult when pulled in many directions. You want to give full attention to every patient and your staff, and sometimes it is just not possible. Within minutes a staffing plan or an "easy" patient can go bad, and you have to constantly change priorities and redirect.

What is the biggest misconception people have about what you do?

In my unit specifically, I think people underestimate the overwhelming knowledge and skill the CVICU bedside nurse has. The challenge of managing a fresh heart transplant, bypass patient, or high-risk surgery can be mentally exhausting but rewarding at the same time. Nurses see the train coming and step in to be a patient advocate over and over again, either with physicians or with other services, without the family or patient knowing.

What was the biggest obstacle you faced in getting to where you are in your career?

Time management and being confident in my assessment skills. I overcame it with time and experience and by asking a lot of questions.

Whom do you admire most in your industry or field? Why?

I admire the bedside nurse I work with on a daily basis who does something small for a family or patient. For example, sneaking in a pet up the back stairs to bring joy to a patient who has been in the hospital for weeks. Or a busy nurse who takes the time to rub the back of an elderly lady who has arthritis. And the nurse who spends hours and hours at the bedside with a grieving family, sometimes only in silence.

What is one piece of advice you would give to someone who is interested in pursuing your career?

Listen to patients and families, read all that you can on your area of interest, and trust your judgment and education to guide you.

Can you please add any additional comments you think might be helpful to someone hoping to pursue your career?

There is not another career with the same type of daily reward.

Dennis Sherrod, Nurse Educator

Professor, Forsyth Medical Center Endowed Chair of Recruitment and Retention, Winston-Salem State University

Barton College, 1979

Major: Nursing

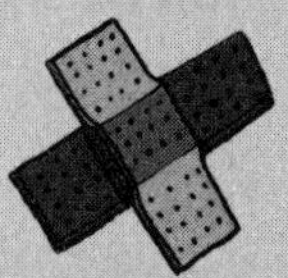

What was your first job after graduation?

Medical surgical nurse.

What criteria did you use when deciding which undergraduate colleges to apply to?

Location, cost, and availability of scholarship funding and financial aid.

What career did you have in mind when you applied to college?

Nurse anesthetist.

How did the school you attended impact on your career choice and opportunities?

I admire the program chair who served as a mentor and helped identify my passion for teaching. She convinced me to return for my MSN in Nursing Education and an EdD in higher education administration and to become a nurse educator.

Can you please describe the "Aha!" moment when you realized what you wanted to do?

I've never actually had an "Aha!" moment. The profession of nursing provides such a variety of opportunities, I've just been fortunate to have a broad educational preparation that allowed me to capitalize on career opportunities as they evolved.

Which classes were most valuable in preparing you for your career or in helping you decide on your career?

Science and mathematics classes.

How did your professors impact your career choice or preparation?

My program chair invited me into her office the semester prior to graduation. She knew I planned to go into anesthesia, but she felt I had strong interpersonal skills that would allow me to be an excellent nurse educator. She hired me as a clinical assistant and helped me enter my MSN program after my spring graduation.

Did you have a job and/or internship during college that influenced your career choice or career preparation in any way?

I worked as a nursing assistant which reassured me that nursing was the right career for me.

Do you have an advanced degree? Is one helpful or required in your field?

Yes, I have my master's and doctorate, and would encourage every nurse to consider advanced education.

What do you love most about your job?

Solving problems and working with excellent colleagues.

What is the most difficult or challenging aspect of your job?

Group problem solving.

What is the biggest misconception people have about what you do?

That nursing does not require smart people and that nurses are not health care leaders.

What was the biggest obstacle you faced in getting to where you are in your career?

Stereotypes. I work diligently to assist colleagues and patients to understand the need for diversity.

What skills are an absolute must for someone interested in pursuing your career?

A career in nursing requires a commitment to improving yourself every day and a dedication to follow through on doing what you say you'll do.

What is one piece of advice you would give to someone who is interested in pursuing your career?

Prepare yourself with strong science and mathematical skills. Contact someone you admire and ask them to serve as a mentor.

If you could do everything all over again, what would you do differently?

In my 27-year career in nursing, there has never been a day I regretted becoming a nurse. I would certainly do it again!

Tere Villot, Registered Nurse
Women Veterans Program Manager/President,
National Association of Hispanic Nurses, Philadelphia VA Medical Center
Catholic University of Puerto Rico, 1983
Major: Nursing Science

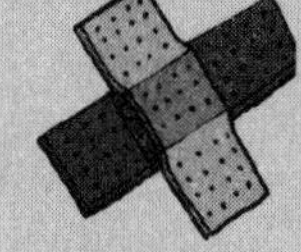

What was your first job after graduation?

Staff nurse.

What criteria did you use when deciding which colleges to apply to?

I based it on my parents' financial status.

What was your first choice school?

Temple University.

What career did you have in mind when you applied to college?

Nursing.

Which college or colleges are turning out the leaders in your profession today?

There are many excellent colleges and universities, but I feel that small community colleges are a good start for students who are not sure of what career they want to pursue.

Can you please describe the "Aha!" moment when you realized what you wanted to do?

Since I was a little girl, I always knew I wanted to be a nurse.

Which classes were most valuable in preparing you for your career or in helping you decide on your career?

Community health.

Do you have an advanced degree? Is one helpful or required in your field?

No, I don't. I think advanced practice is very important, but it is not a requirement to fulfill one's goals.

What do you love most about your job?

The ability to care for people and the flexibility to work in different areas within the health care field.

What is the most difficult or challenging aspect of your job?

Dealing with all types of personalities and characters and being able to keep a positive attitude.

What is the biggest misconception people have about what you do?

They view nursing as someone just cleaning bedpans and bathing patients.

What was the biggest obstacle you faced in getting to where you are in your career?

Relocating to a new country and having to adjust to a completely different way of life. I overcame this by staying focused and knowing that I one day wanted to be a nurse, and the only way I could accomplish this was by studying and getting good grades.

What skills are an absolute must for someone interested in pursuing your career?

Commitment, responsibility, organization, flexibility, and integrity.

Whom do you admire most in your industry or field? Why?

I admire Dr. Idaura Murrillo-Rhodie, the founder of the National Association of Hispanic Nurses, because she blazed the path for all of us Hispanic nurses.

What is one piece of advice you would give to someone who is interested in pursuing your career?

Nursing is a beautiful field. It is difficult, but there are lots of rewards, not only financial but also personal.

If you could do everything all over again, what would you do differently?

Nothing, because everything I have done has made me who I am today.

Can you please add any additional comments you think might be helpful to someone hoping to pursue your career?

To pursue their dreams and don't let anyone get in the way of them accomplishing their goals.

Sue Will, Registered Nurse
School Nurse, Saint Paul Public Schools
College of Saint Teresa, 1969
Major: Nursing

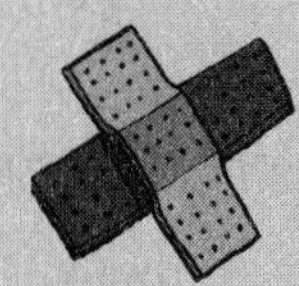

What was your first job after graduation?

Staff nurse.

What criteria did you use when deciding which colleges to apply to?

I looked for a school with a strong, reputable nursing degree program.

What career did you have in mind when you applied to college?

Nursing.

How did the school you attended impact on your career choice and opportunities?

My college experience solidified my choice of nursing as a career.

Which classes were most valuable in preparing you for your career or in helping you decide on your career?

Classes in the humanities were most valuable in preparation for my career.

Did you have a job and/or internship during college that influenced your career choice or career preparation in any way?

A clinical rotation in public health nursing showed me a different aspect of nursing—one that I chose to enter.

Do you have an advanced degree? Is one helpful or required in your field?

I have a master's degree in public health. It is definitely helpful, but it is not required.

What do you love most about your job?

I love the variety of people as well as the continuous challenging issues and needs in school health.

What is the most difficult or challenging aspect of your job?

The most challenging aspect of my job is managing all the issues and needs in the given time.

What is the biggest misconception people have about what you do?

School nursing today is one of the most challenging nursing specialties. School nurses serve students with a broad spectrum of pediatric and young adult health problems (everything from asthma to heart transplants, including management of complex care procedures in the school setting). School nurses practice independently of traditional health care settings and may care for a large number of students. This makes the specialty most challenging, exciting, and rewarding.

What skills are an absolute must for someone interested in pursuing your career?

Someone interested in pursuing a career in school nursing should possess an ability to practice independently, have excellent people skills for relating to adults and children, excellent study skills, and perseverance and determination.

Whom do you admire most in your industry or field? Why?

I admire many of the great nursing leaders but especially Lillian Wald. She began working in the tenements of New York City in the 1890s, where she saw a need in society and founded public health nursing, school nursing, and social work professions to address those needs.

What is one piece of advice you would give to someone who is interested in pursuing your career?

My advice is to study hard, learn well, and connect with excellent mentors.

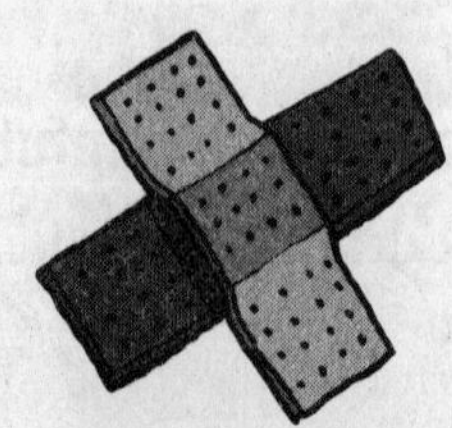

OCCUPATIONAL THERAPY

WHY CHOOSE A CAREER IN OCCUPATIONAL THERAPY

The occupational therapist's primary goal lies in helping people improve cognitive or physical abilities to live a productive, adjusted life. The therapist's work involves skilled assessment and specialized treatment that permits people to maintain independent lives, whatever their situation may be. Many of the challenges in this field involve dealing with diverse individuals. Generally speaking, a health care career is increasingly attractive, as systhe majority of the population continues to age.

Occupational therapists may assist the elderly, who may have disabling physical, mental, or emotional conditions. Therapists provide vital services in developing day-to-day skills, such as cooking, eating, or dressing, that their clients need to enjoy a satisfying life. They may also help clients learn how to use a computer. Assistance is not limited to work with the elderly; therapists may also provide daily care to those with specific disabilities of one kind or another. Work with children or other individuals with special needs is commonplace.

Occupational therapists provide a variety of services, which may include evaluating the home or the workplace, designing comprehensive adaptation programs to help improve quality of life, skill assessment and physical treatment of individual clients, and counseling of related family members. A career in occupational therapy is rich and diverse, with nearly limitless possibilities.

WHERE THE JOBS ARE

The great advantage of a career in occupational therapy is that positions may be found nearly anyplace where there are people. Occupational therapists sometimes work in an institutional setting, such as a large hospital, while others work in schools or universities. Some therapists may find employment in smaller, community-based health care settings. Involvement in the daily lives of clients may sometimes result in meetings or other activities organized outside the boundaries of the workplace as it is commonly understood, whether on weekends, holidays, or during and after the school day. However, due to the unusual nature of the care they provide, occupational therapists may enjoy greater flexibility in their schedules, and more than one-third of them choose to work part-time.

AREAS OF SPECIALTY

Occupational therapists may fulfill a number of roles in the health care field. Areas of specialization include art therapy, massage therapy, physical therapy, respiratory therapy, and rehabilitation counseling, among others. Some therapists may work with clients who have specific disabilities, or they may work exclusively with certain age groups. Activities may include outlining treatment plans, supervising daily activities, and recording the daily progress of the client. Therapists may work with aides, who typically prepare materials and assemble equipment used during treatment and may also assist in administrative duties. However, since aides are not licensed, the law prohibits them from performing the wider range of services that therapists themselves provide. Regardless of their area of expertise, occupational therapists must bring strong people skills and extraordinary patience to their chosen profession.

EDUCATIONAL REQUIREMENTS

A career in occupational therapy requires a master's degree or higher, and full-time educational programs exist at many colleges and universities. In addition, the number of schools offering part-time and weekend study programs continues to grow. Course work in occupational therapy includes a strong core science program as well as a supervised fieldwork requirement.

To obtain licensure as an occupational therapist registered (OTR), all applicants must successfully complete course work at an accredited institution and pass a national certification exam. Some specialized areas in occupational therapy require additional training or licensure, and requirements vary by state.

SALARY RANGE

The job outlook for occupational therapists is excellent. The average starting salary begins at about $38,000 and may approach $60,000 with specialized certification and a master's degree in advanced occupational therapy. Candidates may receive qualification after studying for anywhere from two to six years, depending on their chosen field of expertise.

FAMOUS OCCUPATIONAL THERAPIST

- **Margaret Buchanan** was the first known qualified occupational therapist.

WHERE TO LEARN MORE

The American Occupational Therapy Association

www.aota.org

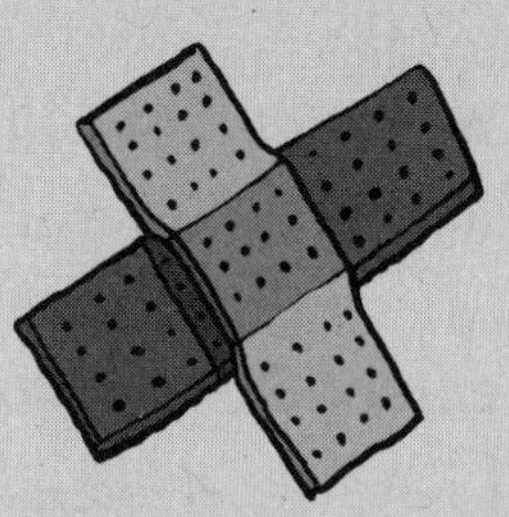

WORDS OF WISDOM

"Volunteer in a variety of settings and observe therapists working with different diagnoses."

—Jennifer L. Tucci, Occupational Therapist

"Try to job-shadow at a variety of locations and in different treatment areas. OT can be based in hospitals, clinics, schools, or in the home, and each setting brings different responsibilities."

—Amy Agasino, Occupational Therapist

Amy Agasino, Occupational Therapist
Pediatric Occupational Therapist
Washington University in St. Louis, 2002
Major: Occupational Therapy

What was your first job after graduation?

I worked in an inclusive day care in St. Louis, Missouri.

What criteria did you use when deciding which colleges to apply to?

Location, reputation of the school.

What was your first choice school?

Washington University in St. Louis was my first choice.

What career did you have in mind when you applied to college?

I did not have a specific career in mind when attending undergraduate school but wanted to be in a health-related profession. I then decided to finish my undergrad degree in psychology and attend Washington University for my master's degree in occupational therapy (OT).

How did the school you attended have an impact on your career choice and opportunities?

Some of the contacts I made through the staff at my school eventually led to job opportunities.

Do you now wish you had attended a different school? Which one and why?

Washington University would still be my number one choice, but I would also consider other schools in the area, for they have now transitioned to master's degree programs.

Which classes were most valuable in preparing you for your career or in helping you decide on your career?

Anatomy, neurology, child development, and professional communication classes were helpful.

How did your professors impact your career choice or preparation?

The professors that I worked with closely on my research project helped me solidify my choice of pediatrics, and they also helped me gain more hands-on experience with dealing with clients and their families.

Did you have a job and/or internship during college that influenced your ultimate career choice or career preparation in any way?

No, I didn't.

How important was your college experience in getting you to where you are today?

Overall, my experience helped me to clarify and refine my career goals and prepare me for the future.

Do you have an advanced degree? Is one helpful or required in your field?

Yes, and master's programs are becoming increasingly more prevalent and necessary.

What do you love most about your job?

Working with kids and their families is very rewarding. I also work with a very motivated and professional team of therapists and teachers.

What is the biggest misconception people have about what you do?

They do not understand what occupational therapy is and confuse the job with either a speech-language or physical therapist.

What was the biggest obstacle you faced in getting to where you are in your career?

There is typically more of a need for OTs in geriatrics. Finding a pediatric job took more time and resources. I overcame this by keeping in contact with some of the people I knew in pediatrics.

What skills are an absolute must for someone interested in pursuing your career?

Good interpersonal skills, creativity, and time efficiency.

Whom do you admire most in your industry or field?

Therapists who have gained expertise in a particular area, such as feeding specialists or splinting specialists.

What is one piece of advice you would give to someone who is interested in pursuing your career?

Try to job-shadow at a variety of locations and in different treatment areas. OT can be based in hospitals, clinics, schools, or in the home, and each setting brings different responsibilities.

Jennifer L. Tucci, Occupational Therapist, Assistive Technology Evaluator
Senior Occupational Therapist
Queens College, 1997
Major: Psychology

What was your first job after graduation?

I worked for the New York City Board of Education.

What criteria did you use when deciding which colleges to apply to?

Academic reputation was very important to me.

What was your first choice school?

For undergrad, Queens College was my first choice.

What career did you have in mind when you applied to college?

I just knew that I wanted to work within the medical field.

How did the school you attended have an impact on your career choice and opportunities?

It helped me feel confident that I possessed a strong knowledge base in the career field that I wanted to pursue.

Do you now wish you had attended a different school? Which one and why?

I would still pursue Queens College.

Which college or colleges are turning out the leaders in your profession today?

I'm not sure.

Which classes were most valuable in preparing you for your career or in helping you decide on your career?

For undergrad, premed sciences and psychology classes were valuable.

How did your professors impact your career choice or preparation?

They didn't really have much of an impact.

Did you have a job and/or internship during college that influenced your ultimate career choice or career preparation in any way?

I did during grad school. It was in mental health, physical disabilities, and pediatrics. It really helped me determine that this was the right career path for me.

Can you please describe the "Aha!" moment when you realized what you wanted to do?

I didn't have one.

Did you change your major? If so, why?

No, I received my bachelor's degree in psychology, which was applicable to my graduate studies.

How important was your college experience in getting you to where you are today?

I felt very prepared and confident leaving my graduate school due to the foundation I learned there.

Do you have an advanced degree? Is one helpful or required in your field?

I have a master's degree in occupational therapy (OT). It is a requirement for the field.

What do you love most about your job?

Knowing I am trying to help a child who is less fortunate than a typically developing child accomplish a developmental milestone or functional task.

What is the most difficult or challenging aspect of your job?

Knowing that sometimes the smallest change is not enough to enhance the child's life.

What is the biggest misconception people have about what you do?

Either that OT focuses on the upper body (waist up) or I help people find jobs.

What was the biggest obstacle you faced in getting to where you are in your career?

I haven't really faced any big obstacles yet.

What skills are an absolute must for someone interested in pursuing your career?

Therapeutic use of self during interactions, knowing how to interact with others, and the theories and skills to address the patient's goals.

Whom do you admire most in your industry or field?

A general admiration for the therapists who work each day with the children and adults who have progressive, degenerative diseases.

What is one piece of advice you would give to someone who is interested in pursuing your career?

Learn from others and work collaboratively.

If you could do everything all over again, what would you do differently?

Not much. Maybe branch out to be a certified hand therapist.

Do you have any additional comments you think might be helpful to someone hoping to pursue your career?

Volunteer in a variety of settings and observe therapists working with different diagnoses.

Sara Beth Holland, Occupational Therapist
Rehabilitation Supervisor
Belmont University, 1997
Major: Occupational Therapy

What was your first job after graduation?

Staff occupational therapist (OT) at Saint Thomas Hospital.

What criteria did you use when deciding which colleges to apply to?

I looked for a school that had a strong science department, was Christian-affiliated, and that was close to home.

What was your first choice school?

Belmont University was my first choice for my undergraduate studies.

What career did you have in mind when you applied to college?

I was interested in working in the health care field and used my college experience to decide between a career in physical therapy and occupational therapy.

How did the school you attended have an impact on your career choice and opportunities?

It didn't have a very strong impact. Rehabilitation professionals are in high demand, so opportunities are readily available.

Do you now wish you had attended a different school? Which one and why?

I wouldn't change my path. Most careers require postgraduate training, so any undergraduate institution with a good reputation is a good starting point.

Which college or colleges are turning out the leaders in your profession today?

Locally, Belmont is well known and respected for turning out great professionals. I don't have my ears to the market nationally to be able to recommend others. As a supervisor responsible for hiring quality people, I'm more interested in fieldwork experience and how someone interviews than I am in institutional reputation.

Which classes were most valuable in preparing you for your career or in helping you decide on your career?

I enjoyed all my science classes.

How did your professors impact your career choice or preparation?

They didn't have a tremendous impact.

Did you have a job and/or internship during college that influenced your ultimate career choice or career preparation in any way?

No.

Can you please describe the "Aha!" moment when you realized what you wanted to do?

In all honesty, I credit my "Aha!" moment to my religious experiences. I really had not looked into OT or known what it was about, but when it came time to apply to graduate schools, I felt a religious and spiritual direction.

Did you change your major? If so, why?

No.

How important was your college experience in getting you to where you are today?

It was extremely important. I met my husband, established excellent close relationships, and shaped my spiritual development during college.

Do you have an advanced degree? Is one helpful or required in your field?

Yes, and one is required in my field.

What do you love most about your job?

I love making other people's job lives easier and giving my staff the support they need to make a difference.

What is the most difficult or challenging aspect of your job?

Dealing with the diverse personalities, needs, and challenges of my staff and different expectations from management.

What is the biggest misconception people have about what you do?

People sometimes think occupational therapists help you get a job, which can be an obstacle in an acute hospital geriatric setting.

What was the biggest obstacle you faced in getting to where you are in your career?

I feel very blessed to have a strong religious and spiritual direction in my career. I was asked in my interview at Saint Thomas why I chose to apply. I said I didn't choose to; I felt that it was chosen for me.

What skills are an absolute must for someone interested in pursuing your career?

Flexibility, compassion, assertiveness, self-confidence, curiosity, drive, creativity, and resourcefulness.

Whom do you admire most in your industry or field?

Mary Warren. She developed a specialty service provision of OT to the low-vision population and is a well-known and respected individual. She saw a need, developed a program, and pursued and disseminated it to others.

What is one piece of advice you would give to someone who is interested in pursuing your career?

If you keep your priorities in line, you can have a wonderful life experience.

If you could do everything all over again, what would you do differently?

I did my thesis on school setting issues, and I would probably switch my focus to business/management issues, which I am much more interested in. More management-specific education would be very helpful for me in my career path.

Bobbie Holden, Occupational Therapist
Director of Occupational Therapy Services
Texas Tech University, 1993
Major: Occupational Therapy

What was your first job after graduation?

I was an occupational therapist at Abilene State School.

What criteria did you use when deciding which colleges to apply to?

Texas Tech is a large school and has a Health Sciences Center that offers degrees in OT. The proximity and size of city where it was located was important, since I wanted to be with my family.

What was your first choice school?

Texas Tech University was my first choice.

What career did you have in mind when you applied to college?

I was fortunate to know early on what I wanted to do. I was sure I wanted to be an occupational therapist.

How did the school you attended have an impact on your career choice and opportunities?

With my degree, I felt that my opportunities were almost unlimited.

Do you now wish you had attended a different school? Which one and why?

I would probably still attend Texas Tech University Health Sciences Center, which was in the best interest of my family. If I only considered the professional issues, I might have considered University of Texas—San Antonio, as their current curriculum best prepares students for my setting.

Which college or colleges are turning out the leaders in your profession today?

Boston University is one well-known school, but there are many others, depending on the region of the United States where one resides.

Which classes were most valuable in preparing you for your career or in helping you decide on your career?

Anatomy and physiology, gross anatomy, psychology, pediatrics, and human development classes.

How did your professors impact your career choice or preparation?

My pediatrics professors and my gross anatomy instructor (an MD) helped me see the impact of the body and its "backup systems" for compensatory strategies.

Did you have a job and/or internship during college that influenced your ultimate career choice or career preparation in any way?

I worked in a pharmacy during college and had two three-month internships. One was in work hardening and the other was a combination of adult/pediatric physical dysfunction. They both helped me gain valuable real-world experience.

Can you please describe the "Aha!" moment when you realized what you wanted to do?

When I saw how occupational therapy was able to make a difference in my family, I knew this was the right career path for me.

Did you change your major? If so, why?

No, I didn't change.

How important was your college experience in getting you to where you are today?

Both my preparatory work (first two years) at McMurry University in my hometown and the formal occupational therapy program at Texas Tech helped me further broaden my knowledge base in both science and the arts. These programs assured me that I had chosen the correct career path and had the skills to work successfully in a profession that requires the training of a generalist. At Texas Tech, I was educated side by side with physicians in psychiatry, gross anatomy, and pharmacology, while also sharing classes with physical therapy students in neurology, physiology, gross anatomy, and research methods.

Do you have an advanced degree? Is one helpful or required in your field?

I don't have one, but it's now required for all new therapists and would be helpful to me.

What do you love most about your job?

The people I work with/for and diversity of my daily duties are what I love most about my job. Working with the physical therapist and orthotics technician, we create specialized positioning equipment, including custom mobility devices (wheelchairs), fabricate splints and other specialized hand care items—and even create some unique adaptive eating equipment. It is exciting to serve on various committees as an expert in a variety of areas, including activities for learning, increasing vocational opportunities for those who need various adaptations to equipment, creating enhanced sensory environments, and physical and nutritional management.

What is the most difficult or challenging aspect of your job?

Making the most of my time and managing staff issues.

What is the biggest misconception people have about what you do?

Many people have only seen or heard about one dimension of occupational therapy, such as rehab after an accident or illness, and don't know that as an OT, you can write your own job description. Occupational therapy is a wide-open field only limited by the imagination of occupational therapists as to the best means to meet the needs of today's world population in the areas of work, play, and leisure.

What was the biggest obstacle you faced in getting to where you are in your career?

Finding a way to get my education completed while supporting my family as a single mom. It required me to be creative and be willing to accept help from groups and individuals that were ready to invest time and money to help me achieve that goal.

What skills are an absolute must for someone interested in pursuing your career?

The ability to think outside the box and be willing to try new things based on the needs/desires of the person they are working with. Also, having the desire to help all kinds of people to gain/regain control of their own lives through the smallest of steps toward independence.

Whom do you admire most in your industry or field?

Jean Ayers and the many therapists who were willing to advance her thoughts and ideas about the importance sensory systems play in the success or failure of many children who have difficulty in a typical school situation. Through confidence in her clinical observations, diligence in documenting these things, and perseverance, she created a new frame of reference for occupational therapists.

What is one piece of advice you would give to someone who is interested in pursuing your career?

After setting the goal to become an occupational therapist, don't let any obstacle stop you. Finding answers in difficult life situations allows you to practice creative problem solving and prepares you for your career.

If you could do everything all over again, what would you do differently?

I would have gotten my education at an earlier age.

Do you have any additional comments you think might be helpful to someone hoping to pursue your career?

Call occupational therapists in your area and ask to observe their practice and visit with them about this career choice.

Michael Zimerman, Occupational Therapist
Temple University, 1998
Major: Occupational Therapy

What was your first job after graduation?

I worked as an occupational therapist (OT) in the New York public school system.

What criteria did you use when deciding which colleges to apply to?

When applying to schools for OT, I primarily considered the quality and reputation of the program, the location of the program, and my eligibility for scholarships offered by the program.

What was your first choice school?

I attended my first choice school.

What career did you have in mind when you applied to college?

I didn't have one in mind when I applied to undergraduate school, but my college experience helped me to recognize and achieve my goal of becoming an OT.

How did the school you attended have an impact on your career choice and opportunities?

I was exposed to a variety of work settings during my internships. I was introduced to work in public schools during one of my internships, and I've worked in public schools for most of my career.

Do you now wish you had attended a different school? Which one and why?

I would apply to the same colleges.

Which college or colleges are turning out the leaders in your profession today?

There are many, such as Columbia University and NYU. There are now many doctoral-level programs that are also producing leaders in the field.

Which classes were most valuable in preparing you for your career or in helping you decide on your career?

In an OT program, all the courses that are focused on preparing you to work in the field of OT are valuable.

How did your professors impact your career choice or preparation?

I had a close relationship with a few professors who were mentors. Marie Anzlone, ScD, was a professor who inspired me to focus my graduate work and clinical internships on pediatric occupational therapy. I have been working with kids ever since.

Did you have a job and/or internship during college that influenced your ultimate career choice or career preparation in any way?

I had many. A few of them included Jamaica Hospital in Queens, Rusk Rehabilitation Institute in Manhattan, Bellevue Hospital in Manhattan, Saint Vincent's Hospital in Manhattan, and New York City Public Schools. I enjoyed my internship with New York City Public Schools. I was able to continue working in the school where I did my internship after graduating. I was there for almost four years before I moved out of state.

Can you please describe the "Aha!" moment when you realized what you wanted to do?

It was more of a gradual process over several years of realizing that OT was the right career for me to pursue.

Did you change your major? If so, why?

Yes. I was attending graduate school for psychology when I realized that OT offered me more opportunities for work and seemed to match my interests and emerging skills as a therapist better.

How important was your college experience in getting you to where you are today?

To become an occupational therapist, you must attend an accredited program and complete specific educational and training requirements. You are also required to obtain a national certification and/or license by most states to work as an occupational therapist.

Do you have an advanced degree? Is one helpful or required in your field?

Yes, I have an MS in occupational therapy. Beginning in 2007, the minimal educational requirement to become an occupational therapist is a master's degree.

What do you love most about your job?

I like the variety of responsibilities and skills that are required to be successful in my job. I do direct occupational therapy with kids with special needs, provide consultation to staff and family, conduct evaluations, make special equipment and materials for kids, train kids to use various types of assistive technology (low-tech as well as high-tech), and develop and conduct training workshops. This list could go on for quite a while!

What is the most difficult or challenging aspect of your job?

There is a high demand for occupational therapists in the area where I live. Thus, salaries and job stability are good. However, my workload is sometimes difficult to manage. Because of the variety of my responsibilities and the number of kids on my caseload, it is difficult to keep up with everything.

What is the biggest misconception people have about what you do?

The name of my profession often leads people to believe that my work is only about vocational rehabilitation or job training. The looks that people give me are quite funny when they don't know what occupational therapy is and I tell them I work with kids. They must think I want to repeal child labor laws!

What was the biggest obstacle you faced in getting to where you are in your career?

Having the finances to afford graduate school. I was fortunate enough to receive a lot of tuition scholarships. However, I still have considerable student debt load.

What skills are an absolute must for someone interested in pursuing your career?

A broad knowledge of the biological, psychological, social, and cultural functioning of people; an understanding of scientific method and research; specific clinical skills and knowledge related to the practice of occupational therapy; the ability to utilize this professional knowledge base and clinical skills in a creative manner.

Whom do you admire most in your industry or field?

Dr. Jane Case-Smith. She is a big inspiration to me.

What is one piece of advice you would give to someone who is interested in pursuing your career?

Speak with an occupational therapist to find out if OT seems right for you. Contact the American Occupational Therapy Association for information about accredited programs. It is quite competitive to get into an occupational therapy program. Thus, plan for your career early by taking the right courses and maintaining a high GPA.

If you could do everything all over again, what would you do differently?

I might have focused more on pursuing OT earlier in my college career. It took me many years until I discovered that OT was the right career path for me.

PHARMACY

WHY CHOOSE TO BECOME A PHARMACIST?

Pharmacists have a desire to help people and to be involved with their health care decisions. Pharmacists work with doctors and other health care providers to decide on the best medicines to prescribe to patients. They also ensure that patients understand the correct usage, effects, and potential side effects of their medications. Pharmacists also keep track of individual patients' drug therapies to be aware of possible drug interactions. It is important that pharmacists have a good grasp of mathematics and science because they have to understand the composition of drugs, including their chemical, biological, and physical properties.

WHERE THE JOBS ARE

Most pharmacists work in retail drugstores or in health care facilities, such as hospitals or nursing homes. Because of the growing older population and advancements in drug therapies, job opportunities for pharmacists are expected to increase substantially. Job openings currently outpace the number of pharmacy degrees being granted and are expected to continue to do so.

AREAS OF SPECIALTY

Beyond the settings in which pharmacists work (hospitals, retail pharmacies, etc.), some specialize in different drug therapies, including intravenous nutrition support, cancer treatment, nuclear pharmacy (used for chemotherapy), geriatric pharmacy, and psychopharmacotherapy (the treatment of mental disorders through drugs).

EDUCATIONAL REQUIREMENTS

The bachelor of pharmacy (B.Pharm.) degree has been replaced by the Doctor of Pharmacy (Pharm.D.) degree, which requires at least six years of postsecondary education. In addition, every state requires that pharmacists be licensed. To obtain a license, students must graduate from an accredited college of pharmacy and pass an exam that tests pharmacy skills and knowledge. Most states also require that students pass an additional exam that tests pharmacy law. A PhD in pharmacy is also available, mainly to those who want to teach pharmacy or conduct research for drug companies.

SALARY RANGE

The median salary for pharmacists in 2004 was $84,900.

Pros: Helping people, high salary

Cons: Dealing with increasingly complicated insurance paperwork, possibly erratic hours

FAMOUS PHARMACISTS

- Before he joined the military, **Benedict Arnold** was a pharmacist.

WHERE TO LEARN MORE

American Association of Colleges of Pharmacy
1426 Prince Street
Alexandria, VA 22314
(703) 739-2330; fax: (703) 836-8982
www.aacp.org

American Pharmacists Association
2215 Constitution Avenue NW
Washington, DC 20037-2985
www.aphanet.org

WORDS OF WISDOM

"I have had many mentors that have instilled a passion for the profession of pharmacy. Many of them helped to instill this in me, as well as instilling in me the importance to stay involved with our profession and to stay involved in the community itself."

—Jennifer L. Tucci, Occupational Therapist

"Don't go into it because you didn't get into medical school or because of the money. Understand the profession and the history. Become a pharmacist because you want to impact patients."

—Kristen Binaso, Director or Strategic Alliances and Business Development

Rick Sain, Pharmacist
Owner/President, Reeves-Sain Drug Store, Inc.
University of Tennessee, 1989
Major: Doctor of Pharmacy

What was your first job after graduation?

My current job.

What criteria did you use when deciding which colleges to apply to?

I wanted to go to a college in Tennessee for in-state tuition.

What career did you have in mind when you applied to college?

At first, agriculture, because I grew up on a farm. I soon realized after taking a part-time job at a local chain pharmacy that pharmacy is what I would pursue.

How did the school you attended impact on your career choice and opportunities

I was in the second class to go all Pharm.D., instead of a B.S. This added an extra year, which was mainly clinical training, and this better prepared me for the future of pharmacy. It also gave me the opportunity to find the job that I have now.

Do you now wish you had attended a different school?

No, the University of Tennessee College of Pharmacy (UTCP) has been ranked in the top ten schools for several years, and I am glad that I had the opportunity to go there.

Which college or colleges are turning out the leaders in your profession today?

Obviously, I am biased to UTCP. There are several deans of colleges of pharmacy around the nation that are UTCP graduates. Our current dean at UTCP has just been elected to the American Pharmacists Association (APhA) Board of Trustees. The president-elect of the APhA is a UTCP graduate. I am currently president of the Tennessee Pharmacists Association (TPA). I could go on and on. I am not sure about other states, but there are a lot of good schools out there.

Can you please describe the "Aha!" moment when you realized what you wanted to do?

It was while working in a chain pharmacy as a clerk/technician. I realized this was a much better profession than being a farmer, which is all I had ever known. I share this story with many students. My points here are that you never know what may lie ahead for you. Take all the classes in different areas that you can so you can be ready for whatever does lie ahead. Also, I recommend getting experience in your field of interest to be sure it is what you want to do.

Which classes were most valuable in preparing you for your career or in helping you decide on your career?

Biology, chemistry, organic chemistry, physics, mathematics.

How did your professors impact your career choice or preparation?

I had many who were a positive influence, simply letting me know that I could do it.

Did you have a job and/or internship during college that influenced your career choice or career preparation in any way?

Yes, I worked for a chain, Revco Drugs, for a while, then later, Super X Drugs, which both later became CVS. As I went through school, I soon realized that I wanted to be a community pharmacist and later, an independent retail pharmacist, in particular.

Do you have an advanced degree? Is one helpful or required in your field?

Yes, a doctor of pharmacy, which is all that is offered now. It used to be a BS degree.

What do you love most about your job?

I love helping people. I love the aspect of helping people with their health. I also love the entrepreneurial business side of owning my own operation.

What is the most difficult or challenging aspect of your job?

Dealing with insurance. Patients have a hard time understanding their insurance, so we spend a lot of time working on their insurance rather than their health. Also, the reimbursement continues to get lower and lower.

What is the biggest misconception people have about what you do?

People think that we simply put their pills in a bottle. Technicians do that. We work on monitoring the patient's drug therapy. We do cholesterol screening. We give immunizations. We compound medications that are customized for patients. We consult with our patients one-on-one to talk about their medications and their health issues.

What was the biggest obstacle you faced in getting to where you are in your career?

The biggest obstacle for me, in particular, was not having any business background. You have to take so many sciences to get through school as a student, but you do not get the business aspect. I have had to learn as I go, but have also surrounded myself with good people.

What skills are an absolute must for someone interested in pursuing your career?

A good background in the sciences. It helps to have good people skills as well.

Whom do you admire most in your industry or field? Why?

I have had many mentors that have such a passion for the profession of pharmacy. Many of them helped to instill this in me, as well as instilling in me the importance of staying involved with our profession and staying involved in the community itself.

What is one piece of advice you would give to someone who is interested in pursuing your career?

First of all, go to work somewhere to see if it is really something you want to do and investigate all of the different areas of pharmacy that are out there.

If you could do everything all over again, what would you do differently?

I would have taken more business classes early in my education.

Can you please add any additional comments you think might be helpful to someone hoping to pursue your career?

Currently, there is a shortage of pharmacists. This has caused the salaries to go up. So know that if you like health care and you like working with people, you can make a good living and that there are numerous opportunities within our profession that are worth exploring.

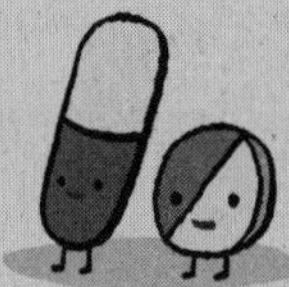

Kristen Binaso, Pharmacist

Director, Strategic Alliances and Business Development, American Pharmacists Association

Rutgers University College of Pharmacy, 1997

Major: Pharmacy

What was your first job after graduation?

Staff pharmacist, CVS Pharmacy.

What criteria did you use when deciding which colleges to apply to?

Ones that had my major of pharmacy.

How did the school you attended impact on your career choice and opportunities

Rutgers University College of Pharmacy (RUCP) was an in-state school, which had lower tuition, and it was highly ranked for its pharmacy program.

Which college or colleges are turning out the leaders in your profession today?

This has changed dramatically. I can't say that there is one specific college that has turned out the leaders in pharmacy—it is more of a collaborative effort.

Can you please describe the "Aha!" moment when you realized what you wanted to do?

When I took a job in my local pharmacy when I was 16.

Which classes were most valuable in preparing you for your career or in helping you decide on your career?

My rotations in pharmacy school solidified my belief that I wanted to be a community pharmacist.

How did your professors impact your career choice or preparation?

My professors taught us a level of organization that I incorporate in my life. You had to be able to juggle 18 to 20 credits in pharmacology, physiology, medicinal chemistry, and therapeutics. They all overlapped each other, and we had tests every week so you had to be organized.

Did you have a job and/or internship during college that influenced your career choice or career preparation in any way?

I was a pharmacy technician.

What do you love most about your job?

That I am helping educate people and changing the profession, which will hopefully lead to better patient care.

What is the most difficult or challenging aspect of your job?

Saying no and not being able to take care of everything on a daily basis.

What is the biggest misconception people have about what you do?

That it is very easy to get funding for projects.

What was the biggest obstacle you faced in getting to where you are in your career?

Not getting intimidated—by being passionate about my job.

What skills are an absolute must for someone interested in pursuing your career?

Communication, political savvy, tact, ability to think out of the box.

Whom do you admire most in your industry or field? Why?

I admire the staff pharmacists who work every day because they are the people that truly deliver patient care day in and out. We have a chance to make a change in how that person feels!

What is one piece of advice you would give to someone who is interested in pursuing your career?

Don't go into it because you didn't get into medical school or because of the money. Understand the profession and the history. Become a pharmacist because you want to impact patients.

Can you please add any additional comments you think might be helpful to someone hoping to pursue your career?

Pharmacy is not limited to just the community environment. There are many facets that include hospital, consultant (pharmacists who work in long-term care), nuclear, federal (VA and U.S. Public Health Service), as well as management opportunities with retailers.

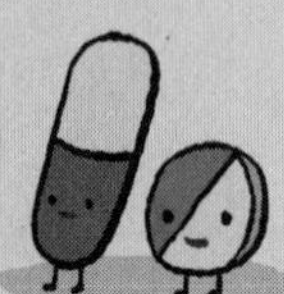

Tim J. Gallagher, Pharmacist
VP Pharmacy Operations, Astrup Drug
South Dakota State University College of Pharmacy, 1985
Major: Pharmacy

What was your first job after graduation?

Pharmacist at Lewis Drug in Huron, South Dakota.

What criteria did you use when deciding which colleges to apply to?

Reputation, location, size of enrollment.

What was your first choice school?

Creighton University.

What career did you have in mind when you applied to college?

Pharmacy.

How did the school you attended impact on your career choice and opportunities

It helped reinforce my decision to become a pharmacist and probably influenced my decision to stay in the Midwest.

Which college or colleges are turning out the leaders in your profession today?

University of Minnesota, University of California—San Francisco, University of the Pacific.

Can you please describe the "Aha!" moment when you realized what you wanted to do?

I didn't really have an "Aha!" moment. I realized in high school that I wanted to be in a health care profession, and I was always intrigued by pharmaceuticals.

Which classes were most valuable in preparing you for your career or in helping you decide on your career?

Chemistry, especially organic chemistry, and biology.

How did your professors impact your career choice or preparation?

Actually my professors encouraged me to go to medical school, which I resisted.

Did you have a job and/or internship during college that influenced your career choice or career preparation in any way?

I worked for two summers during my early college years in a retail pharmacy.

Do you have an advanced degree? Is one helpful or required in your field?

I do not, but it is mandatory now.

What do you love most about your job?

The constant learning and supervising people.

What is the most difficult or challenging aspect of your job?

Managing people, recruiting pharmacists, and firing employees.

What is the biggest misconception people have about what you do?

They don't realize how much driving I do or how many hours I work.

What was the biggest obstacle you faced in getting to where you are in your career?

Paying for college and handling the stress. You have to know when to quit working and find hobbies and a life outside of work. My wife helps a lot.

What skills are an absolute must for someone interested in pursuing your career?

Communication, planning, and organization.

What is one piece of advice you would give to someone who is interested in pursuing your career?

You have to care about patients.

If you could do everything all over again, what would you do differently?

I would finish my MBA.

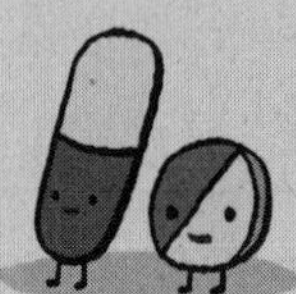

Melinda C. Joyce, Hospital Pharmacist
Corporate Director of Pharmacy, The Medical Center
University of Kentucky, 1982
Major: Pharmacy

What was your first job after graduation?

Pharmacist.

What criteria did you use when deciding which colleges to apply to?

I looked at majors offered, reputation of the school, class size, extracurricular activities, and cost.

What was your first choice school?

Centre College (CC) in Danville, Kentucky, where I attended for two years and then transferred to the University of Kentucky for pharmacy school.

What career did you have in mind when you applied to college?

When I applied to college, I knew that I wanted to be a pharmacist. By attending a liberal arts college, I was keeping my options open. My actual declared major at Centre College was a mathematics major.

How did the school you attended impact on your career choice and opportunities

Attending a private, liberal arts college definitely impacted my career choice. CC is well recognized nationally for its academic programs. There was a highly competitive atmosphere along with a keen desire for excellence. The study skills that I learned at CC were a major advantage once I entered pharmacy school. Plus, my pre-pharmacy work was not just science and mathematics, which has allowed me to have some background in a broad range of topics.

Do you now wish you had attended a different school?

No. I did transfer to the University of Kentucky (UK) after two years at CC in order to attend pharmacy school. I have regretted not graduating from CC, but once I knew that I wanted to attend pharmacy school and had the necessary prerequisites, it was prudent to go ahead and move forward with my chosen profession. My regret stems from not graduating from one of the best small liberal arts colleges in the United States.

Which college or colleges are turning out the leaders in your profession today?

In pharmacy, there are several colleges that are turning out leaders. I am proud to be a graduate of the University of Kentucky College of Pharmacy. It has had many pharmacy leaders and has been consistently ranked in the top ten schools of pharmacy. Other prominent colleges of pharmacy would include University of North Carolina, University of Minnesota, and University of Florida.

Can you please describe the "Aha!" moment when you realized what you wanted to do?

I remember visiting my older brother while he was working in a local independent pharmacy. I was fascinated by the many bottles of medications that were behind the pharmacy counter and what types of illness they would treat. I thought that knowing about those medications and how to help patients would be very interesting work. That "Aha!" moment came while I was in high school and it is still there to this day.

Did you change your major? If so, why?

At CC, there was not a pharmacy school or a pre-pharmacy major. My initial major was mathematics. Once I transferred to UK, my pharmacy major did not change.

Which classes were most valuable in preparing you for your career or in helping you decide on your career?

The science classes were most helpful in preparing for a career in pharmacy since so much that occurs with medication therapy is scientifically studied. Mathematics classes were helpful for teaching me how to think methodically and logically. I also think that some of the liberal arts classes, such as art and literature, helped to make me not just a "mathematics nerd" but more of a well-rounded individual.

How did your professors impact your career choice or preparation?

The professors at UKCP were influential in preparing me as a pharmacist. More importantly, there were professors who instilled a sense of professionalism that I have never lost. These individuals stressed that patient care is of paramount importance. They also showed that one of the ways to impact patient care is to be actively involved with your professional organizations. That is a key part of my daily activities, and I owe that involvement to certain professors.

Did you have a job and/or internship during college that influenced your career choice or career preparation in any way?

Not really. I had several excellent internships while in pharmacy school. Although my main practice setting is in an institution, I have worked in many types of pharmacy positions. Perhaps the fact that I have had multiple positions is because my internships were good and I enjoyed working in many types of pharmacy practice.

Do you have an advanced degree? Is one helpful or required in your field?

Yes and no. When I graduated from pharmacy school, a Pharm.D. degree was considered an advanced degree. Today, it is the entry-level degree from pharmacy school. Other advanced degrees or residencies can be beneficial but are not required at this time.

What do you love most about your job?

As corporate director of pharmacy, I enjoy developing and implementing new programs that have a positive impact on patient care. I like to see what new trends are in health care and then how the pharmacy departments that I oversee can have a key role in these new trends.

What is the most difficult or challenging aspect of your job?

The most challenging part of my job is dealing with the personnel issues that arise. I have direct supervision of more than 60 employees, and there are always personnel issues! I find these challenging because you want to do the right thing for the employee, but patient care must be considered. I believe that it takes time away from more important functions that are more enjoyable.

What is the biggest misconception people have about what you do?

I don't think that most people realize how important a hospital pharmacist is to patient care. A pharmacist in a hospital is usually not a frontline person that a hospital patient or their family deals with directly on a daily basis. But that hospital pharmacist is constantly checking medication orders, discussing medication therapy with physicians and nurses, and ensuring safe medication usage. This is a critical role, and making sure that this critical role is done safely and consistently is my job.

What was the biggest obstacle you faced in getting to where you are in your career?

The biggest obstacle that I have faced was a good obstacle. Because I like so many different types of pharmacy practice, I have worked in a variety of practice settings. The obstacle was learning to say no and to determine what was most important for me. In the past, I would work in the hospital pharmacy while working extra at a community pharmacy and teaching some nursing classes. After a time, I determined that I was not being as effective in any of the positions as I should be. It was necessary for me to determine what was most important and where I should focus.

What skills are an absolute must for someone interested in pursuing your career?

To be a pharmacist, a person must have an interest in mathematics and science, as well as a desire to be part of a team of health care providers. The person must be able to communicate effectively—and a good sense of humor doesn't hurt! To be in an administrative role requires looking at health care globally and then determining how pharmacy fits into that global picture.

Whom do you admire most in your industry or field? Why?

I admire many people in pharmacy: Gloria Niemeyer Francke because she started her career in pharmacy when there were not many women. She was not at all afraid to work in a man's world and to be very successful. She is a role model to many women in pharmacy. John Gans, as executive vice president and CEO of the American Pharmacists Association (APhA), he lives and breathes pharmacy. He is a passionate advocate of how important pharmacists and pharmacy are to patient care. Susan Winckler is a pharmacist who has been extremely active in pharmacy association work and is now working for the FDA. She sees the big picture of health care and how pharmacy can be a key part. Her career has tremendous potential because she is young.

What is one piece of advice you would give to someone who is interested in pursuing your career?

Pharmacy is extremely rewarding! But it is important to pursue what you really want to do. I would not recommend that someone go into pharmacy for the money or for convenient work schedules. A person that wants to be a pharmacist must do it because of wanting to positively impact that patient's health care.

If you could do everything all over again, what would you do differently?

I would probably pay a little bit more attention in school. There were some subjects or topics that I thought (at the time) weren't important, such as some of the business classes. I have since learned that these subjects are important, and I have had to learn them after I graduated.

Can you please add any additional comments you think might be helpful to someone hoping to pursue your career?

I am very proud to be a pharmacist. I would tell anyone with an interest in pharmacy to keep their mind open about their career path. Look at all areas with an interest to learn and then see what interests you the most. Many people are surprised where they may end up.

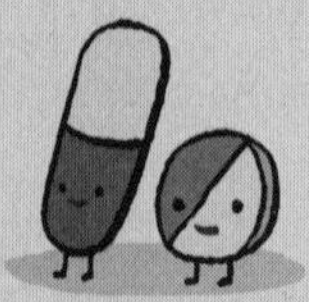

Marlin Weekley, Pharmacist
President, Dot Drug Inc.
St. Louis College of Pharmacy, 1975
Major: Chemistry

What was your first job after graduation?

Pharmacist.

What criteria did you use when deciding which colleges to apply to?

Location and affordability.

What was your first choice school?

St. Louis College of Pharmacy.

What career did you have in mind when you applied to college?

Pharmacist; I wanted to be the owner of an independent pharmacy.

Can you please describe the "Aha!" moment when you realized what you wanted to do?

I was 18 years old and working in the drugstore in my hometown. I had always been fascinated with science and chemistry. I learned from a young pharmacist working with me that pharmacy was all about chemistry and also provided a good income. But I was stuck on the people. I enjoy the people who come into the pharmacy each day and the friendships this allows. I now own four pharmacies and can honesty say I have friends in four counties. I can drive a 60-mile circle from home and tell you who lives in many of the houses or who owns which businesses. Life is good.

Which classes were most valuable in preparing you for your career or in helping you decide on your career?

Chemistry.

Did you have a job and/or internship during college that influenced your career choice or career preparation in any way?

There was nothing formal in those days, just my early work experience in the local drugstore.

What do you love most about your job?

The freedom to run my own business and the friends I have made out of my customers.

What is the most difficult or challenging aspect of your job?

Government regulation, decreasing profit margins, and cash flow.

What is the biggest misconception people have about what you do?

Many believe that pharmacists simply move medicine from big bottles to little bottles, like that Jerry Seinfeld comedy skit.

What was the biggest obstacle you faced in getting to where you are in your career?

Poverty, overcome by hard work and long hours. Some say I was always in the "right place at the right time." The secret: make the right place for yourself and spend a helluva lot of time there.

What skills are an absolute must for someone interested in pursuing your career?

People skills. In short, you must like people, to be happy and fulfilled in the profession of pharmacy. If you don't like people you will be miserable.

Whom do you admire most in your industry or field? Why?

There are many people who come to mind, but honestly I would have to say my wife. She is a pharmacist too and runs one of our busier stores. She is completely committed to her patients (friends) and her practice and does a consistently professional job.

What is one piece of advice you would give to someone who is interested in pursuing your career?

Like science. Love people. Embrace competition. Start early.

If you could do everything all over again, what would you do differently?

Absolutely nothing! I have had and currently have the perfect career and life!

Can you please add any additional comments you think might be helpful to someone hoping to pursue your career?

It's not about you; if it is, you won't be happy.

SPEECH LANGUAGE PATHOLOGY AND AUDIOLOGY

SPEAK
HEAR
S

WHY CHOOSE A CAREER IN SPEECH LANGUAGE PATHOLOGY AND AUDIOLOGY?

Speech-language pathologists and audiologists perform very important work. They enjoy the challenge of working with people with disabilities and the opportunity to establish meaningful relationships with them. Through their dedication and expertise, they help speech- and hearing-impaired individuals who have felt isolated by their disabilities to be understood by others and to communicate their thoughts and ideas freely and clearly.

WHERE THE JOBS ARE

About half of all speech-language pathologists are employed in educational services, primarily in elementary and secondary schools. They collaborate with teachers, special educators, and parents in developing and implementing programs. Others are employed in hospitals, nursing homes, and home health care services. A number are self-employed in private practice, where they contract their services to schools, physicians' offices, or hospitals or work as consultants in various industries.

More than half of all audiologists work in health care facilities (e.g., physicians' offices, hospitals, and outpatient care centers). About 13 percent work in elementary and secondary schools. Others work in health and personal care stores, including hearing aid stores. A small number work in private practice, providing hearing services in their own offices or working under contract for schools or health care facilities.

AREAS OF SPECIALTY

Speech-language pathologists work with people who cannot produce speech sounds or cannot produce them clearly, individuals with rhythm problems like stuttering, people who wish to modify an accent, and others with cognitive communication impairments, such as attention and memory disorders.

With increased clinical experience and continuing education, many speech-language pathologists develop expertise with certain age groups, such as preschoolers or adolescents, or with certain disorders, such as dysphasia or aphasia. Some may obtain board recognition in a specialty area, such as child language, fluency, or feeding and swallowing.

Audiologists examine and identify those who have hearing, balance, and related ear problems.

Many specialize in working with people of all ages, from children to the elderly. Others develop and implement ways to protect workers' hearing from on-the-job injuries by measuring noise levels in workplaces and by conducting hearing-protection programs.

EDUCATIONAL REQUIREMENTS

Most speech-language pathologist jobs require a master's degree. In 2007, 47 states regulated speech-language pathologists through licensure or registration. A passing score on the national examination on speech-language pathology, offered through the Praxis Series of the Educational Testing Service, is required. Other requirements include 300–375 hours of supervised clinical experience and nine months of postgraduate professional clinical experience.

In audiology, individuals must have at least a master's degree to qualify for a job, and a doctoral degree is becoming more common. The professional doctorate in audiology (AuD) requires eight years of university training and supervised professional experience.

In all 50 states, audiologists are regulated by licensure or registration. States set requirements for education, such as mandating a master's or doctoral degree, as well as other requirements. In some states, specific certifications from professional associations satisfy some or all of the requirements for state licensure. Certification can be obtained by earning the certificate of clinical competence in audiology (CCC-A), offered by ASHA and the American Board of Audiology.

SALARY RANGE

In May 2006, the median annual earnings of speech-language pathologists were $57,710. The middle 50 percent earned between $46,360 and $72,410. The lowest 10 percent earned less than $37,970, and the highest 10 percent earned more than $90,400.

In May 2006, the median annual earnings of audiologists were $57,120. The middle 50 percent earned between $47,220 and $70,940. The lowest 10 percent earned less than $38,370, and the highest 10 percent earned more than $89,160.

FAMOUS SPECIAL LANGUAGE PATHOLOGISTS AND AUDIOLOGISTS

- **Dr. Wendell Johnson** (1906–1965) was a prominent American psychologist, speech pathologist, and author. Considered one of the earliest and most influential speech pathologists in the field, he spent most of his life trying to find the cause of and cure for stuttering through teaching, research, and scholarly writing. A stutterer himself, he spent much of his time promoting the need for speech pathologists to schools, the Veterans Administration, and other institutions. He played a major role in the creation ASHA.
- **Dr. Mark Ross**, a principal investigator of the Rehabilitation Engineering Research Center on Hearing Enhancement and a professor emeritus of audiology from the University of Connecticut, has worn a hearing aid for almost 50 years. He writes a regular column for *Hearing Loss Magazine* called "Developments in Research and Technology" and has published and lectured extensively on topics dealing with hearing loss.

WHERE TO LEARN MORE

Speech-language pathology:

SpeechPathology.com

5282 Medical Drive, Suite 150

San Antonio, TX 78229

(800) 242-5183

www.speechpathology.com

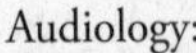

Audiology:

American Board of Audiology

11730 Plaza America Drive, Suite 300

Reston, VA 20190

(800) 881-5410

www.americanboardofaudiology.org

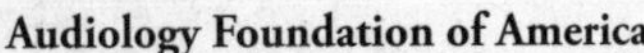

Audiology Foundation of America

8 N. 3rd Street, Suite 406

Lafayette, IN 47901

(765) 743-6283

www.audfound.org

Both speech-language pathology and audiology:

American Speech-Language-Hearing Association (ASHA)

2200 Research Boulevard.

Rockville, MD 20850

(800) 638-8255

www.asha.org

National Student Speech Language Hearing Association (NSSLHA)

2200 Research Boulevard. #450

Rockville, MD 20850

(301) 296-8705

www.nsslha.org

WORDS OF WISDOM

"What I love most about my job are the relationships established with some of my students and the fact that some of my students develop friendships in the speech group setting that may not have been formed had they never had speech together."

—Karen Farrugio,
Speech Improvement Teacher

"Establish yourself as a diligent and compassionate professional who is consistently learning to meet patient's needs."

—Debra Drysdale,
Speech Language Pathologist

Stacey Wilson, Speech-Language Pathologist
East Carolina University, 2002
Major: Communication Sciences and Disorders

What was your first job after graduation?

A speech-language pathologist.

What criteria did you use when deciding which colleges to apply to?

I knew that I wanted to be a speech-language pathologist (SLP). I wanted to find a school that was reputable in, and actually had, my major. I researched the schools in which I was interested and narrowed down my search for undergraduate work. I also knew that I did not want to leave North Carolina.

What was your first choice school?

I attended my first choice school.

What career did you have in mind when you applied to college?

I knew that I wanted to be a speechlanguage pathologist.

How did the school you attended have an impact on your career choice and opportunities?

ECU's Speech and Hearing Sciences program offered education about the normal processes of speech, hearing, and language, along with other academic areas of interest. I knew that my undergraduate studies would ultimately lead to a master's degree. My internship and externships in graduate school helped me become certain that I wanted to practice in the school setting. I worked with adults and did not feel the calling as I did when working with children. I appreciate having had the opportunity to work in a variety of settings in graduate school so that I could feel more confident with my long-term setting choice.

Do you now wish you had attended a different school? Which one and why?

I would apply to and attend the same schools. I feel that the education I received at both schools truly prepared me for the workforce today.

Which college or colleges are turning out the leaders in your profession today?

ECU remains one of only two schools in North Carolina to have a PhD program in communication sciences and disorders. Also, Andrew Stuart, PhD; Joseph Kalinowski, PhD; and Michael Rastatter, PhD, in the Department of Communication Sciences and Disorders at ECU, developed the SpeechEasy device, which has changed a number of lives for people who stutter.

Which classes were most valuable in preparing you for your career or in helping you decide on your career?

All of the classes in my major prepared me for my job. The ones with the most impact on which setting I wanted to practice in would have to be clinical.

How did your professors impact your career choice or preparation?

Ms. Meta Downes at ECU was a wonderful teacher and advisor. She showed genuine care and concern for her students. She was another arrow that pointed me towards education. Dr. Virginia Hinton at UNC—Greensboro was outstanding! She is a lifelong learner and wanted to show everyone else how to enjoy learning as much as she did. She instilled in me the desire to attend as many continuing education events as possible. Through them, I learned that even though the nursing home paid more, I personally would rather be in a school system with children.

Did you have a job and/or internship during college that influenced your ultimate career choice or career preparation in any way?

I had various jobs not relating to my career during undergraduate school (CVS pharmacy tech, inventory for car dealerships). However, I found a job working as a habilitation technician for a child with Down syndrome all throughout graduate school. My internships/externships were during graduate school. I assisted in UNC—Greensboro's clinic one year, a nursing home one semester, and a school another semester. I continued to work as a habilitation technician during my externships as well.

Can you please describe the "Aha!" moment when you realized what you wanted to do?

When he was three years old, my brother had severe speech/language errors that caused almost everyone to not understand him. At 7, I was his interpreter, even for my parents at times. He went to Ms. Karen for a year, and she helped him to correct phonological processes, articulation errors, incorrect use of pronouns, and stuttering. I knew then that I wanted to be able to make that kind of a difference. I feel I have always known that I wanted to work with children, and as I continued to watch old home videos, I saw what an impact Ms. Karen had on my brother (no more speech/language errors to this day, 20 years later).

Did you change your major? If so, why?

No.

How important was your college experience in getting you to where you are today?

My education was very important for the fundamentals of what my job would entail. The internships/externships helped to focus those skills a little more, but you can never be completely prepared for what you may face in the real-life situation.

Do you have an advanced degree? Is one helpful or required in your field?

Yes, I do, in addition to the master's degree. A master's degree is required in order for me to practice solely. If I did not obtain my master's degree, I would have been allowed to be a speech-language pathology assistant. The advanced degree that I received in graduate school allowed me to take extra classes and receive a monthly incentive in my paycheck!

What do you love most about your job?

The children, hands down! They are the reason for coming to work every day. You get to see them progress in leaps and bounds, and you feel as though you have made a difference. When they come running up in the hallway to give hugs, I feel special. Most parents are also extremely supportive. I have had parents thank me for helping their child to communicate. The child used to be hesitant to talk or would become frustrated due to numerous articulation errors that significantly decreased intelligibility. One cried because her child could finally say his name correctly. That in itself is a reward enough for the long hours and huge workload.

What is the most difficult or challenging aspect of your job?

When a child does not make the progress you would expect. That is hard on the child, the parents, and the SLP. You do what you can, but some children, despite their best efforts, cannot attain the skills you teach.

What is the biggest misconception people have about what you do?

Many people think that all I do is tell children to say "ring" instead of "wing." However, speech-language pathology encompasses all areas of speech and language. We work on articulation/phonology (organization of phonemes), morphology (units of meaning), syntax (wordorder/grammar), semantics (wordmeanings/relationships), and pragmatics (social function of language). I also work closely with our exceptional children teacher to form collaborative IEPs so that our goals go hand-in-hand.

What was the biggest obstacle you faced in getting to where you are in your career?

The biggest obstacle was the competitiveness of the college programs. At the end of sophomore year at ECU, you have to apply to get into the undergrad program. Two years later, you apply for grad school. I actually had to take one of my undergrad classes over because I received a C. I took the class again, received a B, and then was accepted into the Communication Sciences and Disorders (CSDI) program.

What skills are an absolute must for someone interested in pursuing your career?

You absolutely have to have patience! The workload (not just caseload) can be stressful. The children can be restless, and the parents can be exasperating. You also have to have the ability to love and adapt. Children are innocent. They may not always learn the way you think they should, so you have to teach them using other means. That is, after all, the reason they come to you in the first place. If they learned the same as typically developing peers, you'd be out of a job.

Whom do you admire most in your industry or field?

All of the people who stick with the job in the public school system. They are often overworked and underpaid, yet they put the needs of the children first.

What is one piece of advice you would give to someone who is interested in pursuing your career?

Go for it! I love my job! Sure, everyone has off days, but it's never boring around here. You have to be a lifelong learner. You must acquire your continuing education units

(CEUs) and maintain state and/or national certification, which requires attendance at workshops or other conferences discussing the latest developments in speech/language.

If you could do everything all over again, what would you do differently?

I can honestly say that I am satisfied. I considered a PhD in SLP, but I couldn't be in school any longer at the time due to my Teaching Fellows scholarship and its stipulations about loan repayment.

Melanie Herzfeld, Audiologist
Lehman College, 1971
Major: Audiology

What was your first job after graduation?

Once I obtained my MA, I worked for the Association for the Help of Retarded Children (AHRC).

What criteria did you use when deciding which colleges to apply to?

Originally for my bachelor's, I did not have much choice since I went to college right after 11th grade, and my parents would not sign a consent for a loan. Therefore, I could go to Hunter (Bronx campus, which became Lehman in my senior year) or another CUNY school.

What was your first choice school?

I wanted to go away and had applications to several schools, but since I was underage, I needed parental approval. I did not attend my first choice school, but it was purely a financial decision.

What career did you have in mind when you applied to college?

I was thinking of a career in medicine or math.

How did the school you attended have an impact on your career choice and opportunities?

There was not the variety available to me at my school, so my career choice was somewhat limited on an undergrad basis.

Do you now wish you had attended a different school? Which one and why?

I really felt I missed having the camaraderie that a dorm school would have given. I would have selected Barnard or Vassar for undergrad, and that might have changed my graduate choices, including my major. I more or less picked a major just to put something on paper, not out of a burning desire to achieve. Perhaps I am mistaken, but from observing my daughters' education, I think that colleges today can offer a lot more in the way of career planning than what I experienced, and I wished that I'd had that.

Which college or colleges are turning out the leaders in your profession today?

Central Michigan for sure. University of Florida as well. As the residential programs get more time under their belts, there will be others assuming outstanding positions. For now, the field is split between those who obtained degrees from distance education (already had MA/MS and went back to school for the doctoral level degree) and those new graduates who must have a doctoral level degree as entry level.

Which classes were most valuable in preparing you for your career or in helping you decide on your career?

I became a speech and hearing major for all the wrong reasons! I was put off by the looks of the women in the other departments, and I was very immature. I actually became a speech and hearing major because the instructors wore attractive clothing and were well groomed. But I enjoyed audiology more than speech in general, and so the hearing science courses were the most appealing to me.

How did your professors impact your career choice or preparation?

When it came time to go for my master's, I had been accepted into a school and given a scholarship, but they insisted I quit a particularly interesting and well-paid part-time job in a school for special needs children. I was hesitant to do that because jobs in the field at that time were scarce, and so I wound up at another college for my degree. At that school, the head of the speech department told me I would have to quit my job, while the head of the audiology department said I could keep it—thus an audiologist was born!

Did you have a job and/or internship during college that influenced your ultimate career choice or career preparation in any way?

As an undergraduate, I worked at various jobs, including one for the speech department, one for a home and pottery shop, and another for a supermarket. Graduate school provided me with an internship for which I taught courses at Queens College and had required placements at hospitals and clinics each semester. While pursuing my doctorate, I was working full-time as the director of audiology for a large, multispecialty medical group.

The various placements gave me experience in a variety of audiology encounters so that I was able to work with the young and old, do electrophysiological testing, as well as work with hearing aids. In those days, one did not dispense hearing aids, so except for dispensing, I had a well-rounded experience. It made it easy for me to take on paid positions requiring a variety of abilities.

Can you please describe the "Aha!" moment when you realized what you wanted to do?

The only "Aha!" moment for me came when I decided that leaving a multispecialty medical group to open a shared practice with some of the physicians with whom I worked was going to be a great idea. Private practice is not for everyone, but for me it has been satisfying.

Did you change your major? If so, why?

I changed it many times. I could not find my niche and did not get good advice from advisors—but I cannot fault the system. In those days, if you did not know what to ask, it was problematic. And so for me, selecting a major was like looking at the Ouija board, rather than having presentations or career placement activities. In fact, I know that my husband took placement tests as a routine part of his college experience, but I do not even know if my school offered anything like that.

How important was your college experience in getting you to where you are today?

Without the college experience, I would not be in audiology. So I guess I would have to give it a 1. Not that I have not learned things along the way, but I felt like it was being on a train—once you picked your major, took your courses, you just kept going, and thus you had to run with the ball. Failure was not an option. As for specific things, one thing I can say is that there was not the choice of electives available then as today, so you did not specialize—you had to learn it all.

Obviously, without the specialization that is so rampant today, one gained as much as possible in all facets. Today the graduates are able to pick and choose which areas interest them the most. So for example, you might choose neonatal audiology and work on infant screenings or testing and become a pediatric audiologist with board certification in that. Or you might become a specialist in intraoperative monitoring. The choices are myriad.

Do you have an advanced degree? Is one helpful or required in your field?

Yes, I do, and it is a requirement in this field.

What do you love most about your job?

Diversity of the population and being my own boss!

What is the most difficult or challenging aspect of your job?

Worrying about finances and/or dealing with insurance issues and reimbursement.

What is the biggest misconception people have about what you do?

That it is easy and/or that anyone can do it.

What was the biggest obstacle you faced in getting to where you are in your career?

Getting up the courage to leave a salaried position for a private practice. Eventually, I just needed to do it for a multitude of reasons. Once I made the decision, it was just a question of satisfying the requirements of physical space and equipment.

What skills are an absolute must for someone interested in pursuing your career?

Outstanding people skills, caring and concern for those who are unable to hear, and the ability to multitask.

Whom do you admire most in your industry or field?

It's hard to pick just one person. Jerry Church, Paul Pessis, Therese Walden, Kris English, and Pat Kricos come to mind. But it is actually the plain old audiologist who works as hard as she/he can who is most inspirational.

What is one piece of advice you would give to someone who is interested in pursuing your career?

Be sure you want to do this for a long time and then become the best you can be—and refer out to others for things you are not an expert at!

If you could do everything all over again, what would you do differently?

I'd probably become a business major.

Karen Farrugio, Speech/Hearing Teacher for the Handicapped
Speech Improvement Teacher
CUNY—Queens College, 1989
Major: Communication Sciences and Disorders

What was your first job after graduation?

I was a speech/language therapist at a group home for mentally challenged adults.

What criteria did you use when deciding which colleges to apply to?

Affordability of the school and the program offerings each college had.

What was your first choice school?

Queens College.

What career did you have in mind when you applied to college?

I had some ideas but none that I pursued.

How did the school you attended have an impact on your career choice and opportunities?

The colleges I attended that did have an impact on me were Queens College and Hunter College, where I studied communication sciences and disorders.

Do you now wish you had attended a different school? Which one and why?

For my master's degree, I would have applied to a college through a scholarship funded by the New York City Board of Education.

Which college or colleges are turning out the leaders in your profession today?

New York City colleges (CUNY).

Which classes were most valuable in preparing you for your career or in helping you decide on your career?

Speech science, phonetics, and speech/language disorders.

How did your professors impact your career choice or preparation?

A writing instructor told me I have what it takes to be a great writer. That statement contributed to my desire to help children with their writing skills and my ongoing wish to write a book/screenplay.

Did you have a job and/or internship during college that influenced your ultimate career choice or career preparation in any way?

I fulfilled my practicum requirements in special education as a speech/language teacher in the New York City public schools. It conveniently facilitated my completion of the master's program, thereby solidifying my eligibility for permanent state certification.

Can you please describe the "Aha!" moment when you realized what you wanted to do?

I didn't really have one.

Did you change your major? If so, why?

Yes. I wanted to help children with their writing skills and/or stroke patients with speaking/comprehension skills (both my mother's parents died after suffering strokes.)

How important was your college experience in getting you to where you are today?

The Queens College Speech Clinic exposed me to individual attending speech therapy sessions and the relevant techniques the clinicians utilized. The Hunter College Special Education Program equally afforded me opportunities to observe professionals in the field and to interview them and participate within classroom settings. These real-world interactions brought definition and clarity to textbook teachings.

Do you have an advanced degree? Is one helpful or required in your field?

Yes, I have an advanced degree, and it's absolutely necessary.

What do you love most about your job?

The relationships established with some of my students and the fact that some of my students develop friendships in the speech group setting that may not have been formed had they never had speech together. I love when students "get" what I teach them and appreciate what they have learned.

What is the most difficult or challenging aspect of your job?

When students are disrespectful, nonappreciative, or disruptive.

What is the biggest misconception people have about what you do?

That the children who receive speech/language services all have speech defects, when in essence, it is their receptive and expressive language abilities that are being targeted/remediated in order to assist with academic performance.

What was the biggest obstacle you faced in getting to where you are in your career?

Working in several schools, some with limited space, before settling down in one school. Years of experience lead to seniority and tenure, which allow you to become more eligible to work in a school of your choice. Also, the notion that you're gaining varied, valuable experience helps to overcome obstacles that you may face.

What skills are an absolute must for someone interested in pursuing your career?

The ability to work with children of all ages, patience, flexibility, creativity in planning lessons, and good behavior management skills.

Whom do you admire most in your industry or field?

Classroom teachers, because of their tremendous influence on the students. They give their all to teach—the struggles they endure in classroom behavior and management and the exciting experiences they impart through field trips, concert participation, after-school activities including sports, etc. I also admire parents who are truly concerned about their children and who've had to overcome odds in raising those who have developmental delays. Finally, I admire my fellow speech clinicians/teachers who have demonstrated such amazing feats as helping to transform a nonverbal, five-year-old boy into a highly verbal, gregarious teenager, and those who, overall, can direct anyone from the young to the old to communicate to the best of their ability.

What is one piece of advice you would give to someone who is interested in pursuing your career?

To persist and not give up if it's what you really want to do in your career.

If you could do everything all over again, what would you do differently?

To have started college sooner after high school.

Do you have any additional comments you think might be helpful to someone hoping to pursue your career?

You may work in a number of different settings depending upon your qualifications. As a state-certified teacher of the speech- and hearing-handicapped, you may work in a school, but as a licensed speech-language pathologist, you may work in not only a school but also a clinic or hospital or in private therapy.

Debra Drysdale, Speech Language Pathologist
Dysphagia Specialist
Pennsylvania State University, 1976
Major: Speech Pathology

What was your first job after graduation?

I was a speech pathologist in the Philadelphia Catholic school system.

What criteria did you use when deciding which colleges to apply to?

For undergraduate schools, I looked at the quality of the programs offered and if the school had an on-site clinic where I could gain experience. For graduate schools, I looked at the quality of the teaching staff and the availability of clinical opportunities.

What was your first choice school?

Penn State was my first choice school.

What career did you have in mind when you applied to college?

Speech pathology.

How did the school you attended have an impact on your career choice and opportunities?

The University of Michigan provided me with an internship at Shady Trails Camp, a speech therapy camp for children between the ages of 5 and 14. The university also gave me the opportunity to work for their Residential Aphasia Program. The program was small, so all of the graduate students were like a little family, and we were all very supportive of each other.

Do you now wish you had attended a different school? Which one and why?

I would have used the same criteria and applied to the same schools.

Which college or colleges are turning out the leaders in your profession today?

I do not know.

Which classes were most valuable in preparing you for your career or in helping you decide on your career?

Classes in anatomy, articulation, voice, philosophy, my clinical experiences—the Residential Aphasia Program, and Stuttering and Fluency Camp.

How did your professors impact your career choice or preparation?

My clinical supervisors for the Residential Aphasia Program helped me to clearly define my role as a therapist, as well as set goals and develop patient activities to meet long-term goals. They would observe my session through a one-way mirror and audio-tape a running commentary on my delivery of service. My written goals and objectives were included in the critique.

Did you have a job and/or internship during college that influenced your ultimate career choice or career preparation in any way?

No.

Can you please describe the "Aha!" moment when you realized what you wanted to do?

I had an opportunity to shadow a social worker and speech pathologist when I was in the 11th grade. I just fell in love with the roles and responsibilities of a speech therapist. I decided then to declare speech pathology as my major in college. Each year, my studies became more interesting and I became more motivated. I have never regretted my decision!

Did you change your major? If so, why?

No, I didn't.

How important was your college experience in getting you to where you are today?

Because of the specialty of the field, I needed to learn the material and techniques to begin work. However, when I finished graduate school, I realized how much more there was to learn. Experience and continuing education has been a significant part of my growth.

Do you have an advanced degree? Is one helpful or required in your field?

Yes, I have a master's degree. It is a necessity. I cannot practice in the medical field without my master's and certificate of clinical competence.

What do you love most about your job?

I work in an acute care setting. I never know what will be waiting for me when I get to work. I am constantly learning after 30 years in the field. I love that I truly make a difference in the lives of my patients and feel as if I give back every day.

What is the most difficult or challenging aspect of your job?

A challenging aspect of my job is dealing with medically compromised patients. Also, determining or recommending decisions that affect the patient's quality of life. It is always difficult telling a patient that their speech may never be the same. I always leave the patient with hope; but realistically, some patients will never again be verbal communicators.

What is the biggest misconception people have about what you do?

That I work with children and just correct their speech. Actually, 80 percent of my work is with adults who have dysphagia (swallowing difficulties).

What was the biggest obstacle you faced in getting to where you are in your career?

Developing expertise and confidence in management of dysphagic and ventilator-dependent patients. I took many continuing education classes and made sure to work in a team environment with nurses, respiratory therapists, and medical doctors, especially pulmonologists.

What skills are an absolute must for someone interested in pursuing your career?

Critical thinking, excellent time management skills, and counseling skills.

Whom do you admire most in your industry or field?

I admire determined patients and all the team members who help these patients, like the rehabilitation team, RNs, respiratory therapists (RTs), and intensivists (physicians who specialize in the care of critically ill patients).

What is one piece of advice you would give to someone who is interested in pursuing your career?

Establish yourself as a diligent and compassionate professional who is consistently learning to meet patients' needs.

If you could do everything all over again, what would you do differently?

I would have participated in more work-study/internships to gain professional experience during my college years.

Ann D. Jablon, College Professor
Professor, Communication Sciences and Disorders
CUNY—Queens College, 1973
Major: Speech Language Pathology

What was your first job after graduation?

Graduate teaching assistant.

What criteria did you use when deciding which colleges to apply to?

Frankly, at the time, most of the students from my high school went to local colleges. So, like many others, I applied to Saint John's University in Queens.

What was your first choice school?

The one I attended, but it turned out not to be the right choice. I knew once I arrived that the school, despite its many fine points, was not the right fit for me.

What career did you have in mind when you applied to college?

I wanted to be a writer and teach English.

How did the school you attended have an impact on your career choice and opportunities?

When I transferred to Queens College (CUNY), I had tried English and psychology at Saint John's. I knew that I wanted to be of service in society (teach or be a psychologist), and I knew I loved words and sentences. When I transferred, the chair of the Communications Arts and Sciences Department suggested speech-language pathology. I had no idea what this profession was, and I still believe there are many young people who do not know anything about this wonderful profession. I loved the humanity of the program, and I still love that about the profession.

I had a strong liberal arts background coupled with a very strong program in speech-language pathology at Queens College. I had the opportunity to serve as a research assistant (in psycholinguistics, the psychology of language) as an undergraduate student. I was selected for a summer clinical internship when I was a senior in college. As a graduate student, I was awarded a teaching assistantship. These were all pivotal experiences that helped me to develop my educational and career goals. I was involved as an undergraduate student with the speech-language pathology honor society, which gave me further exposure through lectures and other activities provided by the society and to many professionals and many points of view about speech-language pathology.

Do you now wish you had attended a different school? Which one and why?

I have absolutely no regrets about my choice of college. Perhaps, if circumstances were different, I might have benefited from living at college rather than commuting. My dream schools are Smith College and Barnard College because they are single-sex schools, as was my high school.

Which college or colleges are turning out the leaders in your profession today?

The leaders in the profession come from various schools all over the country. The Midwest is the seat of the profession, and those schools remain strong in producing leaders. The New York metropolitan schools, such as the school I teach at, Marymount Manhattan College, and the CUNY schools have produced many high-profile professionals in speech-language pathology. But I don't think there is a best choice. There are many, many fine choices, and my belief is that you make the experience worthwhile through your own commitment.

Which classes were most valuable in preparing you for your career or in helping you decide on your career?

All of my classes were valuable. I learned to view life through so many lenses, which in my profession as a speech-language pathologist and a college professor is critical.

How did your professors impact your career choice or preparation?

Two of my professors (my English professor and my Italian professor) at Saint John's advised me to leave! They could see the school was not right for me, and I have treasured their honesty and advice ever since. I try to emulate the integrity and care that they exhibited for me with my own students.

My psycholinguistics professor, who to this day is my mentor and my friend, was perhaps the most influential person in my academic life. I loved her intelligence, her teaching, and her accomplishments in research, which have added to the knowledge we have about human language.

The third influence was the professors in the speech-language pathology program. The head of the program was generous with his advice. In the main, the professors in the program cared about the students' growth and development. They were demanding but available. Queens is a very big university, but I was in what felt like a small community of wonderful people.

Did you have a job and/or internship during college that influenced your ultimate career choice or career preparation in any way?

Not until the summer preceding my senior year. I was selected as a clinical intern for a summer program in the speech and hearing clinic.

Can you please describe the "Aha!" moment when you realized what you wanted to do?

Well, I didn't really have one. I always wanted to teach, first and foremost. I suppose my "Aha!" moment was realizing that I loved the university environment and that was where I wanted to be.

Did you change your major? If so, why?

I changed it twice. I left the English program because at the time, all the young women I knew who graduated with a BA in English, no matter how fine the college they attended, were hired as secretaries. I didn't see this as the right path for me, even as an entry-level position. I left the psychology program because there was a great emphasis at the time and in my school on experimental (behavioral—I thought of it as "rat psych") and not on human dynamics, which is what I thought I wanted.

How important was your college experience in getting you to where you are today?

It was the totality: the people, the rigor, the challenge, the students, and the exposure to so many disciplines. I was so motivated by the goals of my fellow students and the achievements of my professors. That's why I believe that the right fit is the single most important factor in the college experience.

Do you have an advanced degree? Is one helpful or required in your field?

I have a PhD. A master's degree is required to practice as a speech-language pathologist; a PhD is typically required to be a college professor.

What do you love most about your job?

I love the profession of speech-language pathology because of its diversity. I love my job for the same reason. There are many components to my position, and it is always challenging; each day is different. I teach, I advise students, I head the Communication Sciences and Disorders Program, and I chair the Science Division (communication sciences and disorders, psychology, biology, and math). Each of these pieces of my job requires different skills.

What is the most difficult or challenging aspect of your job?

Perhaps the same thing that makes it exciting makes it difficult. In speech-language pathology, you are serving people—no two are alike or have the same needs. As a professor and chair, I am dealing with students and faculty with different needs, goals, strengths, and weaknesses.

What is the biggest misconception people have about what you do?

In speech-language pathology, people are not really aware of the profession. As I mentioned, the field is very broad. Speech-language pathologists serve all ages in many different settings. Commonly, people who do not know the profession think of speech sound production problems (like lisps and stuttering) as all of the work that we do, but that is only a part of the work that we do.

What was the biggest obstacle you faced in getting to where you are in your career?

At times there were no jobs in academia in my field. Since I was married and had a family, I was not flexible and could not relocate. I worked in a school as a speech-language pathologist, and when I acquired experience, I opened my own practice. This was a wonderful learning experience. I treated children and met many lovely families and great children, most of whom are grown-ups now and some of whom I still hear from! The children I treated inform my teaching. This is a cliché of the helping professions, but I learned so much from them.

What skills are an absolute must for someone interested in pursuing your career?

Patience, flexibility, the ability to problem-solve and think on your feet. You must be an excellent writer and have the ability to communicate to people who might be in distress. You must be willing to engage in lifelong learning, because the field changes rapidly as does the technology that supports the work that we do. We are learning more about brain processes, and clinicians must know the current scientific thinking.

Whom do you admire most in your industry or field?

I admire the women (most in the profession are) and men who have devoted their lives to helping others find ways to communicate with the world and achieve goals they might not have thought possible.

What is one piece of advice you would give to someone who is interested in pursuing your career?

Observe professionals in various settings. We have the kindest and most welcoming professionals who want students to learn about the profession and make an informed choice. It is a big educational commitment. But I would also say that studying communication sciences and disorders as an undergraduate can lead to more than one career path. There are few professions where knowledge about human language communication and human language communication breakdown fails to be useful. Certainly any of the helping professions like psychology, social work, counseling, teaching, and nursing.

If you could do everything all over again, what would you do differently?

I suppose there are things I could have done differently, but my life would now be different. I love my work; I love my family and all the friends I have made over the years.

Do you have any additional comments you think might be helpful to someone hoping to pursue your career?

Contact the American Speech-Language-Hearing Association (*www.asha.org*) for information on the profession and about schools that have programs.

SURVEYING TECHNOLOGY

WHY CHOOSE A CAREER AS A GIS SPECIALIST?

Geographic information systems (GIS) specialists use creative and analytical skills, combining the principles of cartography (making visual representations of data) with knowledge of geographic software. They utilize cutting-edge technology to create maps that show—in graphic detail—what's happening in the world. GIS specialists have strong math, research, and communication skills. Using satellite photos, lasers, cameras, thermal scanners, and other remote sensing devices, they create databases of variables like population density, the location of water lines, or potential forest fires. They then display one or more variables on automated maps. In other words, GIS specialists create dynamic "intelligent maps" that offer a sophisticated picture of a geographical area and its characteristics.

WHERE THE JOBS ARE

GIS experts work in a wide variety of exciting fields in both urban and rural areas: scientific investigations, resource and asset management, environmental impact assessment, urban planning, cartography, criminology, history, sales, marketing, and logistics. GIS specialists find the answers to all sorts of questions: Where do most supporters of a political party live? What is the scope of global warming? Which of a city's sewage pipes needs to be repaired? A GIS professional might help find a serial burglar or allow emergency planners to calculate emergency response times in the event of a natural disaster. A GIS specialist might find wetlands that need protection from pollution or help a company find a new business opportunity in an underserved market. GIS specialists are in great demand within many organizations—some doing computer work, some doing fieldwork collecting data. Some become self-employed consultants.

AREAS OF SPECIALTY

GIS professionals have a huge choice of specialty areas, including census work, Web mapping, global change issues, topological or data modeling, geostatistics, map overlay, cartography, and geocoding. Many GIS specialists work for government agencies or utility companies on one large project or several smaller ones. Some work as consultants and technicians to businesses that help public or private groups select the best hardware and software for their GIS needs. There are different levels of GIS specialists, such as technician (junior position, generally with one to five years experience), analyst (a more senior technician, responsible for spatial analysis and more senior responsibilities, generally with three to seven years experience), programmer (educational focus on programming skills), coordinator (with a minimum bachelor's or master's degree, responsible for core GIS staff and some project management), and manager (typically with a master's degree and five to ten years experience, responsible for project management and staff).

EDUCATIONAL REQUIREMENTS

Some entry-level GIS positions require only an associate's degree, but most require a bachelor's degree. GIS specialists usually either pursue a GIS certificate program or have at a BS in geography emphasizing GIS. Some states require licensing or certification for advanced GIS professionals. It is also important for GIS specialists to keep up with new technology and practices through extension courses and professional association seminars. Advancement usually requires a master's degree in geography, cartography, or a related field. With a PhD, specialists can teach at a university or work for a research institution.

SALARY RANGE

GIS specialists' salaries range from about $30,000–$40,000 in entry-level positions to $50,000–$80,000 and beyond for experienced specialists or those with advanced degrees.

FAMOUS GIS SPECIALISTS

- **John Snow** was perhaps the first to use the geographic method in 1854, when he depicted a cholera outbreak in London using points to represent the locations of individual cases. His study of the distribution of cholera led to the source of the disease, a contaminated water pump.
- **Roger Tomlinson** (known as the "father of GIS") and Nicolas Chrisman were tackling the problems of GIS before it was successful commercially.
- **Jack Dangermond** of Environmental Systems Research Institute (ESRI) greatly influenced GIS as we know it today.

WHERE TO LEARN MORE

Association of American Geographers
1710 16th Street N.W.
Washington, DC 20009-3198
(202) 234-1450
www.aag.org

American Society for Photogrammetry and Remote Sensing (ASPRS)
The Imaging and Geospatial Information Society
5410 Grosvenor Lane, Suite 210
Bethesda, MD 20814-2160
(301) 493-0290
www.asprs.org

University Consortium for Geographic Information Science (UCGIS)
43351 Spinks Ferry Road
Leesburg, VA 20176-5631
(888) 850-8533
www.ucgis.org

WORDS OF WISDOM

"For GIS, learn the tools and the software but find a real-world application where you can apply the tools."

—Jason Casanova, Staff Cartographer

"You must have a true passion for cartography, for geographic information, and for quality."

—Gerard Carlier, Senior GIS Analyst

Ali Baird, GIS Specialist
Environmental Scientist
Dickinson College, 1994
Majors: Biological Conservation

What criteria did you use when deciding which colleges to apply to?

I had no idea what I wanted to do when I applied to colleges; I mainly applied to schools that offered a variety of options and had a strong study-abroad component.

What was your first choice school?

Dickinson College.

What career did you have in mind when you applied to college?

I had some vague ideas about a career that involved writing and research. I had little or no exposure to the environmental world and its associated technologies until I began my college course work. While geographic information technologies are not literary, effectively communicating results is critically important.

How did the school you attended have an impact on your career choice and opportunities?

I was exposed to entirely new subject matter. The small liberal arts school that I chose provided me with multiple paths. I was able to pursue my creative interests, as well as develop skills in the sciences. Through this exploration, I learned that there are careers for people like me who enjoy both self-expression and hard science.

The exposure to multiple disciplines helped me enormously. Part of what a GIS person does is to communicate with subject-matter experts in a variety of fields. I've found that my multidisciplinary background has been a tremendous help in these discussions, as well as my own learning process. And graduate school helped me really hone the areas where I needed and wanted more depth.

Do you now wish you had attended a different school? Which one and why?

I don't think I'd do anything differently.

Which college or colleges are turning out the leaders in your profession today?

It's been my experience that the choice of school, while it matters to some extent, doesn't matter nearly as much as the motivation of the student for his or her subject.

Which classes were most valuable in preparing you for your career or in helping you decide on your career?

As an undergraduate, the sciences classes. And to some extent, the English classes, as someone had to teach me how to write. As a graduate student, the GIS course work was good, but I also think that the science classes helped, including social sciences. I knew that I wanted to be in an analytical field, but I didn't want to be stuck wearing a lab coat.

How did your professors impact your career choice or preparation?

The professor who recommended my pursuing geography was obviously influential, but so was the professor who taught the GIS classes. I wound up being a teaching assistant for the GIS course work—I'm pretty sure that I learned more about GIS while teaching than I ever did as a student!

Did you have a job and/or internship during college that influenced your ultimate career choice or career preparation in any way?

As an undergraduate, I was a research assistant with the Environmental Studies Department. In graduate school, I had a GIS internship with a land management agency in Texas. I wouldn't say they had a big impact on my career choices.

Can you please describe the "Aha!" moment when you realized what you wanted to do?

I was applying to graduate schools in biological sciences when a professor handed me a program description for the geography department. I read through it once and thought, "Wow—this is what I'm supposed to be doing!" Prior to that, I'd only had one course in geography, and I hadn't really understood the discipline. Geography perfectly fit my approach to science and my interpretation of the world. Geography is a science, with its own techniques and technologies, that helps us study the distribution of people, things, natural features, philosophies…and interprets what it all means.

Did you change your major? If so, why?

I had started off as an English major. While I love reading and writing, I was fascinated by the natural sciences and wanted more time to explore those.

How important was your college experience in getting you to where you are today?

Although it may sound counterintuitive, the exposure to a multidisciplinary atmosphere really helped me home in on what I did (and did not) want to do with my life.

Do you have an advanced degree? Is one helpful or required in your field?

Yes, I have an MA in geography. It's very helpful to have an advanced degree, but it's not required. It depends on the type of GIS job that you're looking for...an advanced degree in a discipline other than GIS is extremely helpful, as it shows that you can apply the technology in a useful way. However, there are some jobs that are exclusively focused on the technology itself, which may require you to demonstrate more depth in GIS studies.

What do you love most about your job?

The variety of people and disciplines that I get to work with.

What is the most difficult or challenging aspect of your job?

Misperceptions of GIS as cartography. Maps are an effective means of communicating results of GIS analyses, but that's only one facet of the field.

What is the biggest misconception people have about what you do?

Everyone, including my family, is convinced that I am a cartographer.

What was the biggest obstacle you faced in getting to where you are in your career?

Finding a job that reflected my interest in applying technical abilities to multiple fields. As a result, I worked for state and federal government land management agencies, which can provide opportunities for growth in many fields.

What skills are an absolute must for someone interested in pursuing your career?

Attention to detail and a sense of curiosity.

Whom do you admire most in your industry or field?

I've had several coworkers who amaze me with their creativity. From them, I've learned that the simplest, most elegant solutions to problems usually come from those who keep an open mind and maintain excellent technical skills.

What is one piece of advice you would give to someone who is interested in pursuing your career?

Try it. You might like it.

If you could do everything all over again, what would you do differently?

I would probably spend more time developing my skills as a biologist.

Jason Casanova, GIS Specialist
Staff Cartographer
University of Illinois—Champaign-Urbana, 1999
Major: Geography

What was your first job after graduation?

A research associate in a GIS lab.

What criteria did you use when deciding which colleges to apply to?

Proximity to my hometown and reputation.

What was your first choice school?

The school I attended was my first choice.

What career did you have in mind when you applied to college?

I didn't really have a career in mind.

How did the school you attended have an impact on your career choice and opportunities?

As soon as I graduated, I was hired as a research associate in the GIS lab where I had my undergrad internship.

Do you now wish you had attended a different school? Which one and why?

Obviously, those colleges that have the top geography programs would be on the top of my list, but it ultimately comes down to the professors within the department. I didn't necessarily do that research before I started at U of I, but I sort of lucked out. Find a department with professors who have similar research interests, and if nothing else, visit the department and meet the professors (and also other grad students) before applying. Having a good work environment is key to both being successful and enjoying your college experience.

Which college or colleges are turning out the leaders in your profession today?

Penn State, UC—Santa Barbara, University of Wisconsin—Madison, University of Kansas.

Which classes were most valuable in preparing you for your career or in helping you decide on your career?

Surprisingly, my art and math backgrounds eventually helped push me into geography and mapping. The art classes I took helped me better understand design aspects of mapping, and the math background helped with the analytical parts of my job. At the time, I had no idea that they would actually mesh together into a career. After I got into geography as a major, the technical classes (cartography, GIS, remote sensing) were key to giving me some experience with the tools available. And then there were a variety of physical and cultural geography classes that helped me relate GIS to real-world situations.

How did your professors impact your career choice or preparation?

As a kid, I was a huge fan of maps (I always wanted to be the navigator in the car on trips). My cartography instructor, my biggest mentor in school, was the one who eventually sparked my interest in maps again. I was always a perfectionist—that's probably why I could never finish any of my paintings in art class. She was able to take that potential weakness and help me channel it in a positive way by encouraging the attention to detail that is required for map design.

Did you have a job and/or internship during college that influenced your ultimate career choice or career preparation in any way?

Yes, I was a research assistant in the geography department's GIS lab. I also was a line cook at a restaurant on nights and weekends. My research position exposed me to real-world projects in GIS, and I became much more familiarized with the software tools available.

Can you please describe the "Aha!" moment when you realized what you wanted to do?

It actually happened in a world geography class that I was taking as an elective. My professor at the time mentioned a demand for GIS experience in the workforce. Although I didn't understand the nuts and bolts of GIS at the time, I knew it involved analysis of maps. It sounded like something that would tie together my art and math backgrounds.

How important was your college experience in getting you to where you are today?

It gave me a foundation to build on, both the technical skills (learning the applications and methodologies I currently use in my job) and the discipline to complete projects independently.

Do you have an advanced degree? Is one helpful or required in your field?

I don't have one. It is helpful but not required.

What do you love most about your job?

I get to apply my skills to something that hopefully will have some positive effect on the environment.

What is the most difficult or challenging aspect of your job?

Because we are a small nonprofit, I'm sometimes expected to be an expert in all aspects of GIS, graphic design (Web or print), and computer operations in general. I know enough to be dangerous at any of these aspects of my job, but I don't consider myself an expert in any one thing. Because I have no technical support on staff, sometimes it's difficult for me to find answers to many staff problems or questions, and so many of my skills have been self-taught on the job. This tends to take lots of time (and patience).

What is the biggest misconception people have about what you do?

Being a cartographer doesn't necessarily mean I know where everything is located! The other general misconception is that being a geographer doesn't necessarily mean you make maps (although I followed that stereotype to a tee!). Oh and finally, there is a difference between GIS and cartography. One is analytical; the other is design-centric.

What was the biggest obstacle you faced in getting to where you are in your career?

The field I was interested in (cartography more than strictly GIS work) is fairly specialized, so positions are not widely available. I was young and willing to move. So my wife and I decided to pick up and move across country.

What skills are an absolute must for someone interested in pursuing your career?

GIS: software experience, programming/database experience, analytical skills, statistics, project management.

Cartography: being detail-oriented, creative, artistic; good sense of design and use of space.

Whom do you admire most in your industry or field?

As far as my cartographic heroes, Tom Patterson (U.S. National Park Service), Alex Tait (International Mapping Association), and my mentor, Jane Domier (Illinois State Geological Survey). Their attention to detail is incredible, and their maps always inspire me to experiment and work harder.

What is one piece of advice you would give to someone who is interested in pursuing your career?

For GIS, learn the tools and the software, but find a real-world application where you can apply the tools. If you are interested in the technical aspects of GIS, then take programming and database classes either within the department or outside (in the computer science department) if necessary. Many of the jobs offered today desire these skill sets.

For cartography (the design aspects of mapmaking), everything is digital these days, so I encourage folks to take graphic design classes. You become familiar with the software tools and hone your design skills at the same time. Also, GIS classes are useful to understand the tools, but the true cartography classes are where you will learn to make well-designed and aesthetically pleasing maps.

If you could do everything all over again, what would you do differently?

I guess I really don't have any regrets. If there is one thing I'd have to single out, it would be that I didn't pursue grad school right after I finished my undergrad degree. I opted to go for dollars, and now although I'd really like to go back to school, it's a lot more difficult with a mortgage.

What criteria did you use when deciding which colleges to apply to?

Small liberal arts school, strong social science programs, solid financial aid program, significant international student population.

Gerard Carlier, GIS Specialist

Senior GIS Analyst

Macalester College, 1995

Major: Geography

What was your first choice school?

Macalaster College was my first choice.

What career did you have in mind when you applied to college?

I had a few in mind, but not the one I ultimately pursued.

How did the school you attended have an impact on your career choice and opportunities?

Macalester College had a superb geography department with a staff that was truly enthusiastic and passionate about their respective fields of expertise. The field I work in is fairly young, and I am currently working outside the United States, so I would not say that there is a direct correlation between having attended the school I attended and the path my professional career has taken up to this point. However, the quality of my education, the learning environment and resources provided by Macalester, as well as the people I met there have certainly been instrumental in helping me formulate the decisions I made to pursue my career.

Do you now wish you had attended a different school? Which one and why?

I had a superb educational experience at the college I attended, so I have no regrets or reason to say I would have gone elsewhere. I do believe that at the undergraduate level, it is important to select schools that are strong in more than one of your fields of interest.

Which college or colleges are turning out the leaders in your profession today?

Any school with an enthusiastic and properly funded geography, Earth science, or environmental studies department will provide the necessary resources for those students showing a passion for geographic information to explore what it is that they find most relevant to them.

Which classes were most valuable in preparing you for your career or in helping you decide on your career?

I took so many classes, read so much material, and researched so many topics that it would be impossible to say any one particular event was more influential than the other. The whole experience counts more than an individual professor or lecture. In the end, my present career incorporates aspects gleaned from every geography course I've taken. Ironically, the one class I didn't take (Introduction to GIS) ended up being the focus of both my graduate education and present career!

How did your professors impact your career choice or preparation?

Each one of my geography professors did in that they individually exposed me to a different branch of geography and different angles of geographic analysis. Collectively, they encouraged me to take classes outside of the discipline to emphasize how geographic topics in general, as well as my own interests, also related to other fields of study. This type of lateral thinking, and being able to overlay seemingly disparate segments of knowledge, is largely what GIS analysis amounts to.

Did you have a job and/or internship during college that influenced your ultimate career choice or career preparation in any way?

I participated in a work/study financial aid program for the entirety of my college career. The last two years, I was able to work as a teaching aide within the department of my major. I also had a part-time job drafting maps for a local transportation company, and I interned with an NGO (nongovernmental organization) providing sustainable development assistance in third world countries. They were influential in helping me realize how pertinent my study was to numerous situations in various cultural contexts and geographies.

Can you please describe the "Aha!" moment when you realized what you wanted to do?

At a certain point, I realized that I was taking all the classes I thought I should be taking, rather than the classes that interested me. I was not really enjoying these lectures, even though others were. I realized that I was not getting the rewards out of these choices that others were, so I began to focus more on the classes I found to be interesting and more challenging.

Did you change your major? If so, why?

Yes I did. I found the geography classes I took to be far more relevant than the classes in either of my other intended majors. The contact with other students and faculty members was very inspiring, and it didn't take me long to see that my initial choice of majors was based more on what I thought would be practical and financially rewarding than on what I truly found interesting and exciting. In the end, what I do today is still practical and financially rewarding, plus I enjoy what I do.

How important was your college experience in getting you to where you are today?

Without a college education, I could not be doing what I am doing today. It would be very difficult to pursue a graduate degree in GIS without a strong generalist back ground in geography. In turn, my career is entirely reliant on my GIS studies. The liberal arts experience as a whole was also very important to me because I was able to extend my interests to numerous other disciplines.

Do you have an advanced degree? Is one helpful or required in your field?

Yes, an MS in GIS for rural application. An advanced degree incorporating GIS or remote sensing is highly recommended for my particular career path. Geography is a very broad study covering numerous cross-disciplinary areas of interest. Although there is still a wide array of employment opportunities available to the generalist geographer, I found grad school particularly helpful as a foundation upon which to build further specialization.

What do you love most about your job?

I am continually faced with new assignments that allow me to access interesting data sets and use my experiences and creativity to provide solutions that will benefit users of GPS products. There is very little repetition in my work (when it is done correctly!), and thus it always remains challenging and keeps me aware of innovations and developments in the industry.

What is the most difficult or challenging aspect of your job?

In my specific industry, there are many deadlines and dependencies on data providers and other departments. It is important to communicate efficiently and effectively with all stakeholders to ensure that the correct actions are undertaken at the right times. It requires a lot of work, but the results are always very rewarding.

What was the biggest obstacle you faced in getting to where you are in your career?

I had to experience a number of less satisfying work environments before I found my present job. It's a positive thing to build up work experiences and discover for yourself what kind of work environment, organization, or group of colleagues works best for you. I kept working hard but kept my eyes open for a more satisfying job opportunity.

What skills are an absolute must for someone interested in pursuing your career?

Skills can always be learned as long as someone has a will to work hard and has enthusiasm to learn and solve problems. The most important thing is to possess a decent general knowledge and have a true affinity for geographic information.

Whom do you admire most in your industry or field?

I have the most respect for the individuals who get a job done and solve problems creatively and effectively, are proud of their work, and don't mind sharing their ideas with others. This is not really an industry for glamour or heroism.

What is one piece of advice you would give to someone who is interested in pursuing your career?

You must have a true passion for cartography, for geographic information, and for quality. Don't be too specific in your area of specialization; grab onto as many opportunities as you can to find out what work suits you best.

James E. Scott, GIS Specialist
Environmental Planner/Director, Texas Natural Resources Information System
University of Georgia, 1981
Major: Landscape Architecture

What criteria did you use when deciding which colleges to apply to?

Reputation for my course of study.

What was your first choice school?

The University of Georgia was my first choice.

What career did you have in mind when you applied to college?

I knew that I wanted a career in the GIS field.

How did the school you attended have an impact on your career choice and opportunities?

It had a big impact to understand the ins and outs of the field and, career-wise, it opened up a world of opportunities for me.

Do you now wish you had attended a different school? Which one and why?

No, I know that I made the right choice for me.

Which college or colleges are turning out the leaders in your profession today?

Harvard and UPenn.

Which classes were most valuable in preparing you for your career or in helping you decide on your career?

Design.

How did your professors impact your career choice or preparation?

One of my professors learned from the preeminent visionary of environmental planning in the modern era, Ian McHarg, author of *Design with Nature*.

Did you have a job and/or internship during college that influenced your ultimate career choice or career preparation in any way?

I was an intern for the U.S. Bureau of Reclamation in Seminoe, Wyoming. It exposed me to bureaucracy, which I swore never to subject myself to.

Can you please describe the "Aha!" moment when you realized what you wanted to do?

I always knew that I wanted my work to be focused on the environment, and to learn that a profession actually existed to practice design in the environment was a profound discovery!

Did you change your major? If so, why?

I didn't change my major.

How important was your college experience in getting you to where you are today?

It provided an environment of creativity and formalized learning as a process enhanced by open critiques and self-direction.

Do you have an advanced degree? Is one helpful or required in your field?

I don't have one. It's helpful but not required, as my school provided a professional degree program designed to prepare students to immediately enter the profession of landscape architecture.

What do you love most about your job?

It combines leading-edge technology with environmental data and support of citizen awareness of geography's importance in everyday lives.

What is the most difficult or challenging aspect of your job?

Speed of government, meaning its lack of it!

What is the biggest misconception people have about what you do?

People think landscape architects only figure out how to make yards look nice.

What was the biggest obstacle you faced in getting to where you are in your career?

Self-imposed limitations, which on balance did not present severe limits; lack of opportunities in leadership development; business and finance exposure would also have helped.

What skills are an absolute must for someone interested in pursuing your career?

Passion for geography, creative problem-solving skills, communication—listening and translating complex ideas into easy-to-understand concepts.

Whom do you admire most in your industry or field?

The late Ian McHarg, a visionary, humanist, and thoughtful leader.

What is one piece of advice you would give to someone who is interested in pursuing your career?

Consider your true motivations and be sure you want to do it without regard to financial reward.

If you could do everything all over again, what would you do differently?

Not sell my private consulting company that I built from scratch to a venture capital firm.

Shaun Healy, GIS Specialist
Remote Sensing Analyst
CSU—Long Beach, 1999
Major: Geography

What criteria did you use when deciding which colleges to apply to?

I needed to complete my degree as quickly as possible. As a bonus, I fell into GIS and have had the bug ever since.

What was your first choice school?

Loyola Marymount University.

What career did you have in mind when you applied to college?

I didn't really have one.

How did the school you attended have an impact on your career choice and opportunities?

They had a great internship program, which exposed me to a number of opportunities.

Do you now wish you had attended a different school? Which one and why?

I might have chosen to attend Penn State, University of Wisconsin—Madison, or UC—Santa Barbara.

Which college or colleges are turning out the leaders in your profession today?

It's hard to tell since computer sciences host most of the programming talent going into today's GIS fields.

Which classes were most valuable in preparing you for your career or in helping you decide on your career?

Cultural geography. Many problems posed by cultural geographers—while verbose and somewhat cryptic in postmodern parlance—use the notions of scale and research tools required for studying cultural phenomena, which allowed me to think more analytically about the problems of modeling social data in GIS.

How did your professors impact your career choice or preparation?

Most of my professors recognized the power of GIS and were able to bring a different perspective on how one develops a sense of spatial phenomena outside of the computing environment.

Did you have a job and/or internship during college that influenced your ultimate career choice or career preparation in any way?

I worked with Thomas Bros. in Lakewood, Carson, and Boulder County. It didn't have a significant impact on my career.

Can you please describe the "Aha!" moment when you realized what you wanted to do?

I was first in geology at a local community college and was invited to visit a professor at CSU—Dominquez Hills. Once I saw what you could do with satellite imagery and computer mapping systems, everything changed for me.

Did you change your major? If so, why?

Yes, I switched. Geology wasn't exactly exciting for me, nor are there a lot of opportunities to expand your knowledge outside of the discipline.

How important was your college experience in getting you to where you are today?

It helped introduce me to geographic problems, understand the importance of scale and projection, and come to terms with unfamiliar concepts while framing problems in terms of high-level questions.

Do you have an advanced degree? Is one helpful or required in your field?

Almost—I did not complete the thesis. I started working at Cal Tech and had my first-born. Some things in life took precedence over the higher degree. It's absolutely helpful to have one in this field, so I plan to return to school when the kids get older.

What do you love most about your job?

Challenges that are usually based on geographic problems.

What is the most difficult or challenging aspect of your job?

Getting people to understand the underlying issues with how GIS manages their information.

What is the biggest misconception people have about what you do?

That I perform magic tricks in a black box!

What was the biggest obstacle you faced in getting to where you are in your career?

Gaining a better understanding of computing environments and adopting new techniques for building solutions. It helps to break down the problem and reduce the issues to their core.

What skills are an absolute must for someone interested in pursuing your career?

Fundamentals of spatial thinking and understanding the possibilities and the limitations to GIS.

Whom do you admire most in your industry or field?

Roger Tomlinson and Nicholas Chrisman. Some of the biggest minds were tackling the problem of GIS before it was a successful commercial product.

What is one piece of advice you would give to someone who is interested in pursuing your career?

Getting your foot in the door depends on your ability to cope with learning new things rapidly.

If you could do everything all over again, what would you do differently?

Graduate with my master's.

Do you have any additional comments you think might be helpful to someone hoping to pursue your career?

Take the time to learn the basics thoroughly, and you will find that never fails you.

VETERINARY MEDICINE

WHY CHOOSE TO BECOME A VETERINARIAN?

Veterinarians have a love for animals as well as for the study of science. Veterinarians care for the health and well-being of every type of animal, from livestock to companion animals. They provide routine care, including vaccinations and examinations, and also treat the illnesses animals may suffer from. Working with physicians and scientists, veterinarians also sometimes research therapies that may be used to treat human diseases.

WHERE THE JOBS ARE

Veterinarians can work at animal hospitals or clinics and may be in private practice or be employed by a group practice. Some veterinarians also work for the federal government in the Departments of Agriculture, Health and Human Services, and even Homeland Security. In part because veterinary schools turn out so few graduates, job opportunities for those who do graduate will continue to be strong. Other factors, such as the increasing willingness of owners to pay for more advanced medical treatment for their pets as well as the popularity of pet insurance, will also increase demand for veterinarians.

AREAS OF SPECIALTY

Veterinarians often specialize in a specific type of animal: companion animals; large animals, including horses and cattle; or even exotic animals. Most veterinarians, however, treat a variety of animals, and their area of specialty is often connected to the location of their practice. Veterinarians in urban areas, for example, are more likely to treat small companion animals than those in rural areas, who may treat horses or cows.

EDUCATIONAL REQUIREMENTS

Veterinarians are required to graduate from a four-year veterinary school with a doctor of veterinary medicine degree and pass a standard board exam. Most people find the biggest obstacle to becoming a veterinarian is being accepted to graduate school. There are relatively few accredited veterinary schools (there are only 28 in the United States), and competition for entry is keen. An undergraduate degree is not required for entry, but a substantial amount of college course work is. Because schools are so competitive, those without a bachelor's degree are at a serious disadvantage when applying to veterinary school.

SALARY RANGE

The median annual salary for veterinarians in 2006 was $66,590.

Pros: Improving the lives of animals

Cons: Can be somewhat dangerous

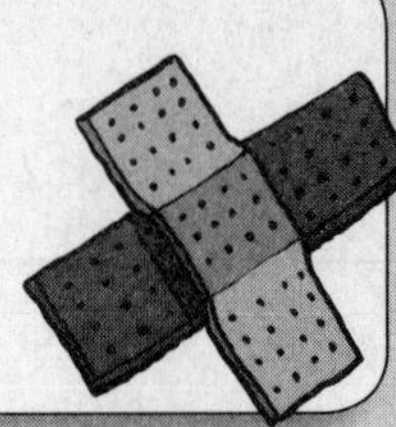

FAMOUS VETERINARIANS

- **James Herriot** (James Alfred Wight) wrote a poular and semiautobiographical series of books, among them *All Creatures Great and Small.*
- **Martin Fettman** was the first veterinarian in outer space.
- **Daniel E. Salmon** was the first U.S. veterinarian to earn a DVM degree; Salmonella is named after him.

WORDS OF WISDOM

"Veterinary medicine is a wonderful profession that allows you the privilege of caring for the health of animals and for protecting public health. It demands a lot physically and mentally, but the rewards for the hard work and job well done are worth the effort."

—Bonnie V. Beaver,
Small Animal Veterinarian

"Do it! Although there is a lot of school involved, it is well worth the effort to have a job that is as much fun as mine. One of the really great things about the veterinary profession is that you can have multiple careers within the profession over your lifetime."

—Lisa C. Freeman, Veterinarian-Scientist

WHERE TO LEARN MORE

American Veterinary Medical Association
1931 N. Meacham Road, Suite 100
Schaumburg, IL 60173-4360
(847) 925-8070; fax: (847) 925-1329
Email: *avmainfo@avma.org*
www.avma.org

The Association of American Veterinary Medical Colleges
1101 Vermont Avenue N.W., Suite 301
Washington, DC 20005
(202) 371-9195; fax: (202) 842-0773
www.aavmc.org

Bonnie V. Beaver, Small Animal Veterinarian
Veterinarian, Texas A&M University
University of Minnesota
Major: Veterinary Medicine

What was your first job after graduation?

Veterinarian.

What criteria did you use when deciding which colleges to apply to?

There really was no choice. I was a resident of Minnesota, and it had a college of veterinary medicine. It was extremely difficult for a person to get into a college of veterinary medicine in any state if they were not a resident.

What career did you have in mind when you applied to college?

Veterinary medicine; it was the only career that I ever seriously considered.

How did the school you attended impact on your career choice and opportunities?

I received an excellent education, both as an undergraduate and in the professional program, so that I could successfully practice veterinary medicine. It provided the foundation upon which all further learning could be built.

Which college or colleges are turning out the leaders in your profession today?

There are currently only 28 colleges of veterinary medicine in the United States, and each, because of accreditation, provides a quality education. Some may excel a little in one area or another, but all provide excellent educational programs at the basic level. Differences are more significant at the graduate/resident training levels.

Which classes were most valuable in preparing you for your career or in helping you decide on your career?

Sciences, mathematics, and English.

How did your professors impact your career choice or preparation?

They provided the quality and current information that provided me with a good basis for the professional knowledge I would need. They were compassionate and good role models of what veterinarians are.

Do you have an advanced degree? Is one helpful or required in your field?

I do have an advanced degree. It was not necessary for the small animal practice, but because I am also working at a university, it was logical that I take additional course work.

What do you love most about your job?

Working with the animals and the people who own them.

What is the most difficult or challenging aspect of your job?

Keeping current with all the new knowledge that is developing.

What is the biggest misconception people have about what you do?

There are two: (1) the amount of education required to become a veterinarian (most people think it just takes a couple of years in a junior college) and (2) the wide variety of things a veterinarian can do in addition to private practice.

What was the biggest obstacle you faced in getting to where you are in your career?

At the time I went through school, it was not common for women to become veterinarians. Fortunately, that has changed, but I knew what my goal was and I had the drive and family support to accomplish that goal.

What skills are an absolute must for someone interested in pursuing your career?

Integrity, enjoyment of working with people and animals, intelligence because the curriculum is very demanding, interest in learning, self-motivation, willingness to work hard.

What is one piece of advice you would give to someone who is interested in pursuing your career?

Volunteer to work with veterinarians so that you get an understanding of what they really do, but remain open-minded to learning about the wide variety of different kinds of opportunities that constitute veterinary medicine.

Can you please add any additional comments you think might be helpful to someone hoping to pursue your career?

Veterinary medicine is a wonderful profession that allows you the privilege of caring for the health of animals and of protecting public health. It demands a lot physically and mentally, but the rewards for the hard work and a job well done are worth the effort.

Lisa C. Freeman, Veterinarian-Scientist
Professor, Associate Dean, Research and Graduate Programs,
Kansas State University
Cornell University, 1985
Majors: Biology; Animal Science

What was your first job after graduation?

Relief veterinarian.

What criteria did you use when deciding which colleges to apply to?

I wanted to go to a research university with a veterinary college on the campus.

What career did you have in mind when you applied to college?

Veterinary medicine.

How did the school you attended impact on your career choice and opportunities?

Cornell University (CU) taught me great time management skills due to the rigor of the classes. CU also offered me unbelievable opportunities to work in research and discovery. In addition, as an Ivy League land grant institution, CU offered incredible diversity in term of students, faculty, and curriculum.

Which college or colleges are turning out the leaders in your profession today?

Cornell University, University of Pennsylvania, University of California—Davis, Ohio State University, University of Missouri.

Can you please describe the "Aha!" moment when you realized what you wanted to do?

I was three years old when I announced that I wanted to be a veterinarian. I think it had something to do with putting a toy stethoscope on my stuffed animals. (I didn't like dolls and didn't have siblings, so that was the logical place to put the stethoscope.) I stuck with that goal over time, although my vision of opportunities within the veterinary profession changed as I matured and learned more about all of things that veterinarians can do.

Did you change your major? If so, why?

I did not change my major, but I took many more laboratory research-related courses than I needed to for veterinary school admissions.

Which classes were most valuable in preparing you for your career or in helping you decide on your career?

In addition to the basic science and animal science courses, which confirmed my interest in veterinary medicine and animal health, there were two experiences that had a significant impact on my career choice. The first was the opportunity to do an undergraduate research project. The second was the chance to serve as an undergraduate teaching assistant for a vertebrate anatomy course. Although my initial interest in these experiences was focused on strengthening my application to veterinary school, they really changed my opinion about what I wanted to do within the veterinary profession.

How did your professors impact your career choice or preparation?

I developed a lot of respect and admiration for my professors, and this influenced me to become one.

Did you have a job and/or internship during college that influenced your career choice or career preparation in any way?

I spent a lot of time working in veterinary practices during high school and college, and I realized that practice becomes very routine after a while. This made me consider other aspects of veterinary medicine.

Do you have an advanced degree? Is one helpful or required in your field?

I have a PhD and postdoctoral research experience. These were important for becoming a faculty member and a federally funded scientist.

What do you love most about your job?

I love everything about my job. No two days are alike, and that keeps me challenged and engaged. I love being able to solve problems and to discover things that will help people. I like interacting with students on a daily basis.

What is the most difficult or challenging aspect of your job?

At this point in my career, I have teaching, research, and administrative responsibility. The last requires me to work with lots of different kinds of people. Understanding and responding to the needs of people with different interests and backgrounds is a challenge and a joy.

What is the biggest misconception people have about what you do?

When I am doing the administrative part of my job well, my efforts are invisible. I often play an unacknowledged role in the success of others. In this sense, people probably think that the administrative part of my job takes less time than it actually does.

What was the biggest obstacle you faced in getting to where you are in your career?

At several stages of my career, there was significant competition for a limited number of positions—most notably when I was admitted to veterinary school and when I was searching for a faculty position in a basic science department. I was successful because I understood the expectations for success in those positions, and I worked hard to demonstrate that I was capable of exceeding those expectations.

What skills are an absolute must for someone interested in pursuing your career?

The abilities to think critically, communicate clearly, and listen carefully.

Whom do you admire most in your industry or field? Why?

I admire Joan Hedricks, the dean of the University of Pennsylvania School of Veterinary Medicine. After a successful career as a veterinarian-scientist, Joan is devoting her talents towards building new positive relationships within and without her college. She is a good listener and a dynamic leader.

What is one piece of advice you would give to someone who is interested in pursuing your career?

Do it! Although there is a lot of school involved, it is well worth the effort to have a job that is as much fun as mine. One of the really great things about the veterinary profession is that you can have multiple careers within the profession over your lifetime.

Paul C. Stromberg, Veterinary Pathologist
Professor, Ohio State University College of Veterinary Medicine
Ohio State University, 1967
Major: Zoology

What was your first job after graduation?

Pathologist at Battelle Columbus Laboratories.

What criteria did you use when deciding which colleges to apply to?

The quality of the program and strength of the department in which I planned my major study.

What was your first choice school?

Ohio State University (OSU).

What career did you have in mind when you applied to college?

I wanted to be a college professor in the area of zoology or biological science.

How did the school you attended impact on your career choice and opportunities?

Greatly. It created terrific opportunities for me to explore my career interest and ultimately led me to get a degree in veterinary medicine.

Which college or colleges are turning out the leaders in your profession today?

There are many good veterinary schools turning out veterinary practitioners. In the medical specialty of veterinary pathology, Ohio State University is the top program in

North America. Other top programs can be found at University of California—Davis; Colorado State University, University of Pennsylvania, North Carolina State University, Iowa State University, and Washington State University.

Can you please describe the "Aha!" moment when you realized what you wanted to do?

I was a sophomore in high school taking biology. My teacher dissected a dead raccoon as an anatomy lesson, and the intestine was filled with tapeworms. I was fascinated that one animal could live inside the body of another animal. I could not understand how that could happen. From that time on, I was interested in studying parasitic diseases, and 45 years later I am still fascinated by it.

Did you change your major? If so, why?

No. I majored in zoology as an undergraduate with a minor in physiology. In graduate school I concentrated on parasitology, and during my training in veterinary school I knew I would specialize in pathology. After graduating from veterinary school, I spent three years in a residency program studying anatomic pathology with special interest on the pathology related to parasitic diseases.

Which classes were most valuable in preparing you for your career or in helping you decide on your career?

Although my classes in zoology, parasitology, medicine, and pathology were of the most interest to me, I also liked the classes in history, literature, and philosophy. It is important for scientists to be well-rounded and have a broad view of our world and society. Science is done within the context of our culture, and studying the arts prepares you for that better than anything else.

How did your professors impact your career choice or preparation?

Greatly. I was fortunate to have inspired teachers in undergraduate and graduate school who saw my interest and supported it by creating extra opportunities to learn.

Did you have a job and/or internship during college that influenced your career choice or career preparation in any way?

I worked as a laboratory assistant for all four years in undergraduate school, which gave me great experience in research laboratories. I learned research techniques and also how research is performed, which is more important.

Do you have an advanced degree? Is one helpful or required in your field?

I have a PhD degree and a doctor of veterinary medicine degree. The PhD degree is not required to be a veterinarian, nor is it required in order to be a veterinary pathologist, but if you want to do research in a university, it helps to have a PhD.

What do you love most about your job?

The diversity of what I do. I teach pathology to students wanting to become veterinarians because pathology is important to practitioners. I also teach pathology to graduate veterinarians who want to specialize in pathology. Part of my job is to provide diagnostic support to the hospital. I perform autopsies on animals to determine why they died, and I "read" surgical biopsies from living animals to help clinical veterinarians make a diagnosis so they know how to treat the disease. I also travel all over the world and give lectures to other veterinarians interested in pathology. I am also engaged in research with other scientists, mostly using my skills and experience to help solve human disease problems by studying similar diseases in animals, such as rats and mice. I have also been involved in developing gene therapy for animals and developing cancer diagnostic reagents for both humans and animals.

What is the most difficult or challenging aspect of your job?

I spend a lot of time keeping up with the newest discoveries in science.

What is the biggest misconception people have about what you do?

When most people find out I am a veterinarian, they think I practice medicine on dogs and cats.

What was the biggest obstacle you faced in getting to where you are in your career?

Getting into veterinary school is difficult. You have to be a good student with good grades. But if you like to learn and study, this is not difficult, so do not be intimidated. You will know if it's right for you.

What skills are an absolute must for someone interested in pursuing your career?

You should love to learn and be a good student. It helps if you are a good reader. If you want to be a good scientist, you should have three attributes: (1) You should be curious; you should have an active imagination. (2) You should be passionate about what you study; you should like to learn new things and desire to contribute to new knowledge.

(3) You should also be critical of everything you see and not accept as truth what others tell you without rigorous proof.

What is one piece of advice you would give to someone who is interested in pursuing your career?

If you want to be what I am, you should work hard at it and be persistent. There are many opportunities. Find the right one for you.

Can you please add any additional comments you think might be helpful to someone hoping to pursue your career?

To be an academic faculty or a professor in any field takes hard work, but do not be intimated by this. If you like to study and are good at learning, you will be successful. It is the same in any academic field.

Guy A. Sheppard, Veterinarian
President, Texas Veterinary Medical Association
Texas A&M University, 1978
Majors: Animal Science; Veterinary Medicine

What was your first job after graduation?

U.S. Army Veterinary Corps.

What criteria did you use when deciding which colleges to apply to?

I wanted to attend a college that emphasized agriculture and veterinary medicine, as well as a college with military training.

What was your first choice school?

Texas A&M University (TAMU).

What career did you have in mind when you applied to college?

Veterinary medicine.

How did the school you attended impact on your career choice and opportunities?

TAMU prepared me for a career in veterinary medicine and solidified that choice for me.

Can you please describe the "Aha!" moment when you realized what you wanted to do?

When I was an elementary student and observed a veterinarian deliver a calf on my family's farm.

Which classes were most valuable in preparing you for your career or in helping you decide on your career?

Animal science courses, physiology, genetics, entomology, biology, chemistry, organic chemistry.

Did you have a job and/or internship during college that influenced your career choice or career preparation in any way?

I worked for a veterinarian and at a feed store between semesters in college. Both jobs reinforced my career choice.

Do you have an advanced degree? Is one helpful or required in your field?

I have a doctor of veterinary medicine degree. A doctorate degree is required for my field.

What do you love most about your job?

I love the challenge of diagnosing and managing the health of animals and humans through medical and surgical procedures. I also enjoy dealing with the humans who own these animals.

What is the most difficult or challenging aspect of your job?

Facing the fact that some conditions cannot be cured and putting animals to sleep (euthanasia).

What is the biggest misconception people have about what you do?

People are usually amazed at how similar veterinary medicine is to human medicine and that veterinary medicine is so advanced. A sizeable number of people are surprised that a veterinarian has a doctorate degree.

What was the biggest obstacle you faced in getting to where you are in your career?

Making the grades required for entry into veterinary school and paying for the costs of the education. I overcame the academic obstacles by studying hard, and I overcame the financial obstacles by obtaining a U.S. Army Health Professions Scholarship to complete veterinary school.

What skills are an absolute must for someone interested in pursuing your career?

If a person is going to enter private veterinary practice, they must possess good people skills and decent business skills, in addition to great study habits and an inquisitive nature.

Whom do you admire most in your industry or field? Why?

The person that I admire the most is one of my veterinary school professors who taught small animal surgery. Dr. Hobson was one of the kindest and most patient men that I have ever known. He was truly concerned and cared for his patients and his students.

What is one piece of advice you would give to someone who is interested in pursuing your career?

If you entertain thoughts of entering the veterinary profession, you must begin to prepare early in school by learning to study and make very good grades. Animal experience and love for the profession will not get you into veterinary school without also having outstanding grades.

If you could do everything all over again, what would you do differently?

I don't think that I would change much, except that I would build a new veterinary hospital sooner in my career than I did.

Can you please add any additional comments you think might be helpful to someone hoping to pursue your career?

Start as early as possible preparing for a career in veterinary medicine. Talk to high school and college counselors as well as veterinarians to find out what is required for entry into the profession.

Kate An G. Hunter, Veterinarian
Carver Lake Veterinary Center
Macalester College, 1990
Majors: Biology; Chemistry; Veterinary Medicine

What was your first job after graduation?

Animal medical clinic.

What criteria did you use when deciding which colleges to apply to?

Quality of education, location, and financial aid.

What was your first choice school?

Macalester College/University of Minnesota.

What career did you have in mind when you applied to college?

I wanted to be either a medical doctor or a veterinarian.

How did the school you attended impact on your career choice and opportunities

Mcalester allowed me to explore many areas of study. I was able to get credit for volunteering at an emergency room. There I learned that I would not enjoy the work of a physician. The University of Minnesota curriculum included everything I needed to apply for a license as a veterinarian.

Can you please describe the "Aha!" moment when you realized what you wanted to do?

I was seven years old and went with my mother to take the dog to the vet for vaccinations. I knew I could do that. Unfortunately, in the early 1970s, girls did not get into veterinary school. After working for eight years as a chemist, I decided that I needed to try to get into veterinary school, as it continued to be what I always wanted to do.

Did you change your major? If so, why?

I started with a major in biology. While working as a chemist, I finished my chemistry major. I also considered and took classes in nursing and chemical engineering.

Can you please list your majors?

Biology, chemistry, veterinary medicine.

Which classes were most valuable in preparing you for your career or in helping you decide on your career?

Biochemistry, anatomy, and physiology taught me that it was possible to understand the workings of a body and therefore treat and prevent disease.

How did your professors impact your career choice or preparation?

Women in chemistry were role models. Their enthusiasm for their subject and how it applied to the world around them made them my favorite professors.

Did you have a job and/or internship during college that influenced your career choice or career preparation in any way?

Independent study working in a human emergency room and in veterinary clinics.

Do you have an advanced degree? Is one helpful or required in your field?

Yes, a four-year medical degree is required for practice.

What do you love most about your job?

The variety of tasks, the ability to improve the lives of animals and people, educating the public, meeting all types of animals.

What is the most difficult or challenging aspect of your job?

Cases that are difficult to diagnose or treat. The time spent on infrastructure as a practice owner—personnel, taxes, regulations, insurance, etc.

What is the biggest misconception people have about what you do?

That anyone who loves animals can be a vet. It is a messy, dangerous, difficult job where we rarely do things to endear ourselves to our patients.

What was the biggest obstacle you faced in getting to where you are in your career?

Getting into veterinary school. I had to retake classes to improve my grades for application and take classes to improve my graduate record examination (GRE) scores.

What skills are an absolute must for someone interested in pursuing your career?

You have to like people! Our patients never come alone. Communication skills; a mathematics and science background. You have to be energetic and motivated.

Whom do you admire most in your industry or field?

Those whose interest in the human-animal bond goes beyond their job and into their personal life. Those who give a little more to the community.

What is one piece of advice you would give to someone who is interested in pursuing your career?

Get to know what the job is really like.

If you could do everything all over again, what would you do differently?

I might have gone to veterinary school earlier.

Can you please add any additional comments you think might be helpful to someone hoping to pursue your career?

It is an accomplishment and an honor to be a veterinarian.